PAGE
52

ON THE ROAD

YOUR COMPLETE DESTINATION GUIDE
In-depth reviews, detailed listings
and insider tips

TOP EXPERIENCES MAP | NEXT PAGE

North Bali
p224

Central Mountains
p207

Gili Islands
p286

West Bali
p241

East Bali
p172

Ubud & Around
p132

Lombok
p256

Kuta & Seminyak
p54

South Bali & the Islands
p90

D1056447

PAGE
365

SURVIVAL GUIDE

YOUR AT-A-GLANCE REFERENCE
How to get around, get a room,
stay safe, say hello

Health

THIS EDITION WRITTEN AND RESEARCHED BY

Ryan Ver Berkmoes

Iain Stewart

❯Bali & Lombok

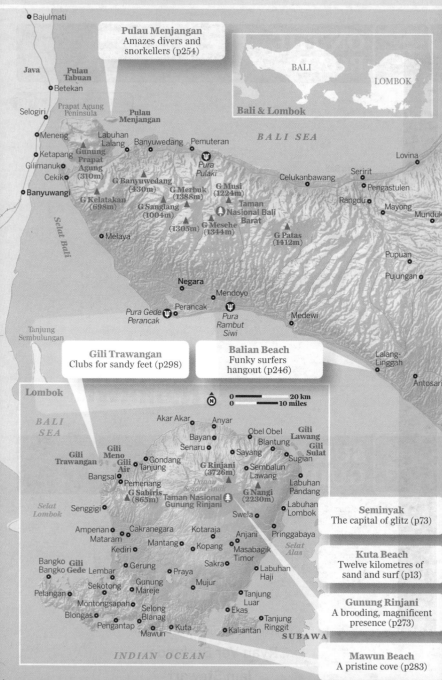

- Bajulmati

Pulau Menjangan
Amazes divers and
snorkellers (p254)

Java

Pulau Tabuan

- Betekan
- Selogiri
Meneng
- Ketapang
Gilimanuk
- Cekik
- **Banyuwangi**

Prapat Agung
Peninsula
- Labuhan
Lalang
- **Pulau Menjangan**

BALI

LOMBOK

Bali & Lombok

BALI SEA

Gunung Prapat Agung (310m)

- Banyuwedang
- Pemuteran

Pura Pulaki

G Banyuwedang (430m)

G Kelatakan (698m)

G Merbuk (1388m)

G Sanglang (1004m)

G Musi (1224m)

Taman Nasional Bali Barat

- Celukanbawang

- Lovina

Seririt

- Pengastulen

Rangdu

Mayong

Munduk

- Melaya

(1305m)

G Mesehe (1344m)

G Patas (1412m)

- Pupuan

- Pujungan

Negara

- Mendoyo
- Perancak

Pura Gede Perancak

Pura Rambut Siwi

- Medewi

Tanjung
Sembulungan

Gili Trawangan
Clubs for sandy feet (p298)

Balian Beach
Funky surfers
hangout (p246)

Lalang-
Linggah

- Antosari

Lombok

BALI SEA

0 ———— 20 km
0 ———— 10 miles

- Akar Akar
- Anyar
- Bayan
- Senaru

Obel Obel

Blantung

Gili Lawang

Gili Sulat

Gili Trawangan

Gili Meno

Gili Air

- Gondang
- Tanjung

- Sayang
- Sembulun
Lawang

- Sugian

- Bangsal
- Pemenang

G Rinjani (3726m)

Danau Segara Anak

G Sabiris (865m)

Taman Nasional Gunung Rinjani

G Nangi (2230m)

- Labuhan
Pandang

Selat Lombok

- Senggigi

- Swela

- Labuhan
Lombok

Seminyak
The capital of glitz (p73)

- Ampenan
- Cakranegara
- Mataram
- Kotaraja
- Anjani
- Pringgabaya

- Kediri
- Mantang
- Kopang

- Masabagik
Timor

Selat Alas

Kuta Beach
Twelve kilometres of
sand and surf (p13)

Bangko
Bangko

Gili Gede

- Lembar
- Gerung
- Praya
- Sakra

- Labuhan
Haji

- Pelangan
- Sekotong
- Gunung
Mareje
- Mujur

- Montongsapah
- Selong
Blanag
- Tanjung
Luar

Gunung Rinjani
A brooding, magnificent
presence (p273)

- Blongas
- Pengantap
- Mawun
- Kuta
- Ekas
- Kaliantan

- Tanjung
Ringgit

SUBAWA

Mawun Beach
A pristine cove (p283)

INDIAN OCEAN

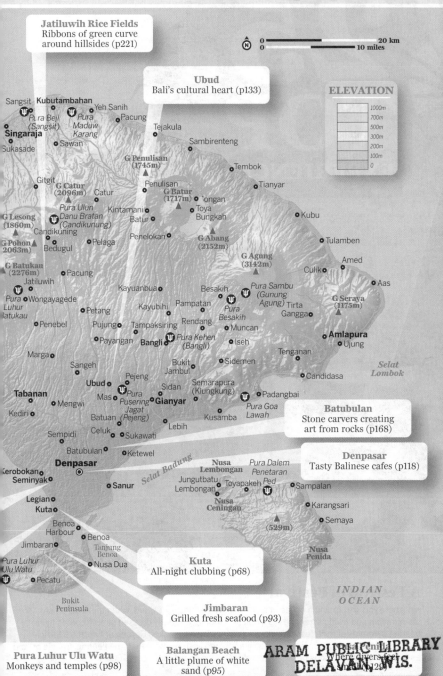

Top Experiences ›

Jatiluwih Rice Fields
Ribbons of green curve
around hillsides (p221)

Ubud
Bali's cultural heart (p133)

ELEVATION

1000m
700m
500m
300m
200m
100m
0

Sangsit · Kubutambahan · Yeh Sanih
Pura Beji · Pura · Pacung
(Sangsit) · Maduw
Singaraja · Karang
Sukasade · Sawan · Tejakula

Sambirenteng

Gitgit · G Catur · Catur · Penulisan · Tembok
(2096m) · G Batur · Tianyar
Pura Ulun · Kintamani · (1717m) · Tongan
G Lesong · Danu Bratan · Batur · Toya
(1860m) · (Candikunung) · Bungkah · Kubu
Candikuning · Penelokan · G Abang
G Pohon · Pelaga · (2152m) · Tulamben
2063m · Bedugul
G Agung · Culik · Amed
G Batukau · Pacung · (3142m)
(2276m)
Jatiluwih · Kayuanbua · Besakih · Pura Sambu · Aas
Pura · Wongayedge · (Gunung · G Seraya
Luhur · Petang · Kayubihi · Pampatan · Agung) Tirta · (1175m)
Batukau · Pujung · Tampaksiring · Rendang · Pura · Gangga
Penebel · Payangan · **Bangli** · Besakih
Muncan · **Amlapura**
Marga · Pura Kehen · Iseh · Ujung
Sangeh · (Bangli)
Tabanan · Ubud · Pejeng · Bukit · Tenganan · Selat
Mas · Pura · Sidan · Jambul · Sidemen · Candidasa · Lombok
Kediri · Mengwi · Pusering · **Gianyar** · Semarapura
Jagat · (Klungkung) · Padangbai
Sempidi · Batuan · (Pejeng) · Kusamba · Pura Goa
Celuk · Sukawati · Lebih · Lawah · **Batubulan**
Batubulan · Ketewel
Stone carvers creating
art from rocks (p168)
Denpasar
Nusa · Pura Dalem
Lembongan · Penetaran · **Denpasar**
Kerobokan · Jungutbatu · Ped · Sampalan · Tasty Balinese cafes (p118)
Seminyak · **Sanur** · Lembongan · Toyapakeh
Legian · Nusa · Karangsari
Kuta · Ceningan
Benoa · Semaya
Harbour · Benoa
Jimbaran · Tanjung · (529m) · Nusa
Benoa · Penida
Pura Luhur · Nusa Dua
Ulu Watu · **Kuta** · INDIAN
Pecatu · All-night clubbing (p68) · OCEAN
Bukit
Peninsula
Jimbaran
Grilled fresh seafood (p93)
Pura Luhur Ulu Watu · **Balangan Beach**
Monkeys and temples (p98) · A little plume of white
sand (p95)

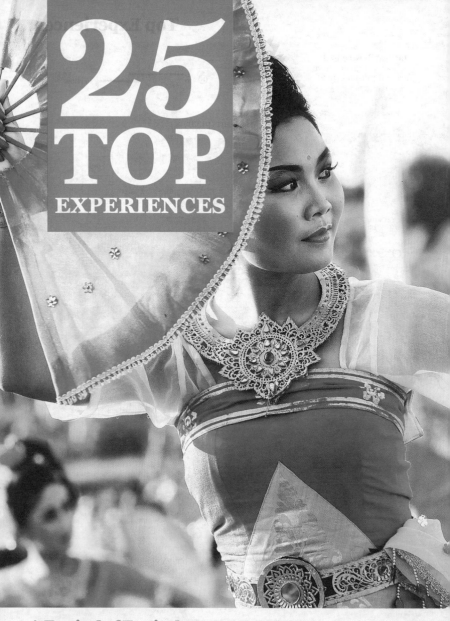

25 TOP EXPERIENCES

A Festival of Festivals

1 There you are sipping a coffee at a cafe in, say, Seminyak or Ubud, when there's a crash of the gamelan and traffic screeches to a halt as a mob of elegantly dressed people comes flying by bearing pyramids of fruit, tasselled parasols and a furred, masked Barong or two. It's a temple procession disappearing as suddenly as it appeared, with no more than the fleeting sparkle of gold and white silk and hibiscus petals in its wake. Dozens occur daily across Bali.

Aaah, a Spa

2 Whether it's a total fix for the mind, body and spirit, or simply the desire for a bit of serenity, visitors to Bali spend many happy hours (sometimes days) being massaged, scrubbed, perfumed, pampered, bathed and blissed out. Sometimes all this attention to your wellbeing happens on the beach or in a garden; other times it's in stylish, even lavish surroundings. As the Balinese massage techniques of stretching, long strokes, skin rolling and palm-and-thumb pressure result in an all-over feeling of calm, it's the perfect holiday prescription. *Aaah...*

Sybaritic Stays

3 On an island that honours art and serenity, is it any wonder you'll find some of the world's finest hotels and resorts? From blissful retreats on south Bali's beautiful beach in Canggu or Seminyak to perches on cliffs above the dazzling white sands that dot the Bukit Peninsula, these stylish hotels are as lovely outside as they are luxurious inside. Further resorts by vaunted architects can be found in Ubud's river valleys and in remote idyllic coastal locations. Amandari hotel, Ubud.

Homestays

4 Off with his head! You won't hear it but you might think it as another chicken is prepared for a meal in a traditional family compound. It's but one of many moments within the daily rhythms of life as three or more generations make offerings, prepare food, come and go from the rice fields or perhaps create a spot of music. Many families have a couple of simple rooms they let out to visitors, so for the price of a night's sleep you can witness this tableau.

JERRY ALEXANDER

Bali's Food

5 'Oh goody!' It's virtually impossible not to say this when you step into a classic warung for lunch to find dozens of freshly made dishes on the counter awaiting you. It shouldn't surprise that this fertile island provides a profusion of ingredients that combine to create fresh and aromatic dishes. Local specialities such as *babi guling*, roast suckling pig that's been marinated for hours in spices, will have you lining up again and again. Try lunch at one of the excellent Balinese cafes in Denpasar (p118).

Offerings

6 A wisp of smoke rises from an incense stick perched in an exquisite array of orange flower petals on a banana leaf no bigger than a deck of cards. You'll quickly realise these Balinese offerings are everywhere – outside your hotel room door, a tiny shrine on the beach, even at the end of the bar. They come in all shapes and sizes and are made throughout the day and night. Some are grand assemblages of fruit and food but most are tiny, appearing as if by magic.

Crafts of the Islands

7 Using a simple knife others might use to cut an apple, a Balinese craftsman sits in the shade of his family compound's frangipani tree and carves a masterpiece. Yes, schlock is sold here in profusion, as it is everywhere, but true local crafts draw on experience handed down for generations and nurtured through the years. Wood carvings are used for temple ceremonies and traditional performances such as the Barong, where colourful, animated wooden masks are integral to the story, while in Batubulan (p168) stone carvers create art from rocks. Butterfly kites, Gianyar.

PAUL BEINSSEN

Balinese Dance

8 The antithesis of Balinese mellow is Balinese dance. It's amazing how people who relish lounging in *bales* (open-sided pavilions) can also produce art that demands complete methodical precision. A performer of the Legong, the most beautiful dance, spends years learning minutely choreographed movements from her eyeballs to her toes. Each movement has a meaning and the language flows with a grace that is hypnotic. Clad in silk and ikat, the dancers tell stories rich with the very essence of Balinese Hindu beliefs and lore.

GREGORY ADAMS

Ubud

9 Famous in books and movies, the artistic heart of Bali exudes a compelling spiritual appeal. The streets are lined with galleries where artists, both humble and great, create. Beautiful performances showcasing the island's rich culture grace a dozen stages nightly. Museums honour the works of those inspired here through the years, while people walk the rice fields to find the perfect spot to sit in lotus position and ponder life's endless possibilities. Ubud is a state of mind and a beautiful state of being. Rice farmer, Ubud.

MICHAEL COYNE

Echoes of the Gamelan

10 Is there anything more stirring than hearing across rice fields the haunting tones of a lone musician practising on the gamelan on a quiet Ubud night? Bali's village orchestras play any of 25 different gamelans, from a solitary bronze gong to long rows of split bamboo that are virtual organs of sound spanning the musical scales. The music is everything from vital and percussive to more intimate syncopations. No dance performance, temple ceremony or procession is complete without this melodic magic.

Bali's Never-Ending Night

11 It starts with stylish cafes and bars in Seminyak, open-air places where everything seems just that bit more beautiful amid the twinkling of candles and enrapturing house beats. Later the world-class clubs of Legian draw you in, with famous international DJs spinning their legendary sets in a glam scene that hints at immediate celebrity. Some time before dawn, Kuta's harder, rawer clubs suck you in like black holes, spitting you out hours later into an unsteady daylight, shattered but happy. *Sky Garden Lounge, Kuta.*

Jatiluwih Rice Fields

12 Ribbons of green sinuously curve around hillsides crested by coconut palms: the ancient rice terraces of Jatiluwih (p221) are as artful as they are elegant, and a timeless testimony to the Balinese rice farmers' love and respect for the land. You'll run out of words for green as you walk, bike or drive the little road that wanders through this fertile bowl of the island's sacred grain. This is one of the few places where the ancient strains grow, standing stout and bounteous in the flowing fields.

WIBOWO RUSLI

Underwater Gilis

13 Taking the plunge? There are few better places than the Gilis, encircled by coral reefs teeming with life and visited by pelagics such as cruising manta rays. Scuba diving is a huge draw – there are several professional schools and all kinds of courses taught (from absolute beginner to nitrox specialist). With easy access from beach to reef, snorkelling is superb too, and you're very likely to see turtles. Want to take snorkelling to the next level? Try freediving – Trawangan is home to one of Asia's only breath-hold diving centres.

FELIX HUG

Diving Bali

14 Feel small as a manta ray blots out the sun's glow overhead, its fluid movement causing barely a disturbance in the surrounding waters as it glides past. And there's another, and another. Just when you think your dive can't get more dramatic, you turn to find a 2.5m sunfish hovering motionlessly, checking you out. Nusa Penida (p130) is but one of the many dive sites ringing Bali. The legendary 30m wall at Pulau Menjangan (p254) thrills, one tank after another.

TIM ROCK

NEIL MCALLISTER / ALAMY

Mawun Beach

15 Southern Lombok's coastline has a wild savage beauty and few visitors, generating lots of talk about the vast tourism potential of the region. When you set eyes on pristine Mawun beach (p283), it's easy to appreciate the hype. With two great headlands, it's perfectly sheltered from the raw power of the ocean, so the swimming is superb, in clear, turquoise-tinged water. At the rear of the bay is a crescent of powdery white sand. Most days this dream of a beach is all but empty.

PAUL KENNEDY

Bukit Peninsula Beaches

16 A little plume of white sand rises out of the blue Indian Ocean and fills a cove below limestone cliffs clad in deep green tropical beauty. It sounds idyllic, and it is. The west coast of the Bukit Peninsula in south Bali is dotted with beaches like that, such as Balangan Beach (p95), Bingin (p96) and Padang Padang. Families run funky surfer bars built on bamboo stilts over the tide, where the only views are the breaks metres away. Grab a lounger and be lulled by the waves. Balangan Beach.

Jimbaran Seafood

17 Enormous fresh prawns marinated in lime and garlic and grilled over coconut husks. Tick. A hint of post-sunset pink on the horizon. Tick. Stars twinkling overhead. Tick. A comfy teak chair settling into the beach while your toes play in the sand. Tick. An ice-cold beer. Tick. A strolling band playing the macarena. OK, maybe not a tick. But the beachside seafood grills in Jimbaran (p93) are a don't-miss evening out, with platters of seafood that came in fresh that morning to the market just up the beach.

DBIMAGES / ALAMY

PAUL KENNEDY

Surfing Bali

18 If it's a month containing the letter 'r', go east; during the other months, go west. Simplicity itself. And on Bali you have dozens of great breaks in each direction. This was the first place in Asia where surfing took off, and like the perfect set, it shows no signs of calming down. Surfers buzz around the island on motorbikes with board racks, looking for the next great break. Waves blown out? Another spot is just five minutes away. The scene at classic surfer hang-outs like Balian Beach is pure funk.

PAUL BEINSSEN

Kuta Beach

19 Tourism on Bali began here and is there any question why? The sweeping arc of sand curves from Kuta into the misty horizon northwest. Surf that started far out in the Indian Ocean crashes to shore in long symmetrical breaks. You can stroll the 12km of sand, enjoying a foot massage and cold beer with thousands of your new best friends in the south, or revel in utter solitude up north. Kuta Beach was and always will be Bali's best beach.

STÉPHANE VICTOR

Seminyak

20 People wander around Seminyak (p73) and ask themselves if they are even in Bali. Of course! On an island that values creativity like few other places, the capital of glitz is where you'll find inventive boutiques run by local designers, the most eclectic and interesting collection of restaurants, and little boutique hotels that break with the island clichés. Expats, locals and visitors alike idle away the hours in its cafes, at ease with the world and secure in their enjoyment of life's pleasures. Oberoi hotel, Seminyak.

Surfing Lombok

21 From Lombok to the Antarctic is virtually half the globe – that's some distance for the azure rollers of the Indian Ocean to build up speed and momentum, so it's no surprise that the island's coastline has some truly spectacular waves. Desert Point is the most famous of these, an incredibly long ride that tubes over a sharp, shallow reef. If that sounds a little too hard core, head to the town of Kuta, where you'll find dozens of challenging surf breaks a short distance away, including Mawi and Gerupak.

Hiking Rinjani

22 Glance at a map of Lombok, and virtually the entire northern half of the island is dominated by the brooding, magnificent presence of Gunung Rinjani (3726m; p273), Indonesia's second-highest volcano. Hiking Rinjani is no picnic, and involves planning, hiring a guide and porters, stamina and sweat. The route winds up the sides of the great peak until you reach the rim of a vast caldera, where there's a jaw-dropping view of Rinjani's sacred crater lake (an important pilgrim site) and the smoking, highly active mini-cone of Gunung Baru below.

Pura Luhur Ulu Watu

23 Just watch out for the monkeys. One of Bali's holiest temples, Pura Luhur Ulu Watu (p98) is perched on tall cliffs in the southwest corner of the island. In the 11th century a Javanese priest first prayed here and the site has only become holier since. Shrines and sacred sites are strung along the edge of the limestone precipice. You'll swear you can see Sri Lanka as you gaze across an ocean rippled by swells that arrive with metronomic precision. Sunset dance performances delight while those monkeys patiently await a banana – or maybe your sunglasses.

Sunrise over Trawangan

24 If you think Gili Trawangan (p288) is a stunner by daylight, you should see it at dawn after a night of dancing to some of the hottest electro, trance, reggae and house music in the region. You won't find slick decor, flashy visuals, door staff and stiff entrance prices in Trawangan, where the parties started as raves on the beach and still have a raw, unorganised spirit. Local DJs normally spin hypnotic tribal sounds and superstar DJs have been known to turn up and play unannounced sets. Parties are held three nights a week but are curtailed during the month of Ramadan.

Snorkelling

25 Swim a short distance from shore and see the eerie ghost of a sunken freighter at Tulamben (p204), or hover a few metres over the marine life teeming around the beautiful reef wall at Pulau Menjangan (p254). Bali and the Gilis have oodles of places where you can slip on fins and mask and enter another beautiful world. The mangroves of Nusa Lembongan (p123) are a smorgasbord for a rainbow of fish that gather in profusion. Or simply slip into the calm waters off a beach such as Sanur (p106) and see what darts off into the distance.

welcome to
Bali &
Lombok

The mere mention of 'Bali' evokes thoughts of a paradise. It's more than a place: it's a mood, an aspiration, a tropical state of mind.

A Place Like No Other

Bali is like no other destination in the world. Its rich culture plays out at all levels of life, from the exquisite flower-petal offerings placed everywhere to the processions of joyfully garbed locals, shutting down major roads as they march to one of the myriad temple ceremonies, to the otherworldly traditional music and dance performed island-wide.

Bali's Essence

Yes, Bali has beaches, surfing, diving, and resorts great and small, but it's the essence of Bali – and the Balinese – that makes it so much more than just a fun-in-the-sun retreat. It is possible to take the cliché of the smiling Balinese too far, but in reality, the inhabitants of this small island are indeed a generous, genuinely warm people. There's also a fun, sly sense of humour behind the smiles; upon seeing a bald tourist, many locals exclaim *'bung ujan'* (today's rain is cancelled) – it's their way of saying that the hairless head is like a clear sky.

One Island, Many Destinations

On Bali you can lose yourself in the chaos of Kuta or the sybaritic pleasures of Seminyak, surf wild beaches in the south or just hang out on Nusa Lembongan. You can go family friendly in Sanur or savour a lavish getaway on the Bukit Peninsula. Ubud is the heart of Bali, a place where the spirit and culture of the island are most accessible. It shares the island's most beautiful rice fields and ancient monuments with east Bali. The middle of Bali is dominated by the dramatic volcanoes of the central mountains and hillside temples such as Pura Luhur Batukau (one of the island's 20,000). North and west Bali are thinly populated but have diving and surfing that make any journey worthwhile.

Lombok & the Gilis, Too

Almost as big as Bali, Lombok is the undiscovered place next door. From its volcanic centre to untrodden idyllic beaches like Mawun, it rewards travellers who want to explore. Many are drawn to mighty Gunung Rinjani, Indonesia's second-highest volcano. Rivers and waterfalls gush down its fissured slopes, while its summit – complete with hot springs and a dazzling crater lake – is the ultimate trekker prize. The fabled Gili Islands – three exquisite droplets of white sand sprinkled with coconut palms and surrounded by coral reefs teeming with marine life – add a dose of south Bali buzz and, on Gili Trawangan, legendary nightlife.

need to know

Currency
» Rupiah (Rp)

Language
» Bahasa Indonesia and Balinese

When to Go

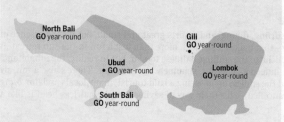

North Bali
GO year-round

Ubud
• **GO** year-round

Gili
GO year-round

South Bali
GO year-round

Lombok
GO year-round

Tropical climate, wet & dry seasons
Tropical climate, rain year-round

Your Daily Budget

Budget less than
US$80
» Room in guesthouse/homestay: less than US$50

» Cheap food and drink, even at fairly nice places

» Can survive on US$20 per day

Midrange
US$80–200
» Room in midrange hotel: US$50–US$150

» Can eat and drink virtually anywhere

» Can enjoy spa treatments and other luxuries

Top end over
US$ 200
» Room in top-end hotel/resort: over US$150

» Major expenses will be lavish spas

» Luxury boutiques await

High Season
(Jul & Aug)

» Rates zip up by 50% or more.

» Many hotels are booked far ahead; the best restaurants need booking in advance.

» Christmas and New Year are equally expensive and crowded.

Shoulder
(May, Jun & Sep)

» Coincides with the best weather (drier, less humid).

» Some deals but last-minute bookings possible.

» Best time for many activities such as diving, since the water is clear and crowds are OK.

Low Season
(Jan–Apr, Oct & Nov)

» Deals everywhere, good airfares.

» Rainy season; however, rainfall is never excessive.

» Can do most activities except volcano treks.

Money

» ATMs in south Bali, Ubud and tourist areas. Credit cards accepted at midrange and top-end hotels and restaurants.

Visas

» Usually a renewable 30 days granted on arrival.

Mobile Phones

» Local SIM cards work with any unlocked GSM phone.

Driving

» Drive on the right; steering wheel is on the right-hand side of the car.

Websites

» **Bali Advertiser** (www.baliadvertiser .biz) Bali's expat journal with insider tips and good columnists.

» **Bali Discovery** (www.balidiscovery .com) Excellent weekly summary of news and features; hotel deals.

» **Bali Paradise** (www .bali-paradise.com) Compendium site of info and links.

» **Lombok Guide** (www.thelombokguide .com) Comprehensive.

» **Lonely Planet** (www.lonelyplanet .com/indonesia) Destination information, hotel bookings, traveller forum and more.

Exchange Rates

Australia	A$1	8760Rp
Canada	C$1	8880Rp
Japan	¥100	10,720Rp
New Zealand	NZ$1	6830Rp
UK	UK£1	14,130Rp
US	US$1	8970Rp

For current exchange rates see www.xe.com.

Important Numbers

Bali has six telephone area codes and Lombok two; these are listed in the relevant chapters of this book. Numbers that begin with 08 are mobiles. Drop the 0 in phone numbers when calling from abroad.

Indonesia country code	✆62
International call prefix	✆001/017
International operator	✆102
Directory assistance	✆108

Arriving in Bali & Lombok

» **Ngurah Rai Airport (DPS; aka Denpasar or Bali) on Bali**
Prepaid 24-hour taxis to all parts of the island:
Kuta 50,000Rp
Seminyak 70,000Rp
Ubud 195,000Rp

» **Selaparang Airport (AMI) on Lombok**
Prepaid 24-hour taxis to all parts of the island:
Mataram 32,000Rp
Senggigi 60,000-75,000Rp
Kuta 240,000Rp

» Note: a new airport may open on Lombok in 2011. See p380.

Bali Is Easy

Forgot something at home? You can get it on Bali. Don't speak the language? They probably speak yours. Afraid to get sick? You don't need shots and clean drinking water and healthy food are readily available. Not sure how you'll get around? Friendly drivers will take care of that. Where to stay? Anywhere, from the world's most luxurious hotels to welcoming family-run guesthouses. Is it safe? Probably safer than your home town. But aren't there touts and scammers? Easily avoided on 98% of the island. How will I stay in touch? Fast wi-fi and mobile service in tourist areas mean friends at home will see pics of every wave you ride. Is the food too hot? The cheeseburgers are always served right off the grill. My biggest concern? Not wanting to leave.

what's new

For this new edition of Bali & Lombok, our authors have hunted down the fresh, the revamped, the transformed, the hot and the happening. Here are a few of our favourites. For up-to-the-minute reviews and recommendations, see lonelyplanet.com/indonesia/bali and lonelyplanet.com/indonesia/lombok.

Let's Eat, Kerobokan

1 The food-universe centre on Bali has shifted to Kerobokan. Superb new restaurants include Biku (p85), an artful, casual cafe; and Sardine (p85), a fantasy of seafood.

Fast Boats to the Gilis

2 It seems there are as many fast boats between Bali and the Gilis as there are dolphins in the ocean on the way. New connections include Nusa Lembongan and Amed (p288).

Book It in Bukit

3 Already home to world-famous surf breaks, the Bukit Peninsula is becoming the place for a break, period. Funky new hotels perch near groovy beaches at Bingin (p96) and Balangan (p95).

Eat, Pray, Love Mania

4 It seems every tour operator is trying to get in on the act spawned by Elizabeth Gilbert's best-selling book (see p140). Meanwhile, some of Bali's traditional healers are available for hype-free consultations (p152).

New Shopping Streets

5 East of retail meccas Seminyak and Kerobokan, a gaggle of new stores lines a meandering string of streets. Some of Bali's best housewares can be found here (p86).

Gili T Arrives

6 Hotter than hot, Gili Trawangan has a great new restaurant, Kokomo (p297), which breaks the backpacker shackles of the island's past, along with one of Asia's best freediving centres, Freedive Gili (p289).

Seminyak Beach Walkway

7 A new walk along the sand links Seminyak's club-lined Jl Abimanyu to Jl Double Six in Legian. At sunset, grab a seat and a cheap beer (p74).

Hidden Luxury

8 The south coast of the Bukit Peninsula is used to surf-tossed drama, but big waves are nothing compared with the splash made by the lavish new Alila Villas (p99).

Sunset Stroll

9 Nusa Lembongan's long beach has a fab new seawall walkway that's ideal for a lazy perambulation before a meal at the hip new hotel-restaurant Indiana Kenanga (p124).

Art with Strings Attached

10 Bali's great tradition of puppets now has a museum worthy of the characters. The Setia Darma House of Masks and Puppets (p171), south of Ubud in Mas, is spectacular.

Balian Ball

11 Alligator hunters once stalked the river nearby, but that's one of the least colourful aspects of Pondok Pitaya, a guesthouse facing the popular surf break at Balian Beach (p247).

if you like...

The Quiet Life

Quiet can take many forms on Bali, but visitors may prefer the kind that comes from staying someplace that defines serenity, where contemplations of life, beauty or your navel can occur in peace. You may wish for a full suite of services – literally – or for simple repose where even the prospect of room service seems like unnecessary bother.

Amed Simple guesthouses on a remote coast in the east where the pursuit of yoga is encouraged (p199)

Ubud You can live at peace in beautiful hotels along the bucolic Sungai Ayung (Ayung River; p154)

Bingin An eclectic collection of guesthouses perches on a cliff overlooking famous surf breaks (p96)

Ungasan New resorts define luxurious getaways at the south end of south Bali (p99)

Munduk Simple guesthouses amid rice terraces and spice plantations are well placed for soul-searching walks (p220)

Diving & Snorkelling

The sunfish stares at you and you stare back. 'Wow' is all you can think. Huge creatures like the sunfish are found at many spots around Bali and Lombok, as are a world of other fish and mammals, from parrot fish to whales.

Pulau Menjangan Coral reefs and 30m cliffs offer some of the finest diving and snorkelling in Southeast Asia. This island falls within Bali's only national park (p254)

Tulamben Shore dive (or snorkel) out to a wrecked WWII freighter in a remote east Bali town that exists entirely to serve divers (p204)

Nusa Lembongan Sites ranging from mangroves to reefs plus good dive shops make this an ideal stay for divers; it's also the best base for diving the cliffs off nearby Nusa Penida (p124)

Gili Trawangan World-class dive shops help you enjoy a range of underwater pleasures (p289)

Surfing

Listen to the accents of the surfers and you'll hear Australian, American, Italian, Dutch, Japanese, Balinese (yes, lots of Balinese!) and many more. People from all over the world come to Bali to surf, which shouldn't surprise anyone. Bali's surf breaks are legendary and there are many.

Ulu Watu A series of breaks that are among the best anywhere. Just look for the morning traffic jams of board-carrying motorbikes heading south from Kuta (p124)

Nusa Lembongan A sort of prototype for funky surfer islands everywhere, with a series of breaks in front of the main beach (p124)

Kuta Bali's premier visitor beach is lined with surf schools, and when it comes time to don the look, there are entire retail empires owned by people who were once just surfers here, dude (p57)

Ekas Bay Head to southeast Lombok for the ultimate away-from-the-crowd breaks (p285)

» Believed to have magical powers, the springs at Tirta Empul (p166) gush through waterspouts into a large bathing pool

Beaches

Beaches ring the islands, but iconic ones with white sand are not as common as you'd think – most are some variation of tan or grey. Surf conditions range from limp to torrid, depending on whether there's an offshore reef.

Seminyak Beach This wide stretch of sand boasts great surf that both swimmers and surfers can frolic in. It's a place enjoyed by locals and visitors alike – especially at sunset (p74)

Balangan Beach This curving white-sand beach on the Bukit Peninsula, backed by an impromptu resort, is ramshackle in an endearing way and perfect for a snooze or booze (p95)

Gili Island beaches The beaches on these three islands are uniformly gorgeous, with circles of white sand, great snorkelling and a timeless traveller vibe (p286)

Mawun Beach An idyllic Lombok wonder that astounds first-time visitors (p283)

Hiking & Walking

It's easy to miss the little things in Bali: simple shrines, an obscured bit of art, a fanciful carving or an exquisite orchid are best appreciated if you slow down enough to take notice. Much of Bali is perfect for walking and hiking.

Ubud The centre for walking. Local guides with a deep knowledge of the surrounding land, plants and spiritual meanings are here; self-guided walks through the rice fields are legion, many surmounting ridges that climb the sky between rivers (p143)

Tirta Gangga Site of the fabled ruins of a water palace. The village is an excellent base for hikes up mountains to isolated yet important temples, and for longer cross-country treks through rice fields and jungle, across the coast and up Gunung Agung (p196)

Munduk Old Dutch colonial mountain retreat with a web of trails through thick forest to hidden waterfalls (p219)

Spas & Massage

Every upmarket hotel worth its stars has spa facilities (almost always open to nonguests) offering health, beauty and relaxation treatments. Day spas are everywhere; many of the best are booked up days in advance during the high season. Costs can be anything from 20,000Rp for a beach rub to US$100 or more for a multihour sybaritic soak. In general, however, the costs are quite low compared with other parts of the world, and the Balinese have just the right cultural background and disposition to enhance the serenity.

Ubud Often the hill town seems like one big spa, and if you can't spa here, you can't spa anywhere (p142)

Kuta Go to the spas favoured by locals. Did you know that many Balinese will only get massages from the blind? You do now (p57)

Seminyak Best mix of spas, including ones that are famous (p75)

If you like... music and dance
Ubud has schools where you can learn to move and groove like the Balinese (p143)

Temples

With over 20,000 temples, Bali has such a variety that you can't even categorise them. The best evoke the great traditions of the island's unique form of Buddhism that has been shaped by priests and prophets for centuries.

Pura Luhur Batukau One of Bali's most important temples is found far up its namesake volcano. It's a misty, remote place that is steeped in ancient spirituality (p221)

Pura Tirta Empul A beautiful temple with holy springs discovered in AD 962 (p166)

Pura Pusering Jagat One of the famous temples at Pejeng, which date to the 14th century empire that once flourished here (p166)

Pura Luhur Ulu Watu As important as it is popular, the temple has sweeping Indian Ocean views, sunset dance performances and monkeys (p98)

Nightlife

Nightclubs on Bali and the Gilis draw acolytes from across Southeast Asia. The large numbers of relatively well-heeled tourists and nonexistent licensing laws have spawned an ever-changing line-up of clubs that book celebrity DJs spinning mixes that are soon heard worldwide. Bouncing from one club to another all night long is a Bali tradition, guaranteeing overheating from the exertion, the mixes, the booze, the companionship or all of the above.

Seminyak Start the evening in hipster/scenester hang-outs where the glow of candles makes everyone beautiful (p81)

Kuta All raw energy and a mad mix of party-goers, from Marg from Melbourne having her first big night out to Made from Munduk enjoying every aspect of modern Balinese life (p68)

Gili Trawangan The place for pounding beats and searing mixes three times weekly (p298)

Religion

The Balinese are deeply spiritual and much of their daily life is devoted to religious matters. Their version of Hinduism is an all-pervasive effort to bring out the best in the gods and spirits. Offerings and shrines are everywhere, and local lives are guided by a complex set of calendars that see to the needs of the gods, temples and spirits.

Nyepi The fabled day of silence occurs once a year and is the one festival you should experience if you can. The airport is closed, nobody may go out and the entire island becomes truly quiet (p325)

Ogoh-Ogoh It's entirely different the night before Nyepi, when parties in every village go until dawn and huge paper sculptures of monsters go up in flames (p325)

Temple Ceremonies Every one of Bali's 20,000-plus temples has a birthday and the celebrations are worth attending (p84)

Offerings You see them everywhere; an iconic delight (p345)

If you like... old things
Gunung Kawi has towering ancient wonders (p166)

If you like... ruins
Semarapura has the remains of a great palace (p177)

If you like... local delicacies
Warung Teges has the best Balinese food in Ubud (p157)

Culture

The island's creative heritage is everywhere you look and there's nothing manufactured about what you see. Dance and musical performances are the result of an ever-evolving culture with a legacy of centuries. Villages save their highest honours for the artists who live there. The culture is vibrant and accessible, and one of the aspects of a trip to Bali that make it like no other.

Dance Rigid choreography and high levels of discipline are hallmarks of beautiful, melodic Balinese dance. No visit is complete without enjoying this purely Balinese art form (p337)

Gamelan The ensemble orchestra makes its unforgettable music on bamboo and bronze instruments, and can be heard at every dance performance and temple celebration (p340)

Painting Balinese and Western styles merged in the 20th century and the results are often extraordinary. See some of the best in Ubud's museums (p136)

Great Food

Balinese food is pungent and lively; there is nothing shy about this cuisine. You'll find shades of South Indian, Malaysian and Chinese flavours in the island's food. It has evolved from years of cross-cultural cook-ups and trading with sea-faring pioneers, and perhaps even pirates, across the seas of Asia. And your dining won't be limited to local fare either: excellent cuisine drawn from around the globe is on offer.

Seminyak Hands down the place with the greatest variety of top restaurants; on a 10-minute stroll you can wander the world of food (p78)

Kerobokan Rapidly becoming the go-to area for the hottest and best restaurants, plus some superb simple Balinese warung (p85)

Denpasar Truly local cafes serve exceptional Balinese and Indonesian food in simple surrounds (p118)

Ubud A profusion of restaurants and cafes, many organic (p154)

Markets

Traditional markets are still the venue of choice for most shoppers. And they should be, with their beautiful and accessible displays of the best Bali and Lombok have to offer. These shady labyrinths are the connection between the people doing the producing and the people consuming. Drop by to see the makings of temple offerings, exotic fruits and everything you need to whip up a 12-course Balinese feast.

Denpasar Bali's capital has the largest markets and you can spend an afternoon wandering the labyrinth of levels across the markets (p119)

Jimbaran Not one but two extraordinary markets: one for produce that draws the best farmers from across Bali, while the other is the island's main fish market, with fresh seafood brought in dripping from the boats on the beach (p92)

Pasar Bertais The intensely local experience at this Lombok market can't be bettered (p260)

>> The popular Barong and Rangda dance (p339) is a battle between good and evil

Volcanoes

Indonesia has a lot of them, and Bali and Lombok have some famous ones. On Bali, volcanoes are the spiritual centre of the island and a local will always know his or her position in relation to them. Houses, even beds, are situated with volcanoes in mind. Climbing one affords sweeping views of the islands and stunning scenery closer in. You may feel some of these huge peaks' spiritual pull yourself.

Gunung Agung The most revered volcano on Bali, the 3142m Agung dominates views of the island from most directions – that is, when it chooses to come out from behind its veil of clouds (p182)

Gunung Batur A volcanic theme park with steaming vents, calderas within calderas and other geological oddities (p208)

Gunung Rinjani Reach the top on a three-day trek that includes a gorgeous lake inside the crater (p273)

Shopping

For some people Bali is a destination for shopping; for others it becomes their destiny. You'll find a plethora of shops and stalls across the island – everything from cheap T-shirt vendors to exquisite boutiques with alluring housewares and fashion by local designers with worldwide followings.

Seminyak It seems you can't run into someone in Seminyak and *not* have them claim to be a designer; the reality is that many actually are. The shopping scene here is constantly changing: new boutiques appear, old ones vanish, some change into something else while others move up the food chain. The odds that you'll stumble upon a star of tomorrow are good (p81)

Kerobokan The next Seminyak in every sense. Just a touch of energy is moving here from its tony neighbour to the south, but there is great promise (p86)

Ubud Excellent for handicrafts and art (p160)

Cooking Courses

Preparing your own Balinese banquet is a fantastic, hands-on way to get acquainted with the ingredients, flavours and techniques of Balinese cooking, and the habits and rituals associated with food. Even if you don't fancy yourself a cook, you'll savour every bite, appreciating the work that went into it. Classes usually start with an early morning market tour to introduce you to the freshness and variety of produce, and the vibrancy of market life.

Ubud There are heaps of schools here in self-learning central; we list the three that are cooked to perfection (p144)

Tanjung Benoa Go to school with one of Bali's best cooks after a visit to the island's best market (p103)

Seminyak A Balinese chef teaches you about his island's cuisine (p75)

month by month

February

The rainy season pours on and the islands take a breather after the Christmas and New Year's high season.

Nyale Festival

The ritual harvesting of wormlike sea fish (*nyale*) takes place on Seger beach near Lombok's Kuta. The evening begins with poetry readings, continues with gamelan performances and carries on until the dawn when the worms start appearing. Usually February but also in March. See p282 for more.

March

The rainy season is ending and there is a lull in the crowds, as this is low season for tourism.

Nyepi (Day of Silence)

Bali's major Hindu festival, Nyepi celebrates the end of the old year and the start of the next. It's marked by inactivity – to convince evil spirits that Bali is uninhabited, so they'll leave the island alone for another year. The night before sees community celebrations with *ogoh-ogoh*, huge papier-mâché monsters that go up in flames. See p325 for more, including dates for coming years. Held in March or early April.

April

The islands dry out after the rainy season, but things remain quiet on the visitor front.

Bali Spirit Festival

A fast-growing yoga, dance and music festival (www.balispiritfestival.com) from the people behind the Yoga Barn (p143). There are over 100 workshops and concerts, plus a market and more. It's usually held in early April but may begin in late March.

Malean Sampi

Buffalo race over waterlogged earth in Narmada, near Mataram on Lombok. Jockeys tear down the track, clinging onto a couple of stampeding yoked buffalo. It's as dangerous, muddy and fun as it sounds. Early in the month.

May

A great month for visiting. It's not high season but the annual rains have stopped (although you'll still get downpours at any time). Trails are drying out for hiking yet the rivers are still high for rafting.

Bali Art Festival of Buleleng

Every year Singaraja hosts this large arts festival in north Bali. During one week, dancers and musicians from some of the region's most renowned village troupes, such as those of Jagaraga, perform.

June

The airport is getting busier, but much of what makes May a good month also applies in June.

Bali Arts Festival

Denpasar's arts festival (www.baliartsfestival.com) is the premier event on Bali's cultural calendar. Based at the Taman Wedhi Budaya arts centre, the festival is a great way to see traditional Balinese dance and music. Village-based dance and musical groups compete fiercely for local pride. Held mid-June to mid-July. See p118 for more.

See p118 for more.

July

Along with August, July is the busiest month for visitors on Bali and the Gilis (Lombok is always rather quiet). Don't expect to have your pick of places to stay, but do plan to enjoy the energy of big happy crowds.

★ Bali Kite Festival

In south Bali scores of kites soar overhead much of the year. Often huge (10m plus), they fly at altitudes that worry pilots. There's a spiritual connection: the kites urge the gods to provide abundant harvests. During this festival the skies fill with these huge creations controlled by dozens of villagers.

October

The skies darken more often with seasonal rains, but mostly the weather is pleasant and the islands go about their normal business.

★ Ubud Writers & Readers Festival

This Ubud festival (www.ubudwritersfestival.com) hosts scores of writers and readers from around the world in a celebration of writing – especially that which touches on Bali.

★ Kuta Karnival

A big beach party on the big beach in Kuta (www.kutakarnival.com); games, art, competitions, surfing and much more on the first October weekend and the days right before.

November

It's getting wetter, but not really so wet that you can't enjoy the islands to the fullest. Usually a quiet month crowd-wise.

★ Perang Topat

This 'rice war' on Lombok is fun. It takes place at Pura Lingsar just outside Mataram and involves a costumed parade, and Hindus and Wektu Telu pelting balls of *ketupat* (sticky rice) at each other. Usually November but also December.

December

Visitors rain down on Bali and the Gilis ahead of the Christmas and New Year's holidays. Hotels and restaurants are booked out and everybody is busy.

◉ Peresean

Martial arts, Lombok-style. Competitors, stripped to the waist, spar with sticks and cowhide shields. The winner is the first to draw blood. It's held annually in Mataram. Late in the month.

★ Galungan & Kuningan

Galungan, which celebrates the death of a legendary tyrant called Mayadenawa, is one of Bali's major festivals. During this 10-day period, all the gods come down to earth for the festivities. Barong prance from temple to temple and village to village, and locals rejoice with feasts and visits to families. The celebrations culminate with the Kuningan festival, when the Balinese say thanks and goodbye to the gods.

Every village in Bali will celebrate Galungan and Kuningan in grand style, and visitors are welcome to join in.

The 210-day *wuku* (or Pawukon) calendar is used to determine festival dates. The calendar uses 10 different types of weeks between one and 10 days long, which all run simultaneously, and the intersection of the various weeks determines auspicious days. Dates for future Galungan and Kuningan celebrations are as follows:

YEAR	GALUNGAN	KUNINGAN
2011	6 Jul	16 Jul
2012	1 Feb & 29 Aug	11 Feb & 8 Sep
2013	27 Mar	6 Apr

Whether you've got three days or 30, these itineraries provide a starting point for the trip of a lifetime. Want more inspiration? Head online to lonelyplanet.com/thorntree to chat with other travellers.

itineraries

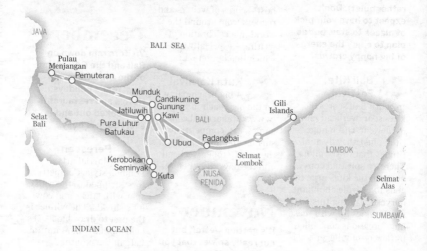

Two Weeks
Bali & the Gilis

> Start your trip in **Seminyak**, which has the best places to go out for a meal, a drink or even a new frock. Allow at least three days to experience the refined charms of **Kerobokan** and the wild nights of **Kuta**. Once you're sated, head west, driving through the rice terraces of **Jatiluwih** and on to **Pura Luhur Batukau**, a holy temple up in the clouds. Head northwest to the crescent of mellow beach resorts at **Pemuteran**. From here, you can snorkel or scuba Bali's best dive site at **Pulau Menjangan**. Driving east, stop in **Munduk** for some hiking to remote waterfalls.

Carry on via **Candikuning** to **Ubud**, the spiritual centre of Bali. Nights of dance and culture are offset by days of walking through the serene countryside. Do a day trip to the ancient monuments at **Gunung Kawi**. Head down to the cute little beach and port town of **Padangbai** and catch a fast boat to the **Gili Islands**. Wander the islands, enjoy Gili T's surprising nightlife and go snorkelling to spot a turtle.

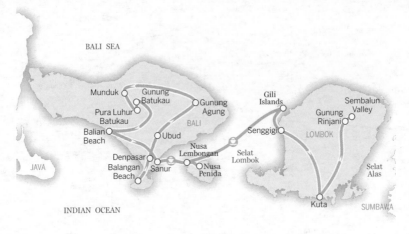

Three Weeks
Total Bali & Lombok

❭ Begin your trip at **Balangan Beach**. Settle back in the sand and let the jetlag vanish. Stop in **Denpasar** for a purely Balinese lunch and then head up the hill to **Ubud** to get a full taste of Balinese culture. Next, tackle **Gunung Agung**, the spiritual centre of the island. Start early to reach the top and take in the views before the daily onslaught of clouds and mist.

Having climbed Bali's most legendary peak, head west to the village of **Munduk**, which looks down to the north coast and the sea beyond. Go for a walk in the area and enjoy waterfalls, truly tiny villages, wild fruit trees and the sinuous bands of rice paddies lining the hills like ribbons. Then head south to the wonderful temple of **Pura Luhur Batukau**, and consider a trek up Bali's second-highest mountain, **Gunung Batukau**. Head down to the newly popular **Balian Beach** on the west coast for some chilled-out time in a funky surfer scene.

Next, bounce across the waves from **Sanur** to **Nusa Lembongan**, the island hiding in the shadow of **Nusa Penida**. The latter is visible from much of the south and east – it's lush, arid and almost unpopulated and makes a good day trip. Take in the amazing vistas from its cliffs and dive under the waves to check out the marine life.

Head to the **Gilis** via the direct boat from Nusa Lembongan for more tranquil time circumnavigating the three islands and diving offshore. Take a boat to **Senggigi**, but ignore the resorts and head south. Well off the beaten path, the south coast near Lombok's **Kuta** has stunning beaches and surfing to reward the intrepid. The seldom-driven back roads of the interior will thrill the adventurous and curious, with tiny villages where you can learn about the amazing local handicrafts. Many of these roads lead up the flanks of **Gunung Rinjani**, the volcanic peak that shelters the lush and remote **Sembalun Valley**. Trekking from one village to the next on the rim can take days, but is one of the great walks.

One Month
Bali at a Slow Pace

❯ Get some accommodation close to the beach in **Kerobokan**. Be sure to get to the trendy restaurants and cafes of **Seminyak** before you leave this part of south Bali behind. Maybe you can learn how to surf, or at least brush up on your skills, before you head south to **Bingin** and its groovy cliff-side inns overlooking fab surfing. Make the short drive down to Bukit Peninsula's spiritual centre (and monkey home) **Pura Luhur Ulu Watu**.

Take a trip through **Denpasar** and stop at the markets and museum. Next, Bali's ancient rice terraces will exhaust your abilities to describe green. Sample these in a drive up to the terraces of **Jatiluwih** followed by the lyrical **Pura Luhur Batukau**. Make your way over the mountains via the **Antosari Road**, pausing at a remote hotel on the way. Head west to **Pemuteran** where the beachside hotels define relaxation. Dive or snorkel nearby **Pulau Menjangan** in the Taman Nasional Bali Barat. It's renowned for its coral and sheer 30m wall.

Lovina is a good break on a route around the coast to **Tulamben**, where scores of people explore the shattered hulk of a WWII freighter. Get some serious chill time on the **Amed Coast** before the short jaunt to **Tirta Gangga** and hikes through rice fields and up jungle-clad hills to remote temples. Continue to **Padangbai**. This fun little port town is an ideal place to hang out for a couple of days before you take backroads to **Ubud**. Find your favourite cafe and let the world wander past, or rid yourself of travel kinks at a spa. You might consider staying at one of the lush hotels in Sayan, taking gentle walks through rice fields by day and marvelling at dance performances at night.

When you're ready and rested, get a fast boat from **Sanur** to **Nusa Lembongan**. This little island still has the classic simple charm of a rural beach town, with a string of hotels – from basic to semi-posh – lining its sands. It's a timeless travellers' scene with a backdrop of excellent surfing and splendid snorkelling and diving.

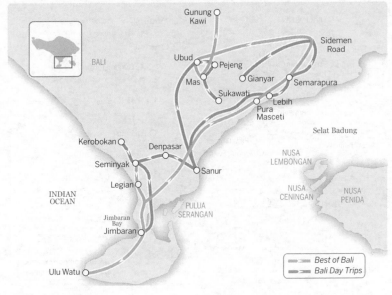

Best of Bali
Bali Day Trips

One Week
Best of Bali

❭ Start at a beachside hotel in **Legian** or **Seminyak**. Shop the streets of the latter and spend time at the beach. Enjoy a seafood dinner on **Jimbaran Bay** as part of a day trip to the monkey-filled temple at **Ulu Watu**.

In the east, take the coast road to wild beaches like the one near **Pura Masceti**, followed by the well-mannered royal town of **Semarapura** with its ruins. Head north up the breathtaking **Sidemen Road**, which combines rice terraces with lush river valleys and cloud-shrouded mountains. Then go west to **Ubud**, the crowning stop on any itinerary.

To spoil yourself, stay in one of Ubud's many hotels with views across rice fields and rivers. Sample the offerings at a spa before you try one of the myriad great restaurants. Bali's rich culture is most celebrated and most accessible in Ubud and you'll be captivated by nightly dance performances. Check out local craft studios, including the woodcarvers of **Mas**. Hike through the surrounding rice fields to river valleys, taking a break in museums bursting with paintings. Finish by heading north to the imposing thousand-year-old rock monoliths at **Gunung Kawi**.

One Week
Bali Day Trips

❭ This is for the traveller who wants to unpack only once, seeing what's possible on Bali during a series of relaxed day trips. Start with a beachside hotel in **Sanur**, such as Hotel La Taverna or Tandjung Sari, both of which have a refined yet relaxed charm.

Day trip one starts with the short drive to **Denpasar**, followed by a visit to the shops of **Seminyak** and **Kerobokan**. Finish up with a sunset seafood grill at **Jimbaran**.

Day trip two heads to **Ubud** for a half day strolling the streets, looking at the shops, galleries and museums. Take different routes there and back so you can enjoy sights such as the temples of **Pejeng**, the carvers of **Mas** and the village market at **Sukawati**.

Day trip three follows the wave-tossed volcanic beaches along the coast road to the northeast. Stop at **Lebih**, which has a temple and mica-infused glittering sand. Go inland to the temple ruins and market at **Semarapura**, then head north along the beautiful **Sidemen Road**. Next loop west and head back down through the tidy regional centre of **Gianyar**, where you can snack at the market and check out large traditional fabric showrooms.

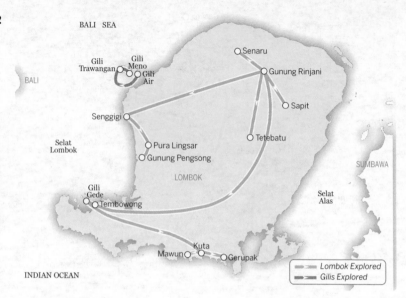

BALI SEA

BALI

Gili Trawangan
Gili Meno
Gili Air

Senaru

Gunung Rinjani

Sapit

Senggigi

Selat Lombok

Pura Lingsar
Gunung Pengsong

Tetebatu

LOMBOK

SUMBAWA

Selat Alas

Gili Gede
Tembowong

Mawun
Kuta
Gerupak

INDIAN OCEAN

Lombok Explored
Gilis Explored

Two Weeks
Lombok Explored

❯ Kick off in gorgeous **Kuta** and spend a day or two finding the perfect beach. East or west of town there are a dozen or so bays to choose from: magnificent **Mawun** is just one. While you're here, it would be rude not to sample the fabled south Lombok surf – tiny **Gerupak** is an excellent place to either take a lesson or hitch a boat ride to an epic break. Tranquil southwest Lombok is not far away for more aqua action – swim in sheltered transparent water or explore the dozen or so islands here by boat. Tiny **Gili Gede** makes a perfect base; you can reach it by boat from Tembowong.

Sacred **Gunung Rinjani** is next up; get here via roads from Tembowong. Either explore its foothills from the rustic bases of **Tetebatu** or **Sapit**, or go the whole hog and trek from **Senaru** to the crater rim, sublime crater lake or summit itself (depending on your time, energy and commitment level). After Rinjani your body will need some serious pampering, and the spas of **Senggigi** are the ideal place to recuperate, with massages and treatments for all budgets. Finish off with a trip or two to the sights around Mataram, such as the intriguing temple of **Pura Lingsar** or the hilltop shrine **Gunung Pengsong**.

One Week
Gilis Explored

❯ The ideal place to get to grips with island life is **Gili Air**, where the main beachfront strip is perfect tropical lounging territory. Here you can wile away a day or two doing nothing but chilling with a book, taking a dip when you need to cool off, snorkelling the offshore coral (maybe you'll spot a turtle) and feasting on inexpensive fresh seafood. OK, now you've acclimatised.

Next up is **Trawangan**, where there's much more action. Here the perfect day could start with a morning dive at a site such as **Shark Point**, followed by a healthy lunch and an afternoon snooze. Then take a gentle cycle round the sandy lanes of the island, slipping in a sunset cocktail on the west coast. After dinner it's time to feel the beat and strut your stuff at one of Trawangan's parties, or catch a reggae band at Sama Sama.

The final stop is idyllic **Gili Meno**, where, once you've secured the perfect place to stay, there's little to do except wonder at the sheer drop-dead beauty of the island and the clarity of the sea. If you can drag yourself away from the beach, you could pop by the turtle hatchery.

Bali & Lombok Outdoors

When to Go

The dry season, April to September, is best for long cycling trips, treks up volcanoes and diving (as there's less silt in the water). But the rest of the year is not that much rainier and people hike, bike and otherwise enjoy themselves. The local bromide for surfing is go east during months containing the letter 'r' and west at other times.

Best Surfing

Ulu Watu (p124) World famous.
Desert Point (p263) Legendary and elusive in Lombok.
Canggu (p88) All-round great.

Best Diving & Snorkelling

Pulau Menjangan (p254) Spectacular 30m wall.
Tulamben (p204) Sunken WWII freighter; snorkelling and diving from shore.
Gilis Islands (p293 & p292) All types of diving and snorkelling in beautiful waters.

Best Hiking

Munduk (p219) Lush, spice-scented, waterfall-riven landscape.
Ubud (p143) Beautiful walks from one hour to one day.
Tirta Gangga (p196) Rice terraces, gorgeous views, temples.

Bali offers so much more than a beach holiday with an overlay of amazing culture – it is an incredible place to get outside and play. Sure, you may have to get up off your beach towel, but the rewards are many.

In waters around the island you'll find world-class diving that ranges from reefs to shipwrecks to huge, rare sea life. When that water hits shore, it creates some of the world's best surfing. No matter what time of year you visit, you'll find legendary surf spots.

On land, hikes abound through the luxuriant green of the rice fields, deep into the river valleys and up the sides of the three main volcanoes. Or you can just whiz through the beautiful scenery on a bike.

Lombok doesn't have the same level of organisation but it has fine diving, surfing (often in remote locations) and hiking, including a famous volcano trek.

Surfing

Surfing kick-started Bali tourism in the 1960s. It's never looked back. Many Balinese have taken to surfing, and the grace of traditional dancing is said to influence their style.

Where to Surf: Bali

Swells come from the Indian Ocean, so the surf is on the southern side of the island and, strangely, on the northwest coast of

Nusa Lembongan, where the swell funnels into the strait between there and the Bali coast.

In the dry season (around April to September), the west coast has the best breaks, with the trade winds coming in from the southeast; this is also when Nusa Lembongan works best. In the wet season, surf the eastern side of the island, from Nusa Dua around to Padangbai. If there's a north wind – or no wind at all – there are also a couple of breaks on the south coast of the Bukit Peninsula.

Balangan

Go through the growing Pecatu Indah resort and follow the road around to the right past Dreamland to reach the Balangan warung. Balangan (p95) is a fast left over a shallow reef, unsurfable at low tide, but good at mid tide with anything over a 4ft swell; with an 8ft swell, this can be one of the classic waves.

Balian

There are a few peaks near the mouth of Sungai Balian (Balian River) in western Bali. The best break here is an enjoyable and consistent left-hander that works well at mid- to high tide if there's no wind. Lots of inns are springing up here.

Bingin

North of Padang Padang and accessible by road, this spot (p124) can get crowded. It's best at mid tide with a 6ft swell, when it manufactures short but perfect left-hand barrels. The cliffs backing the beach are lined with funky accommodation.

Canggu

North of Kerobokan, on the northern extremity of the bay, Canggu has a nice light beach and many surfers. An optimum size for Canggu is 5ft to 6ft. There's a good right-hander that you can really hook into, which works at high tide.

Impossibles

Just north of Padang Padang, this outside reef break (p124) has three shifting peaks with fast left-hand tube sections that can join up if the conditions are perfect.

Ketewel & Lebih

These two beaches (p175) are northeast of Sanur. They're both right-hand beach breaks, and are dodgy at low tide and close out over 6ft.

Kuta Area

For your first plunge into the warm Indian Ocean, try the breaks at Kuta's beach (p57); at full tide, go out near the life-saving club at the southern end of the beach road. At low tide, try the tubes around **Halfway Kuta**, probably the best place in Bali for beginners to practise. Start at the beach breaks if you are a bit rusty, but treat even these breaks with respect.

Further north, the breaks at **Legian Beach** can be pretty powerful, with lefts and rights on the sandbars off Jl Melasti and Jl Padma.

For more serious stuff, go to the reefs south of the beach breaks, about a kilometre out to sea. **Kuta Reef**, a vast stretch of coral, provides a variety of waves. You can paddle out in around 20 minutes, but the easiest way is by boat, for a fee. The main break is a classic left-hander, best at mid- to high tide, with a 5ft to 6ft swell, when it peels across the reef and has a beautiful inside tube section.

As elsewhere, when in doubt here, ask locals.

Medewi

Further along the south coast of western Bali is a softer left called Medewi. It's a point break that can give a long ride right into the river mouth. This wave has a big drop, which fills up then runs into a workable inside section. There's accommodation nearby.

Nusa Dua

During the wet season, you should surf on the east side of the island, where there are some very fine reef breaks. The reef of Nusa Dua has very consistent swells. The main break is 1km off the beach to the south of Nusa Dua – go past the golf course and look for the row of warung, and some boats to take you out. There are lefts and rights that work well on a small swell at low- to mid tide. Further north, in front of the Club Med, there is a fast, barrelling right reef break called **Sri Lanka**, which works best at mid tide.

Nusa Lembongan

In the Nusa Penida group, this island is separated from the southeast coast of Bali by Selat Badung (Badung Strait).

The strait is very deep and generates huge swells that break over the reefs off the northwest coast of Lembongan. **Shipwreck**, clearly visible from the beach, is the most popular break, a longish right that gets a good barrel at mid tide with a 5ft swell.

A bit to the south, **Lacerations** is a very fast, hollow right breaking over a very shallow reef – hence the name. Still further south is a smaller, more user-friendly left-hander called **Playground**. Remember that Lembongan is best with an easterly wind, so it's dry-season surfing. See p124 for more.

Padang Padang

Just Padang (p124) for short, this super-shallow, left-hand reef break is just north of Ulu Watu towards Kuta. Check this place carefully before venturing out. It's a very demanding break that only works over about 6ft from mid- to high tide. It's a great place to watch from the clifftop.

If you can't surf tubes, backhand or forehand, don't go out: Padang is a tube. After a ledgy take-off, you power along the bottom before pulling up into the barrel. Not a wave for the faint-hearted and definitely not a wave to surf when there's a crowd.

Sanur

Sanur Reef (p124) has a hollow wave with excellent barrels. It's fickle, and doesn't even start until you get a 6ft swell, but anything over 8ft will be world-class, and anything over 10ft will be brown-boardshorts material. There are other reefs further offshore and most of them are surfable.

Hyatt Reef, over 2km from shore, has a shifty right peak that can give a great ride at full tide. The classic right is off the Grand Bali Beach Hotel.

Serangan

The development at Pulau Serangan (Turtle Island) has caused huge disruption on the southern and eastern sides of the island; paradoxically, these changes to the shape of the shore have made the surf here much more consistent. In addition, the causeway has made the island more accessible, and several warung face the water, where waves break right and left in anything over a 3ft swell.

South Coast

The extreme south coast, around the end of the Bukit Peninsula (see p99), can be surfed any time of the year provided there is a northerly wind, or no wind at all – get there very early to avoid onshore winds. The peninsula is fringed with reefs, and big swells are produced, but access is a problem; the shoreline is all cliff. Try the steps down to the beach at Pura Mas Suka or charter a boat on a day with no wind and a small swell.

Ulu Watu

When Kuta Reef is 5ft to 6ft, Ulu Watu (p124), the most famous surfing break in Bali, will be 6ft to 8ft with bigger sets. It's way out on the southern extremity of the bay and consequently picks up more swell than Kuta.

Teluk Ulu Watu (Ulu Watu Bay) is a great set-up for surfers – local boys will wax your board, get drinks for you and carry the board down into the cave, which is the usual access to the waves. There are warung and there's accommodation for every budget.

Ulu Watu has about seven different breaks. The **Corner** is straight in front of you to the right. It's a fast-breaking, hollow left that holds about 6ft. The reef shelf under this break is extremely shallow, so try to avoid falling head first. At high tide, the **Peak** starts to work. This is good from 5ft to 8ft, with bigger waves occasionally right on the Peak itself. You can take off from this inside part or further down the line. It's a great wave.

Another left runs off the cliff that forms the southern flank of the bay. It breaks outside this in bigger swells, and once it's 7ft, a left-hander pitches right out in front of a temple on the southern extremity. Out behind the Peak, when it's big, is a bombora (submerged reef) appropriately called the **Bommie**. This is another big left-hander and it doesn't start operating until the swell is about 10ft. On a normal 5ft to 8ft day, there are also breaks south of the Peak.

Observe where other surfers paddle out and follow them. If you are in doubt, ask someone. It is better having some knowledge than none at all. Climb down into the cave and paddle out from there. When the swell is bigger you will be swept to your right. Don't panic – it is an easy matter to paddle around the white water from down along the cliff. Coming back in you have to aim for the cave. When the swell is bigger, come from the southern side of the cave as the current runs to the north.

Where to Surf: Lombok

Lombok has some good surfing and the dearth of tourists means that breaks are uncrowded.

Desert Point

Located in an extremely remote part of Lombok, Desert Point is a legendary if elusive wave that was voted the 'best wave in the world' by *Tracks* magazine. Only suitable for very experienced surfers, it's a fickle beast, in a region known for long, flat spells. On its day this left-handed tube can offer

---

RAFTING BALI'S RAPIDS

Rafting is popular, usually as a day trip from either south Bali or Ubud. Operators pick you up, take you to the put-in point, provide all the equipment and guides, and return you to your hotel at the end of the day. The best time is during the wet season (November to March), or just after; by the middle of the dry season (April to September), the best river rapids may be better described as 'dribbles'.

Some operators use the Sungai Ayung (Ayung River), near Ubud, where there are between 19 and 25 Class II to III rapids (ie potentially exciting but not perilous). The Sungai Telagawaja (Telagawaja River) near Muncan in east Bali is also popular. It's more rugged than the Ayung and the scenery is more wild.

Advertised prices run from US$55 to US$80; discounts are common. Consider the following:

Bali Adventure Tours (☏0361-721 480; www.baliadventuretours.com) Sungai Ayung; also has kayak trips.

Mega Rafting (☏0361-246 724; www.megarafting.net) Sungai Ayung.

Sobek (☏0361-287 059; www.balisobek.com) Trips on both the Sungai Ayung and Sungai Telagawaja.

a 300m ride, growing in size from take-off to close-out (which is over razor-sharp coral). Desert Point only really performs when there's a serious ground swell – May to September offers the best chance. Wear a helmet and boots at low tide. The nearest accommodation is about 12km away in Pelangan, so many surfers either camp next to the shoreline, or cruise in on surf safaris from Bali.

Gerupak

This giant bay 6km east of Kuta boasts four surf breaks, so there's always some wave action no matter what the weather or tide. **Bumbang** is extremely dependable: best on an incoming tide, this right-hander over a flat reef is good for all levels and can be surfed year-round. **Gili Golong** excels at mid- to high tide between October and April. **Don-Don** needs a bigger swell to break but can be great at any time of year. Finally **Kid's Point** (or Pelawangan) only breaks with big swells, but when it does it's barrels all the way. You need to hitch a boat ride (around 70,000Rp) to each wave.

Gili Trawangan

Much better known as a diving mecca, Trawangan also boasts a little-known surf spot off the island's southwestern tip, offshore from the Vila Ombak hotel. It's a quick right-hander that breaks in two sections, one offering a steeper profile, over rounded coral. It can be surfed all year long but is best at high tide.

Mawi

About 18km west of Kuta, the stunning bay of Mawi has a fine barrelling left with a late take-off and a final tube. It's best in the dry season from May to October with easterly offshore winds and a southwest swell. As there are sharp rocks and coral underwater, and the riptide is very fierce, take great care. Unfortunately, thefts have been reported from the beach, so leave nothing of any value behind and tip the locals to look after your vehicle.

Equipment: Pack or Rent?

A small board is usually adequate for the smaller breaks, but a few extra inches on your usual board length won't go astray. For the bigger waves – 8ft and upwards – you'll need a 'gun'. For a surfer of average height and build, a board around the 7ft mark is perfect.

If you try to bring more than two or three boards into the country, you may have problems with customs officials, who might think you're going to try and sell them.

There are surf shops in Kuta (p57) and elsewhere in south Bali. You can rent boards of varying quality (from 30,000Rp to 50,000Rp per day) and get supplies at most popular surf breaks. If you need repairs, ask around: there are lots of places that can help.

Other recommended equipment you might bring:

» Solid luggage for airline travel
» Board-strap for carrying
» Tough shoes for walking down rocky cliffs
» Your favourite wax if you're picky
» Wetsuit or reef booties
» Wetsuit vest or other protective cover from the sun, reefs and rocks
» Surfing helmet for rugged conditions (and riding a motorbike)

Surf Operators

Surf schools operate right off Kuta Beach (see p57). Two other surf operators:

Bali Stand Up Paddle (☎0361-284 260; www.bali-standuppaddle.org; Jl Cemara 72, Sanur) Gear sales and rental plus lessons. Also windsurfing and kite-boarding.

Surf Goddess (☎0858 997 0808; www.surfgoddessretreats.com) Surf holidays for women that include lessons and lodging in a posh guesthouse in Seminyak.

Diving & Snorkelling

With its warm water, extensive coral reefs and abundant marine life, Bali offers excellent diving and snorkelling adventures. Reliable dive schools and operators all around Bali's coast can train complete beginners or arrange challenging trips that will satisfy the most experienced divers. The Gilis provide equally excellent opportunities, while Lombok is close behind with good sites, especially around its northwest coast.

Snorkelling gear is available near all the most accessible spots, but if you're keen, it's definitely worthwhile bringing your own

BEST DIVING & SNORKELLING SITES

The following are Bali and Lombok's most spectacular diving and snorkelling locations, drawing people from near and far.

LOCATION	DETAILS	WHO SHOULD GO?	PAGE
Nusa Penida	Serious diving that includes schools of manta rays and 2.5m sunfish	Skilled divers will enjoy the challenges, but novices and snorkellers will be in over their heads	p129
Pulau Menjangan	Spectacular 30m wall off a small island, good for diving and snorkelling	Divers and snokellers of all skills and ages	p254
Tulamben	Sunken WWII freighter; snorkelling and diving from shore	Divers and snorkellers with good swimming skills	p204
Gilis	All types of diving and snorkelling in beautiful waters	Divers and snokellers of all skills and ages, although some sites may require advanced skills	p293 & p292
Southwest Lombok	Good reefs	Divers and snorkellers with good swimming skills	p263

and checking out some of the less-visited parts of the coasts. The Gilis now have a professional freediving school (p289) if you want to take snorkelling to the next level.

Equipment: Pack or Rent?

If you are not picky, you'll find all the equipment you need in Bali, the Gilis and Lombok (the quality, size and age of the equipment can vary). If you provide your own, you can usually get a discount on your dive. Some small, easy-to-carry things to bring from home include protective gloves, spare straps, silicone lubricant and extra globes/bulbs for your torch/flashlight. Other equipment to consider:

» **Mask, snorkel & fins** Many people bring these as they are not too big to pack and you can be sure they will fit you. Snorkelling gear rents from about 30,000Rp per day and is often shabby.

» **Tanks & weight belt** Usually included with the cost of a dive.

» **Thin, full-length wetsuit** For protection against stinging animals and possible coral abrasions. Bring your own if you are worried about size. If diving off Nusa Penida, be sure you'll be able to use a wetsuit thicker than 3mm, as up-swells bring up deep water that's 18°C.

» **Regulators & BCVs** Most dive shops have decent ones. (BCVs are also known as BCDs or Buoyancy Control Devices.)

Dive Operators

Major dive operators in tourist areas can arrange trips to the main dive sites all around the islands. Distances can be long though, so it's better to stay relatively close to your destination.

For a local trip, count on US$50 to US$90 per person for two dives, which includes all equipment. Note that it is becoming common to price in euros.

Wherever there is decent local diving on Bali and Lombok there are dive shops. Usually you can count on some reefs in fair condition reachable by boat. Recommended sites with shops include the following:

» Amed (p199)

» Candidasa (p191)

» Lovina (p231)

» Nusa Lembongan (p124)

» Padangbai (p185)

» Pemuteran (p238)

» Sanur (p124)

» Gili Air (p302)

» Gili Meno (p299)

Choosing a Dive Operator

In general diving in Bali and Lombok is safe, with a good standard of staff training and equipment maintenance. Here are a few tips to help you select a well set up and safety-conscious dive shop.

» Are its staff fully trained and qualified? Ask to see certificates or certification cards – no reputable shop will be offended by this request. Guides must reach 'full instructor' level to teach. To guide certified divers on a reef dive, guides must hold at least 'rescue diver' or preferably 'dive master' qualifications.

» Do they have safety equipment on the boat? At a minimum, a dive boat should carry oxygen and a first-aid kit. A radio or mobile phone is also important.

» Is the boat's equipment OK and its air clean? This is often the hardest thing for a new diver to judge. A few guidelines:

» Smell the air: open a tank valve a small way and breathe in. Smelling dry or slightly rubbery air is OK. If it smells of oil or car exhaust, that tells you the operator doesn't filter the air correctly.

» When the equipment is put together, are there any big air leaks? All dive centres get some small leaks at some time, however, if you get a *big* hiss of air coming out of any piece of equipment, ask to have it replaced.

» Is it conservation-oriented? Good dive shops explain that you should not touch corals or take shells from the reef, as well as work with local fishers to ensure that certain areas are protected. Some even clean beaches.

Responsible Diving

Please bear in mind the following tips when diving and help preserve the ecology and beauty of reefs:

» Never use anchors on the reef, and take care not to run boats aground on coral.

» Avoid touching or standing on living marine organisms or dragging equipment across the reef.

» Be careful with your fins. Even without contact, the surge from fin strokes near the reef can damage delicate organisms. Don't kick up clouds of sand, which can smother organisms.

» Practise and maintain proper buoyancy control. Major damage can occur from reef collisions.

» Do not collect or buy corals or shells or loot marine archaeological sites (mainly shipwrecks).

» Ensure that you take home all your rubbish and any other litter you may find as well. Plastics are a serious threat to marine life.

» Do not feed the fish.

» Minimise your involvement with marine animals. *Never* ride on the backs of turtles.

Hiking & Trekking

You could wander Bali and Lombok for a year and still not see all the islands have to offer, but their small size means that you can nibble off a bit at a time, especially as day hikes and treks are easily arranged. Guides can help you surmount volcanoes, while tour companies will take you to remote regions and emerald-green valleys of rice terraces.

LEARN TO DIVE

If you're not a qualified diver and you want to try some scuba diving in Bali, you have several options, including packages that include lessons and cheap accommodation in a pretty place.

COURSE	DETAILS	COST
Introductory/orientation	Perfect for novices to see if diving is for them	US$60-100
Basic certification	Three- or four- day limited courses for the basics; popular at resorts	US$300
Open-water certification	The international PADI standard, recognised everywhere	US$300-400

HIKING HIGHLIGHTS

One of Bali's great joys is hiking. You can have good experiences across the island, often starting right outside your hotel. Hikes can last from an hour to a day.

Bali

LOCATION	DETAILS	PAGE
Danau Buyan & Danau Tamblingan	Natural mountain lakes, few people	(p217)
Gunung Agung	Sunrises and isolated temples	(p182)
Gunung Batukau	Misty climbs amid the clouds, with few people	(p220)
Gunung Batur	Hassles but otherworldly scenery	(p208)
Munduk	Lush, spice-scented waterfall-riven landscape	(p219)
Sidemen Road area	Rice terraces, lush hills and lonely temples; comfy lodging for walkers	(p180)
Taman Nasional Bali Barat	Remote, wild scenery, wildlife	(p252)
Tirta Gangga	Rice terraces, gorgeous views, remote mountain temples	(p196)
Ubud	Beautiful walks from one hour to one day; rice fields and terraces, river-valley jungles and ancient monuments	(p143)

Lombok

Like the island itself, Lombok has walks and hikes that are often remote, challenging or both.

LOCATION	DETAILS	PAGE
Air Terjun Sindang Gila	One of many waterfalls	(p271)
Gilis	Beach-bum circumnavigations	(p286)
Gunung Rinjani	Superb for trekking; climb the 3726m summit then drop down into a crater with a sacred lake and hot springs	(p273)
Sembalun Valley	Garlic-scented hikes on the slopes of Rinjani	(p273)

In terms of what to pack, you'll need good boots for mountain treks and solid hiking sandals for walks.

Where to Hike: Bali

Bali is very walkable. No matter where you're staying, ask for recommendations and set off for discoveries and adventures. Even from busy Kuta or Seminyak, you can just head to the beach, turn right and walk north as far as you wish alongside the amazing surf while civilisation seems to evaporate (see p87).

Bali does not offer remote wilderness treks. For the most part, you'll make day trips from the closest village, often leaving before dawn to avoid the clouds and mist that usually blanket the peaks by mid-morning. Most treks don't require camping gear.

Where to Hike: Lombok

Gunung Rinjani draws trekkers from around the world. Expert advice is crucial on the mountain as people die on its slopes every year. You can organise explorations of Gunung Rinjani at Sembalun Valley (p273), Senaru (p271) and Senggigi (p265).

Hiking Tour Operators

Guides and agencies are listed in the relevant destination chapters. In addition to these, Bali-wide agencies include the following:

Bali Culture Tours (☎0813 3827 2777; mur jana70@hotmail.com) Offers highly customisable programs around Ubud and east Bali, including the slopes of Gunung Agung and artists' homes.

Bali Nature Walk (☎0817 973 5914; dade putra@hotmail.com) Walks in isolated areas in the Ubud region. Routes are customisable depending on your desires.

Bali Sunrise Trekking & Tours (☎0818 552 669; www.balisunrisetours.com) Leads treks throughout the central mountains.

Safety Guidelines for Trekking

Before embarking on a trekking trip, consider the following points to ensure a safe and enjoyable experience:

» Pay any fees and carry any permits required by local authorities; often these fees will be rolled into the guide's fee, meaning that it's all negotiable.

» Be sure you are healthy and feel comfortable walking for a sustained period.

» Obtain reliable information about environmental conditions along your intended route, eg the weather can get quite wet and cold in the upper reaches of the volcanoes.

» Confirm with your guide that you will only go on walks/treks within your realm of experience.

» Carry the proper equipment. Depending on the trek and time of year this can mean rain gear or extra water. Carry a torch (flashlight); don't assume the guide will have one.

Cycling

Cyclists are discovering Bali in a big way. The back roads of the island more than make up for the traffic-clogged streets of the south. The main advantage of touring Bali by bike is the quality of the experience – you can be totally immersed in the environment, hearing the wind rustling in the rice paddies or the sound of a gamelan practising, catching the scent of flowers.

Lombok is also good for touring by bicycle. In the populated areas the roads are flat, and the traffic across the island is less chaotic than on Bali.

Some people are put off cycling by the tropical heat, but when you're riding on level ground or downhill, the breeze really moderates the heat.

CYCLING SUGGESTIONS

You can't get too lost on an island as small as Bali. The following are areas good for exploring on two wheels.

LOCATION	DETAILS
Bukit Peninsula	Explore cliffs, coves and beaches along the west and south coasts; beach promenade at Nusa Dua; avoid the area by the airport
Central mountains	Ambitious; explore Danau Bratan, Danau Buyan and Danau Tamblingan; downhill to the north coast via Munduk and to the south via small roads from Candikuning
East Bali	Coast road lined with beaches; north of the coast is uncrowded with serene rice terraces; Sidemen Roadd has lodges good for cyclists
North Bali	Lovina is a good base for day trips to remote waterfalls and temples; the northeast coast has resorts popular with cyclists circumnavigating Bali
Nusa Lembongan	Small; easily done in half a day; nice remote beaches
Nusa Penida	For serious cyclists who bring bikes; nearly traffic-free, with remote vistas of the sea, sheer cliffs, white beaches and lush jungle
Ubud	Many tour companies are based here; narrow mountain roads lead to ancient monuments and jaw-dropping rice-terrace views
West Bali	Rice fields and dense jungle rides in and around Tabanan, Kerambitan and Bajera; further west, small roads off the main road lead to mountain streams, deserted beaches and hidden temples

Where to Cycle: Bali

It's really easier to tell you where *not* to ride in Bali. Denpasar south through Sanur in the east, and Kerobokan to Kuta in the west suffer from lots of traffic and narrow roads.

Where to Cycle: Lombok

East of Mataram are several attractions that would make a good day trip: south to Banyumulek via Gunung Pengsong and then back to Mataram, for example. Some coastal roads have hills and curves like a roller coaster. Try going north from Senggigi to Pemenang along a spectacular, recently improved, paved road, and then (if you feel energetic) return via the steep climb over the Pusuk Pass.

The Gilis are good for riding as well, even if you have to do laps to build up any mileage.

Equipment: Pack or Rent?

Serious cyclists will want to pack personal gear they consider essential. For top-end gear, there's **Planet Bike Bali** (☎0361-746 2858; Jl Gunung Agung 148, Denpasar). It stocks Giant, Trek, Shimano and other brands. Otherwise casual riders can rent bikes and helmets. For details on the practicalities of riding bikes on the islands, including where to rent and get repairs, see p383.

Cycling Tour Operators

Popular tours start high up in the central mountains at places such as Kintamani or Bedugul. The tour company takes you to the top and then you ride down relatively quiet mountain roads soaking up the lush scenery, village culture and tropical scents. The cost including bicycle, gear and lunch is US$35 to US$70. Transport to/from south Bali and Ubud hotels is usually included.

The following are companies to consider:

Archipelago Adventure (☎0361-844 4624; www.archipelago-adventure.com) Offers a range of tours, including ones on Java. In Bali, there are rides around Jatiluwih and Danau Buyan, and mountain biking on trails from Kintamani.

Bali Bike-Baik Tours (☎0361-978 052, 0813 3867 3852; www.balibike.com) Tours run downhill from Kintamani; the emphasis is on cultural immersion and there are frequent stops in tiny villages and at rice farms.

Bali Eco & Educational Cycling Tours (☎0361-975 557; www.baliecocycling.com) Tours start at Kintamani and take small roads through lush scenery south to Ubud.

Banyan Tree Cycling (☎0361-805 1620, 0813 3879 8516; www.banyantree.wikispaces.com) Day-long tours of remote villages in and around Ubud.

C.Bali (☎0813 5320 0251; www.c-bali.com) Unique bike tours around Danau Batur.

Celebrity Cycling Tour (☎0361-912 7686; www.celebritycyclingtour.com) Downhill tours from Penelokan take small roads south through lush scenery.

Lombok Biking Tour (☎0370-660 5792) Guided rides along the Pusuk Pass and in the Lingsar region.

Travel with Children

Children's Highlights

Beaches
Surf schools at Kuta Beach, family-friendly Geger Beach, flying kites at Sanur Beach – kids of all ages will get their kicks.

Water
Play in the ocean at Nusa Lembongan, or dive or snorkel at Pulau Menjangan or in the Gilis. For something different, walk across rice fields – who could resist the promise of muddy water filled with ducks, frogs and other fun critters?

Frolicking
Kids can make like monkeys at Bali Treetop Adventure Park, hit the aquatic playground of Waterbom Park, splash about on a river rafting trip or pedal along on a bike tour.

Animals
It's a jungle out there: Ubud's Monkey Forest, Bali Bird Park, Rimba Reptile Park, Elephant Safari Park and the Bali Safari & Marine Park.

Cool Old Things
Kids will love the Indiana Jones–like pools at Tirta Empul, the ancient water palace and park at Tirta Gangga, and Pura Luhur Ulu Watu, a beautiful temple with monkeys.

Travelling anywhere with *anak-anak* requires energy and organisation, but in Bali these problems are lessened by the Balinese affection for children. They believe that children come straight from God, and the younger they are, the closer they are to God. To the Balinese, children are considered part of the community, and everyone, not just the parents, has a responsibility towards them. If a child cries, the Balinese get most upset and insist on finding a parent and handing the child over with a reproachful look. Sometimes they despair of uncaring Western parents, and the child will be whisked off to a place where it can be cuddled, cosseted and fed. In tourist areas this is less likely, but it's still common in traditional environments. A toddler may even get too much attention!

Bali & Lombok for Kids

Children are a social asset when you travel in Bali, and people will display great interest in any Western child they meet. You will have to learn your child's age and sex in Bahasa Indonesia – *bulau* (month), *tahun* (year), *laki-laki* (boy) and *perempuan* (girl). You should also make polite inquiries about the other person's children, present or absent.

Lombok is generally quieter than Bali and the traffic is less dangerous. People are fond of kids, but less demonstrative about them than the Balinese. The main difference on

Lombok is that services for children are much less developed.

The obvious drawcards for kids are the loads of outdoor adventures available (see p43). But there are also many cultural treats that kids will love.

Dance – A guaranteed snooze right? Wrong. Check out an evening Barong dance at the Ubud Palace or Pura Dalem Ubud, two venues that look like sets from *Tomb Raider* right down to the flaming torches. Sure, the Legong might be tough going for fidgety types, but the Barong has monkeys, monsters, a witch and more. Plus there will be lots of local kids there to befriend.

Markets – If young explorers are going to temples, they will need sarongs. Give them 100,000Rp at a traditional market and let 'em loose. Vendors will be truly charmed as the kids try to assemble the most colourful combo (and nothing is too loud for a Balinese temple).

Temples – Pick the fun ones. Goa Gajah (Elephant Cave; p164) has a deep cavern where hermits lived and you enter through the mouth of a monster. Pura Luhur Batukau (p221) is in dense jungle with a cool lake and a rushing stream.

Planning

The critical decision is deciding where to base yourselves for the holiday.

Where to Stay

A hotel with a swimming pool, air-con and a beachfront location is fun for kids and very convenient, and still provides a good break for parents. Fortunately there are plenty of choices.

Most hotels and guesthouses, at whatever price level, have a 'family plan', which means that children up to about 12 years old can share a room with their parents free of charge. The catch is that hotels may charge for extra beds, although many offer family rooms. It's always worth asking about family rooms or rooms with kitchen facilities when booking.

Large international resorts often offer special programs or supervised activities for kids; where this isn't the case, most hotels can arrange a babysitter.

Hotel staff are usually very willing to help and improvise, so always ask if you need something for your children.

What to Pack

Huge supermarkets and stores in south Bali such as Carrefour (p71) stock most everything you'd find at similar stores at home, including many Western foods; nappies, Western baby food, packaged UHT milk, infant formula and other supplies are easily purchased. Items to bring are personal things your child would miss or favourite books and toys. Suggestions by age:

Babies & Toddlers

» A front or back sling or other baby carrier: Bali's barely walkable streets and paths are not suited to prams and pushchairs.

» A portable changing mat, hand-wash gel et al (baby changing facilities are a rarity).

» Kids' car seats: cars, whether rented or chartered with a driver, are unlikely to come with these.

STAYING SAFE

The main danger to kids – and adults for that matter – is traffic and bad pavement and footpaths in busy areas. If your children can't look after themselves in the water, they must be supervised at all times.

The sorts of facilities, safeguards and services that Western parents regard as basic may not be present. Not many restaurants provide highchairs, many places with great views have nothing to stop your kids falling over the edge, and shops often have breakable things at kiddie height. There are international medical clinics in south Bali (see p392), but medical care elsewhere is simpler. Given the ongoing rabies crisis in Bali, be sure to keep children away from stray dogs.

When it comes to food the same rules apply as for adults – kids should drink only clean water (bottled drinking water is available everywhere) and eat only well-cooked food, or fruit that you have peeled yourself. If you're travelling with a young baby, it's much easier to avoid gastric problems if you're breastfeeding; if bottle feeding, it would pay to bring a portable sterilising unit with you.

Although Bali and Lombok are generally quite kid-friendly, some areas are more accommodating than others.

LOCATION	PROS	CONS
Sanur	Beachside resorts, reef-protected beach with gentle waves, close to many kid-friendly activities, modest traffic	Can be dull, especially for teens and adults
Nusa Dua	Huge beachside resorts, reef-protected beach with gentle waves, modest traffic, quiet	Can be dull for teens and adults, insulated from the rest of Bali
Tanjung Benoa	Beachside resorts, reef-protected beach with gentle waves, close to many kid-friendly activities	Far from the rest of Bali, boring for teens and adults
Lovina	Modest, quiet hotels near the beach, limited traffic, reef-protected beach with gentle waves	Far from the rest of Bali, boring for teens and adults, limited diversions
Kuta	Teens will love it, kids will be able to buy all manner of cheap souvenirs and fake tattoos and get their hair braided, surf lessons	Teens will love it too much, busy road between beach and hotels, crowded, crazy, strong surf
Legian	Much the same as Kuta with beachfront resorts on the sand	Much the same as Kuta without the busy beach road (but there's traffic elsewhere), strong surf
Seminyak	Appealing mix for all ages, large hotels on beach	Traffic, strong surf
Ubud	Quiet in parts, many things to see and do, walks, markets and shops	No beach, evenings may require greater creativity to keep kids amused, adults like it
Gili Trawangan	Small island so kids won't get lost, gentle surf, many tourist amenities and activities such as snorkelling	Can feel cramped and frenetic, teens may discover mushrooms
Senggigi	Modest, quiet hotels on the beach, limited traffic, reef-protected beach with gentle waves	Somewhat isolated, boring for teens and adults, Lombok offers limited kid-specific diversions

Six to 12 Years

» Binoculars for young explorers to zoom in on wildlife, rice terraces, temples, dancers and so on.

» A flip camera to inject newfound fun into 'boring' grown-up sights and walks.

» Activity books, sketchpad and pens, travel journal and kid-sized day pack.

Teens

» Wi-fi device or mobile (check rates; see p374) so young travellers can tell those at home about *everything* they're missing.

» Cool shades and other gear to effect the right look from the minute the plane lands.

Eating with Kids

Eating out as a family is one of the joys of visiting Bali and Lombok. Highchairs are rare, but kids are treated like deities by doting staff who will clamour to grab yours (especially young babies) while mum and dad enjoy some quiet time together. Try not to be too uptight about strangers getting up close and personal with your little ones. Indonesians just cannot help themselves, so sit back, relax and enjoy the opportunity!

Bali especially is so relaxed that kids can just be kids. There are plenty of top-end eateries in Seminyak and elsewhere where kids romp nearby while their parents enjoy a fine meal.

What to Eat

For older babies, bananas, eggs, peelable fruit and *bubur* (rice cooked to a mush in chicken stock) are all generally available.

Obviously, if your children don't like spicy food, show caution in offering them the local cuisine. Many warung will serve food without sauces upon request, such as plain white rice, fried tempeh or tofu, chicken, boiled vegetables and boiled egg.

Otherwise, kid-pleasers like burgers, chicken fingers, pizza and pasta are widespread. Some restaurants have kids' menus but mostly you'll find that staff are happy to try and please the little tykes. And if junior simply refuses to believe that gado gado is the best dish ever, major fast-food chains are found across south Bali.

Regions at a Glance

Kuta and Seminyak are the main towns in the most touristed part of Bali, the segment of the south that runs along the magnificent stretch of sand from Echo Beach almost to the airport. The rest of south Bali defies easy categorisation. The Bukit Peninsula at the bottom combines surf breaks with vast resorts.

Ubud occupies the heart of Bali in many respects and shares some of the island's most beautiful rice fields and ancient monuments with east Bali. The latter has no major centre but does have popular areas such as Padangbai, the Amed Coast and Tulamben.

The middle of Bali is dominated by the dramatic volcanoes of the central mountains. North and west Bali are thinly populated but have fine diving and surfing.

Lombok is largely mountainous, volcanic and rural, while the Gilis are tiny coral islands fringed with white sand.

Kuta & Seminyak

Beaches ✓✓
Nightlife ✓✓✓
Shopping ✓✓

Beaches
Kuta's famous sweep of sand extends for 12km past Legian, Seminyak, Kerobokan and Canggu before finally ending up on the rocks near Echo Beach. It's got beautiful surf the entire length. At Kuta there are beach bars (chairs in the sand) and vendors; these dwindle as you go north-west and eventually you can find an empty stretch of beach all for yourself.

Nightlife
Restaurants and cafes in Seminyak and Kerobokan are some of the best on Bali. Some have gorgeous sunset views, while the bars and clubs have a vaguely sophisticated air. Nightlife becomes manic in Legian and Kuta, where famous clubs draw crowds and DJs from across the globe.

Shopping
Shopping in Seminyak is reason enough to visit Bali; the choice is extraordinary.

p54

South Bali & the Islands

Beaches ✓✓✓
Surfing ✓✓✓
Diving ✓✓

Beaches
Beaches can be found right around south Bali: little coves of white sand like Balangan are idyllic, while those in Nusa Dua, Tanjung Benoa and Sanur are family friendly. The beaches out on Nusa Lembongan offer a funky escape from your Bali holiday.

Surfing
You can't say enough about the surf breaks on the west coast of the Bukit Peninsula; the multitude of breaks around Ulu Watu are world-renowned. Surfer guesthouses let you stay near the action. Nusa Lembongan has some good breaks as well.

Diving
The best diving is out around the islands. Nusa Lembongan has coral and mangroves that attract schools of small fish; Nusa Penida has challenging conditions and deepwater cliffs that bring rays and large pelagics.

p90

Ubud & Around

Culture ✓✓✓
Indulgence ✓✓
Walks ✓✓✓

Culture
Ubud is the heart of Balinese culture. Each night there are at least a dozen performances of traditional Balinese dance, music, puppets and more. Troupes with international reps are found here as are all manner of artists, including superb woodcarvers who make the masks for the shows.

Indulgence
Spas, traditional medicine sessions and yoga classes are just some of the ways you can indulge yourself in Ubud. Practitioners from around the world join local healers to offer services for your mind and body.

Walks
Rice fields surround Ubud and they are some of Bali's most picturesque. You can walk for an hour or an entire day, enjoying river valleys, small villages and enveloping natural beauty.

p132

East Bali

Beaches ✓
History ✓
Hikes ✓✓

Beaches
Beaches are found along much of the east Bali coast. The coast road northeast of Sanur has wave-tossed beaches of dark volcanic sand, many with important temples. Pasir Putih always charms, while the small beach coves of Amed are lined with fishing boats.

History
Taman Kertha Gosa has the moving remains of a palace lost when the royalty committed ritual suicide rather than surrender to the Dutch in 1908. At Tirta Gangga, the atmospheric remains of a raja's water palace always charm.

Hikes
Some of Bali's most alluring rice fields and landscapes are found in the east. You're spoiled for choice along Sidemen Road, or try Tirta Gangga, which excels at remote temple walks. Gunung Agung awaits the ambitious.

p172

Central Mountains

Hikes ✓✓
Culture ✓✓
Solitude ✓✓

Hikes
The centre of the island is all about hiking. The alien landscape of Gunung Batur, an active volcano, thrills many who arise before dawn for sunrise views. In and around Munduk there are misty walks and hikes through spice plantations, coffee orchards and jungle to waterfalls.

Culture
Pura Luhur Batukau never fails to touch the spirit of those who find this important and very old temple on the slopes of Gunung Batukau. Not far away, the perfectly realised rice fields of Jatiluwih embody the deep significance rice has to the Balinese psyche.

Solitude
Cooler than the rest of Bali, the mountains feel lonely. A solitary visit to Pura Luhur Batukau can be followed by retreats to nearby ecolodges or other lodges along the Antosari Road.

p207

North Bali

Resorts ✓✓
Beaches ✓
Diving ✓

Resorts
The crescent of beach hotels at Pemuteran is the real star of north Bali. Beautifully built and with comparatively few rooms, the hotels form a fine human-scaled resort area, and they're close to Pulau Menjangan, west Bali's star. Lovina is good for those looking for a low-cost, quiet getaway.

Beaches
There's a lot of tan and grey sand along Bali's north coast. Much of the coast is protected by reefs and the waves are small; you can stretch out and not worry about the tides.

Diving
The reefs here are in fair shape, but the real draw is the night diving around Lovina. Dive shops run well-managed trips, on which you're likely to see huge amounts of marine life not visible by day.

p224

West Bali

Diving ✓✓✓
Surfing ✓✓
Beaches ✓

Diving
Pulau Menjangan lives up to its many superlatives. A 30m coral wall close to shore delights both divers and snorkellers with a cast of fish and creatures that varies from sardines to whales. The island is part of a national park and is undeveloped; a small temple provides a diversion from the under-sea attractions.

Surfing
Breaks at Balian Beach and Medewi have a following, and at the latter a small surfers' community has sprung up with idiosyncratic guesthouses and a stylish hotel. Other breaks along this remote and wild coast await names and surfers.

Beaches
Balian Beach is the main strand in the west and makes a good place to hang even if you're not surfing. Dig the hep-cat scene, man.

p241

Lombok

Hiking ✓✓
Coastline ✓✓✓
Tropical Chic ✓✓

Hiking
A majestic volcano of mighty dimensions, Gunung Rinjani's very presence overshadows all northern Lombok. Hiking trails sneak up Rinjani's astonishing caldera, where you'll find a shimmering crater lake (a pilgrimage site), hot springs and a smoking minicone to wonder at.

Coastline
Lombok's southern coastline is nature in the raw. There's absolutely nothing genteel about the magnificent shoreline, which is pounded by oceanic waves that make it a surfers' mecca. Here and there the coast relents a little, and sheltered bays such as Mawun allow exceptional swimming in azure waters.

Tropical Chic
Lombok excels at the tropical-chic thing. For total immersion, the Sire area offers uberluxury. Delve into Senggigi's hip hotels and sleek restaurants. Or get a tantalising taster at one of Lombok's magnificent spas.

p256

Gili Islands

Diving ✓✓✓
Adventure ✓✓
Chilling ✓✓✓

Diving
Forming one of Indonesia's most species-rich environments, the Gilis' coral reefs teem with fascinating sea life. The islands are perfect for divers and snorkellers, and you're almost guaranteed to see turtles.

Adventure
They may be miniscule, but the Gilis are loaded with intriguing possibilities. Try kayaking, ride a horse, learn to freedive or surf, energise yourself at a yoga or meditation class or try a tech dive – the islands have it all.

Chilling
We've all dreamt of finding the ultimate beach: a vision of palms trees, blinding white sands and a turquoise sea, perhaps with a seashell or two and a bamboo shack selling cool drinks and fresh fish. Find yours here.

p286

Look out for these icons:

 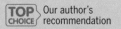 Our author's recommendation

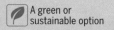 A green or sustainable option

 No payment required

On the Road

Kuta & Seminyak

Best Places to Eat

» Biku (p85)

» Sardine (p85)

» Indo-National (p67)

» Made's Warung II (p78)

Best Places to Stay

» Hotel Tugu Bali (p89)

» Oberoi (p77)

» Un's Hotel (p61)

» Villa Karisa (p75)

Why Go?

Complaining about crowds in Seminyak, an expat said to his friend: 'Maybe it's time to go'. The sceptical friend queried: 'Where would you go?' After a moment the expat shrugged his shoulders and said: 'Nowhere'.

Crowded and frenetic, the swath of south Bali hugging the amazing wide ribbon of beach that begins in Kuta is the place most travellers begin and end their visit to the island. Not a bad choice.

In Seminyak and Kerobokan there is a bounty of restaurants, cafes, designer boutiques, spas and the like that rivals anywhere in the world, while Kuta and Legian are still the choice for rollicking surfer get-downs and carefree family holidays.

Renowned shopping, all-night clubs, fabulous dining, cheap beer, sunsets that dazzle and relentless hustle and bustle are all part of the experience. But just when you wonder what any of this has to do with Bali – the island supposedly all about spirituality and serenity – a religious procession appears and shuts everything down. And then you know the answer.

When to Go

Bali's ever-increasing popularity means that the best time to visit Kuta, Seminyak and their neighbours is outside of the high season, which is July, August and the weeks around Christmas and New Year. Holidays elsewhere mean that visitor numbers spike and it can require actual effort to organise tables in the best restaurants, navigate trendy shops and get a room with a view. Many prefer April to June and September when the weather is driest and slightly cooler, and the crowds manageable.

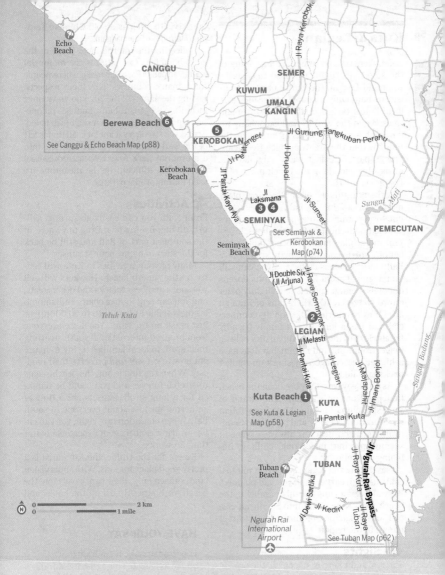

Kuta & Seminyak Highlights

1 Losing your day on **Kuta Beach** (p56)

2 Losing your night in **Legian** (p69)

3 Losing your resolve shopping in **Seminyak** (p81)

4 Losing your tension at a spa in **Seminyak** (p75)

5 Losing your waistline at a fabulous restaurant in **Kerobokan** (p85)

6 Losing the crowds at **Berewa Beach** (p88), north of Seminyak

7 Losing your inhibitions wandering down the first *gang* (alley) you see and discovering a rice field, a little cafe, a new friend.

Kuta & Legian

☑ 0361

Loud, frenetic and brash are just some of the adjectives commonly used to describe Kuta and Legian, the centre of mass tourism in Bali. Only a couple of decades ago, local hotels tacked their signs up to palm trees. Amid the wall-to-wall cacophony today, such an image seems as foreign as the thought that the area was once rice fields. Worse, parts are just plain ugly, like the unsightly strip along the beach north of Jl Poppies Gang II.

Although this is often the first place many visitors hit in Bali, the region is not for everyone. Kuta has narrow lanes jammed with cheap cafes, surf shops, incessant motorbikes and an uncountable number of T-shirt vendors. Its main streets have Bali's most raucous clubs, and you can still find a simple room for US$15 in its dozens of hotels. Legian appeals to a slightly older crowd (wags say it's where fans of Kuta go after they're married). It is equally commercial and has a long row of family-friendly hotels close to the beach. Tuban differs little in feel from Kuta and Legian, but does have a higher percentage of visitors on budget package holidays.

As for the waves, they break on the beach that put Kuta on the map. The strand of sand stretching for kilometres from Tuban north to Kuta, Legian and beyond to Seminyak and Echo Beach is always a scene of surfing, playing, massaging, chilling, imbibing and more.

Navigating the region will drive you to a cold one even earlier than you had planned. Busy Jl Legian runs roughly parallel to the beach from Kuta north into Seminyak. See p64 for information on the changing street names in the region.

◎ Sights

The real sight here is, of course, the **beach**. You can immerse yourself in local life without even getting wet. A pleasant **walkway** runs south from where Jl Pantai Kuta meets the beach. Stretching almost to the airport, it has fine views of the ocean and the efforts to preserve some of Tuban's nearly vanished beach.

Wanderers, browsers and gawkers will find much to fascinate, delight and irritate amid the streets, alleys and constant hubbub. You can even discover the odd non-touristy site, such as an old **Chinese Temple** (Map p58; Jl Blambangan).

Reflecting the international scope of the 2002 bombings (see p318) is the **memorial wall** (Map p58; Jl Raya Seminyak), where people from many countries pay their respects. Listing the names of the 202 known victims, including 88 Australians and 35 Indonesians, it is starting to look just a touch faded. Across the street, a vacant lot is all that is left of the **Sari Club**. Plans to turn the site into a **memorial park** (www.balipeacepark.com.au) are proving difficult; in the meantime it's used for motorbike parking.

⊁ Activities

From Kuta you can easily go surfing, sailing, diving, fishing or rafting anywhere in the southern part of Bali and still be back for the start of happy hour at sunset.

Many of your activities in Kuta will centre on the superb beach. Hawkers will sell you sodas and beer, snacks and other treats, and you can rent lounge chairs and umbrellas (negotiable at 10,000Rp to 20,000Rp) or just crash on the sand. You'll see everyone from bronzed international youth strutting their stuff, to local families trying to figure out how to get wet *and* preserve their modesty. When the tide is out, the beach seems to stretch forever and you could be tempted for a long stroll. Sunsets are a time of gathering for just about everyone in south Bali. When conditions are right, you can enjoy an iridescent magenta spectacle better than fireworks.

Except for the traffic, the Kuta area is a pretty good place for kids. With supervision (and sunscreen!), they can cavort on the beach for hours. Almost all the hotels and

---

HAVE YOUR SAY

Found a fantastic restaurant that you're longing to share with the world? Disagree with our recommendations? Or just want to talk about your most recent trip?

Whatever your reason, head to lonelyplanet.com, where you can post a review, ask or answer a question on the Thorntree forum, comment on a blog, or share your photos and tips on Groups. Or you can simply spend time chatting with like-minded travellers. So go on, have your say.

resorts above the surfer-dude category have pools, and the better ones offer kids' programs. **Amazone** (Map p62; Discovery Shopping Mall, Jl Kartika Plaza, Tuban; ⊙10am-10pm) has hundreds of screeching arcade games on the top floor of the mall.

The very popular **Double Six Beach**, at the north end of Legian, is alive with pickup games of football and volleyball all day long. It's a fine place to meet locals.

Surfing

The beach break called **Halfway Kuta**, offshore near the Hotel Istana Rama, is popular with novices. More challenging breaks can be found on the shifting sandbars off Legian, around the end of Jl Padma, and at Kuta Reef, 1km out to sea off Tuban Beach (see p35 for details).

Shops large and small sell big-brand surf gear and boards. Stalls on the side streets hire out surfboards (for a negotiable 30,000Rp per day) and boogie boards, repair dings and sell new and used boards. Some can also arrange transport to nearby surfing spots. Used boards in good shape average US$200. Check out free surfing magazines such as *Magic Wave*.

Surf schools and shops include the following:

Naruki Surf Shop SURF SHOP
(Map p58; ☑765 772; Jl Lebak Bene; ⊙10am-7pm) One of dozens of surf shops lining the gang of Kuta. The effervescent 'Mr Naruki' will rent you a board, fix your ding, offer advice or give you lessons.

Pro Surf School SURF SCHOOL
(Map p58; ☑744 1466; www.prosurfschool.com; Jl Pantai Kuta; lessons from US$45; ⊙classes from 9am) Right across from Kuta Beach. Facilities include a swimming pool and semiprivate lesson areas where you can first stroke your board.

Rip Curl School of Surf SURF SCHOOL
(Map p58; ☑735 858; www.ripcurlschoolofsurf .com; Jl Arjuna; lessons from US$60; ⊙classes from 8am) Run by the high-profile, local surf-wear conglomerate, the school offers classes for beginners and experts alike. Located right on ever-popular Double Six Beach (transport provided). It also offers lessons in kitesurfing and wakeboarding.

Waterbom Park

This popular **water park** (Map p62; ☑755 676; www.waterbom.com; Jl Kartika Plaza, Tuban; adult/child US$23/13; ⊙9am-6pm), south of

The beach in front of the Bali Mandira Hotel is far from any road, is backed by shady trees, is never crowded and has somnolent vendors, and isn't crossed by a stream with dubious water. You'll have a huge swath of sand to yourself and you'll hear something rarely heard further south in Kuta: the surf.

Kuta, is set on 3.5 hectares of landscaped tropical gardens and has assorted water slides, swimming pools, play areas, a supervised park for children under five years old, and a 'superbowl', where you literally go down the drain. The newest sensation is the **Climax**, where you slide through a 360-degree loop and then shoot through a narrow tube.

Massages & Spas

Spas have proliferated, especially in hotels, and offers are numerous. Check out a few before choosing.

Putri Bali SPA
(Map p58; ☑755 987; Wisata Beach Inn, Jl Padma Utara; massages from 75,000Rp; ⊙10am-9pm) The cream bath here has set the hearts of many spa-o-philes a-flutter with delight. Located off the main street, it's a lovely spa with very competitive prices.

Miracle SPA
(Map p58; ☑769 019; www.miracle-clinic.com; Istana Kuta Galeria, Blok PM 1/20; massages from 220,000Rp; ⊙8.30am-8pm) Who can resist the name? You won't feel a bit of your acid peel here thanks to the Arctic air-con. Waxing, ear candles and much more.

Garbugar MASSAGE VENUE
(Map p58; ☑769 121; Istana Kuta Galleria, Blok OG 09; massages from 75,000Rp; ⊙10am-8pm) Blind masseurs here are experts in sensing exactly where your kinks are located. It's no-frills all the way but hard to beat for a deeply relaxing experience.

Bungy Jumping

AJ Hackett Bungy (Map p58; ☑731 144; Jl Arjuna; from US$100; ⊙noon-8pm Mon-Thu & Sun, noon-8pm & 2-6am Fri & Sat), beside the beach at the Double Six Club in Legian, has a great view of the coast. Late-night hours for boozers give new meaning to 'Look out below!'

Kuta & Legian

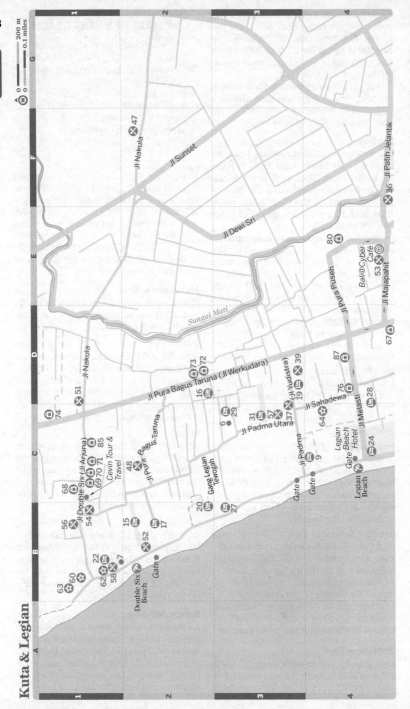

200 m
0.1 miles

Jl Nakula
Jl Sunset
Jl Patih Jelantik
Jl Dewi Sri
Bali@Cyber Café
Jl Majapahit
Jl Pura Puseh
Sungai Mati
Jl Pura Bagus Taruna (Jl Werkudara)
Jl Yudistra
Jl Sahadewa
Jl Nakula
Jl Melasti
Jl Padma Utara
Jl Padma
Legian Beach Hotel
Jl Double Six (Jl Arjuna)
Cevin Tour & Travel
Jl Pura Bagus Taruna
Gang Legian Tewogah
Legian Beach
Gate
Double Six Beach
Gate

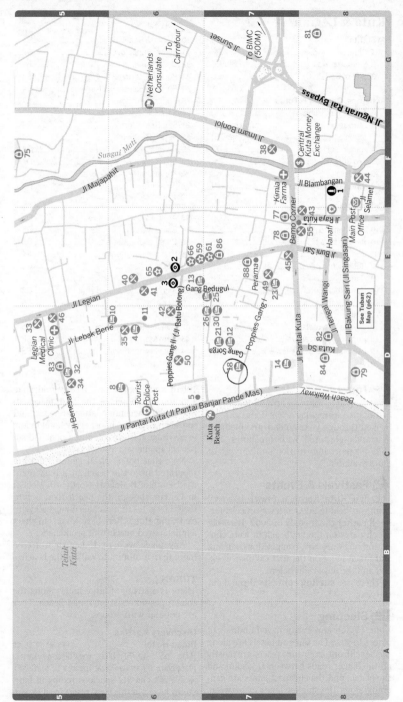

To Carrefour

Jl Sunset

To BIMC (500M)

Jl Ngurah Rai Bypass

Netherlands Consulate

81

Jl Imam Bonjol

Sungai Mati

Central Kuta Money Exchange

Jl Majapahit

38

75

Kimia Farma

Jl Blambangan

77

Benno Corner

Jl Raya Kuta

Hanafi

1

Jl Selamet

44

Main Post Office

43

55

78

Jl Buni Sari

66

59

61

86

2

65

40

41

3

13

Gang Bedugul

45

88

Perama

49

Jl Legian

46

10

42

Jl Batu Bolong

25

23

Poppies Gang I

Jl Pantai Kuta

Jl Lebak Bene

35

4

26

21 30

12

Jl Tengal Wangi

Legian Medical Clinic

33

11

Poppies Gang II

Gang Sorga

Kuta Sq

See Tuban Map (p62)

83

32

50

82

Jl Bakung Sari (Jl Singasari)

34

8

14

84

79

Jl Benesari

Tourist Police Post

5

Jl Pantai Kuta (Jl Pantai Banjar Pande Mas)

Beach Walkway

Kuta Beach

Teluk Kuta

Kuta & Legian

⌂ Tours

A vast range of tours all around Bali, from half-day to three-day excursions, can be booked through your hotel or the plethora of stands plastered with brochures. See p389 for more information on the types of tours available.

✨ Festivals & Events

The first **Kuta Karnival** (www.kutakarnival .com) was held in 2003 as a way of celebrating life after the tragedy of 2002. It's a big beach party on the big beach in Kuta consisting of games, art, competitions, surfing and much more on the first October weekend and the days right before.

There are **surfing contests** throughout the year.

🛏 Sleeping

Kuta, Legian and Tuban have hundreds of places to stay. The top-end hotels are along the beachfront, midrange places are mostly on the bigger roads between Jl Legian and the beach, and the cheapest joints are generally along the smaller lanes in between.

Tuban and Legian have mostly midrange and top-end hotels – the best places to find budget accommodation are Kuta and southern Legian. Almost every hotel in any price range has air-con and a pool. Go super cheap and you also go green.

Note that hotels on Jl Pantai Kuta are separated from the beach by a busy main road south of Jl Melasti. North of Jl Melasti in Legian, though, the beach road is protected by gates that exclude almost all vehicle traffic. Hotels here have what is in effect a quiet, paved beachfront promenade.

Any place west of Jl Legian won't be more than a 10-minute walk to the beach.

TUBAN

There is a string of large hotels along the sometimes-not-existent Tuban Beach. They are popular with groups.

**Discovery Kartika
Plaza Hotel** RESORT HOTEL $$
(Map p62; ☎751 067; www.discoverykartika plaza.com; Jl Kartika Plaza, Tuban; r US$120-240; ❋@☎☎) The 312 spacious rooms in four-storey blocks at this large resort front expan-

sive gardens and a gigantic swimming pool. For a real splurge, rent one of the private villas on the water (units two to seven are best).

KUTA

Wandering the gangs and lanes looking for a cheap room is a rite of passage for many. Options are numerous, so shop and compare. Some of the hotels along Jl Legian are of the type that assume men booking a single actually aspire to a double.

ON THE BEACH

Hard Rock Hotel　RESORT HOTEL **$$$**
(Map p58; ☏761 869; www.hardrockhotels.com; Jl Pantai Kuta; r from US$140; ❋@☈☈) Nothing is understated about this hotel's ostentatious 400 rooms, which, despite various themes, all feel like a retail opportunity. The enormous pool is more fantasyland than amenity. The staff are skilful and you need never wait long to buy a T-shirt in the megastore. It's on the beach.

CENTRAL KUTA

TOP CHOICE **Un's Hotel**　HOTEL **$$**
(Map p58; ☏757 409; www.unshotel .com; Jl Benesari; r US$30-60; ❋☈☈) A hid-

den entrance sets the tone for the secluded feel of Un's. It's a two-storey place with bougainvillea spilling over the pool-facing balconies. The 30 spacious rooms in a pair of blocks (the southern one is quieter) feature antiques, comfy cane loungers and open-air bathrooms. Cheaper rooms are fan only.

Poppies Cottages　HOTEL **$$**
(Map p58; ☏751 059; www.poppiesbali.com; Poppies Gang I; r US$75-100; ❋@☈☈) This Kuta institution has a lush, green setting for its 20 thatch-roofed cottages with outdoor sunken baths. Bed choices include kings and twins. The pool is surrounded by stone sculptures and water fountains in a garden that almost makes you forget you are in the heart of Kuta.

Kuta Puri Bungalows　HOTEL **$**
(Map p58; ☏751 903; www.kutapuri.com; Poppies Gang I; r US$30-50; ❋☈) The 47 bungalow-style rooms here are well maintained and nestled in verdant tropical grounds. The pool has a shallow kids' area. Enjoy the splish-splash of a fountain. Some rooms are fan only.

Bali Bungalo HOTEL **$$**
(Map p58; ☎755 109; www.bali-bungalo.com; off Jl Pantai Kuta; r 450,000-550,000Rp; ✳❂☎) Large rooms close to the beach yet away from irritations are a big part of the appeal of this older, 44-room hotel. It's well maintained and there are statues of prancing horses to inspire horseplay in the pool. Rooms are in two-storey buildings and have patios/porches; not all have wi-fi.

Suji Bungalow HOTEL **$**
(Map p58; ☎765 804; www.sujibglw.com; off Poppies Gang I; r US$30-50; ✳@❂☎) This cheery place offers a choice of 47 bungalows and rooms in two-storey blocks set in a spacious, quiet garden around a pool (which has a slide into the kiddie area). The verandas and terraces are good for relaxing. Not all rooms have wi-fi.

Berlian Inn HOTEL **$**
(Map p58; ☎751 501; off Poppies Gang I; r 120,000-350,000Rp; ✳) A stylish cut above other budget places, the 24 rooms in two-storey buildings here are pleasingly quiet and have ikat bedspreads and an unusual open-air bathroom design. Pricier rooms have air-con and hot water.

Bene Yasa I HOTEL **$**
(Map p58; ☎754 180; Poppies Gang II; r 90,000-200,000Rp; ✳☎) The grounds at this 44-room hotel are large and open, with palms providing some shade. Three-storey blocks overlook the pool area, and the plethora of patios encourages a lively social scene (except at midday, when many guests are passed out on loungers). Better rooms have tubs and air-con. The extended family keeps a close eye on all.

Gemini Star Hotel HOTEL **$**
(Map p58; ☎750 558; aquariushotel@yahoo.com; Poppies Gang II; r 140,000-260,000Rp; ✳☎) Only the monosyllabic mutterings of lounging surfers interrupt the peace at this 12-room hotel on a narrow alley. A pair of two-storey blocks shelter the large and sunny pool area. Cheap rooms have fans and hot water; more money adds air-con and fridges.

Bendesa HOTEL **$**
(Map p58; ☎754 366; www.bendesaaccommodation.com; off Poppies Gang II; r US$15-35; ✳☎) The 42 rooms here are in a three-storey block overlooking a pleasant-enough pool area. The location manages to be quiet amid the greater hubbub. The cheapest rooms – all clean – have cold water (some with bathtubs) and fan.

Mimpi Bungalows HOTEL **$**
(Map p58; ☎751 848; kumimpi@yahoo.com.sg; Gang Sorga; r 150,000-250,000Rp; ✳☎) The

Tuban

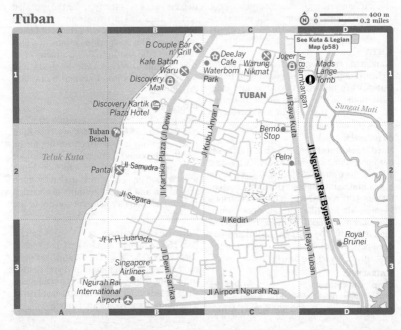

Mads Lange, a Danish copra trader and 19th-century adventurer, set up a successful trading enterprise near modern-day Kuta in 1839. He mediated profitably between local rajahs (lords or princes) and the Dutch, who were encroaching from the north. His business soured in the 1850s and he died suddenly, just as he was about to return to Denmark. It's thought that his death may have been the result of poisoning by locals jealous of his wealth. His restored **tomb** (Map p62; Jl Tuan Langa) is at the site where he used to live in a quiet, tree-shaded area by the river. Lange bred Dalmatians and today locals assume that any dog with a hint of black and white has some of this blood.

Beach tourism got its start in Bali when Bob and Louise Koke – a globetrotting couple from the US – opened a small guesthouse on virtually deserted Kuta Beach in the 1930s. The guests, mostly from Europe and the US, were housed in thatched bungalows built in an idealised Balinese style. In a prescient move, Bob taught the locals to surf, something he'd learned in Hawaii.

Kuta really began to change in the late 1960s when it became a stop on the hippie trail between Australia and Europe. By the early 1970s, it had relaxed losmen in pretty gardens, friendly places to eat, vendors peddling magic mushrooms and a delightfully laid-back atmosphere. Enterprising Balinese seized the opportunity to profit from the tourists and surfers, often in partnership with foreigners seeking a pretext to stay longer.

Legian, the village to the north, sprang up as an alternative to Kuta in the mid-1970s. At first it was a totally separate development, but these days you can't tell where one ends and the other begins.

cheapest of the 10 bungalow-style rooms here are the best value. Private gardens boast orchids and shade, and the pool is a good size. Mimpi's owner, Made Supatra, is a tireless promoter of Kuta.

Ronta Bungalows HOTEL $
(Map p58; ☎754 246; Gang Bedugal; r 80,000-200,000Rp; ✳) One of the best of the budget options, the rooms here are bungalow in name only – all 16 are in a two-storey block that is strenuously maintained. The cheapest are fan only.

Sari Bali Cottages HOTEL $
(Map p58; ☎756 911; Gang Sorga; r US$12-30; ✳) While the term 'cottages' is used very loosely in Bali, the 'cottages' here are in single-storey bungalow-style units, so you could actually say they are at least cottage-like. All 29 rooms span the budget end, from fan only with cold water to air-con and hot water.

LEGIAN

ON THE BEACH
Bali Mandira Hotel HOTEL $$
(Map p58; ☎751 381; www.balimandira.com; Jl Pantai Kuta; r US$110-180; ✳⊛☎) Gardens filled with bird-of-paradise flowers set the tone at this 191-room, full-service resort. Cottages have modern interiors, and the

bathrooms are partly open air. A dramatic pool at the peak of a stone ziggurat (which houses a spa) offers sweeping ocean views, as does the cafe. Popular with older couples and families.

Maharta Beach Resort HOTEL $$
(Map p58; ☎757 688; maharta@indo.net.id; Jl Padma Utara; r US$50-70; ✳⊛) Tucked into a tiny beachfront pocket, the pretension-free Maharta is vintage but solidly maintained. Its real allure is its (admittedly narrow) beach frontage. The 34 rooms, with patios/balconies, have typical Balinese wood furnishings, and some come with bathtubs and tile floors (although none have views). Some beds boast an oddly angled overhead mirror that invites contortions by narcissists.

Sari Beach Inn HOTEL $$
(Map p58; ☎751 635; sbi@indo.net.id; off Jl Padma Utara; r US$60-100; ✳☎⊛) Follow your ears down a long gang to the roar of the surf at this good-value beachside hotel that defines mellow. The 24 rooms have patios and the best have big soaking tubs. Grassy grounds boast many little statues and water features.

Jayakarta Hotel RESORT HOTEL $$
(Map p58; ☎751 433; www.jayakartahotels resorts.com; Jl Pura Bagus Taruna; r US$70-150;

✳@🛜🏊) The Jayakarta fronts a long and shady stretch of beach. The palm-shaded grounds, several pools and various restaurants make it a favourite with groups and families. Hair-braiders by the pool give kids that holiday look. The 277 rooms are large and in two- and three-storey blocks. Wi-fi reception varies by room.

Pullman Bali Legian Nirwana RESORT HOTEL **$$**
(Map p58; ☎762 500; www.accorhotels.com; Jl Melasti 1; r US$120-180; ✳@🛜🏊) The newest thing on Legian Beach, this huge resort is composed of 351 condo units with owners scattered across the globe hoping for good returns. Most units are simply one-room hotel-standard with rich wood furnishings. Note that the resort is shaped like a club on a deck of cards and many of the rooms offer the full *Rear Window* peer-at-your-neighbour experience. Also note that the beach is across the busy street.

CENTRAL LEGIAN

Island HOTEL **$$**
(Map p58; ☎762 722; www.theislandhotelbali .com; Gang Abdi; dm US$25, r US$60-75; ✳@🛜🏊) A real find, literally. Hidden in the attractive maze of tiny lanes west of Jl Legian, this new hotel lies at the confluence of gangs 19, 21 and Abdi. In a rarity for Bali, it has a very deluxe dorm room with eight beds. Regular rooms are stylish and surround a nice pool.

Senen Beach Inn GUESTHOUSE **$**
(Map p58; ☎755 470; Gang Camplung Mas 25; r 60,000-150,000Rp) In a quiet little gang near Jl Melasti, this 18-room place is run by friendly young guys. Most rooms have outdoor bathrooms and are set around a small garden; the better ones have hot water and tubs. There are several other family-run cheapies hidden back here.

Sri Beach Inn GUESTHOUSE **$**
(Map p58; ☎755 897; Gang Legian Tewngah; r 100,000-250,000Rp; ✳) Follow a series of paths into the heart of old Legian; when you hear the rustle of palms overhead, you're close to this homestay with five rooms. More money gets you hot water, air-con and a fridge. The gardens get lovelier by the year; agree to a monthly rate and watch them grow.

Three Brothers Inn HOTEL **$**
(Map p58; ☎751 566; www.threebrothersbun galows.com; off Jl Padma Utara; r US$28-50; ✳🛜🏊) Twisting banyan trees shade scores

---

PICK A NAME, ANY NAME

A small lane or alley is known as a gang, and most of them in Bali lack signs or even names. Some are referred to by the name of a connecting street, eg Jl Padma Utara is the gang going north of Jl Padma.

Meanwhile, some streets in Kuta, Legian and Seminyak have more than one name. Many streets are unofficially named after a well-known temple and/or business place, or according to the direction they head. In recent years there has been an attempt to impose official – and usually more Balinese – names on the streets. But the old, unofficial names are still common.

In this guide, all names are shown on the maps and we give preference to the street name that is most prevalent, eg Jl Arjuna has now surpassed Jl Double Six in common usage. Conversely Poppies Gang II remains just that. Following are the old (unofficial) and new (official) names, from north to south:

OLD (UNOFFICIAL)	CURRENT (OFFICIAL)
Jl Oberoi	Jl Laksmana
Jl Raya Seminyak	Northern stretch: Jl Raya Basangkasa
Jl Dhyana Pura/Jl Gado Gado	Jl Abimanyu
Jl Double Six	Jl Arjuna
Jl Pura Bagus Taruna/Rum Jungle Rd	Jl Werkudara
Jl Padma	Jl Yudistra
Poppies Gang II	Jl Batu Bolong
Jl Pantai Kuta	Jl Pantai Banjar Pande Mas
Jl Kartika Plaza	Jl Dewi Sartika
Jl Segara	Jl Jenggala
Jl Satria	Jl Kediri

KUTA COWBOYS UNSADDLED

You see them all around Bali's southern beaches: young men who are buff, tattooed, long-haired and gregariously courtly. Long known as 'Kuta cowboys', they turn the Asian cliché of a younger local woman with an older Western man on its ear. For decades women of a certain age have found companionship on Bali's beaches (and elsewhere) that meets a need, be it romantic, adventurous or otherwise.

This well-known Bali phenomenon was suddenly thrust into the headlines in 2010 with the release of the documentary *Cowboys in Paradise* (www.cowboysinparadise.com). Director Amit Virmani says he got the idea for the film after he talked to a Balinese boy who said he wanted 'to sex-service Japanese girls' when he grew up. The result looks at the lives of the Kuta cowboys and explores the economics and emotional costs of having fleeting dalliances with female tourists on a schedule. In one memorable scene, a cowboy shows off his collection of flags from foreign 'girl-friends' but can't remember them all. In another, a cowboy admits that when his wife says the kids need something and they're broke (the wife approves of his avocation, by the way) 'I'll email a foreign girlfriend and tell her I need money for school and clothes'.

The film has garnered awards but also outrage on Bali. Police rounded up tanned, buff locals lounging around Bali's beaches for questioning, ignoring the industrial-sized brothels for men found across south Bali.

Men featured in the film have suffered abuse and some have had to leave Bali. Mention Kuta cowboys to locals and some continue angrily denying their existence.

of older brick bungalows holding 83 rooms in the Brothers' sprawling and garden-like grounds. The fan rooms are the best option, but all rooms are spacious and come with tubs, and some have alluring outdoor bathrooms. Not all rooms have wi-fi.

Legian Beach Bungalow HOTEL **$**
(Map p58; ☑751 087; legianbeachbungalow@ yahoo.co.id; Jl Padma; r 100,000-250,000Rp; ❄❄) The entrance here is perfectly suited to the neighbourhood: it's ugly. But inside is a fine, simple budget hotel. The cheapest of the 22 rooms only have cold water but all have air-con; some have bathtubs. The single- and two-storey blocks hem in the pool.

DOUBLE SIX BEACH
Hotel Kumala Pantai HOTEL **$$**
(Map p58; ☑755 500; www.kumalapantai.com; Jl Werkudara; r 600,000-800,000Rp; ❄@✿❄) One of the better deals in Legian. The 108 rooms are large, with marble bathrooms featuring separate shower and tub. The three-storey blocks are set in very lush grounds across from popular Double Six Beach. The breakfast buffet is bountiful; wi-fi charges can be high.

O-CE-N Bali HOTEL **$$$**
(Map p58; ☑737 400; www.outrigger.com; Jl Arjuna 88X; r US$150-300; ❄@✿❄) This flashy

resort looms over a popular stretch of Double Six Beach. The 112 rooms scattered about the concrete complex range from hotel-simple to apartment-deluxe; none are far from the myriad water features.

✖ Eating
There's a profusion of places to eat around Kuta and Legian. Tourist cafes with their cheap menus of Indonesian standards, sandwiches and pizza are ubiquitous. Other forms of Asian fare can be found as well, and there are numerous places serving fresh seafood, steaks and pasta. Look closely and you'll find genuine Balinese warung tucked in amid it all.

If you're looking for the laid-back scene of a classic travellers' cafe, wander the gang and look for the crowds. Often what's busy one night will be quiet the next. For quick snacks and 4am beers, Circle K convenience stores are everywhere and are open 24 hours.

Beware of the big-box restaurants out on Jl Sunset. Heavily promoted, they suffer from traffic noise and are aimed squarely at groups who go where the bus goes.

TUBAN
The beachfront hotels all have restaurants or cafes, which are often good for nonguests to enjoy a snack or a sunset drink.

Kafe Batan Waru
INDONESIAN **$$**

(Map p62; ☑766 303; Jl Kartika Plaza; meals 50,000-150,000Rp) The Tuban branch of one of Ubud's best eateries is a slicked-up version of a warung, albeit with excellent and creative Asian and local fare. There's also good coffee, baked goods and kid-friendly items such as pasta and chicken fingers.

B Couple Bar n' Grill
SEAFOOD **$$**

(Map p62; ☑761 414; Jl Kartika Plaza; meals 60,000-200,000Rp; ⊙24hr) A vibrant mix of upscale local families and a swath of tourists (menus are even in Russian) tuck into Jimbaran-style grilled seafood at this slick operation. Pool tables and live music add to the din while flames flare in the open kitchens.

Warung Nikmat
INDONESIAN **$**

(Map p62; ☑764 678; Jl Banjar Sari; meals 15,000-25,000Rp; ⊙10am-3pm) This Javanese favourite is known for its array of authentic halal dishes, including beef rendang, *perkedel* (fried corn cakes), prawn cakes, *sop buntut* (oxtail soup) and various curries and vegetable dishes. Get there before 2pm or you'll be left with the scraps.

Pantai
SEAFOOD **$$**

(Map p62; ☑753 196; Jl Wana Segara; meals 50,000-150,000Rp) It's location, location, location here at this dead-simple beachside bar and grill. The food is purely stock tourist (seafood, Indo classics, pasta etc) but the setting overlooking the ocean is idyllic. There's none of the pretence (or prices) of the hotel cafes common down here. Follow the beach path south past the big Ramada Bintang Bali resort.

Discovery Mall
FOOD COURT **$**

(Map p62; Jl Kartika Plaza; ❄) This mall is home to many places to eat, including a top-floor food court (meals 15,000Rp to 30,000Rp) with scores of vendors selling cheap, fresh Asian food. You can eat outside on a terrace overlooking Kuta Beach. Elsewhere the mall has several chain cafes and bakeries.

KUTA

Busy Jl Pantai Kuta keeps beachside businesses to a minimum in Kuta. Beach vendors are pretty much limited to drinks.

CENTRAL KUTA

Warung Hanafi
INDONESIAN **$**

(Map p58; ☑765 442; Jl Pantai Kuta 1C; meals from 40,000Rp) The best dish here is straight from the owner's Sumatran mother: *nasi goreng* (the secret is day-old rice). Watch the passing traffic chaos while you try a refreshing – and bright-red – tamarillo juice. The drinks menu is booze free and everything is halal.

Poppies Restaurant
FUSION **$$**

(Map p58; ☑751 059; Poppies Gang I; meals 80,000-200,000Rp; 📶) Right on its namesake gang, long-running Poppies is popular for its lush garden setting, which has a timeless romance. The menu combines upscale Western (avocado and shrimp) and Balinese (your own little grill of satay) tastes.

Made's Warung
INDONESIAN **$$**

(Map p58; ☑755 297; Jl Pantai Kuta; meals 60,000-200,000Rp) Made's was the original tourist warung in Kuta, and through the years the Westernised Indonesian menu has been much copied. Classic dishes such as *nasi campur* (rice with side dishes) are served with colour and flair. Although not the hub it once was, Made's is among the nicest options in the area.

Kuta Night Market
INDONESIAN **$**

(Map p58; Jl Blambangan; meals 15,000-25,000Rp; ⊙6pm-midnight) This enclave of stalls and plastic chairs bustles with locals and tourism workers chowing down on hot-off-the-wok treats, grilled goods and other fresh foods.

ALONG JL LEGIAN

The eating choices along Jl Legian seem endless; avoid tables close to the busy street.

Kopi Pot
CAFE **$$**

(Map p58; ☑752 614; Jl Legian; meals 60,000-150,000Rp; 📶) Shaded by trees, Kopi Pot is a favourite, popular for its coffees, milkshakes and myriad desserts. The multilevel, open-air dining area sits back from noxious Jl Legian.

Ketupat
INDONESIAN **$$**

(Map p58; ☑754 209; Jl Legian; meals 120,000-200,000Rp) Hidden behind the antique-filled Jonathan Gallery, Ketupat is a calm oasis that is an escape from the Kuta clamour. Open-air dining pavilions overlook an azure pool. Dishes originate from across Indonesia, including Javanese curries such as *nasi hijau harum* (fried rice with greens, shrimps and herbs).

Mama's
GERMAN **$$**

(Map p58; ☑761 151; Jl Legian; meals 70,000-250,000Rp; ⊙24hr; 📶) This German classic serves up schnitzel and other pork-heavy dishes around the clock. The menu is so authentic that you'll find dishes such as *Königsberger klopse* (pork meatballs in white sauce). Bintang comes by the litre and the open-air bar is a merry place for enjoying various other imported beers and the excellent local Storm microbrew.

ON & AROUND POPPIES GANG II

Balcony
GLOBAL $$
(Map p58; ☑757 409; Jl Benesari 16; meals 50,000-150,000Rp; ⊘from 5am) The Balcony has a breezy tropical design and sits above the din of Jl Benesari below. Get ready for the day with a long menu of eggs and pancakes. At night it's sort of upscale surfer: pasta, grilled meats and a few Indo classics. It's all nicely done and the perfect place to take your new hook-up from 5am.

Kori Restaurant & Bar
GLOBAL $$
(Map p58; ☑758 605; Poppies Gang II; meals 60,000-180,000Rp) Kori's tables are scattered about a series of gardens and ponds. Definitely a few cuts above its very casual neighbours, this is the place to linger over a gin and tonic and a steak. Enjoy a secluded rendezvous in the flower-bedecked nooks out back. Some nights there's live acoustic music.

Café Local
CAFE $
(Map p58; ☑755 123; Jl Lebak Bene; meals 30,000-70,000Rp) In terms of style, this corner place is classier than the usual surfer joints that line this surfer-filled patch of Kuta. For one, it actually has a colour scheme (a rather pleasing coffee and turquoise) and the food is fresh and modern, with Asian influences throughout a range of sandwiches, salads and other dishes.

Rainbow Cafe
GLOBAL $
(Map p58; ☑765 730; Poppies Gang II; meals from 50,000Rp) Join generations of Kuta denizens quaffing the afternoon away. The vibe at this deeply shaded spot has changed little since people said things like 'I grok that, man'. Many current customers are the offspring of backpackers who met at adjoining tables.

EAST OF JL LEGIAN

Feyloon
CHINESE $$
(Map p58; ☑766 308; Jl Raya Kuta 98; meals 80,000-200,000Rp; ✹) A glossy Hong Kong seafood palace has landed in Bali. All manner of creatures swim in an aquarium's worth of tanks at the entrance, unaware that they will soon become part of your dinner. Presentation is artful and the selec-

tion vast. You can vary your eating with a number of good duck dishes.

Take
JAPANESE $$
(Map p58; ☑759 745; Jl Patih Jelantik; meals from 70,000Rp) Flee Bali for a relaxed version of Tokyo just by ducking under the traditional fabric shield over the doorway here. Hyperfresh sushi, sashimi and more are prepared under the fanatical eyes of a team of chefs behind a long counter. Dine at low tables or hang out in a booth.

Dapur Alam
INDONESIAN $
(Map p58; ☑757 506; Jl Patih Jelantik 81; meals 15,000-40,000Rp; ⊘5-11pm) A real find (if you can find it). The name of this upscale night market means 'natural kitchen'. Spotless tables under two pavilions welcome diners to a shady spot below the road near the river. Various open kitchens serve dishes from across the archipelago. Even standards like the spicy *sate ayam* (chicken satay) are inspired. Kids enjoy a playground.

Kuta Market
MARKET $
(Map p58; Jl Paya Kuta; ⊘6am-4pm) Not big but its popularity ensures constant turnover. Look for some of Bali's unusual fruits here, such as the mangosteen.

LEGIAN
Along the streets of Legian, the ho-hum mix with the good, so browse a bit before choosing.

TOP CHOICE Indo-National
SEAFOOD $$
(Map p58; ☑759 883; Jl Padma 17; meals 60,000-150,000Rp) Kerry and Milton Turner's popular restaurant is a home away from home for legions of fans. Grab a cold one with the crew up front at the bar for a sweeping view of Legian's action. Dine at the well-lit tables or at a secluded one out the back. Order the heaping grilled seafood platter and Bali's best garlic bread; the prawn toast is tops. Toss back a few Bintangs and see how many world monuments you can name amid captivating frescos.

Mang Engking
INDONESIAN $$
(Map p58; ☑882 2000; Jl Nakula 88; meals 100,000-200,000Rp) Serving the food of Indonesia, this large restaurant is a metaphor for the islands themselves, with various thatched dining pavilions set amid ponds and water features. Hugely popular with Bali's emerging middle class, the long menu focuses on fresh seafood. Service is snappy like the jaws of a shark, but far more friendly.

Warung Murah
INDONESIAN $

(Map p58; ☏732 082; Jl Arjuna; meals from 20,000Rp) Lunch goes swimmingly at this authentic warung specialising in seafood. An array of grilled fish awaits; if you prefer fowl over fin, the *sate ayam* is succulent *and* a bargain. It's hugely popular at lunch; try to arrive right before noon.

Warung Asia
ASIAN $

(Map p58; ☏742 0202; off Jl Double Six & Jl Pura Bagus Taruna; meals 20,000-50,000Rp; 🛜) Look down a couple of little gang for this dollhouse of a cafe. Asian dishes such as beef satay, fish curry and ginger chicken are paired with Italian espresso from an authentic machine.

Aroma's Cafe
GLOBAL $$

(Map p58; ☏751 003; Jl Legian; meals 60,000-100,000Rp; 🛜) A gentle garden setting encircled by water fountains is a perfect place to start the day over great juices, breakfasts and coffee. Other times the menu has fresh vegetarian versions of Western and Indonesian classics. A very pleasant place for a time-out from Jl Legian.

Delicioso
GELATO $

(Map p58; Jl Padma) This small stand offers up real Italian gelato that's big on flavour and even bigger on refreshment on a hot south Bali day. A combo of creamy mango and green mint will have you cooing 'aaah'.

Warung Yogya
INDONESIAN $

(Map p58; ☏750 835; Jl Padma Utara; meals 15,000-25,000Rp) A real find in the tourist heart of Legian, this basic warung is spotless and serves up hearty portions of Balinese classics. The gado gado comes with a huge bowl of peanut sauce, while the *nasi campur* is a perfect plate of diverse treats.

Saleko
INDONESIAN $

(Map p58; Jl Nakula 4; meals from 15,000Rp) Just off the madness of Jl Legian, this modest open-front place attracts the discerning with its simple Sumatran fare. Spicy grilled chicken and fish dare you to ladle on the volcanic sambal. Everything is halal.

Pedro's Flying Piano
ECLECTIC $$

(Map p58; ☏763 170; Jl Werkudara; meals US$7-25) Revelling in that noted Swiss-tropical style(!), Pedro's combines fondue with Asian dishes, steaks, seafood and more for a menu that's as eclectic as the decor.

Bands that would do a second-tier cruise ship proud cover old standards on the flying piano itself, along with various other instruments.

DOUBLE SIX BEACH

A strip of restaurants and cafes faces the water at this popular beach, which is always thronging with locals and visitors alike. The following are good come sunset.

Zanzibar
GLOBAL $$

(Map p58; ☏733 529; Jl Double Six; meals 60,000-150,000Rp) Head right to the second level looking out over the shade trees to the surf. The menu is a typical mix of Indo, pasta, sandwiches and decent thin-crust pizzas, but that's not your priority – get a large table with a group and enjoy the sunset views.

Seaside
GLOBAL $$

(Map p58; ☏737 140; Jl Double Six; meals 60,000-180,000Rp) The curving sweep of seating at this sleek place provides beach views for one and all. Upstairs, there's a vast patio with oodles of tables for counting stars after the sun goes down. Seafood and meat dishes come with a touch of style.

☆ Entertainment

Around 6pm every day, sunset on the beach is the big attraction, perhaps while enjoying a drink at a cafe with a sea view. Later on, while the temperature diminishes the action heats up, especially at the happening clubs of Kuta. Many ragers spend their early evening at one of the hipster joints in Seminyak before working their way south to oblivion.

Watching DVDs at a bar with a crowd is a Kuta evening tradition (and much more budget-friendly than a Seminyak club); you'll find scores of places in and around the Poppies. Look for signs during the day or follow your ears at night. Expect anything with lots of guns and unshaven guys.

Check out the free mag the *Beat* (www.beatmag.com) for good club listings and other 'what's on' news.

Bars & Clubs

Bars are free to enter, and often have drink specials; cover charges are uncommon. Ambience ranges from the low-down vibe of the surfer dives to high-concept nightclubs with renowned DJs.

Dodging cars, motorcycles, touts, dogs and dodgy footpaths can make walking through Tuban, Kuta and Legian seem like anything but a holiday. It's intense and can be stressful. You may soon be longing for uncrowded places where you hear little more than the rustling of palm fronds and the call of birds.

Think you need to book a trip out of town? Well, think again. You can escape to the country without leaving the area. All those teeming streets surround vacant swaths of land and once you poke through the wall of commerce, you can be transported back to a Kuta and Legian of 30 years ago. In Kuta, this is hard, as even these can be crowded, but take any alley or lane heading east of Jl Legian and you'll be in the quieter neighbourhood where the locals live.

Better still is Legian. Take any of the narrow gang into the area bounded by Jl Legian, Jl Padma, Jl Padma Utara and Jl Pura Bagus Taruna and soon you'll be on narrow paths that go past local houses and the occasional simple warung or shop. Wander at random and enjoy the silence accented by, yes, the sound of palm fronds and birds.

The stylish clubs of Seminyak are popular with gay and straight crowds, but in general you'll find a mixed crowd anywhere in Kuta and Legian.

TUBAN

DeeJay Cafe
CLUB
(Map p62; ☎758 880; 2nd fl, Kuta Centre, off Jl Kartika Plaza 8X, Tuban; ⏰11pm-9am) The post-midnight hours see this place pulsing in the post-apocalyptic Kuta Centre, the rundown shell of a tourist mall. House DJs play tribal underground, progressive trance, electro house and more. Beware of posers who set their alarms for 5am and arrive all fresh.

KUTA

Jl Legian is lined with interchangeable bars with bar stools moulded to the butts of hard-drinking regulars.

Sky Garden Lounge
BAR
(Map p58; ☎756 362; www.escbali.com; Jl Legian 61; ⏰24hr) This multilevel palace of flash flirts with height restrictions from its rooftop bar where all of Kuta twinkles around you. Look for top DJs, a ground-level cafe and paparazzi wannabes. Munchers can enjoy a long menu of bar snacks and meals (salads, sandwiches, pastas and the like). Most, however, roam from floor to floor posing with posers and having a blast. Despite the gloss, it can get quite rowdy at night when Kuta starts thumping.

Apache Reggae Bar
CLUB
(Map p58; ☎761 212; Jl Legian 146; ⏰11pm-4am) One of the rowdier spots in Kuta, Apache jams in locals and visitors, many of whom are on the make. The music is loud, but that pounding you feel the next day is from the free-flowing *arak* (local spirit) served in huge plastic jugs.

Mbargo
CLUB
(Map p58; ☎756 280; Jl Legian; cover from 10,000Rp; ⏰7pm-4am) This place throbs with the gangsta vibe, and is enjoyed by well-heeled suburbanites. Hard-edged DJs encourage the sweaty throngs to misbehave.

Bounty
CLUB
(Map p58; ☎752 529; Jl Legian; ⏰10pm-6am) Set on a pirate ship in a mini-mall of food and drink, the Bounty is a vast open-air disco that humps, thumps and pumps all night. Play seaman and get down on the poop deck to hip hop, tribal, trance and anything else the DJs come up with.

LEGIAN & DOUBLE SIX BEACH

Most of Legian's bars are smaller and appeal to a more sedate crowd than those in Kuta. The very notable exception is the area at the end of Jl Double Six.

Legend
BAR
(Map p58; ☎755 376; Jl Sahadewa; ⏰3-11pm) A popular open-air spot, the Legend draws nightly crowds for karaoke and vivacious drag shows. Live music spans pop to country.

Double Six Club
CLUB
(Map p58; ☎0812 462 7733; www.doublesixclub .com; Jl Arjuna; ⏰11pm-6am) This legendary club (and namesake of the beach, road and more) continues reinventing itself. The swimming pool is still here and so is the bungy jump. Top international DJs play a mix of dance tunes in a sleek open-air

pavilion. A cafe up front adds glitz to sunset drinks.

De Ja Vu
CLUB

(Map p58; ☑732 777; Jl Arjuna; ⊙5pm-4am; ✳) DJs are on duty from opening every night at this high-concept, glass-fronted club with tables overlooking the beach outside. It's a popular place to go before Double Six.

Bacio
CLUB

(Map p58; ☑756 666; Jl Arjuna; ⊙9pm-dawn) Aims higher than its neighbour Double Six in terms of decor – and drink prices. If you own a Ferrari, you'll go to this house- and concept-heavy club and boast about it. If you don't, you'll lie.

🔒 Shopping

Kuta has a vast concentration of cheap tawdry shops, as well as huge, flashy surf-gear emporiums on Kuta Sq and Jl Legian. As you head north along the latter into Legian, the quality of the shops improves and you start finding cute little boutiques, especially past Jl Melasti. Jl Arjuna is lined with wholesale fabric, clothing and craft stores, giving it a bazaar feel. Continue into Seminyak for absolutely fabulous shopping.

In Tuban, the Discovery Mall is popular, but nearby Kuta Sq and Jl Pantai Kuta are a nightmare of people who put their dukes up if you accidentally call them 'bogan'.

Simple stalls with T-shirts, souvenirs and beachwear are everywhere (especially along the Poppies). See p371 for tips on cutting a deal. Many of these stalls are crowded together in 'art markets' such as the **Kuta Square Art Market** (Map p58) or the **Jl Melasti Art Market** (Map p58), where the 'art' consists of Bintang logo reproductions. The top-selling gift for those left at home are penis-shaped bottle openers in a range of colours and sizes. Bargain hard to avoid paying a stiff price.

Accessories

Earthy Collection
HANDBAGS

(Map p58; ☑748 8400; Jl Legian 456) Handbags in every shape, size and colour imaginable, mostly made from materials woven right on Bali. The staff will be happy to help you realise your fantasy with a custom order.

Djeremi Shop
WOVEN GOODS

(Map p58; ☑0815 578 8169; Jl Legian) Woven goods for yourself and your home. If the idea of a romantic mosquito net draped over your bed gets you all itchy, come here.

Arts & Crafts

Schlocky stuff is the norm but you can find some interesting items that go beyond a gag gift at a stag or hen party.

Jonathan Gallery
ANTIQUE

(Map p58; ☑754 209; Jl Legian 109) Traditional art and antiques are beautifully displayed in this shop.

Kiki Shop
MUSICAL INSTRUMENTS

(Map p58; ☑0819 1612 4351; Jl Pantai Kuta 10) Custom-made musical instruments. Get a bongo drum and drive people mad in hostels worldwide.

Makmur Helmet
HELMETS

(Map p58; ☑486 451; Jl Pura Puseh) Helmets are mandatory for riding motorbikes (a lack thereof is a good way to attract unwanted and potentially costly police interest) and this shop will kit you out in style – even if the helmets may not meet every international standard for safety. Mohawk, Viking and more.

Beachwear & Surf Shops

A huge range of surf shops sells big-name surf gear – including Mambo, Rip Curl and Billabong – although goods may be only marginally cheaper than overseas. Local names include Surfer Girl and Quicksilver. Most have numerous locations in south Bali.

Next Generation Board Bags
SURF GEAR

(Map p58; ☑0813 3700 0523; Jl Benesari) Choose from myriad patterns and colours and then watch your bag (from 250,000Rp) get made on the shop floor in two days or less. There are lots of other family-run surfer shops nearby.

Rip Curl
SURF GEAR

(Map p58; ☑765 035; Kuta Sq) The brightest store on the square. Come here to replace that minimalist black with something eye-popping. Choose from a huge range of beach clothes, water wear and surfboards.

Surfer Girl
SURF WEAR

(Map p58; ☑752 693; Jl Legian 138) The sugary-sweet logo says it all about this Bali-based brand for girls of all ages. Clothes, undies, gear, bikinis and so on.

Bookshops

Small used-book exchanges can be found scattered along the gang and roads, especially the Poppies.

Kerta Bookshop
BOOKSHOP

(Map p58; ☑758 047; Jl Pantai Kuta 6B) A book exchange with a better-than-average selection; many break the Patterson-Brown-Cornwall mould.

Periplus Bookshop
BOOKSHOP

(Map p62; ☑769 757; Discovery Mall, Jl Kartika Plaza, Tuban) Large selection of new books.

Times Bookstore
BOOKSHOP

(Map p58; ☑767 198; Kuta Sq) In Matahari Department Store, this bookshop has a good range of fiction.

Clothing

The local clothing industry has diversified from beach gear to sportswear and fashion clothing. From the intersection with Jl Padma, go north on Jl Legian to Seminyak for the most interesting clothing shops.

Animale
CLOTHING

(Map p58; ☑754 093; Jl Legian 361) One of Bali's top-end international brands, Animale has the full range of its collection at this location (one of many).

Balifu
CLOTHING

(Map p58; ☑490 243; Jl Arjuna 10X) Breezy fashions in brightly coloured cotton and batik. Flouncy sarongs.

Uluwatu
CLOTHING

(Map p58; ☑751 933; Jl Legian) This is where Surfer Girls go when they get old. The largest of numerous locations across Bali, this elegant shop showcases the collection of lace-accented linen and cotton clothing. The items are made in villages around Tabanan in west Bali.

Swell Shop
GIRL'S CLOTHING

(Map p58; ☑751 918; Jl Melasti) Items fit for a little princess, from ultra-frilly frocks to pint-sized bling. Sadly, no T-shirts reading: 'Can I borrow your credit card?'

Desy Shop
FOOTWEAR

(Map p58; ☑733 595; Jl Arjuna 61) Zillions of sandals, all made right here. Show some interest and the owner will offer to make you 100, wholesale.

Department Stores & Malls

Carrefour
HYPERMARKET

(Map p58; ☑847 7222; Jl Sunset; ⊙9am-10pm) This vast outlet of the French discount chain combines lots of small shops (books, computers, bikinis etc) with one huge hypermarket. It's the place to stock up on staples and there's a large ready-to-eat section and a food court as well. The downside, however, is inescapable: it's a mall.

KUTA'S FAVOURITE STORE

The mobs out the front look like they're making a run on a bank. Inside it's simply pandemonium. Welcome to **Joger** (Map p62; Jl Raya, Tuban; ⊙11am-6pm), a Bali retail legend that is the most popular store in the south. No visitor from elsewhere in Indonesia would think of leaving the island without a doe-eyed plastic puppy (4000Rp) or one of the thousands of T-shirts bearing a wry, funny or simply inexplicable phrase (almost all are limited edition). In fact the sign out the front says 'Pabrik Kata-Kata', which means 'factory of words'. When we were there the big seller said 'I love you' in a haiku of English, Chinese and Indonesian. Warning: conditions inside the cramped store are simply insane.

Discovery Mall
MALL

(Map p62; ☑755 522; www.discoveryshoppingmall.com; Jl Kartika Plaza, Tuban; ⊙9am-9pm) Swallowing up a significant section of the shoreline, this huge, hulking and popular enclosed Tuban mall is built on the water and filled with stores of every kind, including the large **Centro** (☑769 629) and trendy **Sogo** (☑769 555) department stores.

Istana Kuta Galleria
MALL

(Map p58; Jl Patih Jelantik) An enormous open-air mall that seems like a dud until you find an interesting shop amid the canyon of glass. There is a hardware store in the rear if your needs run towards rope and duct tape.

Mal Bali Galleria
MALL

(Map p58; ☑758 875; Jl Ngurah Rai) Huge, uninspiring mall at the traffic-congested bypass construction site. The duty-free emporium is big with the group-tour set.

Matahari
DEPARTMENT STORE

(Map p58; ☑757 588; Kuta Sq; ⊙9.30am-10pm) This store has the basics – fairly staid clothing, a floor full of souvenirs, jewellery and a supermarket. Get some decent-quality luggage here should you need extra bags to haul your wretched excess home.

Fabric

Stroll Jl Arjuna in Legian for a festival of open-air wholesalers selling fabric, clothes and housewares. Some recommendations:

Bouchra
FABRIC

(Map p58; ☑733 594; Jl Arjuna 10) Sells fabric with Gauguin-esque designs that has been hand-painted in Denpasar.

Busana Agung
FABRIC

(Map p58; ☑733 442; Jl Arjuna) Here you'll find stacks of vibrant batiks and other fabrics that scream 'sew me!'.

Sriwijaya
FABRIC

(Map p58; ☑733 581; Jl Arjuna 35) Makes batik and other fabrics to order in myriad colours.

Furniture

On Jl Patih Jelantik, between Jl Legian and Jl Pura Puseh, there are scores of furniture shops manufacturing everything from instant 'antiques' to wooden statues. However, a few of the stores make and sell teak outdoor furniture of very high quality at very low prices. A luxurious deckchair goes for about 200,000Rp to 300,000Rp; most of the stores work with freight agencies.

ℹ Information

Dangers & Annoyances

The streets and *gang* are usually safe but there are annoyances. Scooter-borne prostitutes (who hassle single men late at night) cruise after dark. Walking along you may hear 'massage' followed by 'young girl' and the ubiquitous 'transport' followed by 'blow'. But your biggest irritation will likely be the ever-worsening traffic.

HAWKERS Crackdowns mean that it's rare to find carts in the Kuta tourist area, but street selling is common, especially on hassle street, Jl Legian, where selling and begging can be aggressive. The beach isn't unbearable, but the upper part has souvenir sellers and masseurs (who may grab hold of you and not let go). Closer to the water you can sunbake on the sand in peace – you'll see where the invisible line is.

SURF The surf can be dangerous, with a strong current on some tides, especially up north in Legian. Lifeguards patrol swimming areas of the beaches at Kuta and Legian, indicated by red-and-yellow flags. If they say the water is too rough or unsafe to swim in, they mean it. Red flags with skull and crossbones mean no swimming allowed. The lifeguards are very dedicated, as anyone who saw the Bali series of the show *Bondi Rescue* can attest.

THEFT Visitors lose things from unlocked (and some locked) hotel rooms and from the beach. Going into the water and leaving valuables on the beach is simply asking for trouble (in any country). Snatch thefts are uncommon, but valuable items can be left at your hotel reception.

WATER POLLUTION The sea water around Kuta is commonly contaminated by run-off from both built-up areas and surrounding farmland, especially after heavy rain. Swim away from streams, including the often foul one at Double Six Beach.

Emergency

Police station (Map p58; ☑751 598; Jl Raya Kuta; ☺24hr) Next to the Tourist Information Centre.

Tourist police post (Map p58; ☑784 5988; Jl Pantai Kuta; ☺24hr) This is a branch of the main police station in Denpasar. Right across from the beach, the officers have a gig that is sort of like a Balinese *Baywatch*.

Internet Access

There are scores of places to connect to the internet. Most have poky connections and charge about 300Rp a minute.

Bali@Cyber Café (Map p58; ☑761 326; www .balicyber.net; Jl Patih Jelantik; ☺8am-11pm) Fast connections at 250Rp per minute. Has a full range of computer options (including printing), parking and a good menu of snacks, meals and tasty smoothies. Many expats use it as their office.

Medical Services

See p392 for medical clinics serving all of Bali.

Kimia Farma Kuta (Map p58; ☑755 622; Jl Raya Kuta; ☺24hr); Tuban (☑757 483; Jl Raya Kuta 15; ☺24hr) Part of a local chain of pharmacies, it's well stocked and carries hard-to-find items, like that antidote for irksome roosters in the morning: earplugs.

Legian Medical Clinic (Map p58; ☑758 503; Jl Benesari; ☺on call 24hr) Has an ambulance and dental service. It's 500,000Rp for a consultation with an English-speaking Balinese doctor, or 900,000Rp for an emergency visit to your hotel room. It has a well-stocked pharmacy attached to the clinic.

Money

ATMs abound and can be found everywhere, including in the ubiquitous Circle K and Mini Mart convenience stores.

Central Kuta Money Exchange (Map p58; ☑762 970; Jl Raya Kuta) Trustworthy; deals in myriad currencies.

Post

Postal agencies that can send but not receive mail are common.

Main post office (Map p58; Jl Selamet; ☺7am-2pm Mon-Thu, 7-11am Fri, 7am-1pm Sat) On a little road east of Jl Raya Kuta, this small and efficient post office has an easy, sort-it-yourself poste restante service. It's well practised in shipping large packages.

Tourist Information

Places that advertise themselves as 'tourist information centres' are usually commercial travel agents or worse: time-share condo sales operations.

Hanafi (Map p58; ☑756 454; www.hanafi.net; Jl Pantai Kuta 1E) This gay- and family-friendly tour operator and guide operates from a small veterinary clinic he shares with his sister. He's a valuable source of information.

Travel Agencies

Cevin Tour & Travel (Map p58; ☑743 7343; martiflightcentrebali@yahoo.com; Jl Arjuna 23) A reputable agent, popular with expats for airline tickets.

❶ Getting There & Away

Bemo

Bemo regularly travel between Kuta and the Tegal terminal in Denpasar – the fare should be 8000Rp. The route goes from Jl Raya Kuta near Jl Pantai Kuta, looping past the beach, then on Jl Melasti and back past **Bemo Corner** (Map p58) for the trip back to Denpasar.

Bus

For public buses to anywhere in Bali, you'll have to go to the appropriate terminal in Denpasar first; see p122.

Perama (Map p58; ☑751 551; www.perama tour.com; Jl Legian 39; ☉7am-10pm) is the main shuttle-bus operation in town, and will sometimes pick you up from your hotel (confirm this with the staff when making arrangements). It usually has at least one bus a day to its destinations, which are as follows:

DESTINATION	FARE	DURATION
Candidasa	60,000Rp	3½hr
Lovina	100,000Rp	4½hr
Padangbai	60,000Rp	3hr
Sanur	25,000Rp	30min
Ubud	50,000Rp	1½hr

❶ Getting Around

The hardest part about getting around south Bali is the traffic. Besides using taxis, you can rent a motorbike, often with a surfboard rack, or a bike – just ask where you're staying. One of the nicest ways to get around the area is by foot along the beach.

To/From the Airport

An official taxi from the airport costs 35,000Rp to Tuban, 50,000Rp to Kuta and 55,000Rp to

Legian. When travelling *to* the airport, get a metered taxi for much less.

Taxi

As always, the distinctive blue taxis of **Bali Taxi** (☑701 111) are far and away the best.

Seminyak

☑0361

Seminyak is flash, brash, phoney and filled with bony models. It's also the centre of life for hordes of the island's expats, many of whom own boutiques or design clothes, surf, or seem to do nothing at all. It may be immediately north of Kuta and Legian, but in many respects Seminyak feels almost like it's on another island.

It's also a very dynamic place, home to dozens of restaurants and clubs and a wealth of creative shops and galleries. World-class hotels line the beach – and what a beach it is, as deep and sandy as Kuta's but less crowded.

Seminyak seamlessly merges with Kerobokan, which is immediately north – in fact the exact border between the two is as fuzzy as most other geographic details on Bali. Note that despite the hype not every beachfront hotel here is world-class or charges world-class prices. All those restaurants and clubs combine to give travellers the greatest choice of style and budget in Bali. Sure there are exclusive boutiques, but there are also workshops where everything is wholesale. And when it all becomes too much, just head to a quiet corner of the beach and chill.

◉ Sights

North of the string of hotels on Jl Pantai Kaya Aya and across from the beach, **Pura Petitenget** is an important temple and the scene of many ceremonies. It is one of a string of sea temples that stretches from Pura Luhur Ulu Watu on the Bukit Peninsula north to Tanah Lot in western Bali. Petitenget loosely translates as 'magic box', a treasured belonging of the legendary 16th-century priest Nirartha, who refined the Balinese religion and visited this site often. Also in the compound, look for **Pura Masceti**, an agricultural temple where farmers pray for relief from rat infestations, and savvy builders make offerings of forgiveness before planting yet another villa in the rice fields.

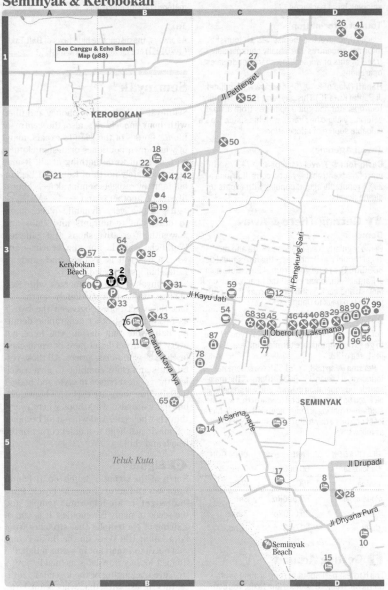

For tips on respecting traditions and acting appropriately while visiting temples, see the boxed text, p329.

The good **beach** here is usually uncrowded and has plenty of parking (2000Rp). Head north towards Kerobokan and, except for a couple of small cafes, you'll have plenty of sand and crashing waves to yourself.

Another good stretch of beach runs south from the end of Jl Abimanyu to Jl Double Six in Legian. The vendors here are especially mellow and a sunset lounger and

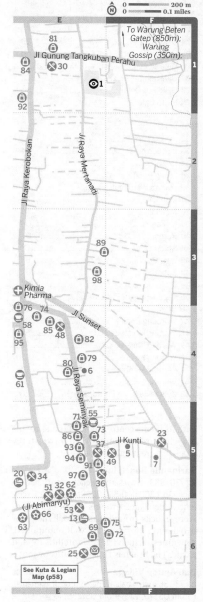

Activities

Because of the limited road access, the beaches in Seminyak tend to be less crowded than further south in Kuta. This also means that they're less patrolled and the water conditions are less monitored. The odds of encountering dangerous rip tides and other hazards are ever-present, especially as you head north.

Massages & Spas

TOP CHOICE **Jari Menari**   SPA
(☏736 740; www.jarimenari.com; Jl Raya Seminyak 47; ☺10am-9pm) This place has won international acclaim. Its name means 'dancing fingers' and your body will be one happy dance floor. The all-male staff use massage techniques that emphasise rhythm. Fees start at 250,000Rp for 75 minutes.

Chill   SPA
(☏734 701; www.thevillas.net; Jl Kunti; ☺10am-10pm) The name says it all. This Zen place embraces reflexology, with treatments starting at US$13. Its sister property **Prana** (☏730 840; Jl Kunti) is a palatial Moorish fantasy that is easily the most lavishly decorated spa in Bali. Massages at Prana start at US$100.

Cooking Schools

Sate Bali (☏736 734; Jl Laksmana 22; course 375,000Rp; ☺9.30am-1.30pm) runs an excellent Balinese cooking course taught by noted chef Nyoman Sudiyasa. Students learn to prepare Balinese spices and sambals, which are then used to flavour duck, fish and pork dishes. Not up to attending school? The restaurant is delicious.

Sleeping

Seminyak has a wide range of places to stay, from world-class resorts such as the Oberoi to more humble hotels hidden away on backstreets. This is also the start of villaland, which runs north from here through the vanishing rice fields. For details on booking a private villa, see p367.

Many of Seminyak's most pleasant hotels are located on small lanes off major roads such as Jl Abimanyu and Jl Laksmana. They are both quiet and close to the action.

JL ABIMANYU & AROUND

Villa Karisa   GUESTHOUSE $$
(☏744 5538; www.villakarisabali.com; Jl Drupadi 100; r US$75-170; ✳@☎☎) It's like visiting the gracious friends on Bali you wish you

ice-cold Bintang cost about 15,000Rp. A new walkway makes wandering this stretch a breeze (note that this has encouraged some of the vendors – like the third of the Three Pigs – to build some pretty substantial 'beach huts'). Come here for sunsets.

had. Ideally located on a little gang off ever-more-popular Jl Drupadi, this large villa-style inn has a row of rooms filled with antiques and many comforts. Guests gather in the common room or around the 12m pool.

Raja Gardens   GUESTHOUSE **$$**
(☑730 494; jdw@eksadata.com; Jl Abimanyu; r 300,000-600,000Rp; ❄❄) Enjoy spacious, grassy grounds in this quiet inn almost on the beach. The nine rooms are fairly bare-bones but there are open-air bathrooms and plenty of potted plants. The basic rate gets you cold water and a fan; more money buys hot water, air-con and a fridge.

Green Room   GUESTHOUSE **$**
(☑731 412; www.thegreenroombali.com; Jl Abimanyu 63B; r US$30-50; ❄❄❄) A new-age cheapie, the Green Room evokes *Robinson Crusoe* from its hammocks to its banana-tree motif. Lounge around the small, ink-blot-shaped pool or chill in the open bale

with its media centre. Some of the 14 rooms (the cheapest are fan only) in a two-storey block feature jungle themes.

Sarinande Beach Inn   HOTEL **$**
(☑730 383; www.sarinandehotel.com; Jl Sari-nande 15; r 300,000-350,000Rp; ❄❄❄) Excellent value. The 24 rooms are in older two-storey blocks around a small pool; the decor is older but everything is well maintained. Amenities include fridges, satellite TV and a cafe. The beach is three minutes by foot.

Bali Agung Village   HOTEL **$$**
(☑730 367; www.bali-agung.com; off Jl Abimanyu; r from US$70, villas from US$150; ❄❄) Off a hidden backstreet, this attractive place has 42 rooms in bungalow-style units that are popular with budget-conscious groups. The grounds are lush and there's a profusion of Balinese wood and stone carvings. Look for the statue of a giraffe as you navigate along the alleys.

Ned's Hide-Away   GUESTHOUSE **$**
(☑731 270; nedshide@dps.centrim.net.id; Gang Bima 3; r from 120,000Rp; ❄) Named after Aussie icon Ned Kelly, this simple, 15-room, two-storey place is popular with those hoping to lie low between bouts of fun. It's down a small gang; look for the sign on Jl Raya Seminyak north of Bintang Supermarket.

JL LAKSMANA & AROUND

TOP CHOICE **Oberoi**   HOTEL **$$$**
(☑730 361; www.oberoihotels.com; Jl Laksmana; r from US$240, villas from US$500; ❄@🛜🏊) One of the world's top hotels, the beautifully understated Oberoi has been a refined Balinese-style beachside retreat since 1971. All accommodations have private verandas, and as you move up the food chain, additional features include private villas, ocean views and private walled pools. From the cafe, overlooking the almost-private sweep of beach, to the numerous luxuries, this is a place to spoil yourself.

Samaya   VILLAS **$$$**
(☑731 149; www.thesamayabali.com; Jl Pantai Kaya Aya; villas from US$300; ❄@🛜🏊) Understated yet cultured, the Samaya is one of the best bets right on the beach in south Bali. The 24 villas in the beachside compound are attractive, roomy and have small pools. The 'Royal Compound' across the road trades location for even larger units. The food, from breakfast onwards, is superb.

Casa Artista   GUESTHOUSE **$$**
(☑736 749; www.casaartistabali.com; Jl Sari Dewi; r from US$85; ❄🛜🏊) You'll literally dance for joy at this cultured guesthouse where the owner, a professional tango dancer, offers lessons. Seven compact rooms in an elegant two-storey house surround a pool. Go for a 2nd-floor room and relax amid flamboyant bling.

Legian
HOTEL $$$

(☏730 622; www.ghmhotels.com; Jl Pantai Kaya Aya; ste from US$350, villas from US$600; ✽@🛜🏊) The Legian is flash and brash – one of the reasons it's a fave with people who use their own jets to reach Bali. All 67 rooms claim to be suites, even if some are just large rooms (called 'studios'). On a little bluff, the views are panoramic. The design mixes traditional materials with contemporary flair. If you're a talent agent, the glam staff will give you their cards.

Mutiara Bali
HOTEL $$

(☏708 888; www.mutiarabali.com; Jl Karang Mas Sejahtera 88; r US$80-120, villas from US$300; ✽@🛜🏊) Although hidden on a small road behind Jl Laksmana, the Mutiara is close to fine dining (two minutes) and the beach (five minutes). There are 29 good-sized and nicely furnished rooms in two-storey blocks around a frangipani-draped pool area. Seventeen large private villas occupy one half of the compound. Wi-fi can be pricey.

✖ Eating

Jl Laksmana is the focus of Seminyak eating but there are interesting choices virtually everywhere. Note that some restaurants morph into clubs as the night wears on. Conversely, some bars and clubs also do decent food.

JL ABIMANYU

Warung Mimpi
INDONESIAN $

(☏732 738; Jl Abimanyu; meals from 40,000Rp) A sweet little open-air shopfront warung in the midst of cacophonous nightlife. A dear husband-and-wife team cook Indo classics simply and well. It's all fresh and tasty.

La Sal
SPANISH $$

(☏738 321; www.lasalbali.com; Jl Drupadi; meals from US$15; ⊘5-11pm) The Manchego cheese comes direct from the Iberian Peninsula at this tapas place, which also has more substantial meals of steaks and paella. Dine in the twinkly garden or in the open-sided room with Moorish hints. A good selection of reds washes it all down.

Zula Vegetarian Paradise
VEGETARIAN $

(☏732 723; Jl Abimanyu 5; meals 25,000-60,000Rp) It's all vegetarian at this large cafe, where you can sample excellent dishes, such as organic red miso soup or pesto pasta, along with a range of smoothies and juices, including a vitamin-fortified number called the 'bone builder'.

ⓘ SEMINYAK'S CURVING SPINE

The thriving heart of Seminyak lines meandering Jl Laksmana (aka Jl Oberoi). It heads towards the beach from bustling Jl Raya Seminyak and then turns north through a part of Seminyak that some people call Petitenget (and where the proper road name is the little-used Jl Pantai Kaya Aya). The road is lined with a profusion of restaurants, upscale boutiques and hotels as it curves through Seminyak and into Kerobokan. Most agree that the name changes to Jl Raya Petitenget when it eventually veers east and intersects Jl Raya Kerobokan. Like so much of Bali, it would be the perfect road for a window-shopping or cafe-hopping stroll if not for the lack of decent footpaths for pedestrians. As you dodge taxis and gaping potholes in front of an exclusive boutique, think of it as an adventure. See p64 for more information on the confusing street names in the region.

Jef Burgers
BURGERS $

(☏0817 473 4311; Jl Abimanyu 24; meals from 30,000Rp; ⊘24hr) Munchies central. Jef cooks up highly customisable burgers around the clock in a Bali version of a diner.

Delicious Onion
ASIAN $$

(☏0813 3789 4243; Jl Drupadi; meals 60,000-90,000Rp; 🛜) A groovy thatched cafe off Jl Abimanyu, Delicious Onion has a long menu of rice and noodle dishes, many featuring the tasty house chicken. The long patio is good for lounging; some nights it morphs into a low-key club replete with DJ.

JL RAYA SEMINYAK

⭐ TOP CHOICE Made's Warung II
INDONESIAN $$

(☏732 130; Jl Raya Seminyak; meals 40,000-150,000Rp) Vastly expanded, the northern branch of Made's has a buzz many thought unlikely for such a long-running veteran. But the well-prepared Indonesian food is delicious as ever and the presentation artful. Even the little bags of Balinese snack crackers are a delight. You'll need to book (or wait) in high season.

Warung Italia
ITALIAN $$

(☏737 437; Jl Kunti 2; meals 40,000-100,000Rp; ⊘8am-7pm; ✽) The climax in any classic warung happens at lunch, when happy diners walk along in front of the display cases and have their plates filled with a wide selection of treats. Here, warung-style meets Italian, as diners select from a range of pastas, salads and more. Next to the open-air warung area, a restaurant section with a wood-burning pizza oven features a long menu.

Mannekepis STEAKS $$
(☎847 5784; Jl Raya Seminyak 2; meals 60,000-200,000Rp; ☎) That little icon of Brussels is permanently peeing out front at this surprisingly good Belgian bistro. Tear your eyes away from the fish swimming in the ceiling tank to peruse a selection of excellent steaks, all served with top-notch *frites*. There is live jazz and blues many nights. Sit on the upper-floor terrace away from the bedlam of the street.

Warung Ibu Made INDONESIAN $
(Jl Raya Seminyak; meals 15,000Rp; ☎7am-7pm) The woks roar almost from dawn to dusk amid the constant hubbub on this busy corner of Jl Raya Seminyak. It's one of a few simple stalls. The meals from this warung couldn't be fresher; they put to shame some of the Western fakery just down the road.

Bali Deli DELI $$
(☎738 686; Jl Kunti 117X; @☎) The lavish deli counter at this upscale market is loaded with imported cheese, meats and baked goods. This is the place to start a special meal. The breezy cafe also has a good fresh menu.

Bintang Supermarket SUPERMARKET $
(☎730 552; Jl Raya Seminyak 17) Always busy, this large supermarket is the grocery favourite among expats (although Carrefour is tough competition). Affordable sunscreen, bug spray and other sundries as well.

JL LAKSMANA
Saddled by some with the unimaginative name 'Eat Street', this restaurant row rewards the indecisive as you can stroll the strip and see what sparks a craving. Prices are uniformly popular.

Ultimo ITALIAN $$
(☎738 720; Jl Laksmana 104; meals 100,000-200,000Rp) *Uno:* find a table overlooking the street action or out the back in one of the gardens. *Due:* choose from the wide-ranging, authentic and tasty Italian fare. *Tre:* marvel at the efficient service from the

army of servers. *Quattro:* smile at the reasonable bill.

Ibu Mangku INDONESIAN $
(☎780 1824; Jl Kayu Jati; meals from 20,000Rp) Where your driver takes lunch. Look for the cabs in front of this bamboo place with a serene garden out the back. The must-have is the superb minced-chicken satay, redolent with lemongrass and other spices.

Sate Bali INDONESIAN $$
(☎736 734; Jl Laksmana 22; meals from 100,000Rp; ☎11am-10pm) Some very fine traditional Balinese dishes are served at this small cafe run by chef Nyoman Sudiyasa (who also has a cooking school here). The multicourse *rijsttafel* (165,000Rp) is a symphony of tastes, including the addictive *babi kecap* (pork in a sweet soy sauce) and *tum bebek* (minced duck in banana leaf).

La Lucciola SEAFOOD $$$
(☎730 838; Jl Pantai Kaya Aya; meals 150,000-300,000Rp) This beachside bistro is near the temple and secluded on all sides except the one that counts: the ocean. Stylish sunset-watchers enjoy good views of the surf from the 2nd floor. The menu is a creative fusion of international fare with an accent on seafood. Beguiling drinks from the bar may have you running across the green lawn to frolic in the ocean.

Tuesday Night Pizza Club PIZZA $$
(☎730 614, 876 6600; Jl Laksmana; pizzas 40,000-150,000Rp; ☎6pm-midnight) Pizzas come in five sizes at this brightly lit joint and have a range of pop culture names like Hawaii Five-O (ham and pineapple). There are only a few tables – fast and efficient delivery to hotels and villas is hugely popular.

Rumours STEAKS $$
(☎738 720; Jl Laksmana 100; meals 70,000-180,000Rp; ☎6pm-midnight) Italian and Indonesian standards are mere supporting cast members for the real stars here: the steaks. There's a range of cuts and preparations, topping out at the 500g T-bone. Terrace tables are tops. Expat characters line the bar.

Trattoria ITALIAN $$
(☎737 082; Jl Laksmana; meals 100,000-200,000Rp; ☎6pm-midnight) Enjoy authentic Italian cuisine at tables inside or out. The menu changes often but always features fresh pasta, grilled meats and seafood. Even the bread sticks – as plentiful as the lines of waiting patrons – score.

Mykonos
GREEK $$

(☎733 253; Jl Laksmana; meals US$10-15) After a lacklustre period, Mykonos is back from Hades and in the land of Apollo. This long-time Greek place has renewed vigour and cheerfully serves up a classic menu of Hellenic standards. The excellent 'Mykonos shrimp' is fragrant with garlic and lemon.

Living Room
FUSION $$$

(☎735 735; www.livingroombali.com; Jl Petitenget; meals 150,000-300,000Rp; ☺noon-late) At night, hundreds of candles twinkle on and about the scores of outdoor tables at this fusion of Balinese thatching and colonial posh. The menu combines French classics with Asian flair – think Saigon before things went pear-shaped. A mature crowd grooves to house, jazz and trance and has earned the place the sobriquet *Cocoon*.

Earth Cafe
VEGETARIAN $

(☎736 645; Jl Laksmana 99; meals from 40,000Rp) The good vibes are organic at this vegetarian cafe and store amid Seminyak's upscale retail precinct. Sweet potato and chickpea soup is a fine lead-in to the creative salads or whole-grain goodies. A retail section sells potions and lotions. While perusing the bookshelves, don't get ahead of yourself in the colonic irrigation section.

🍷 Drinking

Seminyak has developed a full-on cafe culture. The idle masses can while away hours on terraces or overlooking the beach.

JL RAYA SEMINYAK

Café Seminyak
BAKERY

(☎736 967; Jl Raya Seminyak 17; ☻) Right in front of the busy Bintang Supermarket, this cute and casual place has excellent smoothies, and sandwiches made with freshly baked bread.

Café Moka
CAFE

(☎731 424; Jl Raya Seminyak; ❄) Enjoy French-style baked goods (fresh baguettes!) at this popular bakery and cafe. Many escape the heat and linger here for hours over little French treats. The bulletin board spills over with notices for villa rentals.

JL LAKSMANA

Grocer & Grind
CAFE

(☎0817 354 104; Jl Kayu Jati 3X; ❄☻) Keep your vistas limited and you might think you're at just another sleek Melbourne cafe, but look around and you're unmistakably in Bali, albeit one of the trendiest bits. Classic sandwiches, salads and big breakfasts issue forth from the open kitchen. Savour fine coffee in the open air or choose air-con tables in the deli area.

Corner Store
CAFE

(☎730 276; Jl Laksmana 10A; ☺7am-5pm) Seminyak's fashionistas gather here (aka Tuck Shop to the expats) most mornings to dish the gossip and breakfast on upscale healthy fare like organic muesli. Tell everyone you're a 'cushion designer' and look bored under the beautiful frangipani tree.

Vienna Cafe
CAFE

(☎733 265; Jl Drupadi 7) On a strip of road that's fast getting popular, this little cafe combines old-world Vienna with the tropics and pulls it off. Enjoy a schnitzel with a smoothie in the lovely side garden. Baked goods show a Sacher sensibility.

Bali Bakery
BAKERY

(Seminyak Sq, Jl Laksmana; ☻) The best features of the fashionable strip mall in the heart of Seminyak are this bakery's shady tables and long menu of baked goods, salads, sandwiches and other fine fare. A good place to linger before heading back out to shop.

Café Zucchini
CAFE

(☎736 633; Jl Laksmana 49) Hidden behind trees, shrubs and a vivid yellow-striped canopy, this Italian cafe is an ideal refuge from the surrounding retail pressures. Juices and various coffee drinks are the stars. There are a few substantial Italian mains if you need real sustenance.

Collego
CAFE

(☎730 370; Petitenget Beach; ☺10am-8pm) A mostly open-air thatched beach bar, Collego is prime real estate for gay expats and their friends. On Sundays it veritably throbs with life as Liz Taylor lookalikes cruise about. There's a little path from Jl Kayu Jati, but the easiest way to get here the first time is by going to the beach at Pura Petitenget and walking north about 200m.

Mano
CAFE

(☎730 874; Petitenget Beach) Tucked away in a corner of the parking lot behind Pura Petitenget, there is absolutely nothing remarkable about this smallish, barely roofed cafe except for the fabulous views over the water, especially at sunset. Often quiet even at prime time.

★ Entertainment
Bars & Clubs

Like your vision at 2am, the division between restaurant, bar and club blurs in Seminyak. For instance, Living Room and Sarong (in neighbouring Kerobokan) have large and inviting bars that fill with people who never take a crack at a menu. Meanwhile, Ku De Ta and Hu'u serve good food to the partying masses. Although Seminyak lacks any real hardcore clubs where you can greet the dawn (or vice versa), stalwarts can head south to the rough edges of Kuta and Legian in the wee hours.

Numerous bars popular with gay and straight crowds line Jl Abimanyu (aka Jl Dhyana Pura), though noise-sensitive locals complain if things get too raucous.

JL ABIMANYU

Bali Jo CLUB
(☑0819 9910 0445; Jl Abimanyu; ⊙8pm-3am) Simply fun – albeit with falsies. Drag queens rock the house, the crowd lining the street and the entire neighbourhood with songs amped to 11 nightly. Surprisingly intimate, it's a good place to lounge about for a few, even when the boys are busy out the back with their make-up.

Obsession LOUNGE
(☑730 269; Jl Abimanyu; ⊙6pm-2am) It's rather plush and lush at this rather intimate venue. Latin, blues, soul and more add to the pink glow through the night.

Bahiana SALSA CLUB
(☑738 662; Jl Abimanyu 4; ⊙5pm-late) Rum flows almost as freely as the moves on the dance floor at this salsa-themed club. Live music alternates with DJs; there are salsa lessons at 10pm many nights.

JL LAKSMANA

Red Carpet Champagne Bar BAR
(☑737 889; Jl Laksmana 42) The closest most will come to posing for paparazzi is at this over-the-top glam bar on Seminyak's couture strip. Waltz the red carpet and toss back a few namesake flutes while contemplating a raw oyster and displays of frilly frocks. It's open to the street (but elevated, dahling) so you can observe the rabble.

Hu'u LOUNGE
(☑736 443; www.huubali.com; Jl Pantai Kaya Aya; ⊙4pm-late) There's a menu someplace, but really this spot is all about air-kissing, seeing and making the scene, and an enchanting outdoor garden and pavilion. Action

peaks around midnight before the southward club exodus begins.

Ku De Ta LOUNGE
(☑736 969; www.kudeta.net; Jl Laksmana; ⊙7am-1am) Hardly an article gets written about Bali that doesn't mention this beachside lounge, heaving with Bali's beautiful and their attendant scenesters. It's usually packed with people unable to imagine being any place else, although at sunset you'll likely agree.

Zappaz PIANO BAR
(☑742 5534; Jl Laksmana; ⊙11am-midnight) Brit Norman Findlay tickles the ivories nightly at this cheerful piano bar, where he's been not-quite-perfecting his enthusiastic playing for years and years. Why suffer abuse trying to croon your way to idol-dom on TV when you can simply sing at your own bar?

🛍 Shopping

Seminyak shops could occupy days of your holiday. Designer boutiques (Bali has a thriving fashion industry), funky stores, slick galleries, wholesale emporiums and family-run workshops are just some of the choices.

The action picks up in the south from Kuta and Legian and heads north along Jl Legian and Jl Raya Seminyak (there's no exact demarcation between the two and some people call parts of the latter Jl Raya Basangkasa). The retail strip branches off into the prime real estate of Jl Laksmana while continuing north on Jl Raya Kerobokan into Kerobokan itself. Of course, this being Bali, try not to get too overwhelmed by the glitz or you'll step into one of the yawning pavement caverns.

If you need help navigating this retail paradise, check out the 'Retail Therapy' column in the **Bali Advertiser** (www.baliadvertiser.biz). It's written by the singularly named **Marilyn** (retailtherapym@yahoo.com.au), who brings a veteran retailer's keen eye to the local scene. For advanced studies, she's available for consultations.

Accessories

Street Dogs ACCESSORIES
(☑737 819; Jl Laksmana 60) Bracelets made with shells and resin as well as recycled brass demand immediate wearing.

Luna Collection JEWELLERY
(☑0811 398 909; Jl Raya Seminyak) Handmade sterling silver jewellery in a range

of designs. The local craftspeople are quite creative and the mother-of-pearl works are museum quality.

Sabbatha WOMEN'S ACCESSORIES
(✆731 756; Jl Raya Seminyak 97) Mega-bling! The glitter, glam and gold here are almost blinding and that's just what customers want. Opulent handbags and other sun-reflecting accessories are displayed like so much king's ransom.

Beachwear

Blue Glue BATHING SUITS
(✆844 5956; Jl Raya Seminyak) Has a collection of Bali-made bathing suits from teensy to trendy.

Drifter BEACH GEAR
(✆733 274; Jl Laksmana 50) High-end surf fashion, gear, books and brands such as Obey and Rhythm.

Bookshops

Periplus Bookshop BOOKSHOP
Made's Warung II (✆734 843; Jl Raya Seminyak); Seminyak Sq (✆736 851; Jl Laksmana) This island-wide chain of lavishly decorated bookshops has enough design books to have you fitting out even your garage in Bali style. Also stocks bestsellers, magazines and newspapers.

Clothing

Dinda Rella WOMEN'S CLOTHING
(✆734 228; www.dindarella.com; Jl Raya Seminyak) Upscale frocks for women are designed and made on Bali by this much-honoured brand. The place to get that sexy little cocktail dress. There's another location on Jl Laksmana.

Milo's SILK CLOTHING
(✆730 410; www.milos-bali.com; Jl Laksmana) The legendary local designer of silk finery has followed the hordes to designer row and opened this lavish shop. Look for batik-bearing, eye-popping orchid patterns.

Morena WOMEN'S CLOTHING
(✆745 3531; Jl Laksmana 69) Puerto Rican–born Wilma sells her line of sexy, flouncy, comfy and colourful women's clothes here.

Lily Jean WOMEN'S CLOTHING
(✆734 864; www.lily-jean.com; Jl Laksmana 102) Saucy knickers underpin sexy women's clothing that both dares and flirts; most is Bali-made. Now in a lovely new building.

Divine Diva WOMEN'S CLOTHING
(✆731 903; Jl Laksmana 1A) Bali-made breezy styles for fuller female figures. A friend calls it 'the essence of agelessness'.

Paul Ropp CLOTHING
(✆734 208; www.paulropp.com; Jl Laksmana) Elegant main store for one of Bali's premier high-end fashion designers. Rich silks and cottons, vivid to the point of gaudy, effervesce with hints of the tie-dyed '60s.

Biasa CLOTHING
(✆730 308; www.biasabali.com; Jl Raya Seminyak 36) This is Bali-based designer Susanna Perini's premier store. Her line of tropical wear for men and women combines cottons, silks and embroidery. Ex-husband Paul Ropp has a small shop across the street (one of many).

Sacado CHILDREN'S CLOTHING
(✆730 605; Jl Raya Seminyak) Your crazy kid will be a cool kid with the bright and cheery duds from this very cute boutique.

Inti WOMEN'S CLOTHING
(✆733 664; Jl Raya Seminyak 11) Shoppers tired of pawing through racks of size-two clothes will sigh with relief at this shop filled with resort wear aimed at mature women who have something to show for their years of good living.

Bamboo Blonde WOMEN'S CLOTHING
(✆780 5919; Jl Laksmana 61) Frilly, sporty or sexy frocks and more formal wear tempt from this cheery designer boutique.

Bananas Batik CLOTHING
(✆730 938; www.bananasbatik.com; Jl Raya Seminyak) Flouncy clothes for women that you don't have to travel to the source for: the exquisite duds sold here are made at Pondok Pisang, a small inn on the ocean near Candidasa. The batik is very finely made and the muted colours are classy.

Animale Outlet WOMEN'S CLOTHING
(✆737 1544; Jl Raya Seminyak 31) One of Bali's top-end international brands, Animale offers great deals on its lines of casual wear at this outlet store.

ET Club WOMEN'S CLOTHING
(Map p58; ✆730 902; Jl Raya Seminyak 14A) Out-of-this-world prices on designer knock-offs and bohemian bags, belts, shoes and clothes.

Galleries

Theater Art Gallery PUPPETS
(✆732 782; Jl Raya Seminyak) Specialises in vintage and reproduction puppets used in

traditional Balinese theatre. Just browsing the animated faces peering back at you is a delight.

Biasa Art Space
ART GALLERY

(☎744 2902; www.biasaart.com; Jl Raya Seminyak 34) This large, airy and chilly gallery is owned by Biasa designer Susanna Perini. Changing exhibits highlight bold works.

Kemarin Hari Ini
GALLERY

(☎735 262; Jl Raya Seminyak) Glass objects created with laminated Japanese paper sparkle in the light at this airy gallery. Primitive works mix with the starkly modern.

Housewares

TOP CHOICE Ashitaba
WOVEN BASKETS

(☎737 054; Jl Raya Seminyak 6) Tenganan, the Aga village of east Bali, produces the intricate and beautiful rattan items sold here. Containers, bowls, purses and more (from US$5) display the very fine weaving.

Folk Art Gallery
HOUSEWARES

(☎738 113; Jl Laksmana) Tribal and folk art from across Asia are arrayed attractively in this cute little boutique.

DeZine Hammocks
HAMMOCKS

(☎742 2379; Jl Raya Seminyak 34) Talk about a gift that keeps on giving, not to mention swaying. Choose from a rainbow of in-stock hammocks in a multitude of sizes. Or have one custom-made to your exact size using the fabric of your dreams (trust us, you'll be dreaming once you hop aboard). Total cost for the one-day service: about US$20.

St Isador
TEXTILES

(☎738 836; Jl Laksmana 44) The workshops upstairs spew forth lovely bed linens, pillows and other items made of fabrics imported from across Asia.

Heliconia
FLOWERS

(☎732 700; Jl Raya Seminyak) Stunning and exotic floral arrangements out of a Mapplethorpe album – who knew you could do that with a baby pineapple?

You Like Lamp
LAMPS

(☎733 755; Jl Raya Mertanadi) Why yes, we do. All manner of endearing little paper lamps – many good for tea lights – are sold here cheap by the bag full. Don't see what you want? The staff working away on the floor will rustle it up immediately.

Nôblis
DECOR

(☎0815 5800 2815; Jl Raya Mertanadi 54) Feel like royalty here with regal bits of decor from around the globe.

Lucy's Batik
TEXTILES

(☎795 275; Jl Raya Seminyak) Indirect lighting and air-con make this a refined place to shop for batik. Goods are the finest.

Information

Seminyak shares many services with Kuta and Legian.

Dangers & Annoyances

Seminyak is generally a lot more hassle-free than Kuta & Legian. But it's worth reading the warnings on p72, especially those regarding surf and water pollution.

Internet Access

Most hotels have broadband connections for guests, and many cafes offer free wi-fi for patrons, as noted in the listings.

Medical Services

Kimia Pharma (☎916 6509; Jl Raya Kerobokan 140; ◷24hr) At a major crossroads, this pharmacy, part of Bali's best chain of pharmacies, has a full range of prescription medications.

Money

ATMs can be found along all the main roads.

Post

Postal agency (☎761 592; Bintang Supermarket, Jl Raya Seminyak 17)

Getting There & Around

Most transport information is the same as for Kuta. Metered **taxis** are easily hailed. A trip from the airport in an official **airport taxi** costs 70,000Rp, to the airport about half that. A taxi to the heart of Kuta will be about 15,000Rp. You can beat the traffic, save the ozone and have a good stroll by walking south down the beach; Legian is only about 15 minutes away.

Kerobokan

☎0361

Continuing seamlessly north from Seminyak, Kerobokan combines some of Bali's best restaurants, lavish lifestyles and still more – and lonelier – beach. Hotels are upstaged by villas, which sprout from the ground like pustules on an adolescent. At times the mix of commerce and rice fields can be jarring. One notable landmark is the **Kerobokan jail** (Map p74), home to Scha-

TEMPLE FESTIVALS

Temple festivals in Bali are quite amazing, and you'll come across them quite unexpectedly, even in the most remote corners of the island. Each of the thousands of temples on the island has a 'temple birthday' known as an **odalan**. These are celebrated once every Balinese year of 210 days or every 354 to 356 days on the caka calendar.

Odalans are very big deals indeed and even the loneliest temple will suddenly spring to life around these special days. People from villages will travel far to attend, and grumbling business owners in south Bali will automatically give employees time off.

Celebrate!

The most obvious sign of a temple festival is a long line of women in traditional costume, walking gracefully to the temple with beautifully arranged offerings piled in huge pyramids, which they carry on their heads.

Meanwhile, the various *pemangku* (temple guardians and priests for temple rituals) suggest to the gods that they should come down for a visit.

All night long there's activity, music and dancing – it's like a great country fair, with food, amusements, gambling, colour and confusion. Finally, as dawn approaches, the entertainment fades away, the *pemangku* suggest to the gods that it's time they made their way back to heaven and the people wind their weary way back home.

Joining an Odalan

Ask any locals you meet what odalans or temple festivals are happening. Seeing one will be a highlight of your trip, particularly if it is at a major temple (see p356). Foreigners are welcome to watch the festivities and take photographs, but be unobtrusive and dress modestly. See p329 for easy guidelines regarding how to show respect while visiting a temple.

pelle Corby and other prisoners both infamous and unknown.

🏃 Activities

Amo Beauty Spa   SPA

(Map p74; ☎275 3337; www.amospa.com; 100 Jl Raya Petitenget) With some of Asia's top models lounging about it feels like you've stepped into the studios of *Vogue*. A one-hour massage starts at 180,000Rp; other services range from hair care to unisex waxing. Ouch!

Spa Bonita   SPA

(Map p74; ☎731 918; www.bonitabali.com; Jl Petitenget 2000X; ⊙9am-9pm) Part of the delightful Waroeng Bonita, this spa has a range of services in a simply elegant setting. Massages start at 95,000Rp.

Umalas Stables   HORSE RIDING

(☎731 402; www.balionhorse.com; Jl Lestari 9X) Umalas has a stable of 30 horses and ponies and offers 30-minute rice-field rides for US$25, and very popular two-/three-hour beach rides for US$72/102. Lessons can also be arranged.

🛏 Sleeping

Kerobokan is villa country, with walled developments simmering away amid rice fields. Sorting through the myriad options is best done with the help of an agent; see p367 for details.

The opening of the new glitzy **W Hotel** (Map p74) on the beach sometime before 2012 is sure to cause much excitement.

Tony's Villa   HOTEL $$

(Map p74; ☎736 166; www.balitonys.com; Jl Petitenget; r US$55-75, villas US$125-170; ❉@🛜☲) Enjoy no crowds on the beach but big crowds at some of Bali's best restaurants: both are just minutes from Tony's. Fairly modest, lushly planted bungalow-style units are part of a compound with slightly more lavish villas. It's all as unassuming as the price. Some units have no wi-fi.

Taman Ayu Cottage   HOTEL $$

(Map p74; ☎730 111; www.tamanayucottage.com; Jl Petitenget; r US$50-100; ❉@🛜☲) In a fast-growing part of Kerobokan sits this great-value hotel. The cottage in the name here is a bit of a misnomer, as most of the rooms are in two-storey blocks around a pool shaded by mature trees. Everything is a bit frayed around the edges, but all is forgotten when one of the hotel's pet rabbits romps over to say hello.

Grand Balisani Suites HOTEL $$

(Map p88; ☑730 550; www.balisani.com; Jl Batubelig; r US$100-160; ❀@❀❀) Straddling the border between midrange and top end, this elaborately carved complex is right on the beach, midway along the sand between Seminyak and Echo Beach. The 96 rooms are large and have standard teak furniture plus terraces. Once isolated, Batubelig Beach here is becoming popular.

✕ Eating

Kerobokan is attracting some of the most interesting restaurants on Bali. There's one main strip of places to eat: Jl Petitenget, the continuation of Jl Laksmana. But there are also worthy choices scattered about.

At the corner of Jl Raya Kerobokan and Jl Gunung Tangkuban Perahu, there's a scrumptious little **fruit market** (Map p74) where you can research Bali's fruit and vegetables.

JL PETITENGET

TOP CHOICE Sardine SEAFOOD $$$

(Map p74; ☑738 202; www.sardinebali .com; Jl Petitenget 21; meals US$15-35; ⊘closed Mon) Seafood fresh from the famous Jimbaran market is the star at this elegant yet intimate, casual yet stylish restaurant in a beautiful bamboo pavilion. Open-air tables overlook a private rice field that is patrolled by Sardine's own flock of ducks. The inventive bar is a must. The menu changes to reflect what's fresh. Booking is vital.

TOP CHOICE Biku FUSION $$

(Map p74; ☑857 0888; Jl Petitenget; meals 60,000-180,000Rp)

Housed in an old antique shop, uberpopular Biku retains the timeless vibe of its predecessor. But there's nothing old-fashioned about the food, which combines Indonesian, other Asian and Western influences on a casual menu that's served through the day. Dishes, from the exquisite breakfasts to the elegant local choices to Bali's best burger, are artful and delicious. There's a long list of teas and myriad refreshing cocktails. Many swoon upon seeing the cake table.

Warung Sulawesi INDONESIAN $

(Map p74; Jl Petitenget; meals from 30,000Rp; ⊘11am-4pm)

Although seemingly upscale, Kerobokan is blessed with many a fine place for a local meal. Find a table in this quiet family compound and enjoy fresh Balinese and Indonesian food served in classic warung style. Choose a rice, then pick from a captivating array of dishes that are always at their peak at noon. The green beans are yum!

Waroeng Bonita INDONESIAN $$

(Map p74; ☑731 918; www.bonitabali.com; Jl Petitenget 2000X; meals 70,000-180,000Rp) Balinese dishes such as *ikan rica-rica* (fresh fish in a spicy green chilli sauce) and the classic spicy beef rendang are the specialities here. Nab a table under the trees, unless it's Baliwood night when drag queens put on an unmissable and flamboyant spectacle inside.

Cafe Degan ASIAN $$

(Map p74; ☑744 8622; Jl Petitenget 9; meals 80,000-160,000Rp) The young couple running this cultured little warung have created a winner. The menu veers towards Indonesian but overall features dishes from the region you don't often find, such as *daging sambal hijau* (spicy beef with green chillies). A small air-con bakery has an array of delectables for dessert.

Warung Kolega INDONESIAN $

(Map p74; ☑0852 3794 9778; Jl Petitenget; meals 25,000Rp; ⊘11am-3pm) A Javanese halal classic. Choose your rice (we prefer the fragrant yellow), then pick from a delectable array that includes tempeh in sweet chilli sauce, *sambal terung* (spicy eggplant), *ikan sambal* (spicy grilled fish) and other daily specials.

Sarong ASIAN $$$

(Map p74; ☑737 809; www.sarongbali.com; Jl Petitenget 19X; meals US$15-30; ⊘noon-11pm) The food is almost as magical as the setting at this top-end, high-concept restaurant. Largely open to the evening breezes, the dining room has plush furniture and gleaming place settings that twinkle in the candlelight. Opt for tables out the back where you can let the stars do the twinkling. The food focuses on Asian – small plates are popular for an evening spent enjoying the commodious bar.

Bali Catering Co BAKERY $

(Map p74; ☑732 115; Jl Petitenget 45; snacks from 30,000Rp; ❀) Like a gem store of treats, this upscale deli-bakery serves an array of fanciful little delights. Many spend all day battling the temptation of the mango ice cream; others succumb to the croissants.

Café Jemme
FUSION $$

(Map p74; ☑732 392; Jl Petitenget 125; meals US$8-15; ☺8am-4pm; ✱) Ladies who lunch (and men too) sit primly on delicate French chairs here and gaze out at Kerobokan's number-one endangered species: rice terraces. Although there are a few breakfast items on the menu, Jemme is all about long, Italian-accented lunches amid rococo splendour.

Métis
FUSION $$$

(Map p74; ☑737 888; www.metisbali.com; Jl Petitenget 6; meals US$15-40) High-profile – and not just because of the huge building – Métis aims to be one of Bali's finest restaurants. It certainly has the provenance, with roots in the vaunted old Cafe Warisan (the current incarnation under that name bears no resemblance). Set ostentatiously in a surviving rice field, the restaurant and its carefully prepared cuisine work best when filled with buzzing crowds – think high season.

ELSEWHERE IN KEROBOKAN

Warung Sobat
SEAFOOD $$

(Map p88; ☑738 922; Jl Batubelig 11; meals 60,000-150,000Rp; ☺closed Sat) Set in a sort of bungalow-style brick courtyard, this old-fashioned restaurant excels at fresh Balinese seafood with an Italian accent (lots of garlic!). First-time visitors feel like they've made a discovery, and if you have the sensational lobster (a mere 100,000Rp; order in advance), you will too.

🌱 Warung Beten Gatep
INDONESIAN $

(Jl Pengubengan Kauh; meals 20,000Rp; ☺11am-3pm) This warung is run by the Wisnu Foundation, a much-respected environmental group. Enjoy simple, honest Balinese fare, prepared with high-quality and sustainable coconut oil, under palm trees. A shop sells cool handbags made from trash. It's about 500m north of Warung Gossip.

Warung Gossip
INDONESIAN $

(☑0817 970 3209; Jl Pengubengan Kauh; meals from 20,000Rp; ☺noon-4pm; 🛜) Always popular thanks to its Westernised versions of Balinese warung staples. Get a plate, tell the staff what you'd like and you'll soon be enjoying a fine lunch at one of the shady tables. They've opened a new cafe with a fusion menu and long hours across the street. It is about 1km north of the jail.

🛍 Shopping

Look for boutiques to join the trendy restaurants on Jl Petitenget. Jl Raya Kerobokan, extending north from Seminyak, has interesting shops primarily selling decora-

---

SHOPPING SAFARI

East of Seminyak and Kerobokan, a series of streets is lined with all manner of interesting shops selling and manufacturing housewares, baubles, fabric and other intriguing items. Head east of Kerobokan jail for about 2km on Jl Gunung Tangkuban Perahu and then turn south on – get this – a street with the same name (this is Bali, after all).

This particular Jl Gunung Tangkuban Perahu has been called 'the street of amazement' by a shopaholic friend. It meanders south, ending at Jl Gunung Soputan, which has shops in both directions, and then heads east where it ends at the intersection with Jl Sunset and Jl Kunti.

Some recommended shops:

Steven's (☑733 435; Jl Gunung Tangkuban Perahu 199) Dusty treasures from across Indonesia.

Heider (☑0819 1644 7400; Jl Gunung Tangkuban Perahu 100) Vintage bags from Lombok; huge collection of primitive-ish carvings.

IQI (☑733 181; Jl Gunung Tangkuban Perahu 274) Placemats, runners and other woven items made here; outfit your table for about US$5.

Wijaya Kusuma Brass (☑0813 3870 4597; Jl Gunung Soputan) Brass accessories for furniture and your home. Who doesn't want to grab a frog pull to access their undies?

Matrái Shop (☑729 813; Jl Gunung Atena) Smart little shop where intricate containers are made out of wire and beads. Exquisite.

Along the grey-sand beach, it is only 4.5km from Pura Petitenget to Echo Beach. Driving from one to the other can take an hour in traffic and many kilometres, while a walk could be one of your favourite days at the beach on Bali. You'll cover long stretches of empty sand with only the roar of the surf for company. A few villages, temples, expat villas and simple cafes provide interest away from the water.

You can easily spend half a day on this walk or zip along and do it in about an hour. There are a couple of places where rivers run into the ocean; their depth depends on whether it's been raining and can be just a few centimetres or up to a metre for a short distance. So be prepared to get wet (and bring some water to drink).

Following are some highlights, starting at Pura Petitenget. Watch for a couple of Seminyak **beach cafes** near the start of the walk.

The vast new **W Hotel** (Map p74) looms after about 500m, then the mellow sands of **Batubelig Beach** (Map p88) come after a further 1km. A couple of bamboo stands along here usually have cold drinks and plenty of solitude. Another 500m brings you to a river-fed **lagoon** and the deepest potential water crossing. If you can ford this, you're good for the rest of the walk.

If you need a break or the water is too high to cross, take the cool little footbridge over the lagoon to **Warung Agung Kayu Putih** (Map p88; Jl Pura Kayu Putih), which has a basic menu, cold drinks and good views.

One of the most serene swaths of sand is near the vast **Marabito Art Villa**, a private estate that's an architectural wonder. Almost 1km further on, you'll come to another (shallow) water crossing that also marks the large complex of **Pura Dalem Prancak** (Map p88). Turn around and you can see the sweep of the beach all the way to the airport.

A collection of fishing boats and huts is about midway to **Canggu Beach** (Pantai Batu Bolong), where there's the large **Pura Batumejan** (Map p88) complex with a large pagoda-like temple. About 200m further on there's a slightly upscale beach vendor with comfy loungers for rent and drinks.

Construction all along the shore means you've reached **Echo Beach**, where you can reward yourself for having fun and get a taxi back south.

---

tor items and housewares. For a shopping jaunt through the streets east of here towards Denpasar, see p86.

JJ Bali Button ACCESSORIES
(Map p74; ☑730 001; Jl Gunung Tangkuban Perahu) Zillions of beads and buttons made from shells, plastic, metal and more are displayed in what first looks like a candy store (and it *is* for creative types).

Ganesha Bookshop BOOKSHOP
(Map p74; Jl Petitenget) In a corner of the fabulous Biku restaurant, this tiny branch of Bali's best bookstore up in Ubud has all manner of local and literary treats.

Reza Art MARINE ANTIQUES
(Map p74; ☑0813 3705 0548; Jl Kerobokan 22) Brass both gleams and looks aged under green patina at this shop filled with nautical antiques – some newer than others.

Lio HOUSEWARES
(Map p74; ☑780 0942; Jl Raya Kerobokan) A minor empire with shops all along this

stretch of road. Housewares, rattan antiques, reproductions and more.

North of Kerobokan
☑0361

Growth is marching north and west along the coast, much of it anchored by the endless swath of beach, which, despite rampant development, remains blissfully empty in large part. Kerobokan morphs into Canggu, while neighbouring Echo Beach is a big construction site. Cloistered villas lure the well-heeled who whisk past stooped rice farmers in air-con comfort. Traffic may be the ultimate commoner's revenge: road building is a decade or two behind settlement.

Small roads lead off the main clogged artery that runs to Pura Tanah Lot in the north. Alternatively, an ever-growing number of tiny lanes thread through the rice fields and villas allowing you to link up the

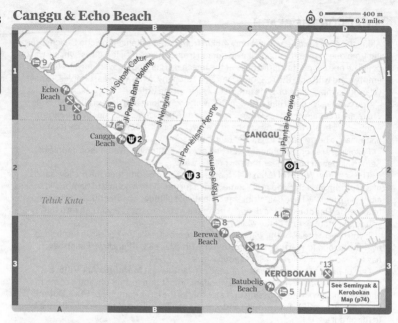

Canggu & Echo Beach

⊙ Sights
1 Canggu Club	C2
2 Pura Batumejan	B2
3 Pura Dalem Prancak	B2

⊜ Sleeping
4 Desa Seni	C2
5 Grand Balisani Suites	C3
6 Green Room	B1
7 Hotel Tugu Bali	B2
8 Legong Keraton	C3
9 Pondok Wisata Nyoman	A1

⊗ Eating
10 Beach House	A1
11 Mandira Cafe	A1
12 Warung Agung Kayu Putih	C3
13 Warung Sobat	D3

beaches without venturing to the Tanah Lot road.

Getting to most of the places listed following can cost 70,000Rp or more by taxi from Kuta or Seminyak.

BEREWA BEACH
This greyish beach, secluded among rice fields and villas, is about 2km up the sand from Seminyak and about 10km by round-about lanes. There are a couple of surfer cafes by the pounding sea. The grey volcanic sand here slopes steeply into foaming waters.

Right on the quiet sands of Berewa, the well-run 40-room **Legong Keraton** (Map p88; ☑730 280; www.legongkeratonhotel.com; Berewa Beach; r US$80-180; ❀@⊛) is the perfect place for a corporate retreat. The grounds are shaded by palms and the pool borders the beach. The best rooms are in bungalow units facing the surf.

CANGGU
A popular surf spot, Canggu draws a lot of locals and expat residents on weekends. Access to the paved parking area costs 2000Rp and there are cafes and warung for those who work up an appetite in the water or watching others in the water.

You can reach Canggu by road from the south by taking Jl Batubelig west in Kerobokan almost to the beach and then veering north past various huge villas and expat shops along a curvaceous road.

Bali's moneyed elite shuttlecock themselves silly at the **Canggu Club** (Map p88; ☑844 6385; www.cangguclub.com; Jl Pantai Berawa; day pass adult/family US$30/65), a new-age version of something you'd expect to find during the Raj. The vast, perfectly virescent lawn is manicured for croquet. Get sweaty with tennis, squash, polo, cricket, the spa or the 25m pool.

🛏 Sleeping

Hotel Tugu Bali   HOTEL $$$
(Map p88; ☏731701; www.tuguhotels.com; Jl Pantai Batu Bolong; r US$200-500; ❄ @ ☎ ☎) Right at Canggu Beach, this is an exquisite hotel surrounded by rice fields and beach. It blurs the boundaries between a museum and a gallery, especially the Walter Spies and Le Mayeur Pavilions, where memorabilia from the artists' lives decorates the rooms. The stunning collection of antiques and artwork begins in the lobby and extends throughout the hotel. There's a spa and numerous customised dining options. Even by day, candles twinkle amid the flowing fabrics in the breezy public areas.

Green Room   HOTEL $$
(Map p88; ☏923 2215; www.thegreenroombali.com; Jl Subak Catur; r US$50-100; ☎ ☎) Popular with surfers, the Green Room exudes hippie chic. Lounge on the 2nd-floor veranda and check out the waves (and villa construction) in the distance. The 14 rooms are comfy and breezy.

Desa Seni   HOTEL $$$
(Map p88; ☏844 6392; www.desaseni.com; Jl Kayu Putih 13; r US$150-360; ❄ @ ☎ ☎) One person described this place as like a hippie Four Seasons, and that's not far from the truth. Desa Seni bills itself as a 'village resort' and what a village it is. Ten classic wooden homes up to 220 years old have been brought to the site from across Indonesia and turned into luxurious quarters. Guests enjoy a menu of organic and healthy cuisine. Nonguests can also enjoy **yoga classes** (per class 90,000Rp), which are offered daily.

ECHO BEACH
Just 500m northwest of Canggu Beach is Echo Beach. One of Bali's most popular surf breaks, it has reached critical mass in popularity and is quite the scene with tourists, expats and locals, who come down to wet their feet at the often spectacular sunsets. Meanwhile huge villa developments are filling the area.

The ever-growing number of cafes includes **Mandira Cafe** (Map p88; Jl Pura Batu Mejan; meals 20,000-50,000Rp), which has a timeless surfer's menu of jaffles, banana pancakes, club sandwiches and smoothies.

Slicker yet, the **Beach House** (Map p88; ☏738 471; Jl Pura Batu Mejan; dishes 30,000-80,000Rp; ☎) faces the waves and draws stylish loungers. It has a variety of couches and picnic tables where you can hang out, watch the waves and enjoy the menu of breakfasts, salads, grilled fare and ambitious dishes such as calamari with aioli. On Sunday nights it offers a hugely popular outdoor barbecue.

A local taxi cooperative has taxis waiting to shuttle you back to Seminyak and the south for about 70,000Rp.

PERERENAN BEACH
Yet to be found by the right developer, this is the beach for you if you want your sand windswept and your waves unridden. It's 300m further on from Echo Beach by sand and rock formations, over 1km by road.

Once you've found it, why leave? The friendly guys at **Pondok Wisata Nyoman** (Map p88; ☏0812 390 6900; pondoknyoman@yahoo.com; Jl Raya Pantai Pererenan; r from 200,000Rp) have four simple rooms (although the bathrooms have a certain colourful flair) just behind the beach. There's a tiny cafe nearby and that's it.

South Bali & the Islands

Best Places to Eat

» Bumbu Bali (p105)

» Cak Asm (p119)

» Teba Mega Cafe (p94)

» Café Smorgås (p112)

Best Places to Stay

» Hotel La Taverna (p110)

» Indiana Kenanga (p124)

» Four Seasons Jimbaran Bay (p93)

» Alila Villas (p99)

Why Go?

You won't have seen Bali if you haven't fully explored south Bali. The island's capital, Denpasar, sprawls in all directions from the centre and is a vibrant place, offering traditional markets, glitzy malls, great eating and plenty of Balinese history and culture, even as it threatens to absorb the tourist hubs of Seminyak, Kuta and Sanur.

The Bukit Peninsula (the southern part of south Bali) has multiple personalities. In the east, Tanjung Benoa is a beach-fronted playground of modest resorts while Nusa Dua attempts to bring order out of chaos with an insulated pasture of five-star hotels. On the west side, however, is where the real action is. Small coves and beaches are dotted with edgy little guesthouses and five-star eco-resorts. The vibe, derived from the fab surfing around Ulu Watu, is funky and free.

To the east, the haunted island of Nusa Penida dominates the horizon but in its lee you'll find Nusa Lembongan, the ultimate island escape from the island of Bali.

When to Go

The best time to visit south Bali is outside the high season, which is July, August and the weeks around Christmas and New Year's Day. Visitor numbers spike and rooms from Bingin to Tanjung Benoa and Sanur to Nusa Lembongan may be filled. Many prefer April to June and September when the crowds are manageable. Surfing is best at the world-class breaks along the west coast of the Bukit Peninsula from February to November, with May to August being especially good.

South Bali & the Islands Highlights

1 Picking a lobster for the grill at a seafood joint in **Jimbaran** (p93)

2 Perching precariously on a bamboo stilt bar at **Balangan Beach** (p95)

3 Surfing **Ulu Watu** (p124), where boards break on the world-class breaks

4 Watching from **Sanur** (p106) as a full moon climbs over Nusa Penida

5 Savouring the best US$1 meal you've ever had in **Denpasar** (p118)

6 Escaping a small island (Bali) for a funkier, smaller one: **Nusa Lembongan** (p123)

7 Diving **Nusa Penida** (p125), where you can swim with manta rays

BUKIT PENINSULA

♫ 0361

Hot and arid, the southern peninsula is known as Bukit (meaning 'hill' in Bahasa Indonesia). It's popular with visitors, from the cloistered climes of Nusa Dua to the sybaritic retreats along the south coast.

One of Bali's new hotspots is the booming west coast with its string-of-pearls beaches. Accommodation sits precariously on the sand at Balangan Beach while the cliffs are dotted with idiosyncratic lodges at Bingin and elsewhere. New places sprout daily and most have views of the turbulent waters here, which have world-famous surf breaks all the way south to the important temple of Ulu Watu.

Jimbaran

Just south of Kuta and the airport, Teluk Jimbaran (Jimbaran Bay) is an alluring crescent of white sand beach and blue sea, fronted by a long string of seafood warung and ending at the southern end in a bushy headland, home to the Four Seasons Jimbaran Bay. Despite its many charms (such as great markets), Jimbaran has been a snoozy place. And that is perfectly fine for many visitors, who enjoy the proximity to the bright lights of Kuta and Seminyak but savour the calm here.

But that's changing. Jimbaran is on the map. Long-running budget hotels by the water have vanished and construction sites for glam condos and villas abound. Whether this will translate into Kuta or Seminyak south remains to be seen.

Facilities are still limited. Jl Raya Ulu Watu has some small stores and Jl Ulu Watu II has ATMs and mini-markets. For most things head north to Kuta.

◉ Sights & Activities

Pura Ulun Siwi   TEMPLE

The temple Pura Ulun Siwi dates from the 18th century. It is different from other Balinese temples in that it faces east, rather than north to Gunung Agung. It's thought this is because the site dates back to the 11th century when Java's Mt Semeru was still the focus of local piety. Look for farmers collecting water here to bless their fields: the anti-rodent powers are considered especially strong.

Produce Market   MARKET

Across from the temple, the **produce market** (Jl Ulu Watu; ◷ 5am-2pm) is small but has one of Bali's best selections of fruit and veg. Many savvy top-end chefs do their shopping here, and farmers from across the island know to bring their best or most unusual items here. Arrive early for the best viewing.

Jimbaran

Fish Market
MARKET

Smelly, lively and frenetic, the open-air fish market heaves with life. Boats land with their hauls and the deal-making, selling and transporting is manic. Watch out for porters carting impossible loads barefoot through the muck.

Surfing
SURFING

Out on the water, Jimbaran is a good place to access the surf breaks off the airport.

Ganeesha Gallery
ART GALLERY

(Four Seasons Jimbaran Bay; ☎701 010; www .fourseasons.com) Ganeesha has exhibitions by international artists and is worth a visit – walk south along the beach.

🛏 Sleeping

Some of south Bali's most luxurious large resorts are found in and around Jimbaran, as well as a few midrange places off the beach. Most offer some form of shuttle through the day to Kuta and beyond. Watch for offers from new beachside resorts.

Being a much more 'real' place (ie it's not an artificially planned resort), Jimbaran makes a good resort alternative to the monoliths of Nusa Dua.

TOP CHOICE Four Seasons Jimbaran Bay
RESORT HOTEL $$$

(☎701 010; www.fourseasons.com; villas from US$800; ✳@🗢🗷) Each of the 147 villas here is designed in a traditional Balinese manner, complete with a carved entrance-way, which opens onto an open-air dining pavilion overlooking a plunge pool. The spa is guests-only, which maintains the very exclusive air. The site is a hillside overlooking Jimbaran Beach, which is a very short walk away; most villas have good views across the bay.

Keraton Jimbaran
HOTEL $$

(☎701 991; www.keratonjimbaranresort.com; Jl Mrajapati; r US$100-150; ✳@🗢🗷) Sharing the same idyllic Jimbaran beach as the neighbouring pricier resorts, the low-key Keraton is a good find. Its 102 rooms are scattered about one- and two-storey bungalow-style units. The grounds are spacious and typically Bali-lush. Turn right as you hit the beach and you're almost immediately at the Middle Seafood Warung.

🍃 Udayana Kingfisher Eco Lodge
LODGE $$

(☎747 4204; www.ecolodgesindonesia.com; r US$70-75; ✳@🗢🗷) Feel like a bird perched in the green canopy from the second-floor common areas of this lodge, which is a bit of a Bukit oasis. There are grand views over south Bali from its perch on a knoll in 70 hectares of bushland. The 10 rooms are comfortable and there is an inviting common area with an excellent library. Much effort has been made to preserve and reuse water. The lodge is inland near Udayana University, off a road that runs uphill from the McDonald's on the bypass.

Jimbaran Puri Bali
HOTEL $$$

(☎701 605; www.jimbaranpuribali.com; Jl Yoga Perkanti; cottages US$250-500; ✳@🗢🗷) Under the umbrella of luxe Orient-Express Resorts, this beachside retreat is set in nice grounds complete with a maze-like pool that looks onto open ocean. The 41 cottages have private gardens, large terraces and a stylish room design with sunken tubs. It's a lavish yet low-key escape.

Hotel Puri Bambu
HOTEL $$

(☎701 377; www.puribambu.com; r US$45-100; ✳@🗢🗷) A mere 200m from the beach, the flash-free Puri Bambu is an older but well-run place – and the best-value option in Jimbaran. The 48 standard rooms (some with tubs) are in three-storey blocks around a large pool.

Hotel Intercontinental Bali
RESORT HOTEL $$$

(☎701 888; www.bali.intercontinental.com; Jl Ulu Watu; r US$250-400; ✳@🗢🗷) With 419 rooms, the Intercontinental is really a little city on the beach. Decorated with Balinese arts and handicrafts, it tries to meld local style to a huge resort. The plethora of pools feed each other and meander through the grounds. There is a good kids' club and the crescent of beach is fine.

🍴 Eating

Jimbaran's three groups of seafood warung cook fresh barbecued seafood every evening (and lunch at many); they draw tourists from across the south. The open-sided affairs are right by the beach and perfect for enjoying sea breezes and sunsets. Tables and chairs are set up on the sand almost to the water's edge.

The usual deal is to select your seafood fresh from iced displays or tanks, and to pay according to weight. Expect to pay around 40,000Rp per 100g of live lobster, 15,000Rp to 25,000Rp for prawns, and 9000Rp for fish, squid and clams. Prices are open to

PASCAL CHEVILLOT: SEAFOOD CHEF

Owner of the very popular Sardine restaurant in Kerobokan, Chevillot is a fixture at the Jimbaran seafood market up to six mornings a week – so he knows what's been brought in fresh.

Best Market

The Jimbaran fish market. New seafood arrives constantly as boats pull up to the beach. You know you'll find certain things like excellent shellfish all the time but it's also an adventure as you are constantly surprised.

Best Fish for Sale Here

Sea bream, mahi mahi, skate, snapper and more.

Best Way to Visit

Get there as early as possible and then stay out of the way. Wander around the dark interior; it's like a warren and you'll be surprised at what Bali's waters yield. The vendors actually are happy to see you there, figuring you'll eat more seafood.

negotiation and the accuracy of the scales is a joke among locals. Agree to a price before ordering. Some places simplify things with fixed menu prices.

The best kitchens marinate the fish in garlic and lime, then douse it with chilli and oil while grilling over coconut husks. Thick clouds of smoke from the coals are part of the atmosphere, as are roaming bands, who perform cheery, dated tunes from the 'Macarena' playlist. Many people actually join in. Almost all take credit cards.

Also right on the beaches, the luxury hotels' cafes and restaurants afford beautiful views of the surf, sea and sunset.

NORTHERN SEAFOOD WARUNG

The longest row of warung is the northern seafood warung, south of the fish market. This is the area you will be taken to by a taxi if you don't specify otherwise. Most of these places are restaurant-like, with tables inside and out on the immaculate raked sand. Call for free transport to/from much of the south. Note that this is the area with

the hardest sell from legions of guys flagging down your driver.

Recommendations:

Ganesha Pudak Cafe   SEAFOOD **$$**
(☑0813 3855 3800; Jl Pantai Kedonganan) Many fish displays of future main courses.

Blue Marlin   SEAFOOD **$$**
(☑702 242; Jl Pantai Kedonganan) This place is built like a brick...warung.

MIDDLE SEAFOOD WARUNG

The middle seafood warung are in a compact group just south of Jl Pantai Jimbaran and Jl Pemelisan Agung. These are the simplest affairs, with old-fashioned thatched roofs and wide-open sides. The beach is a little less manicured, with the fishing boats resting up on the sand. Huge piles of coconut husks await their turn on the fires. Recommendations:

Roman Café   SEAFOOD **$$**
(☑703 124; Jl Pantai Kedonganan) Always seems just a slight cut above the cheek-to-jowl competition.

Warung Bamboo   SEAFOOD **$$**
(☑702 188; off Jl Pantai Jimbaran) Built from just that.

SOUTHERN SEAFOOD WARUNG

The southern seafood warung are just north of the Four Seasons Jimbaran Bay. In many ways the warung groups are like the Three Bears' possessions: this one – not as formal as the northern group, not as rickety as the middle group – is just right. There's a parking area off Jl Bukit Permai and the places are all in a row. The beach here is well groomed with nice trees. Call for transport. Recommendations:

Teba Mega Cafe   SEAFOOD **$$**
(☑703 156; off Jl Bukit Permai) Lots of special platters and a local fave. In fact it's so popular they added 'Mega' to the name. Nice shady beach trees.

Roma   SEAFOOD **$$**
(☑702 387; off Jl Bukit Permai) Redolent with garlic.

🛍 Shopping

Jenggala Keramik Bali   CERAMICS
(☑703 310; www.jenggala-bali.com; Jl Ulu Watu II; ⊙9am-6pm) A modern air-con showroom displays beautiful ceramic homewares. It has a viewing area where you can watch production, and a stylish cafe. The outlet

store for Jenggala is Gudang Keramik in Sanur. This can be a good move if you're buying in bulk, as a simple bowl here costs US$10 and up.

❶ Getting There & Away

Bemo from Tegal terminal in Denpasar go via Kuta to Jimbaran (17,000Rp), and continue to Nusa Dua. They don't run after about 4pm, but plenty of taxis wait around the beachfront warung in the evening to take diners home (about 50,000Rp to Kuta). Some of the seafood warung provide free transport if you call first.

Expect to pay 2000Rp per vehicle to use the beach access roads.

Around Jimbaran

Folding around limestone bluffs, sightly **Tegalwangi Beach**, 4.5km southwest of Jimbaran, is the first of cove after cove holding patches of lovely sand all down the west coast of the peninsula. A small parking area lies in front of **Pura Segara Tegalwangi** temple, a popular place for addressing the ocean gods. There's usually a lone drinks vendor offering refreshment before – or after – you make the short but challenging trip over the bad paths down to the beach. Immediately south, the vast Ayana resort sprawls over the cliffs.

From Jimbaran, follow Jl Bukit Permai past the Four Seasons Jimbaran Bay for 3km until the gates of the Ayana, when it veers west 1.5km to the temple.

Central Bukit

Jl Ulu Watu goes south of Jimbaran, climbing 200m up the peninsula's namesake hill, affording views over southern Bali.

Garuda Wisnu Kencana Cultural Park (GWK; ✆703 603; adult/child 50,000/15,000Rp, parking 5000Rp; ⊙8am-6pm) is the yet-to-be-completed potentially huge cultural park that is meant to be home to a 66m-high statue of Garuda. This Brobdingnagian dream is supposed to be erected on top of a shopping and gallery complex, for a total height of 146m.

So far, however, the only completed part of the statue is the large bronze head. The buildings that do exist are mostly empty. However, besides the perverse fascination with big things gone bad, there's another good reason to visit the site: the **views**. From a small cafe off the parking lot there are sweeping vistas across all of south Bali. And if it's clear enough to see the volcanoes, then GWK is a must-stop off the main Ulu Watu road.

Balangan Beach

Balangan Beach is a real find. A long, low strand at the base of the cliffs is covered with palm trees and fronted by a ribbon of near-white sand, picturesquely dotted with white sun umbrellas. Surfer bars, cafes in shacks and even slightly more permanent guesthouses precariously line the shore where buffed first-world bods soak up rays amid third-world sanitation. Think of it as a bit of the Wild West not far from Bali's glitz.

At the northern end of the beach is a small temple, **Pura Dalem Balangan** (Map p96). Bamboo beach shacks line the southern end, visitors laze away with one eye cast on the action at the fast left surf break here (p34).

🛏 Sleeping & Eating

You have two choices for spending the night at Balangan Beach. Firstly, you can stay up on the bluff at some fairly simple yet quite nice guesthouses that have pools and an air of permanency. The beach is a mere five-minute walk away.

Or you can find a room in one of the beach shacks where many of the bars have small, windowless thatched rooms next to cases of Bintang. It's like Kuta c 1975. Be sure to negotiate and you should be able to pass out to the sounds of alcohol-fuelled hilarity backed by the roar of the surf for under 100,000Rp.

Flower Bud Bungalows GUESTHOUSE $
(✆0828 367 2772; www.flowerbudbalangan.com; r 350,000-450,000Rp; ❄) Eight bamboo bungalows are set on spacious grounds near a classic kidney-shaped pool. There's a certain Crusoe-esque motif, and fans and sprightly pillows are among the 'luxuries'.

Balangan Sea View Bungalows
GUESTHOUSE $
(✆0812 376 1954; robbyandrosita@hotmail.com; r 300,000-650,000Rp; ❄) A cluster of thatched bungalows with 11 rooms surrounds a small pool in an attractive compound. The small cafe has wi-fi. It is directly across from Flower Bud Bungalows.

Nasa Café CAFE $
(✆08180 533 9118; Balangan Beach; r 80,000Rp) Inside the shady bamboo bar built on stilts

SOUTH BALI & THE ISLANDS BUKIT PENINSULA

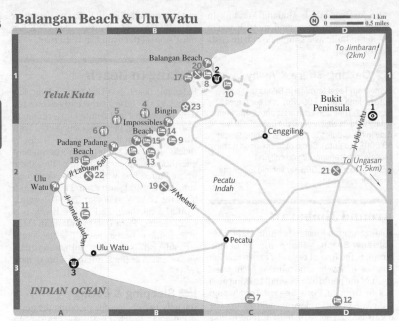

above the sand, a vibrant azure ribbon of crashing surf is the wraparound view through the drooping thatched roof. Simple Indo meals (30,000Rp) set the tone for the bare-bones rooms off the bar, which are little more than a mattress on the floor. It's one of about a dozen similar choices.

Point   GUESTHOUSE $
(☏0857 3951 8317; Balangan Beach; r 200,000-300,000Rp) Built on actual rocks using cement blocks, the Point sits slightly apart from its bamboo-stilted neighbours. The five rooms have fans and windows; a couple look out to the surf, some 10m distant. The porch cafe is shady.

ⓘ Getting There & Away

Balangan Beach is 6.5km off the main Ulu Watu road via Cenggiling. Turn west at the crossroads 1.5km past GWK and immediately in front of Nirmala Supermarket (Map p96), which is a good place to stock up on necessities like water. The road to the beach takes many twists and turns, but it is mostly paved and there are a few signs. When you near the bluff, take the road to the left that goes past Flower Bud Bungalows and ends at a rough dirt parking area close to the beach.

Taxis from the Kuta area cost at least 50,000Rp per hour for the round trip and waiting time.

Pecatu Indah

This 400-hectare **resort complex** (www.balipecatu.com) rises between central Bukit Peninsula and the coast. The land is arid but that hasn't stopped developers from building a huge hotel, condos, houses and a water-sucking 18-hole golf course. Follow the grand boulevards and you can see a lot of tank trucks hauling water all the way in from Denpasar.

Less obvious is the gradual destruction of a sweet little beach community named Dreamland for the construction of **Klapa** (☏848 4581; Pecatu Indah; admission 75,000Rp; ⊙10am-11pm), a brash and heavily promoted beach club where disco lights flash as you enter. There's no arguing with the views, however, which you can enjoy along with a pool and the privatised beach. Note that parking is a stiff 5000Rp. The area is being marketed under the name of 'New Kuta Beach'.

Bingin

An ever-evolving scene, Bingin comprises several funky lodgings scattered across cliffs and on the strip of white sand below. A 1km dirt road turns off the paved road (look for the thicket of accommodation signs),

Balangan Beach & Ulu Watu

which in turn branches off the main Ulu Watu road at the small village of Pecatu.

An elderly resident collects 5000Rp at a T-junction (and will offer you a bootleg DVD) near parking for the trail down to the **beach**. The surf here is often savage but the sands are calm and the roaring breakers mesmerising. For details on the renowned left break, see p34.

The scenery here is simply superb, with sylvan cliffs dropping down to a row of houses and the foaming edge of the azure sea. Several places to stay enjoy the views while more modest places are set back. All have at least simple cafes, although for nightlife – like the rest of this coast – you'll be heading north to Kuta (unless your idea of nightlife is more intimate). Plans for upmarket villas and hotels are constantly rumoured.

🛏 Sleeping & Eating

The places listed are all fairly small and are noninvasive to the overall clifftop Bingin atmosphere. The beach is a five-minute walk down a fairly steep path. A good source for info on the many little guesthouses scattered about here is **Bali Holiday Retreats** (www.baliretreats.com.au).

Mick's Place GUESTHOUSE $$
(☑0812 391 3337; micksplacebali@yahoo.com. au; r US$90-180, villas US$300; ☜❄) The turquoise water in the postage-stamp infinity pool matches the turquoise sea below. Something of a hippie-chic playground, this highly personable place with six artful round huts is set in lush grounds. Candles provide the flickering ambience although each unit has a power point for recharging iPods etc. A lavish walled villa has its own pool.

Mu GUESTHOUSE $$
(☑847 0976; www.mu-bali.com; r €50-190; ❄@☜❄) Turn left after the toll gate for the most stylish option in Bingin. Nine very individual bungalows with round, pointed thatched roofs are scattered about a compound dominated by a cliffside infinity pool. All have open-air living spaces; some have air-con bedrooms and hot tubs with a view.

Kembang Kuning GUESTHOUSE $
(☑743 4424; r 300,000-500,000Rp; ❄) The best-value cliffside option has eight rooms in modern two-storey bungalow-style units. The grounds are thickly landscaped but the real appeal is the infinity swimming pool on the edge of the limestone and the various nearby loungers, all with sensational views. It's down a little path just to the right as you face Mu.

Bingin Garden GUESTHOUSE $
(☑0816 472 2002; tommybarrell76@yahoo.com; r from 250,000Rp) Six basic rooms in bungalows are set around tidy grounds back from the cliffs and 300m north of the toll gate. Each unit sleeps two and has cold water and a fan.

Ulu Watu & Around

Ulu Watu has become the generic name for the southwestern tip of the Bukit Peninsula. It includes the much-revered temple

PILLAGING BUKIT

Many environmentalists consider the always arid Bukit Peninsula a harbinger for the challenges that face the rest of Bali as land use far outpaces the water supply. The small guesthouses that once perched above and on the string of pearls that are the beaches on the west side had a modest impact on the environment. But with the area's exploding popularity have come large developments which in unregulated Bali are having a huge impact. Besides the vast Pecatu Indah development, a growing number of projects are carving away the beautiful limestone cliffs to make way for huge concrete structures housing condos such as the **Anantara** (www.balianantara uluwatu.com), a lavish resort built into the side and above a previously unspoiled stretch of coast.

Now, however, a nascent protest movement has formed and environmental groups are questioning unfettered development. How it plays out will have effects on Bali's future beyond the peninsula.

and the fabled surf breaks at Padang Padang, Suluban and Ulu Watu. Surfers are most common in these parts, although a spate of villa-building is changing that. (In fact, authorities and activists are trying to stop new construction within 2km of the temple.)

Guesthouses, a few hotels and some cafes are scattered along the main road which loops through the area. There is no real centre.

◉ Sights

Pura Luhur Ulu Watu TEMPLE
(admission incl sarong & sash rental 3000Rp, parking 1000Rp; ☺8am-7pm) This important temple is perched precipitously on the southwestern tip of the peninsula, atop sheer cliffs that drop straight into the ceaseless surf. You enter through an unusual arched gateway flanked by **statues of Ganesha**. Inside, the walls of coral bricks are covered with intricate carvings of Bali's mythological menagerie. Only Hindu worshippers can enter the small inner temple that is built onto the jutting tip of land. However, the views of the endless swells of the Indian Ocean from the cliffs are almost spiritual. At **sunset**, walk around the cliff-top to the left (south) of the temple to lose some of the crowd.

Ulu Watu is one of several important temples to the spirits of the sea along the south coast of Bali. In the 11th century the Javanese priest Empu Kuturan first established a temple here. The complex was added to by Nirartha, another Javanese priest who is known for the seafront temples at Tanah Lot, Rambut Siwi and Pura Sakenan. Nirartha retreated to Ulu Watu for his fi-

nal days when he attained *moksa* (freedom from earthly desires).

For tips on respecting traditions and acting appropriately while visiting temples, see the boxed text (p329).

An enchanting and popular **Kecak dance** is held in the temple grounds at sunset; tickets cost 70,000Rp. Although the performance caters for tourists, the gorgeous setting makes it one of the more delightful on the island.

🏃 Activities

Surf Beaches SURFING
From the paved road that goes northwest from Pecatu village (turn right at the small temple), it's easy to access the breaks off the coast at Bingin. **Impossibles** is nearby and **Padang Padang** is about 1km on. There is parking just north of a bridge.

Ulu Watu (Ulu's) is a storied surf spot – the stuff of dreams and nightmares. It's about 1km south of Padang Padang and its legend is matched closely by nearby **Pantai Suluban**. Since the early 1970s these breaks have drawn surfers from around the world. The left breaks seem to go on forever. The area boasts numerous small inns and warung that sell and rent out surfboards, and provide food, drink, ding repairs or a massage – whatever you need most. Pantai Suluban is the best place to swim in the area. From its bluff, you get a good view of all the area surf breaks (for details, see p36).

🛏 Sleeping & Eating

If you're not picky you can count on being able to find accommodation of some sort near the surf break of your choice. Expect to pay at least 100,000Rp for a room with cold water, a fan and a shared bathroom.

Many surfers choose to stay in Kuta and make the commute of less than an hour. Any place there's people on the beach or surfing, you'll find a vendor or two with drinks on ice and snacks.

Thomas Homestay
GUESTHOUSE $

(☑0812 3775 6030; r from 150,000Rp) Enjoy stunning views up and down this spectacular coast. Seven very simple rooms lie at the end of a very rough 400m track off the main road. You can easily walk down to the beach at Padang Padang on a steep path through the palms.

Gong
GUESTHOUSE $

(☑769 976; thegongacc@yahoo.com; Jl Pantai Suluban; r from 175,000Rp) Few stay away long from the Gong. Eight tidy rooms with good ventilation and hot water face a small compound and have distant ocean views. There's also a cafe.

Yeye's Warung
CAFE $

(Jl Labuan Sait; mains 18,000-30,000Rp) A gathering point away from the cliffs, Yeye's has an easygoing ambience, cheapish beers and tasty Western, Indonesian and vegetarian food. But pizza is the perennial number-one attraction at this popular cafe, the closest thing to being the local hangout.

Jiwa Juice
CAFE $

(☑742 4196; Jl Melasti; mains 20,000-30,000Rp; ✳ @) Jiwa means 'soul', and the juices and fresh, light food here are good for the same. This popular stop has internet access, a rarity in these parts.

ⓘ Getting There & Away

The best way to see the west coast is with your own vehicle or by chartering a taxi. Note that the cops often set up checkpoints near Pecatu Indah for checks on motorcycle-riding Westerners. Be aware you may pay a fine for details such as a 'loose' chin strap.

Drivers note: coming from the east to Pantai Suluban you will first encounter a gated parking

---

ⓘ **DAMN MONKEYS**

Pura Luhur Ulu Watu is home to scores of grey monkeys. Greedy little buggers, when they're not energetically fornicating, they snatch sunglasses, handbags, hats and anything else within reach. If you want to start a riot, peel them a banana...

---

area (car/motorcycle 3000/2000Rp), which is about a 400m walk from the water. Continuing over a bridge, there is an older parking area (car/motorcycle 2000/1000Rp), which is a hilly 200m from the water. Watch out for 'gatekeepers' looking for bonuses.

Bemo to Ulu Watu are infrequent and stop running by mid-afternoon. Some from Kuta serve Jimbaran and Ulu Watu – it's best to catch one west of Tuban (on Jl Raya Kuta, outside the Supernova shopping centre).

Ungasan & Around

If Ulu Watu is all about celebrating the surfer vibe, Ungasan is all about celebrating yourself. From crossroads near this otherwise nondescript village, roads radiate to the south coast where some of Bali's most exclusive ocean-side resorts can be found. With the infinite turquoise waters of the Indian Ocean rolling hypnotically in the distance it's hard not to think you've reached the end of the world, albeit a very comfortable one.

◉ Sights

Bali's southernmost **beach** can be found at the end of a 3km-long road from Ungasan village. Here you can look for **Pura Gunung Payung**, a temple that sits on the seaside. New concrete steps lead down the 200m cliff to a sweet swathe of sand on the pounding ocean. Bring a picnic and a good book to enjoy the atmosphere.

Diminutive **Pura Mas Suka** (Map p96) is reached by a twisting narrow road through a mostly barren red-rock landscape that changes dramatically when you reach the Karma Resort, which surrounds the temple. A perfect example of a Balinese seaside temple, it is often closed so consider that before setting off on the rough track from the good resort road to the temple.

See p35 for details of the area's surf breaks.

⌦ Sleeping & Eating

TOP CHOICE / **Alila Villas**
RESORT HOTEL $$$

(☑848 2166; www.alilahotels.com; Pecatu; r from US$725; ✳ @ 🛜 🌊) Visually stunning, this vast new destination resort has the full seal of eco-approval from Green Globe (something others in the area might emulate...). Designed in an artful contemporary style that is at once light and airy while still conveying a sense of wealth, the 85-unit Alila offers gracious service in a setting where the blue of the ocean contrasts with the green of the surrounding (hotel-tended) rice fields. It's 2km off the main Ulu Watu road, about 1km south of Pecatu Indah.

Karma Kandara RESORT HOTEL **$$$**
(☑848 2200; www.karmaresorts.com; Ungasan villas from US$600; ✷@⑱✵) More Mediterranean than Balinese, this beautiful resort clings to the side of hills that roll down to the sea. Stone paths lead between walled villas draped in bougainvillea and punctuated by painted doors, creating the mood of a tropical hill town. Units come with one to four bedrooms. The restaurant, **Di Mare** (meals US$15-30), is linked to the bifurcated property by a little bridge, and is a popular lunch stop for day trippers. The beach cove below is reached via a little elevator. Bear left at the fork in the main Ulu Watu road, about 1km south of the junction with the roads to Balangan Beach and Ungasan, and continue 4km to the Karma.

Nusa Dua

Nusa Dua translates literally as Two Islands – although they are actually small raised headlands, each with a small temple, including Pura Bias Tugal. But Nusa Dua is much better known as Bali's gated compound of resort hotels. It's a vast and manicured place where you leave the rest of the island behind as you pass the guards. Gone are the street vendors, hustle, bustle and engaging chaos of the rest of the island. Here you even talk more quietly.

Built in the 1970s, Nusa Dua was designed to compete with international beach resorts the world over. Balinese 'culture', in the form of attenuated dances and other performances, is literally trucked in for the masses nightly.

With thousands of hotel rooms, Nusa Dua can live up to some of its promise when full, but during slack times it's rather desolate. Certainly it is closer in atmosphere to a generic beach resort than to anything Balinese – although some of the hotels try to apply a patina of Bali style. One side benefit of its isolation is that Nusa Dua is a favoured choice for major international summits.

◎ Sights & Activities

Pasifika Museum MUSEUM
(☑774 559; Bali Collection, Block P, Nusa Dua; admission 60,000Rp; ◷10am-6pm) This large mu-

seum suffers from the same visitor neglect as the rest of the Bali Collection. Good! You'll probably have the place to yourself. Several centuries of art from cultures around the Pacific Ocean are displayed (the tikis are cool). The influential wave of European artists who thrived in Bali in the early 20th century is well represented. Look for works by Arie Smit, Adrien Jean Le Mayeur de Merpes and Theo Meier. Staff will follow you around the wings turning lights on and off. This museum is reason enough to visit Nusa Dua.

Gegar Beach BEACH
Worth a day trip from anywhere in south Bali, Gegar Beach has a string of tidy stands on the sand that offer drinks and snacks plus a few that rent out umbrellas, loungers and **water sports gear** for kayaking, windsurfing etc. Expats in the know mob the place on weekends; on weekdays it's very quiet. Reefs offshore mean the surf close-in is feeble (aka kid-friendly). Wiry seaweed harvesters toil in the sun, blithely ignoring sunbathers.

A short walk south of the St Regis Bali Resort, Gegar Beach is reached by car via a small road over a somewhat askew bridge that runs 300m off the main road south of Nusa Dua. Parking is 2000Rp.

Pura Gegar TEMPLE
Just south of Gegar Beach is a bluff with a good cafe and a path that leads up to Pura Gegar, a compact temple shaded by gnarled old trees. Views are great and you can spy on swimmers who've come south in the shallow, placid waters around the bluff for a little frolic.

Beach Promenade BEACH WALKWAY
One of the nicest features of Nusa Dua is the 5km-long beach promenade that stretches the length of the resort and continues north along much of the beach in Tanjung Benoa. Not only is it a good stroll at any time but it also makes sampling the features of the other beachside resorts easy. The walk is paved for most of its length.

Surf Beaches SURFING
The reef-protected beach at Nusa Dua is shallow at low tide, and the wave action is pretty limp. The surf breaks at Nusa Dua are way out on reefs to the north and south of the two 'islands'. They work best with a big swell during the wet season. **Sri Lanka** is a right-hander in front of Club Med. The so-called **Nusa Dua** breaks are peaks, reached by a boat from Gegar Beach.

Bali Golf & Country Club
GOLF

(✆771 791; www.baligolfandcountryclub.com; green fees US$165) This golf club is an 18-hole course with all the amenities one would expect from a course at a major resort, including a grand new clubhouse. Its popularity has sparked condo development along the fairways, and new resorts have begun opening nearby.

Spas
SPA

All the resort hotels have pricey spas that provide a broad range of therapies, treatments and just plain, simple relaxation. The most lauded of the spas are at the Amanusa, Westin and St Regis hotels in Nusa Dua and at the Conrad in Tanjung Benoa. All are open to nonguests; expect fees for a massage to start at US$100.

🛏 Sleeping

The Nusa Dua hotels are similar in several ways: they are all big (some are huge) and they have long beachfronts. Each has several restaurants and bars, as well as various pools and other resort amenities. But what's most important is the detail, as that's where the real differences lie. Some hotels, such as the Westin and Grand Hyatt, have invested heavily in property, adding loads of amenities (such as elaborate pools and day camps for kids) demanded by travellers today. Other hotels seem little changed from when they were built during the heyday of the Suharto era in the 1970s.

If you're considering a stay at Nusa Dua, prowl the internet looking for deals. During the low season you can get excellent deals that bring nightly rates down by up to half.

Amanusa
RESORT HOTEL $$$

(✆772 333; www.amanresorts.com; villas from US$850; ❄@🛜🏊) Overlooking the golf course and beyond across Selat Badung, the Amanusa is one of Bali's best hotels. The elegant, understated architecture, rich decorations, superb service and brilliant views are the province of just 35 individual villas. Guests enjoy a private beach.

St Regis Bali Resort
RESORT HOTEL $$$

(✆847 8111; www.starwoodhotels.com; ste from US$600; ❄@🛜🏊) This lavish Nusa Dua resort leaves most of the others in the sand. Every conceivable luxury is provided, from the electronics to the furnishings to the marble to a personal butler. Pools abound and units are huge. A golf course and the beach adjoin.

Novotel Nusa Dua
HOTEL $$

(✆848 0555; www.novotelnusaduabali.com; r US$90-160; ❄@🛜🏊) The closest sand to this 188-unit resort is the bunkers on the golf course that surrounds the complex. Large apartments here come with one to three bedrooms and are excellent for families. The beach is a 10-minute walk away.

Grand Hyatt Bali
RESORT HOTEL $$$

(✆771 234; www.bali.grand.hyatt.com; r from US$230; ❄@🛜🏊) A little city, of sorts, the 648-room Hyatt has directional signs displaying up to 21 arrows. As in any city, certain neighbourhoods are better than others. Some rooms in the West Village face the taxi parking lot (of the four Villages, East and South are the best located). The riverlike pool (one of six) is huge and has a fun slide. The children's club will keep 'em busy for days.

Westin Resort
RESORT HOTEL $$$

(✆771 906; www.westin.com/bali; r from US$230; ❄@🛜🏊) Attached to a large convention centre, the Westin has an air-conditioned lobby (a rarity) and vast public spaces. Guests in the 355 rooms enjoy the best pools in Nusa, with waterfalls and other features forming an aquatic playground. The Kids Club has extensive activities and facilities. The landmark 2007 meetings on climate change were held here although, like a phone charger, they were easily forgotten.

🍴 Eating

Restaurants charging resort prices can be found by the dozen in the huge resorts. For people not staying at the hotels, the best reason to venture in is if you want a bounteous Sunday brunch.

South of Nusa Dua, the various warung at the beach serve fresh local standards. Other good **warung** cluster at the corner of Jl Srikandi and Jl Pantai Mengiat. Also along the latter street, just outside the central gate, there is a string of open-air eateries offering an unpretentious alternative to Nusa Dua dining. None will win any culinary awards, but most will provide transport.

Nusa Dua Beach Grill
GLOBAL $

(✆743 4779; Jl Pura Gegar; meals 50,000-150,000Rp) A hidden gem, this warm-hued cafe is just south of Gegar Beach on foot, but a circuitous 1.5km by car. The drink menu is long, the seafood fresh and the

Nusa Dua

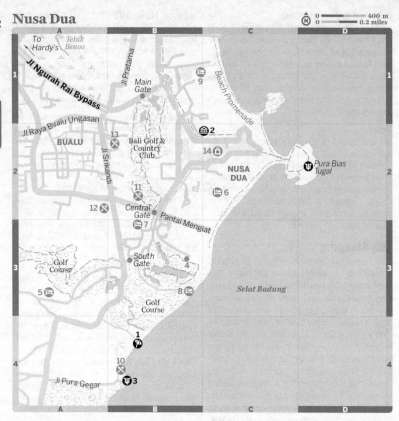

atmosphere heavy with assignations. Lounge your afternoon away in the laid-back bar.

Warung Dobiel   INDONESIAN $
(Jl Srikandi; meals from 15,000Rp; ☺8am-3pm) It's all about pork at this beloved open-front warung. Pork satay, pork soup, and green beans with shredded pork are among the favourites. The sautéd jackfruit will make you a convert; the green sambal is laden with spices. Seating is on stools at long tables.

Nyoman's Beer Garden   GLOBAL $
(☏775 746; Jl Pantai Mengiat; meals 40,000-100,000Rp) Best of the bunch just outside the gates. There's a party atmosphere at the tables inside and out. The menu cuts a broad swathe: Asian, pasta, pizza, burgers and, yes, schnitzel. Order the lobster in advance and it comes with the owner's secret – and tasty – sauce.

☆ Entertainment

Most of the hotels offer Balinese dances on one or more nights, usually as part of a buffet deal. Hotel lounges also often have live music, from crooners to mellow rock bands.

🔒 Shopping

Bali Collection   MALL
(☏771 662) This shopping centre has undergone numerous name changes. Mostly empty except for the dozens of assistants in the glacially air-conditioned Sogo Department Store, it gamely soldiers on. A few souls try to make merry on their Bali holiday at the deserted Starbucks. Good luck. Although the problems can be traced to Nusa Dua's rigorous security and closed nature, the isolation means that the boom other local malls are enjoying is a bust here.

Hardy's   SUPERMARKET
(Jl Ngurah Rai, Bualu; ☺8am-9pm) This huge outlet of the local chain of supermarkets is

Nusa Dua

about 1km west of the main gate. Besides groceries it has most other goods you might need and at real (ie not inflated resort) prices.

ℹ Information

ATMs can be found at the Bali Collection, some hotel lobbies and at the Hardy's supermarket.

Most of the resorts charge outrageous prices for wi-fi access. **Daniel's** (☎0856 9292 7486; Jl Srikandi; 📶) is a cute little place run by a charming family, which offers free wi-fi with coffee and snacks such as banana pancakes.

ℹ Getting There & Around

The fixed taxi fare from the airport is 105,000Rp; a metered taxi to the airport will be much less. Taxis to/from Seminyak average 80,000Rp.

Find out what shuttle-bus services your hotel provides before you start hailing taxis. A free **shuttle bus** (☎771 662; ◷9am-10pm) connects all Nusa Dua and Tanjung Benoa resort hotels with the Bali Collection shopping centre about every hour. Better: walk the delightful beach promenade.

Tanjung Benoa

The peninsula of Tanjung Benoa extends about 4km north from Nusa Dua to Benoa village. It's flat and lined with family-friendly resort hotels, most of midrange calibre. By day the waters buzz with the roar of dozens of motorised water-sports craft. Group tours arrive by the busload for a day's excitement straddling a banana boat among other thrills.

Beaches here are protected from waves by an offshore reef which has allowed a local beach-activities industry to flourish in the placid waters. Overall, Tanjung Benoa is a fairly sedate place and the late-night diversions of Kuta and Seminyak are a bit of a hike.

⊙ Sights

The village of **Benoa** is a fascinating little fishing settlement that makes for a good stroll. Amble the narrow lanes of the peninsula's tip for a multicultural feast. Within 100m of each other are a brightly coloured **Chinese Buddhist temple**, a domed **mosque** with a nicely carved triple entrance. Enjoy views of the busy channel to the port. On the dark side, however, Benoa's back streets hide Bali's illegal trade in turtles (see the boxed text, p361), although regular police raids are helping.

🏃 Activities

Cooking School

TOP CHOICE **Bumbu Bali Cooking School**   COOKING SCHOOL
(☎774 502; www.balifoods.com; Jl Pratama; classes US$80; ◷6am-3pm Mon, Wed & Fri) Heinz von Holzen, who has done much to raise Bali's culinary profile in the greater world, runs a very popular cooking school. It starts with a 6am visit to Jimbaran's fascinating fish and

PRATAMA PERILS

Restaurants and hotels are strung out all along Jl Pratama, which runs the length of the peninsula. The southern end may be one of the most perilous streets in south Bali for a stroll. From Nusa Dua north to the Conrad Hotel, there are no footpaths and in many places nowhere to walk but on the narrow road, which also has blind curves. Fortunately, the **beach promenade** is a wonderful alternative. It continues from Nusa Dua north to the Bali Khama.

Tanjung Benoa

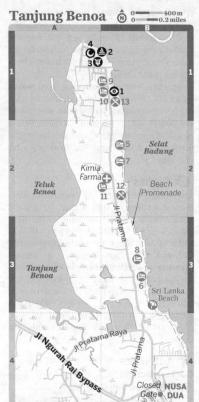

0 —— 400 m
0 —— 0.2 miles

Tanjung Benoa

village markets to buy goods, and finishes with lunch. Von Holzen shares his unique perspectives on life, food and more as the class progresses. It's almost a floor show.

Water Sports
Quite a few water-sports centres along Jl Pratama offer daytime diving, cruises, windsurfing and waterskiing. Check equipment and credentials before you sign up, as a few tourists have been killed here. Most centres have a thatched-roof bar and restaurant where prospective customers are given the hard sell. Each morning convoys of buses arrive from all over south Bali bringing day trippers, and by 10am parasailers float over the water.

Among the established water-sports operators is **Benoa Marine Recreation** (BMR; ☏771 757; www.bmrbali.com; Jl Pratama 99). As if by magic, all operators have similar (negotiable) prices.

Water sports include the following:

Banana-boat rides (per 15min US$30) Wild rides for two as you try to maintain your grasp on the inflatable fruit over the waves.

Diving Diving costs US$80/95 for one/two dives around Tanjung Benoa, including equipment rental.

Glass-bottomed boat trips (60min tour US$25) The non-wet way to see the denizens of the shallows.

Jet-skiing (per 15min US$25) Go fast and belch smoke.

Parasailing (per round US$25) Iconic; you float above the water while towed by a speedboat.

Snorkelling (per hr per person US$25) These trips include equipment and a boat ride to a reef.

One nice way to use the **beach** here is at Tao restaurant, where for the price of a drink, you can enjoy resort-quality loungers and a pool.

🛏 Sleeping
Tanjung Benoa mostly offers midrange low-key resorts aimed at groups. They are family-friendly, offer kids' programs and enjoy repeat business by holidaymakers who are greeted with banners such as 'Welcome

Back Schmidt Family!' There's a couple of simple guesthouses as well.

Rumah Bali GUESTHOUSE **$$**
(☏771 256; www.balifoods.com; Jl Pratama; r US$70-100, villas from US$250; ❄@☎☒) Rumah Bali is a luxurious interpretation of a Balinese village by Heinz von Holzen of Bumbu Bali fame. Guests have large family rooms or individual villas (some with three bedrooms) with their own plunge pools. There's a 'village centre' with a tasty warung, Pasar Malam. Besides a large communal pool, there's also a tennis court. The beach is a short walk away.

Conrad Bali Resort RESORT HOTEL **$$$**
(☏778 788; www.conradhotels.com; Jl Pratama; r from US$250; ❄@☎☒) Tanjung Benoa's flashiest hotel combines a modern Bali look with a refreshing, casual style. The 298 rooms are large and thoughtfully designed. Some units have patios with steps right down into the 33m pool, easing the morning dip. Bungalows have their own private lagoon and there is a large kids' club.

Pondok Agung GUESTHOUSE **$**
(☏771 143; roland@eksadata.com; Jl Pratama; r 250,000-450,000Rp; ❄☎) The nine airy rooms (most with tubs) in a large, house-like building are spotless. Higher-priced rooms come with small kitchens. The gardens are fairly large and attractive.

Pondok Hasan Inn GUESTHOUSE **$**
(☏772 456; hasanhomestay@yahoo.com; Jl Pratama; r 200,000Rp; ❄☎) Back off the main road, this family-run homestay has nine immaculate rooms. The tiles gleam on the outdoor veranda shared by the rooms and there is a small garden.

Club Bali Mirage RESORT HOTEL **$$**
(☏772 147; www.clubbalimirage.com; Jl Pratama 72; r from US$140; ❄☎☒) This compact, J-shaped resort has a good-sized freeform swimming pool and 98 rooms, all with balconies or terraces. Palms shade the grounds and the beach is right out front. Rooms feature bold colours, the better to jolt you out of your jet lag – or hangover (a likely prospect as this is an all-inclusive joint with free-flowing booze and food).

Benoa Beachfront Villas RESORT HOTEL **$$**
(Map p104; ☏771 634; www.thebenoavillas. com; Jl Pratama 15B; r US$100-150; ❄@☎☒) The 18 bungalow-style rooms sport a cream-and-dark-wood motif that you'd find in a Bali Style book and the outdoor

bathrooms are airy. It's a nice, intimately scaled alternative to the big resorts.

Bali Khama RESORT HOTEL **$$$**
(☏774 912; www.thebalikhama.com; Jl Pratama; villas from US$200; ❄@☎☒) Set on its own crescent of sand at the northern end of the beach promenade. The mostly individual walled villas are large, tasteful and – obviously – private.

✖ Eating & Drinking

Each hotel has several restaurants with the Conrad having a good and evolving selection. The usual batch of tourist restaurants can be found along Jl Pratama, with their modestly priced – and modestly good – pasta and seafood for the masses.

TOP CHOICE ⬥ **Bumbu Bali** INDONESIAN **$$$**
(☏774 502; www.balifoods.com; Jl Pratama; meals 150,000-300,000Rp; ⊙noon-9pm) One of the finest restaurants on the island, Bumbu Bali serves the best Balinese food you'll have during your visit. Long-time resident and cookbook author Heinz von Holzen, his wife, Puji, and enthusiastic staff serve exquisitely flavoured dishes. Many diners opt for one of several set menus (from 255,000Rp). The *rijsttafel* (array of Indonesian dishes) shows the range of cooking in the kitchen, from satays served on their own little coconut-husk grill to the tender *be celeng base manis* (pork in sweet soy sauce) and the amazingly tasty and different *jaja batun bedil* (sticky dumpling rice in palm sugar), with a dozen more courses in between. Tables are set under the stars and in small pavilions. The sound of frogs can be heard from the fish ponds. There's complimentary transport in the area. It's wise to book.

Pasar Malam INDONESIAN **$**
(☏771 256; Jl Pratama; meals 40,000-80,000Rp) Inside the Rumah Bali guesthouse, this warung fulfils the role of the village market eatery. There are local coffees, and exhibits and dishes celebrate the many forms of Balinese rice. The food is of the same high standard as that at Bumbu Bali.

Tao ASIAN **$$**
(☏772 902; Jl Pratama 96; meals 80,000-160,000Rp) You'd never know this airy beachfront club was part of the nearby Ramada Resort. The menu is mostly Thai, although that resort menu stalwart, the club sandwich, is there at the bottom. The preparation is inventive. Best of all, for

the mere price of a drink you can use Tao's pool, beach loungers and other facilities.

ℹ️ Information

Kimia Farma (📞916 6509; Jl Pratama) Reliable chain of pharmacies; gives referrals to doctors.

ℹ️ Getting There & Around

Taxis from the airport cost 105,000Rp. Take a bemo to Bualu, then take one of the infrequent green bemo that shuttle up and down Jl Pratama (5000Rp) – after about 3pm bemo become very scarce on both routes.

A free **shuttle bus** (📞771 662; ⊙9am-10pm) connects all Nusa Dua and Tanjung Benoa resort hotels with the Bali Collection shopping centre about every hour. Or stroll the beach promenade.

SANUR

📞0361

Maybe Sanur is the Bali beachfront version of the youngest of the Three Bears, the one that's not too frantic (like Kuta) or too snoozy (like Nusa Dua). Many do indeed consider Sanur 'just right' (and don't suffer the fate of Goldilocks), as it lacks most of the hassles found to the west while maintaining a good mix of restaurants and bars that aren't all owned by resorts.

The beach, while thin, is protected by a reef and breakwaters, so families appreciate the limpid waves. Sanur has a good range of places to stay and it's well placed for day trips around the south, and north to Ubud. Really, it doesn't at all deserve its local moniker, 'Snore'.

Sanur stretches for about 5km along an east-facing coastline, with the lush and green landscaped grounds of resorts fronting right onto the sandy beach. West of the beachfront hotels is the busy main drag, Jl Danau Tamblingan, with hotel entrances and oodles of tourist shops, restaurants and cafes.

Noxious, traffic-choked Jl Ngurah Rai, commonly called Bypass Rd, skirts the western side of the resort area, and is the main link to Kuta and the airport. You don't want to stay out here.

◎ Sights

A few highlights: just north of the Bali Hyatt are the kinds of lavish villas you wished your friends owned. This was the centre of expat life when Donald Friend ruled the roost. Just south of the Hyatt is a long area where multihued **fishing boats** are pulled ashore and repaired under the trees. And look for surprises like a **cow** grazing next to a luxury resort or a bored beach-activities tout tracing beautifully elaborate designs in the sand.

Beachfront Walk   SEAFRONT
Sanur's beachfront walk was the first in Bali and from day one has been delighting locals and visitors alike. Over 4km long, it follows the sand south as it curves to the west. The countless cafes with tables in the sand will give you plenty of reason to pause. Look for ferries crossing Selat Badung between Sanur and mysterious Nusa Penida. Offshore you'll see **gnarled fishermen** in woven bamboo hats standing in the shallows rod-fishing for a living. At the northern end of the beach, elderly men gather at sunrise for *meditasi* – swimming and baking in the black volcanic sand found only at that end of the beach.

Museum Le Mayeur   MUSEUM
(📞286 201; adult/child 2000/1000Rp; ⊙7.30am-3.30pm) The Belgian artist Adrien Jean Le Mayeur de Merpes (1880–1958) arrived in Bali in 1932. Three years later, he met and married the beautiful Legong dancer Ni Polok when she was just 15. They lived in this compound, which houses the museum, when Sanur was still a quiet fishing village. The main house must have been delightful – a peaceful and elegant home filled with art and antiques right by the tranquil beach. After the artist's death, Ni Polok lived in the house until she died in 1985. The house is an interesting example of Balinese-style architecture – notice the beautifully carved window shutters that recount the story of Rama and Sita from the *Ramayana*.

Despite security (some Le Mayeur paintings have sold for US$150,000) and conservation problems, almost 90 Le Mayeur paintings are displayed inside the museum in a naturalistic Balinese interior of woven fibres. Some of Le Mayeur's early works are impressionist paintings from his travels in Africa, India, the Mediterranean and the South Pacific. Paintings from his early period in Bali are romantic depictions of daily life and beautiful Balinese women – often Ni Polok. The works from the 1950s are in much better condition and show fewer signs of wear and tear, displaying the vibrant colours that later became popular with young

Balinese artists. Look for the haunting black-and-white photos of Ni Polok.

Stone Pillar
ANCIENT MONUMENT

The pillar, down a narrow lane to the left as you face Pura Belangjong, is Bali's oldest dated artefact and has ancient inscriptions recounting military victories of more than a thousand years ago. These inscriptions are in Sanskrit and are evidence of Hindu influence 300 years before the arrival of the Majapahit court.

Bali Orchid Garden
GARDENS

(☑466 010; www.baliorchidgardens.com; Coast Rd; admission 50,000Rp; ☺8am-6pm) Given Bali's warm weather and rich volcanic soil, no one should be surprised that orchids thrive in abundance here. At this garden you can see thousands of orchids in a variety of settings. It's 3km north of Sanur along Jl Ngurah Rai, just past the major intersection with the coast road.

🏃 Activities

Sanur Beach
BEACH

In keeping with the local demeanour, the white-sand beach is sheltered by a reef and the surf is sedate. At low tide the beach is wide, but the sea is shallow and you have to pick your way out over rocks and coral through knee-deep water. At high tide the swimming is fine, but the beach is narrow and almost nonexistent in places. The hulking Inna Grand Bali Beach Hotel, located at the northern end of the strip, fronts the best stretch of beach.

Just south of Jl Kesumasari, there are simple warung that rent out loungers for 10,000Rp and battered kayaks for 20,000Rp.

TOP CHOICE Jamu Traditional Spa
SPA

(☑286 595; www.jamutraditionalspa.com; Jl Danau Tamblingan 41; massage from US$45) Jamu has a beautifully carved teak-and-stone entry that sets the mood. This gracious spa offers a range of treatments, including a popular Earth Essence Bust Treatment, a Kemiri Nut Scrub and the ever-popular Fruit Peel.

Most of the large beachside hotels have spas.

Surf Beaches
SURFING

Sanur's fickle breaks (tide conditions often don't produce waves) are offshore along the reef. The best area is called Sanur Reef, a right break in front of the Inna Grand Bali Beach Hotel. Another good spot is known as the Hyatt Reef, in front of, you guessed it, the Bali Hyatt. You can get a fishing boat out to the breaks for 200,000Rp per hour. See p35 for more details on these surf breaks.

Diving
DIVING

The diving near Sanur is not great, but the reef has a variety of fish and offers quite good snorkelling. Sanur is a good departure point for dive trips to Nusa Lembongan.

Among several good options, Crystal Divers (☑286 737; www.crystal-divers.com; Jl Danau Tamblingan 168; intro dives from US$60)

ROYALTY & EXPATS

Sanur was one of the places favoured by Westerners during their pre-WWII discovery of Bali. Artists Miguel Covarrubias, Adrien Jean Le Mayeur de Merpes and Walter Spies, anthropologist Jane Belo and choreographer Katharane Mershon all spent time here. The first tourist bungalows appeared in Sanur in the 1940s and '50s, and more artists, including Australian Donald Friend (whose antics earned him the nickname Lord Devil Donald), made their homes in Sanur. This early popularity made Sanur a likely locale for Bali's first big tourist hotel, the Sukarno-era Grand Bali Beach Hotel.

During this period, Sanur was ruled by insightful priests and scholars, who recognised both the opportunities and the threats presented by expanding tourism. Properly horrified at the high-rise Grand Bali Beach Hotel, they imposed the famous rule that no building could be higher than a coconut palm. They also established village cooperatives that owned land and ran tourist businesses, ensuring that a good share of the economic benefits remained in the community.

The priestly influence remains strong, and Sanur is one of the few communities still ruled by members of the Brahmana caste. It is known as a home of sorcerers and healers, and a centre for both black and white magic. The black-and-white chequered cloth known as *kain poleng*, which symbolises the balance of good and evil, is emblematic of Sanur.

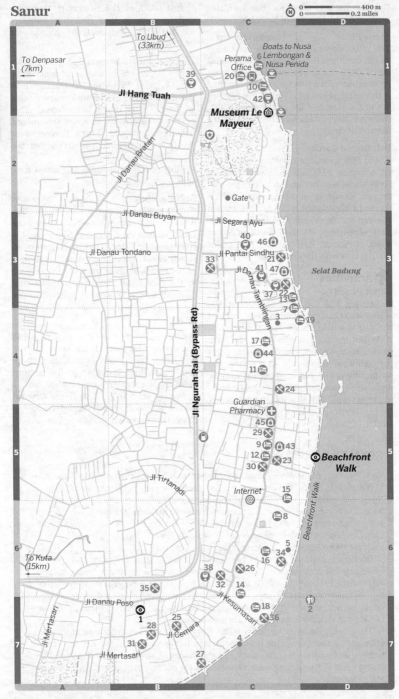

is a slick operation with its own accommodation, Crystal Santai Hotel, and a large diving pool right outside the office. Recommended for beginners, Crystal Divers offers a long list of courses, including PADI openwater for US$450.

Water Sports   WATER SPORTS

Various water sports are offered at kiosks along the beach: close to Museum Le Mayeur; near Sanur Beach Market; and at **Surya Water Sports** (📞287956; www.suryadive.com; Jl Duyung 10), which is the largest. You can go **parasailing** (US$20 per go), **snorkelling** by boat (US$30, two hours), **windsurfing** (US$30, one hour), **kayaking** (50,000Rp per hour), or enjoy a two-tank **dive** at the nearby reef (US$50).

🛏 Sleeping

Usually the best places to stay are right on the beach; however, beware of properties that have been coasting for decades. Modest budgets will find comfort on the nonbeach side of Jl Danau Tamblingan.

When making your choice of where to stay, keep in mind that you can do better than the high-profile Inna Grand Bali, which, despite the hype, is not up to the standards of the best places listed here.

BEACHFRONT

In Sanur you'll find some tasteful smaller beachfront hotels that are surprisingly affordable as well as some plainer beachfront places that are simply very good value.

DON'T MISS

GETTING HIGH OVER SANUR

Travelling through south Bali you can't help but notice scores of kites overhead much of the year. These creations are often huge (10m or more in length, with tails stretching another 100m) and fly at altitudes that worry pilots. Many have noisemakers producing eerie humming and buzzing noises. Like much in Bali there are spiritual roots: the kites are meant to whisper figuratively into the ears of the gods suggestions that abundant harvests might be nice. But for many Balinese, these high-fliers are simply a really fun hobby.

Each July, hundreds of Balinese and international teams descend – as it were – on open spaces north of Sanur for the **Bali Kite Festival**. They compete for an array of honours in such categories as original design and flight endurance. The action is centred around **Padang Galak Beach**, about 2km up the coast from Sanur. You can catch kite-flying Balinese-style here from May to September.

TOP CHOICE **Hotel La Taverna** HOTEL $$
(☑288 497; www.latavernahotel.com; Jl Danau Tambligan 29; r US$80-140, ste US$150-300; ❋@☎❋) One of Sanur's first hotels, La Taverna has awoken from a decades-long slumber utterly rejuvenated. The pretty grounds and simple paths linking buildings now hum with a creative energy that has infused the 36 vintage bungalow-style units with an artful atmosphere. It all seems timeless yet with just a hint of sly youth. Art and antiques abound; views beckon.

Tandjung Sari HOTEL $$
(☑288 441; www.tandjungsari.com; Jl Danau Tamblingan 29; bungalows US$170-270; ❋@☎❋) The mature trees along the shaded driveway set the gracious tone at this Sanur veteran, which was one of the first Balinese boutique hotels. Like a good tree, it has flourished since its start in 1967 and continues to be lauded for its stylish design. The 26 traditional-style bungalows are superbly decorated with crafts and antiques. At night, lights in the trees above the pool are magical. The gracious staff are a delight. Balinese dance classes are taught by one of Bali's best dancers (see p338).

Bali Hyatt RESORT HOTEL $$$
(☑281 234; www.bali.resort.hyatt.com; Jl Danau Tamblingan; r US$150-400; ❋@☎❋) The sprawling Made Wijaya–designed gardens are an attraction in themselves at this 390-room beachfront resort. Hibiscus, wild ginger, lotus and more than 600 species of plants and animals can be found here. Rooms are comfortable; note that balconies shrink on higher floors. Regency Club rooms come with free drinks and food in a serene pavilion. The two pools are oceanic in size,

and one has a waterfall-shrouded snogging cave.

Kesumasari GUESTHOUSE $
(☑287 824; Jl Kesumasari 6; r fan/air-con 200,000/300,000Rp; ❋) The only thing between you and the beach is a small shrine. Beyond the lounging porches, the multihued carved Balinese doors don't prepare you for the riot of colour inside the 10 idiosyncratic rooms at this family-run homestay.

Diwangkara Beach Hotel HOTEL $$
(☑288 577; www.holidayvillahotelbali.com; Jl Hang Tuah 54; r US$65, villas US$90-180; ❋@☎❋) Facing the beach near the end of Jl Hang Tuah, this 38-unit hotel has traditional Balinese architecture. Pool villas have their own plunge pool right off a wooden terrace. Everything here is low-key, from the staff to the regulars snoozing by the small pool. Not all rooms have wi-fi.

Hotel Peneeda View HOTEL $$
(☑288 425; www.peneedaview.com; Jl Danau Tamblingan 89; US$60-140; ❋@❋) Another basic, small beachfront hotel among the many Sanur seems to grow like seaweed, the Peneeda (which is *not* phonetically accurate for Penida) is a good choice for sun, sand and room service at an affordable price. The scope of recent room updates is as narrow as the beach frontage. One false note: expensive wi-fi in the lobby only.

Ananda Beach Hotel GUESTHOUSE $
(☑288 327; Jl Hang Tuah 143; r 225,000-400,000Rp; ❋❋) Built around a large shrine and right on the busy beach, the veteran Ananda has slightly dark rooms that are a jumble of old furniture. Deluxe room num-

ber 7 has a nice balcony with sea views; some of the 16 others are fan-only. Boats to Nusa Lembongan leave nearby.

Anjani
GUESTHOUSE $$

(☏289 567; alit_suarta@hotmail.com; Jl Danau Tamblingan 31; r 500,000Rp; ❀) Nearly lost amid larger beachside hotels (and its own overgrown grounds), the Anjani has six basic bungalow-style rooms on a narrow plot right on the beach. The units are bare bones but do have basic kitchens and padded headboards for headbangers.

OFF THE BEACH

The following are near Jl Danau Tamblingan and are short walks from the beach, cafes and shopping. Lacking sand as a feature, they all tend to try a bit harder than their beachfront brethren (besides being pretty cheap).

TOP CHOICE Flashbacks
GUESTHOUSE $

(☏281 682; www.flashbacks-chb.com; Jl Danau Tamblingan 106; s/d from 150,000/185,000Rp, bungalows 400,000/450,000Rp; ❀❀❀) This welcoming retreat has nine rooms that vary greatly in size. The better ones are bungalows or suites while more modest rooms share bathrooms and have cold water. The lovely design takes a lot of cues from traditional Balinese style. Porch Café is out front.

Hotel Palm Garden
HOTEL $

(Taman Palem; ☏287 041; www.palmgarden-bali.com; Jl Kesumasari 3; r from 350,000Rp; ❀❀) Everything is low-key here, from the 17 large rooms (with satellite TVs and fridges) to the relaxed service and pretty grounds. It's one minute to the beach; there is a nice medium-sized pool with a small waterfall.

Gardenia
GUESTHOUSE $

(☏286 301; www.gardeniaguesthousebali.com; Jl Merta Sari 2; r US$40-50; ❀❀❀) Like its many-petalled namesake, the Gardenia has many facets. The seven rooms are visions in white and sit well back from the road. Nice verandas face a small pool in a pretty courtyard. Up front there is a good cafe.

Hotel Segara Agung
HOTEL $

(☏288 446; www.segaraagung.com; Jl Duyung 43; r US$35-50; ❀@❀❀) Down a quiet, sandy lane lined with villas, this hotel is only a three-minute walk from the beach. The 12 rooms are clean though spartan; the cheapest have fans and cold water only. The big swimming pool is secluded.

Hotel Bali Rita
HOTEL $

(☏282 630; balirita@hotmail.com; Jl Danau Tamblingan 174; r 300,000Rp; ❀) Lovely Rita is tailor-made for those who want a traditional-style bungalow room in a nice garden. The 12 rooms here are large, with big fridges and tubs in open-air bathrooms. This secluded compound is well off busy Jl Danau Tamblingan; the beach is 10 minutes east.

Keke Homestay
GUESTHOUSE $

(☏287 282; Jl Danau Tamblingan 96; r from 100,000Rp; ❀) Set 150m down a *gang* (alley) from the noisy road, Keke welcomes backpackers into its genial family. The seven quiet, clean rooms vary from fan-only to air-con cool.

Watering Hole I
HOTEL $

(☏288 289; www.wateringholesanurbali.com; Jl Hang Tuah 37; r 125,000-250,000Rp; ❀@) In the northern part of Sanur, the Hole is a busy, friendly place close to the Nusa Lembongan boats. It has 20 pleasant, clean rooms; the cheapest have fan cooling and cold water. There's a sister Watering Hole at the southern end of Jl Danau Tamblingan.

Crystal Santai Hotel
HOTEL $

(☏286 737; www.crystal-divers.com; Jl Danau Tamblingan 168; r fan/air-con US$30/35; ❀@❀) HQ for Crystal Dive. A two-storey building forms an L around the pool where divers literally get their feet wet. The 18 rooms are commodious.

🍴 Eating

Dine on the beach in a traditional open-air pavilion or in a genial bar – the choice is yours in Sanur. Although there are plenty of uninspired places on Jl Danau Tamblingan, there are also some gems. Many of the establishments listed under Drinking also do food.

For groceries and personal items, there's a large **Hardy's Supermarket** (☏285 806; Jl Danau Tamblingan 136). Nearby is the gourmet market of Café Batu Jimbar.

On Sundays, there's an **organic market** (Jl Danau Tamblingan; ⊙10am-2pm) in Gudang Keramik parking lot.

The **Pasar Sindhu night market** (off Jl Danau Tamblingan; ⊙6am-midnight) sells fresh vegetables, dried fish, pungent spices and various household goods.

BEACH

The beach path offers restaurants, warung and bars where you can catch a meal, a drink or a sea breeze. There are usually places near the end of each road that leads to the beach. Sunset drink specials are common (though the beach faces east, so you'll need to enjoy the reflected glow off Nusa Penida).

Bonsai Cafe
GLOBAL $

(☑282 908; Jl Danau Tambligan 27; meals 40,000-100,000Rp) Order from a long list of beach-cafe standards while chilling in comfy and shady wicker chairs. Then wander inland for a surprise: hundreds of the cafe's namesake plants growing small in a rather sensational formal garden.

Sanur Bay
SEAFOOD $$

(☑288 153; Jl Duyung; meals 50,000-160,000Rp) You can hear the surf and see the moonlight reflecting on the water at this classic beachside seafood grill, set on the sand amid palm trees and fishing boats.

Donald's Beach Café
GLOBAL $$

(☑287 637; Beachfront Walk; meals 50,000-100,000Rp) If this were owned by Donald Trump, the site would no doubt be condoised in a New York minute. And that would be a shame, as the mature trees provide shade over tables with great views out to sea. The timeless (timeworn?) menu comprises Indo standards, pizza and burgers.

Beach Café
GLOBAL $$

(☑282 875; Beachfront Walk; meals 35,000-80,000Rp; ☎) Brings a bit of Med style to the Sanur beach cliché of palm fronds and plastic chairs. Zone out on wicker sofas or hang on a low cushion on the sand. Enjoy salads and seafood.

Stiff Chili
GLOBAL $$

(☑288 371; Jl Kesumasari; meals 40,000-120,000Rp) Apart from the evocative name, this beachside cafe has fine views through its near lack of walls. Pizza and pasta head the surprisingly ambitious menu.

JL DANAU TAMBLINGAN

TOP CHOICE Café Smorgås
ORGANIC $$

(☑289 361; Jl Danau Tamblingan; meals 35,000-100,000Rp; ✳☎) Set back from traffic, this healthy eatery has nice wicker chairs outside and cool air-con inside. A big local fave for its quiche, salads and sandwiches, the ever-expanding cafe now has a bakery and its own line of deli items.

Char Ming
FUSION $$

(☑288 029; www.charming-bali.com; Jl Danau Tamblingan 97; meals 70,000-200,000Rp) Barbecue with a French accent. A daily menu board lists the fresh seafood available for grilling. Other dishes include plenty of pork and beef. The highly stylised location features lush plantings and carved-wood details, and antiques inside and out. Much of the structure was built from wood reclaimed from old boats and buildings.

Porch Café
GLOBAL $$

(☑281 682; Jl Danau Tamblingan 110; meals 30,000-100,000Rp; ☎) Fronting Flashbacks (a charmer of a small hotel), this inviting cafe is housed in a traditional wooden building complete with the namesake porch. Snuggle up to a table out front or shut it all out in the air-con inside. The menu is a tasty mix of comfort food such as burgers and freshly baked goods. Order from a plethora of fresh juices. It's popular for breakfast.

Massimo
ITALIAN $$

(☑288 942; Jl Danau Tamblingan 206; meals 60,000-200,000Rp) The interior at this authentic Italian restaurant is like an open-air Milanese cafe while the outside is a Balinese garden. The lengthy menu includes wood-fired pizzas. The scent of garlic pours out onto the street, where you can stop and get a perfectly creamy gelato from a window.

Lumut
GLOBAL $$

(☑270 009; Jl Danau Tamblingan; meals 40,000-100,000Rp; ◷10am-10pm) This gracious 2nd-floor open-air cafe is set back from the road. The emphasis is on fresh seafood and Indonesian fare. Service is stylish and should be: part of the complex is a high-end housewares store.

Café Batu Jimbar
GLOBAL $$

(☑287 374; Jl Danau Tamblingan 152; meals 50,000-150,000Rp) This popular top-end cafe has a large wooden patio out front and an airy dining room. The baked goods on display compete for attention with the ice-cream case. As well as having the best banana smoothie in Bali, the menu has pricey Indonesian classics and standards like sandwiches.

SOUTH SANUR
Gardenia
GLOBAL $

(☑286 301; www.gardeniaguesthousebali.com; Jl Merta Sari 2; meals 30,000-80,000Rp; ☎) The streetside cafe of the attractive guesthouse is shaded by large flowering trees. The menu is a mix of traveller favourites (sandwiches, salads, Asian etc) but has a dash of style. The coffee drinks are the best down here.

Mama Putu's
SEAFOOD $$

(②270 572; Jl Mertasari; meals 40,000-120,000Rp) A long-running seafood cafe where the menu changes depending on what's fresh (actually the menu stays the same but what's available changes...). Ask for extra garlic and don't miss – of all things – the sides of coleslaw.

Cat & Fiddle
BRITISH $$

(②282 218; Jl Mertasari 36; meals 30,000-100,000Rp) Look for Brit standards like proper breakfasts and pork pies on the menu at this open-air pub that's – not surprisingly – popular with expats. Surprises include the 'Blarnyschnitzel', which is made with chicken.

Sari Bundo
INDONESIAN $

(②281 389; Jl Danau Poso; meals 15,000-10,000Rp; ⊘24hr) This spotless and simple Padang-style joint serves the best curry chicken in Sanur.

Denata Minang
INDONESIAN $

(Jl Danau Poso; meals 10,000Rp) One of the better Padang-style warung, it's located just west of Café Billiard. Like its brethren, it has fab *ayam* (chicken) in myriad spicy forms – only better.

🍷 Drinking

Many of Sanur's drinking establishments cater to retired expats and are, thankfully for them, air-conditioned. This is not a place where things go late. Note that many places to eat are good for drinks and vice versa.

Less salubriously, Sanur is known as a haven for prostitution. You won't find any in the public bars – except for a couple of dubious ones near Jl Segara Ayu – but along Jl Danau Poso there are numerous huge brothels given away only by the constant traffic.

TOP CHOICE Kalimantan
BAR

(②289 291; Jl Pantai Sindhu 11) Aka Borneo Bob's, this veteran boozer is one of many casual joints on this street. Enjoy cheap drinks under the palms in the large, casual garden or squint at live American football on the satellite TV.

Café Billiard
BAR

(②281 215; Jl Danau Poso; ⊘noon-1am) It's expat heaven! Play billiards and toss down cheap draughts of Heineken until your pension cheque is gone! It's a merry place where you lose your hat on the way home and wake up wishing you were asleep.

Bali Seaman's Club
BAR

(②283 992; Jl Danau Tamblingan 27; ⊘9am-midnight) Hidden away down a small lane, this is where every seaman joke you've ever heard *shouldn't* be repeated. Balinese sailors hang out here between stints on cruise ships. Fascinating stories abound, including one we heard about a vacuum toilet that gives new meaning to 'poop deck'. Simple, gregarious fun.

Street Cafe
BAR

(②289 259; Jl Danau Tamblingan 21; ⊛) A street bar that verges on stylish, with a modern, airy vibe and a choice of loungers, stools or tables. Instead of watching sport on TV, groove to the live piano music here most nights. Sink your teeth into a menu of steaks (average 65,000Rp).

Warung Sunrise
BAR

(②0813 3809 0486; Beachfront Walk) This aptly named beachside bar has tables and chairs on the sand, which will cushion your fall should you over-indulge on the signature – and potent – *arak* drinks. Of course, hearing Bob Marley here – even when played live by a cover band – may drive you to drink.

Jazz Bar & Grille
BAR

(②285 892; Kompleks Sanur 15, Jl Ngurah Rai; ⊘10am-2am; ⊛) Offers live jazz and pop most nights and even a couple of tables out front. The menu features Mexican and Mediterranean dishes (30,000Rp to 80,000Rp).

🛍 Shopping

Sanur is no Seminyak in the shopping department, although a few designers from there are opening branches here. You can kill an afternoon browsing the length of Jl Danau Tamblingan.

Red Camelia
WOMEN'S CLOTHING

(②270 046; www.redcamelia.com; Jl Danau Tamblingan 156) Loose, light resort wear you can't find at home.

Gudang Keramik
CERAMICS

(②289 363; Jl Danau Tamblingan) This outlet store for Jenggala Keramik Bali in Jimbaran has amazing prices on the firm's gorgeous tableware and decorator items. What's called 'seconds' here would be firsts everywhere else.

Nogo
TEXTILES

(②288 765; Jl Danau Tamblingan 100) Look for the wooden loom out front of this classy store, which bills itself as the 'Bali Ikat Centre'. The goods are gorgeous and easy to enjoy in the air-con comfort.

Periplus
BOOKSHOP

(☎282 790; Hardy's Supermarket, Jl Danau Tamblingan 136) Good selection of glossy books, best-sellers and periodicals.

Souvenirs

For souvenirs, try the numerous shops on the main street, or one of the various markets along the beachfront walk. **Sanur Beach Market** (off Jl Segara Ayu) has a wide selection. **Baruna Beach Market** (off Jl Danau Tamblingan) and the maze-like **Shindu Beach Market** (south of Jl Pantai Sindhu) have numerous stalls selling T-shirts, sarongs, woodcarvings and other tatty items.

Hardy's Supermarket (☎285 806; Jl Danau Tamblingan 136) has a range of goods on its 2nd floor at very good prices.

 Information

Most hotels have some form of internet access. Many cafes and bars listed have wi-fi.

Moneychangers here have a dubious reputation. There are numerous ATMs along Jl Danau Tamblingan and several banks.

Guardian Pharmacy (☎284 343; Jl Danau Tamblingan 134) The chain pharmacy has a doctor on call.

Police station (☎288 597; Jl Ngurah Rai)

 Getting There & Away

Bemo

Bemo stop at the southern end of Sanur on Jl Mertasari, and just outside the main entrance to the Inna Grand Bali Beach Hotel on Jl Hang Tuah. You can hail a bemo anywhere along Jl Danau Tamblingan and Jl Danau Poso – although drivers will first try to hail you.

Green bemo go along Jl Hang Tuah to the Kereneng terminal in Denpasar (7000Rp).

Boat

Public boats and the Perama boat to Nusa Lembongan leave from the beach at the end of Jl Hang Tuah. The fast Scoot boat has an office (☎285 522; Jl Hang Tuah) in Sanur; boats depart from a nearby portion of beach. See p128 for details on the trips. None of these services uses a dock – be prepared to wade to the boat.

Gilicat (☎271 680; www.gilicat.com; Jl Danau Tamblingan 51) has a Sanur office for its Padangbai departures to Lombok. See p188 for details.

Tourist Shuttle Bus

The **Perama office** (☎285 592; Jl Hang Tuah 39; ☺7am-10pm) is at Warung Pojok at the northern end of town. It runs shuttles to the following destinations, most only once daily.

DESTINATION	FARE	DURATION
Candidasa	60,000Rp	2¾hr
Kuta	25,000Rp	15min
Lovina	125,000Rp	4hr
Padangbai	60,000Rp	2½hr
Ubud	40,000Rp	1hr

 Getting Around

Official airport taxis cost 95,000Rp.

Bemo go up and down Jl Danau Tamblingan and Jl Danau Poso for 4000Rp, offering a greener way to shuttle about the strip than a taxi. Metered taxis can be flagged down in the street, or call **Bali Taxi** (☎701 111).

AROUND SANUR

Pulau Serangan

Otherwise known as Turtle Island, Pulau Serangan is an example of all that can go wrong with Bali's environment. Originally it was a small (100-hectare) island offshore of the mangroves to the south of Sanur. However, in the 1990s it was selected by Suharto's infamous son Tommy as a site for new development. Much of the original island was obliterated while a new landfill area over 300 hectares in size was grafted on. The Asian economic crisis pulled the plug on the scheme until recently, when the heavy equipment began moving again.

Meanwhile, on the original part of the island, the two small and poor fishing villages, **Ponjok** and **Dukuh**, are still there, as is one of Bali's holiest temples, **Pura Sakenan**, just east of the causeway. Architecturally it is insignificant, but major festivals attract huge crowds of devotees, especially during the Kuningan festival.

Perhaps the best reason to visit is the **Turtle Conservation and Education Centre** (☎0813 3841 2716; donation requested; ☺9am-5pm). Follow the signs to what was once a beach and you'll find a small complex where turtle eggs are hatched for return to the sea, while injured adult turtles are kept in tanks to heal. See p361 for more on the controversies surrounding Bali's turtles.

Benoa Harbour

Bali's main port is at the entrance of Teluk Benoa (Benoa Bay), the wide but shallow body east of the airport runway. Benoa Harbour is on the northern side of the bay – a square of docks and port buildings on reclaimed land, linked to mainland Bali by a 2km causeway. It's referred to as Benoa port or Benoa Harbour to distinguish it from Benoa village, on the southern side of the bay.

Benoa Harbour is the port for tourist day-trip boats to Nusa Lembongan and for Pelni ships to other parts of Indonesia; however, its shallow depth prevents cruise ships from calling.

DENPASAR

☎ 0361

Sprawling, hectic and ever-growing, Bali's capital has been the focus of a lot of the island's growth and wealth over the last five decades. It can seem a daunting and chaotic place but spend a little time on its tree-lined streets in the relatively affluent government and business district of **Renon** and you'll discover a more genteel side. Southeast of the town centre, Renon is laid out on a grand scale, with wide streets, large car parks and huge tracts of landscaped space. You'll find the government offices here, many of which are impressive structures displaying an ersatz Balinese style.

Denpasar might not be a tropical paradise, but it's as much a part of 'the real Bali' as the rice paddies and clifftop temples. This is the hub of the island for over half a million locals and here you will find their shopping malls and parks. Most enticing, however, is the growing range of **fabulous restaurants** and cafes aimed at the burgeoning middle class. You'll also want to sample Denpasar's markets, its excellent museum and its purely modern Balinese vibe. Most visitors stay in the tourist towns of the south and visit Denpasar as a day trip (if traffic is kind you can get here in 10 minutes from Sanur and 20 minutes from Seminyak). Others may pass through while changing bemo or catching a bus to Java.

History

Denpasar, which means 'next to the market', was an important trading centre and the seat of local rajahs (lords or princes) before the colonial period. The Dutch gained control of northern Bali in the mid-19th century, but their takeover of the south didn't start until 1906. After the three Balinese princes destroyed their own palaces in Denpasar and made a suicidal last stand – a ritual *puputan* – the Dutch made Denpasar an important colonial centre. And as Bali's tourism industry expanded in the 1930s, most visitors stayed at one or two government hotels in the city of Denpasar.

The northern town of Singaraja remained the Dutch administrative capital until after WWII when it was moved to Denpasar because of the new airport; in 1958, some years after Indonesian independence, the city became the official capital of the province of Bali.

Many of Denpasar's residents are descended from immigrant groups such as Bugis mercenaries (originally from Sulawesi) and Chinese, Arab and Indian traders. Recent immigrants have come from Java and all over Indonesia, attracted by opportunities in schools, business and the enormous tourist economy. Denpasar's edges have merged with Sanur, Kuta and Seminyak.

◉ Sights

Take time for the Museum Negeri Propinsi Bali, but the real appeal of Denpasar is simply exploring everyday Bali life. Roam the traditional markets and even the air-conditioned malls to see how people live today.

Museum Negeri Propinsi Bali MUSEUM
(☎ 222 680; adult/child 5000/2500Rp; ⊗ 8am-12.30pm Fri, to 4pm Sun-Thu) Think of this as the British Museum or the Smithsonian of Balinese culture. It's all here although, unlike those world-class institutions, you have to work at sorting it out.

This museum was originally established in 1910 by a Dutch resident who was concerned by the export of culturally significant artefacts from the island. Destroyed in a 1917 earthquake, it was rebuilt in the 1920s, but used mainly for storage until 1932. At that time, German artist Walter Spies and some Dutch officials revived the idea of collecting and preserving Balinese antiquities and cultural objects, and creating an ethnographic museum. Today the museum is well organised and most displays are labelled in English. You can climb one of the towers inside the grounds for a better view of the whole complex.

The museum comprises several buildings and pavilions, including many examples of Balinese architecture. The main building, to the back as you enter, has a collection of prehistoric pieces downstairs, including stone sarcophagi and stone and bronze

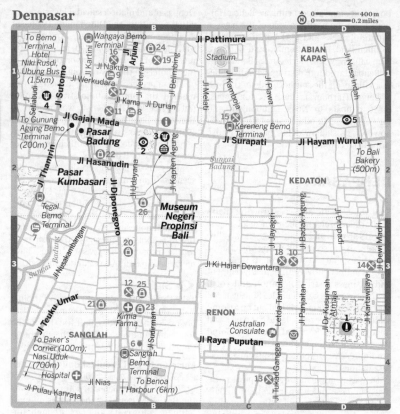

implements. Upstairs are examples of traditional artefacts, including items still in everyday use. Look for the intricate wood-and-cane carrying cases for transporting fighting cocks, and tiny carrying cases for fighting crickets.

The **northern pavilion**, in the style of a Tabanan palace, houses dance costumes and masks, including a sinister Rangda (widow-witch), a healthy-looking Barong (mythical lion-dog creature) and a towering Barong Landung (tall Barong) figure. See p339 for more about these mythical figures.

The **central pavilion**, with its spacious veranda, is like the palace pavilions of the Karangasem kingdom (based in Amlapura), where rajahs held audiences. The exhibits are related to Balinese religion, and include ceremonial objects, calendars and priests' clothing.

The **southern pavilion** (Gedung Buleleng) has a varied collection of textiles, including *endek* (a Balinese method of weaving with pre-dyed threads), double ikat, *songket* (silver- and gold-threaded cloth, hand-woven using a floating weft technique) and *prada* (the application of gold leaf or gold or silver thread in traditional Balinese clothes).

Museum staff often play music on a bamboo gamelan to magical effect; visit in the afternoon when it's uncrowded. Ignore 'guides' who offer little except a chance to part with US$5 or US$10.

Pura Jagatnatha
TEMPLE

Next to the museum, the **state temple**, built in 1953, is dedicated to the supreme god, Sanghyang Widi. Part of its significance is its statement of monotheism. Although the Balinese recognise many gods, the belief in one supreme god (who can have many manifestations) brings Balinese Hinduism into conformity with the first principle of Pancasila – the 'Belief in One God'.

The *padmasana* (shrine) is made of white coral, and consists of an empty throne (symbolic of heaven) on top of the cosmic turtle and two *naga* (mythical serpents), which symbolise the foundation of the world. The walls are decorated with carvings of scenes from the *Ramayana* and *Mahabharata*.

Two major festivals are held here every month, during the full moon and new moon, and feature *wayang kulit* (shadow-puppet plays). You'll need a sarong to enter.

Puputan Square   PARK
Across from Pura Jagatnatha, this classic urban **park** commemorates the heroic but suicidal stand of the rajahs of Badung against the invading Dutch in 1906. A monument depicts a Balinese family in heroic pose, brandishing the weapons that were so ineffective against the Dutch guns. The woman also has jewels in her left hand, as the women of the Badung court reputedly flung their jewellery at the Dutch soldiers to taunt them. The park is popular with locals at lunchtime and with families near sunset.

Pura Maospahit   TEMPLE
Established in the 14th century, at the time the Majapahit arrived from Java, this **temple** (off Jl Sutomo) was damaged in a 1917 earthquake and has been heavily restored since. The oldest structures are at the back of the temple, but the most interesting features are the large statues of Garuda and the giant Batara Bayu.

Bajra Sandhi Monument   MONUMENT
(☑264 517; Jl Raya Puputan; adult/child 10,000/5000Rp; ⊙9am-5pm) Otherwise known as the Monument to the Struggle of the People of Bali, this huge structure is as big as its name and dominates what's already a big park in Renon. Inside this vaguely Borobudur-like structure are dioramas tracing Bali's history. Taking the name as a cue, you won't be surprised that they have a certain jingoistic soap-opera quality. But they're a fun diversion. Note that in the portrayal of the 1906 battle with the Dutch, the King of Badung is literally a sitting target.

Taman Wedhi Budaya   CULTURAL CENTRE
(☑222 776; admission free; ⊙8am-3pm Mon-Thu, to 1pm Fri-Sun) This arts centre is a sprawling complex in the eastern part of Denpasar. Established in 1973 as an academy and showplace for Balinese culture, its lavish architecture houses an art gallery with an interesting collection, but few performances or much else most of the year.

From mid-June to mid-July, however, the centre comes alive for the Bali Arts Festival, with dances, music and craft displays from all over Bali. You may need to book tickets at the centre for more popular events.

☼ Activities

Many Balinese wouldn't think of having a massage from anyone but a blind person. Government-sponsored schools offer lengthy courses to certify blind people in reflexology, shiatsu massage, anatomy and much more. Usually graduates work together in group locations such as **Kube Dharma Bakti** (☏749 9440; Jl Serma Mendara 3; massage per hr 40,000Rp; ⊗9am-9pm). In this airy building redolent with liniments, you can choose from a range of therapies and contribute to a very good cause at the same time.

☆☆ Festivals & Events

The annual **Bali Arts Festival** (www.baliartsfestival.com), based at the Taman Wedhi Budaya arts centre, lasts for about a month starting in mid-June. It's a great time to visit Bali, and the festival is an easy way to see a wide variety of traditional dance, music and crafts from the island. The productions of the *Ramayana* and *Mahabharata* ballets are grand, and the opening ceremony and parade in Denpasar are spectacles.

The festival is the main event of the year for scores of village dance and musical groups. Competition is fierce with local pride on the line at each performance ('our Kecak is better than your stinkin' Kecak' etc). To do well here sets a village on a good course for the year. Some events are held in a 6000-seat amphitheatre, a venue that allows you to realise the mass appeal of traditional Balinese culture. Tickets are usually available before performances, and schedules are available throughout south Bali, in Ubud, at the Denpasar tourist office and online.

🛏 Sleeping

Denpasar has several hotels, but it's hard to think of a compelling reason to stay here unless you want to be close to the bus stations or have some other business in town.

Nakula Familiar Inn GUESTHOUSE $
(☏226 446; nakula_familiar_inn@yahoo.com; Jl Nakula 4; r 70,000-120,000Rp; ✳) The eight rooms at this sprightly urban family compound are clean (some with air-con and cold-water showers only) and have small balconies. The traffic noise isn't too bad and there is a nice little courtyard in the middle. Tegal–Kereneng bemo go along Jl Nakula.

Hotel Taman Suci HOTEL $$
(☏484 445; www.tamansuci.com; Jl Imam Bonjol 45; r from 450,000-600,000Rp; ✳@≋) A good choice for business travellers, this modern, multifloor 45-room hotel insulates you from the hubbub outside the minute you enter its air-con lobby.

Inna Bali HOTEL $$
(☏225 681; www.innabali.com; Jl Veteran 3; r from 400,000-800,000Rp; ✳@≋) The Inna Bali has simple gardens, a huge banyan tree and a certain nostalgic charm; it dates from 1927 and was once the main tourist hotel on the island. Room interiors are standard and a bit frayed, but many have deeply shaded verandas. The hotel is a good base for the *Ngrupuk* parades that take place the day before the Nyepi festival (see the boxed text, p325), as they pass by the front of the hotel. Get the veteran employees talking – they have many stories. Ask about deals: don't pay rack rates here.

Hotel Niki Rusdi HOTEL $
(☏416 397; Jl Pidada XIV; r 100,000-200,000Rp; ✳) Right behind the Ubung bus terminal, the 26 rooms here are a good choice if you have an early or late bus. Rooms are clean, the cheapest fan-only. There are other options nearby if this hotel is full.

🍴 Eating

Denpasar has the island's best range of Indonesian and Balinese food. Savvy locals and expats each have their own favourite warung and restaurants. At the **Pasar Malam Kereneng** (Kereneng Night Market), dozens of vendors dish up food until dawn.

Also good is Jl Teuku Umar, while in Renon there is a phenomenal strip of eating places on Jl Cok Agung Trisna between Jl Ramayana and Jl Dewi Madri. See what you can discover.

Warung Satria INDONESIAN $
(Jl Kedondong; dishes 4000-10,000Rp; ⊗11am-3pm) This is a long-running warung on a quiet street; try the wonderful seafood satay served with a shallot sambal. Otherwise, choose from the immaculate displays of what's fresh, but don't wait too long after lunch or it will all be gone.

Warung Beras Bali ORGANIC $
(☏247 443; Jl Sahedawa 26; mains 7000-15,000Rp) Organic rice underpins organic vegetables and various Chinese dishes at this appropriately green-hued open-front cafe. A long list of fresh juices adds to the healthy patina. Try the unusual – and organic vegetarian – *saté sambal plecina,*

which is a tasty skewer of grilled spinach and tomato. Or buy a bag of rice.

Nasi Uduk
INDONESIAN $
(Jl Teuku Umar; 6000-12,000Rp) Open to the street, this spotless little stall has a few chairs and serves up Javanese treats such as *nasi uduk* (sweetly scented coconut rice with fresh peanut sauce) and *lalapan* (a simple salad of fresh lemon basil leaves).

Bhineka Jaya Café
COFFEE $
(☑224 016; Jl Gajah Mada 80; coffee 4000Rp; ⊙9am-4pm) Home to Bali's Coffee Co, this storefront sells locally grown beans and makes a mean espresso, which you can enjoy at the two tiny tables while watching the bustle of Denpasar's old main drag.

Baker's Corner
GLOBAL $$
(☑243 861; Jl Teuku Umar; meals from 50,000Rp) The crowd of late-model cars crammed into the forecourt indicates you've found one of Bali's new sensations: a thoroughly modern chain of cafes serving all-day Western breakfasts, burgers, luscious baked goods and mainstream Asian fare. It's all very stylish and crowded with local movers and shakers all day long.

Bali Bakery
BAKERY $
(☑243 147; Jl Hayam Wuruk; meals 50,000Rp; ❋🖀) Small branch of the Kuta cafe known for good Western baked goods.

Roti Candy
CANDY $
(☑238 409; Jl Nakula 31; treats 3000Rp) Have a *pia*, a sweet-filled bun, or choose from a variety of other sweets and cakes, plus rolls stuffed with cheesy goodness.

Renon
The slightly gentrified air here temptingly wafts aromas of good cooking.

TOP CHOICE Cak Asm
INDONESIAN $
(☑798 9388; Jl Tukad Gangga; meals 10,000-30,000Rp) No, the name isn't the sound you make after eating here. If that were the case, this simple cafe would be named 'yum'. Join government workers and students from the nearby university for superb dishes at rock-bottom prices. Order the *cumi cumi* (calamari) with *telor asin* sauce (a heavenly mixture of eggs and garlic). The resulting buttery, crispy goodness may be the best dish you have in Bali. And it's under US$1.

Ayam Goreng Kalasan
INDONESIAN $
(☑0812 380 9934; Jl Cok Agung Trisna 6; meals 10,000-30,000Rp) The name here says it

all. Fried chicken (Ayam Goreng) named after a Javanese temple (Kalasan) in a region renowned for its fiery, crispy chicken. The version here falls off the bone on the way to the table; the meat bursts with lemongrass scent from a long marinade prior to the plunge into boiling oil. There are several other excellent little warung in this strip.

Warung Lembongan
INDONESIAN $
(☑236 885; Jl Cok Agung Trisna 62; meals 10,000-30,000Rp) Silver folding chairs at long tables, shaded by a garish green awning out front. These are details you will quickly forget after you have the house speciality: chicken lightly fried yet delicately crispy like the top of a perfect crème brûlée. The special costs 17,000Rp and includes *ayam* (chicken), rice, soup and a beverage. The KFC in Sanur wants over 200,000Rp for its deeply inferior mass-merchandised version.

Café Teduh
INDONESIAN $
(☑221 631; off Jl Diponegoro; meals 10,000-50,000Rp; 🖀) Amid the big shopping malls, this little oasis is hidden down a tiny lane. Hanging orchids, trees, flowers and ponds with fountains create a bucolic feel. There's a menu of meaty mains such as *ayam bakar rica* (barbecued chicken with ratatouille) but the real treats are just that – treats. Try the *es cakalele*, a refreshing sundae of lychee and coconut milk.

Cianjur
SEAFOOD $
(☑230 015; Jl Cok Agung Trisna; meals 15,000-60,000Rp; ❋) Big, airy and cool, this shiny upmarket restaurant has Balinese seafood in an array of preparations (crispy, grilled, steamed or wrapped in a banana leaf). It's hugely popular with families and groups of government workers.

🔒 Shopping
For a complete slice of local life, visit the traditional markets and the large air-con shopping malls.

Markets
Denpasar's largest traditional markets are mostly in a fairly compact area that makes visiting them easy, even if navigating their crowded aisles across multiple floors is not. Like other aspects of Balinese life, the big markets are in flux. Big box supermarkets are biting into their trade and the evolving middle class say they prefer the likes of

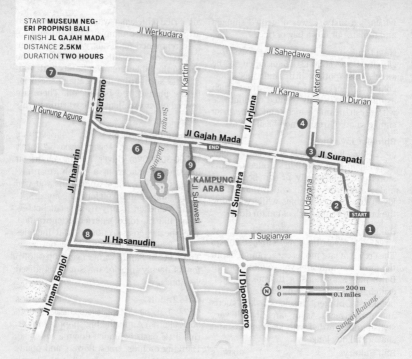

START **MUSEUM NEG-
ERI PROPINSI BALI**
FINISH **JL GAJAH MADA**
DISTANCE **2.5KM**
DURATION **TWO HOURS**

Walking Tour
Denpasar

❯ While Denpasar can seem formidable
and traffic choked, it rewards those who
explore on foot.

This walk includes most attractions in the
historic centre of town and a few vestiges
of when Denpasar – and Bali – moved at a
much slower pace. Allow extra time for visiting the museum or shopping.

Start the walk at ❶ **Museum Negeri
Propinsi Bali** (p115). Opposite is ❷ **Puputan Square** (p117).

Back on the corner of Jl Surapati and Jl
Veteran is the towering ❸ **Catur Muka
statue**, which represents Batara Guru,
Lord of the Four Directions. The four-faced,
eight-armed figure keeps a close eye (or is
it eight eyes?) on the traffic swirling around
him. Head 100m north on Jl Veteran to
the ❹ **Inna Bali** (p118). It was a favourite
of Sukarno – listen for the echoes of his
schemes.

Return to the Catur Muka statue and
head west on Jl Gajah Mada (named after
the 14th-century Majapahit prime minister).

Go past banks, shops and a cafe towards
the bridge over the grubby Sungai Badung
(Badung River). Just before the bridge, on
the left, is the renovated ❺ **Pasar Badung**
(p121), the main produce market. On the
left, just after the bridge, is ❻ **Pasar Kum-
basari** (p121).

At the next main intersection, detour
north up Jl Sutomo, and turn left along a
small *gang* (alley) leading to the ❼ **Pura
Maospahit** temple (p117).

Turn back, and continue south along Jl
Thamrin to the junction of Jl Hasanudin.
On this corner is the ❽ **Puri Pemecutan**,
a palace destroyed during the 1906 Dutch
invasion. It's long since been rebuilt and
you can look inside the compound but don't
expect anything palatial.

Go east on Jl Hasanudin, then north onto
❾ **Jl Sulawesi**, and its markets. Continue
north past Pasar Badung market to return
to Jl Gajah Mada. You could save your visit
to the Museum Negeri Propinsi Bali for the
end, when you'll just want to move slowly.

Carrefour because it has more imported goods (oh my...) and is cleaner (well...). But the big markets aren't down yet. This is where you come for purely Balinese goods, such as temple offerings, ceremonial clothes and a range of foodstuffs unique to the island, including some types of mangosteen.

Pasar Badung
MARKET

A must-see destination: shoppers browse and bargain from 5am to night. It's a retail adventure and you'll find produce and food from all over the island as well as easy-to-assemble temple offerings that are popular with working women. Deals include a half-kilo of saffron for 250,000Rp. Ignore guides who may offer their services. This is one of the better places to see Bali's myriad types of fruit.

Pasar Kumbasari
MARKET

Across the river from Pasar Badung, this huge market has a profusion of handicrafts, a plethora of vibrant fabrics, and costumes decorated with gold. It's a modern, multi-level building of shops and stalls and you should just plunge at random into the canyons of colour.

Pasar Burung
MARKET

Elsewhere in Denpasar, a short distance north on Jl Veteran, Pasar Burung is a bird market with hundreds of caged birds and small animals for sale, including guinea pigs, rabbits and monkeys. There are also gaudy birdcages. An impromptu dog market also operates directly opposite the bird market. While you're here, have a look at the elaborate **Pura Sutriya**, just east of the market.

Kampung Arab
MARKET

(Jl Hasanudin & Jl Sulawesi) Has jewellery and precious-metal stores run by scores of Middle Eastern and Indian merchants.

Shopping Malls

Western-style shopping malls are jammed on Sundays with locals shopping and teens flirting; the brand-name goods are genuine.

Most malls have a food court with stalls serving fresh Asian fare, as well as fast-food joints (which have sated more than one homesick tourist tot).

Bali Mall
MALL

(Jl Dipenegoro) Has the top-end Ramayana Department Store, Bali's largest.

Denpasar Junction
MALL

(Jl Teuku Umar) Newest, glossiest mall with lots of international chains.

JL SULAWESI

Follow Jl Sulawesi north and, just as the glitter of Kampung Arab fades, the street glows anew as you come upon a strip of fabric stores. The textiles here – batiks, cottons, silks – come in colours that make Barbie look like an old purse.

Matahari
MALL

(Jl Teuku Umar) Main branch of the department store plus numerous other shops.

Robinson's
MALL

(Jl Teuku Umar or Jl Sudirman) Matahari's arch-competitor has a large selection of midrange goods.

Tiara Dewata Shopping Centre
MALL

(Jl Udayana) Low-rise place with a good food court.

ℹ Information

Emergency

Police office (☑ 424 346; Jl Pattimura) The place for any general problems.

Tourist police (☑ 224 111)

Medical Services

See p392 for a list of medical providers in and around Denpasar.

Kimia Farma (☑ 227 811; Jl Diponegoro 125; ⊘ 24hr) The main outlet of the island-wide pharmacy chain has the largest selection of prescription medications in Bali.

Money

All major Indonesian banks have offices and ATMs in Denpasar. Several are on Jl Gajah Mada, near the corner of Jl Arjuna, and there are ATMs in the shopping malls.

Post

Main post office (☑ 223 565; Jl Panjaitan; ⊘ 8am-8pm)

Tourist Information

Denpasar tourist office (☑ 234 569; Jl Surapati 7; ⊘ 8am-3.30pm Mon-Thu, to-1pm Fri) Deals with tourism in the Denpasar municipality (including Sanur), but also has some information about the rest of Bali. It's not worth a special trip, but may have the useful *Calendar of Events* booklet. Has an official 'tourist toilet'.

ℹ Getting There & Away

Denpasar is the hub of public transport in Bali – you'll find buses and minibuses bound for all corners of the island.

Air

Sometimes called 'Denpasar' in airline schedules, Bali's Ngurah Rai international airport is 12km south of Kuta. See p379 for details.

Bemo

The city has several bemo terminals – if you're travelling independently around Bali you'll often have to go via Denpasar, and transfer from one terminal to another. The terminals for transport around Bali are Ubung, Batubulan and Tegal, while the Gunung Agung, Kereneng and Sanglah terminals serve destinations in and around Denpasar. Each terminal has regular bemo connections to the other terminals in Denpasar for 7000Rp. See p382 for a full discussion of Bali's sputtering bemo network. And note that bemo fares are approximate and at times seem rather subjective.

UBUNG

Well north of the town, on the road to Gilimanuk, Ubung is the terminal for northern and western Bali and most long-distance bus services. In the complex, there is a **tourist office** (✆427 172) that provides help with fares and schedules. Arriving here by taxi guarantees a reception by baggage and ticket touts.

DESTINATION	FARE
Gilimanuk (for the ferry to Java)	30,000Rp
Kediri (for Tanah Lot)	12,000Rp
Mengwi	12,000Rp
Munduk	27,000Rp
Negara	25,000Rp
Pancasari (for Danau Bratan)	22,000Rp
Singaraja (via Pupuan or Bedugul)	35,000Rp
Tabanan	10,000Rp

BATUBULAN

Located a very inconvenient 6km northeast of Denpasar on a road to Ubud, this terminal is for destinations in eastern and central Bali.

DESTINATION	FARE
Amlapura	25,000Rp
Bangli	17,000Rp
Gianyar	15,000Rp
Kintamani (via Tampaksiring)	24,000Rp
Padangbai (for the Lombok ferry)	24,000Rp
Sanur	7000Rp
Semarapura	23,000Rp
Singaraja (via Kintamani)	35,000Rp
Singaraja (via Semarapura & Amlapura)	35,000Rp
Ubud	13,000Rp

TEGAL

On the western side of town on Jl Iman Bonjol, Tegal is the terminal for Kuta and the Bukit Peninsula.

DESTINATION	FARE
Airport	15,000Rp
Jimbaran	17,000Rp
Kuta	13,000Rp
Legian	13,000Rp
Nusa Dua	25,000Rp
Ulu Watu	22,000Rp

GUNUNG AGUNG

This terminal, at the northwestern corner of town (look for orange bemo), is on Jl Gunung Agung, and has bemo to Kerobokan and Canggu (10,000Rp).

KERENENG

East of the town centre, Kereneng has bemo to Sanur (7000Rp).

SANGLAH

On Jl Diponegoro, near the general hospital in the south of the city, Sanglah has bemo to Suwung and Benoa Harbour (10,000Rp).

WANGAYA

Near the centre of town, this small terminal is the departure point for bemo services to northern Denpasar and the outlying Ubung bus terminal (8000Rp).

Bus

The usual route to Java is by bus (get one with air-con) from Denpasar's Ubung terminal to Surabaya (200,000Rp, 10 hours), which includes the short ferry trip across the Bali Strait. Other buses go as far as Yogyakarta (300,000Rp, 16 hours) and Jakarta (500,000Rp, 24 hours), usually travelling overnight.

Book directly at offices in the Ubung terminal, 3km north of the city centre. To Surabaya or even Jakarta, you may get on a bus within an hour of arriving at Ubung, but at busy times you should buy your ticket at least one day ahead.

Train

Bali doesn't have trains but the state railway company does have an **office** (✆227 131; Jl Diponegoro 150/B4; ✆8.30am-6.30pm) in Denpasar. From here buses leave for eastern Java where they link with trains at Banyuwangi for Surabaya, Yogyakarta and Jakarta among others. Fares and times are comparable to the bus but the air-conditioned trains are more comfortable, even in economy class.

ⓘ Getting Around

Bemo

Bemo take various circuitous routes from and between Denpasar's many bus/bemo terminals.

They line up for various destinations at each terminal, or you can try and hail them from anywhere along the main roads – look for the destination sign above the driver's window. The Tegal–Nusa Dua bemo (dark blue in colour) is handy for Renon; and the Kereneng–Ubung bemo (turquoise) travels along Jl Gajah Mada, past the museum.

Taxi

If you're looking for a taxi, you're in luck – you'll find them prowling the streets of Denpasar looking for fares. As always, the distinctive blue cabs of **Bali Taxi** (☏701 111) are the most reliable choice.

NUSA LEMBONGAN & ISLANDS

Look towards the open ocean southeast of Bali and the hazy bulk of Nusa Penida dominates the view. But for many visitors the real focus is Nusa Lembongan, which lurks in the shadow of its vastly larger neighbour. Here there's great surfing, quiet white beaches and the kind of laid-back vibe travellers cherish. It's a popular destination and justly so – it's the one excursion you should make while in Bali.

Nusa Penida is seldom visited, which means that its dramatic vistas and unchanged village life are yours to explore. Tiny Nusa Ceningan huddles between the larger islands. It is an interesting quick jaunt from Lembongan.

The islands have been a poor region for many years. Thin soils and a lack of fresh water do not permit the cultivation of rice, but other crops such as maize, cassava and beans are staples grown here. The main cash crop, however, has been seaweed (see the boxed text, p129) although the big harvest now on Lembongan comes on two legs.

Nusa Lembongan

☏0366

It's the Bali many imagine but never find outside of perhaps Balangan Beach: simple rooms on the sand, cheap beers with incredible sunsets, days spent surfing and diving, and nights spent riffling through a favourite book or hanging with new friends.

Nusa Lembongan grows in popularity each year, but even though rooms for travellers proliferate, it remains a mellow place. The new-found wealth is bringing changes though: you'll see boys riding motorbikes

300m to school, temples being expensively renovated, higher-end luxuries being introduced, and time being marked by the arrival of tourist boats rather than the crow of a rooster or the fall of a coconut. Concerns include touts starting to hang around where the boats arrive and unfettered villa building on the hillsides.

⊙ Sights

JUNGUTBATU

The **beach** here, a mostly lovely arc of white sand with clear blue water, has views across to Gunung Agung in Bali. The impressive new **seawall walkway** is ideal for strolling, especially – as you'd guess – at sunset.

The village itself is mellow, with quiet lanes, no cars and lots of seaweed production. **Pura Segara** and its enormous banyan tree are the site of frequent ceremonies.

The north end of town holds the proud new **lighthouse**. Follow the road around east for about 1km to **Pura Sakenan**.

PANTAI SELEGIMPAK

The long, straight **beach** is usually lapped by small waves at this remote-feeling spot with a couple of places to stay (one of which has unfortunately built its seawall *below* the low-tide line). About 200m east along the shoreline path where it goes up and over a knoll is a minute **cove** with a nub of sand and a tiny warung. It's cute.

MUSHROOM BAY

This beautiful bay, unofficially named after the mushroom corals offshore, has a crescent of bright white **beach**. By day, the tranquillity can be disturbed by banana-boat rides or parasailing. At other hours, this is a beach of dreams. Look for the enormous **sacred tree** just east of Waka Nusa Resort.

The most interesting way to get here from Jungutbatu is to walk along the trail that starts from the southern end of the main beach and follows the coastline for a kilometre or so (see the boxed text, p128). Alternatively, get a boat from Jungutbatu for about 25,000Rp.

DREAM BEACH

Down a track, on the southern side of the island, this 150m crescent of sand has pounding surf and a warung for sunset beers.

LEMBONGAN

The other main town on the island looks across the seaweed-farm-filled channel to

Nusa Ceningan. It's a beautiful scene of clear water and green hills. You may get some hype for the **underground house**. Ignore it; it's a diversion for day trippers and amounts to little more than somebody's hole in the ground.

🏃 Activities

Most places rent out gear for aquatic fun. Well-used surfboards go for 50,000Rp per day.

Surfing

Surfing here is best in the dry season (April to September), when the winds come from the southeast. It's definitely not for beginners, and can be dangerous even for experts. There are three main breaks on the reef, all aptly named. From north to south are **Shipwreck**, **Lacerations** and **Playground**. Depending on where you are staying, you can paddle directly out to whichever of the three is closest; for others it's better to hire a boat. Prices are negotiable – from about 50,000Rp for a one-way trip. You tell the owner when to return. A fourth break – **Racecourses** – sometimes emerges south of Shipwreck.

The surf can be crowded here even when the island isn't – charter boats from Bali sometimes bring groups of surfers for day trips from the mainland for a minimum of 800,000Rp.

For more on surfing here, see p35.

Diving

World Diving (☏0812 390 0686; www.world -diving.com), based at Pondok Baruna on Jungutbatu Beach, is well regarded. It offers a complete range of courses, including five-day PADI open-water courses for US$395, and dive trips from US$35 to US$50 per dive to sites around all three islands.

Another recommended dive operation is the long-running **Bali Diving Academy** (☏0361-270252; www.scubali.com), which has an office at Bungalow Number 7 on the waterfront.

For details on the area's dive sites, see the boxed text (p125).

Snorkelling

Good snorkelling can be had just off the Mushroom Bay and **Bounty pontoons** off Jungutbatu Beach, as well as in areas off the north coast of the island. You can charter a boat from 150,000Rp per hour, depending on demand, distance and the number of passengers. A trip to the challenging waters of Nusa Penida costs 400,000Rp for three hours; to the nearby mangroves costs about 300,000Rp. Snorkelling gear can be rented for 20,000Rp to 30,000Rp per day. World Diving allows snorkellers to join dive trips and charges 250,000Rp for a four-hour trip.

There's good drift snorkelling along the mangrove-filled channel west of Ceningan Point, between Lembongan and Ceningan.

Cruises

A number of cruise boats offer day trips to Nusa Lembongan from Benoa Harbour in south Bali. Trips include hotel transfer from south Bali, basic water sports, snorkelling, banana-boat rides, island tours and a buffet lunch. Note that with the usually included hotel transfers the following trips can make for a long day.

Bali Hai

(☏0361-720 331; www.balihaicruises.com; adult/child from US$95/48) Cruises use an unsightly offshore pontoon for snorkelling and water play. Offers cash-saving family deals.

Bounty Cruise

(☏0361-726 666; www.balibountycruises .com; adult/child US$95/47.50) Boats dock at a garish yellow offshore pontoon with water slides and other amusements.

Island Explorer Cruise

(☏0361-728 088; www.bali-activities.com; adult/child from US$85/43) Affiliated with Coconuts Beach Resort; uses a large boat that doubles as the base for day-trip aquatic fun.

🛌 Sleeping & Eating

With notable exceptions, rooms and amenities become increasingly posh as you head south and west along the water to Mushroom Bay. A few new places have appeared back from the water on semi-arid patches; we can't imagine staying in these. Almost every property has a cafe serving – unless noted – basic Indonesian and Western dishes for about 30,000Rp.

JUNGUTBATU

Many lodgings in Jungutbatu have shed the surfer shack cliché and are moving upmarket. But you can still find cheapies with cold water and fans.

TOP CHOICE **Indiana Kenanga**   HOTEL $$
(☏0819 1674 6593; www.indiana-kenan ga-villas.com; r from US$130; ❄@🛜🏊) Wow! Jungutbatu will never be the same. Six

There are great diving possibilities around the islands, from shallow and sheltered reefs, mainly on the northern side of Lembongan and Penida, to very demanding drift dives in the channel between Penida and the other two islands. Vigilant locals have protected their waters from dynamite bombing by renegade fishing boats, so the reefs are relatively intact. And a side benefit of seaweed farming is that locals no longer rely so much on fishing.

If you arrange a dive trip from Padangbai or South Bali, stick with the most reputable operators, as conditions here can be tricky and local knowledge is essential (diving accidents have killed people off Penida in recent years). Using one of the recommended operators on Nusa Lembongan puts you close to the action from the start. A particular attraction are the large marine animals, including turtles, sharks and manta rays. The large (3m fin-to-fin) and unusual *mola mola* (sunfish) is sometimes seen around the islands between mid-July and October, while manta rays are often seen south of Nusa Penida.

The best dive sites include **Blue Corner** and **Jackfish Point** off Nusa Lembongan and **Ceningan Point** at the tip of that island. The channel between Ceningan and Penida is renowned for drift diving, but it is essential you have a good operator who can judge fast-changing currents and other conditions. Upswells can bring cold water from the open ocean to sites such as **Ceningan Wall**. This is one of the world's deepest natural channels and attracts all manner and sizes of fish.

Sites close to Nusa Penida include **Crystal Bay, SD, Pura Ped, Manta Point** and **Batu Aba**. Of these, Crystal Bay, SD and Pura Ped are suitable for novice divers and are good for snorkelling. For more on diving in Bali, see p37.

stylish rooms and two posh villas shelter near a pool behind the beach at Lembongan's most-glossy-magazine-ready digs. The French designer-owner has decorated the place with purple armchairs and other whimsical touches. The restaurant (meals US$10 to US$30) has an all-day menu of seafood, sandwiches and various surprises cooked up by the French chef. People have been known to swoon over the chocolate fondant.

Puri Nusa Bungalows GUESTHOUSE $
(☑24 482; r 100,000-450,000Rp; ✱) The 17 rooms here are clean and comfortable (some with hot water and air-con); the two front rooms upstairs have excellent views and there's a good cafe. Comfy loungers are scattered under trees on the manicured grounds.

Pondok Baruna GUESTHOUSE $
(☑0812 394 0992; www.world-diving.com; r 75,000-400,000Rp; ✱@☎) Associated with World Diving, this place offers eight very simple rooms with terraces facing the ocean. They are an excellent budget option. Six new plusher rooms with air-con surround a dive pool off the beach. The restaurant serves first-rate meals. Staff, led by the manager, Putu, are charmers.

Shipwrecks GUESTHOUSE $$
(☑0813 3803 2900; www.nusalembongan .au; r from 550,000Rp ✱☎) This beautiful property is set back from the beach in a coconut-shaded garden, and offers three rooms in a compound constructed in old Balinese style with natural wood. The beds are king sized and the bathrooms open air. The open common area is good for lounging or watching movies. Note that there is a two-night minimum and it's adults only.

Star Two Thousand Cafe & Bungalows
GUESTHOUSE $
(☑0812 381 2775; r 100,000-300,000Rp; ✱☎) Grassy grounds surround 28 rooms in two-storey blocks; some have hot water and air-con. There's a fun cafe-bar right on the sand, with various sunset drink specials.

Nusa Indah Bungalows GUESTHOUSE $
(☑0811 398 553; purnamaindah@hotmail.com; r 150,000-400,000Rp; ✱) This friendly place has classic thatched cottages on a sizeable beachfront and a popular cafe. There are 13 rooms in the cottages and out back in a two-storey block. Fan-only rooms are a good budget option on the beach.

Lembongan Beach Retreat GUESTHOUSE $
(☑0878 6131 3468; r 150,000-400,000Rp) At the northern end of the beach past the end

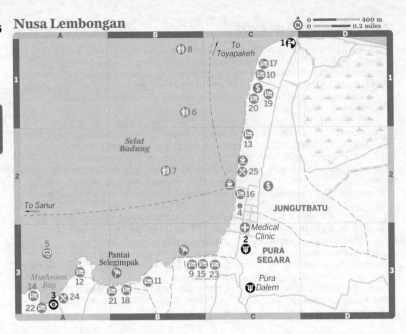

of the breakwater, this little place lives up to its name. A retreat it is, with nothing stirring by day but the ripple of the surf and the imperceptible sound of seaweed drying in the sun.

Scooby Doo Bar & Cafe SEAFOOD $
(meals 30,000-100,000Rp) In a metaphor for the island, the cast-off couches on the sand are gone, replaced by tidy tables with white tablecloths under umbrellas. The menu features fresh seafood brought up from the fishing boats. It still does a good drinks business for sunset, moon or navel gazing.

HILLSIDE

The steep hillside just south of Jungutbatu offers great views and an ever-increasing number of more luxurious rooms. The uppermost rooms at some places have gorgeous views across the water to Bali (on a clear day say hello to Gunung Agung) but such thrills come at a cost: upwards of 120 steep concrete steps. A motorbike-friendly path runs along the top of the hill, good for leg-saving drop-offs.

Playgrounds HOTEL $$
(☏24 524; www.playgroundslembongan.com; r US$75-120; ❄@☞☀) On the hillside, Playgrounds' rooms have good views, satellite TV and fridges. The cheaper ones are fan cooled but do have better views from their long porch. Villas at the top reward climbers with stylish outdoor bathrooms and plenty of space.

Ware-Ware GUESTHOUSE $
(☏0812 397 0572; warewaresurf@yahoo.com; r 250,000-500,000Rp; ❄☀) The units at this hillside place are a mix of traditional square and groovy circular numbers with thatched roofs. The large rooms (some fan only) have rattan couches and big bathrooms. The cafe (meals 30,000Rp to 100,000Rp) scores with a spectacular, breezy location on a cliffside wooden deck. It does well with seafood.

Batu Karang HOTEL $$$
(☏24880; www.batukaranglembongan.com; r from US$220; ❄@☞☀) This upmarket resort has a large infinity pool perched on a terraced hillside with 23 luxury units. Some are villa-style and have multiple rooms and private plunge pools. All have open-air bathrooms and wooden terraces with sweeping views.

PANTAI SELEGIMPAK

Leaving Jungutbatu, the island gets less tame as you go west. If you have backpacks, you may want to avail yourself of the

Nusa Lembongan

boat-meeting luggage carriers for the walk here along the hillside trail. It's a slightly chaotic 15-minute up-and-down scenic walk from the boat-landing area.

Villa Wayan Cottages　　GUESTHOUSE $
(☏745 527, 0811 386 540; r US$25-40) Villa Wayan Cottages has seven varied and unusually decorated rooms; some are suitable for families or groups. Trees give the hillside grounds a remote tropical feel.

Morin Lembongan　　GUESTHOUSE $
(☏0812 385 8396; wayman40@hotmail.com; r US$25-45; @) More lushly planted than many of the hillside places, Morin has four woodsy rooms with views over the water from their verandas. It's cold water and fan only; be sure to bargain.

Ricky's　　GUESTHOUSE $$
(☏0811 394 381; ricky_cruises@hotmail.com; r US$50-70) Local surfer Ricky and his family run this collection of large two-storey bungalow-style rooms. They are large if a tad pricey. But it's a cheery place and, as you'll see, they have room for a lot more bungalows.

MUSHROOM BAY
It's your own treasure island. This shallow bay has a nice beach, plenty of overhanging trees and some of the nicest lodging on Lembongan. Get here from Jungutbatu by road (15,000Rp) or boat (50,000Rp).

Mushroom Beach Bungalows
　　GUESTHOUSE $$
(☏24 515; www.mushroom-lembongan.com; r US$60-90; ✳✳) Perched on a tiny knoll at the eastern end of Mushroom Bay, this family-run place has a great variety of rooms, some fan only. There are good-sized bathtubs and a popular cliffside cafe (meals 40,000Rp to 150,000Rp) for viewing sunsets.

Waka Nusa Resort　　HOTEL $$
(☏0361-723 629; www.wakaexperience.com; bungalows US$110-180; ✳✳) A primitive motif blends with creature comforts at this low-key resort run by the Waka group. Ten thatch-roofed bungalows are set on sandy grounds at the shore. The beachside restaurant and bar are shaded by coconut palms. It's a nice location but new neighbours have hemmed in what was once a rural retreat.

Nusa Lembongan Resort　　HOTEL $$$
(☏0361-725 864; www.nusalembonganresort.com; villas from US$300; ✳✳) Twelve well-appointed and stylish villas overlooking the picture-perfect bay are the draw here. Flowering shrubs and trees highlight the lavish gardens. The resort has a creative terrace **restaurant** (meals US$15 to US$30) with views over the bay.

Bar & Cafe Bali　　GLOBAL $
(☏0828 367 1119, 24536; meals 25,000-60,000Rp) Follow the chicken tracks in the sand to tiered tables under trees above the high-tide mark. Enjoy pizza, pasta, seafood and the Indo usuals. The bar is lively and you can arrange for transport from Jungutbatu.

❶ Information
It's vital that you bring sufficient cash for your stay, as there are no ATMs. **Bank**

You can walk around the entire island in a day, or less on a bike. It's a fascinating journey into remote and rural Balinese life. Start along the hillside trail from **Jungutbatu** and head past the Mutiara Villa; you'll have to do some freelancing as villa developers have screwed up part of the trail. At **Pantai Selegimpak** there are more unnecessary manmade obstacles on the beach. Nature provides the challenges to reach **Mushroom Bay**, but with a little Tarzan spirit, you can stay with the faint trail and be rewarded by refreshments (this is the one segment you can't do by bike: use the roads inland).

From Mushroom Bay, head over to dreamy **Dream Beach**.

Next go to **Lembongan** village where you can take the suspension bridge to **Nusa Ceningen**. Alternatively, from Lembongan village you can take a gentle uphill walk along the sealed road to the killer hill that leads *down* to Jungutbatu, which cuts the circuit to about half a day.

To explore the rest of the island, stick to the paved road that follows the channel between Nusa Lembongan and Nusa Ceningen and then curves north along the mangroves all the way to the lighthouse. Motorbikes won't be able to navigate the trails.

BPD (☉8am-3pm Mon-Thu, 8am-1pm Fri) can exchange travellers cheques and cash but the rates are bad.

If the name **Money Changer** (☉8am-9pm) conjures images of the usurers being chased from the temple, you'd be right. Cash advances here on credit cards incur an 8% service charge. Still, for those exclaiming 'Dude, there's no ATM?!?' this service is a fiscal lifeline.

Pondok Baruna (☏0812 390 0686) has public internet terminals. Wi-fi is becoming common.

Small markets can be found near the bank, but unless you're on a diet of bottled water and Ritz crackers, the selection is small.

The **medical clinic** (consultation 150,000Rp) in the village is well versed in minor surfing injuries and ear ailments.

❶ Getting There & Away

Getting to/from Nusa Lembongan offers numerous choices. In descending order of speed are the fast boats like Scoot, the Perama boat and the public boats. Boats anchor offshore, so be prepared to get your feet wet. And travel light – wheeled bags are comically inappropriate in the water and on the beach and dirt tracks. Porters will shoulder your steamer trunk for 10,000Rp (and don't be like some low lifes we've seen who have stiffed them for their service).

Sanur public boats to Nusa Lembongan leave from the northern end of Sanur beach at 7.45am (45,000Rp, 1¾ to two hours). This is the boat used for supplies, so you may have to share space with a melon.

A **public speed boat** (175,000Rp, one hour) makes the run in under an hour: 3pm from Lembongan, 4pm from Sanur.

The **Perama tourist boat** leaves Sanur at 10.15am (100,000Rp, 1¾ hours). The Lembongan office is near the Mandara Beach Bungalows.

Scoot (☏0361-780 2255; one way/return US$18/30), located on the waterfront, runs speedboats (30 to 40 minutes) that fly over and through the waves. There are several returns daily; check schedules when you book. Note: anyone with money for a speedboat is getting into the fast-boat act; be wary of fly-by-night operators with fly-by-night safety.

For details on the Sanur end of the services, see p114.

Blue Water Express (☏723 479, 310 4558; www.bluewater-express.com), also on the waterfront, has a useful service linking Lembongan with Benoa Harbour on Bali (325,000Rp, 30 minutes) and Gili Trawangan (590,000Rp, 90 minutes).

Nusa Penida boats take locals between Jungutbatu and Toyapakeh (one hour) between 5.30am and 6am for 30,000Rp. Otherwise, charter a boat for 150,000Rp one way.

❶ Getting Around

The island is fairly small and you can easily walk to most places. There are no cars (although pickup trucks are proliferating); bicycles (25,000Rp per day) and small motorbikes (50,000Rp per hour) are widely available for hire. One-way rides on motorbikes or trucks cost 15,000Rp and up.

Nusa Ceningan

There is a narrow suspension bridge crossing the lagoon between Nusa Lembongan and Nusa Ceningan, which makes it quite easy to explore the network of tracks on foot or by bicycle. Besides the lagoon filled with frames for seaweed farming you'll see several small agricultural plots and a fishing village. The island is quite hilly and, if you're up for it, you can get glimpses of great scenery while wandering or cycling around the rough tracks.

To really savour Nusa Ceningan, take an overnight tour of the island with **JED** (Village Ecotourism Network; ☎0361-737447; www .jed.or.id; per person US$120), the cultural organisation that gives people an in-depth look at village and cultural life. Trips include family accommodation in a village, local meals, a fascinating tour with seaweed workers and transport to/from Bali.

There's a **surf break** at Ceningan reef, but it's very exposed and only surfable when the other breaks are too small.

Nusa Penida

☑0366

Largely overlooked by tourists, Nusa Penida awaits discovery. It's an untrammelled place that answers the question: what would Bali be like if tourists never came? There are not a lot of formal activities or sights; rather, you go to Nusa Penida to explore and relax, to adapt to the slow rhythm of life here, and to learn to enjoy subtle pleasures such as the changing colour of the clouds and the sea. Life is simple; you'll still see topless older women carrying huge loads on their heads.

The island is a limestone plateau with white-sand beaches on its north coast, and views over the water to the volcanoes in Bali.

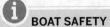

BOAT SAFETY

There have been accidents involving boats between Bali and the surrounding islands. These services are unregulated and there is no safety authority should trouble arise. See the boxed text Travelling Safely by Boat (p384) for information on how to improve your odds for a trouble-free journey.

Most beaches are not great for swimming, as most of the shallows are filled with bamboo frames used for seaweed farming. The south coast has 300m-high limestone cliffs dropping straight down to the sea and a row of offshore islets – it's rugged and spectacular scenery. The interior is hilly, with sparse-looking crops and old-fashioned villages. Rainfall is low and parts of the island are arid.

The population of around 58,000 is predominantly Hindu, although there is a Muslim community in Toyapakeh. The culture is distinct from that of Bali: the language is an old form of Balinese no longer heard on the mainland. It's an unforgiving area: Nusa Penida was once used as a place of banishment for criminals and other undesirables from the kingdom of Klungkung (now Semarapura), and still has a somewhat sinister reputation. Even today there is but one source of water and many hardships.

Services are limited to small shops in the main towns. Bring cash and anything else you'll need.

SEAWEED SUNDAE

The next time you enjoy some creamy ice cream, you might thank the seaweed growers of Nusa Lembongan and Nusa Penida. Carrageenan is an emulsifying agent that is used to thicken ice cream as well as cheese and many other products. It is also used as a fat substitute in 'diet' foods (just look for it on the endless ingredients label). In nature it turns sea water into a gel that gives seaweed its structure.

On Lembongan 85% of the population work at farming seaweed for carrageenan (as opposed to 5% in tourism). It's the island's major industry. Although returns are OK, the work is very intensive and time-consuming. Women are the main labourers.

As you walk around the villages, you'll see – and smell – vast areas used for drying seaweed. Looking down into the water, you'll see the patchwork of cultivated seaweed plots. Small pieces of a marine algae (*Eucheuma*) are attached to strings that are stretched between bamboo poles – these underwater fences can be seen off many of the beaches, and especially in the shallows between Lembongan and Ceningan and at low tide. Growth is so fast that new shoots can be harvested every 45 days. This region is especially good for production, as the waters are shallow and rich in nutrients. The dried red and green seaweed is exported around the world for final processing.

PENIDA'S DEMON

Nusa Penida is the legendary home of Jero Gede Macaling, the demon who inspired the Barong Landung dance. Many Balinese believe the island is a place of enchantment and *angker* (evil power) – paradoxically, this is an attraction. Although few foreigners visit, thousands of Balinese come every year for religious observances aimed at placating the evil spirits.

The island has a number of interesting temples dedicated to Jero Gede Macaling, including Pura Dalem Penetaran Ped, near Toyapakeh. It houses a shrine that is a source of power for practitioners of black magic, and a place of pilgrimage for those seeking protection from sickness and evil.

🏃 Activities

Nusa Penida has world-class **diving**. Make arrangements through a dive shop on Nusa Lembongan. If you plan to go **snorkelling**, bring your own gear.

Between Toyapakeh and Sampalan there is excellent **cycling** on the beautiful, flat coastal road. The hitch is you need to bring a *good* bike with you to Penida. If you really want to explore, bring a mountain bike and camping equipment from the mainland (but remember, Nusa Penida is hilly). Alternatively, plan to do some serious **hiking**, but come well prepared.

SAMPALAN

Sampalan, the main town on Penida, is quiet and pleasant, with a market, schools and shops strung out along the curving coast road. The **market area**, where bemo congregate, is in the middle of town. It's a good place to absorb village life.

🛏 Sleeping & Eating

Not many people stay here, although there are plenty of rooms, so just show up. For meals you'll need to try one of the small warung in town – no more than 10 minutes by foot from any of the inns.

Made's Homestay　　HOMESTAY $
(☑0828 368 6709; r incl breakfast from 100,000Rp) Four small, clean rooms in a pleasant garden. A small side road between the market and the harbour leads here.

Nusa Garden Bungalows　　GUESTHOUSE $
(☑0813 3812 0660; r 100,000-160,000Rp) Crushed-coral pathways running between animal statuary link the 10 rooms here. Rates include a small breakfast. Turn on Jl Nusa Indah just east of the centre.

TOYAPAKEH

If you come by boat from Lembongan, you'll probably be dropped at the beach at Toyapakeh, a pretty village with lots of shady trees. The beach has clean white sand, clear blue water, a neat line of boats, and Gunung Agung as a backdrop. Step up from it and you're at the road where bemo can take you to Ped or Sampalan (10,000Rp).

Offshore, the big grey thing that looks like a tuna-processing plant is the watergames pontoon for **Quicksilver** (☑0361-742 5161; www.quicksilver-bali.com; adult/child US$85/42.50). Day trips from Benoa Harbour include a buffet lunch, snorkelling, rides on a semi-submersible sub for fish spotting and an excursion ashore to an extremely unattractive 'tourist village' of souvenir sellers.

Toyapakeh is ripe for some groovy tourist accommodation, although it's been ripe for a long time. In the meantime, you could be the intrepid traveller and see if rooms have appeared, knowing that you can always go to nearby Sampalan for a simple room.

AROUND THE ISLAND

A trip around the island, following the north and east coasts and crossing the hilly interior, can be completed in half a day by motorcycle or in a day by bike if you're in shape. You could spend much longer, lingering at the temples and the small villages, and walking to less accessible areas, but there's no accommodation outside the two main towns. The following description goes clockwise from Sampalan.

The coastal road from Sampalan curves and dips past bays with rows of fishing boats and offshore seaweed gardens. After about 6km, just before the village of Karangsari, steps go up on the right side of the road to the narrow entrance of **Goa Karangsari** caves. There are usually people who can provide a lantern and guide you through the cave for a small negotiable fee of around 20,000Rp each. The limestone cave is over 15m tall in some sections. It extends more than 200m through the hill and emerges on the other side to overlook a verdant valley.

Continue south past a naval station and several temples to **Suana**. Here the main road swings inland and climbs up into the hills, while a very rough side track goes southeast, past more interesting temples to **Semaya**, a fishing village with a sheltered beach and one of Bali's best dive sites offshore, **Batu Aba**.

About 9km southwest of Suana, **Tanglad** is a very old-fashioned village and a centre for traditional weaving. Rough roads south and east lead to isolated parts of the coast.

A scenic ridge-top road goes northwest from Tanglad. At Batukandik, a rough road and 1.5km track leads to a spectacular **waterfall** *(air terjun)* that crashes onto a small beach. Get a guide (20,000Rp) in Tanglad.

Limestone cliffs drop hundreds of feet into the sea, surrounded by crashing surf. At their base, underground streams discharge fresh water into the sea – a pipeline was made to bring the water up to the top. Look for the remains of the rickety old wooden scaffolding women used to clamber down, returning with large pots of water on their heads.

Back on the main road, continue to Batumadeg, past **Bukit Mundi** (the highest point on the island at 529m; on a clear day you can see Lombok), through Klumpu to Sakti, which has traditional stone buildings. Return to the north coast at Toyapakeh, about one hour after Bukit Mundi.

The important temple of **Pura Dalem Penetaran Ped** is near the beach at Ped, a few kilometres east of Toyapakeh. It houses a shrine for the demon Jero Gede Macaling (see the boxed text, p130). The temple structure is sprawling and you will see many people making offerings for safe sea voyages from Nusa Penida; you may wish to join them.

Across from the temple, the spotless and simple **Depot Anda** (meals 5000-10,000Rp; ☺6am-9pm) is the eating choice on the island, with tasty local standards. Have a banana juice at **Warung Ibu Nur** (dishes from 3000Rp).

WORTH A TRIP

YOUR OWN PERFECT BEACH

South of Toyapakeh, a 10km road through the village of Sakti leads to idyllic **Crystal Bay Beach**, which fronts the popular dive spot. The sand here is the whitest around Bali and you'll likely have it to yourself. Should you somehow have the gear, this would be a fine place to camp.

The road between Sampalan and Toyapakeh follows the craggy and lush coast.

ⓘ Getting There & Away

The strait between Nusa Penida and southern Bali is deep and subject to heavy swells – if there is a strong tide, boats often have to wait. You may also have to wait a while for the public boat to fill up with passengers. Boats to/from Kusamba are not recommended.

PADANGBAI On the beach just east of the car park in Padangbai, you'll find the twin-engine fibre-glass boats that run across the strait to Buyuk, 1km west of Sampalan on Nusa Penida (30,000Rp, 45 minutes, four daily). The boats run between 7am and noon. A large and modern car ferry operates daily (15,000Rp, two hours) from Kusamba.

NUSA LEMBONGAN Boats run between Toyapakeh and Jungutbatu (30,000Rp, one hour) between 5.30am and 6am. Enjoy the mangrove views on the way. Otherwise, charter a boat for 150,000Rp.

ⓘ Getting Around

Bemo regularly travel along the sealed road between Toyapakeh and Sampalan, and sometimes on to Suana and up to Klumpu, but beyond these areas the roads are rough and transport is limited. You should be able to charter your own bemo or private vehicle with driver for about 50,000Rp per hour or rent a motorbike for 100,000Rp per day.

You may also be able to negotiate an *ojek* (motorcycle that takes passengers) for about 30,000Rp per hour.

Ubud & Around

Includes »

Best Places to Eat

» Three Monkeys (p156)

» Café des Artistes (p157)

» Nasi Ayam Kedewatan (p158)

» Warung Teges (p157)

Best Places to Stay

» Swasti Cottage (p153)

» Hotel Tjampuhan (p153)

» Sayan Terrace (p154)

» Bambu Indah (p154)

Why Go?

A dancer moves her hand just so and 200 pairs of entranced eyes follow the exact movement. A gamelan player hits a melodic riff and 200 pairs of feet tap along with it. The Legong goes into its second hour as the bumblebee dance unfolds with its sprightly flair and 200 butts forget they're still stuck in rickety plastic chairs.

So another dance performance works its magic on a crowd in Ubud, the town amid a collection of villages where all that is magical about Bali comes together in one easy-to-love package. From nightly cultural performances to museums showing the works of artists whose creativity flowered here to the unbelievably green rice fields that spill down lush hillsides to rushing rivers below, Ubud is a feast for the soul. Personal pleasures like fine dining, shopping, spas and more only add to the appeal.

When to Go

The weather is slightly cooler but much wetter than in the south; expect it to rain at any time. At night, mountain breezes make air-con unnecessary and let you hear the symphony of frogs, bugs and distant gamelan practices echoing over the rice fields through your screened window. Temps during the day average 30°C and at night 20°C, although extremes are possible. Seasonal variation is muted, given the prevalence of precipitation. The real factor in deciding when to come is peak season: July, August and the Christmas holidays.

UBUD

♪ 0361

Ubud is culture, yes. It's also home to good restaurants, cafes and streets of shops, many selling goods from the region's artisans. There's somewhere to stay for every budget, and no matter what the price you can enjoy lodgings that reflect the local zeitgeist: artful, creative and serene.

Ubud's popularity continues to grow. Tour buses with day trippers can choke the main streets and cause traffic chaos (for a while they even desecrated the iconic Football Field by parking there). Being named the top city in Asia by *Conde Nast Traveler* only added to the hoopla from bestselling *Eat, Pray, Love*. Fortunately Ubud adapts and a brief stroll away from the intersection of Jl Raya Ubud and Monkey Forest Rd can quickly restore sanity. There's nothing like a walk through the verdant rice fields to make all right with the world.

Spend a few days in Ubud to appreciate it properly. It's one of those places where days can become weeks and weeks become months, as the noticeable expat community demonstrates.

History

Late in the 19th century, Cokorda Gede Agung Sukawati established a branch of the Sukawati royal family in Ubud and began a series of alliances and confrontations with neighbouring kingdoms. In 1900, with the kingdom of Gianyar, Ubud became (at its own request) a Dutch protectorate and was able to concentrate on its religious and cultural life.

The Cokorda descendants encouraged Western artists and intellectuals to visit the area in the 1930s, most notably Walter Spies, Colin McPhee and Rudolf Bonnet. They provided an enormous stimulus to local art, introduced new ideas and techniques, and began a process of displaying and promoting Balinese culture worldwide. As mass tourism arrived in Bali, Ubud became an attraction not for beaches or bars, but for the arts.

The royal family is still much a part of Ubud life, helping to fund huge cultural and religious displays such as a memorable cremation ceremony in 2008.

◎ Sights

Palaces & Temples

Ubud Palace and **Puri Saren Agung** (Map p137; cnr Jl Raya Ubud & Jl Suweta) share space

Ubud & Around Highlights

❶ Making like the ubiquitous ducks and wandering the rice fields in and around **Ubud** (p133)

❷ Feeling the rhythm of a traditional Balinese **dance performance** (p159), one of Ubud's great night-time pageants

❸ Making new friends and wiling away the hours at a funky **Ubud cafe** (p154)

❹ Discovering your own hidden talents through an **art or cooking course** (p143) as you draw on the knowledge of talented locals

❺ Exploring the green jungle and white water of the **Sungai Ayung valley** (p146) Sayan)

❻ Making like Indiana Jones at the towering ancient wonders at **Gunung Kawi** (p166)

❼ Exploring the myriad villages in the Ubud region, such as **Mas** (p170), for artworks, crafts, ceremonial objects and other treasures

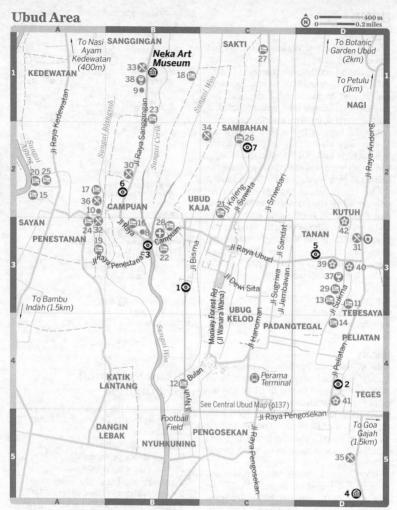

in the heart of Ubud. The compound has many ornate corners and was mostly built after the 1917 earthquake. The local royal family still live here and you can wander around most of the large compound exploring the many traditional and not excessively ornate buildings. If you really like it, you can stay the night. Take time to appreciate the stone carvings, many by noted local artists like I Gusti Nyoman Lempad.

Just north, **Pura Marajan Agung** (Map p137; Jl Suweta) has one of the finest gates you'll find and is the private temple for the royal family.

Pura Desa Ubud (Map p137; Jl Raya Ubud) is the main temple for the Ubud community. It is often closed. Just a bit west is the very picturesque **Pura Taman Saraswati** (Ubud Water Palace; Map p137; Jl Raya Ubud). Waters from the temple at the rear of the site feed the pond in the front, which overflows with pretty lotus blossoms. There are carvings that honour Dewi Saraswati, the goddess of wisdom and the arts, who has clearly given her blessing to Ubud. There are weekly dance performances by night; by day painters set up easels.

UBUD SIGHTS

Natural Sights

Sacred Monkey Forest Sanctuary FOREST
(Map p137; ☎971 304; www.monkeyforestubud
.com; Monkey Forest Rd; adult/child 20,000/
10,000Rp; ☺8am-6pm) This cool and dense
swath of jungle, officially called Mandala
Wisata Wanara Wana, houses three holy
temples. The sanctuary is inhabited by a
band of grey-haired and greedy long-tailed
Balinese macaques who are nothing like
the innocent-looking doe-eyed monkeys
on the brochures. They are ever vigilant for
passing tourists who just might have peanuts and ripe bananas available for a quick
hand-out. Don't hand food directly to these
creatures.

The interesting **Pura Dalem Agung**
(Map p137; Temple of the Dead) is in the forest and has a real Indiana Jones feel to it.

Look for the Rangda figures devouring children at the entrance to the inner temple.

You can enter through one of the three
gates: the main one at the southern end of
Monkey Forest Rd; 100m further east, near
the car park; or from the southern side,
on the lane from Nyuhkuning. The forest
has recently benefited from an infusion of
money. Useful brochures about the forest,
macaques and temples are available. Across
from the main entrance, the forest's **office**
(Map p137) accepts donations for a scheme
to offset the carbon you created getting to
Bali. Get a tree planted for 150,000Rp.

Botanic Garden Ubud GARDENS
(☎970951; www.botanicgardenbali.com; admission
50,000Rp; ☺8am-6pm) Discover the stories behind the many plants that make Bali green at
Botanic Garden Ubud, on the road to Penelokan. Spread over more than 6 hectares, the

UBUD IN...

One Day

Stroll the streets of Ubud, enjoying the galleries and sampling the fine cuisine. Try to get out on one of the short nearby walks through the verdant rice fields. Go to an evening dance performance at the **Ubud Palace**.

Three Days

Take longer walks in the countryside during the mornings, especially the **Campuan Ridge** and **Sayan Valley**. In the afternoons visit the **Museum Puri Lukisan**, **Neka Art Museum** and **Arma**. At night attend **dance performances** not just in Ubud, but also in the nearby villages. Indulge at a local **spa**.

A Week or More

Do everything we've listed but take time to simply chill out. Get in tune with Ubud's rhythm. Take naps, read books, wander about. Think about a **course** in Balinese culture. Compare and choose your favourite cafe, get out to craft villages and ancient sites.

many gardens are devoted to various themes such as orchids (in greenhouses), Bali-grown plants like cinnamon and vanilla, flowering butterfly-friendly gardens, an enormous lotus pond and much more. The work of Stefan Reisner, the gardens are a good counterpoint to art-filled museums. Get lost in the maze and when you finally escape, take comfort from Bali's medicinal plants. The exhibit about the cacti of East Bali is worth the cost of admission alone.

Petulu NATURAL AREA
Every evening at around 6pm, thousands of big **herons** and **egrets** fly in to Petulu, about 2.5km north of Jl Raya Ubud, squabbling over the prime perching places before settling into the trees beside the road and becoming a tourist attraction. The herons, mainly the striped Java pond species, started their visits to Petulu in 1965 for no apparent reason. Villagers believe they bring good luck (as well as tourists), despite the smell and the mess. A few warung (food stalls) have been set up in the paddy fields, where you can have a drink while enjoying the spectacle. Walk quickly under the trees if the herons are already roosting.

Petulu is a pleasant walk or bicycle ride on any of several routes north of Ubud, but if you stay for the birds you'll be heading back in the dark.

Museums

TOP CHOICE **Museum Puri Lukisan** ART MUSEUM
(Map p137; ☑975 136; www.mpl-ubud .com; off Jl Raya Ubud; admission 20,000Rp; ⊙9am-5pm) The Museum of Fine Arts displays fine examples of all schools of Balinese art. Just look at the lush composition of *Balinese Market* by Anak Agung Gde Sobrat to see the vibrancy of local painting.

It was in Ubud that the modern Balinese art movement started, when artists first began to abandon purely religious themes and court subjects for scenes of everyday life. Rudolf Bonnet was part of the Pita Maha artists' cooperative, and together with Cokorda Gede Agung Sukawati (a prince of Ubud's royal family) and Walter Spies they helped to establish a permanent collection.

Building I, straight ahead as you enter, has a collection of early works from Ubud and the surrounding villages. These include examples of classical *wayang*-style paintings (art influenced by shadow puppetry), fine ink drawings by I Gusti Nyoman Lempad and paintings by Pita Maha artists. Notice the level of detail in Lempad's *The Dream of Dharmawangsa*. Classic works from the 1930s heyday of expats are also here.

Building II, on the left, has some colourful examples of the 'Young Artist' style of painting and a good selection of 'modern traditional' works.

Building III, on the right, has classical and traditional paintings and is used for special exhibitions.

The museum's collection is well curated and labelled in English. The museum has a good bookshop and a cafe. The lush, garden-like grounds alone are worth a visit.

0 200 m
0 0.1 miles

A   B   C   D

UBUD SIGHTS

87

Museum Puri Lukisan

UBUD KAJA

Jl Raya Campuran

40
7 77 8
58 5 82 6
60 88
114 91

Jl Bisma

Jl Suweta
Jl Hajeng

Ubud Palace; Puri Saren Agung

Xtrans 2
111 10
26

Jl Sriwedari
Jl Sandat

Jl Jembawan

105 3
68 99
52 11
33

107 73 74
Market
Apotek
Ari Medika 71 59

39 56
37

Jl Anggada
Jl Arjuna

Jl Goutama
Jl Raya Ubud

104 115
108 103
110 96
43
41

Jl Karna
Jl Maruti

98
70

Gang Beji

79 102
57 67
101
50 16 75
95 14 30
90
80 55

Jl Dewi Sita

36 25
20 54
63 64
61 17
112

Jl Hanoman
Jl Sugriwa

Jl Jembawan

97
86
15

1 29

UBUG
KELOD

PADANGTEGAL

31
13 32
69
45 78
84
92

89

113
94
66

49
93 48
38
62 12
51

35
106

24 53

9

Monkey Forest Rd (Jl Wanara Wana)

109

Sacred Monkey Forest Sanctuary

19 18

Jl Nyuh Bulan

4

44

81

Jl Raya Pengosekan

76

46

47 100
72 22

Agung Rai Museum of Art (ARMA)

83 85 21

Neka Art Museum   ART MUSEUM
(Map p134; ☑975 074; www.museumneka.com;
Jl Raya Sanggingan; adult/child 40,000Rp/free;
☉9am-5pm) Quite distinct from Neka Gallery, the Neka Art Museum is the creation of Suteja Neka, a private collector and dealer in Balinese art. It has an excellent and diverse collection and is a good place to learn about the development of painting in Bali.

You can get an overview of the myriad local painting styles in the **Balinese Painting Hall**. Look for the *wayang* works.

The **Arie Smit Pavilion** features Smit's works on the upper level, and examples of the Young Artist school, which he inspired, on the lower level. Look for the Bruegel-like *The Wedding Ceremony* by I Nyoman Tjarka.

The **Lempad Pavilion** houses Bali's largest collection of works by I Gusti Nyoman Lempad.

The **Contemporary Indonesian Art Hall** has paintings by artists from other parts of Indonesia, many of whom have worked in Bali. The upper floor of the **East-West Art Annexe** is devoted to the work of foreign artists, such as Louise Koke, Miguel Covarrubias, Rudolf Bonnet, Han Snel, the Australian Donald Friend, and Antonio Blanco.

The temporary exhibition hall has changing displays, while the **Photography Archive Centre** features black-and-white photography of Bali in the early 1930s and 1940s. The bookshop is noteworthy and there's a cafe.

Agung Rai Museum of Art (ARMA) MUSEUM (Map p137; ☑976 659; www.armamuseum.com; Jl Raya Pengosekan; admission 30,000Rp; ◎9am-6pm) Founded by Agung Rai as a museum, gallery and cultural centre, the impressive Arma is the only place in Bali to see haunting works by the influential German artist Walter Spies.

The museum is housed in several traditional buildings set in gardens with water coursing through channels. It features work by 19th-century Javanese artist Raden Saleh. It exhibits classical Kamasan paintings, Batuan-style work from the 1930s and '40s, and works by Lempad, Affandi, Sadali, Hofker, Bonnet and Le Mayeur. The collection is well labelled in English.

Look for the enigmatic *Portrait of a Javanese Nobleman and His Wife* by Raden Saleh, which predates the similar *American Gothic* by decades.

It's fun to visit ARMA when local children practise **Balinese dancing** (◎3-5pm Mon-Fri, 10.30am-noon Sun) and during **gamelan**

EAT, PRAY, LOVE & UBUD

'That damn book' is a common reaction by many Ubud residents, who fear the town being overrun by *Eat, Pray, Love* fans. *Eat, Pray, Love* is the Elizabeth Gilbert book (and movie) that chronicles the American author's search for self-fulfilment (and fulfilment of a book contract) across Italy, India and, yes, Ubud. It's anyone's guess whether Ubud's surging popularity has everything or just a little to do with EPL – although those who despair over the book enjoyed *Schadenfreude* over the movie's modest box-office results.

Some criticise Gilbert for not offering a more complete picture of Ubud's locals, dance, art, expats and walks, warts and all. And they decry basic factual errors such as the evocative prose about surf spots on the north coast (there are none), which lead you to suspect things might have been embellished a bit for the plot. Meanwhile, others in Ubud have found myriad ways to profit from EPL and are happy to ride the wave (except on the north coast...).

Then there are the genuine fans, those who found a message in EPL that resonated, validating and/or challenging aspects of their lives. For some an ultimately magical journey to Ubud wouldn't have happened without EPL.

People in the Book

Two characters in the book are easily found in Ubud. Both receive large numbers of EPL fans and have lucrative livelihoods because of it.

Ketut Liyer (☏974 092; Pengosekan) The genial and inspirational friend of Gilbert is easily found about a 10-minute walk south of Pengosekan (look for the bright new signs). Any driver will happily bring you here. Hours vary and the ageing Ketut has been in ill health, possibly due to the huge demand for an audience from Westerners. Expect to pay about US$25 for a short and public session, during which you will be told a variation on the theme that you're smart, beautiful, sexy and will live to 101 or 105 etc. Or for US$20 you can spend the night in a very simple room in a guesthouse at the rear of the compound (although the nearby chained and caged birds may detract from this experience). The actual Liyer compound is used in the movie, although Ketut is played by a schoolteacher from Java.

Wayan Nuriasih (Map p137; ☏872 9230, 917 5991; balihealer@hotmail.com; Jl Jembawan 5; ⊕9am-5pm) Another star of *Eat, Pray, Love*, Nuriasih is right in the heart of Ubud. Her open-fronted shop has a table where you can discuss your ailments with her and ponder a treatment. During this time, various buff male assistants will silently wander about and soon an elixir may appear at your elbow. The 'vitamin lunch' is a series of extracts and raw foods that is popular with many. Note that it is important to have a very clear understanding of what you're agreeing to, as it's easy to commit to therapies that can cost US$50 or more. For less, you can enjoy a cleansing, during which time several men whack at your body and give you new pains that make you forget the old ones.

Locations in the Movie

Most of the Bali locations for *Eat Pray Love*, the movie, were filmed in and around Ubud. However, don't be surprised if on your walks in the area, you find beautiful rice fields that surpass those shown in the movie.

The beach scenes were shot at Padang Padang, on south Bali's Bukit Peninsula. Oddly, the real beach is more attractive than the sort of grey version seen in the film. But for those hoping to retire to the beach bar where Julia Roberts meets Javier Bardem, there's no point trying, as the bar was created for the movie. Then again, this being Bali, someone may have created a facsimile by the time you read this.

practice (⊙hours vary). See p159 for details on regular Legong and Kecak performances. See p143 for details on the myriad cultural courses offered here.

You can enter the museum grounds from the southern end of Jl Raya Pengosekan or around the corner on Jl Pengosekan at Kafe Arma, where there's parking.

Museum Rudana ART MUSEUM

(☑975 779; www.museumrudana.com; admission 20,000Rp; ⊙9am-5pm) This large, imposing museum is the creation of local politician and art-lover Nyoman Rudana and his wife Ni Wayan Olasthini. The three floors contain over 400 traditional paintings, including a calendar dated to the 1840s, some Lempad drawings, and more-modern pieces. The museum is beside the Rudana Gallery, which has a large selection of paintings for sale.

Blanco Renaissance Museum ART MUSEUM

(Map p134; ☑975 502; Jl Raya Campuan; admission 50,000Rp; ⊙9am-5pm) The picture of Antonio Blanco mugging with Michael Jackson says it all. His namesake Blanco Renaissance Museum captures the artist's theatrical spirit. Blanco came to Bali from Spain via the Philippines. He specialised in erotic art, illustrated poetry and playing the role of an eccentric artist à la Dali. He died in Bali in 1999, and his flamboyant home is now this museum. More prosaically: enjoy the waterfall on the way in and good views over the river.

Galleries

Ubud is dotted with galleries – every street and lane seems to have a place exhibiting artwork for sale. They vary enormously in the choice and quality of items on display.

Often you will find local artists in the most unusual places, including your place to stay. A good example is **I Wayan Karja**, a painter who has a studio in the grounds of his family's Santra Putra guesthouse.

Neka Gallery ART GALLERY

(Map p137; ☑975 034; Jl Raya Ubud; ⊙9am-5pm) Operated by Suteja Neka, the low-key Neka Gallery is a separate entity from the Neka Art Museum. It has an extensive selection from all the schools of Balinese art, as well as works by European residents such as the renowned Arie Smit.

Seniwati Gallery of Art by Women

ART GALLERY

(Map p137; ⊙975 485; www.seniwatigallery.com; Jl Sriwedari 2B; ⊙9am-5pm Tue-Sun) This gallery exhibits works by more than 70 Balinese, Indonesian and resident foreign women artists. The information on many of the artists makes for fascinating reading. Works span all media.

Symon Studio ART GALLERY

(Map p134; ☑974 721; www.symonbali.com; Jl Raya Campuan; ⊙9am-6pm) 'Danger! Art!' screams the sign in Campuan. With this you know you've found the gallery/studio of the irrepressible American artist Symon. The gallery is a spacious and airy place full of huge, colourful and exotic portraits. The work ranges from the sublime to the profane. Symon, however, is most often found in his gallery in north Bali; see p226.

Komaneka Art Gallery ART GALLERY

(Map p137; ☑976 090; Monkey Forest Rd; ⊙8am-8pm) Exhibiting works from established Balinese artists, this gallery is a good place to see high-profile art, in a large and lofty space.

Agung Rai Gallery ART GALLERY

(Map p134; ☑975 449; Jl Peliatan; ⊙9am-6pm) This gallery is in a pretty compound and its collection covers the full range of Balinese styles. It functions as a cooperative, with the work priced by the artist and the gallery adding a percentage.

Rio Helmi Gallery PHOTOGRAPHY GALLERY

(Map p137; ☑972 304; www.riohelmi.com; Jl Suweta 5; ⊙10am-8pm) Noted photographer and Ubud resident Rio Helmi has a small gallery where you can see examples of journalistic and artistic work. Photos change

---

DON'T MISS

THREADS OF LIFE INDONESIAN TEXTILE ARTS CENTER

This small, professional **textile gallery and educational studio** (Map p134; ☑972 187; www.threadsoflife.com; Jl Kajeng 24; ⊙10am-7pm) sponsors the production of naturally dyed, handmade ritual textiles, helping to recover skills in danger of being lost to modern dyeing and weaving methods. Commissioned pieces are displayed in the gallery, which has good explanatory material. It also runs regular textile appreciation courses and has a good shop.

often and offer beautiful insight into Helmi's travels worldwide and across Bali.

Adi's Gallery
ART GALLERY

(Map p134; ☎977 104; www.adi-s-gallery.com; Jl Bisma 102; ☺10am-5pm) Many of the better local artists display their works here. Adi hosts occasional special events like live music and many popular special exhibits. The gallery is a project of German artist Adi Bachmann.

Pranoto's Art Gallery
ART GALLERY

(Map p134; ☎970 827; Jl Raya Ubud) The husband-wife pair of artists Pranoto and Kerry Pendergrast display their works here. The scenes of Indonesian life are lovely.

Ketut Rudi Gallery
ART GALLERY

(☎974 122; Pengosekan) These sprawling galleries showcase the works of more than 50 Ubud artists with techniques as varied as primitive and new realism. The gallery's namesake is on display as well; he favours an entertaining style best described as 'comical realism'.

Artists' Homes

The 'Spies house' (Map p134) home of German artist Walter Spies, is now part of Hotel Tjampuhan. Aficionados can stay if they book well in advance. Spies played an important part in promoting Bali's artistic culture in the 1930s.

Dutch-born artist **Han Snel** lived in Ubud from the 1950s until his death in 1999, and his family runs his namesake bungalows on Jl Kajeng.

Lempad's House (Map p137; Jl Raya Ubud; admission free; ☺daylight), the home of I Gusti Nyoman Lempad, is open to the public, but it's mainly used as a gallery for a group of artists that includes Lempad's grandchildren. The Puri Lukisan and Neka museums have more extensive collections of Lempad's drawings.

Music scholar **Colin McPhee** is well known thanks to his perennial favourite *A House in Bali*. Although the actual 1930s house is long gone, you can visit the riverside site (which shows up in photographs in the book) at the Sayan Terrace. The hotel's Wayan Ruma, whose mother was McPhee's cook, is good for a few stories.

Arie Smit (1916–) is the best-known and longest-surviving Western artist in Ubud. He worked in the Dutch colonial administration in the 1930s, was imprisoned during WWII, and came to Bali in 1956. In the 1960s, his influence sparked the Young Artists school of painting in Penestanan, earning him an enduring place in the history of Balinese art. His home is not open to the public.

🏃 Activities
Massage, Spas & Salons

Ubud brims with salons and spas where you can heal, pamper, rejuvenate or otherwise focus on your personal needs, physical and mental. Visiting a spa is at the top of many a traveller's itinerary and the business of spas, yoga and other treatments grows each year. Expect the latest trends from any of many practitioners (the bulletin board outside Bali Buddha is bewildering) and prepare to try some new therapies, such as 'pawing'. If you have to ask you don't want to know. You may also wish to seek out a traditional healer or balian (see p152 for details).

Many spas also offer courses in therapies, treatments and activities like yoga.

Bali Botanica Day Spa
SPA

(Map p134; ☎976 739; www.balibotanica.com; massage from 150,000Rp; ☺9am-8pm) Set beautifully on a lush hillside past little fields of rice and ducks, this spa offers a range of treatments including Ayurvedic ones. Will provide transport.

Ubud Sari Health Resort
SPA

(Map p134; ☎974 393; www.ubudsari.com; Jl Kajeng; 1hr massage US$15; ☺8am-8pm) A spa and hotel in one. It is a serious place with extensive organic treatments bearing such names as 'total tissue cleansing'. Besides a long list of daytime spa and salon services, there are packages that include stays at the hotel.

Intuitive Flow
YOGA

(Map p134; ☎977 824; www.intuitiveflow.com; Penestanan; yoga from 90,000Rp) A lovely yoga studio up amid the rice fields – although just climbing the concrete stairs to get here from Campuan may make you too pooped to pop your yoga togs on. Workshops in healing arts.

Zen
SPA

(Map p137; ☎970 976; Jl Hanoman; 1hr massage 100,000Rp; ☺9am-8pm) Offers a 90-minute *mandi lulur* (Javanese body scrub) and a spice bath (160,000Rp).

Nur Salon
SPA

(Map p137; ☎975 352; Jl Hanoman 28; 1hr massage 125,000Rp; ☺9am-8pm) In a traditional

Balinese compound filled with labelled medicinal plants; offers a long menu of straightforward spa and salon services, including a Javanese massage that takes two hours (300,000Rp).

Eve Spa   SPA
(Map p137; ☑747 0910; Monkey Forest Rd; 1hr massage 85,000Rp; ☺9am-9pm) Will cleanse you of toxins. The menu is uncomplicated and affordable, and you can go on something of a spa orgy: an all-day festival of treatments is 410,000Rp.

Kenko Reflexology   MASSAGE
(Map p137; ☑975 293; Monkey Forest Rd; foot massage 40,000Rp; ☺8am-8pm) After a day trekking the beautiful Ubud countryside and listening to all those barking dogs, your own dogs may also be barking. Sessions start with gentle foot cleansing and only get better.

Milano Salon   SALON
(Map p137; ☑973 488; Monkey Forest Rd; 1hr massage 80,000Rp; ☺9am-8pm) Offers facials and massages in a simple setting, plus haircutting (70,000Rp), styling and colouring.

Cycling
Many shops and hotels in central Ubud display mountain bikes for hire. The price is usually a negotiable 35,000Rp per day. If in doubt where to rent, ask at your hotel and someone with a bike is soon likely to appear.

In general, the land is dissected by rivers running south, so any east–west route will involve a lot of ups and downs as you cross the river valleys. North–south routes run between the rivers, and are much easier going, but can have heavy traffic. Most of the sites in Ubud are reachable by bike.

Riding a bike is an excellent way to visit the many museums and cultural sites described in the Around Ubud section, although you'll need to consider your comfort level with traffic south of Ubud.

See p147 for companies offering cycling tours in or near Ubud.

Rafting
The nearby **Sungai Ayung** (Ayung River) is the most popular river in Bali for whitewater rafting. You start north of Ubud and end near the Amandari hotel in the west. Note that depending on rainfall the run can range from sedate to thrilling. See p36 for names of operators.

YOGA BARN

The chakra for the yoga revolution in Ubud, the **Yoga Barn** (Map p137; ☑070 992; www.balispirit.com; off Jl Pengosekan; classes from 100,000Rp; ☺7am-9pm) sits in its own lotus position amid trees back near a river valley. The name exactly describes what you'll find. A huge range of classes in yoga, Pilates, dance and life-affirming offshoots are held through the week. Owner Meghan Pappenheim also organises the fast-growing Bali Spirit Festival (p147).

Walking Tours
The growth of Ubud has engulfed a number of nearby villages, although they have still managed to retain distinct identities. There are lots of interesting walks in the area to surrounding villages or through the paddy fields. You'll frequently see artists at work in open rooms and on verandas, and the timeless tasks of rice cultivation continue alongside luxury villas.

In most places there are plenty of warung or small shops selling snack foods and drinks, but bring your own water. Also bring a good hat, decent shoes and wet-weather gear for the afternoon showers; long trousers are better for walking through thick vegetation.

Try to start walks at daybreak, before it gets too hot. In the walking tours section, the distance is approximate and is measured with the Ubud Palace as the start and end point. Walking time does not include any stops, so you need to factor in your own eating, shopping and rest stops.

Some entrepreneurial rice farmers have erected little toll gates across their fields. You can a) simply detour around them, or b) pay a fee (never, ever accede to more than 10,000Rp).

For information on guided walks, see p147.

⚡ Courses
Ubud is the perfect place to develop your artistic or language skills, or learn about Balinese culture and cuisine. The range of courses offered could keep you busy for a year.

ℹ️ REFILL YOUR WATER BOTTLE

The number of plastic water bottles emptied in Bali's tropical heat daily and then tossed in the trash is appalling. In Ubud there are a few places where you can refill your water bottle (plastic or reusable) for a small fee, usually 3000Rp. The water is the same Aqua brand that is most preferred locally and you'll be helping to save Bali one plastic bottle at a time. A good central location is **Pondok Pecak Library & Learning Centre** (Map p137; ☎976 194; Monkey Forest Rd; ⊙9am-9pm).

TOP CHOICE ARMA   CULTURAL
(Map p137; ☎976 659; www.armamuseum.com; Jl Raya Pengosekan; ⊙9am-6pm) A cultural powerhouse offering classes in painting, woodcarving and batik. Other courses include Balinese history, Hinduism and architecture. Classes cost US$25 to US$55.

Threads of Life Indonesian Textile Arts Center   TEXTILE
(Map p134; ☎972 187; www.threadsoflife.com; Jl Kajeng 24) Textile appreciation courses in the gallery and educational studio last from one to eight days. Some classes involve extensive travel around Bali and should be considered graduate level.

Nirvana Batik Course   TEXTILE
(Map p137; ☎975 415; www.nirvanaku.com; Nirvana Pension & Gallery, Jl Goutama 10; ⊙classes 10am-2pm Mon-Sat) Nyoman Suradnya teaches the highly regarded batik courses. Classes cost US$45 to US$150 depending on duration (one to five days).

IB Anom   CARVING
(☎974 529; Mas) Three generations of some of Bali's best mask-carvers will show you their secrets (from 100,000Rp per day) in a family compound right off the main road; in two weeks you might have something.

Wayan Karja   PAINTING
(Map p134; ☎977 810; Penestanan; classes per hr 100,000Rp) Intensive painting and drawing classes are run by abstract artist Karja, whose studio is on the site of his guesthouse, the Santra Putra.

Wayan Pasek Sucipta   MUSICAL INSTRUMENTS
(Map p137; ☎970 550; Eka's Homestay, Jl Sriwedari 8) Learn the gamelan and bamboo drums from a master (80,000Rp for one hour).

Pondok Pecak Library & Learning Centre
                                       CULTURAL, LANGUAGE
(Map p137; ☎976 194; Monkey Forest Rd; ⊙9am-5pm Mon-Sat, 1-5pm Sun) On the far side of the football field, this centre offers painting, dance, music, language and mask-carving classes; some are geared to kids. One-hour sessions cost from 75,000Rp. Good resource centre for other courses offered locally.

Museum Puri Lukisan   CULTURAL
(Map p137; ☎971 159; www.mpl-ubud.com; Jl Raya Ubud; classes from 100,000Rp) One of Ubud's best museums teaches courses in puppet-making, gamelan, offering-making and much more. There's kite-making for the kids.

Nyoman Warsa   MUSICAL INSTRUMENTS
(Map p137; ☎974 807; Pondok Bamboo Music Shop, Monkey Forest Rd) Noted gamelan musician offers courses in that most basic of Balinese instruments; simple mastery can take six months or more. Less time? Try a flute lesson (per hour 75,000Rp).

Yuliati House   MUSIC & DANCE
(Map p134; ☎973 255; Jl Sukma) The musical family that lives here offers lessons in Balinese dance and gamelan by several generations. If you stay with them, the cost is small.

Studio Perak   JEWELLERY
(Map p137; ☎974 244; www.studioperak.com; Jl Hanoman) Specialises in Balinese-style silversmithing courses. A three-hour lesson, where you'll make a finished piece, costs from 200,000Rp.

Taman Harum Cottages   CULTURAL
(☎975 567; www.tamanharumcottages.com; Mas; lessons per hr from US$10) In the centre of Bali's woodcarving district, this hotel offers a palette of craft, culture, carving and painting courses. You can learn how to make the temple offerings found just about everywhere.

Cooking

One of the most popular activities for visitors to Ubud. Cooking classes usually start at one of the local markets, where you can learn about the huge range of fruits, vegetables and other foods that are part of the Balinese diet.

Amandari   COOKING SCHOOL
(☎975 333; www.amanresorts.com; Kedewatan) Classes begin early (7am) at the produce

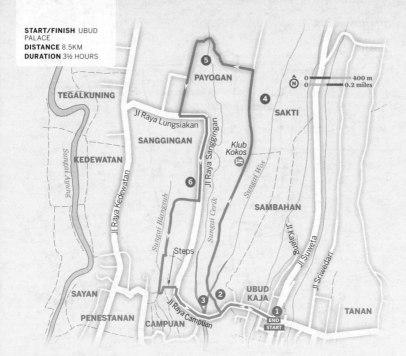

Walking Tour
Campuan Ridge

❯ This walk passes over the lush river valley of Sungai Wos (Wos River), offering views of Gunung Agung and glimpses of small village communities and rice fields.

Begin your walk at ❶ **Ubud Palace** and walk west on Jl Raya Ubud. At the confluence of Sungai Wos and Sungai Cerik (Cerik River) is Campuan, which means 'Where Two Rivers Meet'. This area was among the first to attract Western painters in the 1930s and you'll understand why from the still-lush foliage and the soothing roar of the rivers. The walk leaves Jl Raya Campuan here at the ❷ **Ibah Luxury Villas**. Enter the hotel driveway and take the path to the left, where a walkway crosses the river to the small and serene ❸ **Pura Gunung Lebah**. From there follow the concrete path north, climbing up onto the ridge between the two rivers. Fields of elephant grass, traditionally used for thatched roofs, slope away on either side. You can see the rice fields above Ubud folding over the hills in all directions. Note the myriad plastic bags and other colourful clutter flapping from long

poles. Farmers hope – often in vain – that these will deter rice-hungry birds from having a feast.

Continuing north along Campuan ridge past the Klub Kokos lodging, the road improves as it passes through paddy fields and the village of ❹ **Bangkiang Sidem**. On the outskirts of the village, an unsigned road heads west, winding down to Sungai Cerik (the west branch of Sungai Wos), then climbing steeply up to ❺ **Payogan**. From here you can walk south to the main road, and continue along Jl Raya Sanggingan, which seems to boast one or two more small boutiques and galleries every week. At the restaurant ❻ **Mozaic**, veer to the west onto trails that stay level with the rice fields as the main road drops away. It's a fantasyland of coursing waterways and good views among the rice and villas. If you become entranced with Ubud and decide you can't leave, many of the small bungalows are for rent by the month. When you come to the steep concrete steps, take them down to Campuan and back to Ubud.

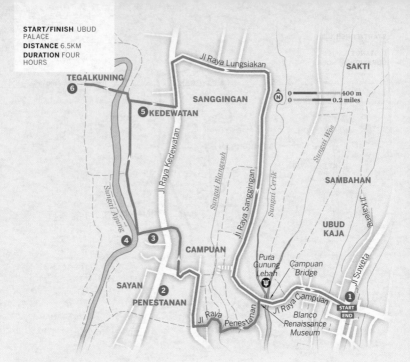

START/FINISH UBUD PALACE
DISTANCE 6.5KM
DURATION FOUR HOURS

Jl Raya Lungsiakan

SAKTI

TEGALKUNING
6

SANGGINGAN

5 KEDEWATAN

N 0 —————— 400 m
   0 —————— 0.2 miles

SAMBAHAN

CAMPUAN

UBUD KAJA

Pura Gunung Lebah

Campuan Bridge

SAYAN
2
PENESTANAN

3

4

Jl Raya Campuan

Blanco Renaissance Museum

Jl Raya Penestanan

START END
1

Walking Tour
Penestanan & Sayan

❯ The wonders of Sungai Ayung (Ayung River) are the focus of this outing, where you will walk below the luxury hotels built to take advantage of the lush, tropical river valley.

Begin your walk at **1** **Ubud Palace** and go west on Jl Raya Ubud. Head west of the Campuan bridge (noting the picturesque old bridge just south of the modern one), past the Blanco Renaissance Museum; here a steep uphill road, Jl Raya Penestanan, bends left and winds across the forested gully of Sungai Blangsuh (Blangsuh River) to the artists' village of **2** **Penestanan**. West of Penestanan, head north on the small road north (it's before the busy main road) that curves around to Sayan. The **3** **Sayan Terrace hotel** was Colin McPhee's home in the 1930s, as chronicled in his book *A House in Bali*. The views over the valley of the magnificent **4** **Sungai Ayung** (Ayung River) are superb. The best place to get to the riverside is just north of the Sayan Terrace hotel – look for the down-

hill path before the gate to the rooms and follow the increasingly narrow tracks down. (This part can be tricky but there are locals who'll show you for a tip of about 5000Rp.)

Following the rough trails north, along the eastern side of the Ayung, you traverse steep slopes, cross paddy fields and pass irrigation canals and tunnels. This is a highlight of the walk for many people, as we're talking about serious tropical jungle here. You don't need to follow any specific trail as you head slowly north along the river; instead just wander and see where your mood takes you. After about 1.5km you'll reach the finishing point for many white-water rafting trips – a good but steep trail goes from there up to the main road at **5** **Kedewatan**, where you can walk back to Ubud. Alternatively, cross the river on the nearby bridge and climb up to the very untouristy village of **6** **Tegalkuning** on the other side. There and back through a lot of tropical forest will add about 1km to your walk. Return to Ubud on Jl Raya Sanggingan, with its shops and cafes offering respite.

market, then move on to a village where you learn how to cook in an actual Balinese home. Instruction is one-on-one and costs from US$150.

Casa Luna Cooking School COOKING SCHOOL
(Map p137; ☑973 282; www.casalunabali.com; Honeymoon Guesthouse, Jl Bisma) There are regular cooking courses at Honeymoon Guesthouse. Half-day courses (300,000Rp) are held six days per week and cover ingredients, cooking techniques and the cultural background of the Balinese kitchen (not all visit the market). Sunday tours cover sea-salt and palm-sugar production (350,000Rp) in East Bali.

Bumbu Bali Cooking School COOKING SCHOOL
(Map p137; ☑976 698; Monkey Forest Rd) Balinese cooking course (250,000Rp) starts at the produce market (9am) and ends with lunch (2pm). Wide list of dishes prepared.

☞ Tours

Specialised tours in Ubud include thematic walks and cultural adventures. Spending a few hours exploring the area with a local expert is a highlight for many.

See also p390 for tours of the Ubud area by companies operating across Bali.

TOP CHOICE **Herb Walks** NATURE
(☑975 051; www.baliherbalwalk.com; walks US$18; ⊙8.30am Mon-Thu) Three-hour walks through lush Bali landscape; medicinal and cooking herbs and plants are identified and explained in their natural environment. Includes herbal drinks. The couple behind the walks also run **Utama Spice** (www.utamaspicebali.com), which makes natural home and spa products.

Banyan Tree Cycling CYCLING
(☑805 1620, 0813 3879 8516; www.banyantree .wikispaces.com) Has day-long tours of remote villages in the hills above Ubud. It's locally owned, and the tours (from 450,000Rp) emphasise interaction with villagers. Very popular.

Bali Bird Walks BIRDS
(Map p134; ☑975 009; www.balibirdwalk.com; Jl Raya Campuan; walks US$33; ⊙9am-12.30pm Tue & Fri-Sun) Started by Victor Mason, this tour, ideal for keen birders, is still going strong. On a gentle morning's walk (from the former Beggar's Bush Bar) you may see up to 30 of the 100-odd local species.

Dhyana Putri Adventures CULTURAL
(☑08123 805 623; www.balispirit.com/tours/bali_tour_dhyana.html) A bi-cultural, tri-lingual couple offer custom cultural tours, with emphasis on Balinese performing arts.

Bali Nature & Medicine Walk CULTURAL
(☑0818 0539 9228; sangtubud@yahoo.com) Lifelong Ubud resident and herbalist leads walks through the countryside explaining how the Balinese interact with nature.

Ubud Tourist Information CULTURAL
(Yaysan Bina Wisata; ☑973 285; Jl Raya Ubud; tours 125,000-200,000Rp; ⊙8am-8pm) Runs interesting and affordable half- and full-day trips to a huge range of places, including Ulu Watu, Mengwi, Alas Kedaton and Tanah Lot, or Goa Gajah, Pejeng, Gunung Kawi and Kintamani.

✯✯ Festivals & Events

One of the best places to see the many religious and cultural events celebrated in Bali each year is the Ubud area. See p26 for details of the events. The tourist office is unmatched for its comprehensive information on events each week.

Bali Spirit Festival (www.balispiritfestival .com) is a fast-growing yoga, dance and music festival from the people behind the Yoga Barn. There are over 100 workshops and concerts plus a market and more. It's usually held in early April.

The **Ubud Writers & Readers Festival** (www.ubudwritersfestival.com) brings together scores of writers and readers from around the world in a celebration of writing – especially writing that touches on Bali. It is usually held in October.

🛏 Sleeping

Ubud has the best and most appealing range of places to stay on Bali, including fabled resorts, artful guesthouses and charming, simple homestays. Choices can be bewildering, so give some thought to where you want to stay.

Generally, Ubud offers good value for money at any price level. Simple accommodation within a family home compound is a cultural experience and costs around US$20. Ubud enjoys cool mountain air at night, so air-con isn't necessary, and with your windows open, you'll hear the symphony of sounds off the rice fields and river valleys.

Guesthouses may be a bit larger and have amenities like swimming pools but are still likely to be fairly intimate, often nestled amid rice fields and rivers. Hotels generally offer swimming pools and other niceties, and the best are often perched on the edges of the deep river valleys, with superb views and service (although even some budget places have amazing views). Some provide shuttle service around the area.

Addresses in Ubud can be imprecise – but signage at the end of a road will often list the names of all the places to stay. Away from the main thoroughfares there are no streetlights and it can be challenging to find your way after dark. If walking, you'll want a torch (flashlight).

CENTRAL UBUD

JL RAYA UBUD & AROUND

Nirvana Pension & Gallery GUESTHOUSE $
(Map p137; ☑975 415; www.nirvanaku.com; Jl Goutama 10; s/d 250,000/350,000Rp) There are *alang-alang* (woven thatch) roofs, a plethora of paintings, ornate doorways and six rooms with modern bathrooms in a shady, secluded locale next to a large family temple. Batik courses are also held.

Puri Saren Agung GUESTHOUSE $$
(Map p137; ☑975 057; fax 975 137; Jl Raya Ubud; r US$65; 图) Part of the Ubud royal family's historic palace. Rooms are tucked behind the courtyard where the dance performances are held. Accommodation is in traditional Balinese pavilions, with big verandas, four-poster beds, antique furnishings and hot water. Give a royal wave to wandering tourists from your patio.

Puri Saraswati Bungalows HOTEL $$
(Map p137; ☑975 164; www.purisaraswati.com; Jl Raya Ubud; r US$60-80; 图 图) Very central and pleasant with lovely gardens that open onto

---

> ### ⓘ FINDING LONG-TERM ACCOMMODATION
>
> There are many houses and flats you can rent or share in the Ubud area. For information about options, check the noticeboards at **Pondok Pecak Library** (Monkey Forest Rd), **Ubud Tourist Information** (Yaysan Bina Wisata; Jl Raya Ubud) and **Bali Buddha** (Jl Jembawan 1). Also look in the free **Bali Advertiser** (www.baliadvertiser. biz) newspaper. Prices start at about US$200 a month and climb as you add amenities.

---

the Ubud Water Palace. The 18 rooms are well back from Jl Raya Ubud, so it's quiet. Some rooms are fan-only; interiors are simply furnished but have richly carved details.

Sania's House GUESTHOUSE $
(Map p137; ☑975 535; sania_house@yahoo.com; Jl Karna 7; r 200,000-300,000Rp; @图) Pets wander about this family-run place, where the large, clear pool, huge terrace and spacious rooms will have you howling at the moon. The 22 rooms are basic but clean; the market is nearly next door.

Agung Cottages HOMESTAY $
(Map p137; ☑975 414; Jl Goutama; r 250,000-350,000Rp, villas 300,000Rp; 图) Follow a short path to reach this slightly rural-feeling family compound. The six huge, spotless rooms (some fan-only) are set in gardens tended by a lovely family. It's well off the already quiet road.

Donald Homestay HOMESTAY $
(Map p137; ☑977 156; Jl Goutama; r 125,000-175,000Rp) The four rooms – some with hot water – are in a nice back corner of the family compound. As in many family-compound places, the chickens running around here have a date with a bamboo skewer.

Raka House GUESTHOUSE $
(Map p137; ☑976 081; www.rakahouse.com; Jl Maruti; r 150,000-250,000Rp; 图) Six bungalow-style rooms cluster at the back of a compact family compound. You can soak your toes in a small trapezoidal plunge pool. More choices nearby.

NORTH OF JL RAYA UBUD

Han Snel Bungalow GUESTHOUSE $$
(☑975 699; www.hansnelbungalow.com; Jl Kajeng 3; bungalows US$35-75; 图 图) Owned by the family of the late Han Snel, a well-known Ubud painter, this quiet compound has eight bungalows with suitably artful stone designs. Some rooms are perched right on the edge of the river gorge and have excellent views; the small pool is partway down.

Padma Accommodation GUESTHOUSE $
(Map p134; ☑977 247; aswatama@hotmail.com; Jl Kajeng 13; r 150,000-200,000Rp) There are five very private bungalows in a tropical garden here (three are new). Rooms are decorated with local crafts and the modern outdoor bathrooms have hot water. Nyoman Sudiarsa, a painter and family member, has a

Do you want to be in the centre or the quiet countryside? Have a rice-field view or enjoy a room with stylish design? Choices are myriad. The main areas of accommodation in Ubud are as follows:

Central Ubud

This original heart of Ubud has a vast range of places to rest your weary head and you'll enjoy a location that will cut down on the need for long walks or 'transport'. If you're near **Jl Raya Ubud**, don't settle for a room with noise from the main drag. Small and quiet streets to the east, including Jl Karna, Jl Maruti and Jl Goutama, have numerous family-style homestays. **North of Jl Raya Ubud**, streets like Jl Kajeng and Jl Suweta offer a timeless tableau, with kids playing in the streets and women bringing home – balanced on their heads – produce from the market. The same advice goes for the long strip of **Monkey Forest Rd**, which has the greatest concentration of lodgings. **Jl Bisma** runs into a plateau of rice fields. New places are popping up all the time and many sit amid the paddies.

Padangtegal & Tebesaya

East of central Ubud, but still conveniently located, **Padangtegal** has several budget lodgings along Jl Hanoman. A little further east, the quiet village of **Tebesaya** comprises little more than its main street, Jl Sukma, which runs between two streams. Cute homestays can be found down small footpaths.

Pengosekan

Pengosekan is good for shopping, dining and activities like yoga.

Nyuhkuning

A very popular area just south of the Monkey Forest, Nyuhkuning has some very creative guesthouses and hotels, yet is not a long walk to the centre.

Sambahan & Sakti

Going north from Jl Raya Ubud, you are soon in rolling terraces of rice fields. Tucked away here you'll find interesting and often luxurious hotels, yet you can have a beautiful walk to the centre in well under an hour.

Campuan & Sanggingan

The long sloping road that takes its names from these two communities has a number of posh properties on its east side that overlook a lush river valley.

Penestanan

Just west of the Campuan bridge, steep Jl Raya Penestanan branches off to the left, and climbs up and around to Penestanan, a large plateau of rice fields and lodgings. Simple rooms and bungalows in the rice fields are pitched at those seeking low-priced, longer-term lodgings. Stroll the narrow paths and you'll find many options – although the owners often find you first. You can also get here via a steep climb up a set of concrete stairs off Jl Raya Campuan but the reward – sweeping views and little coursing streams between the fields – is worth it.

Sayan & Ayung Valley

Two kilometres west of Ubud, the fast-flowing Sungai Ayung has carved out a deep valley, its sides sculpted into terraced paddy fields or draped in thick rainforest. Overlooking this verdant valley are some of Bali's best hotels.

studio here and often shares his knowledge with guests.

Eka's Homestay
HOMESTAY $

(Map p137; ☑970 550; Jl Sriwedari 8; r 100,000Rp) Follow your ears to this nice little family compound with six basic hot-water rooms. Eka's is the home of Wayan Pasek Sucipta, a teacher of Balinese music. It's in a nice sunny spot on a quiet road (well, except during practice).

MONKEY FOREST ROAD

Oka Wati Hotel
HOTEL $$

(Map p137; ☑973 386; www.okawatihotel.com; off Monkey Forest Rd; r US$50-90; ❄@🛜🏊) Oki Wati (the owner) is a lovely lady who grew up near the Ubud Palace. The 19 rooms have large verandas where the delightful staff will deliver your choice of breakfast (do not miss the house-made yoghurt). The decor features vintage details like four-poster beds; some rooms view a small rice field and river valley. Follow narrow footpaths to get here.

Sri Bungalows
GUESTHOUSE $$

(Map p137; ☑975 394; www.sribungalowsubud.com; Monkey Forest Rd; r 500,000-700,000Rp; ❄@🛜🏊) Popular for its free wi-fi and nice views of rice fields (you think you hear it growing but really it's the sound of your soul decompressing). Be sure to get one of the comfy rooms with relaxing loungers that command the views.

Komaneka
HOTEL $$$

(Map p137; ☑976 090; www.komaneka.com; Monkey Forest Rd; r US$150-350; ❄@🛜🏊) The most luxurious hotel close to the centre of Ubud, the Komaneka is gracious yet understated. The grounds hit all the right tropical clichés: coconut palms, a riot of flowers, bamboo this and that. Rooms have marble bathrooms, some with views of private water features. Get one with a balcony looking out over the surrounding verdant lands.

Lumbung Sari
GUESTHOUSE $$

(Map p137; ☑976 396; www.lumbungsari.com; Monkey Forest Rd; r US$65-105; ❄@🛜🏊) Artwork decorates the walls at the stylish Sari, which has a nice breakfast *bale* (traditional pavilion) by the pool. The eight rooms (some fan-only) have tubs in elegant bathrooms finished with terrazzo. Not all rooms have wi-fi.

Mandia Bungalows
GUESTHOUSE $

(Map p137; ☑970 965; Monkey Forest Rd; r 170,000-200,000Rp) It's heliconia heaven in the lush gardens. The four bungalow-style rooms are shaded by coconut palms and cooled by ceiling fans. Porches have comfy loungers, and the guys who run it are sweethearts.

Ubud Inn
HOTEL $$

(Map p137; ☑975 071; www.ubudinn.com; Monkey Forest Rd; r US$20-75; ❄🛜🏊) Lush loses its meaning in Ubud, but this place takes it to a new level. The 30 rooms are barren compared to the gardens and span several budgets: basic are fan-only; the rest are large and have fridges. The L-shaped pool has a children's area. Not all rooms have wi-fi.

Wenara Bali
GUESTHOUSE $

(Map p137; ☑977 384; wenarabali@hotmail.com; Monkey Forest Rd; r 180,000-280,000Rp; ❄) All but one of the 12 rooms here have serene views of rice terraces. Porches have chairs for lounging and the simple rooms are spotless and cooled by fans. That bump you hear in the night is the namesake residents of the adjoining Monkey Forest making new namesakes. Watching the macaques frolic is major fun here.

Warsa's Garden Bungalows
GUESTHOUSE $

(Map p137; ☑971 548; warsagallery@yahoo.com; Monkey Forest Rd; r 250,000-350,000Rp; ❄🏊) A good-sized pool with fountains enlivens this comfy but simple place in the heart of Monkey Forest action. The 15 rooms are reached through a traditional family-compound entrance. Some have tubs; some are fan-only.

Pande Permai Bungalows
GUESTHOUSE $

(Map p137; ☑971 332; www.pandepermai.com; Monkey Forest Rd; r 300,000-450,000Rp; ❄🏊) A walk down a short and unpromising lane leads to a verdant oasis of 27 rooms in two-storey blocks surrounding a pool. View options include a river valley and rice fields.

Loka House
GUESTHOUSE $

(Map p137; ☑973 326; off Monkey Forest Rd; r 125,000-150,000Rp) The lush entrance sets the mood at this peaceful place, where the two-storey main building overlooks a small carp pond in the garden. The three rooms (one with a tub) have hot water and fans.

Warsi's House
HOMESTAY $

(Map p137; ☑975 311; Monkey Forest Rd; r 120,000-160,000Rp) Look for a tailor and then enter through the retail building's breezeway. Tucked away out back is this ideally located little homestay with eight rooms. It's very clean, there is hot water and if you need a suit, you're set.

JL BISMA

Sama's Cottages
GUESTHOUSE $

(Map p137; ☑973 481; samascottagesubud@hot mail.com; Jl Bisma; r 200,000-350,000Rp; ☎) This lovely little hideaway is terraced down a hill. The 10 bungalow-style rooms have lashings of Balinese style layered on absolute simplicity. The oval pool feels like a jungle oasis. Ask for low-season discounts.

Honeymoon Guesthouse
GUESTHOUSE $$

(Map p137; ☑973 282; www.casalunabali.com; Jl Bisma; r 350,000-600,000Rp; ✳@☎☎) Run by the Casa Luna clan, the 30 rooms here have terraces and tubs. There's a play area for kids. Avoid the dark rooms; some rooms have air-con, not all have wi-fi. Eleven of the rooms are in an annexe and are quite spacious.

Pondok Krishna
GUESTHOUSE $

(Map p137; ☑08155 821 8103; kriz_tie@yahoo .com; Jl Bisma; r 250,000-300,000Rp; ✳@☎☎) This light and airy family compound has four rooms set among the frog-filled rice fields west of Jl Bisma. The open common area with its sunny location is good for nailing that tan.

Ina Inn
GUESTHOUSE $

(Map p137; ☑971 093; Jl Bisma; r 250,000-300,000Rp; ☎) Stroll the thickly planted grounds and climb the steps to the rooftop swimming pool for views across Ubud and the rice fields. Rooms are basic but clean and comfy. If you want to take the plunge closer to your bed, they have tubs.

PADANGTEGAL & TEBESAYA

Matahari Cottages
GUESTHOUSE $

(Map p137; ☑975 459; www.matahariubud.com; Jl Jembawan; r US$35-60; ✳☎) This delightful place has six flamboyant, themed rooms, including the 'Batavia Princess' and the 'Indian Pasha'. The library is a vision out of a 1920s fantasy. It also boasts a self-proclaimed 'jungle jacuzzi' and a multi-course breakfast and high tea elaborately served on silver (free for guests, 60,000Rp others). And in a nod to the modern day, the hotel recycles.

Ni Nyoman Warini Bungalows
HOMESTAY $

(Map p137; ☑978 364; Jl Hanoman; r 80,000-100,000Rp) There's a whole pod of simple family compounds with rooms for rent

back on a little footpath off Jl Hanoman. It's quiet, and without even trying you'll find yourself enjoying the rhythms of family life. The three rooms here have hot water and traditional bamboo furniture.

Yuliati House
HOMESTAY $

(Map p134; ☑974 044; yuliahouse10@yahoo.com; Jl Sukma 10; r 70,000-170,000Rp) Some of the nine rooms here are cold-water only; others have tubs and some even have river valley views. But the real draw is this talented-as-all-heck family that offers lessons in gamelan, dance and more.

Artini Cottages 1
HOMESTAY $

(Map p137; ☑975 348; www.artinicottage.com; Jl Hanoman; r US$17-25) The Artini family runs a small empire of good-value guesthouses on Jl Hanoman. This, the original, is in an ornate family compound with many flowers. The three bungalows have hot water and large bathtubs. The more upscale Artini 2, with rice-field views and a pool, is opposite.

Nick's Homestay
HOMESTAY $

(Map p137; ☑975 526; www.nickshotels-ubud .com; Jl Hanoman 57; r 230,000Rp) Nick has a network of three Ubud budget hotels. This, his simplest, is the best. Beds in the six bungalow-style hot-water rooms are made from bamboo logs. Watch family life from the copious porches.

Dewi Sri Bungalows
GUESTHOUSE $

(Map p137; ☑975 300; Jl Hanoman 69; r with fan/air-con 250,000/300,000Rp; ✳☎) The best value here are the split-level, fan-only rooms, which have cute, open-air bathrooms below and a terrace with glimpses of rice above. The air-con rooms are daggy and strictly for those who think they need cool air – in Ubud nature supplies it at night.

Family Guest House
HOMESTAY $

(Map p134; ☑974 054; familyhouse@telkom.net; Jl Sukma; r 250,000-350,000Rp; ☎) There's a bit of bustle from the busy family at this charming homestay. Healthy breakfasts featuring brown bread from Café Wayan are served. The nine rooms are cold water only at the low end of the price range; as you reach the middle range, rooms also include tubs; and at the top, they have a balcony with a valley view.

Biangs
HOMESTAY $

(Map p134; ☑976 520; Jl Sukma 28; r 120,000Rp) In a little garden, Biangs (meaning 'mama') has six well-maintained rooms, with hot water. The best rooms have views of a small valley.

Aji Lodge
HOMESTAY $

(Map p134; ☑973 255; ajilodge11@yahoo.com; Tebesaya 11; r 150,000Rp) A group of comfortable family compounds line a footpath east of Jl Sukma. Get a room down the hill by the river for the full bedtime symphony of birds, bugs and critters.

SAMBAHAN & SAKTI

Waka di Ume
HOTEL $$$

(Map p134; ☑973 178; www.wakadiumeubud.com; Jl Suweta; r US$200-250, villas from US$300; ❄@☎☒) Located a gentle 1.5km uphill from the centre, this elegant compound enjoys engrossing verdant views across rice fields.

New and old styles mix in the large units; go for a villa with a view. Service is superb yet relaxed. Listening to gamelan practice echoing across the fields at night is quite magical.

Ketut's Place
GUESTHOUSE $$

(☑975 304; www.ketutsplace.com; Jl Suweta 40; r US$25-75; ❄@☒) The nine rooms here range from basic with fans to deluxe versions with air-con and bathtub. All have artful accents and enjoy a dramatic pool shimmering down the hillside and river-valley views. On some nights, an impressive Balinese feast is served by Ketut, a local luminary.

Ubud Sari Health Resort
GUESTHOUSE $$

(Map p134; ☑974 393; www.ubudsari.com; Jl Kajeng; r US$60-80; ❄☒) Like your colon

BALI'S TRADITIONAL HEALERS

Bali's traditional healers, known as balian (dukun on Lombok), play an important part in Bali's culture by treating physical and mental illness, removing spells and channelling information from the ancestors. Numbering about 8000, balian are the ultimate in community medicine, making a commitment to serve their communities and turning no one away.

Lately, however, this system has come under stress in some areas due to the attention brought by *Eat, Pray, Love* and other media coverage of Bali's healers. Curious tourists are turning up in village compounds, taking balians' time and attention from the genuinely ill. However, that doesn't mean you shouldn't visit a balian if you're genuinely curious. Just do so in a manner that befits the experience: gently.

Consider the following before a visit:

» Make an appointment before visiting a balian.

» English is rarely spoken.

» Dress respectfully (long trousers and a shirt, better yet a sarong and sash).

» Women should not be menstruating.

» Never point your feet at the healer.

» Bring an offering into which you have tucked the consulting fee, which will range from 100,000Rp to 200,000Rp per person.

» Your treatment will be very public and probably painful. It may include deep tissue massage, being poked with sharp sticks or having chewed herbs spat on you.

Finding a balian can take some work. Ask at your hotel, which can probably help with making an appointment and providing a suitable offering for stashing your fee. Or consider the following, who do see visitors to Bali:

Ketut Gading (☑0361-970 770; Ubud)

Man Nyoman (☑0813 3893 5369; Ubud)

Sirkus (☑0361-739 538; Kuta)

Made Surya (www.balihealers.com) is an authority on Bali's traditional healers and offers one- and two-day intensive workshops on healing, magic, traditional systems and history, which include visits to authentic balian. His website is an excellent resource on visiting healers on Bali.

after a week of treatments here, this 10-room health resort has been spiffed up (it's now called a Zen Village). The plants in the gardens are labelled for their medicinal qualities and the cafe serves organic, vegetarian fare. Guests can use the health facilities, including the sauna and whirlpool.

Klub Kokos
GUESTHOUSE $$

(Map p134; ☑978 270; www.klubkokos.com; r US$60-120; ❋@☎) A beautiful 1.5km walk north along the Campuan ridge, Klub Kokos is a ridge-top hideaway with a big pool and seven spotless bungalow-style rooms. It's reachable by car from the north; call for directions. Rates include breakfast and snacks and there's a cafe.

NYUHKUNING

TOP CHOICE ### Swasti Cottage
GUESTHOUSE $$

(Map p137; ☑974 079; www.bali swasti.com; Jl Nyuh Bulan; r 350,000-700,000Rp; @☎) One of Ubud's most inventive and appealing places to stay is just five minutes' walk from the south entrance to the Monkey Forest. Run by a French-Balinese couple, this 12-room guesthouse has large, manicured grounds that feature a bounteous organic garden (produce is used in the excellent cafe). Some rooms are in simple two-storey blocks; others are in vintage traditional bungalows brought here from across Bali.

Alam Indah
HOTEL $$

(Map p134; ☑974 629; www.alamindahbali.com; Jl Nyuh Bulan; r US$55-115; ❋☎) Just south of the Monkey Forest in Nyuhkuning, this isolated and spacious resort has 10 rooms that are beautifully finished in natural materials to traditional designs. The Wos Valley views are entrancing, especially from the multilevel pool area. The walk in at night follows a driveway lined with tea candles.

Saren Indah Hotel
HOTEL $$

(Map p137; ☑971 471; www.sarenhotel.com; Jl Nyuh Bulan, Nyuhkuning; r US$45-95; ❋☎) South of the Monkey Forest, this 15-room hotel sits in the middle of rice fields – be sure to get a 2nd-floor room to enjoy the views. Rooms are spotless; better ones have TVs, fridges and baths with stylish tubs.

PENGOSEKAN

Arma Resort
HOTEL $$

(Map p137; ☑976 659; www.armaresort.com; Jl Raya Pengosekan; r US$90-175, villas from US$375; ❋@☎) Get full Balinese cultural immersion at the hotel enclave of the Arma compound. The expansive property has a large library and elegant gardens. Villas come with private pools. Not all rooms have wi-fi.

Tegal Sari
HOTEL $$

(Map p137; ☑973 318; www.tegalsari-ubud.com; Jl Raya Pengosekan; r US$35-70; ❋@☎) Set back from the main road, this hotel is almost an aquatic park. Water from the surrounding rice fields seems to flow almost everywhere. The 21 rooms are set in two-storey, bungalow-style blocks. Get a room on a higher level for decent views of ducks and more. Units in brick buildings are stark; those in wooden buildings are richly panelled.

Artini 3 Cottages
HOTEL $$

(Map p137; ☑974 147; www.artinicottage.com; Jl Raya Pengosekan; r US$40-60; ❋☎) The top choice of the Artini empire, the 16 rooms here are in attractive stone buildings arrayed around a spectacular pool area down by a stream. Get a room facing east for the best views through the palms. Room decor is comfortable but standard.

CAMPUAN & SANGGINGAN

Hotel Tjampuhan
HOTEL $$

(Map p134; ☑975 368; www.tjampuhan-bali.com; Jl Raya Campuan; r US$90-160; ❋@☎) This venerable place overlooks the confluence of Sungai Wos and Campuan. The influential German artist Walter Spies lived here in the 1930s, and his former home, which sleeps four people (US$240), is now part of the hotel. Bungalow-style units spill down the hill and enjoy mesmerising valley views.

Warwick Ibah Luxury Villas & Spa
HOTEL $$$

(Map p134; ☑974 466; www.warwickibah.com; off Jl Raya Campuan; ste US$200-300, villas US$400-600; ❋@☎) Overlooking the rushing waters of the Wos Valley, the Ibah offers refined luxury in 15 spacious, stylish individual suites and villas that combine ancient and modern details. The swimming pool is set into the hillside amid gardens and lavish stone carvings.

Pita Maha
HOTEL $$$

(Map p134; ☑974 330; www.pitamaha-bali.com; Jl Raya Sangginган; villas US$300-600; ❋@☎) Broad, open views across a valley to the rice fields beyond are the highlight of this understated but luxurious hotel. The traditional-style villas are large and built with real attention to detail. More money gets you good views and a private plunge pool – although the main curving infinity pool may seduce you.

Pager Bungalows GUESTHOUSE $$
(Map p134; ☑975 433; Jl Raya Campuan; r 250,000-500,000Rp, villas 600,000Rp) Run by painter Nyoman Pageh and his family, this cute homestay hugs a verdant hillside location that feels like you're lost in the bottom of the spinach bowl on a salad bar. Two large bungalows face the compound; five more rooms are comfortable and have views. The family villa is a fully appointed apartment.

PENESTANAN

Indo French Villa GUESTHOUSE $$
(Map p134; ☑790 4518, 08133 866 9028; nengah kuntia@hotmail.com; villa US$35-80; ☀) Wander a series of lanes through rice fields and you'll find yourself at this very homey two-villa complex. The small one is a steal, with a small pool and two levels plus a kitchen. The second is also great value, with a pool you can train in, plus many more posh details.

Santra Putra GUESTHOUSE $
(Map p134; ☑977 810; karjabali@yahoo.com; off Jl Raya Campuan; r US$20-30; ☎) Run by internationally exhibited abstract artist I Wayan Karja (whose studio/gallery is also on site), this place has nine big, open, airy rooms with hot water. Enjoy paddy-field views from all vantage points. Painting and drawing classes are offered by the artist.

Melati Cottages HOTEL $$
(Map p134; ☑974 650; www.melati-cottages.com; Jl Penestanan; r US$30-60; ☀☎☀) Set back among the rice fields, the deeply shaded Melati has somewhat spartan rooms in two-storey bungalow-style buildings. All have porches for listening to the sounds of the fields and taking the cool night air.

SAYAN & AYUNG VALLEY

TOP CHOICE Sayan Terrace HOTEL $$
(Map p134; ☑974 384; www.sayanterrace resort.com; Jl Raya Sayan; r US$115-160, villas from US$220; ☀@☎☀) Gaze into the Sayan Valley from this venerable hotel and you'll understand why this was the site of Colin McPhee's *A House in Bali;* see p142 for details. Stay here while your neighbours – distant neighbours it should be said – are housed in luxury resorts paying far more.

Here the 11 rooms and villas are simply decorated but are large and have *that* view. Rates include afternoon tea.

Bambu Indah GUESTHOUSE $$$
(☑975 124; www.bambuindah.com; Baung; house US$180-500; @☎☀) Famed expat entrepreneur John Hardy sold his namesake jewellery company in 2007 and became a hotelier. On a ridge near Sayan and his beloved Sungai Ayung, he's assembled a compound of seven 100-year-old royal Javanese houses, each furnished with style and flair. Several outbuildings create a timeless village with underpinnings of luxury. The entire compound is run to a very 'green' standard.

Amandari HOTEL $$$
(☑975 333; www.amanresorts.com; Kedewatan; ste from US$800; ☀@☎☀) In Kedewatan village, the storied Amandari does everything with charm and grace – sort of like a classical Balinese dancer. Superb views over the jungle and down to the river – the 30m green-tiled swimming pool seems to drop right over the edge – are just some of the inducements. The 30 private pavilions may prove inescapable.

Four Seasons Resort HOTEL $$$
(Map p134; ☑977 577; www.fourseasons.com; Sayan; ste from US$600, villas from US$700; ☀@☎☀) Set below the valley rim, the curved open-air reception area looks like a Cinerama screen of Ubud beauty. Many villas have private pools and all share the same amazing views and striking modern design. At night you hear just the water rushing below. The service wins rave reviews.

Novus Tamen Bebek HOTEL $$$
(Map p134; ☑975 385; www.novushotels.com; Jl Raya Sayan; r US$140-320; ☀☎☀) A spectacular, verdant location overlooking the Sayan Valley may keep you glued to your terrace throughout the day. Eleven rooms and villas here wrap around the Sayan Terrace and enjoy a stylish new common area and entrance. All have understated yet classic Balinese wood-and-thatch architecture.

🍴 Eating

Ubud's cafes and restaurants are some of the best in Bali. Local and expat chefs produce a bounty of authentic Balinese dishes, as well as inventive Asian and other international cuisines.

Many eateries make beautiful use of natural design elements and some offer serene settings with views out over the rice fields. Cafes where you can sip an excellent coffee or juice are common – some people never seem to leave. There are also many inexpensive warung serving fresh and tasty authentic Indonesian dishes. Note: Ubud's nightlife fades fast after the last note of gamelan music; don't wait past 9pm to eat or you won't. Better restaurants will provide transport to and from; call to arrange.

Good **organic farmers markets** are held each week, at **Pizza Bagus** (Jl Raya Pengosekan; ◎9.30am-2pm Sat) and at the **Arma Museum** (Jl Raya Pengosekan; ◎9.30am-2pm Wed). **Bali Buddha** (Jl Jembawan 1) is another good source. And in keeping with the local ethos, organic produce is a feature on many menus.

Delta Mart convenience stores are common but are not recommended (eg they often claim they only have expensive imported water). The ubiquitous Circle Ks are more reliable and sell Bintang around the clock. **Delta Dewata Supermarket** (Map p134; ☏973 049; Jl Raya Andong) has a huge selection of goods. **Bintang Supermarket** (Map p134; Bintang Centre, Jl Raya Campuan) is well located and has a large range of food and other essentials. The traditional **produce market** (Map p137) is a multi-level carnival of tropical foods and worth exploring despite the crowds.

CENTRAL UBUD

JL RAYA UBUD & AROUND
There are busy and tasty choices on Ubud's main street while nearly traffic-free Jl Goutama has a good range of options.

Kué   GLOBAL $
(Map p137; ☏976 7040; Jl Raya Ubud; meals 30,000-80,000Rp; ✳🅏) A top-end organic bakery and chocolate shop with a couple of stools downstairs; climb the side stairs for a lovely cafe that sits above the road chaos. Good baked items as well as sandwiches, organic wraps and Indo mains make it a great casual stop.

🖊 Bali Buddha   GLOBAL $
(Map p137; ☏976 324; Jl Jembawan 1; meals 40,000-80,000Rp) A local institution, Bali Buddha has a mostly veggie cafe with a long list of healthy foods upstairs and a health-food store and bakery downstairs (the blueberry muffins are mighty fine). Raw foodists

and vegans will find much to like here – but so will carnivores and those simply in search of tasty food and drink. The bulletin board out front is a community resource.

Nomad   ASIAN $$
(Map p137; ☏977 169; Jl Raya Ubud; meals 60,000-150,000Rp) Offers a daily barbecue, often with a gamelan player providing the soundtrack. Balinese food is served in tapas-sized portions. Assume the position – lotus that is – at low Japanese-style tables.

Rendezvousdoux   FRENCH $
(Map p137; ☏747 0163; Jl Raya Ubud 14; meals 30,000-80,000Rp; ✳) How to define it? A fusion of French-accented forms: cafe, library and bookshop, Rendezvousdoux is the most interesting spot on the street. Bonuses include global music (at times live) and historic films about Ubud on loop.

Casa Luna   INDONESIAN $$
(Map p137; ☏977 409; Jl Raya Ubud; meals 80,000-160,000Rp) Janet de Neefe of cooking school and writers' festival fame runs this ever-popular Indonesian-focused restaurant (the seafood satay, yum!), which also has a delicious range of bakery items. Recent renovations have softened the edges; live jazz some nights.

Café Moka   BAKERY $
(Map p137; ☏972 881; Jl Raya Ubud; meals 40,000-60,000Rp; ✳) Slick outpost for the Bali chain of French-accented coffee shops and bakeries, Café Moka has a front terrace well back from the busy road. Inside, you can cool off with a juice or rev up with an array of coffee drinks.

Clear   FUSION $$
(Map p137; ☏0818 553 015; Jl Hanoman; meals US$4-15) You'll love it or hate it. This high-concept restaurant brings a bit of Hollywood glitz and ditz to Ubud. The dishes are relentlessly healthy but also creative – think soba noodles meets raw food meets curried tofu etc. It's all done rather artfully, which may help you forget the very uncommon BYOB policy and demands that you leave your shoes outside.

Café Lotus   GLOBAL $$
(Map p137; ☏975 357; Jl Raya Ubud; meals 80,000-180,000Rp) A meal at this Ubud veteran, overlooking the lotus pond at Pura Taman Saraswati, is a relaxing treat for many when they first arrive in Ubud. The menu features well-prepared Western and Indonesian fare. Paying extra for front-row seats for dance

performances at Pura Taman Saraswati is not worth it, the dancers are still tiny.

NORTH OF JL RAYA UBUD

Rumah Roda
BALINESE $

(Map p134; ☎975 487; Jl Kajeng 24; meals 15,000-30,000Rp) Above Threads of Life, Roda serves astonishingly cheap Balinese dishes with a wonderful overlay of local culture. The extended Roda family live here and prepare dishes handed down for generations. You can order a delectably authentic feast in advance for a mere 35,000Rp per person. (Note: the family is the subject of the cult favourite *A Little Bit One O'clock*, by William Ingram.)

Terazo
FUSION $$

(Map p137; ☎978 941; Jl Suweta; meals 60,000-200,000Rp) A classy escape, Terazo restaurant serves creative and organic Balinese fusion cuisine. The wine list is decent and features French, Italian and Australian choices. The spare interior is accented by evocative vintage travel posters and furnished with plush cane chairs.

Warung Ibu Oka
BALINESE $

(Map p137; Jl Suweta; meals 30,000Rp; ⏱11am-3pm) Join the lunchtime lines opposite Ubud Palace waiting for one thing: the eponymous Balinese-style roast suckling pig. Those in the know travel far for meat they say is the most tender and tasty on the island. Order a *spesial* to get the best cut. Popularity has caused prices to zoom.

MONKEY FOREST ROAD

TOP CHOICE Three Monkeys
ASIAN $$

(Map p137; ☎974 830; Monkey Forest Rd; mains 20,000-50,000Rp) Mellow music and artworks set a cultured mood. The tables overlooking the rice field out back make it magical and the place for romance. By day there are sandwiches, salads and gelato. At night there's a fusion menu of Asian classics, including addictive Vietnamese summer prawn rolls.

Warung Aja
INDONESIAN $$

(Map p137; ☎973 398; Monkey Forest Rd; meals 30,000-50,000Rp) A real find amid the often fair-to-middlin' food scene of Monkey Forest Rd, this little bamboo hut is set well back from the clogged traffic. Get there early because the groovy young staff only cook so much and when stuff runs out, that's it.

Laughing Buddha
INDONESIAN $

(Map p137; ☎970 928; Monkey Forest Rd; meals 40,000-70,000Rp; 📶) More stylish than your average warung, this casual cafe serves good Indonesian food aimed at the discriminating Western palate. Get a table at a bench in front and enjoy the passing Monkey Forest parade.

Bumbu Bali
INDONESIAN $$

(Map p137; ☎976 698; Monkey Forest Rd; meals 60,000-150,000Rp) A good place for Balinese food in the heart of Ubud. The menu features dishes such as *lawar* (green bean salad), *ayam pelalah* (spicy shredded chicken salad) and *sambal goreng udang* (prawns in a tangy coconut-milk sauce). Like your food? You can also learn to cook it.

Coffee & Silver
TAPAS $$

(Map p137; ☎975 354; Monkey Forest Rd; meals 40,000-120,000Rp; ⏱10am-midnight; 📶) Tapas and more substantial items make up the menu at this comfortable cafe with seating inside and out. Vintage photos of Ubud line the walls. Many patrons linger over the good coffee and other drinks for hours.

Sjaki's Warung
GLOBAL $

(Map p137; off Monkey Forest Rd; meals 20,000-30,000Rp; ⏱9am-6pm Mon-Fri) The best Bintang you'll ever have – in terms of helping others – is right here at this modest cafe with a prize position overlooking the Football Field. Run by a charity that helps developmentally disadvantaged kids, the staff are all learning the ropes while serving classic Indo fare like *nasi goreng*.

JL DEWI SITA & JL GOUTAMA

East of Monkey Forest Rd, a short stroll takes you past many fine and diverse options.

TOP CHOICE Cafe Havana
LATIN $$

(Map p137; ☎972 973; Jl Dewi Sita; meals 50,000-150,000Rp) All that's missing is Fidel. Actually, the decrepitude of its namesake city is also missing from this smart and stylish cafe on smart and stylish Dewi Sita. The menu boasts many a dish with Latin flair, including some tasty pork numbers, but expect surprises such as a *crème brûlée* oatmeal in the morning. The dining room upstairs is a baroque wonder; watch for salsa dance nights.

Juice Ja Café
ORGANIC $

(Map p137; ☎971 056; Jl Dewi Sita; snacks from 20,000Rp) Glass of spirulina? Dash of wheatgrass with your papaya juice? Organic fruits and vegetables go into the food at this funky bakery-cafe. The cashew banana muffin and passion-fruit juice are a killer combo.

Tutmak Café
GLOBAL $$

(Map p137; ☏ 975 754; Jl Dewi Sita; meals 30,000-90,000Rp; ☏) The breezy multilevel location here, facing both Jl Dewi Sita and the football field, is a popular place for a refreshing drink or a meal. Local comers on the make huddle around their laptops plotting their next move; others enjoy long-planned rendezvous.

Dewa Warung
INDONESIAN $

(Map p137; Jl Goutama; meals 15,000-20,000Rp) When it rains, the tin roof sounds like a tap-dance convention and the bare lightbulbs sway in the breeze. A little garden surrounds tables a few steps above the road where diners tuck into plates of sizzling fresh Indo fare.

Kafe Batan Waru
INDONESIAN $$

(Map p137; ☏ 977 528; Jl Dewi Sita; meals 40,000-180,000Rp) This ever-popular cafe has an expanded outdoor terrace. It serves consistently excellent Indonesian food, stylishly presented. The *mie goreng* noodles are made fresh daily – a noteworthy detail given the number of places that substitute pot noodles. Western dishes include sandwiches and salads.

Devilicious
GLOBAL $$

(Map p137; ☏ 745 972; Jl Goutama; meals 40,000-120,000Rp) Jl Goutama is a delightful street for a stroll and this cafe is one of the reasons why. Cajun, grilled steaks, pasta and good Indonesian headline at this tasty and attractive cafe. Be sure to ask for your food 'spicy'.

Biah Biah
INDONESIAN $

(Map p137; ☏ 978 249; Jl Goutama 13; meals 30,000-70,000Rp) A tidy little warung with some nice dining along walker-friendly Jl Goutama. A varied menu of Indo classics that are artfully served atop banana leaves. The 'romantic dinner' for two may be stretching it; think 'I like you' dinner.

JL BISMA

TOP CHOICE ## Café des Artistes
BELGIAN $$

(Map p137; ☏ 972 706; Jl Bisma 9X; meals 70,000-220,000Rp; ☏10am-midnight) In a quiet perch up off Jl Raya Ubud, the popular Café des Artistes serves elaborate Belgian-accented food, superb steaks and daily specials. Local art is on display and the bar is refreshingly cultured. Enjoy the enveloping wicker seating inside or in front in a small garden. Book.

157

LILI MOLLOY: DEDICATED SNACKER

Ubud teenager, fashion model and dedicated snacker, Lili comes from a family known for their food. Her mother owns Cafe Havana.

Favourite place to eat that's pure Ubud

Warung Teges (Map p134; Jl Cok Rai Pudak, Peliatan; meals 20,000Rp) It has the best Balinese food.

Why?

The *nasi campur* is better here than anywhere. They get every dish just right, from the pork sausage to the chicken, the *babi* (marinated suckling pig) and even the tempeh.

PADANGTEGAL

TOP CHOICE ## Kafe
GLOBAL $

(Map p137; ☏ 970 992; www.balispirit.com; Jl Hanoman 44; dishes 15,000-40,000Rp) Kafe has an organic menu great for veggie grazing or just having a coffee, juice or house-made natural soft drink. Breakfasts are healthy while lunch meals feature excellent salads and burritos, with many raw items. One of *the* places to meet in Ubud, it's always busy.

Bebek Bengil
INDONESIAN $$

(Map p137; Dirty Duck Diner; ☏ 975 489; Jl Hanoman; dishes 70,000-200,000Rp; ☏11am-10pm) This pretty, rambling place is popular for one reason: its crispy Balinese duck, which is marinated for 36 hours in spices and then fried up hot. The ducks on the few surviving rice fields outside the open-air dining pavilions look worried.

Matahari Cottages
ENGLISH $

(Map p137; ☏ 975 459; Jl Jembawan; high tea 60,000Rp; ☏2-5pm certain days) 'Never do anything by half' is the motto at this almost-goofy over-the-top inn, which serves extravagant high tea in open-air pavilions. Call to confirm.

Masakan Padang
INDONESIAN $

(Map p137; Jl Hanoman; dishes 6000-15,000Rp; ☏noon-1am) The bright-orange exterior at this Padang-style eatery – where you choose from the plates on display – hints at the fresh and spicy food within.

PENGOSEKAN

Many highly regarded restaurants are found along the curves of Jl Raya Pengosekan. It's always worth seeing what's new.

Pizza Bagus
PIZZA $$
(Map p137; ☑978 520; www.pizzabagus.com; Jl Raya Pengosekan; meals 40,000-100,000Rp; ✴︎✳︎☎) Ubud's best pizza with a crispy thin crust is baked here. Besides the long list of pizza options, there's pasta and sandwiches – all mostly organic. Tables are in and out, there's a play area, and they deliver.

Warung Enak
INDONESIAN $$
(Map p137; ☑972 911; www.warungenakbali.com; Jl Raya Pengosekan; meals 40,000-180,000Rp) A breezy two-level restaurant with a winsome logo, Enak specialises in Indonesian food. The *rijstafel* (array of Indonesian dishes) is justifiably popular or you can go modest by choosing from the long menu of satays and variations on *mie goreng*.

NYUHKUNING

Swasti
GLOBAL $
(Map p137; ☑974 079; Jl Nyuh Bulan; meals 30,000-70,000Rp) This cafe attached to the excellent guesthouse of the same name is reason enough to take a stroll through the Monkey Forest. Indonesian and Western dishes prepared from the large in-house organic garden are fresh and tasty. Have a glass of fresh juice with the beloved chocolate crepes. Watch for children's dance performances.

CAMPUAN & SANGGINGAN

Mozaic
FUSION $$$
(☑975 768; www.mozaic-bali.com; Jl Raya Sanggingan; menus from 600,000Rp; ⊙6-10pm Tue-Sun) Chef Chris Salans oversees this much-lauded top-end restaurant. Fine French fusion cuisine features on a constantly changing seasonal menu that takes its influences from tropical Asia. Dine in an elegant garden or ornate pavilion. Most people leave the driving to Salans and order a tasting menu with wine pairings.

Naughty Nuri's
BARBECUE $$
(Map p134; ☑977 547; Jl Raya Sanggingan; meals 40,000-100,000Rp) This legendary expat hang-out is more sizzle than steak. Hugely popular with martini-drinkers of a certain age who wolf down chewy grilled steaks, ribs and burgers. Thursday-night grilled-tuna specials are something of a mob scene

of long-lost cronies. Come for the camaraderie and ignore the lapses in the kitchen (which is mostly a barbecue out front).

🌿 Warung Bodag Maliah
ORGANIC $
(Map p134; ☑780 1839; meals from 30,000Rp; ⊙11am-4pm) In a beautiful location on a plateau overlooking rice terraces and river valleys, this small cafe is in the middle of a big organic farm. The food's healthy but more importantly, given that half the fun is getting here, the drinks are cool and refreshing. Look for a little track off Jl Raya Ubud that goes past Abangan Bungalows, then follow the signs along footpaths for another 800m.

PENESTANAN

Yellow Flower Cafe
INDONESIAN $
(Map p134; ☑889 9865; meals from 30,000Rp; ☎) New Age Indonesian right up in Penestanan along a little path through the rice fields. Nearby views look out over Ubud but you'll be happier concentrating on organic mains like a good *nasi campur* (rice with side dishes) and rice pancakes. Snackers will delight in the good coffees, cakes and smoothies.

Lala & Lili
INDONESIAN $
(Map p134; ☑0812 398 8037; off Jl Raya Campuan, Penestanan; mains 15,000-40,000Rp) Fields of rice stretch away like waves of green from this simple cafe set on a path on a plateau. The menu is a familiar mix of Indo and sandwiches. Many local expat artists hang out here while others living in the numerous nearby cheap rentals spring for delivery.

KEDEWATAN

TOP CHOICE Nasi Ayam Kedewatan
BALINESE $
(☑742 7168; Jl Raya Kedewatan; meals 15,000Rp; ⊙9am-6pm) Few locals making the trek up the hill on the main road through Sayan pass this open-air place without stopping. The star is *sate lilit* (minced chicken satay), which here reaches heights that belie the common name. Chicken is minced, combined with an array of spices including lemongrass, then moulded onto bamboo skewers and grilled. Simply amazing, as are the traditional Balinese road snacks: fried chips combined with nuts and spices.

🍷 Drinking

Ubud. Bacchanalia. Mutually exclusive. No one comes to Ubud for wild nightlife. A few bars get lively around sunset and later in the night, but the venues certainly don't aspire to the extremes of beer-swilling debauchery and club partying found in Kuta and Seminyak.

Bars close early in Ubud, often by 11pm. Many eating places listed earlier are also good just for a drink, including Nomad, Terazo, Laughing Buddha and Naughty Nuri's.

Jazz Café   LIVE MUSIC
(Map p134; ☑976 594; www.jazzcafebali.com; Jl Sukma 2; ☺5pm-midnight) Always popular, Jazz Café has a relaxed vibe in a garden of coconut palms and ferns. It offers good Asian fusion food (mains 35,000Rp to 70,000Rp), a long cocktail list and live jazz in various forms, as well as blues and more, Tuesday to Saturday from 7.30pm. Transport around Ubud provided.

Blue Cat   BAR
(Map p137; ☑0878 6058 3574; Jl Pengosekan; ☺3pm-late) As unadorned as an empty garage, this live music venue has local expat garage bands, better bands of locals and even, shudder, karaoke. Bintang specials at happy hour.

Napi Orti   BAR
(Map p137; ☑970 982; Monkey Forest Rd; ☺noon-sunrise) This upstairs place is your best bet for a late-night drink. Get boozy under the hazy gaze of Jim Morrison and Bob Marley. Been known to go till dawn.

Ozigo   DANCE CLUB
(Map p134; ☑0812 367 9736; Jl Raya Sanggingan; ☺9pm-2am) Ubud's late-night action – such as it is – is right here at this small and friendly club up by Naughty Nuri's. DJs are in residence nightly with edgy mixes plus lots of dance competitions and prizes.

☆ Entertainment

Few travel experiences can be more magical than attending a Balinese dance performance, especially in Ubud. Cultural entertainment keeps people returning and sets Bali apart from other tropical destinations. Ubud is a good base for the nightly array of performances and for accessing events in surrounding villages.

Dance

Dances performed for visitors are usually adapted and abbreviated to some extent to make them more enjoyable, but usually have appreciative locals in the audience (or peering around the screen!). It's also common to combine the features of more

than one traditional dance in a single performance.

In a week in Ubud, you can see Kecak, Legong and Barong dances, *Mahabharata* and *Ramayana* ballets, *wayang kulit* puppets and gamelan orchestras. For details on these classic Balinese arts, see p337. One of your first stops in town should be the tourist office for the weekly performance schedule.

Venues will usually host a variety of performances by various troupes through the week and aren't tied to a particular group. Some venues to consider:

Ubud Palace
(Map p137; Jl Raya Ubud) Near-nightly performances in a royal setting.

Pura Dalem Ubud
(Map p137; Jl Raya Ubud) Perfect for the fire dance, one of the prettiest venues.

Pura Taman Saraswati
(Water Palace; Map p137; Jl Raya Ubud) A beautiful location.

Arma Open Stage
(Map p137; ☑976 659; Jl Raya Pengosekan) Has among the best troupes.

Puri Desa Gede
(Map p134; Jl Peliatan) Good, well-lit venue.

Padangtegal Kaja
(Map p137; Jl Hanoman) Simple, open venue.

Pura Dalem Puri
(Map p134; Jl Raya Ubud) Opposite Ubud's main cremation grounds.

Semara Ratih
(Map p134; Kutuh) Stage with a name that means 'Spirit of Bali'; usually one performance per week.

Ubud Wantilan
(Map p137; Jl Raya Ubud) Unadorned meeting *bale* across from Ubud Palace.

Other performances can be found in nearby towns such as Batuan, Mawang and Kutuh.

Ubud Tourist Information (Yaysan Bina Wisata; ☑973 285; Jl Raya Ubud; ☺8am-8pm) has performance information and sells tickets (usually 80,000Rp). For performances outside Ubud, transport is often included in the price. Tickets are also sold at many hotels, at the venues and by street vendors who hang around outside Ubud Palace – all charge the same price.

Vendors sell drinks at the performances, which typically last about 1½ hours. Before the show, you might notice the musicians checking out the size of the crowd – ticket

DANCE TROUPES: GOOD & BAD

All dance groups on Ubud's stages are not created equal. You've got true artists with international reputations and then you've got some who really shouldn't quit their day jobs. If you're a Balinese dance novice, you shouldn't worry too much about this; just pick a venue and go.

But after a few performances, you'll start to appreciate the differences in talent, and that's part of the enjoyment. Clue: if the costumes are dirty, the orchestra seems particularly uninterested and you find yourself watching a dancer and saying 'I could do that', then the group is B-level. For more perspective on the good and bad of Balinese dancers, see p338.

Excellent troupes who regularly perform in Ubud include the following:

» **Semara Ratih** High-energy, creative Legong interpretations.

» **Gunung Sari** Legong dance; one of Bali's oldest and most respected troupes.

» **Semara Madya** Kekac dance; especially good for the hypnotic monkey chants.

» **Sekaa Gong Wanita Mekar Sari** An all-woman Legong troupe from Peliatan.

» **Tirta Sari** Legong dance.

» **Sadha Budaya** Barong dance.

sales fund the troupes. Also watch for potential members of the next generation of performers: local children avidly watch from under the screens, behind stage and from a musician's lap or two.

One note about your mobile phone: nobody wants to hear it; nor do the performers want flash in their eyes. And don't be rude and walk out loudly in the middle (we're shocked at how many boors do this).

Shadow Puppets

You can also find shadow-puppet shows – although these are greatly attenuated from traditional performances, which often last the entire night. Regular performances are held at **Oka Kartini** (Map p134; ☎975 193; Jl Raya Ubud; tickets 50,000Rp), which has bungalows and a gallery.

Musician **Nyoman Warsa** (Map p137; ☎974 807; Pondok Bamboo Music Shop, Monkey Forest Rd) orchestrates highly recommended puppet shows (75,000Rp) on certain evenings.

🔒 Shopping

Ubud has myriad art shops, boutiques and galleries. Many offer clever and unique items made in and around the area. Ubud is the ideal base for exploring the enormous number of craft galleries, studios and workshops in villages north and south.

The euphemistically named **Pasar Seni** (Art Market; Map p137; cnr Jl Raya Ubud & Monkey Forest Rd) is a tourist-mobbed two-storey place that sells a wide range of clothing,

sarongs, footwear and souvenirs of highly variable quality at negotiable prices. Decent items *may* include leather goods, batiks, baskets, textiles such as bedspreads, and silverware. You can bet they will have lots of penis-shaped bottle openers.

Much more interesting is Ubud's bountiful **produce market**, which operates to a greater or lesser extent every day and is buried within Pasar Seni. It starts early in the morning and winds up by lunch.

What to Buy

You can spend days in and around Ubud shopping. Jl Raya Ubud, Monkey Forest Rd, Jl Hanoman and Jl Dewi Sita should be your starting points.

You'll find **art** for sale everywhere. Check the gallery listings for recommendations. Prices range from cheap to collector-level, depending on the artist. Surrounding villages are also hotbeds for arts and crafts – as you'll have noticed on your drive to Ubud.

Ubud has a few **clothing designers**. Look along Monkey Forest Rd, Jl Dewi Sita and Jl Hanoman. Many will make or alter to order. In these same areas, look for **housewares**, especially local goods such as weaving and antiques.

Ubud is the best place in Bali for **books**. Selections are wide and varied, especially for tomes on Balinese art and culture. Many sellers carry titles by small and obscure publishers. Shops typically offer newspapers such as the *International Herald Tribune*.

JL RAYA UBUD & AROUND

Ganesha Bookshop BOOKSHOP

(Map p137; ☑970 320; www.ganeshabooksbali.com; Jl Raya Ubud) Bali's best bookshop has an amazing amount of stock jammed into a small space, with an excellent selection of titles on Indonesian studies, travel, arts, music and fiction (including used titles). Good recommendations and mail-order service.

Toko HOUSEWARES

(Map p137; ☑975 979; Jl Raya Ubud) High-end Balinese-made housewares, antiques and handicrafts; they're quite stylish, and some, like the exquisite small picture frames, just might fit into your already-full luggage.

Smile Shop CHARITY

(Map p137; ☑233 758; www.senyumbali.org; Jl Sriwedari) All manner of creative goods for sale in a shop to benefit the Smile Foundation of Bali.

Threads of Life Indonesian Textile Arts Center TEXTILES

(Map p134; ☑972 187; Jl Kajeng 24) The small store here stocks exquisite handmade traditional fabrics.

Moari MUSICAL INSTRUMENTS

(Map p137; ☑977 367; Jl Raya Ubud) New and restored Balinese musical instruments are sold here.

Ary's Bookshop BOOKSHOP

(Map p137; ☑978 203; Jl Raya Ubud) Good for art books and maps.

MONKEY FOREST ROAD

Ashitaba HOUSEWARES

(Map p137; ☑464 922; Monkey Forest Rd) Tenganan, the Aga village of East Bali, produces the intricate and beautiful rattan items sold here (and in Seminyak). Containers, bowls, purses and more (from US$5) display the fine and intricate weaving.

Macan Tidur HOUSEWARES

(Map p137; ☑977 121; Monkey Forest Rd) Amid a string of trashy places, this elegant store stands out like Audrey Hepburn amid the Spice Girls. Silks, art, antiques and more are beautifully displayed.

Kou Cuisine HOUSEWARES

(Map p137; ☑972 319; Monkey Forest Rd) Give the gift of exquisite little containers of jams made with Balinese fruit or containers of sea salt made along Bali's shores. Afterwards, clean up with their soap.

Pondok Bamboo Music Shop MUSICAL INSTRUMENTS

(Map p137; ☑974 807; Monkey Forest Rd) Hear the music of a thousand bamboo wind chimes at this store owned by noted gamelan musician Nyoman Warsa, who offers music lessons and stages shadow-puppet shows.

Pusaka CLOTHING

(Map p137; ☑978 619; Monkey Forest Rd 71) 'Modern ethnic clothing' is the motto here, which translates into cool, comfy yet stylish cottons. Need a gift for somebody small (or not so small)? Adorable house-made plush toys are 50,000Rp.

Zarong CLOTHING

(Map p137; ☑977 601; Monkey Forest Rd) An offbeat, hippie-chic fashion store that brings a patchouli of elegance. There are lots of cool cottons here that will be at home in any Balinese situation.

Calico HOUSEWARES

(Map p137; ☑971 354; Monkey Forest Rd) The wooden Balinese cow bell of your dreams is among the fun and intriguing merch here.

Bali Opiqkids CHILDREN'S CLOTHING

(Map p137; ☑238 743; Monkey Forest Rd) Bright clothes for kids, super-colourful.

Periplus BOOKSHOP

(Map p137; ☑975 178; Monkey Forest Rd) Typically glossy.

JL DEWI SITA

Kou COSMETICS

(Map p137; ☑971 905; Jl Dewi Sita) Luxurious handmade organic soaps produced locally. Put one in your undies drawer and smell fine for weeks.

Kertas Lingsir PAPER

(Map p137; ☑973 030; Jl Dewi Sita) Specialises in interesting paper handmade from banana, pineapple and taro plants. If you're a real fan, ask about factory visits.

Destynation WOMEN'S CLOTHING

(Map p137; ☑0812 3643 9591; Jl Dewi Sita) Create your own breeze in these sheer, cool cottons and silks.

Alamkara JEWELLERY

(Map p137; ☑972 213; Monkey Forest Rd) On display are unusual but very wearable designs in gold and silver, featuring black pearls and gems, some made locally.

SOS Jungle Shop CHARITY

(Map p137; ☑972 906; Jl Goutama) Run for the Ubud-based **Sumatran Orangutan**

Society (www.orangutans-sos.org), this small shop has crafts made in Sumatra and clothes good for the jungle; many orangutan-related items.

Cinta Bookshop
BOOKSHOP

(Map p137; ☑973 295; Jl Dewi Sita) Nice assortment of used novels and vintage books about Bali.

PADANGTEGAL & PENGOSEKAN

Namaste
NEW AGE

(Map p137; ☑796 9178; Jl Hanoman 64) Just the place to buy a crystal to get your spiritual house in order, Namaste is a gem of a little store with a top range of New Age supplies. Incense, yoga mats, moody instrumental music – it's all here.

Tegun Galeri
HOUSEWARES

(Map p137; ☑973361; Jl Hanoman 44) It's everything the souvenir stores are not, with beautiful handmade items from around the island plus ancient art.

Gemala Jewelry
JEWELLERY

(Map p137; ☑0811 392 058; Jl Raya Pengosekan) One of Ubud's top places for locally designed and produced jewellery.

Goddess on the Go!
WOMEN'S CLOTHING

(Map p137; ☑976 084; Jl Raya Pengosekan) Clothes for adventure. Super-comfortable, easy-to-pack and made eco-friendly.

Bali Spirit Yoga Shop
CLOTHING

(Map p137; ☑970 992; Jl Hanoman 44) Stretchy cottony clothes, mats, yoga gear, music to move by, etc.

Ading
MUSICAL INSTRUMENTS

(Map p137; Jl Hanoman) One of several small workshops in a row where you can have musical instruments and puppets made to order.

Galaxyan Atelier
JEWELLERY

(Map p137; ☑971 430; Jl Hanoman 3) In-house creations in silver and gold, flashy designs.

Arma
BOOKSHOP

(Map p137; ☑976 659; www.armamuseum.com; Jl Raya Pengosekan; ☉9am-6pm) Large selection of cultural titles.

ELSEWHERE

Neka Art Museum
BOOKSHOP

(Map p134; ☑975 074; www.museumneka.com; Jl Raya Sanggingan; ☉9am-5pm) Good range of art books.

Periplus
BOOKSHOP

(Map p134; ☑976 149; Bintang Centre, Jl Raya Campuan) Large store with a small cafe.

❶ Information

Visitors will find every service they need and then some along Ubud's main roads. Bulletin boards at **Bali Buddha** (Jl Jembawan 1) and **Kafe** (Jl Hanoman 44) have info on housing, jobs, classes and much more.

Ubud is home to many non-profit and volunteer groups; see p376 for details.

Emergency

Police station (☑975 316; Jl Raya Andong; ☉24hr) Located east, at Andong.

Internet Access

Many of Ubud's cafes and hotels offer wi-fi as noted in the listings.

@Highway (☑972 107; Jl Raya Ubud; per hr 30,000Rp; ☉24hr; ✳☜) Full-service and very fast.

Libraries

Pondok Pecak Library & Learning Centre (Map p137; ☑976 194; Monkey Forest Rd; ☉9am-9pm) On the far side of the football field, this relaxed place is a fitting tribute to its late founder, Laurie Billington. Charges membership fees for library use. Small cafe and a pleasant reading area.

Medical Services

See Health (p392) for details on international clinics and hospitals in Bali.

Apotek Ari Medika (Map p137; Jl Raya Ubud; ☉8am-9pm) Pharmacy with a limited selection.

Ubud Clinic (Map p134; ☑974 911; www.ubud-clinic.com; Jl Raya Campuan 36; ☉24hr) Charges begin at 300,000Rp for a clinical consultation; has a pharmacy.

Money

Ubud has numerous banks, ATMs and money-changers along Jl Raya Ubud and Monkey Forest Rd.

Post

Main post office (Jl Jembawan; ☉8am-5pm) Has a sort-it-yourself poste restante system. Address poste restante mail to Kantor Pos, Ubud 80571, Bali, Indonesia.

Tourist Information

Ubud Tourist Information (Yaysan Bina Wisata; ☑973 285; Jl Raya Ubud; ☉8am-8pm) The one really useful tourist office in Bali has big new digs, a good range of information and a noticeboard listing current happenings and activities. The staff can answer most regional questions and have up-to-date information on ceremonies and traditional dances held in the area; dance tickets are sold here.

Getting There & Away

Many people get to Ubud from other parts of Bali via a car and driver arranged with a hotel at either end of the trip. The cost can vary between 200,000Rp and 600,000Rp, depending on whether you're making a day of it (or you've simply cut a bad deal). Given all the outlying points of interest around Ubud, making a day of it can be enjoyable indeed.

Bemo

Ubud is on two bemo routes. Orange bemos travel from Gianyar to Ubud (10,000Rp) and larger brown bemos from Batubulan terminal in Denpasar to Ubud (13,000Rp), and then head to Kintamani via Payangan. Ubud doesn't have a bemo terminal; there are bemo stops on Jl Suweta near the market in the centre of town.

Tourist Shuttle Bus

Perama (973 316; Jl Hanoman; ⊙9am-9pm) is the major tourist-shuttle operator, but its terminal is inconveniently located in Padangtegal; to get to your final destination in Ubud will cost another 15,000Rp.

DESTINATION	FARE	DURATION
Candidasa	50,000Rp	1¾hr
Kuta	50,000Rp	1¼hr
Lovina	100,000Rp	3hr
Padangbai	50,000Rp	1¼hr
Sanur	40,000Rp	1hr

Getting Around

Many better restaurants and hotels offer free local transport for guests and customers. Ask.

To/From the Airport

Official taxis from the airport to Ubud cost 195,000Rp. A taxi or car with driver *to* the airport will cost much less.

Xtrans (287 555; www.xtrans.co.id; Jl Raya Ubud; one-way 40,000Rp; ⊙10am-9pm) New airport shuttle via Sanur and Kuta; confirm all details in advance.

Bemo

Bemo don't directly link Ubud with nearby villages; you'll have to catch one going to Denpasar, Gianyar, Pujung or Kintamani and get off where you need to. Bemo to Gianyar travel along eastern Jl Raya Ubud, down Jl Peliatan and east to Bedulu. To Pujung, bemo head east along Jl Raya Ubud and then north through Andong and past the turn-off to Petulu.

To Payangan, bemo travel west along Jl Raya Ubud, go up past the many places on Jl Raya Campuan and Jl Raya Sanggingan and turn north at the junction after Sanggingan. Larger brown-coloured bemo to Batubulan terminal go east along Jl Raya Ubud and down Jl Hanoman.

The fare for a ride within the Ubud area shouldn't be more than 7000Rp.

Bicycle

Shops renting out bikes have their cycles on display along the main roads; your accommodation can always arrange bike hire. For more info, see p143.

Car & Motorcycle

With numerous nearby attractions, many of which are difficult to reach by bemo, renting a

UBUD GETTING THERE & AWAY

SAVING BALI'S DOGS

Mangy curs. That's the only label you can apply to many of Bali's dogs. As you travel the island – especially by foot – you can't help but notice dogs that are sick, ill-tempered, uncared for and victims to a litany of other maladies.

How can such a seemingly gentle island have Asia's worst dog population (which now has a huge rabies problem; see p394)? The answers are complex, but benign neglect has a lot to do with it. Dogs are at the bottom of the social strata; few have owners and local interest in them is nil.

Some non-profits in Ubud are hoping to change the fortunes of Bali's maligned best friends through rabies vaccinations, spaying and neutering, and public education. Donations are always greatly needed.

Bali Adoption Rehab Centre (BARC; 790 4579; www.freewebs.com/balidogs) Cares for dogs, places strays with sponsors and operates a mobile clinic for sterilisation.

Bali Animal Welfare Association (BAWA; 977 217; www.bawabali.com) Runs lauded mobile rabies vaccination teams, organises adoption, promotes population control. In addition, this group in Denapasar works island-wide.

Yudisthira Bali Street Dog Foundation (742 4048; www.balistreetdogs.com) Cares for thousands of strays a year and has vaccination and population-control programs.

vehicle is sensible. Ask at your accommodation or hire a car and driver. See p385 for details.

Taxi

There are very few taxis in Ubud – those that honk their horns at you have usually dropped off passengers from southern Bali in Ubud and are hoping for a fare back. Instead, you'll be stuck using one of the ubiquitous drivers with private vehicles hanging around on the street corners hectoring passersby (the better drivers simply hold up signs that say 'transport').

Many of the drivers are very fair; others – often from out of the area – not so much. If you find a driver you like, get his number and call him for rides during your stay. From central Ubud to, say, Sanggingan should cost about 20,000Rp – rather steep actually.

AROUND UBUD

📞 0361

The region east and north of Ubud has many of the most ancient monuments and relics in Bali. Some of them predate the Majapahit era and raise as-yet-unanswered questions about Bali's history. Others are more recent, and in other instances, newer structures have been built on and around the ancient remains. They're interesting to history and archaeology buffs, but not that spectacular to look at – with the exception of Bali's own bit of Angkor at Gunung Kawi. Perhaps the best approach is to plan a whole day walking or cycling around the area, stopping at the places that interest you, but not treating any one as a destination in itself.

The area is thick with excursion possibilities. Besides the Elephant Cave, there's the Crazy Buffalo Temple. Heading north you find Bali's most important ancient site at Tampaksiring and a nearly forgotten shrine nearby, Pura Mengening, that rewards the adventurous.

Bedulu

Bedulu was once the capital of a great kingdom. The legendary Dalem Bedaulu ruled the Pejeng dynasty from here, and was the last Balinese king to withstand the onslaught of the powerful Majapahit from Java. He was defeated by Gajah Mada in 1343. The capital shifted several times after this, to Gelgel and then later to Semarapura (Klungkung). Today Bedulu is absorbed into the greater Ubud sprawl.

⊙ Sights

Goa Gajah ANCIENT SITE
(Elephant Cave; adult/child 6000/3000Rp, parking 2000Rp; ⊙8am-6pm) There were never any elephants in Bali (until tourist attractions changed that); Goa Gajah probably takes its name from the nearby Sungai Petanu, which at one time was known as Elephant River, or perhaps because the face over the cave entrance might resemble an elephant. Some 2km southeast of Ubud on the road to Bedulu, a large car park with clamorous souvenir shops indicates that you've reached a big tourist attraction.

The origins of the cave are uncertain – one tale relates that it was created by the fingernail of the legendary giant Kebo Iwa. It probably dates to the 11th century, and was certainly in existence during the Majapahit takeover of Bali. The cave was rediscovered by Dutch archaeologists in 1923, but the fountains and pool were not found until 1954.

The cave is carved into a rock face and you enter through the cavernous mouth of a demon. The gigantic fingertips pressed beside the face of the demon push back a riotous jungle of surrounding stone carvings.

Inside the T-shaped cave you can see fragmentary remains of the *lingam,* the phallic symbol of the Hindu god Shiva, and its female counterpart the *yoni,* plus a statue of Shiva's son, the elephant-headed god Ganesha. In the courtyard in front of the cave are two square bathing pools with

THE LEGEND OF DALEM BEDAULU

A legend relates how Dalem Bedaulu possessed magical powers that allowed him to have his head chopped off and then replaced. Performing this unique party trick one day, the servant entrusted with lopping off the king's head and then replacing it unfortunately dropped it in a river and, to his horror, watched it float away. Looking around in panic for a replacement, he grabbed a pig, cut off its head and popped it upon the king's shoulders. Thereafter, the king was forced to sit on a high throne and forbade his subjects to look up at him; Bedaulu means 'he who changed heads'.

water trickling into them from waterspouts held by six female figures.

From Goa Gajah you can clamber down through the rice paddies to Sungai Petanu (Petanu River), where there are crumbling **rock carvings** of stupas (domes for housing Buddhist relics) on a cliff face, and a small **cave**.

Try to get here before 10am, when the big tourist buses begin lumbering in like, well, elephants. Sarong rental is 3000Rp.

Yeh Pulu ANCIENT SITE
(adult/child 6000/3000Rp) A man having his hand munched by a boar is one of the scenes on the 25m-long carved cliff face known as Yeh Pulu, believed to be a hermitage from the late 14th century. Apart from the figure of Ganesha, the elephant-headed son of Shiva, most of the scenes deal with everyday life, although the position and movement of the figures suggests that it could be read from left to right as a story. One theory is that they are events from the life of Krishna, the Hindu god.

One of the first recognisable images is of a man carrying a shoulder pole with two jugs, possibly full of *tuak* (palm wine). He is following a woman whose jewellery suggests wealth and power. There's a whimsical figure peering round a doorway, who seems to have armour on his front and a weapon on his back.

The hunting scene starts with a horseman and a man throwing a spear, while a frog takes on a snake with a club. Above the frog, two figures kneel over a pot, while to the right, two men carry off a slain animal on a pole.

The Ganesha figures of Yeh Pulu and Goa Gajah are quite similar, indicating a close relationship between them. You can walk between the sites, following small paths through the paddy fields, but you might need to pay a local to guide you. By car or bicycle, look for the signs to 'Relief Yeh Pulu' or 'Villa Yeh Pulu', east of Goa Gajah.

Even if your interest in carved Hindu art is minor, this site is quite lovely and rarely will you have much company. From the entrance, it's a 300m lush, tropical walk to Yeh Pulu.

Pura Samuan Tiga TEMPLE
The majestic Pura Samuan Tiga (Temple of the Meeting of the Three) is about 200m east of the Bedulu junction. The name is possibly a reference to the Hindu trinity, or it may refer to meetings held here in

the early 11th century. Despite these early associations, all the temple buildings have been rebuilt since the 1917 earthquake. The imposing main gate was designed and built by I Gusti Nyoman Lempad, one of Bali's renowned artists and a native of Bedulu.

ⓘ Getting There & Away

About 3km east of Teges, the road from Ubud reaches a junction where you can turn south to Gianyar or north to Pejeng, Tampaksiring and Penelokan. Ubud–Gianyar bemo will drop you off at this junction, from where you can walk to the sights. The road from Ubud is reasonably flat, so coming by bicycle is a good option.

Pejeng

Continuing up the road towards Tampaksiring you soon come to Pejeng and its famous temples. Like Bedulu, this was once an important seat of power, as it was the capital of the Pejeng kingdom, which fell to the Majapahit invaders in 1343.

⊙ Sights

Museum Purbakala MUSEUM
(☏942 354; Jl Raya Tampaksiring; admission by donation; ⊙8am-3pm Mon-Thu, 8am-12.30pm Fri) This archaeological museum has a reasonable collection of artefacts from all over Bali, and most displays are in English. The exhibits in several small buildings include some of Bali's first pottery from near Gilimanuk, and sarcophagi dating from as early as 300 BC – some originating from Bangli are carved in the shape of a turtle, which has important cosmic associations in Balinese mythology. The museum is about 500m north of the Bedulu junction, and is easy to reach by bemo or by bicycle. It's a sleepy place and you'll get the most out of it if you come with a knowledgeable guide.

Pura Kebo Edan TEMPLE
(Jl Raya Tampaksiring) Who can resist a sight called Crazy Buffalo Temple? Although not an imposing structure, it's famous for its 3m-high statue, known as the **Giant of Pejeng**, thought to be approximately 700 years old. Details are sketchy, but it may represent Bima, a hero of the *Mahabharata*, dancing on a dead body, as in a myth related to the Hindu Shiva cult. There is some conjecture about the giant's giant genitalia – it has what appear to be pins on the side. Some claim this was to give the woman more pleasure – an early version of

what is often sold by vending machines in public toilets.

Pura Pusering Jagat TEMPLE

(Jl Raya Tampaksiring) So that's what it looks like? The large Pura Pusering Jagat is said to be the centre of the old Pejeng kingdom. Dating from 1329, this temple is visited by young couples who pray at the stone *lingam* and *yoni*. Further back is a large stone urn, with elaborate but worn carvings of gods and demons searching for the elixir of life in a depiction of the *Mahabharata* tale 'Churning the Sea of Milk'. The temple is on a small track running west of the main road.

Pura Penataran Sasih TEMPLE

(Jl Raya Tampaksiring) This was once the state temple of the Pejeng kingdom. In the inner courtyard, high up in a pavilion and difficult to see, is the huge bronze drum known as the **Fallen Moon of Pejeng**. The hourglass-shaped drum is 186cm long, the largest single-piece cast drum in the world. Estimates of its age vary from 1000 to 2000 years, and it is not certain whether it was made locally or imported – the intricate geometric decorations are said to resemble patterns from places as far apart as West Papua and Vietnam. Even in its inaccessible position, you can make out these patterns and the distinctive heart-shaped face designs.

Balinese legend relates that the drum came to earth as a fallen moon, landing in a tree and shining so brightly that it prevented a band of thieves from going about their unlawful purpose. One of the thieves decided to put the light out by urinating on it, but the moon exploded and fell to earth as a drum, with a crack across its base as a result of the fall.

Although the big noise here is all about the drum, be sure to notice the **statuary** in the temple courtyard that dates from the 10th to the 12th century.

Tampaksiring

Tampaksiring is a small village about 18km northeast of Ubud with a large and important temple, Tirta Empul, and the most impressive ancient site in Bali, Gunung Kawi. It sits in the Pakerisan Valley, and the entire area has been nominated for Unesco recognition.

◎ Sights

TOP CHOICE Gunung Kawi ANCIENT MONUMENT

(adult/child 6000/3000Rp, sarong 3000Rp, parking 2000Rp; ⊘7am-5pm) On the northern outskirts of town, a sign points east off the main road to Gunung Kawi and its ancient monuments. From the end of the access road, a steep, stone stairway leads down to the river, at one point cutting through an embankment of solid rock. There, in the bottom of this lush green river valley, is one of Bali's oldest and largest ancient monuments.

Gunung Kawi consists of 10 rock-cut *candi* (shrines) – memorials cut out of the rock face in imitation of actual statues. They stand in awe-inspiring 8m-high sheltered niches cut into the sheer cliff face. A solitary *candi* stands about a kilometre further down the valley to the south; this is reached by a trek through the rice paddies on the western side of the rushing river. Be prepared for long climbs up and down – it is over 270 steps, although these are broken up into sections and at times the views as you walk through ancient terraced rice fields are as fine as any on Bali.

Each *candi* is believed to be a memorial to a member of the 11th-century Balinese royalty, but little is known for certain. Legends relate that the whole group of memorials was carved out of the rock face in one hardworking night by the mighty fingernails of Kebo Iwa.

The five monuments on the eastern bank are probably dedicated to King Udayana, Queen Mahendradatta, their son Airlangga and his brothers Anak Wungsu and Marakata. While Airlangga ruled eastern Java, Anak Wungsu ruled Bali. The four monuments on the western side are, by this theory, to Anak Wungsu's chief concubines. Another theory is that the whole complex is dedicated to Anak Wungsu, his wives, concubines and, in the case of the remote 10th *candi,* to a royal minister.

As you wander between monuments, temples, offerings, streams and fountains, you can't help but feel a certain ancient majesty here.

Tirta Empul ANCIENT MONUMENT

(adult/child 6000/3000Rp, parking 2000Rp; ⊘8am-6pm) A well-signposted fork in the road north of Tampaksiring leads to the popular holy springs at Tirta Empul, discovered in AD 962 and believed to have magical powers. The springs bubble up into

---

ⓘ BEST TIME TO VISIT GUNUNG KAWI

Get to Gunung Kawi as early as possible for the best experience. If you start down the steps by 7.30am, you'll avoid all the vendors and you'll still see residents going about their morning business in the swift-flowing streams such as ablutions and cleaning ceremonial offerings. You can hear the birds, the flowing water and your own voice going 'ooh' and 'aah' without the distractions that come later when large groups arrive. In addition, you'll still have cool air when you start back up the endless steps. Be sure to have a sarong in case there is nobody yet offering them for use. If the ticket office is closed, you can pay on your way out.

---

a large, crystal-clear pool within the temple and gush out through waterspouts into a bathing pool – they're the main source of Sungai Pakerisan (Pakerisan River), the river that rushes by Gunung Kawi only 1km or so away. Next to the springs, Pura Tirta Empul is one of Bali's most important temples.

Come in the early morning or late afternoon to avoid the tourist buses. You can also use the clean, segregated and free public baths here.

Other Sights

There are other groups of *candi* and monks' cells in the area once encompassed by the ancient Pejeng kingdom, notably **Pura Krobokan** and **Goa Garba**, but none so grand as Gunung Kawi. Between Gunung Kawi and Tirta Empul, **Pura Mengening** temple has a freestanding *candi,* similar in design to those at Gunung Kawi and much less visited.

The road running north to Penelokan is lined with a growing number of **agritourism attractions**. In reality these are mostly gift shops selling coffee and the usual carvings plus a few plants out back in labelled gardens. They give groups a reason to stop and shop.

Tegallalang

There are lots of shops and stalls in this busy market town you're likely to pass through on your visit to the area's temples. Stop for a stroll and you may be rewarded by hearing the practice of one of the local noted gamelan orchestras. Otherwise, plenty of carvers stand ready to sell you a carved fertility doll or the like.

You can pause at **Cafe Kampung & Cottages** (☏901 201; dishes 20,000-50,000Rp), an attractive warung (perfect for lunch) and upmarket guesthouse (rooms from US$90) with jaw-dropping rice-terrace views. The design makes great use of natural rock. Nearby, scores of carvers produce works from albesia wood, which is easily turned into simplistic, cartoonish figures. The wood is also a favourite of wind-chime makers.

Go about 3km west of town on a small, very green road to **Keliki**, and you'll pass **Alam Sari** (☏240 308; www.alamsari.com; r US$70-120; ❈@☎☞), a small hotel in a wonderfully isolated location where the bamboo grows like grass. There are 12 luxurious yet rustic rooms, a pool and a great view. The hotel treats its own wastewater, among other environmental initiatives.

North of Ubud

Abused and abandoned logging elephants from Sumatra have been given refuge in Bali at the **Elephant Safari Park** (☏721 480; www.baliadventuretours.com; adult/child US$16/8; ☉8am-6pm). Located in the cool, wet highlands of **Taro** (14km north of Ubud), the park is home to almost 30 elephants. Besides seeing a full complement of exhibits about elephants, most people will probably want to *ride* an elephant (adult/child US$45/32). The park has received praise for its conservation efforts; however, be careful you don't end up at one of the rogue parks, designed to divert the unwary to unsanctioned displays of elephants.

The surrounding region produces ochre-coloured paint pigment. The gentle uphill drive from Ubud is a lush attraction in itself.

The usual road from Ubud to Batur is through Tampaksiring, but there are other lesser roads up the gentle mountain slope. One of the most attractive goes north from Peliatan, past Petulu and its birds, and through the rice terraces between Tegallalang and Ceking, to bring you out on the crater rim between Penelokan and Batur. It's a sealed road all the way and you also pass through **Sebatu**, which has all manner of artisans tucked away in tiny villages.

The one off-note will be **Pujung**, where the rice terraces are beautiful but have attracted a strip of ugly tourist traps overlooking them. A few years ago, the farmers got fed up with looking up at others profiting from their labours and installed picture-ruining mirrors until they were cut in on the take.

South of Ubud

The road between south Bali and Ubud is lined with little shops making and selling handicrafts. Many visitors shop along the route as they head to Ubud, sometimes by the busload, but much of the craftwork is actually done in small workshops and family compounds on quiet back roads. You may enjoy these places more after visiting Ubud, where you'll see some of the best Balinese arts and develop some appreciation of the styles and themes.

For serious shopping and real flexibility in exploring these villages, it's worth arranging your own transport, so you can explore the back roads and carry your purchases without any hassles. Note that your driver may receive a commission from any place you spend your money – this can add 10% or more to the cost of purchases (think of it as his tip). Also, a driver may try to steer you to

---

BALI'S VILLAGE ARTISTS

In small villages throughout the Ubud region, from Sebatu to Mas and beyond across Bali, you'll see small signs for artists and crafts people, often near the local temple. As one local told us, 'we are only as rich of a village as our art,' so the people who create the ceremonial costumes, masks, kris (swords), musical instruments and all the other beautiful aspects of Balinese life and religion are accorded great honour. It's a symbiotic relationship, with the artist never charging the village for the work and the village in turn seeing to the welfare of the artist. Often there are many artists in residence because few events would bring more shame to a village than having to go to another village to procure a needed sacred object.

---

workshops or artisans that he favours, rather than those of most interest to you.

The roads form a real patchwork and you'll be rewarded with surprises if you take some time to wander the lesser routes.

From the **Batubulan bus/bemo terminal**, stop at the craft villages along the main road through Negari on your way to Ubud. The following points of interest are presented in the order you'll encounter them on the way to Ubud from the south.

BATUBULAN

The start of the road from south Bali is lined with outlets for stone sculptures – **stone carving** is the main craft of Batubulan (moonstone). Workshops are found right along the road to Tegaltamu, with another batch further north around Silakarang. Batubulan is the source of the stunning temple-gate guardians seen all over Bali. The stone used for these sculptures is a porous grey volcanic rock called *paras,* which resembles pumice; it's soft and surprisingly light. It also ages quickly, so that 'ancient' work may be years rather than centuries old.

The temples around Batubulan are, naturally, noted for their fine stonework. Just 200m to the east of the busy main road, **Pura Puseh Batubulan** is worth a visit for its moat filled with lotus flowers and perfectly balanced overall composition. Statues draw on ancient Hindu and Buddhist iconography and Balinese mythology; however, they are not old – many are copied from books on archaeology. An attenuated **Barong dance show** (admission 80,000Rp; ☺9.30am) about the iconic lion-dog creature is performed in an ugly hall; it's a bus-tour-friendly one-hour-long show. Note that Pura Puseh means 'central temple' – you'll find many around Bali. Some translations have 'Puseh' meaning 'navel', which is apt.

Batubulan is also a centre for making 'antiques', textiles and woodwork, and has numerous craft shops.

BALI BIRD PARK & RIMBA REPTILE PARK

More than 1000 birds from 250 species flit about this **bird park** (☎299 352; www.bali-bird-park.com; both parks adult/child US$24/12; ☺9am-5.30pm), including rare *cendrawasih* (birds of paradise) from West Papua and the all-but-vanished Bali starlings. Many of these birds are housed in special walk-

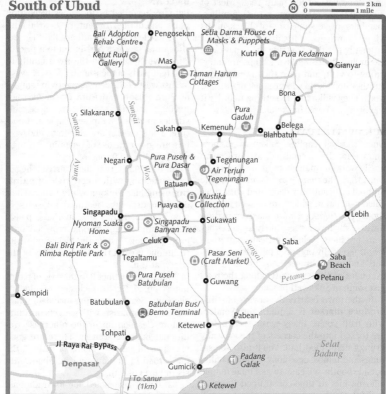

through aviaries; in one of them you follow a walk at tree-level, or what some with feathers might say is bird-level. The 2 hectares of landscaped gardens feature a fine collection of tropical plants.

Next door, **Rimba Reptile Park** (☑299 344) has about 20 species of creatures from Indonesia and Africa, as well as turtles, crocodiles, a python and a solitary Komodo dragon. The parks are popular with kids; allow at least two hours.

Tours stop at the parks, or you can take a Batubulan–Ubud bemo, get off at the junction at Tegaltamu, and follow the signs north for about 600m. There is a large parking lot.

SINGAPADU

The centre of Singapadu is dominated by a huge **banyan tree**. In the past, these were community meeting places. Even today the local meeting hall is just across the road. The surrounding village has a traditional

appearance, with walled family compounds and shady trees. You can visit the **Nyoman Suaka Home** (requested donation 10,000Rp; ⊙9am-5pm), which is 50m off the main road, just south of the big tree. Pass through the old carved entrance to the walled family compound and you'll discover a classic Balinese home. While you snoop about, the family goes about its business. Many pestles are in use in the kitchen producing spices and some of the roofs are still made from thatch on bamboo frames.

Singapadu's dancers now perform mostly at large venues in tourist areas – there are no regular public performances.

CELUK

Celuk is the **silver** and **gold** centre of Bali. The flashier showrooms are on the main road, and have marked prices that are quite high, although you can always bargain.

Hundreds of silversmiths and goldsmiths work in their homes on the backstreets north and east of the main road. Most of these artisans are from *pande* families, members of a sub-caste of blacksmiths whose knowledge of fire and metal has traditionally put them outside the usual caste hierarchy. Their small workshops are interesting to visit, and have the lowest prices, but they don't keep a large stock of finished work. They will make something to order if you bring a sample or sketch.

SUKAWATI & PUAYA

Once a royal capital, Sukawati is now known for its specialised artisans, who busily work in small shops along the roads. One group, the *tukang prada,* make temple umbrellas, beautifully decorated with stencilled gold paint, which can be seen in their shops. The *tukang wadah* make cremation towers, which you're less likely to see. Other craft products include intricate patterned *lontar* (specially prepared palm leaves) baskets and wind chimes. Look for some fine examples of all these crafts along the road just south of Sukawati proper.

In the town centre, the always-bustling **produce market** is a highlight. Vendors with fruit you've likely never seen before are tucked into the corners of the typically grungy main food hall. You'll also see sarongs and temple ceremony paraphernalia; outside booths sell easy-to-assemble temple offering kits to time-constrained Balinese faithful. On the surrounding streets, you'll find some stalls with high-quality handicrafts mixed in with those peddling 'I Love Bali' handbags. Should you get inspired, there are ATMs at the ready.

About 2km south of town, the much-hyped and very touristy **Pasar Seni** is a two-storey market where every type of knick-knack and trinket is on sale.

Puaya, about 1km northwest of Sukawati, specialises in high-quality **leather shadow puppets** and **masks** for Topeng and Barong dances. On the main street, look for a small sign that reads **Mustika Collection** (☑299 479; Kubu Dauh 62), or ask anyone. Inside the family compound you'll find a workshop for masks and puppets where you can see how cow hide is transformed into these works of art. Nearby, **Baruna Art Shop** (☑299 490; Kubu Duah) has *barongs* aplenty. Other workshops nearby are in shadowing rooms behind open doorways; look inside and you might see a fearsome mask staring at you.

BATUAN

Batuan's recorded history goes back 1000 years, and in the 17th century its royal family controlled most of southern Bali. The decline of its power is attributed to a priest's curse, which scattered the royal family to different parts of the island.

Just west of the centre, the twin temples of **Pura Puseh** and **Pura Dasar** (donation 10,000Rp, includes sarong) are accessible studies in classic Balinese temple architecture. The carvings are elaborate and visitors are given the use of vermilion sarongs, which look good in photos.

In the 1930s two local artists began experimenting with a new style of **painting** using black ink on white paper. Their dynamic drawings featured all sorts of scenes from daily life – markets, paddy fields, animals and people crowded onto each painting – while the black-and-white technique evoked the Balinese view of the supernatural.

Today, this distinct Batuan style of painting is noted for its inclusion of modern elements. Sea scenes often include a windsurfer, while tourists with gadgets or riding motorcycles pop up in the otherwise traditional Balinese scenery. There are good examples in galleries along, or just off, the main road in Batuan, and in Ubud's Museum Puri Lukisan.

Batuan is also noted for its traditional dance, and is a centre for carved wooden relief panels and screens. The ancient Gambuh dance is performed in the Pura Puseh every full moon. (The carvers also keep busy making all manner of stylish teak furnishings.)

MAS

Mas means 'gold' in Bahasa Indonesia, but **woodcarving** is the principal craft in this village. The great Majapahit priest Nirartha once lived here, and **Pura Taman Pule** is said to be built on the site of his home. During the three-day Kuningan festival, a performance of *wayang wong* (an older version of the *Ramayana* ballet) is held in the temple's courtyard.

Carving was a traditional art of the priestly Brahmana caste, and the skills are said to have been a gift of the gods. Historically, carving was limited to temple decorations, dance masks and musical instruments, but in the 1930s carvers began to depict people and animals in a naturalistic way. Today it's hard to resist the oodles of winsome creatures produced here.

This is the place to come if you want something custom-made in sandalwood – just be prepared to pay well (and check the wood's authenticity carefully). Mas is also part of Bali's booming furniture industry, producing chairs, tables and antiques ('made to order!'), mainly from teak imported from other Indonesian islands.

Three generations of carvers produce some of Bali's most revered **masks** in the family compound of **IB Anom** (☎974 529), right off the main road in Mas. There is a small showroom with their works, but mostly the appeal is visiting with the family while they create something out of cedar. You can take lessons (from 100,000Rp per day) and expect to have something half-good in about two weeks.

Along the main road in Mas are the **Taman Harum Cottages** (☎975 567; www .tamanharumcottages.com; r from US$35, villas US$50-80; ✸@✉). There are 17 rooms and villas – some quite large. By all means get one overlooking the rice fields. They're behind a gallery, which is also a venue for a huge range of art and cultural courses. Ubud shuttles are free.

North of Mas, woodcarving shops make way for the art galleries, cafes, hotels and lights of Ubud.

Alternative Routes

From Sakah, along the road between Batuan and Ubud, you can continue east for a few kilometres to the turn-off to Blahbatuh and continue to Ubud via Kutri and Bedulu. In Blahbatuh, **Pura Gaduh** has a 1m-high stone head, believed to be a portrait of Kebo Iwa, the legendary strongman and minister to the last king of the Bedulu kingdom. Gajah Mada – the Majapahit strongman – realised that it wouldn't be possible to conquer Bedulu (Bali's strongest kingdom) while Kebo Iwa was there. So Gajah Mada lured him away to Java (with promises of women and song) and had him murdered. The stone head possibly predates the Javanese influence in Bali, but the temple is simply a reconstruction of an earlier one destroyed in the earthquake of 1917.

See looms busily making ikat and batik fabrics at **Putri Ayu** (☎225 533; Jl Diponegoro). The workshops and showroom are a good complement to the textile shops in Gianyar and are just across from the temple.

A MAGICAL KINGDOM OF PUPPETS

Setia Darma House of Masks and Puppets (Map p169; ☎977 404; Jl Tegal Bingin; admission by donation; ◷8am-4pm) is both the newest and one of the best museums in the Ubud area. Over 4600 ceremonial masks and puppets from Indonesia and across Asia are beautifully displayed in a series of renovated historic buildings. Among the many treasures, look for the golden **Jero Luh Mask** as well as the faces of royalty, mythical monsters and even the common man. Puppets are unnervingly lifelike. The museum is about 2km northeast of the main Mas crossroads.

West of here, there are A-list views of **rice terraces** off the main road near the village of **Kemenuh**.

About 2km southwest of Blahbatuh, along Sungai Petanu (Petanu River), is **Air Terjun Tegenungan** (Tegenungan Waterfall; aka Srog Srogan). Follow the signs from Kemenuh for the best view of the falls, from the west side of the river.

KUTRI

Heading north from Blahbatuh, Kutri has the interesting **Pura Kedarman** (aka Pura Bukit Dharma). If you climb up Bukit Dharma behind the temple, there's a great panoramic view and a **hilltop shrine**, with a stone statue of the six-armed goddess of death and destruction, Durga, killing a demon-possessed water buffalo.

BONA & BELEGA

On the back road between Blahbatuh and Gianyar, Bona is a **basket-weaving** centre and features many articles made from *lontar* leaves. It is also known for fire dances. (Note: most road signs in the area read 'Bone' instead of Bona, so if you get lost, you'll have to ask: 'Do you know the way to Bone?') Nearby, the village of Belega is a centre for bamboo furniture production.

UBUD & AROUND SOUTH OF UBUD

East Bali

Best Places to Eat

» Cafe Garam (p203)

» Merta Sari (p184)

» Amankila (p189)

Best Places to Stay

» Tirta Gangga Villas (p197)

» Turtle Bay Hideaway (p195)

» Meditasi (p203)

» Alam Anda (p206)

» Pondok Wisata Lihat Sawah (p180)

Why Go?

Wandering the roads of east Bali is one of the island's great pleasures. Rice terraces spill down hillsides under swaying palms, wild volcanic beaches are washed by pounding surf, and age-old villages soldier on with barely a trace of modernity.

Watching over it all is Gunung Agung, the 3142m volcano known as the 'navel of the world' and 'Mother Mountain', which has a perfect conical shape you might glimpse on hikes from lovely Tirta Gangga.

You can find Bali's past amid evocative ruins in the former royal city of Semarapura. Follow the rivers coursing down the slopes on the Sidemen road to find vistas and valleys that could have inspired Shangri-La. Down at the coast, Padangbai and Candidasa cater to the funky and frowsy respectively.

Resorts and hidden beaches dot the seashore and cluster on the Amed Coast. Just north of there, Tulamben is all about external exploration: the entire town is geared for diving.

When to Go

The best time to visit east Bali is during the dry season April to September, although recent weather patterns have made the dry season wetter and the wet season drier. Hiking and trekking in the lush hills from Gunung Agung over to Tirta Gangga is much easier when it isn't muddy. Along the coast, however, there's little reason to pick one month over another; it's usually just tropical. Top-end resorts may book up in peak season (July, August and Christmas), but it's never jammed like south Bali.

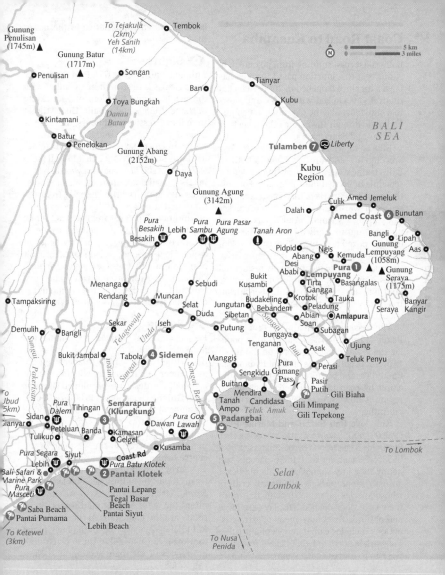

East Bali Highlights

1 Counting the shades of green on the longest and best climb of your life at **Pura Lempuyang** (p197), one of many hikes around Tirta Gangga

2 Marvelling at the combination of the sacred and the sublime and lots of black sand at **Pantai Klotek** (p175)

3 Sensing Bali's violent past and proud traditions of sacrifice at Semarapura's **Kertha Gosa** (p177)

4 Trekking the picture-perfect valley at **Sidemen** (p180)

5 Chilling with new friends at the mellow cafes and laid-back beaches of **Padangbai** (p185)

6 Finding your perfect lotus position at an inn perched along the **Amed Coast** (p198)

7 Plunging into the blue waters at **Tulamben** (p204) to explore the famous shipwreck right off the beach

Coast Road to Kusamba

🎵0361

Bali's coast road running from just north of Sanur east to a junction past Kusamba has been a hit since it opened in 2006. In fact at times it gets choked with traffic and slows to a crawl just like the old route, which meandered through towns far inland such as Gianyar and Semarapura.

Efforts to widen the two lanes to four are ongoing and are emblematic both of Bali's traffic woes and the at-times sclerotic schedule of needed improvements. For now the road has sparked the construction of scores of warung (food stalls) and trucker cafes along its length. And it has opened up numerous formerly inaccessible beaches (see the boxed text, p175). Tourism development hasn't yet caught up, but as you drive the road you'll see plenty of new residential villas aimed at foreigners and even more land for sale (signs promising 'beachfront freeholds' are as common as tyre-repair shops).

The coast road (formally the Prof Dr Ida Bagus Mantra Bypass – named for a popular 1980s Balinese governor who did much to promote culture) has brought Padangbai, Candidasa and points east one to two hours closer by road to south Bali. Much of the region is now an easy day trip, depending on traffic.

Kids love **Bali Safari and Marine Park** (🎵950 000; www.balisafarimarinepark.com; Prof Dr Ida Bagus Mantra Bypass; admission from US$35; ☺9am-5pm) and their parents are happy they love *someplace*. This big-ticket animal theme park is filled with critters whose species never set foot in Bali until their cage door opened. Displays are large and naturalistic. A huge menu of extra-cost options includes camel and elephant rides. The park is north of Lebih Beach; free shuttles run to tourist centres across south Bali.

Gianyar

🎵0361

This is the affluent administrative capital and main market town of the Gianyar district, which also includes Ubud. The town has a number of factories producing batik and ikat fabrics, and a compact centre with some excellent food. With so much traffic now diverted to the coast road, the once-busy route east through town is now a relaxed and scenic alternative to the newer road.

👁 Sights

Although dating from 1771, **Puri Gianyar** (Jl Ngurah Rai) was destroyed in a conflict with the neighbouring kingdom of Klungkung in the mid-1880s and rebuilt. Under threat from its aggressive neighbours, the Gianyar kingdom requested Dutch protection. A 1900 agreement let the ruling family retain its status and palace, though it lost all political power. The *puri* (palace) was damaged in a 1917 earthquake, but was restored soon after and appears little changed from the time the Dutch arrived. It's a fine example of traditional palace architecture. While tourists are not usually allowed inside, if you report to the guard you may be given a quick look around, which makes for a bit of illicit fun (otherwise the views are good through the wrought-iron gate). The huge banyan tree across from the compound is considered sacred and is a royal symbol.

🍴 Eating

People come to Gianyar to sample the market food, like *babi guling* (spit-roast pig stuffed with chilli, turmeric, garlic and ginger – delicious), for which the town is noted. The descriptively named **Gianyar Babi Guleng** (Jl Jata; meals 15,000-20,000Rp; ☺7am-4pm) is favoured by locals among many competitors. (There are lots of cops and bemo drivers here – they know.) It's in a tiny side street at the west end of the centre behind the bemo parking area.

Nearby are numerous stands selling fresh food, including delectable *piseng goreng* (fried banana). Also worth sampling for *babi guling* and other local treats are the food stalls in the **food market** (☺11am-2pm) as well as the busy **night market** (☺6-11pm). All of these places line both sides of the main section of Jl Ngurah Rai.

🛍 Shopping

At the western end of town on the main Ubud road are textile factories, including the large **Tenun Ikat Setia Cili** (🎵943 409; Jl Astina Utara; ☺9am-5pm) and **Cap Togog** (🎵943 046; Jl Astina Utara 11; ☺8am-5pm). Both are on the main drag west of the centre, about 500m apart.

Connoisseurs of handwoven fabrics will be fit to be tied (dyed?). These places have showrooms where you can buy material

The coast road from Sanur heads east past long stretches of shore that until recently were reached only by long and narrow lanes from roads well inland. Development has yet to catch on here – excepting a few villas – so take advantage of the easy access to enjoy the often-quiet beaches and the many important temples near the sand.

The shoreline the coast road follows is striking, with beaches in volcanic shades of grey and pounding waves. The entire coast has great religious significance and there are oodles of temples. At the many small coastal-village beaches, cremation formalities reach their conclusion when the ashes are consigned to the sea. Ritual purification ceremonies for temple artefacts are also held on these beaches.

Ketewel and **Lebih** are good spots for surfing; see p34 for details. Swimming in the often pounding surf is dangerous. You'll need your own transport to reach these beaches. Except where noted, services are few, so bring your own drinking water and towels. On some access roads, locals will charge you a modest fee, say 2000Rp.

From west to east, beaches include the following:

» **Pantai Purnama** is small but has the blackest sand, which the sun studs with billions of reflected sparkles. Religion is big here. The temple, **Pura Erjeruk**, is important for irrigation of rice fields, while some of Bali's most elaborate full-moon purification ceremonies are held here each month.

» **Saba Beach** has a small temple, covered shelters, a shady parking area and a twisting 1.1km, junglelike drive from the coast road; it's about 12km east of Sanur. A few drink vendors recline on the burnt-umber-hued sand.

» **Pura Masceti Beach**, 15km east of Sanur, has a few drink vendors. **Pura Masceti** is one of Bali's nine directional temples. Right on the beach, it is architecturally significant and enlivened with gaudy statuary. There are vendors, which contributes to some litter. A large building back behind the temple is used for cockfights.

» **Lebih Beach** has glittering mica-infused sand. Just off the main road, a strip of shacky warung and cafes leads to the surf. The large Sungai Pakerisan (Pakerisan River), which starts near Tampaksiring, reaches the sea near here. Fishing boats line the shore. North, just across the coast road, impressive **Pura Segara** looks across the strait to Nusa Penida, home of Jero Gede Macaling (p130) – the temple helps protect Bali from his evil influence.

» **Pantai Siyut**, a mere 300m off the road, and often deserted, is a good place for a parasol, there's no shade otherwise.

» **Tegal Basar Beach** is a turtle sanctuary (don't expect to see any, though) with no shade but offering a good view of Nusa Lembongan. The 600m drive in runs through a dense forest of palms.

» **Pantai Lepang** is worth visiting just for the little slice of rural Bali you pass through on the 600m drive from the main road. Rice and corn grow in profusion. Down at the carbon-coloured sand you'll find small dunes, a few vendors and a lot of reason to snap some pics.

» **Pantai Klotek** offers another lovely drive on an 800m hilly access road and is the most interesting of the beaches. The quiet at **Pura Batu Klotek** belies its great significance: sacred statues are brought here from Pura Besakih for ritual cleansing. Look for a man with a *bakso ayam* (chicken soup) cart. He makes fresh noodles by hand all day.

by the metre, or have it tailored. You can at times see weavers at work and observe how the thread is dyed before being woven to produce the vibrantly patterned weft ikat, which is called *endek* in Bali. Prices are 50,000Rp to 100,000Rp per metre for handwoven ikat, depending on how fine the weaving is – costs will rise if it contains silk. You can get a batik sarong for 50,000Rp. Note that the industry is struggling from competition with machine-made Javanese fabric, so your arrival will be welcomed.

ⓘ Getting There & Away

Regular bemo run between Batubulan terminal near Denpasar and Gianyar's main terminal (15,000Rp), which is behind the main market. Bemo from Gianyar's main terminal also serve Semarapura (10,000Rp) and Amlapura (20,000Rp). Bemo to and from Ubud (10,000Rp) use the bemo stop across the road from the main market.

Sidan

When driving east from Gianyar you come to the turn-off to Bangli about 2km out of Peteluan. Follow this road for about 1km until you reach a sharp bend, where you'll find Sidan's **Pura Dalem**. This good example of a temple of the dead has very fine carvings. In particular, note the sculptures of Durga with children by the gate and the separate enclosure in one corner of the temple – this is dedicated to Merajapati, the guardian spirit of the dead.

Bangli

☑ 0366

Halfway up the slope to Penelokan, Bangli, once the capital of a kingdom, is a humble market town noteworthy for its sprawling temple, Pura Kehen, which is on a beautiful jungle road that runs east past rice terraces and connects at Sekar with roads to Rendang and Sidemen.

History

Bangli dates from the early 13th century. In the Majapahit era it broke away from Gelgel to become a separate kingdom, even though it was landlocked, poor and involved in long-running conflicts with neighbouring states.

In 1849 Bangli made a treaty with the Dutch that gave it control over the defeated north-coast kingdom of Buleleng, but Buleleng then rebelled and the Dutch imposed direct rule there. In 1909 the rajah (lord or prince) of Bangli chose for it to become a Dutch protectorate rather than face suicidal *puputan* (a warrior's fight to the death) or complete conquest by the neighbouring kingdoms or the colonial power.

◉ Sights & Activities

Pura Kehen   TEMPLE
The state temple of the Bangli kingdom, **Pura Kehen** (adult/child 6000/3000Rp; ⊙9am-5pm), one of the finest temples in eastern Bali, is a miniature version of Pura Besakih. It is terraced up the hillside, with a flight of steps leading to the beautifully decorated entrance. The first courtyard has a huge banyan tree with a *kulkul* (hollow tree-trunk warning drum) entwined in its branches. Chinese porcelain plates were set into the walls as decoration, but most of the originals have been damaged or lost. The inner courtyard has an 11-roof *meru* (multitiered shrine), and there are other shrines with thrones for the Hindu trinity – Brahma, Shiva and Vishnu. The carvings are particularly intricate. See if you can count all 43 altars.

There's a counter opposite the temple entrance where you pay your admission.

Pura Dalem Penunggekan   TEMPLE
The exterior wall of this fascinating temple of the dead features vivid relief carvings of wrong-doers getting their just desserts in the afterlife. One panel addresses the lurid fate of adulterers (men in particular may find the viewing uncomfortable). Other panels portray sinners as monkeys, while another is a good representation of evil-doers begging to be spared the fires of hell. It's to the south of the centre.

Sasana Budaya Giri Kusuma   VENUE
Supposedly a showplace for Balinese dance, drama, gamelan and the visual arts, this large arts centre is mostly quiet. But it's well maintained, so it's worth popping by in case one of the large ceremonies held here is on, or just to admire the grounds.

Bukit Demulih   NATURAL FEATURE
Three kilometres west of Bangli is the village of Demulih, and a hill called Bukit Demulih. If you can't find the sign pointing to it, ask local children to direct you. After a short climb to the top, you'll see a small temple and good views over south Bali.

On the way to Bukit Demulih, a steep side road leads down to Tirta Buana, a **public swimming pool** in a lovely location deep in the valley, visible through the trees from the road above. You can take a vehicle most of the way down, but the track peters out and you'll need to walk the last 100m or so.

🛏 Sleeping & Eating

A *pasar malam* (night market), on the street beside the bemo terminal, has some good warung, and you'll also find some in the market area during the day.

Bangli Inn   GUESTHOUSE $
(☑91 419; Jl Rambutan 1; r 150,000Rp) Somewhat modern and popular with locals,

the 10 cold-water rooms are clean and include breakfast. You'd only stay here if you wanted to hang at the night market for the evening, which – given the freshness of the food and the lack of other visitors – might be a good thing indeed.

❶ Information

The compact centre has a **Bank BRI** (Jl Kutai) with ATM. There's also a police station and a post office. The shambolic market makes a diverting stroll; watch where you step.

❶ Getting There & Away

Bangli is located on the main road between Denpasar's Batubulan terminal (17,000Rp) and Gunung Batur, via Penelokan.

Semarapura (Klungkung)

☏0366

A tidy regional capital, Semarapura should be on your itinerary for its fascinating Kertha Gosa complex, a relic of Bali from the time before the Dutch. Once the centre of Bali's most important kingdom, Semarapura is still commonly called by its old name, Klungkung.

It's a good place to stroll and get a feel for modern Balinese life. The markets are large, the shops many and the streets are almost pleasant now that the coast road has diverted a lot of the traffic away.

History

Successors to the Majapahit conquerors of Bali established themselves at Gelgel (just south of modern Semarapura) around 1400, the Gelgel dynasty strengthening the growing Majapahit presence on the island. During the 17th century the successors of the Gelgel line established separate kingdoms, and the dominance of the Gelgel court was lost. The court moved to Klungkung in 1710, but never regained a pre-eminent position.

In 1849 the rulers of Klungkung and Gianyar defeated a Dutch invasion force at Kusamba. Before the Dutch could launch a counter-attack, a force from Tabanan arrived and the trader Mads Lange was able to broker a peace settlement.

For the next 50 years, the south Bali kingdoms squabbled, until the rajah of Gianyar petitioned the Dutch for support. When the Dutch finally invaded the south, the king of Klungkung had a choice between a suicidal *puputan,* like the rajah of Denpasar, or an ignominious surrender, as Tabanan's rajah

had done. He chose the former. In April 1908, as the Dutch surrounded his palace, the Dewa Agung and hundreds of his relatives and followers marched out to certain death from Dutch gunfire or the blades of their own kris (traditional daggers). It was the last Balinese kingdom to succumb and the sacrifice is commemorated in the large **Puputan Monument**.

◉ Sights

TOP CHOICE **Taman Kertha Gosa**   HISTORIC SITE
(adult/child 12,000/6000Rp, parking 2000Rp; ⊙7am-6pm) When the Dewa Agung dynasty moved here in 1710, the Semara Pura was established. The palace was laid out as a large square, believed to be in the form of a mandala, with courtyards, gardens, pavilions and moats. The complex is sometimes referred to as Taman Gili (Island Garden). Most of the original palace and grounds were destroyed by Dutch attacks in 1908 – the **Pemedal Agung**, the gateway on the south side of the square, is all that remains of the palace itself (but it's worth a close look to see the carvings). Two important buildings are preserved in a restored section of the grounds, and, with a museum, they comprise the Taman Kertha Gosa complex. Although vendors are persistent, parking is easy and it's easy to explore the town from here.

Kertha Gosa
In the northeastern corner of the complex, the 'Hall of Justice' was effectively the supreme court of the Klungkung kingdom, where disputes and cases that could not be settled at the village level were eventually brought. This open-sided pavilion is a superb example of Klungkung architecture. The ceiling is completely covered with fine paintings in the Klungkung style. The paintings, done on asbestos sheeting, were installed in the 1940s, replacing cloth paintings that had deteriorated.

The rows of ceiling panels depict several themes. The lowest level illustrates five tales from Bali's answer to the *Arabian Nights,* where a girl called Tantri spins a different yarn every night. The next two rows are scenes from Bima's travels in the afterlife, where he witnesses the torment of evil-doers. The gruesome tortures are shown clearly, but there are different interpretations of which punishment goes with what crime. (There's an authoritative explanation in *The Epic of Life – A Balinese Journey of the Soul* by Idanna Pucci, available

Semarapura

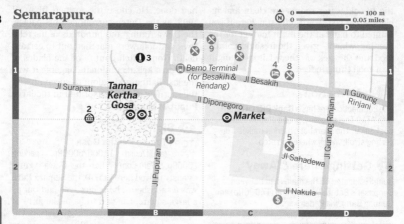

Semarapura

⊙ Top Sights
Market...C1
Taman Kertha Gosa............................B1

⊙ Sights
1 Kertha Gosa..............................B1
2 Museum Semarajaya....................A1
3 Puputan Monument......................B1

🛏 Sleeping
4 Klungkung Tower Hotel.................C1

✗ Eating
5 Bali Indah.................................C2
6 Market Stalls.............................C1
7 Pasar Senggol...........................B1
8 Puri Ajengan.............................C1
9 Tragia......................................C1

for reference in the pavilion.) The fourth row of panels depicts the story of Garuda's (mythical man-bird) search for the elixir of life, while the fifth row shows events on the Balinese astrological calendar. The next three rows return to the story of Bima, this time travelling in heaven, with doves and a lotus flower at the apex of the ceiling.

Bale Kambang
The ceiling of the beautiful 'Floating Pavilion' is painted in Klungkung style. Again, the different rows of paintings deal with various subjects. The first row is based on the astrological calendar, the second on the folk tale of Pan and Men Brayut and their 18 children, and the upper rows on the adventures of the hero Sutasona.

Museum Semarajaya
This diverting museum has an interesting collection of archaeological and other pieces. There are exhibits of *songket* (silver- or gold-threaded cloth) weaving and palm toddy (palm wine) and palm-sugar extraction. Don't miss the moving display about the 1908 *puputan*, along with some interesting old photos of the royal court. The exhibit on salt-making gives you a good idea of the hard work involved (see the boxed text, p202).

Pura Taman Sari   TEMPLE
The quiet lawns and ponds around this temple, northeast of the Taman Kertha Gosa complex, make it a relaxing stop and live up to the translation of its name: Flower Garden Temple. The towering 11-roofed *meru* indicates that this was a temple built for royalty, today it seems built for the geese who wander the grounds.

🛏 Sleeping & Eating
Klungkung Tower Hotel (☑25637; Jl Gunung Rinjani 18; r 225,000-375,000Rp; ❄@) is a recently built hotel aimed at business travellers; its 20 rooms are fairly slick and include satellite TV. Bathrooms have walk-in showers.

The best bet for food locally is the **market stalls** with all manner of lunch items. **Tragia** (☑21997; Jl Gunung Batukaru) is a rather tragic supermarket but vital if you need water, while **Pasar Senggol** (☺5pm-midnight) is a night market and by far the best spot to eat if you're in town late. It's the usual flurry of woks, customers and noise.

Since 1943, **Bali Indah** (☑21056; Jl Nakula 1; dishes 10,000-20,000Rp) has served a classic Chinese and local menu of cheap rice dishes, fresh juices and iced treats. Klungkung Tower Hotel's restaurant, **Puri Ajengan** (mains 7000-16,000Rp), has a simple menu of Indonesian and Balinese fare. The bar has popular pool tables.

ℹ Information

Jl Nakula and the main street, Jl Diponegoro, have several banks with ATMs.

ℹ Getting There & Away

The best way to visit Semarapura is with your own transport and as part of a circuit taking in other sites up the mountains and along the coast.

Bemo from Denpasar (Batubulan terminal) pass through Semarapura (23,000Rp) on the way to points further east. They can be hailed from near the Puputan Monument.

Bemo heading north to Besakih (12,000Rp) leave from the centre of Semarapura, a block northeast of Kertha Gosa. Most of the other bemo leave from the inconvenient Terminal Kelod, about 2km south of the city centre.

Around Semarapura

East of Semarapura, the main road dramatically crosses Sungai Unda (Unda River), then swings south towards Kusamba and the sea. Lava from the 1963 eruption of Gunung Agung destroyed villages and cut the road here, but the lava flows are now overgrown.

TIHINGAN

Several workshops in Tihingan are dedicated to producing **gamelan instruments**. Small foundries make the resonating bronze bars and bowl-shaped gongs, which are then carefully filed and polished until they produce the correct tone. Some pieces are on sale, but most of the instruments are produced for musical groups all over Bali.

Workshops with signs out front are good for visits. Look for the welcoming **Tari Gamelan** (☑22339) amid many along the main strip. The often hot work is usually done very early in the morning when it's cool, but at other times you'll still likely see something going on.

From Semarapura, head west along Jl Diponegoro and look for the signs.

SEMARAPURA MARKET

Semarapura's sprawling **market** is one of the best in east Bali. It's a vibrant hub of commerce and a meeting place for people of the region. You can easily spend an hour wandering about the warren of stalls on three levels. It's grimy, yes, but also endlessly fascinating. Huge straw baskets of lemons, limes, tomatoes and other produce are islands of colour amid the chaos. Glittering jewellery stalls crowd up against shops selling nothing but plastic buckets. On breezeways out back, climb to the top for **views** of multicultural Semarapura, where mosque minarets crowd the sky along with Balinese temples. Mornings are the best time to visit.

The market merges into Jl Diponegoro, where you'll find dusty **curio shops** seemingly as old as the battered goods inside.

NYOMAN GUNARSA MUSEUM

Dedicated to classical and contemporary Balinese painting, this beautiful **museum complex** (☑22256; adult/child 25,000Rp/free; ⊘9am-4pm Mon-Sat) was established by Nyoman Gunarsa, one of the most respected and successful modern artists in Indonesia. A vast three-storey building exhibits an impressive variety of well-displayed older pieces, including stone carvings and woodcarvings, architectural antiques, masks, ceramics and textiles.

Many of the classical paintings are on bark paper and are some of the oldest surviving examples. Check out the many old puppets, still seemingly animated even in retirement. The top floor is devoted to Gunarsa's own bold, expressionistic depictions of traditional life. Look for *Offering*.

A large space nearby features regular performances – check for times. Enjoy some fine examples of traditional architecture in the compound, a serene place where visitors are always outnumbered by flocks of songbirds.

The museum is about 4km west from Semarapura, near a bend on the Gianyar road – look for the dummy policemen at the base of a large statue nearby.

KAMASAN

This quiet, traditional village is the place where the classical **Kamasan painting style** originated, and several artists still practise this art. You can see their workshops and small showrooms along the main street. **Suar Gallery** (☏22064) is a good starting place; its owner, Gede Wedasmura, is a well-known painter.

The local painting style is often a family affair, with one person inking the outlines while another mixes the paints and yet another applies the colours. Paintings depict traditional stories or Balinese calendars, and although they are sold in souvenir shops all over Bali, the quality is better here. Look for smooth and distinct linework, evenly applied colours and balance in the overall composition. The village is also home to families of *bokor* artisans, who produce the silver bowls used in traditional ceremonies.

To reach Kamasan, go about 2km south of Semarapura and look for the turn-off to the east.

GELGEL

Situated about 2.5km south of Semarapura on the way to the coast road and 500m south of Kamasan, Gelgel was once the seat of Bali's most powerful dynasty. The town's decline started in 1710, when the court moved to present-day Semarapura, and finished when the Dutch bombarded the place in 1908.

Today the wide streets and the surviving temples are only faintly evocative of past grandeur. **Pura Dasar Bhuana** has huge banyan trees shading grassy grounds where you may feel the urge for a quiet contemplative stroll. The vast courtyards are a clue to its former importance, and festivals here attract large numbers of people from all over Bali.

About 500m to the east, the **Masjid Gelgel** is Bali's oldest mosque. Although modern-looking, it was established in the late 16th century for the benefit of Muslim missionaries from Java, who were unwilling to return home after failing to make any converts.

BUKIT JAMBAL

The road north of Semarapura climbs steeply into the hills via Bukit Jambal, which is understandably popular for its magnificent views. Several restaurants here provide buffet lunches for tour groups. This road continues to Rendang and Pura Besakih.

SUNGAI UNDA & SUNGAI TELAGAWAJA

East of Semarapura, the main road crosses the dammed-up Sungai Unda. Further upstream, Sungai Telagawaja (Telagawaja River) is used for white-water rafting trips (see the boxed text, p36).

Sidemen Road

☏0366

Winding through one of Bali's most beautiful river valleys, the Sidemen road offers marvellous paddy-field scenery, a delightful rural character and extraordinary views of Gunung Agung (when the clouds permit). It's getting more popular every year as a verdant escape, where a walk in any direction is a communion with nature.

German artist Walter Spies lived in Iseh for some time from 1932 in order to escape the perpetual party of his own making in Ubud. Later the Swiss painter Theo Meier, nearly as famous as Spies for his influence on Balinese art, lived in the same house.

The village of Sidemen has a spectacular location and is a centre for culture and arts, particularly *endek* cloth and *songket*. **Pelangi Weaving** (☏23012; Jl Soka 67; ☉8am-6pm) has a couple of dozen employees busily creating downstairs, while upstairs you can relax with the Sidemen views from comfy chairs outside the showroom.

There are many **walks** through the rice fields and streams in the multihued green valley. One involves a spectacular 2½-hour climb up to **Pura Bukit Tageh**, a small temple with big views. No matter where you stay, you'll be able to arrange guides for in-depth trekking (about 45,000Rp per hour), or just set out on your own exploration.

🛏 Sleeping & Eating

Views throughout the area are sweeping, from terraced green hills to Gunung Agung. Most inns have restaurants; it can get cool and misty at night.

Near the centre of Sidemen, a small road heads west for 500m to a fork and a signpost with the names of several places to stay. Meals can be arranged at all of these guesthouses, which are quite spread out.

TOP CHOICE Pondok Wisata
Lihat Sawah   GUESTHOUSE $
(☏530 0516; www.lihatsawah.com; r 250,000-600,000Rp) Take the right fork in the road

to this ever-expanding place with lavish gardens. All 12 rooms have views of the valley and mountain (the best have hot water and bathtubs, nice after an early morning hike). Water courses through the surrounding rice fields. A cafe offering Thai and Indo menu items shares the views (dishes 12,500Rp to 30,000Rp). It's worth stopping here just for their useful map of the area.

Subak Tabola Inn HOTEL $
(☎530 0648; r 350,000Rp-800,000Rp; ☀) Set in an impossibly green amphitheatre of rice terraces, nine rooms here have a bit of style and open-air bathrooms, while two very large bungalows are the real stars. Verandas have mesmerising views down the valley to the ocean. The grounds are spacious and there's a cool pool with frog fountains. It's nearly 2km from the hotel signpost.

Nirarta GUESTHOUSE $$
(Centre for Living Awareness; ☎24122; www .awareness-bali.com; Br Tabola; r €25-50) Guests here partake in serious programs for personal and spiritual development, including meditation intensives and yoga. The 11 comfortable rooms are split among six bungalows, some right on the babbling river.

Tanto Villa GUESTHOUSE $
(☎0812 395 0271; www.tanto-villa.com; r US$35-60) Views of the Luwah Valley are the appeal at this modern house, which has six large and comfortable rooms with hot water. Upstairs rooms have the best views of the surrounding chilli, bean and peanut fields.

Patal Kikian GUESTHOUSE $$
(☎530 0541; patalkikian@gmail.com; villas US$55-60; ☀) Two kilometres north of Sidemen look for a steep driveway on the eastern side of the road. This retreat has three spacious villas with verandas overlooking terraced hillsides; one of the best views in east Bali. Rooms have hot water, simple furnishings and tubs; there is a small pool.

Uma Agung GUESTHOUSE $
(☎41672; Jl Tebola; r 250,000-350,000Rp) With impossibly green views, this six-room inn is a tidy and well-run affair. A good cafe sits amongst the flower-filled gardens. Deluxe rooms have open-air bathrooms and greenstone tubs for soaking away the healthy glow from your walks.

Kubu Tani GUESTHOUSE $$
(☎530 0519; Jl Tebola; r 450,000-600,000Rp) There are three apartments at this two-storey house in a quiet location well away from other buildings. Open-plan living rooms have good views of the rice fields and mountains as well as large porches with loungers. Kitchens allow for cooking; there's no cafe close.

❶ Getting There & Away

The Sidemen road can be a beautiful part of any day trip from south Bali or Ubud. It connects in the north with the Rendang–Amlapura road just west of Duda. The road is in good shape and regular bemo shuttle up and down from Semarapura. A less-travelled route to Pura Besakih goes northeast from Semarapura, via Sidemen and Iseh, to another scenic treat: the Rendang–Amlapura road.

Pura Besakih

Perched nearly 1000m up the side of Gunung Agung is Bali's most important temple, Pura Besakih. In fact, it is an extensive complex of 23 separate but related temples, with the largest and most important being Pura Penataran Agung. Unfortunately, many people find it a disappointing (and dispiriting) experience due to the avarice of various local characters. See the boxed text, p183, for details that may help you decide whether to skip it.

The multitude of hassles aside, the complex comes alive during frequent ceremonies.

History
The precise origins of Pura Besakih are not totally clear, but it almost certainly dates from prehistoric times. The stone bases of Pura Penataran Agung and several other temples resemble megalithic stepped pyramids, and date back at least 2000 years. It was certainly used as a Hindu place of worship from 1284, when the first Javanese conquerors settled in Bali. By the 15th century, Besakih had become a state temple of the Gelgel dynasty.

◉ Sights
The largest and most important temple is **Pura Penataran Agung**. It is built on six levels, terraced up the slope, with the entrance approached from below, up a flight of steps. This entrance is an imposing *candi bentar* (split gateway), and beyond it, the even more impressive *kori agung* is the gateway to the second courtyard. You will find that it's most enjoyable during one of the frequent festivals, when

hundreds or even thousands of gorgeously dressed devotees turn up with beautifully arranged offerings. Note that tourists are not allowed inside this temple.

The other Besakih temples – all with individual significance and often closed to visitors – are markedly less scenic. Just as each village in Bali has a *pura puseh* (temple of origin), *pura desa* (village temple) and *pura dalem* (temple of the dead), Pura Besakih has three temples that fulfil these roles for Bali as a whole – Pura Basukian, Pura Penataran Agung and Pura Dalem Puri, respectively.

When it's mist-free, the view down to the coast is sublime.

For tips on respecting traditions and acting appropriately while visiting temples, see the boxed text, p329. For a directory of important temples, see p356.

ℹ Information

The temple's main entrance is 2km south of the complex on the road from Menanga and the south. Admission is 10,000Rp per person plus 5000Rp per vehicle. The fact that the vehicle fee is charged but not posted, nor a ticket dispensed for it, gives a taste of things to come.

About 200m past the ticket office, there is a fork in the road with a sign indicating Besakih to the right and Kintamani to the left. Go left, because going to the right puts you in the main parking area at the bottom of a hill some 300m from the complex. Going past the road to Kintamani, where there is another ticket office, puts you in the north parking area only 20m from the complex, and away from scammers at the main entrance.

ℹ Getting There & Away

The best way to visit is with your own transport, which allows you to explore the many gorgeous drives in the area.

You can visit by bemo from Semarapura (12,000Rp) but from other parts of Bali this can make the outing an all-day affair. Be sure to ask the driver to take you to the temple entrance, not to the village about 1km from the temple complex. Make certain you leave the temple by 3pm if you want to return to either Semarapura or Denpasar by bemo.

Gunung Agung

Bali's highest and most revered mountain, Gunung Agung is an imposing peak seen from most of south and east Bali, although it's often obscured by cloud and mist. Many sources say it's 3142m high, but some say it lost its summit in the 1963 eruption. The summit is an oval crater, about 700m across, with its highest point on the western edge above Besakih.

As it's the spiritual centre of Bali, traditional houses are laid out on an axis in line with Agung and many locals always know where they are in relation to the peak, which is thought to house ancestral spirits. Climbing the mountain takes you through verdant forest in the clouds and rewards with sweeping (dawn) views.

Climbing Gunung Agung

It's possible to climb Agung from various directions. The two shortest and most popular routes are from Pura Besakih, on the southwest side of the mountain, and from Pura Pasar Agung, on the southern slopes.

Points to consider for a climb:

» Use a guide.
» Respect your guide's pauses at shrines for prayers on the sacred mountain.

Pura Besakih Complex

AN UNHOLY EXPERIENCE

So intrusive are the scams and irritations faced by visitors to Besakih that many wish they had skipped the complex altogether. What follows are some of the ploys you should be aware of before a visit.

» Near the main parking area at the bottom of the hill is a building where guides hang around looking for visitors. Guides here may emphatically tell you that you need their services and quote a ridiculously high price of US$25 for a short visit. You don't: you may always walk among the temples, and no 'guide' can get you into a closed temple.

» Other 'guides' may foist their services on you throughout your visit. There have been reports of people agreeing to a guide's services only to be hit with a huge fee at the end.

» Once inside the complex, you may receive offers to 'come pray with me'. Visitors who seize on this chance to get into a forbidden temple can face demands of 100,000Rp or more.

» Get to the top before 8am – the clouds that often obscure the view of Agung also obscure the view *from* Agung.

» Take a strong torch (flashlight), extra batteries, plenty of water (2L per person), snack food, waterproof clothing and a warm jumper (sweater).

» The descent is especially hard on your feet, so wear strong shoes or boots and have manicured toes.

» Climb during the dry season (April to September); July to September are the most reliable months. At other times, the paths can be slippery and dangerous and the views are clouded over (especially true in January and February).

» Climbing Gunung Agung is not permitted when major religious events are being held at Pura Besakih, which generally includes most of April.

Guides

Trips with guides on either of the routes up Gunung Agung generally include breakfast and other meals as well as a place to stay, but be sure to confirm all details in advance. Guides are also able to arrange transport.

Most of the places to stay in the region, including those at Selat, along the Sidemen road and Tirta Gangga, will recommend guides for Gunung Agung climbs. Expect to pay a negotiable 450,000Rp to 800,000Rp for one or two people for your climb.

The following guides are recommended:

Gung Bawa Trekking (☑0812 387 8168; www.gb-trekking.blogspot.com) Experienced and reliable.

Ketut Uriada (☑0812 364 6426; Muncan) This knowledgeable guide can arrange transport for an extra fee (look for his small sign on the road east of Muncan).

Wayan Tegteg (☑0813 3852 5677; Selat) Wins reader plaudits.

Yande (☑0366-530 0887; Pura Agung Inn, Selat) Has many years on the mountain.

From Pura Pasar Agung

This route involves the least walking, because Pura Pasar Agung (Agung Market Temple) is high on the southern slopes of the mountain (around 1500m) and can be reached by a good road north from Selat. From the temple you can climb to the top in three or four hours, but it's a pretty demanding trek, so use a guide.

Start climbing from the temple at around 3am. There are numerous trails through the pine forest but after an hour or so you'll climb above the treeline. Then you're climbing on solidified lava, which can be loose and broken in places, but a good guide will keep you on solid ground. At the top (2900m), you can gawk into the crater, watch the sun rise over Lombok and see the shadow of Agung in the morning haze over southern Bali, but you can't make your way to the very highest point and you won't be able to see central Bali.

Allow at least six hours total for this trek.

From Pura Besakih

This climb is much tougher than the southern approach and is only for the very physically fit. For the best chance of a clear view before the clouds close in, you should start at midnight. Allow at least six hours for the climb, and four to six hours for the descent. The starting point is Pura Pengubengan, northeast of the main temple complex; attempting this without a guide would be folly.

Rendang to Amlapura

☑0366

A fascinating road goes around the southern slopes of Gunung Agung from Rendang almost to Amlapura. It runs through some superb countryside, descending more or less gradually as it goes east. Water flows everywhere and there are rice fields, orchards and carvers of stones for temples most of the way.

Cyclists enjoy the route and find going east to be a breezier ride.

You can get to the start of the road in Rendang from Bangli in the west on a very pretty road through rice terraces and thick jungle vegetation. **Rendang** itself is an attractive mountain village; the crossroads are dominated by a huge and historic banyan tree. After going east for about 3km, you'll come into a beautiful small valley of rice terraces. At the bottom is **Sungai Telagawaja**, a popular river for white-water rafting. Some companies (see the boxed text, p36) have their facilities near here.

The old-fashioned village of **Muncan** has quaint shingle roofs. It's approximately 4km along the winding road. Note the statues at the west entrance to town showing two boys: one a scholar and one showing the naked stupidity of skipping class. Nearby are scores of open-air factories where the soft lava rock is carved into temple decorations.

The road then passes through some of the most attractive rice country in Bali before reaching **Selat**, where you turn north to get to Pura Pasar Agung, a starting point for climbing Gunung Agung. **Puri Agung Inn** (☑530 0887; r 125,000-175,000Rp) has six clean and comfortable rooms; the inn has views of rice fields and stone carvers. You can arrange rice-field walks here or climbs up Gunung Agung with local guide Yande.

Just before **Duda**, the very scenic Sidemen road branches southwest via Sidemen to Semarapura. Further east, a side road (about 800m) leads to **Putung**. This area is superb for hiking: there's an easy-to-follow track from Putung to **Manggis**, about 8km down the hill.

Continuing east, **Sibetan** is famous for growing *salak,* the delicious fruit with a curious 'snakeskin' covering, which you can buy from roadside stalls. This is one of the villages you can visit on tours and homestays organised by **JED** (Village Ecotourism Network; ☑0361-735 320; www.jed.or.id; tours US$75-105), the non-profit group that organises rural tourism.

Northeast of Sibetan, a poorly signposted road leads north to Jungutan, with its **Tirta Telaga Tista** – a decorative pool and garden complex built for the water-loving old rajah of Karangasem.

The scenic road finishes at **Bebandem**, which has a cattle market every three days, and plenty of other stuff for sale as well. Bebandem and several nearby villages are home to members of the traditional metalworker caste, which includes silversmiths and blacksmiths.

Kusamba to Padangbai

The coast road from Sanur crosses the traditional route to the east at the fishing town of Kusamba before joining the road near Pura Goa Lawah.

KUSAMBA

A side road leaves the main road and goes south to the fishing and salt-making village of Kusamba, where you will see rows of colourful *prahu* (outrigger fishing boats) lined up all along the grey-sand beach. The fishing is usually done at night and the 'eyes' on the front of the boats help navigate through the darkness. The fish market in Kusamba displays the night's catch.

Local boats travel to Nusa Penida and Nusa Lembongan, which are clearly visible from Kusamba (boats from Padangbai are faster and safer). Both east and west of Kusamba, there are small salt-making huts lined up in rows along the beach – see the boxed text, p202.

East of Kusamba and 300m west of Pura Goa Lawah, **Merta Sari** (meals 15,000Rp; ☉10am-3pm) is renowned for its *nasi campur* (steamed rice with mixed goodies), which includes juicy, pounded fish satay; a slightly sour, fragrant fish broth; fish steamed in banana leaves; snake beans in a fragrant tomato-peanut sauce; and a firered sambal. The open-air pavilion is 300m north of the coast road in the village of Bingin. Look for the Merta Sari signs.

Also good is archrival **Sari Baruna** (meals 10,000-15,000Rp; ⊘10am-6pm), which also grills fish with attitude and authority. It's in a rickety bamboo hut about 200m west of Pura Goa Lawah. A large, modern car ferry links Kusamba daily with Nusa Penida (15,000Rp, two hours).

PURA GOA LAWAH

Three kilometres east of Kusamba is **Pura Goa Lawah** (Bat Cave Temple; adult/child 6000/3000Rp, car park 2000Rp; ⊘8am-6pm), which is one of nine directional temples in Bali. The cave in the cliff face is packed, crammed and jammed full of bats, and the complex is equally overcrowded with tour groups, foreign and local. You might exclaim 'Holy Bat Guano, Batman!' when you get a whiff of the odours emanating from the cave. Superficially, the temple is small and unimpressive, but it is very old and of great significance to the Balinese.

Legend says the cave leads all the way to Pura Besakih, some 19km away, but it's unlikely that you'd want to try this route. The bats provide sustenance for the legendary giant snake, the deity Naga Basuki, which is also believed to live in the cave.

Padangbai

☑ 0363

There's a real backpacker vibe about this funky little beach town that is also the port for the main public ferry connecting Bali with Lombok.

Padangbai is on the upswing. It sits on a small bay and has a nice little curve of beach. A whole compact seaside travellers' scene offers cheap places to stay and some fun cafes. A town beautification drive has cleaned up the beach and added a market area nearby.

The pace is slow, but should ambition strike there's good snorkelling and diving plus some easy walks and a couple of great beaches. Meanwhile you can soak up the languid air punctuated by the occasional arrival and departure of a ferry.

◐ Sights

Padangbai is interesting for a stroll. At the west end of town near the post office there's a small **mosque** and a temple, **Pura Desa**. Towards the middle of town are two more temples, **Pura Dalem** and **Pura Segara**,

and the central **market**, which is home to numerous vendors and cafes.

On a headland at the northeast corner of the bay, a path leads uphill to three temples, including **Pura Silayukti**, where Empu Kuturan – who introduced the caste system to Bali in the 11th century – is said to have lived. It is one of the four oldest in Bali.

Beaches

With its protected bay, Padangbai has a good beach right in front. Others are nearby; about 500m up and over the headland in the east is the small, light-sand **Blue Lagoon Beach**, an idyllic place with a couple of cafes and gentle, family-friendly surf.

To the southwest, you can drive 1.3km on a curving route past the mosque and Pura Desa or you can do a shadeless 800m hike up and over a hill past a failed hotel project to the grey sand of **Bias Tugal**, on the exposed coast outside the bay. It rewards the effort with a pretty cove setting and a couple of warung to sate your thirst. Note that the water here is subject to strong currents.

🏃 Activities

The Topi Inn arranges cultural workshops for guests and non-guests. The fee is 100,000Rp for a course of two to four hours.

Diving

There is good diving on the coral reefs around Padangbai, but the water can be a bit cold and visibility is not always ideal. The most popular local dives are **Blue Lagoon** and **Teluk Jepun** (Jepun Bay), both in Teluk Amuk, the bay just east of Padangbai. There's a good range of soft and hard corals and varied marine life, including sharks, turtles and wrasse, and a 40m wall at Blue Lagoon.

Several good local outfits offer diving trips in the area, including to Gili Tepekong and Gili Biaha, and on to Tulamben and Nusa Penida. All dive prices are competitive, costing US$70 for dives in the area to US$110 for trips out to Nusa Penida. This would be a cool town to hang out in while you get your PADI open-water certificate (US$400).

Recommended operators:

Geko Dive (☑41516; www.gekodive.com; Jl Silayukti) The longest-established operator; has a nice cafe across from the beach.

Water Worx (☑41220; www.waterworxbali.com; Jl Silayukti) Another good dive operator.

Snorkelling

One of the best and most accessible walk-in snorkel sites is off Blue Lagoon Beach. Note

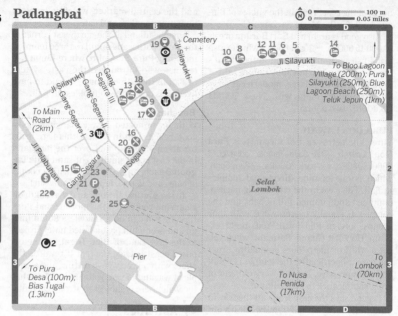

that it is subject to strong currents when the tide is out. Other sites such as Teluk Jepun can be reached by local boat (or check with the dive operators to see if they have any room on their dive boats). Snorkel sets cost about 30,000Rp per day.

Local *jukung* (boats) offer snorkelling trips (bring your own gear) around Padangbai (50,000Rp per person per hour) and as far away as Nusa Lembongan (400,000Rp for two passengers).

🛏 Sleeping

Accommodation in Padangbai – like the town itself – is pretty laid-back. Prices are fairly cheap and it's pleasant enough here that there's no need to hurry through to or from Lombok if you want to hang out on the beach and in cafes with other travellers. It's easy to wander the town comparing rooms before choosing one.

VILLAGE

In the village, there are several tiny places in the alleys, some with a choice of small, cheap downstairs rooms or bigger, brighter upstairs rooms.

Pondok Wisata Parta GUESTHOUSE **$**
(☏41 475, 0817 975 2668; off Gang Segara III; r 60,000-250,000Rp; ✼) The pick of the nine rooms in this hidden and snoozy spot is the 'honeymoon room', which has a harbour view and good breezes. The most expensive rooms have air-con and have a common terrace and views.

Zen Inn GUESTHOUSE **$**
(☏41 418; www.zeninn.com; Gang Segara; r 130,000-150,000Rp; ✼🛜) Close to the ferry terminal, Zen's three rooms are eclectically decorated with bamboo and rattan interiors and both indoor and outdoor showers. Extra money gets hot water and air-con. The cafe is faded hip.

Darma Homestay GUESTHOUSE **$**
(☏41 394; Gang Segara III; r with fan/air-con 100,000/200,000Rp; ✼@) A classic Balinese family homestay. The more expensive of the 12 rooms have hot showers and air-con; go for the private room on the top floor.

Kembar Inn GUESTHOUSE **$**
(☏41 364; kembarinn@hotmail.com; r 100,000-250,000Rp; ✼) There are 11 rooms (some with fans) at this inn linked by a steep and narrow staircase. The best awaits at the top and has a private terrace with views.

JL SILAYUKTI

On this little strip at the east end of the village, places are close together and right across from the sand.

Topi Inn GUESTHOUSE $

(☎41 424; www.topiinn.com; Jl Silayukti; r from 90,000Rp; @ 🛜) Sitting at the end of the strip in a serene location, Topi has five pleasant rooms, some of which share bathrooms. The enthusiastic owners offer courses in cooking, among other diversions. The cafe is excellent.

Padangbai Beach Resort HOTEL $

(☎41 417; Jl Silayukti; r US$35-52; ⊛ 🛋) The bungalows are attractive, with open-air bathrooms, and set in a classic Balinese garden setting that boasts a large pool across from the beach. The top rooms have air-con and the ones in front have nice, easy-going beach views.

Padangbai Billabong GUESTHOUSE $

(☎41 399; Jl Silayukti; r 100,000-250,000Rp) We prefer the bungalows right up front at this scrupulously tidy place, which has 12 rooms set amid immaculate gardens. It often seems to have rooms when others on the strip are full.

Hotel Puri Rai HOTEL $

(☎41 385; purirai_hotel@yahoo.com; Jl Silayukti 3; r with fan/air-con 300,000/400,000Rp; ⊛ 🛋) The Puri Rai has 30 rooms, some with fans, in a two-storey stone building pleasantly facing the good-sized pool. Other rooms en-

joy harbour views or overlook a yucky parking area. Ask to see a couple.

Padangbai Beach Inn GUESTHOUSE $

(☎41 439; Jl Silayukti; r 100,000-180,000Rp) The 18 cold-water rooms in cute bungalows are the pick, but try to avoid the rice-barn-style two-storey cottages, which can get hot and stuffy. Breakfast omelettes are a treat.

Made's Homestay GUESTHOUSE $

(☎41 441; Jl Silayukti; r 80,000-1200,000Rp) Four basic, clean and simple rooms are behind the Gilicat office.

BLUE LAGOON BEACH

Bloo Lagoon Village HOTEL $$

(☎41 211; www.bloolagoon.com; r from US$120; ⊛ @ 🛋) Perched above Blue Lagoon Beach, the 25 cottages and villas here are all designed in traditional thatched style and the compound is dedicated to sustainable practices. Units come with one, two or three bedrooms and are well thought out and stylish.

✕ Eating & Drinking

Beach fare and backpacker staples are what's on offer in Padangbai – lots of fresh seafood, Indonesian classics, pizza and, yes, banana pancakes. Most of the places to stay have a cafe. You can easily laze away a few hours soaking up the scene at the places along Jl Segara and Jl Silayukti, which have harbour views during the day and cool breezes in the evening.

TOP CHOICE **Ozone Café** GLOBAL $
(📞41 501; dishes 15,000-35,000Rp) This popular travellers' gathering spot has more character than every other place in east Bali combined. Slogans cover the walls, including this example from a wall of dating advice: 'Men are like chocolate, first they are sweet but then they make stomach fat.' Ozone has pizza and live music, sometimes by patrons.

Topi Inn CAFE $
(📞41 424; Jl Silayukti; mains 18,000-40,000Rp) Juices, shakes and good coffees served up throughout the day. Breakfasts are big, and whatever is landed by the fishing boats outside the front door during the day is grilled by night. The seats right out on the sandy road are conducive to permanent hanging out.

Depot Segara SEAFOOD $
(📞41 443; Jl Segara; dishes 10,000-30,000Rp) Fresh seafood such as barracuda, marlin and snapper is prepared in a variety of ways at this popular cafe. Enjoy harbour views from the slightly elevated terrace. In a town where casual is the byword, this is the slightly nicer option.

Zen Inn GLOBAL $
(📞41 418; Gang Segara; dishes 18,000-30,000Rp; 🛜) Burgers and other meaty mains with a Dutch accent are served in this dark cafe that goes late by local standards – often until 11pm. Lose yourself on the loungers.

Joe's Bar GLOBAL $
(📞0819 3307 2907; Jl Segara; mains 25,000Rp) A menu of martinis gets you ready for the Lombok ferry. Recline on sofas or sit erect for typical Indo and Western chow.

Babylon Bar (Jl Silayukti) and **Kinky Reggae Bar** (Jl Silayukti) are tiny adjoining bars in the market area back off the beach. They have a few chairs, tables and pillows scattered about and are perfect places to while away the evening with new friends.

🛍 Shopping

Year after year, **Ryan Shop** (📞41 215; Jl Segara 38) is still the name you can trust for quality. It has a fair selection of secondhand paperbacks and sundries.

ⓘ Information

Bank BRI (Jl Pelabuhan) exchanges money and has an ATM.

You can find public internet access (per minute 300Rp) at Darma Homestay.

ⓘ Getting There & Away

Bemo

Padangbai is 2km south of the main Semarapura-Amlapura road. Bemo leave from the car park in front of the port; orange bemo go east through Candidasa to Amlapura (10,000Rp); blue or white bemo go to Semarapura (10,000Rp).

Boat

Anyone who carries your luggage on or off the ferries at the piers will expect to be paid, so agree on the price first or carry your own stuff. Also, watch out for scams where the porter may try to sell you a ticket you've already bought.

LOMBOK & GILI ISLANDS There are many ways to travel between Bali and Lombok.

Public ferries (adult/child 31,000/19,000Rp) travel nonstop between Padangbai and Lembar on Lombok. Motorbikes cost 86,000Rp and cars cost 555,000Rp – go through the weighbridge at the west corner of the Padangbai car park. Passenger tickets are sold near the pier. Boats supposedly run 24 hours and leave about every 90 minutes, but the service is often unreliable – boats have caught on fire and run aground.

Perama has a 40-passenger boat (300,000Rp, six hours), which usually leaves at 9am for Senggigi, where you can connect to the Gilis, although at times it runs there direct. Check details at the **Perama office** (📞41419; Café Dona, Jl Pelabuhan; ⊙7am-8pm).

Gilicat (📞0361-271 680; www.gilicat. com) serves Gili Trawangan in a fast boat (660,000Rp, 90 minutes). Its local agent is at **Made's Homestay** (Jl Silayukti).

NUSA PENIDA On the beach just east of the car park, you'll find the twin-engine **fast boats** that run across the strait to Buyuk (40,000Rp, 45 minutes), 1km west of Sampalan on Nusa Penida. The boats run between 7am and noon. A modern car ferry makes the run in about two hours (passenger fare 15,000Rp) from nearby Kusamba.

Bus

To connect with Denpasar, catch a bemo out to the main road and hail a bus to the Batubulan terminal (18,000Rp).

Tourist Buses

Perama (📞41419; Café Dona, Jl Pelabuhan; ⊙7am-8pm) has a stop here for its services around the east coast.

DESTINATION	FARE	DURATION
Candidasa	25,000Rp	30min
Kuta	60,000Rp	3hr
Lovina	150,000Rp	5hr
Sanur	60,000Rp	2¼hr
Ubud	50,000Rp	1¼hr

Padangbai to Candidasa

☑0363

It's 11km along the main road from the Padangbai turn-off to the tourist town of Candidasa. Between the two towns is an attractive stretch of coast, which has some tourist development, and a large oil-storage depot in Teluk Amuk.

A short way east, the new cruise-ship port at Tanah Ampo has proved a flop. Visions of mega-ships docking and spewing 5000 free-spending tourists into east Bali were fantasies after it was discovered that the new dock had been built in water too shallow for cruise ships. Blame is going around and around (Benoa Harbour is also too shallow for large cruise ships.)

It's worth prowling some of the beachside lanes off the main road for places to stay.

MANGGIS

A pretty village inland from the coast, Manggis is the address used by several luxury resorts hidden along the water.

Two of the island's best hotels are off the main road along here.

One of Bali's best resorts, the **Amankila** (☑41 333; www.amankila.com; villas from US$800; ❄@☎☲), is perched along the jutting cliffs. About 5.6km beyond the Padangbai turn-off and 500m past the road to Manggis, a discreetly marked side road leads to the hotel. It features an isolated seaside location with views to Nusa Penida and even Lombok. The renowned architecture boasts three main swimming pools that step down to the sea in matching shades of blue that actually doesn't seem real. Of the restaurants here, the casual yet superb **Terrace** (lunch 100,000-200,000Rp) has a creative and varied menu with global and local influences. Service vies with the view for your plaudits.

About 1km further on from the Amankila, the **Alila Manggis** (☑41 011; www.alilahotels.com; r US$170-300; ❄@☎☲) has elegant, white, thatch-roofed buildings in spacious lawn gardens facing a beautiful stretch of secluded beach. The 55 rooms are large with stylish interiors that are heavy on creams with muted wood accents; go for deluxe ones on the upper floor to enjoy the best views. The restaurant, **Seasalt** (meals US$15-30), features much-lauded organic fusion and Balinese cuisine. Activities include a kids' camp, a spa and cooking courses.

MENDIRA & SENGKIDU

Coming from the west, there are hotels and guesthouses well off the main road at Mendira and Sengkidu, before you reach Candidasa. Although the beach has all but vanished and unsightly sea walls have been constructed, this area is a good choice for a quiet getaway if you have your own transport. Think views, breezes and a good book.

🛏 Sleeping

All of the following are on small tracks between the main road and the water; none are far from Candidasa but all have a sense of isolation that makes them seem far from everywhere. They are reached via narrow roads from a single turn-off from the main road 1km west of Candidasa. Look for a large sign listing places to stay, a school and a huge banyan tree.

Amarta Beach Inn Bungalows GUESTHOUSE **$**
(☑41 230; r 150,000-170,000Rp; @) In a panoramic seaside setting, the 10 units here are right on the water and are great value. The more expensive ones have hot water and interesting open-air bathrooms. At low tide there is a tiny beach; at other times you can sit and enjoy the views out to Nusas Lembongan and Penida.

Pondok Pisang GUESTHOUSE **$$**
(☑41 065; www.pondokpisang.com; r US$50-65) The name here means 'Banana Hut', and there's plenty of appeal (and plenty of banana trees). Six spacious two-level bungalows face the sea in a large compound. Each has an artful interior, including mosaic-tiled bathrooms. Yoga intensives are held at various times. In a small workshop local ladies sew textiles, which are then sold at the Bananas Batik boutique in Seminyak.

Anom Beach Inn HOTEL **$$**
(☑419 024; www.anom-beach.com; r US$25-60; ❄☲) This older resort from a simpler time has 24 rooms in a variety of configurations. The cheapest are fan-only – not a problem given the constant offshore breezes. The

WORTH A TRIP

MANGGIS TO PUTUNG ROAD

Winding up a lush hillside scented with cloves, the little-used road linking Manggis on the coast with the mountain village of Putung is worth a detour no matter which way you are heading: east or west, up or down. Heading up you'll round curves to see east Bali and the islands unfolding before you. After stopping for photos, you'll feel good until you round another curve and the views are even better. At some scenic points, adorable families will appear offering beautiful handmade baskets for about 30,000Rp. It's hard not to exceed your basket-buying quota.

Coming from Manggis the road is in good shape for the first half but then deteriorates the rest of the way. It remains just OK for cars but you'll want to go slow for the views anyway; give it an hour.

best are bungalow-style with air-con and fridges. Many customers have been coming for years and couldn't imagine staying anyplace else.

TENGANAN

Step back several centuries with a visit to Tenganan, home of the Bali Aga people – the descendants of the original Balinese who inhabited Bali before the Majapahit arrival in the 11th century.

The **Bali Aga** are reputed to be exceptionally conservative and resistant to change. Well, that's only partially true: TVs and other modern conveniences are hidden away in the traditional houses. But it is fair to say that the village has a much more traditional feel than most other villages in Bali. Cars and motorcycles are forbidden from entering. It should also be noted that this a real village, not a creation for tourists.

The most striking feature of Tenganan is its postcard-like beauty, with the hills providing a photogenic backdrop. The village is surrounded by a wall, and consists basically of two rows of identical houses stretching up the gentle slope of a hill. As you enter the village (5000Rp donation), you'll likely be greeted by a guide who will take you on a tour – and generally lead you back to his family compound to look at textiles and *lontar* (specially prepared palm leaves) strips. Unlike Besakih, however, there's no pressure to buy anything, so you won't need your own armed guards. For more on *lontar* books, see the boxed text, p228.

A peculiar, old-fashioned version of the gamelan known as the *gamelan selunding* is still played here, and girls dance an equally ancient dance known as the Rejang. There are other Bali Aga villages nearby, including Tenganan Dauh Tenkad, 1.5km west off the Tenganan road, with a charming old-fashioned ambience and several weaving workshops.

⚘ Festivals

Tenganan is full of unusual customs, festivals and practices. At the month-long **Usaba Sambah Festival**, which usually starts in May or June, men fight with sticks wrapped in thorny *pandanus* leaves. At this same festival, small, hand-powered Ferris wheels are brought out and the village girls are ceremonially twirled around.

☞ Tours

To really experience the ambience and culture of the village, consider one of the tours offered by **JED** (Village Ecotourism Network; ☑ 0361-735 320; www.jed.or.id; tours US$75-105). These highly regarded excursions (some overnight) feature local guides who explain the culture in detail and show how local goods are produced. Tours include transport from south Bali and Ubud.

🛍 Shopping

A magical cloth known as *kamben gringsing* is woven here – a person wearing it is said to be protected against black magic. Traditionally this is made using the 'double ikat' technique, in which both the warp and weft threads are 'resist dyed' before being woven. MBAs would be thrilled studying the integrated production of the cloth: everything, from growing the cotton to producing the dyes from local plants to the actual production, is accomplished here. It's very time-consuming, and the exquisite pieces of double ikat available for sale are quite expensive (from 600,000Rp). You'll see cheaper cloth for sale but it usually comes from elsewhere in Bali.

Many baskets from across the region, made from *ata* palm, are on sale. Another local craft is traditional Balinese calligraphy, with the script inscribed onto *lontar* palm strips in the same way that the ancient *lontar* books were created. Most of these books are Balinese calendars or depictions of the *Ramayana*. They cost 150,000Rp to 300,000Rp, depending on quality.

Tenganan weaving is also sold in Ashitaba shops in Seminyak and Ubud.

❶ Getting There & Away

Tenganan is 3.2km up a side road just west of Candidasa. At the turn-off where bemo stop, motorcycle riders offer *ojek* (motorcycles that take passengers) rides to the village for about 10,000Rp. A nice option is to take an *ojek* up to Tenganan, and enjoy a shady downhill walk back to the main road, which has a Bali rarity: wide footpaths.

Candidasa

☏ 0363

Candidasa is a relaxed spot on the route east, with hotels and some decent restaurants. However, it also has problems stemming from decisions made three decades ago that should serve as cautionary notes to any previously undiscovered place that suddenly finds itself on the map.

Until the 1970s, Candidasa was just a quiet little fishing village, then beachside losmen (small hotels) and restaurants sprang up and suddenly it was *the* new beach sensation in Bali. As the facilities developed, the beach eroded – unthinkingly, offshore barrier-reef corals were harvested to produce lime for cement in the orgy of construction that took place – and by the late 1980s Candidasa was a beach resort with no beach.

Mining stopped in 1991, and concrete sea walls and breakwaters (newly beautified in 2008) have limited the erosion and now provide some tiny pockets of sand. The relaxed seaside ambience and sweeping views from the hotels built right on the water appeal to a more mature crowd of visitors. Candidasa is a good base from which to explore the interior of east Bali and the east coast's famous diving and snorkelling sites. As such it's a place to spend some quiet time; during the day you inevitably see people wandering around looking for something to do.

◉ Sights

Candidasa's temple, **Pura Candidasa** (admission by donation), is on the hillside across from the lagoon at the eastern end of the

village strip. It has twin temples devoted to the male-female gods Shiva and Hariti. The fishing village, just east of the lagoon, has colourful *prahu* (outrigger fishing boats) drawn up on what's left of the beach. In the early morning you can watch the boats coasting in after a night's fishing. By day the owners offer snorkelling trips to the reef and the nearby islets.

Apart from the Bali Aga village of Tenganan, there are several traditional villages inland from Candidasa and attractive countryside for walking.

Ashram Gandhi Chandi (☏41 108; Jl Raya Candidasa), a lagoon-side Hindu community, follows the pacifist teachings of Mahatma Gandhi. Guests may stay for short or extended periods, but are expected to participate in community life. Simple guest cottages by the ocean (about 300,000Rp) are handy after a long day of yoga here.

🏃 Activities

Diving and snorkelling (followed by sleeping) are the most popular activities in Candidasa. **Gili Tepekong**, which has a series of coral heads at the top of a sheer drop-off, is perhaps the best dive site. It offers the chance to see lots of fish, including some larger marine life. Other features include an underwater canyon, which can be dived in good conditions, but is always potentially hazardous. The currents here are strong and unpredictable, the water is cold and visibility is variable – it's recommended for experienced divers only.

Other dive sites are beside Gili Mimpang, further east at Gili Biaha, and Nusa Penida. A recommended and popular dive operator is **Dive Lite** (☏41 660; www.divelite.com; Jl Raya Candidasa; dives US$40-105), which dives the local area plus the rest of the island. An intro to diving course is an excellent deal: US$80 gets you a dive for basic instruction followed by a supervised fun dive. It's a great way to see if diving is for you. Snorkelling trips are US$30.

Hotels rent snorkel sets for about 30,000Rp per day. For the best snorkelling, take a boat to offshore sites or to Gili Mimpang (a one-hour boat trip should cost about 100,000Rp for up to three people).

On shore, you can catch up on your beauty treatments at the modest **Dewi Spa** (☏41 042; Jl Raya Candidasa; massage from US$8; ⊙9am-7pm). Waxing, steaming, rubbing, braiding and more are offered.

A more posh option is the **Alam Asmara Spa** (☏41929; ⊙9am-9pm) at the hotel of the

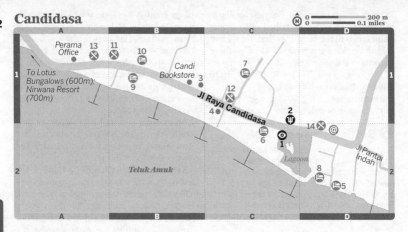

Candidasa

same name. Organic and natural products are used for a variety of traditional massages (from 150,000Rp) and treatments in a gently restful setting.

🛏 Sleeping

Candidasa's busy main drag is well supplied with seaside accommodation, as well as restaurants and other tourist facilities. Another group of places can be found immediately east of the centre along quiet Jl Pantai Indah. These are nicely relaxed and often have a sliver of beach. West of town also offers quiet lodging amid the flaccid lapping of the waves.

WEST OF CANDIDASA

The following pair is a short walk from Candidasa.

Nirwana Resort　　　　HOTEL **$$**
(☎41 136; www.thenirwana.com; r US$100-150; ❄@🛜☲) A dramatic walk across a lotus pond sets the tone at this intimate older resort that was given a massive refit. The 18 units (with DVD players and other niceties) are all near the now-standard infinity pool by the ocean. Rates are often discounted; go for one of six units right on the water.

Lotus Bungalows　　　　HOTEL **$$**
(☎41 104; www.lotusbungalows.com; half-board US$75-150; ❄@☲) Managed by earnest Europeans, the 20 rooms here (some with air-con, some completely remodelled) are in well-spaced, bungalow-style units. Four (numbers 101, 102, 113 and 114) are right on the ocean. The decor is bright and airy, and there is a large and inviting pool area. There is free nitrox at the dive centre here.

CENTRAL CANDIDASA

Kubu Bali Bungalows　　　HOMESTAY **$$**
(☎41 532; www.kububali.com; r US$50-65; ❄☲) Behind Kubu Bali restaurant and up a lane, this garden spot has streams, ponds and a swimming pool landscaped into a valley in the hillside. The 20 units have views over palm trees, the coast and the sea. Large porches have daybeds and the open-air marble bathrooms have tubs.

Hotel Ida's
GUESTHOUSE **$**

(☑41 096; jsidas1@aol.com; Jl Raya Candidasa; bungalows 150,000-280,000Rp) Set in a dense seaside grove of coconut trees so perfectly realised that it looks like a set for *South Pacific,* Ida's has five thatched bungalows with open-air bathrooms. Rustic balcony furniture, including a daybed, gets you to thinking just what you'd choose for 'Desert Island Discs' – for yet more tropical cliché.

Seaside Cottages
GUESTHOUSE **$**

(☑41 629; www.balibeachfront-cottages.com; Jl Raya Candidasa; cottages 100,000-450,000Rp; ❄@) The 15 rooms here are scattered in cottages and span the gamut from cold-water basic to restful units with air-con and tropical bathrooms. The seafront has loungers right along the breakwater. The Temple Café is a mellow place.

Alam Asmara
HOTEL **$$**

(☑41 929; www.alamasamara.com; r US$70-115; ❄@🛜❄) Walk on paths lined with little waterways at this private compound. The pool is on the ocean; the 12 rooms have a traditional yet stylish design with lots of space and details such as stone tubs and satellite TV. Ask about diving packages.

Watergarden
HOTEL **$$**

(☑41 540; www.watergardenhotel.com; Jl Raya Candidasa; r US$125-155; ❄🛜❄) The Watergarden lives up to its name with a swimming pool and fish-filled ponds that wind around the buildings. The gardens are lush and worth exploring. Each of the 13 rooms has a veranda projecting over the lily ponds, which are fresher than the somewhat dated interiors. The cafe is good for breakfast.

Rama Bungalows
GUESTHOUSE **$**

(☑41778; r with fan/air-con 260,000/360,000Rp) On a little road near the lagoon and ocean, the eight rooms are split between a two-storey stone structure and bungalows. Upstairs rooms have views of the lagoon and its birdlife.

EAST OF THE CENTRE
A small road winds through banana trees passing several low-key lodgings that span the budget categories. This is the nicest area for lodging in Candidasa as you are less than 10 minutes by foot from the centre yet there is no traffic noise. And you might find a ripe banana...

Sekar Orchid Beach Bungalows
GUESTHOUSE **$**

(☑41 086; www.sekar-orchid.com; Jl Pantai Indah 26; bungalows 250,000-400,000Rp) The grounds here live up to the name with orchids and bromeliads growing in profusion. There's a small beach; the six large rooms are good value with nice views from the 2nd floor. The site feels isolated but is only a short walk from the centre.

Puri Oka Bungalows
GUESTHOUSE **$**

(☑41 092; www.purioka.com; Jl Pantai Indah; r 200,000-600,000Rp; ❄❄) Hidden by a banana grove east of town. The cheapest of the 17 rooms here are fan-cooled and small, while the better ones have water views and extras like DVD players. The beachside pool is small and is next to a cafe; at low tide there's a small beach out front. Two new roomy bungalows are the pick here.

Villa Sasoon
VILLA **$$$**

(☑0818 0567 1467; www.villasasoon.com; Jl Pantai Indah; villas US$250-350; ❄@🛜❄) Four large private villas are in a quiet spot about a two-minute walk from the rocky shore. Each unit is a small compound with large open living areas (you can arrange for a chef) plus smaller bedroom units (you can use one or two). All are set around small pools behind walls, so your frolics stay private.

Puri Bagus Candidasa
HOTEL **$$**

(☑41 131; www.bagus-discovery.com; Jl Pantai Indah; r US$80-160; ❄❄) At the eastern end of the shore near an outcropping of outriggers, this mainstream resort is hidden away in the palm trees. The large pool and restaurant have good sea views; the beach is illusory. The 46 rooms have open-air bathrooms; look for deals.

✗ Eating

Some of the hotels, such as Lotus Bungalows, have seafront restaurants and cafes that are good for views at lunch and great for sea breezes and moonlight at night.

The places to eat along Jl Raya Candidasa are mostly simple and family-run, but you should beware of traffic noise, although it abates after dark. Where noted, many of these places are also good for a drink (but don't plan on staying out past, say, 10pm). If you're out of town, some places will provide transport, in which case, call.

Vincent's
GLOBAL **$$**

(☑41 368; www.vincentsbali.com; Jl Raya Candidasa; meals 50,000-150,000Rp) Candi's best is a deep and open place with several distinct rooms and a lovely rear garden with rattan lounge furniture. The bar is an oasis of jazz.

The menu combines excellent Balinese, fresh seafood and European dishes.

Toke Café
SEAFOOD $$

($\boxed{\nearrow}$41 991; Jl Raya Candidasa; meals 60,000-120,000Rp; $\widehat{\boxed{\approx}}$) The glass-enclosed kitchen at this mellow place turns out some good grilled seafood, including *ikan pepes* (fish with Balinese spices); there are also Indo specialties. It's got a nice old bar and is a good place for a cocktail or a glass of wine.

Candi Bakery & Bistro
GERMAN $$

($\boxed{\nearrow}$41883; Jl Tenganan; meals 40,000-150,000Rp) About 100m up from the Tenganan turn-off west of town, this smart cafe is worth the slight detour. The bakery specialises in delicious pastries, cakes and croissants. You can enjoy a menu of local and German meals plus steaks out on the tree-shaded veranda. Or just savour a Bavarian beer. A small **cafe** (Jl Raya Candidasa) in town has baked goods.

Kubu Bali Restaurant
ASIAN $$

($\boxed{\nearrow}$41 532; Jl Raya Candidasa; meals 40,000-120,000Rp) The open kitchen out the front at this airy, open-air dining pavilion (the roaring woks drown out the trucks) prepares Indonesian and Chinese dishes – including excellent seafood.

Temple Café
GLOBAL $

($\boxed{\nearrow}$41 629; Seaside Cottages, Jl Raya Candidasa; meals 30,000-70,000Rp) Global citizens can get a taste of home at this cafe attached to the Seaside Cottages. It has a few menu items from the owner's native Oz, such as Vegemite. The popular bar has a long drink list.

ⓘ Information

The closest ATMs are inconveniently located in Padangbai and Amlapura. For any serious shopping you'll need to visit the latter.

Candi Bookstore ($\boxed{\nearrow}$41 272; Jl Raya Candidasa 45) is a used-book shop run by a cute family.
Mr Grumpy's (Jl Raya Candidasa; $\widehat{\boxed{\approx}}$) belies its name with friendly service, internet access and computers plus drinks.

ⓘ Getting There & Away

Candidasa is on the main road between Amlapura and south Bali, but there's no terminal, so hail bemo as buses probably won't stop. You'll need to change in either Padangbai or Semarapura.

You can hire a ride to Amed in the far east for about 150,000Rp, and Kuta and the airport for 250,000Rp. Ask at your accommodation about vehicle and bicycle rental.

Perama ($\boxed{\nearrow}$41 114; Jl Raya Candidasa; $\odot$7am-7pm) is at the western end of the strip.

DESTINATION	FARE	DURATION
Kuta	60,000Rp	3½hr
Lovina	150,000Rp	5¼hr
Padangbai	25,000Rp	30min
Sanur	60,000Rp	2¾hr
Ubud	50,000Rp	1¾hr

Candidasa to Amlapura

The main road east of Candidasa curves up to **Pura Gamang Pass** (*gamang* means 'to get dizzy' – an overstatement), from where you'll find fine views down to the coast and lots of greedy-faced monkeys. If you walk along the coastline from Candidasa towards Amlapura, a trail climbs up over the headland, with fine views over the rocky islets off the coast. Beyond this headland there's a long sweep of wide, exposed black-sand beach.

PASIR PUTIH

No longer a secret, **Pasir Putih** is an idyllic white-sand beach whose name indeed means 'White Sand'. When we first visited in 2004, it was empty, save for a long row of fishing boats at one end. Just a few years, it is sort of an ongoing lab in seaside economic development.

A dozen thatched beach **warung** and **cafes** have appeared. You can get *nasi goreng* (fried rice) or grilled fish. Bintang is of course on ice and loungers await bikini-clad bottoms. The beach itself is truly lovely: a long crescent of white sand backed by coconut trees. At one end cliffs provide shade. The surf is often mellow; bring your own snorkelling gear to explore the waters.

The one thing saving Pasir Putih from being swamped is the difficult access. Look for crude signs with either 'Virgin Beach Club' or 'Jl Pasir Putih' near the village of Perasi. Turn off the main road (5.6km east of Candidasa) and follow a pretty paved track for about 1.5km to a temple where locals will collect a fee (2500Rp). You can park here and walk the gentle hill down or drive a further 600m directly to the beach on a road that barely qualifies as such.

As for any qualms you might have about furthering the commercialisation of this beach, here's what the locals told us: 'The money you pay us for a ticket we spend on our school and medicine.'

Meanwhile, the economic lab may be in its final semester: in 2010 we saw engineers carrying clipboards, taking measurements and talking about a resort.

TELUK PENYU

A little bend in the coast has earned the moniker Teluk Penyu, or Turtle Bay. The shelled critters do indeed come here to nest and there have been some efforts made to protect them. About 5km south of Amlapura, the area has attracted a few expats and villas. It also has one of the most interesting places to stay in this part of Bali.

 Turtle Bay Hideaway
(☎23611; www.turtlebayhideaway.com; Jl Raya Pura Mascime; cottages US$140-270; 🛜🌊) comprises a compound built from old wooden tribal houses brought over from Sulawesi. There are three units, all with ocean views, near a large tiled pool. Interiors combine exotic details and modern comforts – there are fridges and organic food is served. There are enough shady verandas, decks and loungers to keep you busy doing nothing for a week.

Amlapura

☎0363

Amlapura is the capital of Karangasem district, and the main town and transport junction in eastern Bali. The smallest of Bali's district capitals, it's a multicultural place with Chinese shophouses, several mosques, and confusing one-way streets (which are the tidiest in Bali). It's worth a stop to see the royal palaces but a lack of options means you'll want to spend the night elsewhere, such as Tirta Gangga.

Sights

Amlapura's three palaces, on Jl Teuku Umar, are decaying reminders of Karangasem's period as a kingdom at its most important when supported by Dutch colonial power in the late 19th and early 20th centuries.

Outside the orderly **Puri Agung Karangasem** (Jl Teuku Umar; admission 10,000Rp; ⊙8am-5pm), there are beautifully sculpted panels and an impressive three-tiered entry gate. After you pass through the entry courtyard (note how all entrances point you towards the rising sun in the east), a left turn takes you to the main building, known as the Maskerdam (Amsterdam), because it was the Karangasem kingdom's acquies-

cence to Dutch rule that allowed it to hang on long after the demise of the other Balinese kingdoms.

Inside you'll be able to see several rooms, including the royal bedroom and a living room with furniture that was a gift from the Dutch royal family. The Maskerdam faces the ornately decorated Bale Pemandesan, which was used for the royal tooth-filing ceremonies. Beyond this, surrounded by a pond, is the Bale Kambang, still used for family meetings and for dance practice.

Borrow one of the new English-language info sheets and think about what this compound must have been like when the Karangasem dynasty was at its peak in the 19th century, having conquered Lombok.

Across the street, **Puri Gede** (Jl Teuku Umar; donation requested; ⊙8am-6pm) is still used by the royal family. Surrounded by long walls, the palace grounds feature many brick buildings dating from the Dutch colonial period. Look for 19th-century stone carving and woodcarvings. The **Rangki**, the main palace building, has been returned to its glory and is surrounded by fish ponds. Catch the stern portrait of the late king AA Gede Putu, while his descendents laughingly play soccer nearby.

The other royal palace building, **Puri Kertasura**, is not open to visitors.

Eating & Shopping

Options are few in Amlapura; there are various **warung** around the market and the main bus/bemo terminal as well as a good **night market** (⊙5pm-midnight). A vast **Hardy's** (☎22 363; Jl Diponegoro) supermarket has groceries, sundries of all kinds and

---

ⓘ KARANGASEM INFO

The regency of Karangasem, which includes the coast from Pandangbai right around to an area north of Tulamben and all of Gunung Agung, has an excellent website (www.karangasem tourism.com) in English for travellers. Besides listing resources and businesses, it has a detailed calendar that is good at showing cultural listings, especially small ones that are easily overlooked. There's more info available at the tourist office in Amlapura.

a row of stalls cooking up good fresh Asian food fast. It has the best range of supplies, like sunscreen, east of Semarapura and south of Singaraja.

ℹ️ Information

The friendly staff at the **tourist office** (☎ 21 196; www.karangasemtourism.com; Jl Diponegoro; ⊙7am-3pm Mon-Thu, 7am-noon Fri) offer the booklet *Agung Info*, which is filled with useful detail, as is the website.

Bank BRI (Jl Gajah Mada) will change money. **Hardy's** (☎ 22 363; Jl Diponegoro) has ATMs. There is a **pharmacy** (Apotik; Jl Ngurah Rai 47; ⊙24hr) and a small hospital across the street.

ℹ️ Getting There & Away

Amlapura is a major transport hub. Buses and bemo regularly ply the main road to Denpasar's Batubulan terminal (25,000Rp; roughly three hours) via Candidasa, Padangbai and Gianyar. Plenty of minibuses also go around the north coast to Singaraja (about 20,000Rp) via Tirta Gangga, Amed and Tulamben.

Around Amlapura

Five kilometres south of Amlapura, **Taman Ujung** is a major complex that may leave you slack-jawed – and not necessarily with wonder. In 1921 the last king of Karangasem completed the construction of a grand water palace here, which was extensively damaged by an earthquake in 1979. A tiny vestige of the old palace is surrounded by vast modern ponds and terraces built for untold billions of rupiah. Today, the wind-swept grounds are seldom trod by visitors. It's a bit sad really and you can see all that you'd want to from the road. Just a bit further on is the interesting fishing village of **Ujung** (Edge) and the alternative road to Amed (see the boxed text, p199).

Tirta Gangga

☎ 0363

Tirta Gangga (Water of the Ganges) is the site of a holy temple, some great water features and some of the best views of rice fields and the sea beyond in east Bali. Capping a sweep of green flowing down to the distant sea, it is a relaxing place to stop for an hour. With more time you can hike the surrounding terraced countryside, which ripples with coursing water and is dotted with temples. A small valley of rice

terraces runs up the hill behind the parking area. It is a majestic vision of emerald steps receding into the distance.

◉ Sights

Amlapura's water-loving rajah, after completing his lost masterpiece at Ujung, had another go at building the water palace of his dreams. He succeeded at **Taman Tirta Gangga** (adult/child 5000/3000Rp, parking 2000Rp; ⊙site 24hr, ticket office 6am-6pm), which has a stunning crescent of rice-terrace-lined hills for a backdrop.

Originally built in 1948, the water palace was damaged in the 1963 eruption of Gunung Agung and again during the political events that rocked Indonesia two years later. Today it is an aquatic fantasy with several swimming pools and ornamental ponds filled with huge koi and lotus blossoms, which serve as a fascinating reminder of the old days of the Balinese rajahs. 'Pool A' (adult/child 6000/4000Rp) is the cleanest and is in the top part of the complex. 'Pool B' is pond-like. Look for the 11-tiered fountain and plop down under the huge old banyans.

🏃 Activities

Hiking in the surrounding hills transports you far from your memories of frenetic south Bali. This far east corner of Bali is alive with coursing streams through rice fields and tropical forests that suddenly open to reveal vistas taking in Lombok, Nusa Penida and the lush green surrounding lands stretching down to the sea. The rice terraces around Tirta Gangga are some of the most beautiful in Bali. Back roads and walking paths take you to many picturesque traditional villages.

Sights that make a perfect excuse for day treks are scattered in the surrounding hills. See p198 for a few. Or for the Full Bali, ascend the side of Gunung Agung. Among the possible treks is a six-hour loop to Tenganan village, plus shorter ones across the local hills, which include visits to remote temples and all the stunning vistas you can handle.

Guides for the more complex hikes are a good idea, as they help you plan routes and see things you simply would never find otherwise. Ask at any of the accommodation we've listed, especially Homestay Rijasa where the owner I Ketut Sarjana is an experienced guide. Another local guide who comes with good marks is **Komang Gede Sutama** (☎ 0813 3877 0893). Rates average about 50,000Rp per hour for one or two people.

cal classics which you enjoy overlooking the palace.

🛏 Sleeping & Eating

You can overnight in luxury in old royal quarters overlooking the water palace or lodge in humble surrounds in anticipation of an early morning trek. Many places to stay have cafes with mains under 20,000Rp and there's a cluster by the sedate fruit vendors near the shady parking area (2000Rp).

With the exception of Tirta Ayu Hotel and Tirta Gangga Villas, hot water is not a universal option.

Tirta Gangga Villas　　　VILLAS $$$
(🗷21 383; www.tirtagangga-villas.com; villas US$120-400; ☀) Built on the same terrace as the Tirta Ayu Hotel, the villas are parts of the old royal palace. Thoroughly updated – but still possessing that classic Bali-style motif – the villas look out over the water palace from large shady porches. Private cooks are available and you can arrange to rent the entire complex and preside over your own court under a 500-year-old banyan tree.

Tirta Ayu Hotel　　　HOTEL $$
(🗷22 503; www.hoteltirtagangga.com; villas US$125-200; ❋🛜☀) Right in the palace compound, this has four pleasant villas that are clean and have basic, modern decor in the limited palette of creams and coffees. Flop about like a fish in the hotel's private pool or use the vast palace facilities. The restaurant is a tad upscale (mains from 50,000Rp) and serves creative takes on lo-

Homestay Rijasa　　　HOMESTAY $
(🗷21 873, 0813 5300 5080; r 100,000-200,000Rp) With elaborately planted grounds, this well-run, nine-room homestay is a recommended choice opposite the water palace entrance. Better rooms have hot water, good for the large soaking tubs. The owner, I Ketut Sarjana, is an experienced trekking guide.

Good Karma　　　HOMESTAY $
(🗷22 445; r 120,000-200,000Rp) A classic homestay, Good Karma has four very clean and simple bungalows and a good vibe derived from the surrounding pastoral rice field. The good cafe's gazebos look towards the parking lot; often you'll see the winsome Nyoman playing bamboo flute music out front.

Puri Sawah Bungalows　　　GUESTHOUSE $
(🗷21 847; r 250,000-300,000Rp) Just up the road from the palace, Puri Sawah has four comfortable and spacious rooms and a family bungalow that sleeps six (with hot water). Besides Indo classics, the restaurant has some interesting sandwiches like 'avocado delight'.

Dhangin Taman　　　GUESTHOUSE $
(Friendly Hotel; 🗷22 059; r 60,000-100,000Rp) Adjacent to the water palace, this characterful place features elaborate tiled artworks in a garden. It has a range of 13 coldwater rooms – the cheapest ones facing the rice paddies are the best – and a simple

EAST BALI TIRTA GANGGA

DON'T MISS

PURA LEMPUYANG

We swear, you'll thank us for this.

One of Bali's nine directional temples and the one responsible for the east, **Pura Lempuyang** is perched on a hilltop on the side of 1058m Gunung Lempuyang, a twin of neighbouring 1175m Gunung Seraya. Together, the pair form the distinctive double peaks of basalt that loom over Amlapura to the south and Amed to the north. The Lempuyang temple is part of a compact complex that looks across the mottled green patchwork that is east Bali. Its significance means there are always faithful Balinese in meditative contemplation and you may wish to join them as you recover from the one key detail of reaching the temple: the 1700-step climb up the side of the 768m hill.

Reaching the base of the stairs is about a 30-minute walk from Tirta Gangga. Take the turn south off the Amlapura–Tulamben road to Ngis (2km), a palm-sugar and coffee-growing area, and follow the signs another 2km to Kemuda (ask for directions if the signs confuse you). From Kemuda, climb those steps to Pura Lempuyang, allowing at least two hours, one way. If you want to continue to the peaks of Lempuyang or Seraya, you should take a guide.

cafe with tables overlooking the palace. You leave your breakfast order hanging on the door, just like at the Hilton.

Pondok Lembah Dukah　　GUESTHOUSE **$**

(r from 100,000Rp) Down the path to the right of Good Karma, follow the signs for 300m along the rice field and then up a steep set of steps. Three basic bungalows are clean and have fans plus sweeping views over bougainvillea from their porches. Warning: you may go all the way and find no one.

Genta Bali　　INDONESIAN **$**

(☑22 436; meals 15,000-25,000Rp) Across the road from the parking area, you can find a fine yoghurt drink here, as well as pasta and Indonesian food. It has an impressive list of puddings, including ones with banana and jackfruit. Try out the black-rice wine.

ⓘ Getting There & Away

Bemo and minibuses making the east-coast haul between Amlapura and Singaraja stop at Tirta Gangga. The fare to Amlapura should be 7000Rp.

Around Tirta Gangga

The main road running from Amlapura through Tirta Gangga and on to Amed and the coast doesn't do the local attractions justice – although it is an attractive road. To appreciate things, you need to get off the main road or go hiking.

Throughout the area the *rontal* palms all look like new arrivals at army boot camp, as they are shorn of their leaves as fast as they grow them in order to meet the demand for inscribed *lontar* books.

BUKIT KUSAMBI

This small hill has a big view – at sunrise Lombok's Gunung Rinjani throws a shadow on Gunung Agung. Bukit Kusambi is easy to reach from Abian Soan – look for the obvious large hill to the northwest, and follow the tiny canals through the rice fields. On the western side of the hill, a set of steps leads to the top.

BUDAKELING & KROTOK

Budakeling, home to several Buddhist communities, is on the back road to Bebandem, a few kilometres southeast of Tirta Gangga. It's a short drive, or a pleasant three-hour walk through rice fields, via Krotok, home of traditional blacksmiths and silversmiths.

TANAH ARON

This imposing monument to the post-WWII Dutch resistance is gloriously situated on the southeastern slopes of Gunung Agung. The road is quite good, or you can walk up and back in about six hours from Tirta Gangga.

Amed & the Far East Coast

☑0363

Stretching from Amed to Bali's far eastern tip, this once-remote stretch of semi-arid coast draws visitors to a succession of small, scalloped, black-sand beaches, a relaxed atmosphere and excellent diving and snorkelling.

The coast here is often called simply 'Amed' but this is a misnomer, as the coast is a series of seaside *dusun* (small villages) that start with the actual Amed in the north and then run southeast to Aas. If you're looking to get away from crowds, this is the place to come and try some yoga. Everything is spread out, so you never feel like you're in the middle of anything much except maybe one of the small fishing villages.

Traditionally this area has been quite poor, with thin soils, low rainfall and very limited infrastructure. Salt production is

DECODING AMED

The entire 10km stretch of far east coast is often called 'Amed' by both tourists and marketing-minded locals. Most development at first was around three bays with fishing villages: **Jemeluk**, which has cafes and a few shops; **Bunutan**, with both a beach and headlands; and **Lipah**, which has warung, shops and a few services. Development has marched onwards through tiny **Lehan**, **Selang**, **Bayuning** and **Aas**, each a minor oasis at the base of the dry, brown hills. To appreciate the narrow band of the coast, stop at the viewpoint at Jemeluk, where you can see fishing boats lined up like a riot of multihued sardines on the beach.

Besides the main road via Tirta Gangga, you can also approach the Amed area from the Aas end in the south; see the boxed text for details.

still carried out on the beach at Amed. Villages further east rely on fishing, and colourful *jukung* (traditional boats) line up on every available piece of beach. Inland, the steep hillsides are generally too dry for rice – corn, peanuts and vegetables are the main crops.

🏃 Activities

Diving & Snorkelling

Snorkelling is excellent along the coast. Jemeluk is a protected area where you can admire live coral and plentiful fish within 100m of the beach. There's a few bits of wood remaining from a **sunken Japanese fishing boat** at Bayuning – just offshore from Eka Purnama bungalows – and coral gardens and colourful marine life at Selang. Almost every hotel rents snorkelling equipment for about 30,000Rp per day.

Scuba diving is also excellent, with dive sites off Jemeluk, Lipah and Selang featuring coral slopes and drop-offs with soft and hard corals, and abundant fish. Some are accessible from the beach, while others require a short boat ride. The *Liberty* wreck at Tulamben is only a 20-minute drive away.

Three good dive operators have shown a commitment to the communities by organising regular beach clean-ups and educating locals on the need for conservation. All have similar prices for a long list of offerings (eg local dives from about US$70, open-water dive course about US$375).

Eco-dive (☑23 482; www.ecodivebali.com; Jemeluk; ☎) Full-service shop with simple, free accommodation for clients. Has led the way on environmental issues.

Euro Dive (☑23 605; www.eurodivebali.com; Lipah) Has a large facility and offers packages with hotels.

Jukung Dive (☑23 469; www.jukungdivebali .com; Amed) Pushes its eco-credentials and has a dive pool.

Trekking

Quite a few trails go inland from the coast, up the slopes of **Gunung Seraya** (1175m) and to some little-visited villages. The countryside is sparsely vegetated and most trails are well defined, so you won't need a guide for shorter walks – if you get lost, just follow a ridge-top back down to the coast road. Allow a good three hours to get to the top of Seraya, starting from the rocky ridge just east of Jemeluk Bay, near Prem Liong Art Bungalows. To reach the top for sunrise, you'll need to start in the dark, so a guide is a good idea – ask at your hotel.

🛌 Sleeping

The Amed region is very spread out, so take this into consideration when choosing accommodation. If you want to venture to restaurants beyond your hotel's own, for example, you'll have to walk or find transport.

You will also need to choose between staying in the little beachside villages or on the sunny and dry headlands connect-

---

WORTH A TRIP

DETOUR TO AMED

Typically travellers bound for the coast of **Amed** travel the inland route through Tirta Gangga. However, there is a longer, twistier and more adventurous road much less travelled that runs from **Ujung** right around the coast to the Amed area. The road climbs up the side of the twin peaks of Seraya and Lempuyang, and the views out to sea are breathtaking. Along the way it passes through numerous small villages where people are carving fishing boats, bathing in streams or simply standing a bit slack-jawed at the appearance of *tamu* (visitors or foreigners). Don't be surprised to see a pig, goat or boulder on the road. After the lush east, it's noticeably drier here and the people's existence thinner; corn replaces rice as the staple.

Near **Seraya** (which has a cute market) look for weavers and cotton-fabric-makers. For lots of the time, you'll just be in the middle of fruit-filled orchards and jungle. About 4km south of **Aas** there's a lighthouse.

The road is narrow but paved, and covering the 35km to Aas will take about one hour without stops. Combine this with the inland road through Tirta Gangga for a good circular visit to Amed from the west.

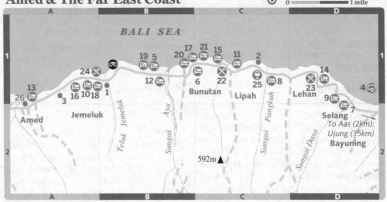

ing the inlets. The former puts you right on the sand and offers a small amount of community life while the latter gives you broad, sweeping vistas and isolation.

Accommodation can be found in every price category; almost every place has a restaurant or cafe. Places with noteworthy dining are indicated in the listings.

EAST OF AMED VILLAGE

TOP CHOICE **Hotel Uyah Amed** HOTEL $$
(☎23 462; www.hoteluyah.com; r €30-45; ✳✳) This cute place features four-poster beds set in stylish, conical interiors bathed in light. From all 16 rooms (two with air-con) you can see the saltworks on the beach. The hotel makes the most of this by offering fascinating and free salt-making demonstrations (see the boxed text, p202). The tasty Cafe Garam is appropriately named for salt.

JEMELUK

You might say what's now called Amed started here.

Pondok Kebun Wayan GUESTHOUSE $
(☎23 473; www.amedcafe.com; r €10-50; ✳✳) This Amed empire features a range of 23 bungalow-style rooms mostly on a hillside across from the beach. The most expensive rooms have views, terraces and amenities like air-con while the cheapest have cold water and showers. The cafe has a good grilled seafood menu.

Sama Sama Bungalows HOMESTAY $
(☎0813 3738 2945; r 150,000-400,000Rp) Choose from a cold-water room with fan or

something a scotch more posh (hot water) in a bungalow here (and a good seafood cafe) across from the beach. The family that runs things is often busy making kites.

Galang Kangin Bungalows GUESTHOUSE $
(☎23 480; bali_amed_gk@yahoo.co.jp; r 150,000Rp-600,000Rp; ✳) Set on the hill side of the road amid a nice garden, the 10 rooms here mix and match fans, cold water, hot water and air-con. The beach is right over the pavement, as is the cafe.

BANUTAN BEACH

This is a classic little swathe of sand and fishing boats between arid headlands.

Santai HOTEL $$
(☎23 487; www.santaibali.com; r US$50-120; ✳✳) This lovely option is on a slight hill down to the beach. The name means 're-lax' and you'll have a hard time not taking the hint. A series of authentic traditional thatched bungalows gathered from around the archipelago hold 10 rooms with four-poster beds, timber floors, open-air bathrooms and big comfy balcony sofas. A swimming pool, fringed by purple bougain-villea, snakes through the property. The cafe is good.

Aiona Garden of Health GUESTHOUSE $
(☎0813 3816 1730; www.aionabali.com; r US$25-45) This eccentric place has enough signs outside that it qualifies as a genuine roadside attraction. The simple bungalows are shaded by mango trees and the natural food may be the healthiest of your trip. You can partake of organic potions and lotions, classes in yoga, meditation, tarot reading

Amed & Far East Coast

etc. If you don't get a natural high, your inner peace might improve with the high-fibre diet or try the fermented tea, pow! A small **shell museum** (open 2pm to 4pm) boasts that no bivalves died in its creation.

Hotel Prema Liong
GUESTHOUSE $

(☑23 486; www.bali-amed.com; bungalows 280,000-380,000Rp) Large Javanese-style two-storey bungalows are terraced amid trees up a hillside and have a New-Age ethos. The cold-water, open-air bathrooms (showers only) are lush and feel like extensions of the garden, while the balconies have daybeds for snoozing away the afternoons.

BUNUTAN

These places are on a sun-drenched, arid stretch of highland. Most are on sloping hillsides and spill down to the water.

Onlyou Villas
VILLAS $$

(☑23 595; www.onlyou-bali.com; villas €50-90; ❈ ❑) You could go nuts trying to find the missing y in the name of this three-villa complex. Happily it is such a good deal that you'll go 'y not!'. Villas are large and have many amenities such as DVD players, multiple beds, luxurious teak furniture and an array of genial pets.

Wawa-Wewe II
HOTEL $$

(☑23 522, 23 506; wawawewevillas@yahoo.com; r 300,000-600,000Rp; ❈ ❑) From the headlands, this restful place has 10 bungalow-style rooms on lush grounds that shamble down to the water's edge. The natural-stone infinity pool is shaped like a Buddha and is near the water, as are two rooms with delectable ocean views.

Anda Amed
HOTEL $$

(☑23 498; www.andaamedresort.com; villas €50-90; ❈ ❑) This whitewashed hillside hotel feels like it could be on Mykonos. The infinity pool is an ahhh-inducing classic of the genre and has a waterfall and sweeping views of the sea from well above the road. The four villas are a good deal; each has one or two bedrooms and lots of posh details like deep soaking tubs.

Waeni's Sunset View Bungalows
GUESTHOUSE $

(☑23 515; www.baliwaenis.com; r US$30-60; ❈) Waeni's is a hillside place with eight unusual rustic stone cottages that have gorgeous views of the mountains behind and the bay below. Some feature hot water and air-con, others are fan-cooled with cold water. The cafe is a good place for a sunset drink.

Puri Wirata
HOTEL $$

(☑23 523; www.puriwirata.com; r US$48-85, villas US$75-260; ❈ ❑ ❑) The most mainstream Amed choice, this 30-room resort has two pools and rooms ambling down the hill to the rocky ribbon at the waterline. Service is professional and there are many dive packages on offer.

LIPAH

This village is just large enough for you to go wandering – briefly.

WORKING IN THE SALT BRINE

For a real day at the beach, try making some salt. You start by carrying, say, 500L of ocean water across the sand to bamboo and wood funnels, which filter the water after it is poured in. Next the water goes into a *palungan* (shallow trough), made of palm-tree trunks split in half and hollowed out, or cement canisters where it evaporates, leaving salt behind. And that's just the start, and just what you might see in Kusamba or on the beach in Amed.

In the volcanic areas around the east coast between Sanur and Yeh Sanih in the north, a range of salt-making methods is used. What is universal is that the work is hard, very hard, but is also an essential source of income for many families.

In some places the first step is drying sand that has been saturated with sea water. It's then taken inside a hut, where more sea water is strained through it to wash out the salt. This very salty water is then poured into a *palungan*. Hundreds of these troughs are lined up in rows along the beaches during the salt-making season (the dry season), and as the hot sun evaporates the water, the almost-dry salt is scraped out and put in baskets. There are good exhibits on this method at the Museum Semara-jaya in Semarapura.

Most salt produced on the coast of Bali is used for processing dried fish. And that's where Amed has an advantage: although its method of making salt results in a lower yield than that using sand, its salt is prized for its flavour. In fact there is a fast-growing market for this 'artisan salt' worldwide. The grey and cloudy crystals are finding their way into many top-end kitchens.

Visitors to the Amed area can learn all about this fascinating process at the adjoining Hotel Uyah Amed and Cafe Garam. Many of the staff here also work in salt production. Tours are offered, and you can buy big bags of the precious stuff (per kilogram 10,000Rp) for a tiny fraction of what it costs once it's gone through many hands and made its way to your local gourmet market.

Bayu Cottages GUESTHOUSE **$$**
(☏23495; www.bayucottages.com; r €25-50; ❈☂☄) Bayu has six large, comfortable rooms with balconies overlooking the coast from the hillside above the road. There's a small pool and many amenities including open-air marble bathrooms and satellite TV.

Hidden Paradise Cottages HOTEL **$$**
(☏23514; www.hiddenparadise-bali.com; r US$60-120; ❈☂☄) The 16 simply decorated bungalow-style rooms at this older beach-side resort have large patios and open-air bathrooms. The pool is the classic kidney shape in a natural garden setting. Several dive packages are available.

LEHAN
Life in Amed GUESTHOUSE **$$**
(☏23152, 0813 3850 1555; www.lifebali.com; r US$60-100, villas US$100-170; ❈@☄) Life here is posh. The six bungalow-style units are in a slightly cramped compound around a sinuous pool; two villas are directly on the beach. The cafe concentrates on seafood and showy local dishes (meals 50,000Rp to 120,000Rp).

SELANG
Blue Moon Villas GUESTHOUSE **$$**
(☏0817 4738 100; www.bluemoonvilla.com; r from US$60-75; ❈☄) On the hillside across the road from the cliffs, Blue Moon is a small and upmarket place, complete with a cute pool. The nine rooms set in villa-style buildings have open-air stone bathrooms. Rooms can be combined into larger multi-bedroom suites. The restaurant serves good Balinese classics and grilled seafood.

Aquaterrace GUESTHOUSE **$$**
(☏0813 3791 1096; www.bbamed.exblog.jp; r 200,000-550,000Rp; ❈) Perched on the headland, this two-unit Japanese-themed guesthouse has a beautiful unit with balconies and views to Gili T. A simpler fan-cooled room has nearly the same views. Both have fridges and the tiny cafe serves Japanese-style food.

AAS
Once you've reached Aas, hole up for a spell and give your butt a rest.

TOP CHOICE **Meditasi** GUESTHOUSE **$**
(fax 22 166; r 250,000-300,000Rp) Get off the grid and take a respite from the pressures of life at this chilled-out hideaway. Meditation and yoga help you relax, and the four rooms are close to good swimming and snorkelling. Open-air baths allow you to count the colours of the bougainvillea and frangipani that grow in profusion. The owners are lovely.

Eating & Drinking

As noted, most places to stay have cafes. Ones worth seeking out are listed here.

Cafe Garam INDONESIAN **$**
(23 462; Hotel Uyah Amed, east of Amed; meals 20,000-50,000Rp) There's a relaxed feel here, with pool tables and Balinese food plus the lyrical and haunting melodies of live genjek music at 8pm on Wednesday and Saturday. *Garam* means salt and the cafe honours the local salt-making industry. Try the *salada ayam,* an addictive mix of cabbage, grilled chicken, shallots and tiny peppers.

Sama Sama Café SEAFOOD **$**
(0813 3738 2945; Jemeluk; meals 20,000-50,000Rp) Super-fresh prawns, calamari and whatever else was caught on the nearby boats is grilled however you like at this beachside joint, located right on the sand on this pint-sized bay.

Wawa-Wewe I BAR **$**
(23 506; Lipah) Spend the evening here and you won't know your wawas from your wewes, if you try the local *arak* (fermented spirit) made with palm fronds. This is the coast's most raucous bar – which by local standards means that sometimes it gets sorta loud. Local bands jam on many nights. You can also eat here (mains from 15,000Rp).

Restaurant Gede CHINESE **$**
(23 517; Bunutan; meals 25,000-50,000Rp) The menu is typical of those found in Chinese restaurants everywhere: long. Views are good from this spot halfway up the hill from the cove. Artwork by the owner decorates the walls.

Sails FUSION **$$**
(22 006; Lehan; meals 50,000-100,000Rp) A high-concept restaurant with high standards for food, Sails is one big terrace with 180-degree views from its cliffside perch. Settle back in the chic blonde furniture and enjoy fusion hits like lamb medallions, spare ribs and grilled fillets of fresh fish with Balinese accents.

ℹ️ Information

You may be charged a tourist tax. Enforcement of a 5000Rp per-person fee at a tollbooth on the outskirts of Amed is sporadic. When collected, the funds go in part to develop the infrastructure at the beaches.

Pondok Kebun Wayan (23 473; east of Amed) changes US-dollar travellers cheques and has a small market with groceries and a few sundries.

There are moneychangers in Lipah but the closest ATMs and banks are in Amlapura. Many places don't take credit cards.

ℹ️ Getting There & Around

Most people drive here via the main highway from Amlapura and Culik. The spectacular road going all the way around the twin peaks from Aas to Ujung makes a good circle. See the boxed text, p199 for details.

You can arrange for a driver and car to/from south Bali and the airport for about 400,000Rp.

Public transport is difficult. **Minibuses** and **bemo** between Singaraja and Amlapura pass through Culik, the turn-off for the coast. Infrequent bemo go from Culik to Amed (3.5km), and some continue to Seraya until 1pm. Fares average 8000Rp.

You can also charter transport from Culik for a negotiable 50,000Rp (by *ojek* is less than half). Specify which hotel you wish to go to – agree on 'Amed' and you could come up short in Amed village.

Perama (www.perama.com) offers charter tourist-bus services from Candidasa or Padangbai; the cost is 125,000Rp each for a minimum of two people. This is similar to the cost of hiring a car and driver.

Amed Sea Express (80 852, 0819 3617 6914; Amed; per person 600,000Rp) makes 75-minute crossings to Gili Trawangan on a 20-person speedboat. This makes many interesting itineraries possible.

Many hotels rent bicycles for about 35,000Rp per day.

Kubu Region

Driving along the main road you will pass through vast old lava flows from Gunung Agung down to the sea. The landscape is strewn with a moonscape of boulders, and is nothing like the lush rice paddies elsewhere.

Tulamben

☎ 0363

The big attraction here sunk over 60 years ago. The wreck of the US cargo ship *Liberty* is among the best and most popular dive sites in Bali and this has given rise to an entire town based on scuba diving. Other great dive sites are nearby and even snorkellers can easily swim out and enjoy the wreck and the coral.

But if you don't plan to explore the briny waves, don't expect to hang out on the beach either. The shore is made up of rather beautiful, large washed stones, the kind that cost a fortune at a DIY store.

🏃 Activities

Diving and snorkelling are the reason Tulamben exists.

The **shipwreck** *Liberty* is about 50m directly offshore from Puri Madha Bungalows (where you can park); look for the schools of black snorkels. Swim straight out and you'll see the stern rearing up from the depths, heavily encrusted with coral and swarming with dozens of species of colourful fish – and with scuba divers most of the day. The ship is more than 100m long, but the hull is broken into sections and it's easy for divers to get inside. The bow is in quite good shape, the midships region is badly mangled and the stern is almost intact – the best parts are between 15m and 30m deep. You will want at least two dives to really explore the wreck.

Many divers commute to Tulamben from Candidasa or Lovina, and in busy times it can get quite crowded between 11am and 4pm, with up to 50 divers at a time around

THE WRECK OF THE LIBERTY

In January 1942 the US Navy cargo ship USAT *Liberty* was torpedoed by a Japanese submarine near Lombok. Taken in tow, it was beached at Tulamben so that its cargo of rubber and railway parts could be saved. The Japanese invasion prevented this and the ship sat on the beach until the 1963 eruption of Gunung Agung broke it in two and left it just off the shoreline, much to the delight of scores of divers.

the wreck. Stay the night in Tulamben or in nearby Amed and get an early start.

Most hotels have their own diving centre, and some will give a discount on accommodation if you dive with their centre. If you are an inexperienced diver, see p39 for tips on choosing a dive operation.

Among the many dive operators, **Tauch Terminal** is one of the longest-established operators in Bali. A four-day PADI open-water certificate course costs about €350. Expect to pay about €30/50 for one/two dives at Tulamben, and a little more for a night dive or dives around Amed.

Snorkelling gear is rented everywhere for 30,000Rp.

🛏 Sleeping & Eating

Tulamben is a quiet place, and is essentially built around the wreck – the hotels, all with cafes and many with dive shops, are spread along a 3km stretch either side of the main road. You have your choice of roadside (cheaper) or by the water (nicer). At high tide even the rocky shore vanishes but hotels situated on the water always have great views of the surf.

Mimpi Resort   HOTEL **$$**
(☎21 642; www.mimpi.com; r US$75-110, cottage US$125-200; ❋@☒) The choice for a traditional resort experience, Mimpi has a lavish spa, room service, loungers by the shore, a refined restaurant and more. The 13 rooms open onto lush gardens as do 12 large cottages. Four more are on the water. The crashing waves should pound the jet lag right out of your head.

Tauch Terminal Resort   HOTEL **$$**
(☎0361-774 504, 22 911; www.tauch-terminal .com; r US$50-100; ❋☎☒) Down a side road, this sprawling waterfront hotel has 27 rooms in several categories. Many of the rooms are newly built and all are comfortable in a modern, motel-style way. Expect amenities like satellite TV and fridges. Of the two waterfront pools, one is reserved for swimming only. The cafe serves a fine breakfast.

Puri Madha Bungalows   GUESTHOUSE **$**
(☎22 921; r 100,000-300,000Rp; ❋) Refurbished bungalow-style units are directly opposite the wreck on shore. The best of the 11 rooms have air-con and hot water. The spacious grounds feel like a public park and you can't beat getting out of

bed and paddling right out to a famous shipwreck.

Paradise Palm Beach Bungalows HOTEL $
(✆22 910; paradisetulamben@yahoo.co.id; r 150,000-450,000Rp; ❄) An older but very well-maintained property, there are 30 bungalow-style units arrayed on a long, narrow plot down to the water. The cheapest rooms can be a bit dark but those by the water are bright and enjoy the view.

Deep Blue Studio GUESTHOUSE $
(✆22 919; www.diving-bali.com; r 200,000Rp; ❄) Owned by Czechs, this dive operation has eight rooms in two-storey buildings on the hill side of the road. Rooms have fans and balconies.

Bali Coral Bungalows GUESTHOUSE $
(✆22 909; r with fan/air-con 200,000/300,000Rp; ❄) Ten basic, clean bungalows with modern bathrooms are built back from the shore near Tauch Terminal. The cafe has views of the ocean.

Ocean Sun GUESTHOUSE $
(✆0813 3757 3434; www.ocean-sun.com; r from 100,000Rp) Ocean Sun has four bungalow-style rooms on the hill side of the road. Units are clean and basic. Feel like some head-bangin'? The beds have thickly cushioned headboards.

ℹ Information
You can change cash at a few signposted places at the eastern end of the main road; otherwise services are sparse. For dial-up internet access, try **Tulamben Wreck Divers Resort** (per min 500Rp).

ℹ Getting There & Away
Plenty of buses and bemo travel between Amlapura and Singaraja and will stop anywhere along the Tulamben road, but they're infrequent after 2pm. Expect to pay 12,000Rp to either town.

Perama offers charter tourist-bus services from Candidasa; the cost is 125,000Rp each for a minimum of two people. This is similar to the cost of hiring a car and driver.

If you are driving to Lovina for the night, be sure to leave by about 3pm, so you will still have a little light when you get there. There's a petrol station just south of town.

If you are just going to snorkel the wreck and are day tripping with a driver, don't let them park at a dive shop away from the wreck where you'll get a sales pitch.

Tulamben to Yeh Sanih

North of Tulamben, the road continues to skirt the slopes of Gunung Agung, with frequent evidence of lava flows from the 1963 eruption. Further around, the outer crater of Gunung Batur slopes steeply down to the sea. The rainfall is low and you can generally count on sunny weather. The scenery is very stark in the dry season and it's thinly populated. The route has public transport, but it's easier to make stops and detours with your own wheels.

There are regular markets in **Kubu**, a roadside village 5km northwest of Tulamben. At **Les**, a road goes inland to lovely **Air Terjun Yeh Mampeh** (Yeh Mampeh Waterfall), at 40m one of Bali's highest. Look for a large sign on the main road and then turn inland for about 1km. Walk the last 2km or so on an obvious path by the stream, shaded by rambutan trees. A 5000Rp donation is requested; there's no need for a guide.

The next main town is **Tejakula**, famous for its stream-fed public bathing area, said to have been built for washing horses and often called the 'horse bath'. The renovated bathing areas (separate for men and women) are behind walls topped by rows of elaborately decorated arches, and are regarded as a sacred area. The baths are 100m inland on a narrow road with lots of small shops – it's a quaint village, with some finely carved *kulkul* (hollow tree-trunk warning drum) towers. Take a stroll above the baths, past irrigation channels flowing in all directions.

At Pacung, about 10km before Yeh Sanih, you can turn inland 4km to **Sembiran**, which is a Bali Aga village, although it doesn't promote itself as such. The most striking thing about the place is its hillside location and brilliant coastal views.

🛏 Sleeping
Bali's remote northeast coast has a growing number of resorts where you can indeed get away from it all. These are places to settle in for a few days and revive your senses. Getting here from the airport or south Bali can take three hours or more via two routes: one up and over the mountains via Kintamani and then down a rustic, scenic road to the sea near Tejakula; the other going right round east Bali on the coast road via Candidasa and Tulamben.

SAVING BALI'S FORGOTTEN

Long the poorest region of Bali, the arid lands far up the northeast slopes of Gunung Agung were so poor for so long that as recently as the 1990s, government bureaucrats wouldn't even admit that people lived there. Diseases from malnutrition were common, education was nil, incomes were under US$30 a year and so on. It was poverty at its worst on an island that already 20 years ago was experiencing an economic boom from tourism.

Amazingly, this bleak scene no longer exists and although it sounds like a cliché, the tireless efforts of one man, David Booth, are responsible. Irascible, idiosyncratic and relentless, the British-born Booth turned his engineering background on the region (which extends from the tiny village of Ban) starting in the 1990s. A tireless organiser, he rallied the locals, badgered the government, charmed donors and turned his **East Bali Poverty Project** (www.eastbalipovertyproject.org) into an amazing force of change.

There are schools, electricity, clinics and a sense of accomplishment that have liberated the people from their past. Now moving into a sustainable phase of development, the project has built the **Bamboo Centre** in the hamlet of Daya. It shows the possibilities for bamboo as a renewable resource. The now-supportive Balinese government has greatly improved a road running over the mountain from a point near Pura Besakih, all the way down to the coast at Tianyar, 20km northwest of Tulamben. If you're not worried about getting lost, this can make a fascinating day's outing. There may not be anyone at the centre, but if there is, the welcome is warm.

Alam Anda   HOTEL $$

(☑0361-750 444; www.alamanda.de; r €40-170; ✸ ✿) The tropical architecture at this oceanside resort, near Sambirenteng, is striking thanks to the efforts of the German architect-owner. A reef just offshore keeps the dive shop busy. The 30 units come in various sizes, from losmen rooms to cottages with views. All are well-equipped and have artful thatch and bamboo motifs. The resort is 1km north of Poinciana Resort, roughly between Kubu and Tejakula.

Poinciana Resort   HOTEL $$

(☑0812 398 6458; www.poincianaresortbali.com; villas US$50-180; ✸ ✿) A remote retreat, isolated from the coast road amid palms, Poinciana is absolutely spotless and has seven villas on large, lavishly planted grounds. Beach villas (US$60) are excellent value and have large tubs, fridges and relaxing indoor/outdoor seating. Many cyclists stay here as they circumnavigate the island. It is roughly between Kubu and Tejakula.

Siddhartha Dive Resort   HOTEL $$

(☑0363-23034; www.siddhartha-bali.de; Kubu; r €80-160; ✸ ✿) With 30 separate bungalows that are stylish and modern, these German-owned units have Euro-style clean lines within a Balinese architectural vibe. Most people staying here plan to join the Tulamben crowd diving.

Tembok Spa Village Resort   HOTEL $$$

(☑0362-32033; www.spavillage.com; full board r from US$400; ✸ @ ✿) When you arrive at this beachside resort, you realise you're in for an experience. Guests are asked to choose a path: balance, creativity or vigour (there's no 'leave me alone'). Extensive spa treatments and daily activities are geared to your path. The 27 rooms have a traditional feel with a coffee-and-cream theme accented by carving. Meals are healthful and focus on simple, local ingredients. It is between Kubu and Tejakula, northwest of Tembok.

Central Mountains

Includes »

Best Places to Eat

» Strawberry Hill (p215)

» Strawberry Stop (p217)

» Puri Lumbung Cottages
(p220)

Best Places to Stay

» Puri Lumbung Cottages
(p220)

» Lumbung Bali Cottages
(p220)

» Sarinbuana Eco-Lodge
(p222)

» Bali Mountain Retreat
(p222)

» Sanda Bukit Villas &
Restaurant (p223)

Why Go?

Bali has a hot soul. The volcanoes stretching along the island's spine are more than just cones of silence; their active
spirits are literally just below the surface, eager for expression.

Gunung Batur (1717m) is constantly letting off steam.
The otherworldly beauty of the place may overwhelm the
attendant hassles of a visit. Danau Bratan has sacred Hindu
temples and its shore is lined with strawberry farms. The
village of Candikuning has an engrossing botanic garden.

The old colonial village of Munduk, a hiking centre, has
views down the hills to the coast of north Bali that match
the beauty of the many nearby waterfalls and plantations.
In the shadow of Gunung Batukau (2276m), you'll find
one of Bali's most mystic temples. Just south, the Unesco-
nominated ancient rice terraces in and around Jatiluwih
bedazzle.

Amid it all, little roads lead to untouched villages and
the occasional hidden retreat where you can truly get away
from it all. Start driving north from Antosari for one surprise after another.

When to Go

Bali's central mountains can be cool and misty throughout the year. They also get a lot of rain: this is the starting
point for the water that courses through rice terraces and
fields all the way to Seminyak. Although you can expect
more rain from October to April, it can pour any time. Tem-
peratures show few seasonal variations, although it can get
down to 10°C at night at high elevations – it's no wonder
locals wander around bundled up. There's no peak tourist
season in the hills.

GUNUNG BATUR AREA

🎵0366

This area is like a giant bowl, with the bottom half covered by water and a set of volcanic cones jutting out of the middle. Sound a bit spectacular? It is. On clear days – vital to appreciating the spectacle – the turquoise waters wrap around the newer volcanoes, which have obvious old lava flows oozing down their sides.

The road around the southwestern rim of the Gunung Batur crater is one of Bali's most important north–south routes and has one of Bali's most stunning vistas. Most people intending to do some trekking stay in the villages around the shores of Danau Batur and plan an early start to climb the volcano.

Even day trippers should bring some sort of wrap in case the mist closes in and the temperature drops to 16°C.

The villages around the Gunung Batur crater rim have grown together in a continuous untidy strip. The main village is Kintamani, though the whole area is often referred to by that name. Coming from the south, the first village is **Penelokan**, where tour groups stop to gasp at the view, eat a buffet lunch and be hassled by souvenir sellers.

Penelokan is also where you can take a short road down into the crater. From here, a road loosely follows the shore of Danau Batur, linking the villages of **Kedisan** and **Toya Bungkah**. You can travel between the Gunung Batur and Danau Bratan areas using a beautiful mountain lane (see the boxed text, p215).

Dangers & Annoyances

The Gunung Batur area has a reputation as an avaricious place and many visitors leave vowing never to return. One travel agent told us that he gets more complaints about this area than the rest of Bali combined, which is a shame, as if properly briefed you can enjoy the stunning natural beauty of this region.

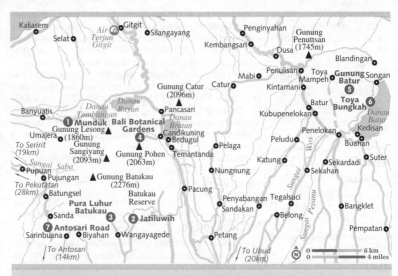

Central Mountains Highlights

❶ Claiming your own waterfall while trekking around **Munduk** (p219)

❷ Identifying each ancient variety of rice grown at the magnificent ancient terraces of **Jatiluwih** (p221)

❸ Hearing the chant of priests at one of Bali's holiest temples, **Pura Luhur Batukau** (p221)

❹ Luxuriating among the hundreds of rare plants at Candikuning's **Bali Botanical Gardens** (p216)

❺ Beholding the otherworldly, lava-strewn side of **Gunung Batur** (p208)

❻ Finding your own serenity in the lakeside village of **Toya Bungkah** (p214), in the shadow of steaming Gunung Batur

❼ Exploring the region's maze of back roads, such as the one north from **Antosari** (p222)

Keep an eye on your gear and do not leave any valuables in your car, especially at the start of any trail up the volcano. Break-ins are common. This is also ground zero for the car con, where miscreants surreptitiously damage your car, then offer to fix it for money (tyres are a favourite target).

Be wary of touts on motorcycles, who will attempt to steer you to a hotel of *their* choice as you descend into the Danau Batur area from the village of Penelokan. Vendors in the area can be highly aggressive and irritating.

❶ Information

Services are few in the Gunung Batur area. Bring anything you might need, including cash, from the lowlands.

❶ Getting There & Around

From Batubulan terminal in Denpasar, bemo travel regularly to Kintamani (24,000Rp). Buses on the Denpasar–(Batubulan)–Singaraja route will stop in Penelokan and Kintamani (about 24,000Rp). Alternatively, you can just hire a car or use a driver (which is a good way to avoid falling prey to the car con).

Bemo regularly shuttle back and forth around the crater rim, between Penelokan and Kintamani (10,000Rp for tourists). Bemo from Penelokan down to the lakeside villages go mostly in the morning (the tourist price is about 8000Rp to Toya Bungkah). Later in the day, you may have to charter transport (40,000Rp or more).

Arriving by private vehicle, you will be stopped at Penelokan and Kubupenelokan to buy an entry ticket (5000Rp per person) that's good for the whole Gunung Batur area. You shouldn't be charged again – save your stub.

Trekking Gunung Batur

Volcanologists describe Gunung Batur as a 'double caldera', ie one crater inside another. The outer crater is an oval about 14km long, with its western rim about 1500m above sea level. The inner is a classic volcano-shaped peak that reaches 1717m. Activity over the last decade has spawned several smaller cones on its western flank, unimaginatively named Batur I, II, III and IV. More than 20 minor eruptions were recorded between 1824 and 1994, and there were major eruptions in 1917, 1926 and 1963. Geological activity and tremors have continued to occur regularly.

Statistics aside, you really have to see it to believe it. One look at this otherworldly

spectacle and you'll understand why people want to go through the many hassles and expenses of taking a trek. Note that the odds of clouds obscuring your reason for coming are greater from July to December, but any time of year you should check conditions with a trekking agency before committing to a trip, or even coming up the mountain.

HPPGB

The **HPPGB** (Mt Batur Tour Guides Association; ☑52 362; ☉3am-noon) has a monopoly on guided climbs up Gunung Batur. It requires that all trekking agencies that operate on the mountain hire at least one of its guides for trips up the mountain. In addition, the cartel has developed a reputation for intimidation in requiring climbers to use its guides and during negotiations for its services.

Reported tactics have ranged from dire warnings given to people who inquired at its offices to threats against people attempting to climb without a guide. That said, many people use the services of HPPGB guides without incident, and some of the guides win plaudits from visitors for their ideas in customising trips.

The following strategies should help you have a spectacular climb:

» Be absolutely clear in your agreement with the HPPGB about the terms you're agreeing to, such as whether fees are per person or group and include breakfast, and exactly where you will go.

» Deal with one of the trekking agencies. There will still be an HPPGB guide

❶ UNPLANNED EXCITEMENT

The volcanically active area west of the main peak of Gunung Batur can be deadly, with explosions of steam and hot lava, unstable ground and sulphurous gases. To find out about current conditions, ask at the trekking agencies or look at the website of the **Directorate of Volcanology & Geographical Hazard Mitigation** (www.vsi.esdm.go.id), although much of this site is in Bahasa Indonesia. The active areas are sometimes closed to visitors for safety reasons.

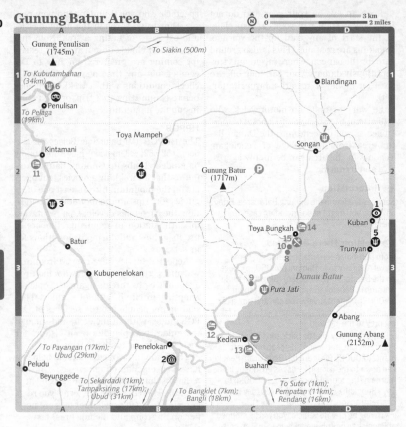

along, but all arrangements will be done through the agency.

HPPGB rates and times are posted at its Pura Jati office. The **Batur Sunrise trek** (400,000Rp) goes from 4am to 8am, the **Gunung Batur Main Crater trek** (500,000Rp) from 4am to 10am.

Trekking Agencies

Even reputable and highly competent adventure-tour operators cannot take their customers up Gunung Batur without paying the HPPGB to have one of their guys tag along, so these tours are relatively expensive.

Most of the accommodation in the area can help you put together a trek. As with the trekking agencies, they can recommend alternatives to the classic Batur climb, such as the outer rim of the crater, or treks to other mountains such as Gunung Agung.

All of the agencies listed here can get you up Gunung Batur starting from about US$30 (not including HPPGB fees); everything is negotiable.

TOP CHOICE **Jero Wijaya Tourist Service** (☑51 249; Lakeside Cottages, Toya Bungkah) Wijaya is an expert and he can organise and lead memorable treks and hikes across the central mountains.

Hotel Miranda (☑52 022; Jl Raya Kintamani, Kintamani) Will take solo climbers; the owner Made Senter is a gem.

Hotel Segara (☑51 136; hotelsegara@plasa. com; Kedisan) Popular with larger groups.

Volcano Breeze (☑51 824; Toya Bungkah) Located in the cafe of the same name; offers many treks.

Equipment

If you're climbing before sunrise, take a torch (flashlight) or be absolutely sure that

Gunung Batur Area

your guide provides you with one. You'll need good strong footwear, a hat, a jumper (sweater) and drinking water.

Trekking Routes

The climb to see the sunrise from Gunung Batur is still the most popular trek, even with the various hassles.

Ideally, trekkers should get to the top for sunrise (about 6am), before mist and cloud obscure the view. It is a magnificent sight, although hardly a wilderness experience – it's not uncommon for there to be 100 people present for the sunrise in the tourist season. It isn't even necessary to be at the top for sunrise – a halfway point is fine. If you start at 5am, you'll avoid the crowds.

Guides will provide breakfast on the summit for a fee (50,000Rp), which often includes the novelty of cooking an egg or banana in the steaming holes at the top of the volcano. There are several pricey refreshment stops along the way.

The basic trek is to start climbing from Toya Bungkah at about 4am, reach the summit for sunrise, and possibly walk right around the main cone, then return to Toya Bungkah. The route is pretty straightforward – walk out of the village towards Kedisan and turn right just after the car park. After about 30 minutes, you'll be on a ridge with a well-defined track; keep going up. It gets pretty steep towards the top and it can be hard walking over the loose volcanic sand. Allow about two hours to reach the top, which is at the northern edge of the inner crater.

Climbers have reported that they've made the journey without a HPPGB guide, though this has risks as a hiker fell to his death at night in 2010. Don't try this when it's dark; by day you can see the paths easily.

You can follow the rim to the western side, where you can view the most recent volcanic activity, continue to the southern edge, and then return to Toya Bungkah by the route you climbed up.

Longer trips go around the recent volcanic cones southwest of the summit. This has the most exciting volcanic activity, with smoking craters, bright-yellow sulphur deposits, and steep slopes of fine black sand. If the activity is *too* exciting, the area may be closed for trekking, although the summit can still be OK.

Climbing up Gunung Batur, spending a reasonable time on the top and then strolling back down takes four or five hours; for the longer treks around the newer cones, allow around eight hours.

FROM PURA JATI
A huge parking lot (and HPPGB office) near Pura Jati makes this the main entrance for groups and day trippers. The shortest trek is basically across the lava fields, then straight up (allow about two hours to the top). If you want to see the newer cones west of the peak (assuming the area is safe to visit), go to the summit first – do not go walking around the active area before sunrise.

FROM THE NORTHEAST
The easiest route is from the northeast – that is if you can get transport to the trailhead at 4am. From Toya Bungkah take the road northeast towards Songan, then take the left fork after about 3.5km. Follow this small road for another 1.7km to a badly

signposted track on the left – this climbs another kilometre or so to a parking area. From here, the walking track is easy to follow to the top, and should take less than an hour.

FROM KINTAMANI

From the western edge of the outer crater, trails go from Batur and Kintamani down into the main crater, then up Gunung Batur from the west side. This route passes close to the rather exciting volcanically active area and may be closed for safety reasons. Check the current status with Made Senter at Hotel Miranda.

THE OUTER CRATER

A popular place to see the sunrise is on the outer crater rim northeast of Songan. You'll need transport to Pura Ulun Danu Batur, near the northern end of the lake. From there you can climb to the top of the outer crater rim in under 30 minutes, from where you can see Bali's northeast coast, about 5km away. At sunrise, the silhouette of Lombok looms across the water, and the first rays strike the great volcanoes of Batur and Agung.

Villages Around Gunung Batur Crater

There are several small villages on the ridge around Gunung Batur crater. The Penelokan area is lined with bus-tour restaurants (many of which have failed, leaving their forgotten hulks littering the roadside like the forgotten egg rolls within). Generally places on the west side of the road enjoy views down to south Bali, while those on the east side look into the double caldera.

PENELOKAN

Appropriately, Penelokan means 'place to look' and you'll be stunned by the view across to Gunung Batur and down to the lake at the bottom of the crater. Apart from the vista (check out the large lava flow on Gunung Batur), the **Museum Gunungapi Batur** (☏51 152; admission 10,000Rp; ☉8am-5pm) combines the serious with the hokey. In the former category there are OK displays about the volcanoes and the legends around them. In the latter, there's a model volcano that erupts on command in a manner that would do Peter Brady proud.

✖ Eating

Bring a shovel for the chow served at a lot of the ugly monolithic restaurants lining the crater rim. These places are geared for tourists and have fine views. Buffet lunches cost 60,000Rp to 80,000Rp or more (your guide often gets half of that as a commission) and the food is usually of the bucket-of-slop school of cuisine.

But there are some acceptable choices, including many humble places where you can sit on a plastic chair and have a simple, freshly cooked meal while enjoying a priceless view. Spotting an *ikan mujair* sign is almost as rewarding as spotting Gunung Agung on a clear day: these vendors sell small sweet fish that are caught in the lake below and then barbecued to a crisp with onion, garlic and bamboo sprouts.

BATUR & KINTAMANI

The villages of Batur and Kintamani now virtually run together. Kintamani is famed for its large and colourful **market**, which is held every three days. The town is like a string bean: long, with pods of development. Activity starts early, and by 11am everything's all packed up. If you don't want to go on a trek, the sunrise view from the road here is pretty good.

The original village of Batur was in the crater, but was wiped out by a violent eruption in 1917. It killed thousands of people before the lava flow stopped at the entrance to the village's main temple. Taking this as a good omen, the village was rebuilt, but Gunung Batur erupted again in 1926. This time, the lava flow covered everything except the loftiest temple shrine. Fortunately, there were evacuations and few lives were lost.

The village was relocated up onto the crater rim, and the surviving shrine was also moved up there and placed in the new temple, **Pura Batur** (admission 6000Rp; sarong & sash rental 3000Rp). Spiritually, Gunung Batur is the second most important mountain in Bali (only Gunung Agung outranks it), so this temple is of considerable importance. It's a great stop, as there are always a few colourful mountain characters hanging around. Within the complex is a Taoist shrine.

Hotel Miranda (☏52 022; Jl Raya Kintamani, Kintamani; s/d 40,000/70,000Rp) is the only accommodation here. The six rooms are clean and very basic with squat toilets. It has good food and a welcome open fire at night. The informative owner, Made Senter, is an excellent trekking guide.

PENULISAN

The road gradually climbs along the crater rim beyond Kintamani, and is often shrouded in clouds, mist or rain. Penulisan is where the road bends sharply and heads down towards the north coast and the remote scenic drive to Bedugul (see the boxed text, p215). A viewpoint about 400m south from here offers an amazing panorama over three mountains: Gunung Batur, Gunung Abang and Gunung Agung. If you're coming from the north, this is where you'll first see what all the tourism fuss is about.

Near the road junction, several steep flights of steps lead to Bali's highest temple, **Pura Puncak Penulisan** (1745m). Inside the highest courtyard are rows of old statues and fragments of sculptures in the open bale. Some of the sculptures date back to the 11th century. The temple views are superb: facing north you can see over the rice terraces clear to the Singaraja coast (weather permitting).

Villages Around Danau Batur

The little villages around Danau Batur have a crisp lakeside setting and views up to the surrounding peaks. There's a lot of fish farming here, and the air is pungent with the smell of onions from the tiny vegetable farms in the area. You'll also see chillies, cabbage and garlic growing, a festival for those who like assertively flavoured food.

A hairpin road winds its way down from Penelokan to the shore of Danau Batur. At the lakeside you can go left along the good road that twists through lava fields to Toya Bungkah, the usual base for climbing Gunung Batur.

KEDISAN & BUAHAN

The villages around the southern end of the lake have a few inns available for stays in a fairly isolated setting. Buahan is a pleasant 15-minute stroll from Kedisan, and has market gardens going right down to the lakeshore.

Beware of the motorcycle touts who will follow you down the hill from Penelokan, trying out the various guide and hotel scams. Local hotels ask that you call ahead and reserve so that they have your name on

record and thus can avoid paying a bounty to the touts.

🏃 Activities

TOP CHOICE **C.Bali** (☑0813 5320 0251; www.c-bali .com; Hotel Segara, Kedisan) Operated by an Australian-Dutch couple, C. Bali offers you bike tours around the craters and canoe tours on the lake. Prices start at US$40 and include pick-up across south Bali (discounts are available if you're already staying in the area). Packages include multiday trips. The pair also sponsors charity drives for local schools and neighbourhood clean-ups. A very important note: these tours often fill up in advance, so book ahead.

🛏 Sleeping & Eating

The restaurants at the following two hotels are good places to sample the garlic-infused local fish.

Kedisan Floating Hotel   GUESTHOUSE **$$**
(☑51 627; www.kedisan.com; r US$30-100) OK, so nothing floats here – except maybe your rubber duck from home in the soaking tubs – but this newish hotel on the shores of the lake is an appealing place to stay. The most expensive rooms are cottages at the water's edge, then there are some airy upper-level bungalow-style units. Budgeteers can seek out the dark rooms below the bungalows. The restaurant does well with lake fish.

Hotel Segara   GUESTHOUSE **$**
(☑51 136; hotelsegara@plasa.com; Kedisan; r 80,000-200,000Rp; @) The Segara has bungalows set around a courtyard. The cheapest rooms have cold water, the best rooms hot water and bathtubs – perfect for soaking away the hypothermia.

TRUNYAN & KUBAN

The village of Trunyan is squeezed between the lake and the outer crater rim. It is inhabited by Bali Aga people, but unlike Tenganan in east Bali, it is not a welcoming place.

Trunyan is known for the **Pura Pancering Jagat**, with its 4m-high statue of the village's guardian spirit, but tourists are not allowed to go inside. Touts and guides, however, hang about soliciting exorbitant tips. Our advice: don't go.

A little beyond Trunyan, and accessible only by boat, is the **cemetery** at Kuban. The people of Trunyan do not cremate or bury their dead – they lay them out in bamboo cages to decompose. If you do decide to visit the cemetery you'll be met by characters demanding huge fees (it is a tourist trap). Our advice again: don't go.

Boats leave from a jetty near Kedisan. The price for a four-hour return trip (Kedisan–Trunyan–Kuban–Toya Bungkah–Kedisan) depends on the number of passengers, with a maximum of seven people (the boat costs 400,000Rp, although extra 'fees' may be added). Our advice? You guessed it: don't go. However, if you'd like to spend time out on the lake, take one of the canoe trips with C.Bali.

TOYA BUNGKAH

The main tourist centre is Toya Bungkah (also known as Tirta), which boasts hot springs (*tirta* and *toya* both mean water). It's a simple village, and travellers stay here so they can climb Gunung Batur early in the morning. But if you take a moment to smell the onions (and take in the azure lake view), you may decide to stay awhile, even if you don't climb the mountain.

🏃 Activities

Hot springs bubble in a couple of spots, and have long been used for bathing pools.

Batur Natural Hot Spring HOT SPRINGS
(☑0813 3832 5552; admission 80,000Rp; ⊘8am-6pm) Walk down a cinder path and you'll reach this low-key complex of pools on the edge of the lake. Different pools have different temps, so you can simmer yourself successively. The overall feel of the hot springs rather nicely matches the slightly shabby feel of the entire region. Lockers and towels are included with admission, and the simple cafe has good views.

Toya Devasya HOT SPRINGS
(☑51 204; admission 150,000Rp; ⊘8am-8pm) This glossy retreat is built around springs. A huge hot pool is 38°C while a comparatively brisk lake-fed pool is 20°C. Admission includes refreshments and the use of loungers. Villas ring the site. You can camp here – a rarity in Bali – for US$50, which includes two days of soaking and one night shivering in a provided tent.

🍴 Sleeping & Eating

Avoid rooms near the noisy main road through town, opting for placid ones with lake views instead. Unless noted, hotels only have cold water, which can be a boon for waking up before a sunset climb.

Small, sweet lake fish (*ikan mujair*) are the local delicacy.

Lakeside Cottages & Restaurant
GUESTHOUSE $
(☑51 249; r US$10-35; ⊠) The home of recommended guide Jero Wijaya has a lakeside pool on the water's edge that makes it a top pick. Of the 11 rooms, the best have hot water and satellite TV. The restaurant serves home-style Japanese dishes. Renovations may be in the offing.

Under the Volcano III GUESTHOUSE $
(☑0813 386 0081; r 150,000Rp) With a lovely, quiet lakeside location opposite chilli plots, this inn has six clean and pretty rooms; go for room 1 right on the water. There are two other nearby inns in the Volcano empire, all run by the same lovely family.

Hotel Puri Bening Hayato & Restaurant
HOTEL $
(☑51 234; www.indo.com/hotels/puribening hayato; r 350,000-450,000Rp; ⊠) An incongruously modern place for rustic Toya Bungkah. The 21 rooms are motel-like and basically fine. The pool is small, but there's also a hot-spring-fed whirlpool. Free use of mountain bikes is a brilliant amenity.

Volcano Breeze INDONESIAN $
(☑51 824; dishes 15,000-25,000Rp) This sociable travellers cafe with local art on the walls serves fresh lake fish in many forms. It's a good place to just hang out, enjoy the gardens and to gather and plan volcano treks.

SONGAN

Two kilometres around the lake from Toya Bungkah, Songan is a large and interesting village with market gardens extending to the lake's edge. At the lakeside road end is **Pura Ulun Danu Batur**, under the edge of the crater rim.

A turn-off in Songan takes you on a rough but passable road around the crater floor. Much of the area is very fertile, with bright patches of market garden and quite strange landforms. On the northwestern side of the volcano, the village of **Toya Mampeh** (Yeh Mampeh) is surrounded by a vast field of chunky black lava – a legacy of the 1974 eruption. Further on, **Pura Bukit Mentik** was completely surrounded by molten lava from this eruption, but the temple itself, and its impressive banyan tree, were quite untouched – it's called the 'Lucky Temple'.

DANAU BRATAN AREA

As you approach from the south, you gradually leave the rice terraces behind and ascend into the cool, often misty mountain country around Danau Bratan. Candikuning is the main village in the area, and has an important and picturesque temple. Bedugul is at the south end of the lake, with the most touristy attractions. Danau Buyan and Danau Tamblingan are pristine lakes northwest of Danau Bratan that offer good trekking possibilities, while marvellous Munduk anchors the region with fine trekking to waterfalls and cloud-cloaked forests.

The choice of accommodation near the lake is limited, as much of the area is geared towards domestic, not foreign, tourists. On Sundays and public holidays, the lakeside can be crowded with courting couples and Toyotas bursting with day-tripping families. Many new inns have opened around Munduk.

Wherever you go, you are likely to see the blissfully sweet local strawberries on offer. Note that it is often misty and can get chilly up here.

Bedugul

☎0368

'Bedugul' is sometimes used to refer to the whole lakeside area, but strictly speaking it's just the first place you reach at the top of the hill when coming from south Bali, and even then, you might not pause long as it's small.

◉ Sights & Activities

Lakeside eateries, a souvenir market and a selection of water sports – parasailing, water- and jet-skiing plus speedboats – are the features at **Taman Rekreasi Bedugul** (☎21 197; admission 8000Rp, parking 2000Rp), a recreation park that attracts busloads of locals to its timeless carnival charms.

From the water-sports area, a trail around the south side of the lake goes to the mundane **Goa Jepang** (Japanese Cave), which was dug during WWII. From there, a difficult path ascends to the top of **Gunung Catur** (2096m), where the old **Pura Puncak Mangu** temple is popular with monkeys. Allow about four hours to hike up and back from Taman Rekreasi Bedugul.

🛏 Sleeping & Eating

Upmarket hotels on the slope 9km south of Bedugul offer outstanding views to the south, and they're also good choices for a snack or a refreshment if you're just passing by. Beware of a string of rundown places up at the ridge around Bedugul.

Strawberry Hill GUESTHOUSE $
(Bukit Stroberi; ☎21 265; www.strawberryhillbali .com; r 250,000-350,000Rp) Five conical little cottages are arrayed on a hill, each with a deep soaking tub and nice views down to south Bali (although some have better views than others, so compare). The cafe has polished floorboards and on a clear day you can see Kuta. The Indo menu includes soul-healing *soto ayam* (chicken soup) and *gudeg yogya* (jackfruit stew); meals are about 50,000Rp. Hot drinks chase away

---

THE ROAD NEVER TRAVELLED

A series of narrow roads links the Danau Bratan area and the Gunung Batur region. Few locals outside of this area even know the roads exist, and if you have a driver, you might need to do some convincing. Over a 30km route you not only step back to a simpler time, but also leave Bali altogether for something resembling less-developed islands such as Timor. The scenery is beautiful and may make you forget you had a destination.

South of Bedugul, you turn east at Temantanda and take a small and winding road down the hillside into some lush ravines cut by rivers. After about 6km you'll come to a T-junction: turn north and travel about 5km to reach the pretty village of **Pelaga**. This area is known for its organic coffee and cinnamon plantations, which you'll both see and smell. Consider a tour and homestay in Pelaga organised by **JED** (Village Ecotourism Network; ☎0361-735 320; www.jed.or.id; tours US$75-105), a nonprofit group that offers rural tourism experiences (see p390).

From Pelaga, ascend the mountain, following terrain that alternates between jungle and rice fields. Most of the bridges are modest except for a recent one, the highest in Bali, over a deep gorge. Continue north to Catur, then veer east to the junction with the road down to north Bali and drive east again for 1km to Penulisan.

Expect arm and smile fatigue, as you'll be doing a lot of waving to the locals.

the mists. It's opposite the Taman Rekreasi turn-off on the main road.

Pacung Indah
HOTEL $$

(21 020; www.pacungbali.com; r 260,000-830,000Rp; ≋) Across the road from the slightly more upscale Saranam Eco-Resort, this hotel has rice-terrace views and the walled rooms have some style – all include a private courtyard. Those at the top end have decks and views. Treks are offered in the green, green, green countryside.

ⓘ Getting There & Away

Any minibus or bemo between south Bali and Singaraja will stop at Bedugul on request (for more detail, see p217).

Candikuning

☑0368

Dotting the western side of the lake, Candikuning is a haven for plant lovers. Its **market** (parking 2000Rp) is touristy, but among the eager vendors of tat, you'll find locals shopping for fruit, veg, herbs, spices and potted plants. There are also good cafes hidden in the corners and a few worthwhile stalls, such as Smile for Life, a T-shirt shop run by widows of the 2002 Kuta bombings. Privately run toilets (5000Rp) in the southwest corner are the cleanest for miles.

◎ Sights

TOP CHOICE **Bali Botanical Gardens**
GARDENS

(Kebun Raya Eka Karya Bali; ☑21 273; admission walking/driving 7000/12,000Rp, car parking 6000Rp; ⊙7am-6pm) This garden is a showplace. Established in 1959 as a branch of the national botanical gardens at Bogor, near Jakarta, it covers more than 154 hectares on the lower slopes of Gunung Pohen. The garden boasts an extensive collection of trees and flowers. Some plants are labelled with their botanical names, and a booklet of self-guided walks (20,000Rp) is helpful. The gorgeous orchid area is often locked to foil flower filchers; you can ask for it to be unlocked.

Within the park, you can cavort like a bird or a squirrel at the **Bali Treetop Adventure Park** (www.balitreetop.com; adult/child US$20/13). Winches, ropes, nets and the like let you explore the forest well above the ground. And it's not passive – you hoist, jump, balance and otherwise circumnavigate the park. Special programs are geared to different ages.

Coming northwest from Bedugul, at a junction conspicuously marked with a large, phallic corn-cob sculpture, a small side road goes 600m west to the garden. It gets crowded on Sundays with local families.

Pura Ulun Danu Bratan
TEMPLE

(adult/child 10,000/5000Rp, parking 5000Rp; ⊙tickets 7am-5pm, site 24hr) This very important Hindu-Buddhist temple was founded in the 17th century. It is dedicated to Dewi Danu, the goddess of the waters, and is actually built on small islands, which means it is completely surrounded by the lake. Pilgrimages and ceremonies are held here to ensure that there is a supply of water for farmers all over Bali.

The tableau includes classical Hindu thatch-roofed meru reflected in the water and silhouetted against the often cloudy mountain backdrop – a classic Bali photo opportunity. A large banyan tree shades the entrance, and you walk through manicured gardens and past an impressive Buddhist stupa to reach the lakeside.

There's a bit of a sideshow atmosphere, however. Animals in small cages and opportunities to caress a snake or hold a huge bat amuse the punters.

🏃 Activities

At the temple gardens, you can hire a four-passenger **speedboat** with driver (150,000Rp per 30 minutes), a five-person **rowboat** with rower (100,000Rp per 30 minutes), or a two-person **pedal boat** (35,000Rp per 30 minutes).

🛏 Sleeping

Pondok Wisata Dahlia Indah GUESTHOUSE $

(☑21 233; Jl Kebun Raya Bedugul; r 100,000-200,000Rp) In the village along a lane near the road to the botanical gardens, this is a decent budget option whose 17 comfortable, clean rooms have hot-water showers set in a garden of mountain flowers.

Enjung Beji Resort HOTEL $$

(☑21 490; cottages 300,000-600,000Rp) Just north of the temple and overlooking Danau Bratan is this peaceful pleasant option. The 23 cottages are modern and clean, the nicest with outdoor showers and sunken baths.

🍴 Eating

From simple market snacks to meals featuring the region's fresh strawberries, you'll have much to choose from. At the entrance to Pura Ulun Danu Bratan are several Padang warung, and there's a cafe with a view on the grounds.

Strawberry Stop
SWEETS $
(☎21 060; snacks 7000-20,000Rp; ☺8am-7pm) Locally grown strawberries star in milkshakes, juices, pancakes and other sweet treats here. Bananas are used when berries are out of season, which might drive you to drink the self-proclaimed 'dry' – ha! – strawberry wine (100,000Rp).

Top Deck
INDONESIAN $
(☎0811 388 697, 0361-877 9633; meals 20,000-50,000Rp; ☺9am-5pm) Hovering above Crackers, and with the same Australian owners, this airy cafe with an open kitchen looks over the market and has a full menu of creative Indo fare. At lunch there's a buffet option.

Cafe Teras Lempuna
GLOBAL $
(☎0362-29312; meals 25,000-60,000Rp; ❄) North of the temple, this indoor/outdoor cafe is stylish and modern. The menu ranges from burgers to Japanese, and the coffee, tea and juices refresh no matter what the temperature. When it's sunny, enjoy the inviting covered patio; when it's cool, put on the heat with the hot chilli soup.

Crackers
BAR $
(☎0811 388 697; ☺9am-5pm) A small sports bar hidden in the back of the market; it has barbecued mains and comfy wicker seating.

Roti Bedugul
BAKERY $
(☎21 838; snacks 5000Rp; ☺8am-4pm) Just north of the market, this tiny bakery produces fine versions of its namesake, as well as croissants and other treats all day.

❶ Getting There & Away
Danau Bratan is along the main north–south road from south Bali or Singaraja.

Although the main terminal is in Pancasari, most minibuses and bemo will stop along the road in Bedugul and Candikuning. There are frequent connections from Denpasar's Ubung terminal (20,000Rp) and Singaraja's Sukasada terminal (20,000Rp). For Gunung Batur, you have to connect through Singaraja or hire transport.

Pancasari
The broad green valley northwest of Danau Bratan is actually the crater of an extinct volcano. In the middle of the valley, on the

SUNRISE JOY
For an almost surreal experience, take a quiet paddle across Danau Bratan and see Pura Ulun Danu Bratan at sunrise – arrange it with a boatman the night before. The mobs see it by day, but you'll see something entirely different – and magical – in the mists of dawn.

main road, Pancasari is a nontourist town with a bustling market and the main terminal for public bemo.

Just south of Pancasari, you will see the entrance to **Bali Handara Kosaido Country Club** (☎0362-22646; www.balihandarakosaido.com; greens fees US$150), a well-situated (in that, compared with south Bali courses, there's plenty of water here), top-flight 18-hole golf course. It also offers comfortable accommodation (rooms from US$95) in the sterile atmosphere of a 1970s resort, reminiscent of the villain's grand lair in an old James Bond movie.

Danau Buyan & Danau Tamblingan
Also northwest of Danau Bratan are two more lakes, Danau Buyan and Danau Tamblingan – neither has been developed for tourism, which is a plus. There are several tiny villages and abandoned temples along the shores of both lakes, and although frequently swampy ground makes it unpleasant in parts to explore, this is still a good place for a hike.

❂ Sights & Activities
Danau Buyan (admission 5000Rp, parking 2000Rp) has parking right at the lake, a pretty 1.5km drive off the main road – when you park, an attendant will find you for the fees. The entire area is home to market gardens growing strawberries and other high-value crops, such as the orange and blue flowers used in offerings.

A 4km **hiking** trail goes around the southern side of Danau Buyan from the car park, then over the saddle to Danau Tamblingan, and on to Asan Munduk. It combines forest and lake views.

Danau Tamblingan (adult/child 6000/3000Rp, parking 2000Rp) also has parking

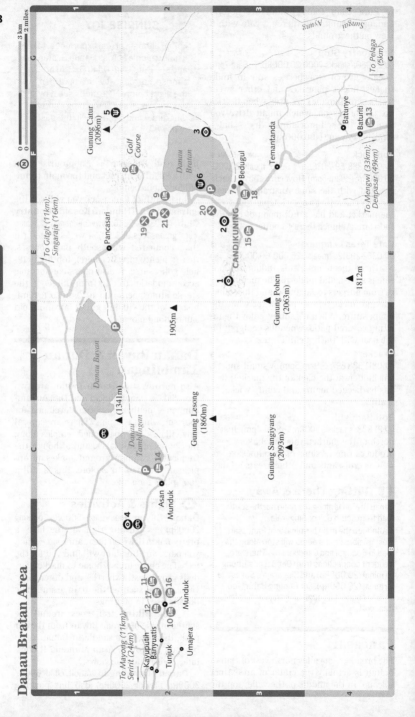

Danau Bratan Area

CENTRAL MOUNTAINS DANAU BRATAN AREA

0   3 km
0   2 miles

To Gitgit (11km);
Singaraja (16km)

To Mayong (11km);
Seririt (24km)

Gunung Catur
(2096m)

Danau Bratan

Golf Course

Bedugul

Temantanda

Baturiti

To Pelaga
(5km)

Sungai Ayung

To Mengwi (33km);
Denpasar (49km)

Pancasari

CANDIKUNING

Gunung Pohen
(2063m)

1812m

1905m

Danau Buyan

Danau
Tamblingan

(1341m)

Asan
Munduk

Gunung Lesong
(1860m)

Gunung Sangiyang
(2093m)

Munduk

Kayuputih
Banyuatis

Tunjuk

Umajera

Danau Bratan Area

at the end of the road from the village of Asan Munduk. The lake is a 400m walk from where you park. From here you can catch the trail to Danau Buyan. If you have a driver, walk this path in one direction and be met at the other end.

There are usually a couple of guides hanging around the car park (you don't need them for the lake path) who will gladly take you up and around **Gunung Lesong** (per 6hr 350,000Rp).

🛏 Sleeping & Eating

Pondok Kesuma Wisata　GUESTHOUSE $
(☑0852 3856 7944; r from 250,000Rp) This nice guesthouse features clean rooms with hot water and a pleasant cafe (meals 15,000Rp to 30,000Rp). It's just up from the Danau Tamblingan parking lot. The owners are charmers and have good hiking advice.

Munduk & Around
☑0362

The simple village of Munduk is one of Bali's most appealing mountain retreats. It has a cool misty ambience set among lush hillsides covered with jungle, rice, fruit trees and pretty much anything else that grows on the island. **Waterfalls** tumble off precipices by the dozen. There are hikes and treks galore and a number of really nice places to stay, from old Dutch summer homes, to retreats where you can plunge full-on into local culture. Many people come for a day and stay for a week.

Archaeological evidence suggests there was a developed community in the Munduk region between the 10th and 14th centuries. When the Dutch took control of north Bali in the 1890s, they experimented with commercial crops, establishing plantations for coffee, vanilla, cloves and cocoa. Quite a few **Dutch colonial buildings** are still intact along the road in Munduk and further west. Look for shrines nestled in the crooks of hills.

⊙ Sights & Activities

Heading to Munduk from Pancasari, the main road climbs steeply up the rim of the old volcanic crater. It's worth stopping to enjoy the views back over the valley and lakes – show a banana and the swarms of monkeys here will get so excited they'll start spanking themselves with joy. Turning right (east) at the top will take you on a scenic descent to the coastal town of Singaraja, via the Gitgit waterfalls (p229). Taking a sharp left turn (west), you follow a ridgetop road with Danau Buyan on one side and a slope to the sea on the other. Coffee is a big crop in the area.

At Asan Munduk, you'll find another T-junction. If you turn left, a trail leads to near Danau Tamblingan, among forest and market gardens. Turning right takes you along beautiful winding roads to the main village of Munduk. Watch for superb panoramas of north Bali and the ocean. Consider a stop at **Ngiring Ngewedang** (☑0828 365146; snacks 15,000-40,000Rp; ⊙10am-5pm), a coffeehouse 5km east of Munduk that grows its own beans on the surrounding slopes. Staff are happy to show you the process that puts the coffee in your cup.

Wherever you stay, staff will fill you in on **walking** and **hiking** options. Numerous trails are suitable for treks of two hours or much longer to coffee plantations, rice paddies, waterfalls, villages, or around both Danau Tamblingan and Danau Buyan. Most are easy to do on your own, but guides will take you far off the beaten path to waterfalls and other delights that are hard to find. Almost everything in the Munduk area is at an elevation of at least 1000m. You will be able to arrange a guide through your lodgings.

🛏 Sleeping & Eating

The hikes around Munduk draw many visitors and consequently there are many places for them to stay. Enjoy simple old Dutch houses in the village or more naturalistic places in the countryside. Most have cafes, usually serving good local fare. There are a couple of cute warung along the road down to Seririt and north Bali, and a few stores with very basic supplies (including bug spray) have now opened.

TOP CHOICE **Puri Lumbung Cottages**

GUESTHOUSE **$$**
(☑0812 383 6891, 0812 387 3986; www.purilum bung.com; cottages US$75-160; @�{?}) Founded by Nyoman Bagiarta to develop sustainable tourism, this lovely hotel has 33 bright two-storey cottages and rooms set among rice fields. Enjoy intoxicating views (units 3, 8, 10, 11, 14A and 14B have the best) down to the coast from the upstairs balconies. Dozens of trekking options and courses, including dance and cooking, are offered. The hotel's restaurant, **Warung Kopi Bali**, is sponsored by a Swiss cooking school. The menu includes a local dish *timbungan bi siap* (chicken soup with sliced cassava and fried shallots), as well as a Cobb salad. The hotel is on the right-hand side of the road coming from Bedugul, 700m before Munduk.

DON'T MISS

MUNDUK'S EASIEST WATERFALL

About 2km east of Munduk, look for signs indicating parking for a 15m waterfall near the road; this is the most accessible of many in the immediate area. A very short walk along a decent path brings you to the source of the enticing roar. Clouds of mist from the water add to the already misty air; drips come off every leaf. If you felt wilted in south Bali, you'll feel fully refreshed here.

Lumbung Bali Cottages GUESTHOUSE **$$**
(☑700 5211, 0828 372 6458; www.lumbung-bali .com; r US$55-90) About 800m east of Munduk, this country inn has nine traditional cottages overlooking the lush local terrain. The open-air bathrooms (with tubs) are as refreshing as the porches are relaxing. A short trail leads to a small waterfall. There are cooking classes and guided walks.

Meme Surung & Mekel Ragi GUESTHOUSE **$**
(☑0812 383 6891, 0812 387 3986; r 200,000Rp) These atmospheric old Dutch houses adjoin each other in the village and have two rooms. There are seven more rooms – all with hot showers – in a small building next door to the pair. Meme Surung has views.

Puri Alam Bali GUESTHOUSE **$**
(☑0812 465 9815; www.purialambali.com; r 250,000Rp) Perched on a precipice at the east end of the village, Puri Alam Bali's eight rooms (all with hot water) have better views the higher you go. The rooftop cafe is newly expanded and worth a visit; it surveys the local scene from on high. Think of the long concrete stairs down from the road as trekking practice.

Guru Ratna GUESTHOUSE **$**
(☑0813 3852 6092; r 150,000-300,000Rp) The cheapest place in the village has seven comfortable hot-water rooms in a colonial Dutch house. The best rooms have some style, carved wood details and nice porches. Ponder the distant ocean from the cafe.

Munduk Sari GUESTHOUSE **$$**
(☑0361-297 123; www.munduksari.com; r from 500,000Rp) The polished rooms at this modern, slightly soulless inn have classic views of the hills and large tubs with hot water. It's just east of the village.

ℹ Getting There & Away

Bemo leave Ubung terminal in Denpasar for Munduk (22,000Rp) frequently. Morning bemo from Candikuning also stop in Munduk (13,000Rp). If you're driving to the north coast, a decent road west of Munduk goes through a number of picturesque villages to Mayong (where you can head south to west Bali; see p222). The road then goes down to the sea at Seririt in north Bali.

GUNUNG BATUKAU AREA

☑0361

Gunung Batukau is Bali's second-highest mountain (2276m), the third of Bali's three major mountains and the holy peak of the island's western end. It's often overlooked, which is probably a good thing given what the vendor hordes have done to Gunung Agung.

You can climb its slippery slopes from one of the island's holiest and most under-rated temples, Pura Luhur Batukau, or just revel in the ancient rice-terrace greenery around Jatiluwih, which would be a fantasy if it wasn't real. Extend your stay at lodges far up the slopes of the volcano.

There are two main approaches to the Gunung Batukau area. The easiest is via Tabanan: take the Pura Luhur Batukau road north 9km to a fork in the road, then take the left-hand turn (towards the temple) and go a further 5km to a junction near a school in Wangayagede village. Here you can continue straight to the temple or turn right (east) for the rice fields of Jatiluwih.

The other way is to approach from the east. On the main Denpasar–Singaraja road, look for a small road to the west, just south of the Pacung Indah hotel (p216). Here you follow a series of small paved roads west until you reach the Jatiluwih rice fields. You'll get lost, but locals will quickly set you right and the scenery is su-perb anyway. Combine the two routes for a nice circle tour.

◉ Sights & Activities

TOP CHOICE **Pura Luhur Batukau** TEMPLE
(donation 10,000Rp) On the slopes of Gunung Batukau, Pura Luhur Batukau was the state temple when Tabanan was an in-dependent kingdom. It has a seven-roofed meru dedicated to Maha Dewa, the moun-tain's guardian spirit, as well as shrines for Bratan, Buyan and Tamblingan lakes. The main meru in the inner courtyard have lit-tle doors shielding small ceremonial items. This is certainly the most spiritual temple you can easily visit in Bali.

The temple is surrounded by forest and the atmosphere is cool and misty; the chants of priests are backed by birds sing-ing. Facing the temple, take a short walk around to the left to see a small white-water stream where the air resonates with tumbling water. Get here early for the best chance of seeing the dark and foreboding slopes of the volcano.

There's a general lack of touts and other characters here – including hordes of tour-ists. A sign indicates that 'mad ladies/gen-tlemen' are not allowed to visit. Look sane.

DON'T MISS

JATILUWIH RICE FIELDS

At Jatiluwih, which means 'truly marvellous' (or 'real beautiful' depending on the translation), you will be rewarded with vistas of centuries-old rice terraces that ex-haust your ability to describe green. Emerald ribbons curve around the hillsides, step-ping back as they climb to the blue sky.

The terraces have been nominated for Unesco status for being emblematic of Bali's ancient rice-growing culture. You'll understand the nomination just viewing the panorama from the narrow, twisting 18km road, but getting out for a rice-field walk is even more rewarding, following the water as it runs through channels and bamboo pipes from one plot to the next. Much of the rice you'll see is traditional, rather than the hybrid versions grown elsewhere on the island. Look for heavy short husks of red rice.

Take some time, leave your driver behind and just find a place to sit and enjoy the views. It sounds like a cliché, but the longer you look the more you'll see. What at first seems like a vast palette of greens reveals itself to be rice at various stages of growth. See how many you can count, from the impossibly iridescent emerald hues of the young shoots to the lazy green-yellows of the rice-laden stalks ready for harvest.

There are a couple of simple cafes for refreshments along the drive, which won't take more than an hour – unless you get so caught up in the beauty you can't leave. Because the road is sharply curved, vehicles are forced to drive slowly, which makes the Jatiluwih route a good one for bikes. There is a road toll for visitors (10,000Rp per person, plus 5000Rp per car).

You can access the road in the west off the road to Pura Luhur Batukau from Ta-banan, and in the east off the main road to Bedugul near Pacung. Drivers all know this road well and locals offer directions.

For tips on respecting traditions and acting appropriately while visiting temples, see p329. Sarongs can be borrowed.

Gunung Batukau
VOLCANO

At Pura Luhur Batukau you are fairly well up the side of Gunung Batukau, and you may wish to go for a climb. But to trek to the top of the 2276m peak, you'll need a guide, which can be arranged at the temple ticket booth. Expect to pay 1,000,000Rp (for two people) for a muddy and arduous journey that will take at least seven hours in one direction. The rewards are amazing views alternating with thick dripping jungle, and the knowledge that you've taken a trail that is much less travelled than the ones on the eastern peaks. You can get a taste of the adventure on a two-hour mini-jaunt (200,000Rp for two).

🛏 Sleeping

Two remote lodges are hidden away on the slopes of Gunung Batukau. You reach both via a spectacular small and twisting road that makes a long inverted V far up the mountain from Bajera and Pucuk on the main Tabanan–Gilimanuk road in west Bali.

Sarinbuana Eco-Lodge   LODGE **$$**
(☏743 5198; www.baliecolodge.com; Sarinbuana; €110-140) These beautiful two-level bungalows are built on the side of a hill just a 10-minute walk from a protected rainforest preserve. Notable amenities include fridges, marble bathrooms and handmade soap. There are extensive cultural workshops and trekking opportunities. A delightful treehouse bungalow in the village costs €22 to €30. The lodge has a long list of green practices.

Bali Mountain Retreat   LODGE **$$**
(☏789 7553; www.balimountainretreat.com; Biyahan; r US$20-200; 🗐🏊) Luxurious rooms set in refined cottages are arrayed artistically at this hillside location. A pool and gardens mix with mannered architecture that combines new and old influences. The rooms have video and music systems, plus large verandas perfect for contemplating the views. Budget options include a bed in a vintage rice-storage barn.

ℹ Getting There & Away

The only realistic way to explore the Gunung Batukau area is with your own transport.

THE ANTOSARI ROAD

☏0361

Although most people cross the mountains via Candikuning or Kintamani, there is a very scenic third alternative that links Bali's south and north coasts. From the Denpasar–Gilimanuk road in west Bali, a road goes north from **Antosari** through the village of **Pupuan** and then drops down to Seririt, west of Lovina in north Bali.

Starting through rice paddies, after 8km the road runs alongside a beautiful valley of rice terraces. Another 2km brings you to **Sari Wisata** (☏0812 398 8773), where a charming family has created what should be the model for roadhouses everywhere. Gorgeous gardens line the bluff and only enhance the already remarkable vistas. (Did somebody tell the rice farmers to wear red so they pop from the fields of green?) Snacks and drinks are available, and outside you'll

WORTH A TRIP

THE OTHER ROAD TO PUPUAN

You can reach the mountain village of Pupuan on the road from Antosari but there is another route, one that wanders the back roads of deepest mountain Bali. Start at Pulukan, which is on the Denpasar–Gilimanuk road in west Bali. A small road climbs steeply up from the coast providing fine views back down to west Bali and the sea. It runs through spice-growing country – you'll see (and smell) spices laid out to dry on mats by the road. After about 10km and just before Manggissari, the narrow and winding road actually runs right through **Bunut Bolong** – an enormous tree that forms a complete tunnel (the *bunut* is a type of ficus; *bolong* means 'hole').

Further on, the road spirals down to Pupuan through some of Bali's most beautiful rice terraces. It's worth stopping off for a walk to the magnificent **waterfalls** near Pujungan, a few kilometres south of Pupuan. Follow signs down a narrow rough road and then walk 1.5km to the first waterfall; it's nice, but before you say 'is that all there is?' follow your ears to a second that's 50m high.

find some remarkably healthy and furry bats literally hanging around in the sun.

Once you're deep in the foothills of Gunung Batukau, 20km north of Antosari, you'll smell the fragrant spice-growing village of **Sanda** before you see it. Look for the old wooden elevated rice barns that still feature in every house.

After another 8km north through coffee plantations, you'll reach Pupuan. From here it is 12km or so to Mayong, where you can turn east to Munduk and on to Danau Bratan or go straight on to Seririt.

🛏 Sleeping & Eating

TOP
CHOICE **Sanda Bukit Villas & Restaurant**
LODGE **$$**

(☑0828 372 0055; www.sandavillas.com; bungalows from US$75; ✳ ☒) This boutique hotel

offers a serene escape. Its large infinity pool seems to disappear into the rice terraces, while the seven bungalows are really quite luxe. It's well run and the fusion cafe is excellent (dinner from US$5). The engaging owners will recommend walks among the coffee plantations and rice fields. It is just north of the village of Sanda.

Kebun Villas LODGE **$$**

(☑0361-780 6068; www.kebunvilla.com; r US$60-85; ☒) Eight cottages here are scattered down a hillside and make the most of the sweeping view over rice fields in the valley. The pool area is a hike down to the valley floor but is huge, and once there you may just linger all day. The cafe serves tasty food.

North Bali

Includes »

Best Places to Eat

» Damai (p235)

» Jasmine Kitchen (p235)

» Akar (p235)

Best Places to Stay

» Taman Sari Bali Cottages (p238)

» Pondok Sari (p239)

» Puri Ganesha Villas (p239)

» Damai (p234)

» Cilik's Beach Garden (p226)

Why Go?

The land on the other side, that's north Bali. Although one-sixth of the island's population lives here, the vast region is overlooked by many visitors who stay trapped in the south Bali–Ubud axis.

The two big draws are Lovina, the sleepy beach town with cheap hotels and even cheaper sunset beer specials; and Pemuteran. The latter is everything a mellow beach resort should be, with appealing hotels arrayed around a small bay. The major draw is diving and snorkelling at nearby Pulau Menjangan in west Bali.

Getting to north Bali for once lives up to the cliché: it's half the fun. Routes follow the thinly populated coastlines east and west, or you can go up and over the mountains by any number of routes, marvelling at crater lakes and maybe stopping for a misty trek on the way.

Once north, sacred temples, waterfalls and many other seldom-visited treasures await. Pick a back road for a ride or a drive, wave to the villagers and discover a new, more relaxed side of Bali.

When to Go

Most of north Bali doesn't have a high season in terms of visitors. The exception is Pemuteran, which is busy July, August and the weeks around Christmas and New Year. Weather-wise it's always drier in the north as opposed to south Bali. Days of perpetual sun are the norm year-round (most visitors like air-con for sleeping). The only real variation will be found when you venture back into the hills for waterfalls or hikes; mornings will be cool.

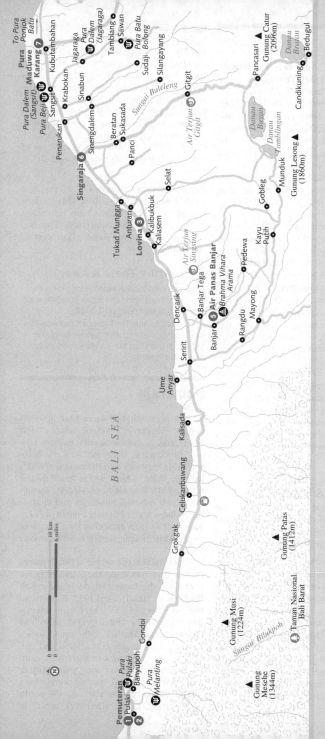

North Bali Highlights

1 Exploring underwater marvels while staying at **Pemuteran** (p238), an idyllic beach town

2 Wandering the beach in front of **Pemuteran's resorts** (p238), trying to choose where to have dinner

3 Losing track of time at **Lovina** (p230), but not of your budget

4 Going for a hike in the lush hills that line north Bali, especially to **hidden waterfalls** (p231) for a swim

5 Getting dirty in the healthy mud of **Air Panas Banjar** (p237)

6 Savouring Buleleng's rich culture at the museums of **Singaraja** (p226), which has a long royal history

7 Marvelling at the carving all around the artful temple **Pura Maduwe Karang** (p230)

Yeh Sanih

☎ 0362

On the coast road to the beach and diving towns of east Bali, Yeh Sanih (also called Air Sanih) is a hassle-free seaside spot with a few guesthouses on the beachfront. It's named for its fresh-water springs, **Air Sanih** (adult/child 3000/1000Rp; ⊗8am-6pm), which are channelled into large swimming pools before flowing into the sea. The pools are particularly picturesque at sunset, when throngs of locals bathe under blooming frangipani trees – most of the time they're alive with frolicking kids. It's about 15km east of Singaraja.

Pura Ponjok Batu has a commanding location between the sea and the road, some 7km east of Yeh Sanih. It has some very fine limestone carvings in the central temple area. Legend holds that it was built to provide some spiritual balance for Bali, what with all the temples in the south.

Between the springs and the temple, the road is often close to the sea. It's probably Bali's best stretch of coast driving, with waves crashing onto the breakwater and great views out to sea.

Completely out of character for the area is a place run by quite a character: **Art Zoo** (www.symonstudios.com; ⊗8am-6pm) is 5.7km east of Yeh Sanih on the Singaraja road. Symon, the irrepressible American artist (who also has a gallery in Ubud), owns this gallery and studio, which are fairly bursting with a creativity at times vibrant, exotic and erotic.

🛏 Sleeping & Eating

A few warung (food stalls) hover near the entrance of Yeh Sanih and do a brisk business with the local trade. Otherwise, options are few and scattered.

Cilik's Beach Garden   GUESTHOUSE $$
(☎26 561; www.ciliksbeachgarden.com; r €50-80, villas €80-110; @) Coming here is like visiting your rich friends, albeit ones with good taste. These custom-built villas, 3km east of Yeh Sanih, are large and have extensive private gardens. Other accommodation is in stylish *lumbung* (rice barns with round roofs) set in a delightful garden facing the ocean. There's a real emphasis on local culture; the owners have even more remote villas further south on the coast.

Pondok Sembiran   GUESTHOUSE $$
(☎0813 3852 8874; www.sembiran.com; r 500,000-850,000Rp; ❅ ✉) This inn is bifurcated: one wing is 20m from the sea and has a pool and four rooms, the other has seven bungalows and is located right on the seawall. All habitations are large, good for families, have full kitchens and are well off the main road in a grove of coconut palms. The hotel is off the main road in Alassari, 1km east of the temple and 8.3km east of Yeh Sanih. It's popular with frugal Dutch travellers.

Pondok Wisata Cleopatra   GUESTHOUSE $
(☎0812 362 2232; r 200,000Rp) This modern budget place has nine clean, cold-water rooms with showers and tubs. The big, flowery grounds are about 1.1km west of the springs.

ℹ Getting There & Away

Yeh Sanih is on the main road along the north coast. Frequent bemo and buses from Singaraja stop outside the springs (10,000Rp).

If heading to Amed or Tulamben, make certain you're on your way south from here by 4pm in order to arrive while there's still some light to avoid road hazards.

Singaraja

☎ 0362

With a population of more than 100,000 people, Singaraja (which means 'Lion King' and somehow hasn't caused Disney to demand licensing fees) is Bali's second-largest city and the capital of Buleleng Regency, which covers much of the north. With its tree-lined streets, surviving Dutch colonial buildings and charmingly sleepy waterfront area north of Jl Erlangga, it's worth exploring for a couple of hours. Most people stay in nearby Lovina, however.

Singaraja was the centre of Dutch power in Bali and remained the administrative centre for the Lesser Sunda Islands (Bali through to Timor) until 1953. It is one of the few places in Bali where there are visible traces of the Dutch period, as well as Chinese and Muslim influences. Today, Singaraja is a major educational and cultural centre, and its two university campuses provide the city with a substantial, and sometimes vocal, student population.

The village of **Beratan**, to the south of Singaraja, is the silverwork centre of

northern Bali. You'll find a few traditional pieces such as *cucuk* (gold headpieces) on display, but otherwise it's mostly uninspiring tourist jewellery. A few workshops in and around Singaraja produce hand-woven sarongs – especially *songket* (cloth woven with silver or gold threads).

◎ Sights & Activities

Old Harbour & Waterfront   HISTORIC AREA
The conspicuous **Yudha Mandala Tama monument** commemorates a freedom fighter killed by gunfire from a Dutch warship early in the struggle for independence. Close by, there's the colourful Chinese temple, **Ling Gwan Kiong**. There are a few old canals here as well and you can still get a little feel of the colonial port that was the main entrance to Bali before WWII; check out the cinematically decrepit **old Dutch warehouses** opposite the water. Some warung have been built on stilts over the

water. Walk up Jl Imam Bonjol and you'll see the art deco lines of late-colonial Dutch buildings.

Gedong Kirtya Library & Museum Buleleng MUSEUM

(☎22 645; admission 10,000Rp; ☺8am-4pm Mon-Thu, 8am-1pm Fri) This small historical library was established in 1928 by Dutch colonialists and named after the Sanskrit for 'to try'. It has a collection of *lontar* (dried palm leaves) books (see the boxed text), as well as some even older written works in the form of inscribed copper plates called *prasasti*. Dutch publications, dating back to 1901, may interest students of the colonial period. On our visit they were carefully copying the text from a beautiful example from 1933.

The nearby **Museum Buleleng** (admission free; ☺9am-3.30pm Mon-Fri) recalls the life of the last Radja (rajah; prince) of Buleleng, Pandji Tisna, who is credited with developing Lovina's tourism. Among the items here is the Royal (brand) typewriter he used during his career as a travel writer (obviously, the rajah was a smart, if poorly remunerated guy) before his death in 1978. It also traces the history of the region back to when there was no history.

Down a small lane in the compound you'll find displays of local weaving.

Pura Jagat Natha TEMPLE

Singaraja's main temple, the largest in northern Bali, is not usually open to foreigners. You can appreciate its size and admire the carved stone decorations from the outside.

LONTAR BOOKS

Lontar is made from the fan-shaped leaves of the *rontal* palm. The leaf is dried, soaked in water, cleaned, steamed, dried again, then flattened, dyed and eventually cut into strips. The strips are inscribed with words and pictures using a very sharp blade or point, then coated with a black stain which is wiped off – the black colour stays in the inscription. A hole in the middle of each *lontar* strip is threaded onto a string, with a carved bamboo 'cover' at each end to protect the 'pages', and the string is secured with a couple of pierced Chinese coins, or *kepeng*.

The Gedong Kirtya Library in Singaraja has the world's largest collection of lontar works.

✦✦ Festivals & Events

Every May or June, the **Bali Art Festival of Buleleng** is held in Singaraja and surrounding villages. Over one week dancers and musicians from some of the region's most renowned village troupes, such as those of Jagaraga, perform. In August, the **North Bali Festival** is a celebration of the traditional arts of the regency. Consult with the Diparda tourist office for details on both.

🛏 Sleeping & Eating

There are slim accommodation pickings in Singaraja, and there's no real reason to stay here, as it's just a short drive from Lovina.

For supplies and sundries, head to **Hardy's Supermarket** (Jl Pramuka; ☺6am-10pm). Join the villa-owning expats for gourmet and imported food stuffs at **ABD Food Mart** (☎700 1400; Jl Udayana Barat 2). In the evening, there are food stalls in the **night market** (Jl Durian; ☺5pm-1am).

Hotel Wijaya GUESTHOUSE **$**

(☎21 915; Jl Sudiman 74; r 75,000-250,000Rp; ✱) This is the most comfortable place in town and now sports a fresh look; economy fan rooms have an outside bathroom. It also has a small cafe. The bus terminal is a three-minute walk.

Warung Kota CAFE **$**

(☎700 9737; Jl Ngurah Rai 22; meals 8000-15,000Rp) The kool kats' hang-out, this ebullient cafe is popular with students from the university. Grab a table amid the bamboo decor and make some friends. There's live music some nights, movies others.

Istana Bakery BAKERY **$**

(☎21 983; Jl Jen Achmed Yani; snacks 3000Rp; ☺8am-6pm) Fallen in love in Lovina? Get your wedding cake here. For lesser life moments like the munchies, choose from an array of tasty baked goods.

Dapur Ibu INDONESIAN **$**

(☎24 474; Jl Jen Achmed Yani; meals 8000-15,000Rp) A nice local cafe with a small garden off the street. The *nasi goreng* (fried rice) is fresh and excellent; wash it down with a fresh juice or bubble tea.

ℹ Information

Medical Services

RSUP Hospital (☎22 046; Jl Ngurah Rai; ☺24hr) Singaraja's hospital is the largest in northern Bali.

Money

There are numerous banks that will change money and have ATMs on Jl Jen Achmed Yani.

Post

Post office (Jl Imam Bonjol)

Tourist Information

Diparda (25 141; www.northbalitourism.com; Jl Ngurah Rai 2; ⊙7.30am-3.30pm Mon-Fri) Near the museum, the regional tourist office has some OK maps. Good information if you ask specifically about dance and other cultural events. Useful website.

❶ Getting There & Away

Singaraja is the main transport hub for the northern coast, with three bemo/bus terminals. From the **Sukasada terminal**, 3km south of town, minibuses go to Denpasar (Ubung terminal, 35,000Rp) via Bedugul/Pancasari sporadically through the day.

The **Banyuasri terminal**, on the western side of town, has buses heading to Gilimanuk (25,000Rp, two hours) and Java, and plenty of bemo to Lovina (10,000Rp).

The **Penarukan terminal**, 2km east of town, has bemo to Yeh Sanih (10,000Rp) and Amlapura (about 20,000Rp, three hours) via the coastal road; and also minibuses to Denpasar (Batubulan terminal, 35,000Rp, three hours) via Kintamani.

TO JAVA From Singaraja, several companies have services, which include the ferry trip across the Bali Strait. Buses go as far as Yogyakarta (350,000Rp, 16 hours) and Jakarta (500,000Rp, 24 hours), usually travelling overnight – book at Banyuasri terminal a day before.

❶ Getting Around

Bemo link the three main bemo/bus terminals and cost about 7000Rp. The green Banyuasri–Sukasada bemo goes along Jl Gajah Mada to the Gedong Kirtya Library & Museum Buleleng; this bemo, and the brown one between Penarukan and Banyuasri terminals, also goes along Jl Jen Achmed Yani.

Around Singaraja

The interesting sites around Singaraja include some of Bali's most important temples.

SANGSIT

A few kilometres northeast of Singaraja you can see an excellent example of the colourful architectural style of north Bali. Sangsit's **Pura Beji** is a temple for the *subak* (village association of rice-growers),

dedicated to the goddess Dewi Sri, who looks after irrigated rice fields. The over-the-top sculptured panels along the front wall set the tone with cartoonlike demons and amazing *naga* (mythical snake-like creatures). The inside also has a variety of sculptures covering every available space. It's 500m off the main road towards the coast.

The **Pura Dalem** (Temple of the Dead) shows scenes of punishment in the afterlife, and other humorous, sometimes erotic, pictures. You'll find it in the rice fields, about 500m northeast of Pura Beji.

Buses and bemo going east from Singaraja's Penarukan terminal will stop at Sangsit.

JAGARAGA

It was the capture of the local rajah's stronghold at Jagaraga that marked the arrival of Dutch power in Bali in 1849. The village, a few kilometres south of the main road, also has a **Pura Dalem**. The small, interesting temple has delightful sculptured panels along its front wall, inside and out. On the outer wall, look for a vintage car driving sedately past, a steamer at sea and even an aerial dogfight between early aircraft. Jagaraga is also famous for its Legong troupe – said to be the best in north Bali – but performances are irregular.

Bemo from the Penarukan terminal in Singaraja stop at Jagaraga on the way to Sawan.

SAWAN

Several kilometres inland from Jagaraga, Sawan is a centre for the manufacturing of gamelan gongs and instruments. You can see the gongs being cast and the intricately carved gamelan frames being fashioned. **Pura Batu Bolong** (Temple of the Hollow Stone) and its baths are also worth a look. Around Sawan there are cold-water springs believed to cure all sorts of illnesses.

Regular bemo to Sawan leave from Penarukan terminal in Singaraja.

GITGIT

Around about 11km south of Singaraja, a well-signposted path goes 800m west from the main road to the touristy waterfall, **Air Terjun Gitgit** (adult/child 6000/3000Rp). The path is lined with souvenir stalls and guides to nowhere. The 40m waterfalls pound away and the mists are more refreshing than any air-con.

BALI'S FIRST CYCLIST

Pura Maduwe Karang (Temple of the Land Owner) is one of the most intriguing temples in north Bali and is particularly notable for its sculptured panels, including the famous stone-carved **bicycle relief** that depicts a gentleman riding a bicycle with a lotus flower serving as the back wheel. It's on the base of the main plinth in the inner enclosure. The cyclist may be WOJ Nieuwenkamp, a Dutch artist who, in 1904, brought what was probably the first bicycle to Bali.

Like Pura Beji at Sangsit, this temple of dark stone is dedicated to agricultural spirits, but this one looks after nonirrigated land. The temple is easy to find in the village of Kubutambahan – seek the 34 carved figures from the *Ramayana* outside the walls. Kubutambahan is on the road between Singaraja and Amlapura, about 1km east of the turn-off to Kintamani. Regular bemo and buses pass through.

About 2km further up the hill, there's a multitiered **waterfall** (donation 5000Rp) about 600m off the western side of the main road. The path crosses a narrow bridge and follows the river up past several small sets of waterfalls, through verdant jungle.

Regular bemo and minibuses between Denpasar (Ubung terminal) and Singaraja (Sukasada terminal) stop at Gitgit. Gitgit is also a major stop on organised tours of central and north Bali.

Lovina

📞 0362

'Relaxed' is how people most often describe Lovina and they are correct. This low-key, low-rise beach resort is the polar opposite of Kuta. Days are slow and so are the nights. The waves are calm, the beach is thin and over-amped attractions nil.

This is where you catch up on your journal and get plenty of R&R, finish a book or simply let one day disappear into the next. There's some good diving in the area, and if you want to get your motor revving, literally, there's dolphin watching in the early morning. The beaches are made up of washed-out grey and black volcanic sand, and while they're mostly clean near the hotel areas, they're not spectacular. Reefs protect the shore, calming the waves and keeping the water clear.

While not arid, Lovina is also not a tropical jungle. It's sun-drenched, with patches of shade from palm trees. A highlight every afternoon at fishing villages like Anturan is watching *prahu* (traditional outrigger canoes) being prepared for the night's fishing; as sunset reddens the sky, the lights of the fishing boats appear as bright dots across the horizon.

The Lovina tourist area stretches over 8km, and consists of a string of coastal villages – Kaliasem, Kalibukbuk, Anturan, Tukad Mungga – collectively known as Lovina. The main focus is Kalibukbuk, 10.5km west of Singaraja and the heart of Lovina. The main street is also the main east–west road. It goes by various names, including Jl Raya Lovina and Jl Raya Kaliasem. Traffic in the daytime can be loud and constant.

For trips to Singaraja, back roads offer scenic alternatives.

◉ Sights & Activities

Beaches

A paved **beach footpath** runs along the sand in Kalibukbuk and extends in a circuitous path along the seashore; it ranges from clean to grubby. Enjoy the postcard view to the east of the mountainous north Bali coast. You'll also enjoy that the sleepy vibe extends to the vendors, who are mostly somnolent.

The best beach areas include the main beach east of the **Dolphin Monument**, as well as the curving stretch a bit west. The cluster of cheap hotels in Anturan also enjoy fun on the sand. While moored near shore, the fishing boats can fascinate with their large, bare engines, menacing-looking props and individual paint schemes.

Dolphin Watching

Sunrise boat trips to see dolphins are Lovina's much-hyped tourist attraction, so much so that a large, concrete-crowned monument was erected in their honour.

Some days no dolphins are sighted, but most of the time at least a few surface.

Expect pressure from your hotel and touts selling dolphin trips. The price is fixed at 50,000Rp per person by the boat-owners' cartel. Trips start at a non-holiday-like 6am and last about two hours. Note that the ocean can get pretty crowded with loud, roaring powerboats.

There's great debate about what all this means to the dolphins. Do they like being chased by boats? If not, why do they keep coming back? Maybe it's the fish, of which there are plenty off Lovina.

Diving

Scuba diving on the local reef is better at lower depths and night diving is popular. Many people stay here and dive Pulau Menjangan, a two-hour drive west.

Spice Dive (☏41 509; www.balispicedive .com) is a large operation. It offers snorkelling trips (€23), local intro dives (€45) and popular Menjangan trips (€60). It's based at the west end of the beach path.

Snorkelling

Generally, the water is clear and some parts of the reef are quite good for snorkelling, though the coral has been damaged by bleaching and, in places, by dynamite fishing. The best place is to the west, a few hundred metres offshore from Billibo Beach Cottages. A boat trip will cost about 50,000Rp per person for two people for two hours, including equipment. Snorkelling gear costs about 30,000Rp per day.

Hiking

Komang Dodik (☏0819 3631 6701; lovina .tracking@gmail.com) leads highly recommended hikes in the hills along the north coast. Trips start at 250,000Rp per person and can last from three to seven hours. The highlight of most is a series of waterfalls, over 20m high, in a jungle grotto. Routes can include coffee and vanilla plantations.

Cycling

The roads south of Jl Raya Lovina are excellent for biking, with limited traffic and enjoyable rides amid the rice fields and into the hills for views. Many of the sites beyond Lovina to the west are easily reached by bike.

Most hotels can rent you a bike. **Sovina Shop** (☏41 402; Jl Ketapang) has a good selection of bicycles for hire from 20,000Rp per day. Motorbikes are 35,000Rp per day.

Massage & Spas

Araminth Spa (☏0812 384 4655; Jl Ketapang; massage from 150,000Rp; ☺10am-7pm) offers Balinese, Ayurveda and foot massage in a simple but soothing setting. It promotes 'vagina steaming', which involves dry, herbal smoke (120,000Rp).

🛏 Sleeping

Hotels are spread out along Jl Raya Lovina, and on the side roads going off to the beach. Overall, choices tend to be more budget-focused; don't come here for a luxe experience. Be wary of hotels right on the main road – however, those with rooms down by the water are just fine.

Anturan is largely a backpackers' beach with a mellow charm. There are a variety of choices from Anturan to Kalibukbuk, which is jammed with accommodation and places to drink. West of Kalibukbuk the hotel density again diminishes right along with the beach.

During slow periods in Lovina, all room prices are negotiable.

ANTURAN

A few tiny side tracks and one proper sealed road, Jl Kubu Gembong, lead to this lively little fishing village, busy with swimming locals and moored fishing boats. It's a real travellers' hang-out. But it's a long way from Lovina's evening delights – expect to pay around 20,000Rp for transport back to Anturan from Kalibukbuk after 6pm when the bemo stop operating.

Puspa Rama   GUESTHOUSE $
(☏42 070; agungdayu@yahoo.com; Jl Kubu Gembong; r 150,000Rp) The best budget option on this street, Puspa Rama has grounds a few cuts above the others. The six rooms have hot water. Fruit trees abound – why not pick your own breakfast?

Gede Home Stay Bungalows   HOMESTAY $
(☏41526; Jl Kubu Gembong; r 100,000-200,000Rp; ❄) Don't forget to shake the sand off your feet as you enter this beachside eight-room homestay. Cheap rooms have cold water while better ones have hot water and air-con.

ANTURAN TO KALIBUKBUK

Jl Pantai Banyualit has many hotels, although the beach is not very inspiring. There is a little park-like area by the water and the walk along the shore to Kalibukbuk is quick and scenic.

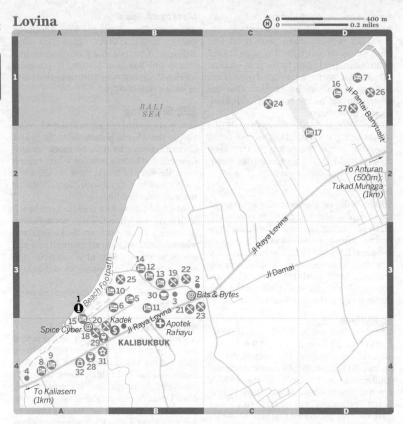

Hotel Banyualit HOTEL **$$**
(☑41 789; www.banyualit.com; Jl Pantai Banyualit; r 300,000-800,000Rp; ✳❄) About 100m back from the beach, the Banyualit has a lush garden, statues and a large pool. The 23 rooms offer great choice; best are the good-value villas with whirlpools, fridges and large, shady patios. There's also a small spa.

Suma GUESTHOUSE **$**
(☑41 566; www.sumahotel.com; Jl Pantai Banyu-alit; r 150,000-700,000Rp; ✳@❄) In this mannered stone building behind a newly enlarged temple, you'll find views of the sea from its upstairs rooms; the best of the 13 have air-con and hot water; newish bungalows are quite nice. The pool is large and naturalistic; there's also a pleasant cafe. A much-renovated temple is nearby.

Sunari HOTEL **$$**
(☑41 775; www.sunari.com; r US$40-100, villas US$70-200; ✳@❄) Off Jl Raya Lovina, the imposing entrance of this 83-room place leads to a large resort with many room choices. Decor is not lavish and the garden-view rooms are basic, but the deluxe private villas with whirlpools and views of the ocean give a lot of bang for the buck. The beach here is one of the better in Lovina.

KALIBUKBUK

A little over 10km from Singaraja, the 'centre' of Lovina is the village of Kalibukbuk. Mellow Jl Ketapang is quieter and more pleasant than Jl Bina Ria. Small gang (alleys) lined with cheap places to stay lead off both streets.

Rambutan Hotel HOTEL **$$**
(☑41 388; www.rambutan.org; Jl Ketapang; r US$25-80, villas from US$95-190; ✳@❄❄) The hotel, on one hectare of lush gardens, features two pools, a playground and games for all ages. The 28 rooms are tasteful and decorated with Balinese style. The very

Lovina

cheapest have fans and cold water. Villas are good deals and have a sense of style. The largest are good for families and have kitchens. Wi-fi is best near the restaurant.

Harris Homestay   HOMESTAY $
(☎41 152; Gang Binaria; r from 150,000Rp) Sprightly and white, Harris avoids the weary look of some neighbouring cheapies. The charming family live in back; guests enjoy bright, modern rooms up front.

Sea Breeze Cabins   GUESTHOUSE $
(☎41 138; r 350,000-400,000Rp; ❄☀) One of the best choices in the heart of Kalibukbuk and right off Jl Bina Ria, the Sea Breeze has five appealing bungalows by the pool and beach, some with sensational views from their verandas. Two economy rooms have fans and hot water.

Nirwana Seaside Cottages   HOTEL $
(☎41 288; www.nirwanaseaside.com; r 150,000-600,000Rp; ❄☀) On large and deeply shaded beachfront grounds, the 30-unit Nirwana offers a wide range of rooms. The bungalows are a bit fusty but have hot water; those with beach views are a great deal. A modern two-storey wing has hotel-style air-con rooms with satellite TV. The pool areas are made from natural stone and have a dash of tropical style.

Puri Bali Hotel   HOTEL $
(☎41 485; www.puribalilovina.com; Jl Ketapang; r 150,000-300,000Rp; ❄☀) The pool area is set deep in a lush garden – you could easily hang out here all day and let any cares wander off to the ether. The better of the 24 rooms, with hot water and air-con, are simple but comfortable. The cheapest, with fans and cold water, are simply simple.

Padang Lovina   GUESTHOUSE $
(☎41 302; padanglovina@yahoo.com; Gang Binaria; r 100,000-350,000Rp; ❄☀) Down a narrow lane in the very heart of Kalibukbuk. There's no pretension at all around the 14 comfortable bungalow-style rooms set around spacious grounds teeming with flowers. The best rooms have air-con and bathtubs.

Rini Hotel   HOTEL $
(☎41 386; rinihotel@telkom.net; Jl Ketapang; r 180,000-350,000Rp; ❄☀) This tidy 30-room place has a large saltwater pool. Cheaper rooms have fans and cold water but the

more expensive ones are huge, with air-con and hot water. In fact, should you come across a keg, you could have a party. A big one.

Hotel Angsoka
HOTEL $

(☑41 841; www.angsoka.com; Gang Binaria; r 40,000-400,000Rp; ✳ ✵) The 44 rooms here span quite a range, from cold-water, fan singles to large units with air-con and tubs for you and a fridge for your beer. All enjoy a good-sized pool, cafe and quiet gardens.

WEST OF KALIBUKBUK
Aditya Beach Resort
HOTEL $$

(☑41 059; www.adityalovina.com; r US$35-100; ✳ ✵) There are 64 rooms at this big hotel on a sandy beach. The best have views of the ocean and all have a good range of amenities and attractive bathrooms. Swim in the large pool, or in the ocean? Sit on your patio while you're deciding.

Hotel Purnama
HOMESTAY $

(☑41 043; Jl Raya Lovina; r 50,000Rp) One of the best deals on this stretch, Hotel Purnama has seven clean cold-water rooms, and the beach is only a two-minute walk away. This is a family compound, and a friendly one at that.

Lovina Beach Hotel
HOTEL $

(☑41005; www.lovinabeachhotel.com; Jl Raya Lovina; r 100,000-250,000Rp, bungalows 300,000Rp; ✳ ✵) This older beach hotel hasn't changed in years and neither have its prices. The 24 rooms, in a two-storey block, are clean if a bit frayed. Bungalows feature carving and Balinese details, the ones on the beach are a bargain. The grounds feel like a park.

SOUTH OF LOVINA
Damai
HOTEL $$$

(☑41 008; www.damai.com; villas US$210-450; ✳ 🛈 ✵) Set on a hillside behind Lovina, Damai has the kind of sweeping views you'd expect. Its 14 luxury villas mix antiques and a modern style accented by beautiful Balinese fabrics. The infinity pool seemingly spills onto a landscape of peanut fields, rice paddies and coconut palms. Larger villas have private pools and multiple rooms that flow from one to another. The restaurant is lauded for its organic fusion cuisine. Call for transport or, at the main junction in Kalibukbuk, go south on Jl Damai and follow the road for about 3km.

Eating
Just about every hotel has a cafe or restaurant. Close to the centre of Lovina you can find several modest cafes that manage to go beyond the usual travellers' fare. Beachside places are good just for drinks if you're planning to do some hopping.

A small **night market** (Jl Raya Lovina; ⊙5-11pm) is a good choice for fresh and cheap local food.

ANTURAN
Warung Rasta
SEAFOOD $

(meals 15,000-50,000Rp) Right on a strip of beach, a growing number of tables, chairs and picnic benches mix with fishing boats. The menu not surprisingly leans towards simply grilled fresh seafood; given the name, the endless loop of music shouldn't surprise either. It's run by dudes who have clearly realised that lounging around here all day beats fishing. That snorting you hear is a nearby pen housing worried-looking pigs.

Babi Guling
BALINESE $

(Jl Raya Lovina; meals 20,000Rp; ⊙11am-4pm) Generically named for the dish it offers, this simple stand is 1km east of Anturan beside the main road to Singaraja. Highly spiced roasted baby pig is served on platters with rice.

ANTURAN TO KALIBUKBUK
Warung Dolphin
SEAFOOD $

(☑0813 5327 6985; Jl Pantai Banyualit; meals 25,000-70,000Rp) Right on the beach, this cheery hang-out for dolphin-tour skippers serves a killer grilled seafood platter (which was probably caught by the guy next to you). There's live acoustic music many nights and a few other cheery warung nearby.

Spunky's
INDONESIAN $

(☑41 134; Jl Pantai Banyualit; meals 20,000-70,000Rp) A real comer in the sunset drinks department, sprightly Spunky's serves Indonesian classics right on the beach. Like Lovina, it's a snoozy place day and night; walk here from anywhere along the sand.

Warung Peni
INDONESIAN $

(☑0813 5323 4636; Jl Pantai Banyualit; meals 15,000-40,000Rp) One of a few tropical hideaway warung on this quiet street. The long menu is mostly Indonesian with a few Chinese, Western and Balinese (grilled tuna with spicy sauce) dishes for variety; the mushroom omelette is just the thing after days of rice.

KALIBUKBUK

This is ground zero for nightlife. There's a good range of restaurants, beachside cafes, bars where you can get a pizza and maybe hear some music, or fun places that defy description.

TOP CHOICE Jasmine Kitchen · THAI $$

(✆41 565; Gang Binaria; meals 40,000-100,000Rp) The Thai fare at this elegant two-level restaurant lives up to the promise of the trays of chillies drying out front: it's excellent. The menu is long and authentic and the staff gracious. While soft jazz plays, try the homemade ice cream for dessert. You can refill water bottles here for 2000Rp.

Akar · VEGETARIAN $

(✆0817 972 4717; Jl Bina Ria; meals 30,000-50,000Rp) The many shades of green at this cute-as-a-baby-frog cafe aren't just for show. They reflect the earth-friendly ethics of the owners. Refill your water containers here and then enjoy organic smoothies and fresh and tasty noodle dishes that include Asian sesame, beetroot and cheese lasagne and chilli garlic spaghetti. A tiny back porch overlooks the river.

Khi Khi Restaurant · CHINESE $

(✆41 548; meals 8000-100,000Rp) Well off Jl Raya Lovina and behind the night market, this barn of a place specialises in Chinese food and grilled seafood, including lobster. It's always popular in a rub-elbows-with-your-neighbour kind of way.

Sea Breeze Café · INDONESIAN $

(✆41 138; meals 25,000-60,000Rp) Right by the beach off Jl Bina Ria, this breezy cafe has a range of Indonesian and Western dishes and excellent breakfasts. It's a good spot for sunset drinks and ocean views.

Le Madre · ITALIAN $

(✆0817 554 399; Jl Ketapang; meals 40,000-70,000Rp) Two married chefs who worked at some of south Bali's best Italian restaurants run this cute little polished bistro that looks like somebody's home (actually it is). Enjoy fresh pasta and seafood with crusty Italian bread that's baked daily.

Pappagallo · GLOBAL $

(✆41 163; Jl Binaria; meals 40,000-60,000Rp) A three-level travellers' cafe in the heart of town – the views from the top are good at sunset. Wood-fired ovens on the ground floor produce pizzas and fresh baguettes for sandwiches. There's also pasta and Indo classics.

Barcelona Bar & Restaurant · INDONESIAN $$

(✆41 894; Jl Ketapang; meals 40,000-90,000Rp) This quiet and restful restaurant has a shady garden area out the back that is the preferred seating option. Despite the name, it has an ambitious and good Balinese menu.

Tropis Club · GLOBAL $

(✆42 090; Jl Ketapang; meals 25,000-60,000Rp) The long menu at this beachside place is right out of the traveller rulebook: there's Indo, Western, sandwiches and wood-fired pizza. Choose a table under the soaring roof or out along the beach walkway. Sunset specials include cheap Bintang.

SOUTH OF LOVINA

TOP CHOICE Damai · FUSION $$$

(✆41 008; www.damai.com; lunch US$5-15, 5-course dinner from US$50) Enjoy the renowned organic restaurant at the boutique hotel in the hills behind Lovina. Tables enjoy views across the north coast. The changing menu draws its fresh ingredients from the hotel's organic farm and the local fishing fleet. Dishes are artful and the wine list one of the best in Bali. Sunday brunch is a new local sensation (from 245,000Rp). Call for pick-up.

🍷 Drinking

Plenty of places to eat are also good for just a drink, especially those on the beach. Happy hours abound. The following are some of the top picks in Kalibukbuk.

Kantin 21 · BAR

(✆0812 460 7791; Jl Raya Lovina; ⏱11am-1am) Funky open-air place where you can watch traffic by day and groove to acoustic guitar or garage-band rock by night. There's a long drinks list (jugs of Long Island iced tea for 75,000Rp), fresh juices and a few local snacks.

Triple 9 · CAFE

(✆0813 3708 4318; Jl Ketapang; 🛜) It's almost too appropriate: an oldies bar with sleepy crooners from the 1950s lilting out from the sound system. This attractive open-sided cafe boasts that you can hear conversations and, yes, you can. Or be a grump and use the wi-fi (every table has a power point).

Poco Lounge · BAR

(✆41 535; Jl Bina Ria; dishes 12,000-25,000Rp; ⏱11am-1am) Movies are shown at various times, and cover bands perform at this popular bar-cafe. Classic travellers' fare is served at tables open to street life in front and the river in back.

☆ Entertainment

Some of the joints on Jl Bina Ria have live music.

Volcano Club   CLUB
(Jl Raya Lovina; ⊗9pm-late Wed-Sat) There's nothing fancy about this big tropical disco in Anturan, where local and visiting parties mix it up to local DJs until all hours.

Pashaa   CLUB
(www.pashaabalinightclub.com; Jl Raya Lovina; ⊗8pm-late Tue-Sat) A small but high-concept club near the centre, where noted DJs from around the island mix it up and bikini-clad dancers seem utterly tireless.

🛍 Shopping

Shops on the main streets of Kalibukbuk sell a range of souvenirs, sundries and groceries.

Zakia's   HOUSEWARES
(☎0819 1560 2928; Jl Raya Lovina) Wood from the hills behind town is carved into all sorts of fascinating items and furniture. It's artful in a primitive way and much better than the typical tourist trash everywhere.

ℹ Information

If you're planning a reading holiday in Lovina, come prepared. Other than some used-book stalls, there's no good source for books or newspapers.

Internet Access

Fast internet access is common.
Bits and Bytes (☎0817 552 511; Jl Raya Lovina; per hr 25,000Rp; ⊗8am-8pm; 🛜) Fast connections.
Spice Cyber (☎41 305; Jl Bina Ria; per min 200Rp; ⊗8am-midnight; ✳🛜) Printing and burning services.

Medical Services

Apotek Rahayu (Jl Raya Lovina) Decent pharmacy run by a local doctor.

Money

There is a **Bank BCA ATM** at the corner of Jl Bina Ria and Jl Raya Lovina in Kalibukbuk, plus many more in Singaraja.

ℹ Getting There & Away

Bus & Bemo

To reach Lovina from south Bali by public transport, you'll need to change in Singaraja. Regular

blue bemo go from Singaraja's Banyuasri terminal to Kalibukbuk (about 10,000Rp) – you can flag them down anywhere on the main road.

If you're coming by long-distance bus from the west you can ask to be dropped off anywhere along the main road.

Tourist Shuttle Bus

Perama buses stop at its office, in front of **Hotel Perama** (☎41 161) on Jl Raya Lovina in Anturan. Passengers are then ferried to other points on the Lovina strip (10,000Rp).

DESTINATION	FARE	DURATION
Candidasa	150,000Rp	5½hr
Kuta	100,000Rp	4hr
Padangbai	150,000Rp	4¾hr
Sanur	100,000Rp	3¾hr
Ubud	100,000Rp	2¾hr

ℹ Getting Around

The Lovina strip is *very* spread out, but you can easily travel back and forth on bemo (5000Rp). Bikes are easily rented around town for about 30,000Rp per day.

Kadek (☎0818 0544 2907; Jl Raya Lovina) has a small office and he can arrange for all transport including a car and driver or motorbike (30,000Rp per day).

West of Lovina

The main road west of Lovina passes temples, farms and towns while it follows the thinly developed coast. You'll see many vineyards, where the grapes work overtime producing the sugar used in Bali's very sweet local vintages. The road continues to Taman Nasional Bali Barat (West Bali National Park) and the port of Gilimanuk.

AIR TERJUN SINGSING

About 5km west of Lovina, a sign points to **Air Terjun Singsing** (Daybreak Waterfall), and 1km from the main road, there's a warung on the left and a car park on the right. Walk past the warung and along the path for about 200m to the lower falls. The waterfall isn't huge, but the pool underneath is ideal for swimming, though not crystal-clear. The water, cooler than the sea, is very refreshing.

Clamber further up the hill to another, slightly bigger fall, **Singsing Dua**. It has a mud bath that is supposedly good for the skin (we'll let you decide about this). These falls also cascade into a deep swimming pool.

The area is thick with tropical forest and makes a nice day trip from Lovina. The falls are more spectacular in the wet season (October to March), and may be just a trickle other times.

BRAHMA VIHARA ARAMA

Bali's single Buddhist monastery is only vaguely Buddhist in appearance, with colourful decorations, a bright orange roof and statues of Buddha – it also has very Balinese decorative carvings and door guardians plus elaborately carved dark stones. It is quite a handsome structure in a commanding location, with views that reach down into the valley and across rice fields to the sea. You should wear long pants or a sarong, which can be hired for a small donation. The monastery does not advertise any regular courses or programs, but visitors are more than welcome to meditate in special rooms.

The temple is 3.3km off the main road – take the obvious turn-off in Dencarik. If you don't have your own transport, arrange it with an *ojek* (motorcycle) driver at the turn-off (10,000Rp). The road continues past the monastery, winding further up into the hills to Pedewa, a Bali Aga village.

AIR PANAS BANJAR

☏ 0362

Not far from Brahma Vihara Arama, these **hot springs** (adult/child 6000/3000Rp, parking 2000Rp; ☺8am-6pm) percolate amid lush tropical plants. You can relax here for a few hours and have lunch at the restaurant, or even stay the night.

Eight fierce-faced carved stone *naga* (mythical serpents) pour water from a natural hot spring into the first bath, which then overflows (via the mouths of five more *naga*), into a second, larger pool. In a third pool, water pours from 3m-high spouts to give you a pummelling massage. The water is slightly sulphurous and pleasantly hot (about 38°C), so you might enjoy it more in the morning or evening than in the heat of the Balinese day. You must wear a swimsuit and you shouldn't use soap in the pools, but you can do so under an adjacent outdoor shower.

In a verdant setting on a hillside very close to the baths, the rooms at **Pondok Wisata Grya Sari** (☏92 903; r 100,000-150,000Rp) are rustic at best and have outdoor bathrooms. Treks into the surrounding densely grown countryside can be organised from here.

Overlooking the baths, a casual **cafe** (dishes 8000-20,000Rp) has the usual Indonesian menu, which only gets better thanks to the view.

It's only about 3km from the Buddhist monastery to the hot springs if you take the short cut – go down to Banjar Tega, turn left in the centre of the village and follow the small road west, then south to Banjar village. From there, it's a short distance uphill before you see the 'Air Panas 1km' sign on the left (on the corner by the police station). From the bemo stop on the main road to the hot springs you can take an *ojek;* going back is a 2.4km downhill stroll.

SERIRIT

☏ 0362

This town is a junction for roads that run south through the central mountains to Munduk or to Papuan and west Bali via the beautiful Antosari Road or an equally scenic road to Pulukan.

The road continuing west along the coast towards Gilimanuk is in good shape. In Seririt, there's a Bank BCA ATM at the Lovina end of town and a large Hardy's supermarket. There are many warung in the market area, just north of the bemo stop, and you can find petrol stations on the main road. Temple-offering stalls here brim with orange and pale-blue beauty.

The name says it all, albeit very calmly, at **Zen Resort Bali** (☏93 578; www.zen resortbali.com; r €65-95; ☒), a seaside resort devoted to your internal and mental well-being. Rooms in traditional bungalows have a minimalist look designed to not tax the synapses, gardens are dotted with water features and the beach is 200m away. Activities start with yoga and end with a good Ayurvedic cleansing. It's just west of Seririt in the seaside village of Ume Anyar.

CELUKANBAWANG

Celukanbawang is the main cargo port for north Bali, and has a large wharf. Bugis schooners, the magnificent sailing ships that take their name from the seafaring Bugis people of Sulawesi, can sometimes be seen anchoring here.

PULAKI

Pulaki is famous for its grape vines, watermelons and for **Pura Pulaki**, a coastal temple that was completely rebuilt in the early 1980s, and is home to a large troop of monkeys, as well as troops at a nearby army base.

Pemuteran

☎ 0362

This oasis in the far northwest corner of Bali has a number of artful resorts set on a little dogbone-shaped bay that's alive with local life such as kids playing soccer until dark. The villagers, once impoverished, have realised that healthy reefs and sea life draw visitors, so they've found relative prosperity as good stewards of the local environment.

This is the place to come for a real beach getaway. Most people dive or snorkel the underwater wonders at nearby Pulau Menjangan while here.

◉ Sights

Strolling the beach is popular, especially at sunset, as you'd expect. The little fishing village is interesting, and if you walk around to the eastern end of the dogbone, you escape a lot of the development – although new projects are being contemplated.

Pemuteran is home to the non-profit **Reef Seen Turtle Project**, run by **Reef Seen Aquatics** (☎ 93 001; www.reefseen.com). Turtle eggs and small turtles purchased from locals are looked after here until they're ready for ocean release. More than 7000 turtles have been released since 1994. You can visit the small hatchery and make a donation to sponsor and release a tiny turtle. It's just off the main road, along the beach just east of Taman Selini Beach Bungalows.

🏊 Activities

The extensive coral reefs are about 3km offshore. Coral that's closer in is being restored as part of a unique project (see the boxed text). **Diving** and **snorkelling** are universally popular. Local dives cost from US$50; snorkelling gear rents from 40,000Rp.

Reef Seen DIVING

(☎ 93 001; www.reefseen.com) Right on the beach in a large compound, Reef Seen is active in local preservation efforts. It is a PADI dive centre and has a full complement of classes. It also offers sunset and sunrise cruises aboard glass-bottomed boats (per person from 250,000Rp), and pony rides on the beach for kids (from 200,000Rp for 30 minutes).

Easy Divers DIVING

(☎ 94 736; www.easy-divers.eu) The founder, Dusan Repic, has befriended many a diver new to Bali and this shop is well recommended. It is on the main road near the Taman Sari Bali Cottages and Pondok Sari hotel.

K&K Dive Centre DIVING

(☎ 94 747, 0813 3856 8000; rareangon@yahoo .co.id) In the Rare Angon homestay, this diver operation has a loyal following of annual regulars.

🛏 Sleeping & Eating

Pemuteran has one of the nicest selections of beachside hotels in Bali. Many have a sense of style and all are low-key and relaxed, with easy access to the beach, which has nice sand and is good for swimming. There are small warung along the main drag, otherwise all the hotels have good, mostly modestly priced, restaurants. You can wander between them along the beach debating which one to choose.

Some of the hotels are accessed directly off the main road, others are off of a small road that follows the west side of the bay.

TOP CHOICE **Taman Sari Bali Cottages** HOTEL $$

(☎ 93 264; www.balitamansari.com; bungalows US$50-200; ❄ @ 🛜 ☯) Thirty-one rooms are set in gorgeous bungalows that feature intricate carvings and traditional artwork inside and out. The open-air bath-

---

WORTH A TRIP

THE TEMPLE FOR BUSINESS

About 600m east of Pura Pulaki, a well-signposted 1.7km paved road leads to **Pura Melanting**. This temple has a dramatic setting with steps leading up into the foothills. It's dedicated to good fortune in business. A donation is expected as entry to the complex, although you're not permitted in the main worship area. Look for the dragon statue with the lotus blossom on its back near the entrance as well as villa owners hoping for rentals. Sarong rentals are 5000Rp.

Pemuteran is set among a fairly arid part of Bali where people have always had a hardscrabble existence. In the early 1990s, tourism began to take advantage of the excellent diving in the area. Locals who'd previously been scrambling to grow or catch something to eat began getting language and other training to welcome people to what would become a collection of resorts.

But there was one big problem: dynamite and cyanide fishing was rampant. After a few fits and starts, however, the community managed to control this. Then came the late 1990s and the El Niño warming of the water, which bleached and damaged large parts of the reef.

A group of local hotels, dive-shop owners and community leaders hit upon a novel solution: charge a new reef! Not with plastic, of course, but with electricity. The idea had already been floated by scientists internationally, but Pemuteran was the first place to implement it on a wide – and hugely successful – scale.

Using local materials, the community built dozens of large metal cages that were placed out along the threatened reef. These were then hooked to *very* low-wattage generators on land (you can see the cables running ashore near the Taman Sari Bali Cottages). What had been a theory became a reality. The low current stimulated limestone formation on the cages which in turn quickly grew new coral. All told, Pemuteran's small bay is getting new coral at five to six times the rate it would take to grow naturally.

The results are win-win all around. Locals and visitors are happy and so are the reefs. The efforts have gained international attention and are now called **Reef Gardeners of Pemuteran** (www.pemuteranfoundation.com); you can find interesting and detailed information at local businesses. An info booth with a sign reading 'Bio Rocks' is sometimes open on the beach by Pondok Sari.

rooms inspire extended ablutions. Most rooms are under US$100 – those over are quite palatial. It's located on a long stretch of quiet beach on the bay, and part of the reef restoration project.

Pondok Sari HOTEL **$$**
(☏92 337; www.pondoksari.com; r US$50-160; ✳ ✉) There are 36 rooms here set in densely planted gardens that assure privacy. The pool is down by the beach; the cafe has sweet water views through the trees. Traditional Balinese details abound; bathrooms are open-air and a calling card for the stone-carvers. Deluxe units have elaborate stone tubs among other details. The resort is just off the main road.

Puri Ganesha Villas GUESTHOUSE **$$$**
(☏94 766; www.puriganeshabali.com; villas US$400-500; ✳ ✉ @) Four two-storey villas on sweeping grounds at the west end of the bay are the basics at Puri Ganesha. Ahh, but the details: each has a unique style that mixes antiques with silks and relaxed comfort. Outside the air-con bedrooms, life is in the open air, including time in your private pool. Dine in the small restaurant or in your

villa; the spa is lavish. It is located on the western point of the bay, near Taman Sari.

Taman Selini Beach Bungalows HOTEL **$$**
(☏94 746; www.tamanselini.com; r US$90-200; ✳ 🛜 ✉) The 11 bungalows recall an older, refined Bali, from the quaint thatched roofs down to the antique carved doors and detailed stonework. Rooms, which open onto a large garden running to the beach, have four-poster beds and large outdoor bathrooms. The outdoor daybeds can be addictive. It's immediately east of Pondok Sari, on the beach and right off the main road.

Amertha Bali Villas HOTEL **$$**
(☏94 831; www.amerthabalivillas.com; r US$75-150, villas US$175-400; ✳ 🛜 ✉) A slightly older resort with spacious grounds, the Amertha benefits from having large mature trees that give it that timeless tropical cliché. The 14 units are large, with a lot of natural wood and spacious covered patios. Showers are open-air.

Adi Assri HOTEL **$$**
(☏94 838; www.adiassri.com; r US$36-77; ✳ 🛜 ✉) Amid the village just east of the other hotels,

DIVING & SNORKELLING PULAU MENJANGAN

Besides having the best selection of lodgings, Pemuteran is also well placed for diving and snorkelling Menjangan (p254). A dock for boats out to the island is just 7km west of town, so you have only a short ride before you're on a boat for the relaxing and pretty 45-minute journey to Menjangan. Besides the dive shops, all of the Pemuteran hotels run snorkelling trips that cost US$35 to US$50, and dive trips from US$90.

the 60 bungalow-style units here have nice porches and views to the beach. A large double pool goes right to the sand. The young garden is growing at a tropical pace (today's shrub is tomorrow's tree).

Reef Seen GUESTHOUSE $

(☏93 001; www.reefseen.com; r 450,000Rp; ✳🛜) Five simple Balinese-style brick bungalows have open-air bathrooms with showers. This is a well-regarded dive centre and there are room discounts for clients.

Rare Angon Homestay HOMESTAY $

(☏94 747, 0813 3856 8000; rareangon@yahoo.co.id; r 200,000-350,000Rp; ✳) Good basic rooms in a homestay located on the south side of the main road. K&K Dive Centre is here.

❶ Getting There & Away

Pemuteran is served by any of the buses and bemo on the Gilimanuk–Lovina run. Labuhan Lalang and Taman Nasional Bali Barat are 12km west. It's a three- to four-hour drive from south Bali, either over the hills or around the west coast.

West Bali

Best Places to Eat

» Pondok Pitaya (p247)

» Tom's Garden Cafe (p247)

Best Places to Stay

» Mimpi Resort Menjangan (p255)

» Waka Shorea (p255)

» Pondok Pitaya (p247)

» Pondok Pisces (p247)

» Gajah Mina (p247)

» Taman Wana Villas & Spa (p250)

Why Go?

Few who dive or snorkel the rich and pristine waters around Pulau Menjangan forget the experience. It's part of Taman Nasional Bali Barat (West Bali National Park), the only protected place of its kind on the island. Many take the challenge of trekking through the savannah flats, mangroves and hillside jungles.

On the coast, waves pound the rocky shore and surfers hit the breaks at funky beaches like Balian and Medewi. Some of Bali's most sacred sites are also here, from the ever-thronged Pura Tanah Lot to the Unesco-nominated Pura Taman Ayun and on to the wonderful isolation of Pura Rambut Siwi.

The tidy town of Tabanan is at the apex of Bali's *subak*, the system of irrigation that ensures everybody gets a fair share of the water. The lush green fields all around attest to its success. On narrow backroads you can cruise beside rushing streams with bamboo arching overhead and fruit piling up below. Or go for the spectacle of huge beasts and flying mud: a bull race.

When to Go

The best time to visit west Bali is during the dry season in April to September, although recent weather patterns have made the dry season wetter and the wet season drier. Hiking and trekking in Taman Nasional Bali Barat is much easier when it isn't muddy, and the waters of Pulau Menjangan are at their world-class best for diving when clear. Along the coast, however, the west has yet to develop a peak season – although surfing is best in months without an R.

West Bali Highlights

1 Plunging into the depths at Bali's best dive spot, **Pulau Menjangan** (p254), or enjoying the show while snorkelling

2 Revelling in the classic beach-funk vibe of **Balian**

Beach (p246), where surfer dives and stylish digs rub shoulders

3 Nailing the long left break at **Pantai Medewi** (p247)

4 Finding your own corner of serenity at **Pura Taman Ayun** (p243)

5 Discovering, by foot or boat, Bali's national park, **Taman Nasional Bali Barat**

(p243) before it's replaced by afternoon avarice

7 Discovering your own **backroad paradise** of low-hanging fruit, arching bamboo and rushing water

(p251) and hoping against hope to discover Bali's sole unique species, the possibly extinct Bali starling

6 Enjoying the morning spirituality of **Pura Tanah Lot**

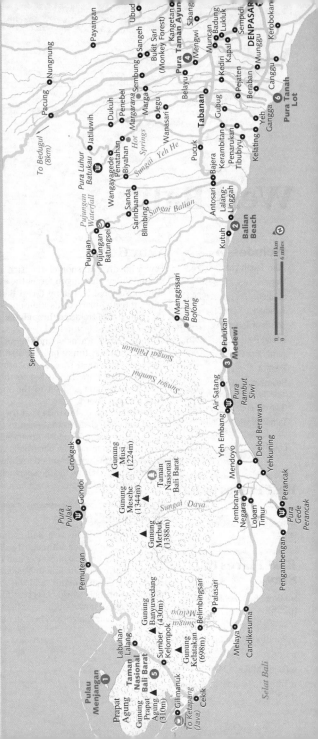

Pura Tanah Lot

 0361

One of the most popular day trips from south Bali, **Pura Tanah Lot** (adult/child 10,000/5000Rp, car park 5000Rp) is the most visited and photographed temple in Bali. It's an obligatory stop, especially at sunset, and a very commercialised one. It has all the authenticity of a stage set – even the tower of rock that the temple sits upon is an artful reconstruction (the entire structure was crumbling). Over one-third of the rock you see is artificial.

For the Balinese, Pura Tanah Lot is one of the most important and venerated sea temples (p356). Like Pura Luhur Ulu Watu, at the tip of the southern Bukit Peninsula, and Pura Rambut Siwi to the west, it is closely associated with the Majapahit priest Nirartha. It's said that each of the sea temples was intended to be within sight of the next, so they formed a chain along Bali's southwestern coast – from Pura Tanah Lot you can usually see the cliff-top site of Pura Ulu Watu far to the south, and the long sweep of sea shore west to Perancak, near Negara.

But at Tanah Lot itself you may just see from one vendor to the next. To reach the temple, a walkway runs through a sideshow of souvenir shops down to the sea. To ease the task of making purchases, there is an ATM.

You can walk over to the temple itself at low tide, but non-Balinese people are not allowed to enter. One other thing: local legend has it that if you bring a partner to Tanah Lot before marriage, you will end up as split as the temple. Let that be a warning – or an inducement.

Since you really want to just drop in on Tanah Lot, there's no need to worry about food or drink – although there's no shortage of warung (food stalls). You won't be able to miss the looming Le Meridien Nirwana resort with its water-sucking golf course. It has been controversial since the day it was built, as many feel its greater height shows the temple disrespect.

For info about respecting traditions and acting appropriately while visiting temples, see p329.

❶ Getting There & Away

Coming from south Bali take the coastal road west from Kerobokan and follow the signs or,

near sunset, the traffic. From other parts of Bali, turn off the Denpasar–Gilimanuk road near Kediri and follow the signs. During the pre- and post-sunset rush, traffic is awful.

Kapal

About 10km north of Denpasar, Kapal is the garden-feature and temple-doodad centre of Bali. If you need a green tiger or other decorative critter (we saw a pink beaver) rendered in colours not found in nature, then this your place! (Although shipping might be a bitch.) This is on the main road to the west, so it might be worth getting out of the traffic just to walk with the animals.

The most important temple in the area is **Pura Sadat**. It was possibly built in the 12th century, then damaged in an earthquake early in the 20th century and subsequently restored after WWII.

Throughout this part of Bali you will see peanuts and corn growing in rotation with rice. Bananas and other fruits grow wild alongside the roads.

Pura Taman Ayun

The huge state temple of **Pura Taman Ayun** (adult/child 5000/2500Rp; ⊙8am-6pm), surrounded by a wide, elegant moat, was the main temple of the Mengwi kingdom, which survived until 1891, when it was conquered by the neighbouring kingdoms of Tabanan and Badung. The large, spacious temple was built in 1634 and extensively renovated in 1937. It's a spacious place to wander around and you can get away from speed-obsessed group-tour mobs ('Back on the bus, pilgrims!'). The first courtyard is a large, open, grassy expanse and the inner

ENJOYING TANAH LOT

So why not skip Tanah Lot? Because it is an important spiritual site and does have an innate beauty. The secret is to arrive before noon: you'll beat the crowds and the vendors will still be asleep. You'll actually hear birds chirping rather than buses idling and people carping. Besides, you can see the sunset from many other places – like a beachfront bar south towards Seminyak.

courtyard has a multitude of *meru* (multi-tiered shrines).

Owing to its heritage, the temple has been nominated for Unesco recognition.

❶ Getting There & Away

This is an easy stop on a drive to/from Bedugal and Singaraja. And bemo (small minibuses) on this route (from Denpasar's Ubung terminal) can drop you off at the roundabout in Mengwi, where signs indicate the road (250m) to the temple. Pura Taman Ayun is a stop-off on many organised tourist tours.

Belayu

Traditional *songket* sarongs are intricately woven with gold threads. These are for ceremonial use only and not for everyday wear. You'll find them in the small village of Belayu (or Blayu), 3km north of Mengwi.

Marga

Between the walls of traditional family compounds in the village of Marga, there are some beautifully shaded roads – but this town wasn't always so peaceful. On 20 November 1946, a much larger and better-armed Dutch force, fighting to regain Bali as a colony after the departure of the Japanese, surrounded a force of 96 independence fighters. The outcome was similar to the *puputan* (warrior's fight to the death) of 40 years earlier – Ngurah Rai, who led the resistance against the Dutch (and later had the airport named after him), was killed, along with every one of his men. There was, however, one important difference – this time the Dutch suffered heavy casualties as well, and this may have helped weaken their resolve to hang on to the rebellious colony.

The independence struggle is commemorated at the **Margarana** (admission 5000Rp; ☉9am-5pm), northwest of Marga village. Tourists seldom visit, but every Balinese schoolchild comes here at least once, and a ceremony is held annually on 20 November. In a large compound stands a 17m-high pillar, and nearby is a **museum** with a few photos, homemade weapons and other artefacts from the conflict (Ngurah Rai's quoteworthy last letter includes the line: 'Freedom or death!'). Behind is a smaller compound with 1372 small stone memorials to those who gave their lives for the cause of

independence – they're headstone markers in a military cemetery, though bodies are not actually buried here. Each memorial has a symbol indicating the hero's religion, mostly the Hindu swastika, but also Islamic crescent moons and even a few Christian crosses. Look for the memorials to 11 Japanese who stayed on after WWII and fought with the Balinese against the Dutch.

❶ Getting There & Away

Even with your own transport it's easy to get lost finding Marga and the memorial, so, as always, ask for directions. You can easily combine this with a tour of the amazing Jatiluwih rice terraces.

Sangeh

If you love monkeys, you will love the 14-hectare monkey forest of **Bukit Sari**. But if you're put off by the thieving, copulating little buggers, than perhaps you should give it a miss. Actually we're among the former, and the monkeys here are all rather workmanlike: they eat three square meals a day (breakfast is bananas, lunch is cassava and dinner is rice – a very Balinese diet, in fact), and when tourists leave they relax after a day of high jinks ('Those glasses you stole make you look fat').

Also noteworthy, but not as exciting, are a rare grove of **nutmeg trees** in the monkey forest and a temple, **Pura Bukit Sari**, with an interesting old Garuda (mythical man-bird) statue. This place is touristy, but the forest is cool, green and shady. The souvenir sellers are restricted to certain areas and hence are easy to avoid.

❶ Getting There & Away

Most people visit on an organised tour or drive themselves; it's about 20km north of Denpasar.

Tabanan

☎ 0361

A renowned centre for dancing and gamelan playing, Tabanan, like most regional capitals in Bali, is a large, well-organised place. Mario, the renowned dancer of the prewar period, hailed from Tabanan and is featured in Miguel Covarrubias' classic book, *Island of Bali*. His greatest achievement was to perfect the Kebyar dance. Nowadays it's hard for visitors to find performances here on a regular basis, but you can enjoy the vibrant rice fields and related museum.

◎ Sights

Playing a critical role in rural Bali life, the *subak* is a village association that deals with water, water rights and irrigation. The **Mandala Mathika Subak** (☑810315; Jl Raya Kediri; admission 5000Rp; ◷7am-4.30pm) is quite a large complex devoted to Tabanan's *subak* organisations. Within this is the **Subak Museum**, which has displays about the irrigation and cultivation of rice and the intricate social systems that govern it. Staff here are very sweet and will show you around; the exhibits themselves could use a little love.

With water passing through many, many scores of rice fields before it drains away for good, there is always the chance that growers near the source would be water-rich while those at the bottom would be selling carved wooden critters at Tanah Lot. Regulating a system that apportions a fair share to everyone is a model of mutual cooperation and an insight into the Balinese character. (One of the strategies used is to put the last person on the water channel in control.)

Exhibits are housed in a large building with water streaming by right out front. For more, see p327.

⊨ Sleeping & Eating

You can sample village life as part of the ☑**Bali Homestay Program** (☑0817 067 1788; www.bali-homestay.com; Jegu, Penebel; r from US$30), an innovative program that places travellers in the homes of residents of the rice-growing village of Jegu, 9km north of Tabanan. Guests (who normally stay at least three nights, packages from US$130) participate in activities like making offerings and go on cultural tours with locals. All meals are included.

There are plenty of warung in the town centre and at the bustling regional market; a tasty **night market** (◷5pm-midnight) sets up on the south side. Out on the main road, a **babi guling stall** (dishes 5000-15,000Rp; ◷7am-7pm) has batches of fresh-roasted seasoned young pork throughout the day. It's a savoury treat Balinese love.

Hardy's (☑819850), also on the main road, is a huge, modern supermarket with groceries and sundries. It's good if you're heading to one of the surf sites in the west.

⊕ Information

The main road bypasses the centre, where you'll find ATMs and solid blocks of shops.

⊕ Getting There & Away

All bemo and buses between Denpasar (Ubung terminal) and Gilimanuk stop at the terminal at the western end of Tabanan (10,000Rp). If you're driving, note that most main streets are one way, with traffic moving in a clockwise direction around the central blocks.

The road to Pura Luhur Batukau and the amazing rice terraces of Jatiluwih heads north from the centre of town.

South of Tabanan

Driving in the southern part of Tabanan district takes you though many charming villages and past a lot of vigorously growing rice. The fields are revered by many as the most productive in Bali.

Just south of Tabanan, **Kediri** has Pasar Hewan, one of Bali's busiest cattle markets. About 10km south of Tabanan is **Pejaten**, a centre for the production of traditional pottery, including elaborate ornamental roof tiles. Porcelain clay objects, which are made purely for decorative use, can be seen in a few workshops in the village. Check out the small showroom of **CV Keramik Pejaten** (☑0361-831997), one of several local producers. The trademark pale-green pieces are lovely, and when you see the prices, you'll at least buy a toad.

A little west of Tabanan, a road goes 8km south via Gubug to the secluded coast at **Yeh Gangga**, where there are some good accommodation choices and **Island Horse** (☑0361-730218; www.baliislandhorse.com; rides from US$56), which offers horse rides along the long flat beach and surrounding countryside.

The next road west from Tabanan turns down to the coast via **Kerambitan**, a village noted for its dance troupe and musicians who perform across the south and in Ubud. Banyan trees shade beautiful old buildings, including two 17th-century palaces. **Puri Anyar Kerambitan** accepts guests and is an attraction in itself with a vast shambolic compound filled with antiques and populated by genial characters. The other palace, **Puri Agung Kerambitan**, is tidy and dull.

South of Kerambitan, you will pass through **Penarukan**, known for its stone carvers and woodcarvers, and also its dancers. Continue to the coast, where you'll find the beach at **Kelating** wide, black and usually deserted.

About 4km from southern Kerambitan is **Tibubiyu**. For a lovely drive through huge bamboo, fruit trees, rice paddies and more, take the scenic road northwest from Kerambitan to the main Tabanan–Gilimanuk road.

🛏 Sleeping

Bali Wisata Bungalows GUESTHOUSE $
(☎0361-7443561; www.baliwisatabungalows.com; Yeh Gangga; bungalows 300,000-450,000Rp; ✸)
West of Tabanan and on the coast at Yeh Gangga, this attractive accommodation has excellent views in a superb setting on 15km of rock and black-sand beach. The cheapest of the 12 rooms have cold water; the best have dramatic oceanfront vistas. It's family-run, and there's nothing fancy here. It is 9km southwest of Tabanan.

Puri Anyar Kerambitan HOMESTAY $
(☎0361-812668; giribali@yahoo.co.id; r from 400,000Rp; ✸) Join Anak Agung, the leader of the royal family that lives sit-com style in this intriguing compound. Anak will teach you about kite culture while his son the prince will offer to paint you or do a figure study. Children wandering about provide cute punchlines. The four rooms are filled with royal antiques and vary in tidiness. At your command, Balinese feasts and cultural shows fit for a king will be arranged.

North of Tabanan

The area north of Tabanan is good to travel around with your own transport. There are some strictly B-level attractions; the real appeal here is just driving the fecund back-roads where the bamboo arches templelike over the road.

About 9km north of Tabanan the road reaches a fork. The left road goes to Pura Luhur Batukau, via the **hot springs** at Penatahan. Here you'll find the simple **Yeh Panas Resort** (☎0361-262356; espa_yeh panes@telkom.net; r from 300,000Rp; ✸) 4km from the fork, by Sungai Yeh He (Yeh He River). The resort has a small, cool pool, which nonguests can enjoy for 30,000Rp. Another pool has water from the hot springs and costs 150,000Rp. Rooms are basic; you may just want to literally dip in...

Antosari & Bajera

At Antosari, the main road takes a sharp turn south to the welcoming breezes of the ocean. Turn north and you enjoy a scenic drive to north Bali (see p222). Nearby Bajera is renowned for the quality of its market and warung. The *nasi campur* (steamed rice with mixed goodies) is much vaunted. A narrow road goes north up the river valley and eventually reaches tiny villages on the side of Gunung Batukau with rather luxurious and ecologically sound places to stay.

Balian Beach
☎0361
Rapidly emerging as one of the new hot surf spots, Balian Beach has the slight pioneer charm of a place that's still on the brink of discovery. A rolling area of dunes and knolls overlooks the pounding surf here (see p34 for details). A sort of critical mass

---

LOCAL KNOWLEDGE

MADE SUARNATA: RICE FARMER

'When I was little, rice was special, something you added to the daily diet of cassava. Now you can have rice for every meal and we have money for things like meat and better houses', says Made Suarnata, a rice farmer in the tiny village of **Tegalambengam** south of Tabanan. Although you might expect him to say this, he says his region is 'the best place for growing rice in Bali. You see the green fields everywhere you look. My whole family lives near each other as we've always done for hundreds of years.'

And pride aside, he is correct. Rice from the area south of Tabanan is prized across Bali. Why? 'Sun, soil, water.' And how can the visitor experience this? 'Just look around here', Suarnata says, noting that it's hard to get too lost wandering these back roads and that through your driver or guide you'll find people working the land are more than happy to stop and talk about it. 'People here love their land', he says. But when they do sell, say for an expat's villa, it's purely for practical reasons. 'It is sad to see rice fields disappear but the farmers need money. They never had any at all.'

of villas and beach accommodation has appeared and you can wander between a few cafes and join other travellers for a beer, sunset and talk of waves. Nonsurfers will simply enjoy the wild waves and good cafes.

Balian Beach is right at the mouth of the wide Sungai Balian (Balian River). It is 800m south of the town of **Lalang-Linggah,** which is on the main road 10km west of Antosari.

🛏 Sleeping & Eating

All of the accommodation listed below is fairly close together. The way things are going, there will be more choices by the time you arrive. Warung and simple cafes mean a bottle of Bintang is never more than a one-minute walk away.

TOP CHOICE **Pondok Pitaya** GUESTHOUSE $
(☑0819 9984 9054; www.baliansurf .com; r per person US$10-50; ☀) A lodge as memorable as its spray-scented location right on wave-tossed Balian Beach. The work of hilariously creative Michael Canada and family, the complex combines vintage Indonesian buildings (including a 1950 Javanese house and an 1860 Balinese alligator hunter's shack) with more modest accommodation. Room choices are like the surf: variable. Budgeteers can bunk down in the bare-bones 'Chicken Wing' for US$10 each, couples have a choice of rather lavish king-bed rooms, and a tribe can occupy a vast house that sleeps eight in one room. The **bar** is a hoot and food includes tasty burritos and pizza.

Pondok Pisces GUESTHOUSE $$
(☑780 1735, 0813 3879 7722; www.pondok piscesbali.com; r 380,000-650,000Rp) You can certainly hear the sea, even if you can't see it, at this tropical fantasy of thatched cottages and flower-filled gardens. The five bungalows and rooms have hot-water showers, fans and large patios. A large beach house goes for the top rate. That blockbuster you missed five years ago awaits in the DVD library. In-house **Tom's Garden Cafe** has grilled seafood and surf views. Down by the river and slightly upstream, there are three large villas and bungalows in **Balian Riverside Sanctuary** (380,000-680,000Rp), lushly set in a teak forest.

Gajah Mina HOTEL $$
(☑0812 381 1630; www.gajahminaresort.com; bungalows US$100-170; ❄☀) Designed by the French architect-owner, this 11-unit boutique hotel is close to the ocean. The private, walled bungalows march out to a dramatic outcrop of stone surrounded by surf. The grounds are vast and there are little trails for wandering and pavilions for relaxing. The restaurant overlooks its own little bowl of rice terraces.

Kubu Balian Beach GUESTHOUSE $
(☑0815 5801 1707; r from 350,000Rp; ☀) You might decide to stay a spell at these four apartments based in two villas at the start of the road to Gajah Mina hotel. The large units are cheap for what you get: full kitchens, satellite TV, huge porches, stylish furniture and more. Stay on the upper level and you can see the sea through the palms. There are deals if you want to rent out the whole complex for a memorable bash.

Warung Ayu HOMESTAY $
(☑0812 399 353; r 150,000-200,000Rp) Like some vast surfer shack, the 11 rooms in this two-storey cold-water block look down the road to the surf, dude.

Made's Homestay HOMESTAY $
(☑0812 396 3335; r 150,000Rp) Four basic bungalow-style units are surrounded by banana trees back from the beach. The rooms are basic, clean, large enough to hold numerous surfboards, and have cold-water showers.

Jembrana Coast

About 34km west of Tabanan you cross into Bali's most sparsely populated district, Jembrana. The main road follows the south coast most of the way to Negara. There's some beautiful scenery, but little tourist development, with the exception of the surfing action at Medewi. At Pulukan you can turn north and enjoy a remote and scenic drive to north Bali; see p222.

MEDEWI
☑0365
The surf scene at Medewi is centred on one short lane from the road down to the waves. There are a couple of guesthouses aimed at surfers plus internet and board rental/ repair shops. Along the coast nearby, a few more inns lie scattered amid the rice fields.

On the main road, a large sign points down the paved road (200m) to the surfing mecca of **Pantai Medewi** and its *long* left-hand wave. The 'beach' is a stretch of huge, smooth grey rocks interspersed among

PURA RAMBUT SIWI

Picturesquely situated on a clifftop overlooking a long, wide stretch of black-sand beach, this superb temple shaded by flowering frangipani trees is one of the important sea temples of west Bali. Like Pura Tanah Lot and Pura Ulu Watu, it was established in the 16th century by the priest **Nirartha**, who had a good eye for ocean scenery. Unlike Tanah Lot, it remains a peaceful and little-visited place.

Legend has it that when Nirartha first came here, he donated some of his hair to the local villagers. The hair is now kept in a box buried in a three-tiered *meru* (multitiered shrine), the name of which means 'Worship of the Hair'. Although the main *meru* is inaccessible, you can view it easily through the gate.

The caretaker rents sarongs for 2000Rp and is happy to show you around the temple and down to the beach. He then opens the guestbook and requests a donation – a suitable sum is about 10,000Rp (regardless of the much higher amounts attributed to previous visitors). A path along the cliff leads to a staircase down to a small and even older temple, **Pura Penataran**.

Getting There & Away

The temple is between Air Satang and Yeh Embang, at the end of a 500m side road. You'll find it's well signposted, but look for the turn-off near a cluster of warung on the main road. Any of the regular bemo and buses between Denpasar and Gilimanuk will stop at the turn-off.

round black pebbles. Think of it as free reflexology. Cattle graze by the shore, paying no heed to the spectators watching the action out on the water.

On the main road, Medewi proper is a classic market town with shops selling all the essentials of west Bali life.

Sleeping & Eating

You'll find accommodation along the main lane to the surf break and down other lanes about 2km east. For a casual meal, some of the finest fare is freshly stir-fried and served up at a cart right by the beach/rocks.

Puri Dajuma Cottages   HOTEL **$$**
(☎43955; www.dajuma.com; Pulukan; cottages from US$110; ❖@☎☀) Coming from the east, you won't be able to miss this seaside resort, thanks to its prolific signage. Happily, the 18 cottages actually live up to the billing. Each has a private garden, an ocean view and a walled outdoor bathroom. The Medewi break is 2km west.

Homestay CSB   GUESTHOUSE **$**
(☎0813 3866 7288; Pulukan; r 150,000-200,000Rp; ❖) Some 900m east of the Medewi surf break at Pulukan, look for signs along the main road. Venture 300m down a track and you'll find a great family with the beginnings of an empire. The best of their 18 simply furnished rooms have air-con, hot water and balconies with views

that put anything in south Bali to shame. The coast and churning surf curve to the east, backed by jade-green rice fields and rows of palm trees. It's rather idyllic.

Mai Malu Restaurant & Guesthouse
GUESTHOUSE **$**
(☎470 0068, 0813 3795 8866; s/d 70,000/90,000Rp) Near the highway on the Medewi side road, Mai Malu is a popular (and almost the only) hang-out, serving crowd-pleasing pizza, burgers and Indonesian meals in its modern, breezy upstairs eating area. Eight cold-water rooms have the basics plus fans.

Medewi Beach Cottages   HOTEL **$$**
(☎40029; r US$60-80; ❖☀) A large pool anchors 27 modern, comfortable rooms (with satellite TV) scattered about nice gardens right down by the surf break. The one off-note: security measures obstruct what should be a good view. Across the lane there's a lively two-storey building ostensibly called 'the party wing' with seven second-rate cold-water rooms (150,000Rp) aimed at surfers.

Negara
☎0365

Set amid the broad and fertile flatlands between the mountains and ocean, Negara is a prosperous little town, and a useful pit stop. Although it's a district capital, there's not much to see. The town springs to life, however, for the region's famous bull races. Banks on the main commercial road (south of the Tabanan–Gilimanuk road), Jl Ngurah Rai, change money and have international ATMs.

Eating

Numerous choices for meals line Jl Ngurah Rai. There are assorted warung in the market area at the traffic circle with Jl Pahlawan.

Natalia　　　　CHINESE INDONESIAN $
(🖉42669; Jl Ngurah Rai 107; dishes 5000-20,000Rp) In front of Hotel Wira Pada, Natalia is the stop for a sit-down Indonesian meal.

Hardy's Supermarket　　　INDONESIAN $
(🖉40709; Jl Ngurah Rai; ✸) Hardy's has a popular albeit cacophonous indoor food court serving fresh, cheap chow. Dishes are generally under 8000Rp. This large supermarket has the best selection of goods in western Bali.

❶ Getting There & Away

Most bemo and minibuses from Denpasar (Ubung terminal) to Gilimanuk drop you in Negara (25,000Rp).

Around Negara

At the southern fringe of Negara, **Loloan Timur** is a largely Bugis community (originally from Sulawesi) that retains 300-year-old traditions. Look for a few distinctive houses on stilts, some decorated with wooden fretwork.

To reach **Delod Berawan**, turn off the main Gilimanuk–Denpasar road at Mendoyo and go south to the coast, which has a black-sand beach and irregular surf. You can see bull-race practices Sunday mornings at the nearby football field.

Perancak is the site of Nirartha's arrival in Bali in 1546, commemorated by a

---

BULL RACES

The Negara region is famous for bull races, known as *mekepung*, which culminate in the Bupati Cup in Negara in early August. The racing animals are actually the normally docile water buffalo, which charge down a 2km stretch of road or beach pulling tiny chariots. Gaily clad riders stand or kneel on top of the chariots forcing the bullocks on, sometimes by twisting their tails to make them follow the curve of the makeshift racetrack. The winner, however, is not necessarily first past the post. Style also plays a part and points are awarded for the most elegant runner. Gambling is not legal in Bali, but locals do sometimes indulge.

Important races are held during the dry season, from July to October. Races are staged for tourists, including regular ones listed below and more occasional ones at more traditional venues, such as at Perancak on the coast. Minor races and practices are held at several sites around Perancak and elsewhere on Sunday mornings, including Delod Berawan and Yeh Embang. However, actually finding these events can be somewhat like seeking the Holy Grail. If you're in Negara on a bull-race Sunday, people will gladly direct you. But trying to obtain info remotely is often a quest best not started. You can try three different strategies:

» See if the **Jembrana Government Tourist Office** (🖉0365-41210, ext 224) has details.

» Show up in Negara on a Sunday morning from July to October and hope to get lucky by asking around.

» Go to the weekly **Bull Races** (🖉0361-886 6483; www.westbalibuffalorace.com; adult/child US$35/17; ⏲10.30am Thu) staged for tourists. These 3½-hour spectacles include musical accompaniment by bamboo instruments and *kendang mebarung* (huge wooden drums). The site is about 3km north of Negara along a series of roads that are, well, impossible to find. Expect to ask directions often, allow extra time and confirm details in advance. Or take a tour from south Bali with **Suta Tours** (🖉0361-741 6665, 788 8865; www.sutatour.com; bull races tour US$60). Buses leave from south Bali at 7am.

limestone temple, **Pura Gede Perancak**. Bull races are run at **Taman Wisata Perancak** (☎0365-42173), and Balinese buffets are sometimes staged for organised tours from south Bali. If you're travelling independently, give the park a call before you go there. In Perancak, ignore the sad little zoo and go for a walk along the fishing harbour.

Once capital of the region, **Jembrana** is the centre of the *gamelan jegog,* a gamelan using huge bamboo instruments that produce a low-pitched, resonant sound. Performances often feature gamelan groups engaging in musical contest. To hear them in action, time your arrival with a local festival, or ask in Negara where you might find a group practising.

Belimbingsari & Palasari

Two fascinating religious towns north of the main road are reason enough for a detour.

Christian evangelism in Bali was discouraged by the secular Dutch, but sporadic missionary activity resulted in a number of converts, many of whom were rejected by their own communities. In 1939 they were encouraged to resettle in Christian communities in the wilds of west Bali.

Palasari is home to a Catholic community, which boasts a huge church largely made from white stone and set on a large town square. It is really rather peaceful, and with the gently waving palms it feels like old missionary Hawaii rather than Hindu Bali. The church does show Balinese touches in the spires, which resemble the *meru* in a Hindu temple, and features a facade with the same shape as a temple gate.

Nearby **Belimbingsari** was established as a Protestant community, and now has the largest Protestant church in Bali, although it doesn't reach for the heavens the way the church in Palasari does. Still, it's an amazing structure, with features rendered in a distinctly Balinese style – in place of a church bell there's a *kulkul* (hollow tree-trunk warning drum) like those in a Hindu temple. The entrance is through an *aling aling*-style (guard wall) gate, and the attractive carved angels look very Balinese. Go on Sunday to see inside.

For a near-religious experience you might consider staying at **Taman Wana Villas & Spa** (☎0365-40970; www.bali-taman wana-villas.com; Palasari; r US$150-325; ❋ 🗷),

a striking 2km drive through a jungle past the Palasari church. This architecturally stunning boutique resort has 27 rooms in unusual round structures. Posh only starts to describe the luxuries at this cloistered refuge. Views are panoramic; get a view of the rice fields.

The two villages are north of the main road, and the best way to see them is on a loop with your own transport. About 17km west from Negara, look for signs for the Taman Wana Villas. Follow these for 6.1km to Palasari. From the west, look for a turn for Belimbingsari, some 20km southeast of Cekik. A good road leads to the village. Between the two towns, only divine intervention will allow you to tackle the thicket of narrow but passable lanes unaided. Fortunately directional help is readily at hand.

Cekik

At this junction one road continues west to Gilimanuk and another heads northeast towards north Bali. All buses and bemo to and from Gilimanuk pass through Cekik.

Archaeological excavations here during the 1960s yielded the oldest evidence of human life in Bali. Finds include burial mounds with funerary offerings, bronze jewellery, axes, adzes and earthenware vessels from around 1000 BC, give or take a few centuries. Look for some of this in the Museum Situs Purbakala Gilimanuk.

On the southern side of the junction, the pagoda-like structure with a spiral stairway around the outside is a **war memorial**. It commemorates the landing of independence forces in Bali to oppose the Dutch, who were trying to reassert control of Indonesia after WWII.

Cekik is home to the **park headquarters** (☎0365-61060; ☉7am-5pm) of the Taman Nasional Bali Barat.

Gilimanuk

☎0365

Gilimanuk is the terminus for ferries that shuttle back and forth across the narrow strait to Java. Most travellers to or from Java can get an onward ferry or bus straight away, and won't hang around. The museum is the only attraction – the town is really a place one passes through quickly. It does have the closest accommodation to the national park, however, if you want to start a trek early.

◉ Sights

This part of Bali has been occupied for thousands of years. The **Museum Situs Purbakala Gilimanuk** (☏61328; donation 5000Rp; ◷8am-4pm Mon-Fri) is centred on a family of skeletons, thought to be 4000 years old, which were found locally in 2004. The museum is 500m east of the ferry port.

Stop anywhere along the north shore of town to see the huge clash of waves and currents in the strait. It's dramatic and a good reason *not* to have that dodgy curry dish if you're about to board a ferry.

🛏 Sleeping

Good sleeping choices are thin on the ground. With one exception, there's nothing worthwhile here. However, there are choices aplenty in Pemuteran. The freshest food sizzles up at the bus station warung. Yikes.

Hotel Lestari   GUESTHOUSE $
(☏61504; r 70,000-350,000Rp; ❄) From fan-cooled singles to air-con suites, you have your choice of basic accommodation at this 21-room hotel, which feels strangely 1950s suburban. It has a cafe.

ⓘ Information

There is a Bank BRI ATM, a post office and a police station on Jl Raya Gilimanuk, but not many shops or other services.

ⓘ Getting There & Around

Frequent buses hurtle along the main road between Gilimanuk's huge bus depot and Denpasar's Ubung terminal (30,000Rp, two to three hours), or along the north-coast road to Singaraja (25,000Rp).

To get to and from Ketapang on Java (30 minutes), car ferries (adult/child 6000/4500Rp, car and driver 95,000Rp, motorbike 31,000Rp) run around the clock.

If you have wheels, watch out for police checkpoints around the terminal where commas are counted and the number of dots on i's checked on vehicle documents. Freelance 'fines' are common.

Taman Nasional Bali Barat

☏0365

Call it nature's symphony. Most visitors to Bali's only national park, Taman Nasional Bali Barat (West Bali National Park), are struck by the mellifluous sounds from myriad birds with a nice riff from the various rustling trees.

The park covers 19,000 hectares of the western tip of Bali. An additional 55,000 hectares is protected in the national park extension, as well as almost 7000 hectares of coral reef and coastal waters. Together this represents a significant commitment to conservation on an island as densely populated as Bali.

It's a place where you can hike through forests, enjoy Bali's best diving at Pulau Menjangan and explore coastal mangroves.

Although you may imagine dense jungle, most of the natural vegetation in the park is not tropical rainforest, which requires rain year-round, but rather coastal savannah, with deciduous trees that become bare in the dry season. The southern slopes receive more-regular rainfall, and so have more tropical vegetation, while the coastal lowlands have extensive mangroves.

There are more than 200 species of plants growing in the park. Local fauna includes black monkeys, leaf monkeys and macaques (seen in the afternoon along the main road near Sumber Kelompok); rusa, barking, sambar, Java and mouse deer *(muncak);* and some wild pigs, squirrels, buffalo, iguanas, pythons and green snakes. There were once tigers, but the last confirmed sighting was in 1937 – and that one was shot. The bird life is prolific, with many of Bali's 300 species found here, including the possibly extinct Bali starling (p253). For more on the park's wildlife, see p360.

Just getting off the road a bit on one of the many trails transports you into the heart of nature. One discordant note: hikes in fuel prices have seen lots of vendors along the road selling firewood snatched from the forest.

🐾 Activities

By land, by boat or underwater, the park awaits exploration.

Boat Trips

The best way to explore the mangroves of Teluk Gilimanuk (Gilimanuk Bay) or the west side of Prapat Agung is by chartering a boat (maximum of five people) for about 250,000Rp per boat per hour, including guide and entrance fees. You can arrange this at either of the park offices in Cekik or Labuhan Lalang. This is the ideal way to see bird life, including kingfishers, Javanese herons and more.

Trekking

All trekkers must be accompanied by an authorised guide. It's best to arrive the day before you want to trek, and make inquiries at the park offices in Cekik or Labuhan Lalang.

The set rates for guides in the park depend on the size of the group and the length of the trek – with one or two people it's 340,000Rp for one or two hours, 420,000Rp for two to three hours, 750,000Rp for five to seven hours and so on; extra persons cost 100,000Rp. Food (a small lunchbox) is included but transport is extra and all the prices are *very* negotiable. Early morning, say 6am, is the best time to start – it's cooler and you're more likely to see some wildlife.

Although you can try to customise your hike, the guides are most familiar with the four options listed here. If, once you're out, you have a good rapport with your guide, you might consider getting creative.

Gunung Kelatakan (Mt Kelatakan) From Sumber Kelompok, go up the mountain (698m), then down to the main road near Kelatakan village (six to seven hours). You may be able to get permission from park headquarters to stay overnight in the forest – if you don't have a tent, your guide can make a shelter from branches and leaves which will be an adventure in itself. Clear streams abound in the dense woods.

Kelatakan Starting at the village, climb to the microwave tower, go down to Ambyasari and get transport back to Cekik (four hours). This takes you through the forested southern sector of the park. From the tower you get a feel for what much of Bali looked like centuries ago.

Prapat Agung From Sumber Kelompok, you can trek around here, via the Bali Starling Pre-Release Centre and Batu Lucin – but only from about June to September, when the sensitive Bali starlings move further inland (allow at least five hours). It's easier and quicker to access the peninsula by chartered boat from Gilimanuk where you will see the mangroves and drier savannah landscape.

Teluk Terima (Terima Bay) From a trail west of Labuhan Lalang, hike around the mangroves here. Then partially follow Sungai Terima (Terima River) into the hills and walk back down to the road along the steps at Makam Jayaprana. You might see grey macaques, deer and black monkeys. The most popular hike, it takes three to four hours.

Sleeping

Park visitors will want to spend the night close to the park to get an early start. Gili-

Taman Nasional Bali Barat

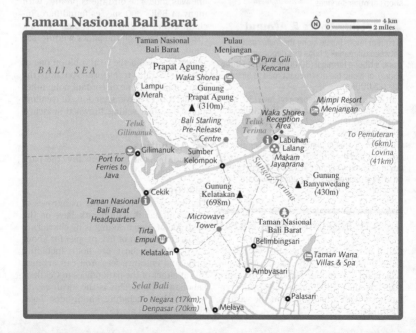

Also known as the Bali myna, Rothschild's mynah, or locally as *jalak putih,* the Bali starling is perhaps Bali's only endemic bird (opinions differ – as other places are so close, who can tell?). It is striking white in colour, with black tips to the wings and tail, and a distinctive bright-blue mask. These natural good looks have caused the bird to be poached into virtual extinction. On the black market, Bali starlings command US$7000 or more.

The wild population (maybe in the park) has been estimated at a dozen or none. In captivity, however, there are hundreds if not thousands.

It's possible to visit the **Bali Starling Pre-Release Centre** (◷8am-3pm), which is a holdover from failed efforts to reintroduce the bird into the wild. Some 6km off the main road through the park, you can see starlings in cages for a negotiable 50,000Rp.

Near Ubud, the Bali Bird Park (p168) has large aviaries where you can see Bali starlings. The park was one of the major supporters of efforts to reintroduce the birds into the wild.

manuk is closest and has basic choices. Much nicer are the luxury hotels in Labuhan Lalang, with the best all-round choices in Pemuteran (p238), 12km further east.

There is free camping at the park headquarters in Cekik. The grounds are not pristine, but the bathroom is clean enough and the toilets decent. A gratuity to the staff is greatly appreciated. You'll need some sort of gear, however.

ℹ️ Information

The **park headquarters** (☏61060; ◷7am-5pm) at Cekik displays a topographic model of the park area, and has a little information about plants and wildlife. The **Labuhan Lalang visitors centre** (◷7.30am-5pm) is in a hut located on the northern coast, where boats leave for Pulau Menjangan. Park guides on hand usually include **Nyoman Kawit** (☏0852 3850 5291), who is very knowledgeable.

You can arrange trekking guides and permits at either office; however, there are always a few characters hanging around, and determining who is an actual park official can be like spotting a Bali starling: difficult.

The main roads to Gilimanuk go through the national park, but you don't have to pay an entrance fee just to drive through. If you want to stop and visit any of the sites within the park, you must buy a ticket (20,000Rp).

ℹ️ Getting There & Away

The national park is too far for a comfortable day trip from Ubud or south Bali, though many dive operators do it. Better to consider the options outlined under Sleeping.

If you don't have transport, any Gilimanuk-bound bus or bemo from north or west Bali can drop you at park headquarters at Cekik (those from north Bali can also drop you at the Labuhan Lalang visitors centre).

Labuhan Lalang

To catch a boat to visit or snorkel Pulau Menjangan, head to the **jetty** at this small harbour in the national park. There's also a useful park **visitors centre** in a hut at the main parking lot. There are warung and a pleasant **beach** 200m to the east. The resorts and dive shops of Pemuteran are 12km northeast.

◉ Sights

Makam Jayaprana   TEMPLE

A 20-minute walk up some stone stairs from the southern side of the road, a little west of Labuhan Lalang, will bring you to Jayaprana's grave. There are fine views to the north at the top. Jayaprana, the foster son of a 17th-century king, planned to marry Leyonsari, a beautiful girl of humble origins. The king, however, also fell in love with Leyonsari and had Jayaprana killed. Leyonsari learned the truth of Jayaprana's death in a dream, and killed herself rather than marry the king. This Romeo and Juliet story is a common theme in Balinese folklore, and the grave is regarded as sacred, even though the ill-fated couple were not gods.

🛌 Sleeping

The closest choices are quite luxurious and have dive operations for your days at Pulau Menjangan.

DIVING & SNORKELLING PULAU MENJANGAN

Bali's best-known underwater attraction, **Pulau Menjangan** has a dozen superb dive sites. The experience is excellent – iconic tropical fish, soft corals, great visibility (usually), caves and a spectacular drop-off. *Sportdiver* magazine said this:

> *'Nothing prepares me for just how vibrant the coral is down the length of the sheer walls here. Dozens of species of hard and soft corals overrun each other in a glorious abundance of shades and textures that continually bewitch the eye.'*

Lacy sea fans and various sponges provide both texture and myriad hiding spots for small fish that together form a colour chart for the sea. Few can resist the silly charms of parrotfish and clownfish. Among larger creatures, you may well see whales, whale sharks and manta rays swimming gracefully past.

Of the dozen of so named sites here, most are close to shore and suitable for snorkellers or diving novices. Some decent snorkelling spots are not far from the jetty – ask the boatman where to go. Venture a bit out, however, and the depths turn inky black as the shallows drop off in dramatic cliffs, a magnet for experienced divers looking for wall dives. The Anker Wreck, a mysterious sunken ship, challenges even experts.

This uninhabited island boasts what is thought to be Bali's oldest temple, **Pura Gili Kencana**, dating from the 14th century and about 300m from the pier. You can walk around the island in about an hour and most people who take to the waters here take a break on the unfortunately not-entirely-unblemished beaches.

Practicalities

Divers have more scope to customise their experience, although it inevitably begins – as it should – at the extraordinary 30m wall. **Snorkellers**, however, may find themselves conveyed along the underwater beauty by guides who do this day-in and day-out and are just as happy to go home. This can happen with both top-end hotel-sponsored tours and the boats from Labuhan Lalang. Keep the following in mind to maximise what will likely be a highlight of your Bali trip.

» Boats usually tie up to the pier at Palau Menjangan. The wall, which is where you'll find all the action (even while just floating on the surface), is directly out from the shore. Currents tend to flow gently southwest (the shore is on your right) so you can just literally go with the flow and enjoy the underwater spectacle.

» Your guide (who you really don't need) may try to get you to swim back to the boat at some point along the less-interesting bleached coral near the shore, this turns out to be for their break. Instead, suggest that the boat come down and pick you up when you're ready, thus avoiding the swim against the current followed by downtime at the pier.

» The wall extends far to the southwest and gets more pristine and spectacular as you go. If you're overcome with joy and can't stop, you could get to the end in one go or you can break up the experience by having the boat pick you up and then drop you off again.

» North of the pier, you can snorkel from shore and cover the wall in a big circle. This lets your boat crew take their lunch.

» Try to hover over some divers along the wall. Watching their bubbles sinuously rise in all their multi-hued silvery glory from the inky depths is just plain spectacular.

» If your guide really adds to your experience, tip accordingly.

Getting There & Away

The closest and most convenient dive operators are found at **Pemuteran**, where the hotels also arrange diving and snorkelling trips. Independent snorkellers can arrange for a boat (three-hour trip for two, 325,000Rp) from the tiny dock at **Labuhan Lalang** just across the turquoise water from Menjangan. Warung here rent snorkelling gear (a pricey 50,000Rp for four hours; negotiate).

Mimpi Resort Menjangan HOTEL $$
(☏0362-94497, 0361-701070; www.mimpi.com; r US$85-130, villas US$185-400; ✳@≋) At isolated Banyuwedang, this 54-unit resort extends down to a small, mangrove-fringed, white-sand beach. The rooms have an unadorned monochromatic motif with open-air bathrooms. Hot springs feed communal pools and private tubs in the villas. The grand villas with a private pool and a view of the lagoon are one of the best tropical fantasy escapes on Bali.

Waka Shorea HOTEL $$
(☏0362-94666; www.wakaexperience.com; r US$130-260, villas US$250-375; ✳≋) Located in splendid isolation in the park, Waka Shorea is a 10-minute boat ride from the hotel's reception area 100m east of Labuhan Lalang. The 16 naturalistic units are hidden in the forest, with decks above the trees and a dreamy pool.

Lombok

Best Places to Eat

» Astari (p281)

» Oberoi Lombok (p271)

» De Quake (p268)

Best Places to Stay

» Qunci Pool Villas (p267)

» Tugu Lombok (p270)

» Heaven on the Planet (p285)

» Yuli's Homestay (p280)

Why Go?

Long overshadowed by its superstar neighbour across the water, there's a steady hum about Lombok that's beginning to turn into a distinct buzz. Blessed with exquisite white-sand beaches, epic surf, a lush forested interior, and hiking trails through tobacco and rice fields, Lombok is fully loaded with tropical allure. Oh, and you'll probably notice mighty Gunung Rinjani, Indonesia's second-highest volcano, its summit complete with hot springs and a dazzling crater lake.

And there's much more. Lombok's southern coastline is nature on a very grand scale indeed: breathtaking turquoise bays, world-class surf breaks and massive headlands.

For years Lombok has been touted as Indonesia's next hot destination. Finally the reality seems to have caught up with the hype, and with a new international airport and renewed interest from around the globe, Lombok's time seems to be nigh.

When to Go

Lombok is hot, sticky and tropical throughout the year, with a marked rainy season (roughly between late October and April). The driest months coincide with the peak period in July and August. The rainy season offers an excellent time to catch a local festival, such as the spectacular rice-throwing event called Perang Topat (held at Pura Lingsar in November or December), Peresean stick-fighting competitions (in December) or the Narmada buffalo races (in April). For more on Sasak festivals see the boxed text, p284.

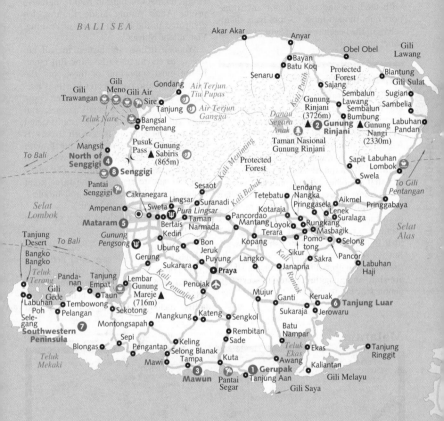

Lombok Highlights

❶ Surfing (or learning to surf) the ride of your life in **Gerupak** (p283)

❷ Scaling **Gunung Rinjani** (p273), Lombok's incomparable sacred peak

❸ Setting eyes on idyllic **Mawun beach** (p283) for the very first time

❹ Picking your own deserted-cove beach **north of Senggigi** (p270)

❺ Catching a **Sasak festival** (p284), such as Peresean near Mataram

❻ Soaking up the incredible scene at the unique **fish market** (p283) of Tanjung Luar

❼ Exploring the off-the-beaten-track beaches and islands of the **Southwestern Peninsula** (p263)

❽ Indulging in a blissful treatment or massage in a **Senggigi spa** (p265)

WEST LOMBOK

☎ 0370

This region is dominated by the sprawling city of Mataram, which is well endowed with facilities and is an important transport hub, though most visitors base themselves in the beach resort of Senggigi, just a short hop away.

Mataram

Lombok's capital is a conurbation of several (once separate) towns: Ampenan (the port); Mataram (the administrative centre); Cakranegara (the business centre, often called simply 'Cakra') and Bertais and Sweta to the east, where you'll find the bus terminal. It's a quintessentially Indonesian city that stretches 12km from east to west and is home to over a million people. As far as developing-world towns go, it's a relatively attractive place, with broad tree-lined avenues, grand municipal buildings and little in the way of squalor or shanty towns. But it's resolutely provincial, with little in the way of metropolitan culture. As sights are slim, and Senggigi is close by, very few people stay here.

◉ Sights

Pura Meru
HINDU TEMPLE

(off Jl Selaparang; admission by donation; ⊗8am-5pm) Lombok's largest and most important Hindu temple was built in 1720 by Balinese prince Anak Agung Made Karang. It's dedicated to the Hindu trinity of Brahma, Vishnu and Shiva.

Wooden drums are beaten to call believers to ceremonies (the June full moon is the most important of these, but the grounds are also packed on Christmas Eve) in the outer courtyard. The inner court has one large and 33 small shrines, and three thatched, teak *meru* (multi-tiered shrines). The central *meru,* with 11 tiers, is Shiva's house; the *meru* to the north, with nine tiers, is Vishnu's; and the seven-tiered *meru* to the south is Brahma's. The *meru* are also said to represent the three great mountains – Rinjani, Agung and Bromo – and the mythical Mount Meru.

The caretaker will lend you a sash and sarong.

Po Hwa Kong
BUDDHIST TEMPLE

(Jl Sudarso, Ampenan; ⊗open 24hr) Reflecting the religious diversity of the island, this historic Chinese Buddhist temple (built in 1806) acts as a spiritual centre for believers of all faiths, including Hindus, Christians and

Mataram

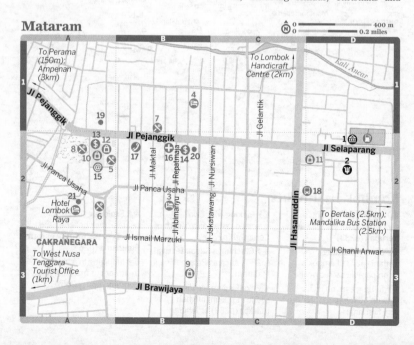

N ↑ 0 ───────── 400 m
     0 ───────── 0.2 miles

To Perama (150m); Ampenan (3km)

Jl Pejanggik

To Lombok Handicraft Centre (2km)

Kali Ancar

Jl Gelantik

Jl Selaparang

Jl Pejanggik

Jl Maktal
Jl Repatmaja
Jl Nursiwan

Jl Panca Usaha

Jl Panca Usaha

Jl Jakatawang
Jl Abimanyu

Jl Hasanuddin

Hotel Lombok Raya

Jl Ismail Marzuki

To Bertais (2.5km); Mandalika Bus Station (2.5km)

CAKRANEGARA

To West Nusa Tenggara Tourist Office (1km)

Jl Chanil Anwar

Jl Brawijaya

Muslims. Inside the compound there's a classically Chinese combination of dragons, gods and clouds of sweet incense. Make a donation and the whippet-thin, *kretek* cigarette-puffing guardian will give you a personal fortune reading (in Bahasa Indonesia only). It's just east of the port in Ampenan.

Museum Negeri Nusa Tenggara Barat
MUSEUM
(☑632 519; Jl Panji Tilar Negara 6; admission 20,000Rp; ⊙8am-2pm Tue-Thu & Sat & Sun, 8-11am Fri) This museum, about 1km from the coast, houses an interesting, eclectic collection that includes many fine kris (traditional daggers), *songket* (silver- or gold-threaded cloth), and some very precious palm-leaf manuscripts of the *Mahabharata*. Pay an extra 40,000Rp to see the royal collection of gold swords and jewellery.

Mayura Water Palace
PALACE
(Jl Selaparang; admission by donation; ⊙7am-7.30pm) Built in 1744, this palace encom-

passes the former king's family temple, which is a pilgrimage site (on December 24) for Lombok's Hindus. In 1894 it was the location of bloody battles between the Dutch and the Balinese. It's now a somewhat neglected public park with an artificial lake.

🛏 Sleeping

Most folks nest among Cakranegara's quiet streets off Jl Pejanggik/Selaparang, east of Mataram Mall.

Hotel Melati Viktor 1
LOSMEN $
(☑633 830; Jl Abimanyu 1; r with fan/air-con 70,000/90,000Rp; ✸) Offering excellent value for money, this place has neat, very clean rooms with high ceilings, tiled floors and TV. On the other side of the street there's a second branch, Viktor 2, which resembles a Balinese courtyard. Inexpensive laundry is available.

Karthika II Hotel
BUDGET HOTEL $
(☑641 776; Jl Subak I 16; s/d/tr 80,000/95,000/110,000Rp; ✸) All rooms have front verandas at the Karthika, which has been designed like a Balinese temple compound. Rooms do vary in quality – some of the standard rooms are in better shape than the VIPs. Air-con costs extra.

Grand Legi Mataram
HOTEL $$
(☑636 282; www.grandlegihotels.co.id; Jl Sriwijaya 81; r/deluxe 575,000/625,000Rp + 21% tax; ✸@☲) Formerly the Sahid Legi, this landmark hotel combines Western and Indonesian design influences and boasts full facilities including three restaurants and a large pool. Rooms have been recently renovated and are comfortable if a little bland. No alcohol is available.

🍴 Eating

The Mataram Mall (and the streets around it) are loaded with Western-style fast-food outlets, Indonesian noodle bars and warung.

Aroma
CHINESE $$
(☑632 585; Jl Palapa 1-2; meals from 30,000Rp; ⊙9am-9.30pm) Spotless, well-run and highly popular family-run Chinese restaurant around the corner from the Mataram Mall. The surrounds are functional; the emphasis is all on the freshness and flavour of the cooking here, particularly the seafood. Crab with black pepper and chilli sauce is the signature dish, or try *cumi saos tiram* (squid with oyster sauce).

Bakmi Raos NOODLE BAR $
(☑661 0499; Jl Panca Usaha; dishes 10,000-22,000Rp; ☺10am-10pm, closed Fri 11am-2pm) A modern take on the tried-and-tested Indonesian noodle joint, this modern place serves up delicious *mie* (noodles) cooked in a multitude of sauces.

Melissa Bakery DELI $
(☑628 446; Jl Pejanggik; snacks from 2000Rp; ☺8am-8pm) A squeaky-clean bakery-cum-deli that pumps out the full monty of Indonesian street snacks (such as smoked beef roti) and *nasi kuning* (yellow rice) as well as Western treats such as brownies and cheesecake.

Rumah Makan Dirgahayu INDONESIAN $
(☑637 559; Jl Cilinaya 19; rice dishes from 7000Rp, seafood from 25,000Rp) No-frills Makassar-style dining hall opposite the mall. Try the *ikan laut bakar* (baked fish).

Mie Ayam Jakarta INDONESIAN $
(☑623 965; Jl Yos Sudarso 112, Ampenan; dishes 12,000-25,000Rp) Just east of the Po Hwa Kong temple, this simple place scores for chicken noodle dishes.

🛍 Shopping

For handicrafts try the many stores on Jl Raya Senggigi, the road heading north from Ampenan towards Senggigi.

Pasar Bertais MARKET
(☺7am-5pm) A vast, scruffy-but-fascinating market near the bus terminal. Virtually anything under the Lombok sun is traded including spices and herbs, palm sugar and fresh tobacco leaves; enormous, pungent bricks of shrimp paste; and cheaper handicrafts than anywhere else on Lombok.

Mataram Mall MALL
(Jl Pejanggik) Multi-storey shopping mall with a Hero supermarket, kids' play area and loads of electrical, mobile-phone and clothes stores and restaurants. An outdoor pool complex, **Waterboom** (☺8am-6pm; entrance 15,000Rp), adjoins the mall too.

Lombok Handicraft Centre CRAFT CENTRE
(Jl Hasanuddin) At Sayang Sayang (2km north of Cakra), there's a wide range of crafts, including masks, textiles, and ceramics from across Nusa Tenggara.

Royal Surf CLOTHING
(☑629 927; Mataram Mall) Skate and surf wear, including genuine sunglasses and hip headgear.

Galeria Nao FURNITURE
(☑626 835; Jl Raya Senggigi 234) Contemporary hardwood furniture and artefacts that wouldn't look out of place in *Wallpaper* magazine.

Lombok Pottery Centre POTTERY
(☑640 351; Jl Sriwijaya 111) Classy, stylish Fair Trade pottery and ceramics. Six hundred designs are available, including fruit bowls and elegant vases, all made on Lombok.

Pasar Cakranegara MARKET
(cnr Jl Hasanuddin & Jl Selaparang) Collection of quirky stalls, some of which sell good-quality ikat, as well as an interesting food market.

ℹ Information

Emergency
Police station (☑631 225; Jl Langko) In an emergency, dial ☑110.
Rumah Sakit Risa (☑625 560; Jl Pejanggik) The best private hospital on Lombok with English-speaking doctors and modern facilities.

Internet Access
Elian Internet (www.elianmedia.net; 1 Panca Usaha Komplek, Mataram Mall; per hr 5000Rp; ☺24hr)

Money
You'll find plenty of banks with ATMs scattered along Cakra's main drag. Moneychangers in Mataram Mall and on Jl Pejanggik often provide the best rates for cash.

Post
Post office (Jl Langko; ☺8am-4.30pm Mon-Thu, 8-11am Fri, 8am-1pm Sat)

Telephone
Wartel (public telephone offices) are on Jl Pejanggik and at the airport.
Telkom (☑633 333; Jl Pendidikan 23; ☺24hr) Offers phone and fax services.

Tourist Information
West Lombok tourist office (☑621 658; Jl Suprato 20; ☺7.30am-2pm Mon-Thu, 7.30-11am Fri, 8am-1pm Sat) Stocks a few maps and leaflets, though not much in the way of practical information.
West Nusa Tenggara tourist office (☑634 800; Jl Singosari 2; ☺8am-2pm Mon-Thu, 8-11am Fri, 8am-12.30pm Sat) Offers limited information about Lombok and Sumbawa.

ℹ Getting There & Away

Air
Lombok's new airport near Praya should open in 2011; when it's operational all international and

domestic flights will be routed there. Until then, all flights arrive at Selaparang Airport (AMI) in north Mataram. Domestic departure tax from Selaparang is 20,000Rp; international departure tax is 100,000Rp.

Batavia Air (☑021 3899 9888; www.batavia -air.com) Daily to Jakarta via Surabaya.

Garuda Indonesia (☑0804 180 7807; www .garuda-indonesia.com; Jl Pejanggik 42) Three daily flights to Jakarta, one daily flight to Bali.

Lion Air (☑629 333, www.lionair.co.id; Grand Legi Mataram, Jl Sriwijaya 81) Flights to Jakarta and Surabaya twice daily.

Merpati Airlines (☑621 111; www.merpati .co.id; Jl Pejanggik 69, Mataram) Flies to Kuala Lumpur daily and Bali at least four times daily. Connections to most parts of Indonesia via Denpasar, Surabaya or Jakarta.

Silk Air (☑628 254; www.silkair.com; Jl Panca Usaka 11, Hotel Lombok Raya) Serves Singapore direct three times a week.

Trans Nusa (☑616 2428; www.transnusa .co.id) Flies to Bali three times daily, plus daily to Bima and Sumbawa Besar.

Trigana Airlines (☑616 2433; www.trigana-air .com) Two or three daily flights to Bali.

Wings Air (☑629 333, www.lionair.co.id; Grand Legi Mataram, Jl Sriwijaya 81) A subsidiary of Lion Air, sometimes covers the Denpasar and Surabaya route.

Bus

The sprawling, dusty Mandalika bus station in Bertais is the main bus and bemo (minibus) terminal for the entire island, and also for long-distance buses to Sumbawa, Bali and Java (p381).

It's a chaotic, badly organised place, so be sure to keep a level head to avoid the 'help' of the commission-happy touts. Long-distance buses leave from behind the main terminal building, while bemo and smaller buses leave from one of two car parks on either side.

Some distances and fares for buses and bemo from Mandalika terminal:

DESTINATION	DISTANCE	FARE	DURA-TION
Kuta (via Praya & Sengkol)	54km	13,000Rp	90min
Labuhan Lombok	69km	15,000Rp	2hr
Lembar	22km	5000Rp	30min
Pemenang (for Bangsal)	30km	8000Rp	40min
Praya	27km	6000Rp	30min

Kebon Roek bemo terminal in Ampenan has bemo to Bertais and Senggigi (both 3000Rp).

Tourist Shuttle Bus

Perama (☑635 928; www.peramatour.com; Jl Pejanggik 66) operates shuttle buses to popular destinations on Lombok (including Bangsal, Senggigi and Kuta), and to Bali.

ℹ Getting Around
To/From the Airport

Lombok's (old) Selaparang Airport is due to be phased out during the lifetime of this guidebook, and a new airport near Praya will probably be open by the time you read this. Selaparang is 5km north of Cakra. A taxi desk here sells prepaid tickets to locations around the island: 32,000Rp to Mataram; 60,000Rp to 75,000Rp to Senggigi; 125,000Rp to Bangsal; 240,000Rp to Kuta; 380,000Rp to Senaru. Alternatively, walk out of the airport and taxis wait right by the gate on Jl Adi Sucipto – from here Senggigi

---

LOMBOK'S NEW AIRPORT

A high-tech, visually arresting vision of modernity rising out of the rustic flatlands of Praya in the south of the island, **Lombok International Airport** (Bandara Internasional Lombok) is slated for a much-delayed official opening ceremony in 2011. It will boast international and domestic terminals and slick shopping facilities. Indonesia's tourism officials hope its emergence will really put Lombok on the map and divert air traffic away from clogged Bali. Its 2750m runway will be able to accommodate aircraft as large as the Boeing 747-400.

The striking new glass, steel and concrete edifice will certainly present a modern face of Lombok, yet for tourists bound for the Gilis or Senggigi its location is inconvenient (though Kuta is now very close). And as the island government was still struggling to come to agreement on compensation with landowners to widen key access roads as late as November 2010, expect a long slow journey to the north of the island behind *cidomo* (pony carts) and chugging trucks for some time.

Until it opens, all air traffic will continue to use **Mataram's Selaparang Airport** (AMI). For the latest airport news consult *The Lombok Guide* (www.thelombokguide.com).

costs about 40,000Rp using a meter; bemo 7 also leaves from here to Ampenan.

Bemo

Mataram is *very* spread out. Yellow bemo shuttle between Kebon Roek bemo terminal in Ampenan and Mandalika terminal in Bertais (10km away), along the two main thoroughfares. Outside the Pasar Cakranegara there is a handy bemo stop for services to Bertais, Ampenan, Sweta and Lembar. Fares cost 2000 to 3000Rp.

Car & Motorcycle

Car hire rates are much cheaper in Senggigi.

Trac Astra Rent-a-Car (📞 626 363; www.trac .astra.co.id; Jl Adi Sucipto 5, Rembiga Mataram) Toyota Avanza self-drive/with driver per day from 360,000/570,000Rp.

Taxi

For a reliable taxi with a meter, call **Lombok Taksi** (📞 627 000).

Around Mataram

There are some gorgeous villages, temples and scenery east of Mataram. You can easily visit all of the following places in half a day with your own transport.

PURA LINGSAR

This large **temple compound** (admission by donation; ⏰7am-6pm) is the holiest on Lombok. Built in 1714 by King Anak Agung Ngurah, and nestled beautifully in lush rice paddies, it's multi-denominational, with a temple for Balinese Hindus and one for followers of Lombok's mystical take on Islam, Wektu Telu (see the boxed text, p272). It's not uncommon to happen upon pilgrims of both religions making offerings and sipping holy water.

The Hindu temple (Pura Gaduh) has four shrines: one oriented to Gunung Rinjani (seat of the gods on Lombok), one to Gunung Agung (seat of the gods in Bali) and a double shrine representing the union between the two islands.

The Wektu Telu temple is noted for its enclosed pond devoted to Lord Vishnu, and the holy eels, which can be enticed from their hiding places with hard-boiled eggs (available at stalls outside) – it's considered good luck to feed them. Follow the temple etiquette and rent a sash and/or sarong (available outside).

A huge ritual battle, Perang Topat, is held here every year in November or Decem-

ber (the exact date depends on the lunar month). After a costumed parade, Hindus and Wektu pelt each other with *ketupat* (sticky rice in coconut leaves).

Pura Lingsar is 9km northeast of the Mandalika terminal in Bertais. First take a bemo from the terminal to Taman Narmada, and another to Lingsar.

SURANADI

Suranadi is an attractive village in lush countryside with a forest reserve, temple and natural swimming pool. It's a popular spot for locals on weekends and holidays but wonderfully peaceful at other times.

◉ Sights

Pura Suranadi (admission by donation; ⏰7.30am -6pm) is one of the holiest Hindu temples on Lombok, a pilgrimage site with temples set against a dramatic background of towering tropical trees. A bubbling, cool natural spring feeds the lovely pool here – ideal for a refreshing, if chilly dip. Watch out for the cheeky troupe of resident monkeys.

Just opposite the village market, **Hutan Wisata Suranadi** (admission 3000Rp; ⏰8am-5pm) is a quiet forest sanctuary good for a short hike and birdwatching.

WORTH A TRIP

GUNUNG PENGSONG

This Balinese **hilltop temple** (admission by donation; ⏰7am-6pm), 9km south of Mataram, has spectacular views across undulating rice fields towards distant volcanoes and the sea. Japanese soldiers hid here towards the end of WWII, and remnants of cannons can be found, as can plenty of playful monkeys.

Once a year, generally in March or April, a buffalo is taken up the steep slope and sacrificed to give thanks for a good harvest. The Desa Bersih festival also occurs here at harvest time – houses and gardens are cleaned, fences whitewashed, and roads and paths repaired. Once part of a ritual to rid the village of evil spirits, it's now held in honour of the rice goddess, Dewi Sri.

It's a 15-minute walk up to the temple top from the entrance. You'll need your own wheels to get here.

Several restaurants and warung line the approach road to the temple. Pura Suranadi is 6km northwest of Taman Narmada and served by frequent public bemo.

SESAOT & AROUND

Some 4km northeast of Suranadi is Sesaot, a charming market town with an ice-cold holy river that snakes from Gunung Rinjani into the forest. There are some gorgeous picnic spots and enticing swimming holes here. Regular transport connects Taman Narmada with Sesaot, and you'll find warung along the main street.

Further east, **Air Nyet** is another pretty village with more options for swimming and picnics. Ask for directions to the unsigned turn-off in the middle of Sesaot. The bridge and road to Air Nyet are rough, but it's a lovely stroll (about 3km) from Sesaot.

Lembar

Lembar is Lombok's main port for ferries, tankers and Pelni liners coming in from Bali and beyond. Though the ferry port itself is scruffy, the setting – think azure inlets ringed by soaring green hills – is stunning. However, there's no reason to linger, with good transport connections to Mataram and Senggigi. If you really don't want to move on, or need a feed, **Hotel Tigar** (☑681 444; Jl Raya Pelabuhan; meals from 12,000Rp, s/d 70,000Rp, cottages 150,000Rp, all incl breakfast), 1km north of the ferry port, is a clean, hospitable place.

Bemo shuttle regularly between Lembar and the Mandalika terminal in Bertais (5000Rp), or you can catch one at the market stop in Cakra. See p188 for details on boats between Bali and Lembar.

Southwestern Peninsula

The sweeping coastline that stretches west of Lembar is blessed with deserted beaches and tranquil offshore islands set in pellucid, shallow waters. It's long been touted as Lombok's next big tourist destination, but though a couple of resorts have opened in recent years, it's still a very laid-back area, dotted with fishing villages and Hindu temples. The only blot on the landscape is the gold-rush town of **Sekotong**. The hills above Sekotong are rich in the precious metal, and up to 6000 locals mined illegally here in huge open-cast pits (using mercury)

until a crackdown in December 2009. Clandestine mining still continues despite official opposition and severe environmental damage, but it's hoped that a community mine will open in the future.

None of this is visible from the narrow (but paved) coastal road, which hugs the contours of the peninsula, passing white-sand beaches and perfect coves. The roads loops past a succession of tiny settlements to Bangko Bangko and Tanjung Desert, one of Asia's legendary surf breaks (see p36).

A few of the palm-dappled offshore islands with silky beaches are inhabited. Gili Nanggu and Gili Gede both have accommodation. There's much better snorkelling and diving from the islands than from the mainland, as the sea is extremely shallow along most of the peninsula. Gili Gede has a sea turtle conservation project you can visit, where tanks of young turtles are fed before being released.

🛏 Sleeping & Eating

Places to stay and restaurants are thin on the ground in this region, and be aware that some close in the rainy season.

MAINLAND

Bola Bola Paradis   BEACH HOTEL **$**
(☑0817 578 7355; www.bolabolaparadis.com; Pelangan; r 300,000-415,000Rp) A classy hotel, with very well-kept facilities and gardens that stretch down to a lovely sandy beach (though swimming is impossible at low tide). Rooms are either in delightful colonial-style 12-sided bungalows or in the tall-roofed main building; all have private verandas. There's a good restaurant (mains 38,000Rp to 70,000Rp) and a pool is planned.

Cocotino's   RESORT HOTEL **$$**
(☑0813 4024 7788; www.cocotinos-sekotong .com; Tanjung Empat; r/villas from US$90/220; ✹@) New in 2010, this resort hotel has an oceanfront location, private beach and high-quality bungalows (some with lovely outdoor bathrooms), though not all have sea views. There's a professional dive shop, and many visitors stay here on scuba packages. Rack rates are quite steep – check the website for offers.

ISLANDS

Via Vacare   ISLAND HIDEAWAY **$**
(☑0819 1590 4275; www.viavacare.com; budget bed €5, bungalow s/d €20/30, 3 meals €15) Via

Vacare is a very welcoming, Dutch-owned place on lovely Gili Gede that feels more like a secret retreat dedicated to the essence of life than a hotel. It's located on a charming crescent beach (though sea access is tricky at low tide). The four spacious bungalows are simple yet stylish, with thatched roofs, quality beds and outdoor bathrooms. Backpacker digs are a comfy mattress on the floor and a mosquito net, in a large open-sided room. There's no electricity, but the power of nature is intense here, with ocean vistas and starry, starry nights to enjoy. There's a yoga space, and fine home-cooked fresh food in the restaurant.

Secret Island Resort BUNGALOWS $
(✆0818 0376 2001; www.secretislandresort .com; r 200,000Rp, bungalow 250,000Rp; ❀) Gili Gede's only other option, Secret Island has attractive accommodation (including a bungalow over the reef) scattered around a lovely garden, with sea views to die for. Kayak, sport-fishing, surfing, diving and three-island boat trips (200,000Rp) are offered. Snorkelling is quite good just offshore. Airport/Lembar pick-ups are offered as are free boat transfers from Tembowong beach.

Gili Nanggu Cottages ISLAND BUNGALOWS $
(✆623 783; www.gilinanggu.com; cottages 250,000Rp, bungalows 350,000Rp, meals from 20,000Rp; ❀) Leave all your worldly worries behind on serene and peaceful Gili Nanggu. This place offers rustic two-storey *lumbung* (rice barn) cottages and air-conditioned bungalows just off the beach, with fabulously clear water for snorkelling and beach volleyball games during the main tourist season. A boat transfer from Lembar costs 150,000Rp one way.

❶ Getting There & Away

Bemo run between Lembar and Pelangan (1½ hours) via Sekotong every 30 minutes until 5pm. West of Pelangan, transport is less regular, but the route is still served by infrequent bemo services until Selegang.

To reach Gili Nanggu, a return boat charter from Taun costs 275,000Rp. Chartered boats also connect Tembowong with the islands of Gili Gede and Gili Ringit (250,000Rp return).

Senggigi

Lombok's only bona fide tourist resort, Senggigi enjoys a spectacular location along a series of sweeping bays interrupted by headlands, with white-sand beaches sitting pretty below a backdrop of jungle-clad mountains and coconut palms. During the day everyone gravitates to the beach, but in the late afternoon all eyes face west to take in one of Indonesia's most dramatic sights. The setting sun creates a blood-red vision of the orient, as a tumbling ball of fire sinks into the ocean next to the giant triangular cone of Bali's Gunung Agung.

Tourist numbers are relatively modest here, except in high season, and you'll find some excellent-value hotels and restaurants. The main strip, with its empty storefronts, could look more appealing, and the resident beach hawkers can be an over-persistent bunch at times. Fortunately, Senggigi's wellness scene is really on the up, and the ever-growing selection of blissful massage and treatment rooms in the resort's many spas are the ideal place to revitalise and rediscover that serene side to your nature.

The Senggigi area spans 10km of coastal road; Mangsit is 3km north of central Senggigi.

⊙ Sights

Pura Batu Bolong HINDU TEMPLE
(admission by donation; ⊙7am-7pm) This small Hindu temple enjoys a spectacular position on the southern fringes of Senggigi, its 14 altars and mini-pagodas clinging to a rocky volcanic outcrop that spills into the foaming sea. The temple is oriented towards Gunung Agung, Bali's holiest mountain, and is a perfect sunset spot. The rock underneath the temple has a natural hole that gives it its name – *batu bolong* (literally, 'rock with hole').

⪢ Activities
Snorkelling, Diving & Surfing
There's reasonable snorkelling off the point in Senggigi and in front of Windy Cottages, 3km north of the town. You can rent snorkelling gear (25,000Rp per day) from several spots on the beach.

Diving trips from Senggigi usually visit the Gili Islands. Note there are a couple of dive centres in town that should be more professional. Don't compromise your safety: use a recommended scuba school.

There's some surfing in the Senggigi area, including one break by Qunci Villas. However, if you're really wave-hungry head to south Lombok for world-class surf.

Blue Marlin (📞0812 375 6012; www.bluemar lindive.com; Holiday Resort Lombok & Alang Alang, Jl Raya Senggigi)

Dream Divers (📞692 047; www.dreamdivers .com; Jl Raya Senggigi)

New Surf Senggigi (📞693 312; Jl Raya Senggigi) Sells, repairs and rents surfboards (100,000Rp per day) and surf gear. Lessons with an instructor cost 350,000Rp a day.

Cycling & Hiking

Lombok Biking Tour (📞660 5792; www .lombokbiking.com; Jl Raya Senggigi; half-day excursions per person from US$22) Runs well-planned guided rides, including trips along the Pusuk Pass and in the Lingsar region.

Rinjani Trek Club (📞693 202; rtc.senggigi@ gmail.com; Jl Raya Senggigi) Well informed about routes and trail conditions on Gunung Rinjani and has a wide choice of guided hikes.

Massages, Spas & Salons

Very determined local masseurs armed with mats, oils and attitude hunt for business on Senggigi's beaches. Expect to pay about 60,000Rp for one hour after bargaining. Most hotels can arrange a masseur to visit your room; rates start at about 75,000Rp.

Senggigi has a burgeoning spa scene, with everything from simple set-ups to Zen-like wellness centres.

Royal Spa (📞686 6577; Jl Raya Senggigi; ☺10am-9pm) A professional yet inexpensive spa with a tempting range of scrubs, massages (from 85,000Rp) and treatments. The *lulur* massage is a real treat and includes a body mask. It's always popular so book ahead.

Qambodja Spa (📞693 800; Qunci Pool Villas, Mangsit; ☺10am-10pm) Gorgeous spa where you select your choice of oil (uplifting, harmony) depending on the effect and mood you require from your massage (from US$30), which includes Thai, Balinese and shiatsu. There's a huge Java stone tub for really luxuriant bath treatments.

Laguna Beach Spa (📞693 333; Sheraton Senggigi Beach Resort; ☺9am-9pm) Has a Sasak massage that relieves tension (one hour, US$37) and a complete foot-care spa treatment (one hour, US$30).

Aero Spa (📞693 210; Senggigi Beach Hotel; ☺10am-9pm) Revitalising aromatherapy oil massages (from US$32) as well as reflexology, and beauty treatments.

Stylist Salon (📞619 4240; Senggigi Plaza Blok 1 No 4; ☺10am-8pm) For a manicure, pedicure, beauty treatment or massage (from 60,000Rp) in humble environs, this friendly place is ideal.

🛏 Sleeping

Senggigi's accommodation is very spread out. But even if you're located a few kilometres away (say, in Mangsit) you're not isolated as many restaurants offer free rides to diners and taxis are very inexpensive.

Heavy discounts of up to 50% are common in midrange and top-end places outside the July–August peak season.

SENGGIGI

Beach Club BEACH HOTEL $
(📞693 637; Jl Raya Senggigi; s/d with fan 105,000/160,000Rp, bungalows from 410,000Rp; ❄🅿🛜🏊) A new, well-run, Australian-owned place with a great beachfront location, a lovely pool area shaded by palms, plenty of greenery and a spacious bar-restaurant (try the rotisserie chicken). The tastefully decorated, well-equipped bungalows have all mod cons, including fridge, TV/DVD and outdoor bathrooms. There are also a couple of very good-value backpacker rooms with private cold-water bathroom. Beach Club is just south of central Senggigi.

Villa Pantai HIP VILLAS $$
(📞0817 970 8534; villas 650,000-800,000Rp; ❄🛜🏊) Three gorgeous, very spacious and well-designed contemporary villas, just off the beach about 3km south of central Senggigi (Villa 1 has sea views). All are finished to a very high standard and boast a nice combination of modern and Indonesian decor, with lovely tropical gardens and full kitchen facilities. A cook prepares a full breakfast for you every day.

Raja's Bungalows BUDGET $
(📞0812 377 0138; d 120,000Rp) Up a little lane behind the mosque, this very attractive place has a village-style location surrounded by fields and free-range chickens. It offers lovely, very clean, detached bungalows, all with mosquito nets, high ceilings, bedside lights, cane furniture, private bathrooms and front porches. There's a small lounge for socialising and a shady garden.

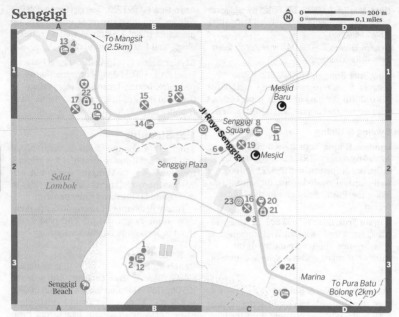

Batu Bolong Cottages BUNGALOWS **$**
(☎693 065; Jl Raya Senggigi; s/d 150,000/
300,000Rp; ❀❀) A good choice, this place occupies two large garden plots on either side
of the coastal road just south of central Senggigi. There's a wide range of traditional-style
bungalows to choose from, all with lovely
hand-carved furniture. Those on the beachside are the most desirable but even the fan-
cooled rooms are perfectly acceptable.

Sunset House HOTEL **$$**
(☎692 020; Jl Raya Senggigi 66; www.sunset
house-lombok.com; r 450,000Rp; ❀❀) Six
tastefully simple yet elegant, well-equipped
rooms on a quiet stretch of shoreline near
the Batu Bolong temple; the upper-floor
ones have sweeping ocean views towards
Bali. There's a lovely garden to enjoy, and
staff are very welcoming.

Hotel Elen BACKPACKERS **$**
(☎693 077; Jl Raya Senggigi; r 100,000Rp) The
faded sign on the street is a giveaway: this is
a long-time backpackers' choice. The clean
rooms are basic but represent fair value, all
have en-suite bathrooms with Western toi-
lets and fans and there's a little lounge area
with sofas. However, pack those earplugs,
as it's right next to the mosque.

Pondok Shinta BUDGET **$**
(☎693 563; Jl Raya Senggigi; r 85,000Rp) Set
just off the main drag, this little homestay
has an accommodation block of nine simple
rooms, all with fan, private bathroom and
a double bed. There's a shady garden and a
bar-restaurant here too.

Sheraton Senggigi Beach Resort
RESORT HOTEL **$$**
(☎693 333; www.sheraton.com; r from 775,000Rp;
❀❀@❀❀) A lovely palm-fringed swimming pool and the well-regarded spa and
health club are the positives at the beachfront Sheraton. The rooms are looking a
little dated though and wi-fi is a hefty US$12
per day in rooms (though free in the lobby).

Senggigi Beach Hotel RESORT HOTEL **$$**
(☎693 210; http://senggigibeachhotel.com; r from
US$80, beach bungalows from US$140 plus 21%
tax; ❀❀@❀❀) Large hotel with deluxe bun-
galows spread around a large palm-studded
garden just off the beach. The complex in-
cludes a large pool, spa and tennis courts.
The buffet breakfast is a veritable banquet.

Sonya Homestay BUDGET **$**
(☎0813 3989 9878; Jl Raya Senggigi; r 65,000Rp)
The dark rooms are looking tatty these
days, with lino floors and a foam slab for
a bed. At least the owners are friendly and
helpful.

LOMBOK SENGGIGI

Lina Hotel HOTEL $

(☑693 237; Jl Raya Senggigi; r 150,000-250,000Rp; ✸) Staff wear worn 1980s-style uniforms at this faded beachside resort and the rooms are equally dated. Those facing the beach are best.

MANGSIT

TOP CHOICE Qunci Villas CONTEMPORARY HOTEL $$

(☑693 800; www.quncivillas.com; r US$80-125, villas from US$165 plus 21% tax; ❂✸@☎✸) Lombok's hippest hotel enterprise now occupies two (almost) neighbouring beachfront plots, with a third venture forthcoming and a couple of amazing villas in the hills to boot. This is the most popular address on Lombok: the hotels exude contemporary élan while maintaining excellent levels of comfort and service, and value for money. Rooms are sleek and modern, with impressive attention to detail and modern artistic flourishes; the gardens are gorgeous (with a 30m pool and vistas of Bali). Qunci Pool Villas (home to one of Lombok's best spas) is a little more upmarket than the original Qunci. Both places have a great restaurant.

Windy Beach Resort BEACH COTTAGES $$

(☑693 191; www.windybeach.com; cottages 400,000-450,000Rp, lumbung 500,000Rp; ✸☎✸) Deservedly popular place on a fine sandy beach. Attractive traditional-style thatched cottages (with bamboo walls and mosquito nets) and two-storey *lumbung* are scattered around a wonderful garden, and there's a bar-restaurant and decent snorkelling offshore. Staff are very helpful indeed, and the bright lights of Senggigi are a short taxi ride away.

Alang Alang HOTEL $$

(☑693 518; www.alang-alang-villas.com; bungalows from US$100; ✸✸@) This classic Indonesian-style hotel has spacious rooms with stately teak furniture, lots of hand-carved detailing and marble floors. Alang Alang is professionally run and boasts a good restaurant, and an oceanfront location, with a sandy beach a short walk away.

Bulan Baru HOTEL $

(☑693 785; r 280,000Rp; ✸✸) A welcoming hotel with spacious bungalows, all with minibars and hot-water bathrooms. It's about 7km from central Senggigi; no children are permitted.

✗ Eating

Senggigi's dining scene ranges from fine dining to simple warung. Many places offer free transport for evening diners – phone for a ride.

For authentic Indonesian street food, head to the hillside night stalls on the route north to Mangsit where *sate* (satay) sizzles, pots of noodles bubble, and corn on the cob roasts.

SENGGIGI

De Quake
ASIAN $

(☎693 694; www.dequake.com; mains from 23,000Rp) Part lounge bar, part contemporary restaurant, De Quake is one of the most enjoyable places to eat in Senggigi, with a modern menu that features tapas-style Asian dishes such as Malay-style chicken laksa. The upper level has tables with direct ocean views. It's right on the beach behind the art market.

Asmara
INTERNATIONAL $$

(☎693 619; www.asmara-group.com; Jl Raya Senggigi; mains 38,000-100,000Rp; 🛜) For a memorable meal, this elegant two-storey structure set back from the road is a treat, with a menu that spans the culinary globe, from Greek salads and steaks to authentic Indonesian dishes such as *gulai lemak* (beef curry cooked with turmeric). There's a (partly) open kitchen, and a bar at the rear.

Kayu Manis
INTERNATIONAL $

(☎693 561; mains 30,000-45,000Rp) This exciting new restaurant has a casual vibe (think polished-wood bench seating) and an East-meets-West menu that reflects the life of chef-patron Berri, an Indonesian who lived in Australia for years. Dishes such as beer-battered calamari and snapper fillet topped with green veggies are superb.

Bumbu Café
INDONESIAN $

(Jl Raya Senggigi; mains 35,000Rp) One of the best restaurants on Senggigi's central strip, Bumbu has delicious Asian cooking, including a fine seafood coconut curry. You can also catch the live bands at Papaya Café from the front tables.

Café Alberto
ITALIAN $$

(☎693 039; www.cafealberto.com; mains from 45,000Rp; 🛜🏊) Munch on authentic pizza (from a wood-fired oven) and Italian food right next to the waves. There's a pool too, so it's ideal for daytime lounging.

Square
INTERNATIONAL $$

(☎693 688; Senggigi Square; mains 40,000-150,000Rp 🛜) Destination restaurant with beautifully crafted seating, and a menu that features Western and Indonesian food such as fried king prawns with Worcester-shire sauce. The atmosphere is perhaps a little too formal, though the cooking is certainly very accomplished.

LOCAL KNOWLEDGE

BARBARA LUCAS CAHYADI: LOMBOK JOURNALIST

Originally from Western Australia, Barbara is a journalist on *The Lombok Guide* (online at www.thelombokguide.com). She lives near Senggigi with her Sasak husband.

Best Restaurants

Asmara restaurant in Senggigi is always consistent. Clean and fresh, with a great selection of international and Indonesian meals, the tuna carpaccio is delicious and their local dishes like *urap* salad are authentic. I also love De Quake for its laid-back flair and cool beachfront location. The Thai food here is fantastic.

Cheap Bites

When I want a cheap bite, I eat at one of the Padang cafes in Senggigi – there's one just before the bridge at the south end of town. They're not fancy, but the food is good and the price is right! Also you can't go wrong at Kayu Manis – top-value meals, beautifully presented and very easy on the pocket.

Splurge

For a splurge, I usually head to Quali Restaurant at Qunci Pool Villas in Mangsit. Elegant dining, delicious meals and excellent service. If I'm out on Gili Trawangan, a visit to Kokomo is a must. The very best oysters Kilpatrick, crab ravioli, Tahitian-style tuna and desserts to die for – fine dining on a perfect beach!

Warung Manega   SEAFOOD **$$**
(Jl Raya Senggigi 6; meals 90,000-350,000Rp)
This deceptively simple-looking beachside place (4km south of central Senggigi) is renowned for its seafood (fish, squid, lobster and prawns), which is grilled over coconut husks and served to you on candlelit tables in the sand. It's wonderful here at sunset.

NORTH OF SENGGIGI

Coco Beach   ORGANIC **$**
(0817 578 0055; Pantai Kerandangan; mains from 25,000Rp; noon-10pm) About 2km north of central Senggigi, this beachside restaurant features a healthy menu that includes lots of salads and choices for vegetarians (and uses organic produce wherever possible). It's a wonderful setting with low tables (you sit on a mat to eat at them) and the waves surging against the shoreline close by.

Quali Restaurant   INTERNATIONAL **$$**
(693 800; Qunci Pool Villas, Mangsit; www
.quncivillas.com; mains from 52,000Rp) This terrific, hip hotel-restaurant has a well-selected modern menu of Asian and European dishes. Book ahead and bag a table right on the shore; it's an incredibly romantic setting.

🍷 Drinking & Entertainment

Senggigi's bar scene is pretty middle-of-the-road by nature and revolves around a few bars that feature live bands playing rock and pop covers, plus a couple of clubs. De Quake and Quali at Qunci Pool Villas are also great for a drink; both have a happy hour and great cocktails.

Papaya Café   MUSIC BAR
(Jl Raya Senggigi) A touch classier than most bars in Senggigi, Papaya has a live band every night of the week and a fully stocked bar.

Marina   CLUB
(www.marinasenggigi.com; Jl Raya Senggigi; admission usually free) The most popular club in town, though musically it serves up pretty mainstream dance and pop sounds interspersed with live bands and dance routines. Weekends are the best bet, when there's a good mix of locals and visitors.

🛍 Shopping

Pasar Seni (Art Market; Jl Raya Senggigi) This market mainly consists of perfunctory souvenir stalls, though there are a few decent

LOMBOK DURING RAMADAN

Ramadan, the month of fasting, is the ninth month of the Muslim calendar. During daylight hours, many restaurants are closed in the capital and in conservative east and south Lombok. Foreigners eating, drinking (especially alcohol) and smoking in public may attract a negative reaction in these areas. In Senggigi, resort areas and most of north Lombok, cultural attitudes are far less strict.

handicrafts too. The warehouses and craft shops along the main road to Ampenan are also worth stopping for.

Asmara Collection (693 619; Jl Raya Senggigi) A cut above the rest, this store has well-selected tribal art, including wonderful carvings and textiles from Sumba and Flores. Also stocks great jewellery, antiques and ceramics.

Cikolata (0812 375 0086; Jl Raya Senggigi) Boutique selling gorgeous dresses and accessories, using bold colours and local fabrics; many are one-off original pieces. Also sells pearl jewellery.

Little Shop (693 647; Pasar Seni) Offers good-quality souvenirs including hand-carved wooden objects, tasteful sarongs and bags and shell-inlaid bowls. All prices are fixed.

ℹ Information

The nearest hospitals are in Mataram.
BCA (Jl Raya Senggigi) Bank with ATM.
Millennium Internet (Jl Raya Senggigi; per hr 8000Rp; 24hr)
Police station (110)
Post office (Jl Raya Senggigi; 8am-6pm)
Senggigi Medical Clinic (693 856; 8am-7pm) At the Senggigi Beach Hotel.
Tourist police (632 733)

ℹ Getting There & Away

Boat
Perama (693 007; www.peramatour.com; Jl Raya Senggigi) operates daily boats to Padang-bai in Bali (300,000Rp, four to five hours) at 7am and to the Gili Islands (100,000Rp, 75 minutes) at 9am. For Gili Island connections see p288.

Bus

Regular bemo travel between Senggigi and Ampenan's Kebon Roek terminal (3000Rp). You can easily wave them down on the main drag. Heading to the Gilis? There's no public bemo service north to Bangsal harbour; a taxi costs 75,000Rp.

Perama has tourist shuttle bus/boat services between Senggigi and Bali.

DESTINATION	FARE
Bangsal	60,000Rp
Kuta Bali or Ubud by ferry/Perama boat	150,000/350,000Rp
Kuta Lombok	125,000Rp
Mataram	25,000Rp
Tetebatu	125,000Rp

Getting Around

The central area is easy to negotiate on foot. If you're staying further away remember that many restaurants offer a free lift for diners.

MOTORBIKES are readily available for hire in Senggigi, starting from 50,000Rp per day for a moped.

CAR HIRE is cheap. There are many places on the main drag with rates starting at 150,000Rp for an ageing Suzuki Jimny to around 350,000Rp for a newish Kijang. **E-One**(☏0819 0722 9053; Jl Raya Senggigi; www.lomboktoursandtravel.com) is run by Ewan, a fluent English speaker who lived in the UK for years. Car rental per day with driver costs 400,000Rp.

NORTH & CENTRAL LOMBOK

☏0370

Lush and fertile, Lombok's scenic interior is stitched together with rice terraces, lush forest, undulating tobacco fields and fruit and nut orchards, and is crowned by sacred Gunung Rinjani, which initiates springs, rivers and waterfalls. Entwined in all this big nature are traditional Sasak settlements, some of which are known for their handicrafts. Public transport is not frequent or consistent enough to rely on, but the main roads are in good condition. With your own wheels you can explore the black-sand fishing beaches, inland villages and waterfalls, and if you're here in August you can attend the annual Sasak stick-fighting tournament. Bottom line: if you get bored here you may need to seek psychological help.

Bangsal to Bayan

Bangsal is a hassle (see the boxed text, p271), and public transport north from here is infrequent. Several minibuses a day go from Mandalika terminal in Bertais (Mataram) to Bayan, but you'll have to get connections in Pemenang and/or Anyar, which can be difficult to navigate. Simplify things and get your own wheels.

SIRE

Fast becoming Lombok's most upmarket enclave, the Sire (or Sira) area is blessed with insanely gorgeous, sweeping white-sand beaches and some snorkelling offshore. Four opulent hotels are now established here, alongside a couple of fishing villages and some amazing private villas. Look out for the small **Hindu temple**, just beyond the Oberoi, which has shrines built into the coastal rocks and sublime ocean views. There's also the **Lombok Golf Kosaido Country Club** (☏640 137; per round incl caddy & cart US$80), an attractive 18-hole seaside course. Holes 10 to 18 have exceptional Gunung Rinjani views.

Sleeping & Eating

TOP CHOICE ⮕ **Tugu Lombok**   LUXURY HOTEL $$$

(☏620 111; www.tuguhotels.com; villas from US$210, plus 21% tax; ❄❀@☎⊠) An astonishing fantasy of a hotel that's like no other on Lombok, this outrageous amalgamation of luxury accommodation, wacky design and spiritual Indonesian heritage sits on a wonderful white-sand beach. In aesthetic terms, some of the soaring structures clash somewhat, but overall the effect is quite something and the sheer ambition compelling. Room decor reflects Indonesian tradition, the exquisite spa is modelled on Java's Buddhist Borobudur temple and

WORTH A TRIP

DETOUR

North of Senggigi is a succession of wonderful, near-deserted fishermen's coves where you are pretty much guaranteed to have a beach all to yourself. Cruise north of the Bulan Baru hotel, about 7km from central Senggigi, for some beautiful beaches; Pantai Setangi is one fine example. The road slaloms the coastal contours and serves up sweeping ocean views.

Scruffy Bangsal is the port for public boats to the Gili Islands. It's not a threatening place but it's home to plenty of small-time hustlers eager to earn a crust by selling overpriced boat tickets or some item they dream up you might need. All supplies can be bought in the Gilis, and all boat tickets should only be bought at the (filthy) Koperasi office on the harbourfront.

Most travellers are aware of Bangsal's reputation, but now the town has introduced a kind of official entrance-ticket fee, which applies to all cars, taxis and motorbikes. Yes, all vehicles have to pay 5000Rp to 15,000Rp for the privilege of driving to the port. You can avoid this by walking from the barrier to the port (it's only 500m), or taking a *cidomo* (from 10,000Rp). Buses only run as far as Pemenang, 1km inland from the port.

Public boats (roughly 8am to 5pm) leave when full (about 20 people) and cost 8000Rp to Gili Air, 9000Rp to Gili Meno and 10,000Rp to Gili Trawangan. If you don't want to wait, a charter costs 155,000/170,000/180,000Rp respectively.

You can avoid Bangsal completely by booking a speedboat via a Gili dive school or luxury hotel, or by taking one of the fast boat services direct from Bali.

the main restaurant is like a rice barn on steroids. Service is spot on. Drop by for a meal or drink if you can't afford to stay.

Oberoi Lombok   LUXURY HOTEL **$$$**
(☏638 444; www.oberoihotels.com; r from US$240, villas from US$350, plus 21% tax; meals around US$40; 🖼✳️@🛜🏊) For sheer get-away-from-it-all bliss the Oberoi simply excels. The hotel's core is a triple-level pool which leads the eye to a lovely private beach. Indonesian rajah-style luxury is the look: sunken marble bathtubs, teak floors, antique entertainment armoires and oriental rugs. The whole place seems to tick over effortlessly, thanks to the flawless service, and facilities are superb (tennis court, diving and sailing, spa and gym). The restaurant here probably serves the best Western food on Lombok, including memorable seafood creations.

Lombok Lodge   LUXURY HOTEL **$$$**
(☏0858 5717 6746; www.thelomboklodge.com; r from US$240 plus 21% tax; 🖼✳️@🛜🏊) Eight modernist villas built into a hillside cascade down to an infinity pool and beach. Straight out of the luxe minimalist design school, each villa comes complete with stunning white furnishings. There's a spa and restaurant too.

GONDANG & AROUND
Just northeast of Gondang village, a 6km trail heads inland to **Air Terjun Tiu Pupas**, a 30m waterfall that's only worth seeing in the wet season. Trails continue from here to other wet-season waterfalls, including

Air Terjun Gangga, the most beautiful of all. A guide is useful to navigate the confusing trails in these parts. Don't worry, they'll find you.

BAYAN
Wektu Telu (p272), Lombok's animist-tinted form of Islam, was born in humble thatched mosques nestled in these Rinjani foothills. The best example is **Masjid Kuno Bayan Beleq**, next to the village of Baleq. Its low-slung roof, dirt floors and bamboo walls reportedly date from 1634, making this mosque the oldest on Lombok. It's built on a square platform of river stones with a pagoda-like upper section. Inside is a huge old drum which served as the call to prayer before PA systems. Ah, the good old days. The mosque is kept closed, except for Islamic festivals. Some of the outlying buildings are tombs, including one for the mosque's founding haji.

SENARU & BATU KOQ
These scenic villages merge into one along a steep road with sweeping Rinjani and sea views. Most visitors here are volcano-bound but the beautiful walking trails and spectacular waterfalls are worth a day or so anyway.

👁 Sights & Activities
Air Terjun Sindang Gila (2000Rp) is a spectacular set of falls 20 minutes' walk from Senaru via a lovely forest and hillside trail. Locals love to picnic by Sindang Gila. The hearty and the foolish make for the creek, edge close and then get pounded by the

WEKTU TELU

Wektu Telu is a complex mixture of Hindu, Islamic and animist beliefs, though it's now officially classified as a sect of Islam. At its forefront is a rather physical concept of the Holy Trinity. The sun, moon and stars represent heaven, earth and water, while the head, body and limbs represent creativity, sensitivity and control.

As recently as 1965, the vast majority of Sasaks in northern Lombok were Wektu Telu, but under Suharto's 'New Order' government, indigenous religious beliefs were discouraged, and enormous pressure was placed on Wektu Telu to become Wektu Lima (Muslims who pray five times a day).

Most of the Wektu Telu religious festivals take place at the beginning of the rainy season (from October to December), or at harvest time (April to May), with celebrations held in villages all over the island. Though these ceremonies and rituals are annual events, they are based on a lunar calendar and do not fall on specific days.

In the Wektu Telu heartland around Bayan, locals have been able to maintain their unique beliefs by differentiating their cultural traditions (Wektu Telu) from religion (Islam). Most do not fast for the full month of Ramadam, only attend the mosque for special occasions, and there's widespread consumption of *brem* (alcoholic rice wine).

hard foaming cascade that explodes over black volcanic stone 40m above.

A further 50 minutes or so uphill is **Air Terjun Tiu Kelep**, another waterfall with a swimming hole. The track is steep and tough at times. Guides are compulsory (40,000Rp). Long-tailed macaques (locals call them *kera*) and the much rarer silvered leaf monkey are sometimes seen here.

In the traditional village of **Dusun Senaru** at the top of the road locals will invite you to chew betel nut (or tobacco) and show you around (for a donation).

Guided walks and community tourism activities can be arranged in most guesthouses – they include a **rice-terrace and waterfalls walk** (per person 215,000Rp), which takes in Sindang Gila, rice paddies and an old bamboo mosque, and the **Senaru Panorama Walk** (185,000Rp), which incorporates stunning views, insights into local traditions and the national park entrance fee.

🍽 Sleeping & Eating

Most of the dozen or so places here are simple mountain lodges, and since the climate's cooler, you won't need fans. All the following are dotted along the road from Bayan to Senaru.

TOP CHOICE **Horizon**   MOD LODGE $
(☑0817 576 0936; www.horizonsenaru .com; r from 300,000Rp) This is a chic new Australian-owned place with stylish contemporary rooms (in one, you can gaze over the Senaru valley from your bed), pebble-

floored bathrooms and very high standards of cleanliness. It's well run and also home to a small restaurant.

Pondok Senaru & Restaurant
MOUNTAIN LODGE $
(☑0818 0363 0668; r 200,000-600,000Rp) A class act, this place has lovely little cottages with terracotta-tiled roofs, and some well-equipped and comfortable suites. The restaurant, with tables perched on the edge of a rice-terraced valley, is a sublime place for a bite (dishes 20,000Rp to 35,000Rp).

Bukit Senaru Cottages   BUDGET BUNGALOWS $
(☑0818 0368 7215; r 100,000Rp) Shortly before Dusun Senaru, this very peaceful place has four decent semi-detached bungalows in a lush garden. It's run by a house-proud woman who also cooks up tasty, cheap meals.

Rinjani Homestay   BUNGALOWS $
(☑0817 575 0889; r 60,000Rp) These simple bamboo-and-tile bungalows have twin beds and amazing views.

Emy Cafe   BUDGET $
(☑0817 575 0889; r from 100,000Rp) Eight functional rooms in a two-storey block, plus tasty Sasak, Indonesian and Western food in the vista-rich restaurant.

ℹ Information

Rinjani Trek Centre (☑0868 1210 4132; www .info2lombok.com), at the southern end of the village, has good information on Rinjani and the surrounding area.

ⓘ Getting There & Away

From Mandalika terminal in Bertais (Mataram), catch a bus to Anyar (20,000Rp, 2½ hours). Bemo leave Anyar for Senaru (7000Rp) about every 20 minutes until 4.30pm. Very few bemo run east from Bayan to eastern Lombok.

Sembalun Valley

☑0376

High on the eastern side of Gunung Rinjani is the beautiful Sembalun Valley, a rich farming region where the golden foothills turn vivid green in the wet season. When the high clouds part, Rinjani goes full frontal from all angles. The valley has two main settlements, Sembalun Lawang and Sembalun Bumbung, tranquil places primarily concerned with growing cabbage and potatoes and, above all, garlic – though trekking tourism brings in a little income too, as this is the best access point for an attempt on Rinjani's summit.

🏃 Activities

The **Rinjani Information Centre** (RIC; ⊙6am-6pm) has well-informed English-speaking staff and lots of fascinating information panels about the area's flora, fauna, geology and history. Treks, such as a four-hour **Village Walk** (180,000Rp, minimum 2 people) and a two-day rambling **Wildflower Walk** (per person 650,000Rp incl a guide, porters, meals & all camping gear) past flowery grasslands, can be set up here. There is camping and trekking gear for hire.

🛏 Sleeping & Eating

All these places in Sembalun Lawang village are rustic and will heat up water for a fee. Alcohol is very rarely available.

Lembah Rinjani   HOTEL $
(☑0818 0365 2511; r 225,000Rp, meals from 17,000Rp) A pleasant mountain lodge, this place has 10 tidy bungalows with queen-size beds set in grounds planted with chilli bushes and fruit trees. The open-sided restaurant serves good Indonesian food.

Pondok Sembalun   BUNGALOWS $
(☑0852 3956 1340; r 75,000Rp) Four charming little bamboo-and-thatch bungalows with front porches (though the adjacent mobile phone tower is an eyesore). There's also a restaurant here (open May to December) too.

Maria Guesthouse   GUESTHOUSE $
(☑0852 3956 1340; r 220,000Rp) New place with smart-ish tin-roofed bungalows at the rear of a family compound, though they are a little overpriced.

Paer Doe Homestay   HOMESTAY $
(☑0819 1771 4514; r 100,000Rp; meals from 15,000Rp) Very simple family-run affair in Sembalun Bumbang, with two rooms (and four more being constructed). Bintang beer is sold.

ⓘ Getting There & Away

From Mandalika bus terminal (in Bertais, Mataram), take a bus to Aikmel (12,000Rp) and change there for a bemo to Sembalun Lawang (10,000Rp). Regular pick-ups connect Lawang and Bumbang.

There's no public transport between Sembalun Lawang and Senaru, so you'll have to charter an *ojek* (motorcycle that takes passengers), or a bemo for around 120,000Rp. Roads to Sembalun Lawang and Sembalun Bumbung are sometimes closed in the wet season due to landslides.

Sapit

☑0376

On the southeastern slopes of Gunung Rinjani, Sapit is a tiny, very relaxed village with views across to Sumbawa. Tobacco-drying *open* (tall red-brick buildings) loom above the beautifully lush landscape. Sapit makes a delightful, peaceful rural base for a few days well off the tourist trail. You can hike to hot-water springs and small waterfalls nearby or visit **Taman Lemor** (admission 3000Rp; ⊙8am-4pm), a park with a spring-fed swimming pool located between Swela and Sapit.

Hati Suci Homestay (☑0818 545 655; www.hatisuci.tk; s 40,000-45,000Rp, d 75,000-85,000Rp; meals from 14,000Rp) is a good budget place with a selection of bungalows set in a blossoming garden with stunning views over the sea to Sumbawa. Hikes to Rinjani can be organised here.

Gunung Rinjani

Lording it over the northern half of Lombok, 3726m Gunung Rinjani is Indonesia's second-tallest volcano. It's an astonishing peak, a sacred cone for Hindus and Sasaks (both Muslims and Wektu Telu) who make pilgrimages to its peak and lake to leave offerings for the gods and spirits. To the Balinese, Rinjani is one of three sacred mountains, along with Bali's Agung and Java's Bromo. Sasaks ascend throughout the year around the full moon.

The mountain also has climatic significance. Its peak attracts a steady stream of swirling rain clouds, while its ash emissions bring fertility to the island's rice fields and tobacco crops, feeding a tapestry of rice paddies, tobacco fields, cashew and mango trees.

Inside the immense caldera, sitting 600m below the rim, is a stunning, 6km-

CLIMBING GUNUNG RINJANI

The most popular way to climb Gunung Rinjani is the five-day trek (described below) that starts at Senaru and finishes at Sembalun Lawang. Other possibilities include a summit attempt from Sembulan (which is extremely tough but can be done as a two-day return hike). A guide is essential from the hot springs to Sembalun Lawang, as the path is indistinct. This trek is outlined on the Gunung Rinjani map. Another good map is issued by the Rinjani Trek Centre (RTC) – it's large, in colour, glossy and easy to understand.

It's usually forbidden to climb Rinjani during the wet season (November to March), due to the threat of landslides and rockslides.

Day One: Senaru Pos I to Pos III (Five to Six Hours)

At the southern end of Senaru is the Rinjani Trek Centre (Pos I, 601m), where you register and pay the park fee. Just beyond the post, the trail forks – continue straight ahead on the right fork. The trail climbs steadily through scrubby farmland for about half an hour to the entrance of Taman Nasional Gunung Rinjani (Gunung Rinjani National Park). The wide trail climbs for another 2½ hours until you reach Pos II (1500m), where there's a shelter. Water can be found 100m down the slopes from the trail, but it should be treated or boiled.

Another 1½ hours' steady walk uphill brings you to Pos III (2000m), where there are two shelters in disrepair. Pos III is usually the place to camp at the end of the first day.

Day Two: Pos III to Danau Segara Anak & Aiq Kalak (Four Hours)

From Pos III, it takes about 1½ hours to reach the rim, Pelawangan I, at an altitude of 2641m. Set off very early for the stunning sunrise. It's possible to camp at Pelawangan I, but there are drawbacks: level sites are limited, there's no water and it can be very blustery.

It takes about two hours to descend to Danau Segara Anak and around to the hot springs, Aiq Kalak. The first hour is a very steep descent and involves low-grade rock climbing in parts. From the bottom of the crater wall it's an easy 30-minute walk across undulating terrain around the lake's edge. There are several places to camp, but most locals prefer to be near the hot springs to soak their weary bodies and recuperate. There are caves nearby, but these are not adequate for shelter. The nicest campsites are at the lake's edge, and fresh water can be gathered from a spring near the hot springs. (The climb back up the rim is certainly taxing – allow at least three hours and you'll have to start early to make it back to Senaru in one day.) Instead of retracing your steps, it's best to continue to Sembalun Lawang and arrange transport back to Senaru.

Day Three: Aiq Kalak to Pelawangan II (Three to Four Hours)

The trail starts beside the last shelter at the hot springs and heads away from the lake for about 100m before veering right. It then traverses the northern slope of the crater, and it's an easy one-hour walk along the grassy slopes before you hit a steep, unforgiving rise; from the lake it takes about three hours to reach the crater rim (2639m). At the rim, a sign points the way back to Danau Segara Anak. Water can be found down the slope near the sign. The trail forks here – go straight on to Lawang or continue along the rim to the campsite of Pelawangan II (2700m). It's only about 15 minutes more to the campsite, which is located on a bare ridge (that's strewn with rubbish).

wide, cobalt-blue crescent lake, **Danau Segara Anak** (Child of the Sea). The Balinese toss gold and jewellery into the lake in a ceremony called *pekelan,* before they slog their way towards the sacred summit.

The mountain's newest cone, the minor peak of Gunung Baru, only emerged a couple of hundred years ago, its scarred, smouldering profile rising above the lake as an ominous reminder of the apocalyptic power of nature. This peak has been erupting fitfully for the last decade, periodically belching out plumes of smoke and ash over the entire Rinjani caldera. Also in the cra-

Day Four: Pelawangan II to Rinjani Summit (Five to Six Hours Return)

Gunung Rinjani's summit arcs above the campsite and looks deceptively close. Start the climb very early (around 3am) in order to reach the summit in time for sunrise and before the clouds roll in. Depending on wind conditions, it may not be possible to attempt the summit at all, as the trail is along a very exposed ridge.

It takes about 45 minutes to clamber up a steep, slippery and indistinct trail to the ridge that leads to Rinjani. Once on the ridge it's a relatively steady walk uphill. After about an hour heading towards what looks like the peak, the real summit of Rinjani (3726m) looms behind, and as you gain altitude you'll see it towering above you.

The trail then gets steeper and steeper. About 350m before the summit, the scree is composed of loose, fist-sized rocks – it's easier to get along by scrambling on all fours. This section can take about an hour. The views from the top are truly magnificent – west to the volcanoes of Bali, and in the east Gunung Tambora (in distant Sumbawa) may be visible on very clear days. In total it takes around three hours to reach the summit, and two to return.

Day Four/Five: Pelawangan II to Sembalun Lawang (Six to Seven Hours)

After negotiating the peak, it's possible to reach Lawang the same day. From the campsite, it's a tough descent to the village, as the steep downhill profile puts a lot of pressure on your knee joints. From the campsite, head back along the crater rim. Shortly after the turn-off to Danau Segara Anak, there's a signposted right turn down to Pada Balong (also called Pos 3). Once on the trail, it's easy to follow and there's plenty of forest shade; it takes around two hours to reach Pada Balong shelter (at 1800m).

The trail then levels out and crosses through riverbeds, undulating to flat grassland all the way to Sembalun Lawang. After less than an hour you'll hit Tengengean (or Pos 2) shelter at 1500m – it's beautifully situated in a river valley surrounded by ferns and mosses. It's then another 30 minutes through long grass to lonely Pemantuan (or Pos 1) shelter, a tin roof at 1300m. From here it's two hours to Sembalun Lawang, crossing bridges and through pastureland, along a dirt track that turns into a muddy road after rain.

Variations

There are a few possible variations to the route described above. They're outlined here:

» Compress the last two days into one (racking up a hefty 11 to 12 hours on the trail).

» Start trekking from Sembalun Lawang (a guide is essential), from where it takes around seven hours to get to Pelawangan II. This is a much shorter walk to the summit than from Senaru.

» Retrace your steps to Senaru after climbing to the summit, making a five-day circuit that includes another night at the hot springs.

» Another popular route, because the trail is well defined and (if you're experienced) can be trekked with only a porter, is a three-day trek from Senaru to the hot springs and back. The first night is spent at Pos III and the second at the hot springs. The return to Senaru on the final day takes eight to nine hours.

» For (almost) instant gratification (if you travel light and climb fast) you can reach the crater rim from Senaru in about six hours. You'll gain an altitude of approximately 2040m in 10km. Armed with a torch, some moonlight and a guide, set off at midnight to arrive for sunrise. The return takes about five hours.

ter are natural hot springs known as **Aiq Kalak**. Locals suffering from skin diseases trek here with a satchel of medicinal herbs to bathe and scrub in the bubbling mineral water.

Organised Treks

Treks to the rim, lake and peak should not be taken lightly, and guides are mandatory. Climbing Rinjani during the wet season (November to March) is usually completely forbidden due to the risk of landslide. June to August is the only time you are (almost) guaranteed minimal rain or clouds. Be prepared with layers and a fleece because it can get cold at the rim (and near-freezing at the summit) at any time of year.

The easiest way to organise a trip is to head to the Rinjani Trek Club (RTC; offices in Senaru and Senggigi) or the Rinjani Information Centre (RIC) in Sembalun Lawang. These centres use a rotation system so that all local guides get a slice of the trekking purse (and consequently most are laid-back and easy to work with, in contrast with the aggressive guiding that taints Bali's Agung).

Roughly the same trek packages are offered by all operators, though some have 'budget' and 'luxury' options. Treks from Senaru to Sembalun Lawang via the lake summit are very popular, and the return

hike from Sembalun Lawang to the summit is another well-trodden trail.

Trek prices get cheaper the larger the party. A three-day hike (including food, equipment, guide, porters, park fee and transport back to Senaru) to the summit and lake costs around US$190 per person based on a group of two to four. An overnight trek to the crater rim costs from US$150.

OPERATORS

Agencies in Mataram, Senggigi and the Gili Islands can organise Rinjani treks too, with return transport from the point of origin. **Perama** (www.peramatour.com), with offices in all of these locations, uses official RTC guides and has rates from 2.5 million rupiah per person (minimum two people).

John's Adventures (☑0817 578 8018; www.rinjanimaster.com) Very experienced organiser which has toilet tents, thick sleeping mats and starts hiking from Sembalun.

Galang Ijo Expedition (☑0819 1740 4198; www.galangijo.com) An outfitter with competitive prices and experienced guides.

Guides & Porters

Hiking independently is simply not allowed, and deeply unwise. If you don't want to do an all-inclusive trekking package you can hire guides (about 125,000Rp per day) and porters (90,000Rp per day) from RTC or RIC. You'll have to organise camping gear, supplies, radio and mobile phone. Use guides and porters directly from the centres in Senaru or Sembalun Lawang, as they are licensed for your security. Guides are knowledgeable and informative, but will usually only carry a light day pack for you, so you'll need to take at least one porter. Obviously, ample food and water is vital.

Entrance Fee & Equipment

Entrance to Taman Nasional Gunung Rinjani (Gunung Rinjani National Park) is a hefty 150,000Rp – you register and pay at the RTC in Senaru or the RIC in Sembalun Lawang before you start your trek.

Sleeping bags and tents are essential and can be hired at either RTC or RIC. Decent footwear, warm clothing, wet-weather gear, cooking equipment and a torch (flashlight) are important (all can be hired if necessary). Expect to pay upwards of 100,000Rp a head per day for all your gear. Muscle balm (to ease aching legs) and a swimming costume (for the lake and hot springs) could also be packed.

Poaching firewood at high altitude is an environmental no-no, so take a stove. And bring home your rubbish, including toilet tissue. Sadly several Rinjani camps are litter-strewn.

Food & Supplies

Trek organisers at RTC and RIC will arrange trekking food. Mataram is cheapest for supplies but many provisions are available in Senaru and Sembalun Lawang. Take more water than seems reasonable (dehydration can spur altitude sickness) and a lighter.

Tetebatu

✍ 0376

Laced with Rinjani mountain-spring-fed streams and blessed with rich volcanic soil, Tetebatu is a Sasak breadbasket. The surrounding countryside is quilted with tobacco and rice fields, fruit orchards and cow pastures that fade into remnant monkey forest where you'll find some fabulous waterfalls. Tetebatu is ideal for long country walks (at 400m it's high enough to mute that hot, sticky coastal mercury). Dark nights come saturated with sound courtesy

RINJANI BASE CAMPS 277

There are two main starting points for an ascent on Gunung Rinjani. Most people base themselves in **Senaru**, which has the best facilities, or **Sembalun Lawang**, which is much closer if you want to attempt the summit. It's also possible to set up a trip in Senggigi (from where trekking operators will shuttle you to the Rinjani trailhead, usually for no extra cost). The mountain villages of Tetebatu and Sapit are other places where treks can be organised.

of a frog orchestra accompanied by countless gurgling brooks. Even insomniacs snore here.

The town is spread out, with facilities on roads north and east (nicknamed 'waterfall road') of the central *ojek* stop. The internet has yet to colonise tiny Tetebatu.

⊙ Sights & Activities

A shady 4km track leading from the main road, just north of the mosque, heads into the **Taman Wisata Tetebatu** (Monkey Forest) with black monkeys and waterfalls – you'll need a guide to find both.

Waterfalls WATERFALLS
On the southern slopes of Rinjani, there are two waterfalls. Both are accessible by private transport or a spectacular two-hour walk (one way) through rice fields from Tetebatu. If walking, hire a guide (around 100,000Rp) through your hotel.

A steep 2km hike from the car park at the end of the access road to Taman Nasional Gunung Rinjani, beautiful **Air Terjun Jukut** (Jeruk Manis, Air Temer; admission 20,000Rp) has an impressive 20m drop to a deep pool and is surrounded by lush forest.

Northwest of Tetebatu, **Air Terjun Joben** (Otak Kokok Gading; admission 20,000Rp) is more of a public bathing pool, so less alluring.

🛏 Sleeping & Eating

TOP CHOICE **Cendrawasih Cottages** BUNGALOWS $
(✍ 0818 0372 6709; r 125,000Rp) About 500m east of the intersection, these dinky thatched *lumbung*-style cottages, some with two storeys, are set in a lovely garden. The fantastic stilted restaurant is a real bonus – here you can gaze out over rice fields from floor cushions and feast on Sasak,

SASAK LIFE

Lombok's indigenous Sasak people comprise about 90% of the island's population. Virtually all are now orthodox Muslims, though before 1965 many Sasaks in remote areas were Wektu Telu (see the boxed text, p272).

Traditional Sasak houses are made of bamboo, and sit on a base of compacted mud and cow dung; they have a steeply angled and rather low-slung thatched roof, which forces guests to bow humbly before their hosts. Husbands and wives share a home, but not a bed (ie bamboo mat). They only spend the night together when they are trying to get pregnant. Once the job is done, the men sleep outside, and the women and children huddle indoors. Villages in northern Lombok still maintain a caste system, which heavily influences courtship, and marriage between the highest castes – *Datu* (men) and *Denek Bini* (women) – and lower castes are quite rare.

Each village will have *lumbung*, stilted rice-storage barns, to keep rodents at bay. They look like little thatched cottages, and have been mimicked by bungalow resorts throughout Lombok.

There are several examples of traditional villages, including Sade and Rembitan near Kuta.

Indonesian or Western grub (meals from 15,000Rp).

Wisma Soedjono RUSTIC HOTEL $
(☑21309; r 85,000-165,000R; ☒) Centred around a Dutch colonial house that was built in 1913, this hotel has a row of spartan but clean rooms that share a slim terrace overlooking over a river valley plus a few cottages that vary in quality. The gigantic pool is cleaned up for high-season months only. Jaya, a good guide, is based here. The hotel is 2km north of the intersection.

Green Orry COTTAGES $
(☑632 233; cottages 150,000-250,000Rp) Well-run place where the sweet, tiled cottages (some with hot water) are very homely and have ikat wall hangings. There's table tennis and a large restaurant (try the pasta and a lassi). It's just along the waterfall road.

Pondok Tetebatu BUDGET BUNGALOWS $
(☑632 572; s/d 80,000/100,000Rp) North of the intersection, these simple, tile-floored little cottages are a good budget bet, especially as the Sasak-specialising restaurant here (meals from 14,000Rp) is a key place to hook up with guides and find transport.

❶ Getting There & Around

Public transport to Tetebatu is infrequent. All cross-island buses pass Pomotong (10,000Rp from Mandalika terminal) on the main east–west highway, from where bemo run regularly to Kotaraja (2000Rp). Here you can get an *ojek* (5000Rp) to Tetebatu.

Private cars (with drivers) can be arranged at Pondok Tetebatu to all Lombok destinations (300,000Rp to 500,000Rp); bicycles (from 20,000Rp) and motorbikes can be rented here too.

South of Tetebatu

The nearest market town to Tetebatu is **Kotaraja**, the transport hub of the area, which hosts an annual **Sasak stick-fighting** festival each August. The fights are both fierce and real, and end gracefully at the first sight of blood. Market day in Kotaraja is Monday and Wednesday mornings.

Loyok, heading south, is noted for its fine basketry and **Rungkang** is known for its pottery made from local black clay. You'll find home workshops in both villages.

Masbagik is a large town on Lombok's east–west highway with a daily morning market, an imposing new mosque and the region's only reliable ATMs. **Masbagik Timor**, 1km east, is a centre for black-clay pottery and ceramic production.

Lendang Nangka is a pretty Sasak village, 3km north of the highway, famous for its blacksmiths (who make knives, hoes and other tools) and silversmiths.

SOUTH LOMBOK

☑0370

Beaches just don't get much better: the water is warm, striped turquoise and curls into barrels, and the sand is silky and snow-white, framed by massive headlands and sheer cliffs that recall Bali's Bukit Peninsula 30 years ago. Village life is still vibrant in south Lombok as well, with unique festivals and an economy based on seaweed and tobacco harvests. The south is noticeably drier than the rest of Lombok and more sparsely populated, with limited roads and public transport. But, with Lombok's new state-of-the-art international airport opening here changes will surely come. Get here quick, as the coast is clear for now.

Praya

Sprawling Praya is the main town in the south, with tree-lined streets and the odd crumbling Dutch colonial relic. Lombok's new airport is around 5km south of the centre, but there's no real reason to drop by the town itself except to hit an ATM or perhaps the bemo terminal, on the northwest side of Praya.

Around Praya

SUKARARA

The main street here is the domain of textile shops, where you can watch weavers work their old looms. **Dharma Setya** (☑660 5204; ⊙8am-5pm) has an incredible array of hand-woven Sasak textiles, including ikat and *songket*.

To reach Sukarara, take a bemo to Puyung along the main road. From there, hire a *cidomo* or walk the 2km to Sukarara.

PENUJAK

Penujak is well known for its traditional *gerabah* pottery. Made from chocolatey terracotta-tinted local clay, it's hand-burnished and topped with braided bamboo. Huge floor-stander vases cost US$6 or so, and there are also plates and cups on offer from the potters' humble home studios. **Wadiah** (☑0819 3316 0391) is a friendly, talented local potter who is all smiles and has a terrific selection. Her home is across from the cemetery.

Any bemo from Praya to Kuta will drop you off here.

REMBITAN & SADE

The area from Sengkol down to Kuta is a centre for Sasak culture – traditional villages full of towering *lumbung* and *bale tani*, homes made from bamboo, cow and

buffalo dung, and mud. Regular bemo cover this route.

Rembitan, aka Sasak Village, boasts an authentic cluster of houses and *lumbung* and very nearby is **Masjid Kuno**, an ancient thatched-roof mosque that is a pilgrimage destination for Lombok's Muslims.

A little further south, Sade village has been extensively renovated and has some fascinating *bale tani*.

Both villages are worth a look but unfortunately local boys offering tours can be a little over-pushy and it's not possible to look around without a guide (around 40,000Rp).

Kuta

Imagine a crescent bay – turquoise in the shallows and deep blue further out. It licks a huge, white-sand beach, wide as a football pitch and framed by headlands. It's deserted, save for a few fishermen, seaweed farmers and their children. Now imagine a coastline of nearly a dozen such bays, all backed by a rugged range of coastal hills spotted with lush patches of banana trees and tobacco fields, and you'll have a vague idea of the Kuta region's majesty.

Southern Lombok's incredible coastline of giant bite-shaped bays is startling, its beauty immediate, undeniable and arresting. Yet this region has historically been the island's poorest, its sun-blasted soil parched and unproductive. Kuta itself consists of no more than a few hundred houses, a likeable but scruffy-around-the-edges place with a ramshackle market area, and a seafront lined with simple seafood shacks and barefoot bars (and some very persistent, if sweet, child hawkers).

For years it's been an under-the-radar surf spot, thanks to the limitless world-class breaks within a short ride of town. And while a vast Dubai-backed scheme has been called off, other resort developers have purchased huge swaths of coastline here. For now everyone seems to be sitting on their land, but with the new airport a 30-minute ride away, the town's real-estate agents are betting on change real soon.

🏃 Activities

Surfing

Plenty of good waves break on the reefs, including lefts and rights, in Teluk Kuta (Kuta Bay), and more on the reefs east of Tanjung Aan. If you're after a reef break,

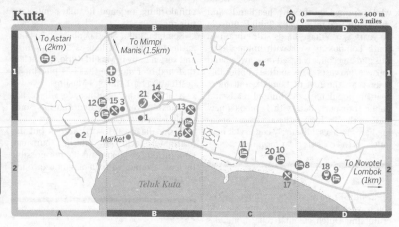

get local boatmen to tow you out for around 100,000Rp. About 7km east of Kuta, **Gerupak** also has a good surf school and no fewer than five breaks, including some ideal for beginners. West of Kuta, gorgeous **Mawi** offers consistent world-class surf.

Kimen Surf (☑655 064; www.kuta-lombok .net) Offers swell forecasts, tips, surf trips, board rental (from 50,000Rp per day), repairs and lessons (360,000Rp, four hours).

Gloro (☑0818 0576 5690) Rents boards (35,000Rp per day) and offers lessons (250,000Rp, four hours) and surf trips.

Diving

Dive Zone (☑660 3205; www.divezone-lombok .com) runs trips to spectacular ocean pinnacles in Belongas bay (famous for schooling hammerheads and pelagic fish, including tuna and eagle rays). Currents and conditions can be very challenging so some sites are for experienced divers only. Rates start from US$65 for two fun dives.

Horse Riding

Kuta Horses (☑0819 1599 9436; 1hr ride 300,000Rp; ⊘rides 8am & 4pm) offers great horseback riding, through Sasak villages and Kuta's country lanes at sunrise and sunset.

Fishing Trips

Made (☑0818 369 950) offers ocean fishing trips (600,000Rp, four hours), including boat, bait, tackle, lunch and a delicious fish dinner at the end of the day.

🛏 Sleeping

Prices increase markedly in the (short) July–August high season at some places.

TOP CHOICE Yuli's Homestay MODISH HOMESTAY **$** (☑0819 1710 0983; www.yulishomestay. com; r 300,000Rp; ❄🗢🏊) A wonderful new place, Yuli's is owned by a very hospitable and friendly Indonesian-Kiwi couple. The three rooms are immaculately clean, extremely spacious and nicely furnished with huge beds and wardrobes (and have big front terraces, though cold-water bathrooms). There's a guests' kitchen for good measure and a huge garden to enjoy. It really is a home away from home.

Sekar Kuning BUDGET **$** (☑654 856; r 130,000Rp; @) Offering excellent value, this attractive place has 12 spotless if spartan renovated rooms with nice wooden window shutters, good-quality mattresses and mosquito nets; numbers 9 and 12 have coastal views. You'll find good food available too.

Mimpi Manis BACKPACKERS **$** (☑0818 369 950; www.mimpimanis.com; r 80,000-150,000Rp; ❄) About 2km inland from the beach on the road to Praya, this is an extremely welcoming English-Balinese-owned backpacker stronghold. It offers two spotless, bright rooms and a separate little two-storey house, each with en-suite shower and TV/DVD player. There's a little terrace for breakfast and socialising, a dartboard, book exchange and DVDs to borrow.

Novotel Lombok RESORT HOTEL **$$** (☑653 333; www.novotel-lombok.com; r from US$90, villas from US$180, plus 21% tax; ❄🏊@🗢🏊) Top dog in Kuta, the Novotel is an efficiently run resort that's popular with European families and spills onto a

Kuta

superb beach. Accommodation is modish, smart and immaculately presented; some villas have private pools. There's a gym, dive school, spa and good restaurant – the breakfast spread is fit for a sultan. Book via the web for special promotional rates.

Surfers Inn SURF HOTEL **$**
(☑655 582; www.lombok-surfersinn.com; r with fan 130,000Rp; air-con 200,000-450,000Rp; ❉❊❋) It's lost a little lustre in the tropical sun, but this stylish, well-run place is still a good bet, with five classes of modern rooms, each with huge windows and large beds. The lovely pool area is perfect for post-surf chilling.

Melon Homestay APARTMENTS **$**
(☑0817 367 892; r/apt 150,000/250,000Rp) Two very spacious apartments with lounge and self-catering facilities (one with sea views from its balcony); plus a couple of good-value plain rooms.

Seger Reef Homestay HOMESTAY **$**
(☑655 528; r 150,000Rp) Run by Ani and Ahmedi, this family homestay has four cute little bungalows, some with two beds, that face a pretty garden. Prices rise steeply according to demand.

Kutah Indah Hotel HOTEL **$**
(☑653 781; kutaindah@indonet.id; r 150,000-300,000Rp; ❉❊) Ageing resort that's worth considering for its magnificent garden setting and supremely relaxing pool area. All four classes of accommodation are spacious if plain and in fair shape.

Puri Rinjani BUNGALOWS **$**
(☑654 849; bungalow/r 150,000/400,000Rp; ❉) The traditional bungalows here are good value and have character; the rooms boast all mod cons but are overpriced.

Matahari Inn HOTEL **$**
(☑655 000; r US$18-50; ❉❊) Lush gardens and all accommodation is loaded with Balinese artefacts.

Eating & Drinking

There's not too much fancy cooking in Kuta so it's best to stick to tried-and-tested Indo nosh, or fresh seafood.

TOP CHOICE **Astari** HEAVENLY GLOBAL **$**
(dishes 18,000-38,000Rp; ⏰8.30am-6pm Tue-Sun) Head-and-shoulders above the rest, Australian-owned Astari (3km west of town) really has no competition in south Lombok. The location is astonishing: high, high above the town with stunning vistas of the ocean rollers and a succession of beaches. The menu raids Italy and the Middle East, India and Indonesia for influence – with samosas, focaccia sandwiches and stupendous desserts (try the vanilla and cardamom cake). Plenty of people lose all track of time here, mesmerised by the view, food and serene atmosphere.

Ketapang Café BEACHFRONT RESTAURANT **$**
(☑0878 654 15209; meals 13,000-55,000Rp; ❂) Friendly, efficiently run local place that enjoys a prime beachfront plot with dining pagodas shaded by grass umbrellas. The *ayam pelicitan* (Lombok-style chilli chicken) is fiery and authentic here and the pizzas are decent and popular too. Also has a full bar, including some of the best cocktails in Kuta.

Family Cafe INDONESIAN **$**
(☑653 748; mains 12,000-35,000Rp) Large family-run place where the house special-

NYALE FESTIVAL

On the 19th day of the 10th month in the Sasak calendar (generally February or March), hundreds of Sasaks gather on the beach at Kuta, Lombok. When night falls, fires are built and teens sit around competing in a Sasak poetry slam, where they spit rhyming couplets called *pantun* back and forth. At dawn the next day, the first of millions of *nyale* (wormlike fish that appear here annually) are caught, then teenage girls and boys take to the sea separately in decorated boats, and chase one another with lots of noise and laughter. The *nyale* are eaten raw or grilled, and are considered to be an aphrodisiac. A good catch is a sign that a bumper crop of rice is coming too.

ity, *sate pusut* (minced fish, chicken or beef mixed with fresh coconut, chilli and spices, moulded and grilled on lemongrass stalks), is simply divine.

Shore Beach Bar　　　　　　MUSIC BAR **$**
This happening bar with a breezy seafront terrace and a dance-hall interior is where local bands rock the house a couple of times a week. They also serve up (so-so) food here too.

Bong's　　　　　　　　　INDONESIAN **$**
(meals 18,000-40,000Rp) *Lumbung*-style restaurant that scores highly for Sasak food, including *olah olah* (vegetables cooked in coconut milk), seared fish and lemon chicken.

Cafe 7　　　　　　　　　　　CAFE **$**
(meals 38,000-70,000Rp) The style is lounge bar, the menu is mainly Western (sandwiches, steaks and smoothies) and the vibe is friendly. It's a little pricey, though the cocktails are worth a splurge.

Rumah Makan Hidayah　　INDONESIAN **$**
(mains from 12,000Rp) Honest, inexpensive local food including Sasak specials and *kangkung pelecing* (sautéd water spinach) in a family-run beachside shack. The sandy courtyard at the rear has direct ocean views.

ⓘ Information

The market fires up on Sunday and Wednesday. There's a wartel close to the junction.

Lombok International Medical Service
(☑655 155; ⏱4-9pm) Doctor and pharmacy.

Perama (☑654 846; at Segare Anak Cottages) Shuttle buses all over Lombok.

Segare Anak Cottages (☑654 846) Postal agency and internet.

Danger & Annoyances

If you decide to rent a bicycle or motorbike, take care whom you deal with – arrangements are informal and no rental contracts are exchanged. We have received occasional reports of some visitors having motorbikes stolen, and then having to pay substantial sums of money as compensation to the owner (who may or may not have arranged the 'theft' himself). Renting a motorbike from your guesthouse is safest.

As you drive up the coastal road west of Kuta, watch your back – there have been reports of muggings in the area.

ⓘ Getting There & Away

Kuta is tricky to reach by public transport – from Mataram you'll have to go via Praya (5000Rp), then to Sengkol (3000Rp) and finally to Kuta (2000Rp), usually changing buses at all these places. Perama run shuttle buses to/from Kuta and Mataram (110,000Rp, two hours), Senggigi (125,000Rp, 2½ hours), and the Gilis (220,000Rp, 3½ hours).

ⓘ Getting Around

Irregular bemo go east of Kuta to Awang and Tanjung Aan (5000Rp), and west to Selong Blanak (10,000Rp), or can be chartered to nearby beaches. Guesthouses rent motorbikes for about 50,000Rp per day (see p282 for information about bike-hire scams). *Ojek* congregate around the main junction as you enter Kuta.

East of Kuta

A decent paved road snakes along the coast to the east, passing a seemingly endless series of beautiful bays punctuated by headlands. It's a terrific motorbike ride.

Pantai Segar, a lovely beach about 2km east around the first headland, has unbelievably turquoise water, decent swimming (though no shade) and a break 200m offshore. The spherical sand granules resemble white peppercorns. Continuing 3km east, **Tanjung Aan** is a spectacular sight: a giant horseshoe bay with two sweeping arcs of fine sand. Swimming is good here and there's a little shade under trees and shelters, plus safe parking (for a small charge).

The huge Dubai-backed resort project planned here is moribund.

Gerupak, another kilometre further on, is a fascinating little coastal village where the thousand or so local souls earn their keep from fishing, seaweed harvesting and lobster exports. It's on the west side of a huge bay, with five exceptional surf breaks, a couple of hotels and warung popular with Japanese and Aussie surfers. **Edhu's** (☑ 655 369; r 120,000Rp, meals from 15,000Rp) is a hotel-cum-restaurant-cum-surf-shack run by a very amiable local with five clean rooms, honest surf advice and moderate prices for lessons (120,000Rp including boat ride to break), board hire, repairs and trips. For more comfort check out the comfy seaview *lumbung* at **Lakuen** (☑ 0817 470 4161; r 550,000Rp; ✷ ✈).

Northeast just before Tanjung Aan, a side road leads to **Awang**, another busy fishing village. Boatmen will ferry you across the bay from here to Ekas (a charter costs around 160,000Rp) or to surf spots.

West of Kuta

West of Kuta is yet another series of awesome beaches and sick surf breaks. Developers are nosing around here, and land has changed hands, but for now it remains almost pristine and the region has a raw beauty. The road is badly rutted and potholed (and very steep in places), detouring inland and skirting tobacco, sweet potato and rice fields in between turn-offs to the sand.

WORTH A TRIP

SHARK CITY

Tanjung Luar is a dusty, unremarkable port town in many ways, but it does have one star attraction: perhaps Indonesia's most astonishing fish market. Northerly ocean currents from the Pacific cut through the Alas Strait just offshore, bringing spectacular pelagic fish. Wander the town's lanes in the early morning and you'll have to step over a who's who of marine exotica – giant tuna, eagle rays, 2m-long wahoo, barracuda and dozens of sharks, including hammerheads – all arranged in neat rows on the dirt lanes, without an ice block in sight, then gutted on the street.

The first left after Astari leads to **Mawun** (or Mawan), truly a vision of paradise. This half-moon cove is framed by soaring headlands with azure water and a swath of empty sand (save a fishing village of a dozen thatched homes). There's safe parking (motorbike/car 1000/5000Rp), and a woman who sells fresh coconuts and instant noodles. It's a terrific swimming beach.

The very next left – although it's quite a bit further down the road – leads through a gate (admission 5000Rp) down a horribly rutted track to **Mawi**, 16km from Kuta, with safe parking. This is a surf paradise, a stunning scene, with legendary barrels and several beaches scattered around the great bay. Watch out for the strong riptide though.

Further west from Mawi is **Selong Blanak** village. Park and cross the rickety pedestrian bridge to a wide, sugar-white beach with water streaked a thousand shades of blue, ideal for swimming.

From **Pengantap**, the road climbs across a headland then descends to a superb bay; follow this around for 1km then look out for the turn-off west to **Blongas**, the road to which is steep, rough and winding with breathtaking scenery.

EAST LOMBOK

☑ 0376

All most travellers see of the east coast of Lombok is Labuhan Lombok, the port for ferries to Sumbawa. But the road around the northeast coast is pretty good, and can be traversed if you're hoping to complete a circumnavigation. The real highlight here is the remote southeastern peninsula. If you've ever wondered what Bali's Bukit looked like before all the villas and surf rats, here's your chance.

Labuhan Lombok

Labuhan Lombok (Labuhan Kayangan) is the port for ferries and boats to Sumbawa. The town centre of Labuhan Lombok, 3km west of the ferry terminal, is a scruffy place but it does have great views of Gunung Rinjani. There's only one decent place to stay here, **Losmen Lima Tiga** (☑ 23316; Jl Raya Kayangan; r 90,000Rp), 2.5km inland from the port with small rooms and shared bathrooms.

SASAK FESTIVALS & CEREMONIES

As more and more Sasaks have adopted orthodox Islam, many ancient cultural rituals and celebrations based on animist and Hindu traditions have dwindled in popularity. Nevertheless, some festivals and events have endured, and are being promoted by local authorities. In addition to these festivals, there are also events celebrating the harvesting of a sea worm called *nyale* (p282) in Kuta, and the riotous Hindu-Wektu Telu 'rice war' known as **Perang Topat** held at Pura Lingsar (p262).

Lebaran Topat, held in the seven days after the end of the fasting month (Idul Fitri; Ramadan) in the Islamic calendar, is a Sasak ceremony thought to be unique to west Lombok. Relatives gather in cemeteries to pour water over family graves, and add offerings of flowers, betel leaves and lime powder. Visitors can observe ceremonies at the Bintaro cemetery on the outskirts of Ampenan.

Malean Sampi (meaning 'cow chase' in Sasak) are highly competitive buffalo races held over a 100m waterlogged field in Narmada, just east of Mataram. Two buffalo are yoked together and then driven along the course by a driver brandishing a whip. The event takes place in early April, and commemorates the beginning of the planting season.

Gendang Beleq (big drum) performances were originally performed before battles. Today many villages in central Lombok have a *gendang* battery, some with up to 40 drummers, who perform at festivals and ceremonies. The drums themselves are colossal, up to a metre in length and not unlike an oil drum in shape or size. The drummers support the drums using a sash around their necks.

Peresean (stick fighting) are martial-art performances by two young men stripped to the waist, armed with rattan sticks and square shields made of cowhide. The Sasak believe that the more blood shed on the earth, the better the rainfall will be in the forthcoming wet season. In late July, demonstrations can be seen in Senggigi, and in late December there's a championship in Mataram.

ℹ️ Getting There & Away

Bus & Bemo

Very regular buses and bemo buzz between Mandalika terminal in Mataram and Labuhan Lombok (also known as Labuhan Kayangan or Tanjung Kayangan); the journey takes two hours (14,000Rp). Some buses will only drop you off at the port entrance road – catch another bemo to the ferry terminal. Don't walk – it's too far.

Ferry

See p382 for details of ferry connections between Lombok and Sumbawa and p261 for bus connections between Mataram and Sumbawa.

North of Labuhan Lombok

This road has limited public transport and becomes very steep and winding as you near Anyar. There are isolated black-sand beaches along the way, particularly at **Obel Obel**.

Leaving Labuhan Lombok, look out for the giant mahogany trees about 4km north of the harbour. From Labuhan Pandan, or from further north at Sugian, you can charter a boat to **Gili Sulat** or **Gili Pentangan**.

Both islands have lovely white beaches and good coral for snorkelling, but no facilities.

South of Labuhan Lombok

Selong, the capital of the East Lombok administrative district, has some dusty Dutch colonial buildings. The transport junction for the region is just to the west of Selong at **Pancor**, where you can catch bemo to most points south.

Tanjung Luar is one of Lombok's main fishing ports and has lots of Bugis-style houses on stilts. From here, the road swings west to **Keruak**, where wooden boats are built, and continues past the turn to **Sukaraja**, a traditional Sasak village where you can buy woodcarvings. Just west of Keruak a road leads south to **Jerowaru** and the spectacular southeastern peninsula. You'll need your own transport; be warned that it's easy to lose your way around here and that the roads go from bad to worse.

A sealed road branches west past Jerowaru to **Ekas**, where you'll find a huge bay framed by stunning sheer cliffs on both sides. There are two sensational surf breaks (Inside and Outside) at Ekas and boat charters to Awang across the bay. Or just head on to the aptly named, Kiwi-owned **Heaven on the Planet** (☏0812 370 5393; www.heavenontheplanet.co.nz; bed per person AU$40, all-inclusive per person AU$120-225; ⊜@⊠). Chalets, huts and villas (some with three bedrooms and marble flooring) are scattered among the cliffs, from where you'll have mind-blowing bird's-eye views of the sea and swell lines. Heaven is primarily a surf resort (you can even surf at night here thanks to ocean spotlights) but kitesurfing, scuba diving (fun dives and courses) and snorkelling is possible –

southern Lombok's first artificial reef has been installed in Ekas bay. Yes, this is ocean adrenalin junkie heaven (on the planet).

A second resort, **Ocean Heaven** (www .heavenontheplanet.co.nz; r AU$30-50, all-inclusive per person AU$120-150; ⊜), with chalets right on the sands at Ekas beach, is under the same ownership. Both resorts have tasty food, a full bar and friendly staff, and guests receive free airport or ferry transfers and massages (every second day).

The road to Heaven is rough and rocky (!); if you're already in Kuta it's easiest to head to Awang and charter a boat from there rather than loop round overland.

Gili Islands

Best Places to Eat

» Kokomo (p297)

» Blu d'Mare (p297)

» Wiwin Café (p304)

Best Places to Stay

» Karma Kayak (p296)

» Shack 58 (p299)

» Good Heart (p299)

» Scallywags (p297)

Why Go?

Picture three miniscule desert islands, fringed by white-sand beaches and coconut palms, sitting in a turquoise sea: the Gilis are a vision of paradise. These islets have exploded in popularity, and are booming like nowhere else in Indonesia – speedboats zip visitors direct from Bali and a new hip hotel opens every month.

It's not hard to understand the Gilis' unique appeal, for a serenity endures (no motorbikes or dogs!) and a green consciousness is growing. Most development is incredibly tasteful and there are no concrete eyesores.

Each island has its own special character. Trawangan is by far the most cosmopolitan, its bar and party scene vibrant, its accommodation and restaurants close to definitive tropical chic. Gili Air has the strongest local character, a mellow atmosphere and a lovely Rinjani-facing coastline. Meno is simply tranquillity on earth. But all have one thing in common: they are incredibly hard to leave.

When to Go

The wet season is approximately late October until late March. But even in the height of the rainy season, when it's lashing it down in Mataram or Bali, the Gilis can be dry and sunny. High season is between June and late August, when rooms are very hard to find and prices can double (though great weather is almost guaranteed). Perhaps the perfect times of year to visit are April to June and September. There's no cyclone season to worry about.

Dangers & Annoyances

There are no **police** on any of the Gilis (though this may change soon as tourism continues to boom). Report thefts to the island *kepala desa* (village head) immediately, who will deal with the issue; staff at the dive schools will direct you to him. On Gili Trawangan, contact **Satgas**, the community organisation that runs island affairs, via your hotel or dive centre. Satgas are usually able to resolve problems and track down stolen property.

Trawangan (and Air to a lesser degree) have a resident population of wannabe local gigolos, much like the Kuta cowboys of Bali. Girls can expect plenty of interest and comments from these chancers as they walk around. If you'd rather avoid their attentions holding a mobile phone to your ear is a good tactic. Although it's rare, some

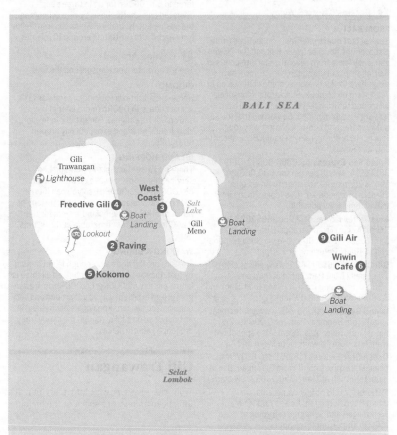

Gili Islands Highlights

① Snorkelling with hawksbill and green sea **turtles** (p289)

② Raving all night at one of Trawangan's **(in)famous parties** (p298)

③ Finding serenity on **Gili Meno's west coast** (p299)

④ Learning to **freedive** in paradise (p289)

⑤ Savouring a seafood platter at **Kokomo** (p297)

⑥ Munching authentic Indonesian food right by the waves at **Wiwin Café** (p304)

⑦ **Cycling** around Gili Trawangan, then climbing the hill for unbeatable sunset views (p291)

⑧ Diving with reef sharks at **Shark Point** (p293)

⑨ Enjoying the sheer thrill of eye-dazzling white sand and pellucid sea on **Gili Air** (p302)

foreign women have experienced sexual harassment and even assault while on the Gilis – it's best to walk home in pairs to the quieter parts of the islands.

Jellyfish can plague the coast (particularly in June and July), the larger ones leave a painful rash. See p395.

In stark contrast to Bali, there are no **dogs** on the Gilis. That's right, the islands are completely pooch-less.

Getting There & Away

FROM BALI

Several **fast boats** offer fast connections (from just over one hour) between Bali and Gili Trawangan. They leave from several departure points in Bali, all stop on Trawangan (where you'll have to disembark for Air or Meno), some continue on to Teluk Nare on Lombok. Shop around for special offers and return ticket discounts; hotel transfers are usually included. Be warned that the sea between Bali and Lombok can get very rough (particularly during rainy season). Book ahead in July and August.

Amed Sea Express (☑0363-80852, 0819 3617 6914; Amed; per person 600,000Rp) Makes 75-minute crossings to Amed on a 20-person speedboat. This makes many interesting itineraries possible.

Blue Water Express (☑0361-895 1082; www .bwsbali.com) From Serangan, Bali direct at 8am (US$77, 2¼ hours); also via Nusa Lembongan at 10am. Returning at 1.30pm.

Gili Cat (☑0361-271 680; www.gilicat.com) Twice daily from Padangbai at 9am and 1.30pm, returning from Trawangan at 11am and 3.30pm (660,000Rp, 1½ hours)

Island Getaway (☑753 241; www.gili-fastboat .com) From Benoa at 8am (660,000Rp, 2½ hours), returning at 11.30am. Also speedboat transfers from Trawangan to Meno and Air.

Ocean Star Express (☑0811 385 6037; http:// oceanstarexpress.com) From Serangan, Bali at 8am, returning at 11am (650,000Rp, 2½ hours).

Perama (☑638 514; www.peramatour .com) From Serangan, Bali at 7am via Nusa Lembongan and Senggigi, returning at noon (500,000Rp, from three hours).

Red Line (☑634 893; www.redlinexpress.com) From Benoa at 8am, returning at 12.30pm (700,000Rp, 2½ hours).

There's also a cheaper **slow boat** service from Bali (from 350,000Rp) operated by Perama, which involves a shuttle bus to Padangbai, and a slow boat (departing 1.30pm, four to five hours) to the Gilis. Finally, if your budget is really stretched, Perama sell a **shuttle bus–ferry– shuttle bus** ticket (160,000Rp) that leaves Kuta Bali at 6am and gets you to Mataram for around

2pm, from where you can get a connection to Bangsal and the Gilis.

FROM LOMBOK

The cheapest route involves travelling by public boat from **Bangsal** (p271), a dirty little port with a big rep for hassle. Catch a bus or bemo to Pemenang, from where it's about 1km to Bangsal.

From Senggigi there's a daily Perama shuttle bus–boat connection at 9am (100,000Rp).

Finally, there are various **speedboat** options (around 500,000Rp for up to three people), operated on a charter basis by dive schools and the posher hotels, that will whisk you from Teluk Nare harbour to the Gilis in around 10 minutes.

Getting Around

There's no motorised transport on the Gilis.

CIDOMO

Horse-and-cart taxis (*cidomo*) operate as taxis. A short ride is 15,000Rp (more later at night and on Gili Trawangan). For an hour-long clip-clop around an island expect to pay around 90,000Rp.

ISLAND-HOPPING

There's a twice-daily island-hopping boat service that loops between all three islands (20,000Rp to 23,000Rp), so you can hit the ATM on Trawangan if you're based on Meno or Air, or snorkel another island's reefs for the day. Check the latest timetable at the islands' docks.

WALKING & BIKING

The Gilis are flat and easy enough to get around by foot. Bicycles, available for hire on all three islands (per day 40,000Rp; 60,000Rp on Trawangan) are an excellent way to get around and very popular. You can circumnavigate each island in an hour or so on a bike, though the sandy trails are tough going in places.

Gili Trawangan
☑0370

Well, the secret is well and truly out. It's long been an obscure speck in the big blue,

BOAT SAFETY

There have been accidents involving boats between Bali and the Gilis. These services are unregulated and there is no safety authority should trouble arise. See the boxed text Travelling Safely by Boat (p384) for information on how to improve your odds for a trouble-free journey.

but Gili Trawangan's zeitgeist is right here, right now. Today it's a paradise of global repute, ranking alongside Bali and Borobudur as one of Indonesia's essential destinations.

Gili T's rise has been meteoric, for it was only settled 50 years ago (by Bugis fishermen from Sulawesi). Travellers arrived in the 1980s, seduced by the white-sand beaches, coral reefs and simplicity of life. By the 1990s Trawangan had mutated into a kind of tropical Ibiza, famed for its entrenched weed and *shrooms* trade, a boho idyll where you could rave away from the eyes of the Indonesian police. And then the island began to grow up – resident Western hedonists metamorphosised into entrepreneurs and diving became more important to the island economy than partying.

Today Trawangan's main drag boasts a glittering roster of lounge bars, hip hotels and cosmopolitan restaurants, mini-marts and dive schools. And yet behind this glitzy facade, a bohemian character endures, with rickety warung and reggae joints surviving between the cocktail tables. Head just inland and the village is a little-changed scene of free-range roosters, sandy lanes, simple backpacker-geared losmen and wild-haired kids playing hopscotch. Here the call of the *muezzin*, not happy hour, defines the time of day. And for real serenity, escape the crowds completely on the island's north-western coast, where birdsong and not banging beats are the soundtrack to life.

◉ Sights & Activities

There's a **turtle hatchery** right on the main beach on Trawangan, with pools full of juvenile turtles. These are released when they're over six months old. Pak Dino who runs the place appreciates donations.

Diving & Snorkelling

Trawangan is a diver's paradise, with eight professional scuba schools and one of Asia's only freediving schools. See p293 and p292.

Big Bubble (☑625 020; www.bigbubblediving .com)

Blue Marlin Dive Centre (☑632 424, 0813 3993 0190; www.bluemarlindive.com)

Buddha Dive (☑644 175; www.buddhadive .com)

Dream Divers (☑634 496; www.dreamdivers .com)

Freedive Gili (☑0858 5718 7170; www.free divegili.com)

Lutwala Dive (☑689 3609; www.lutwala.com)

Manta Dive (☑643 649; www.manta-dive .com)

Trawangan Diving (☑649 220, 0813 3770 2332; www.trawangandive.com)

Vila Ombak Diving Academy (☑638 531; www.hotelombak.com)

There's fun **snorkelling** off the beach north of the boat landing – the coral isn't in the best shape here, but there are tons of fish. The reef is in better shape close to the lighthouse off the northwest coast, but you'll have to scramble over some low coral to access it (take some rubber footwear). At certain times offshore currents can be very strong, so take care.

Boat Trips

Sailing trips around the Gilis and to Komodo on a beautiful Indonesian wooden *phinisi* (dead-ringer for a pirate ship) are run by **Bulan Purnama** (☑0819 1774 8883; www.bulan-purnama.com) on Trawangan. Day cruises start at US$30 per person.

Glass-bottomed boat trips (80,000Rp per person, including snorkelling equipment) to coral reefs can be booked at many stores on the main strip. We've had reports that some boat captains have harassed turtles on snorkelling trips by encouraging snorkellers to try to touch them. Turtles can easily get alarmed by such antics; please encourage all to keep a respectful distance from these magnificent marine creatures.

FREEDIVING THE GILIS

Freediving is an advanced breath-hold technique that allows you to explore much deeper depths than snorkelling (to 30m and beyond!). Trawangan is one of Asia's premier freediving centres, with a professional school, Freedive Gili, offering two-day (US$185) and advanced (US$275) courses that include theory sessions, breathing techniques and depth-training sessions. There's no better way to feel at one with the ocean, and as you're not expelling clouds of bubbles you can observe fish very closely. After a two-day course many students are able to get down to 15m on a single breath of air.

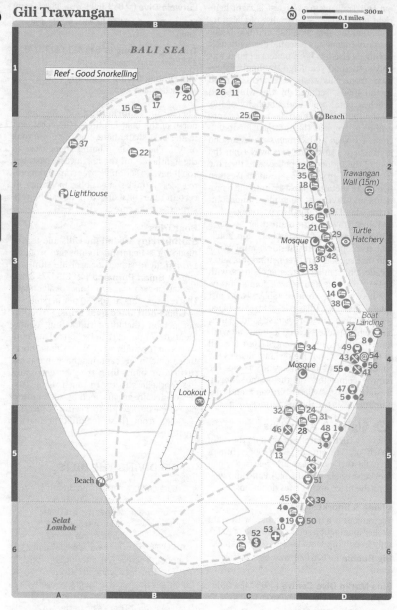

BALI SEA

Reef - Good Snorkelling

Trawangan Wall (15m)

Lighthouse

Mosque

Turtle Hatchery

Mosque

Boat Landing

Lookout

Beach

Selat Lombok

GILI ISLANDS

Surfing & Kayaking

Trawangan has a fast right reef break that can be surfed year-round and at times swells overhead. The central section of the reef is not that sharp. It's just south of Hotel Villa Ombok; for details, see p37.

Abdi Surf (☎0878 6508 1108) Abdi is a friendly soul who rents boards (from 50,000Rp) and offers instruction (per day 300,000Rp, including gear and laughter!).

Karma Kayak (☎0818 0559 3710; www .karmakayak.com; trips from €20) Karma

GILI ISLANDS GILI TRAWANGAN

Kayak offers professional guides for sea-kayaking trips and courses. The company is run by Astrid, a former champion stunt kayaker (she took silver at the 1991 world championships).

Walking, Cycling & Horse Riding

Trawangan is perfect for exploring on foot or by bike. You can walk around the whole island in a couple of hours or so – if you finish at the hill on the southwestern corner (which has the remains of an old Japanese gun placement c WWII), you'll have terrific sunset views of Bali's Gunung Agung.

Bikes (per day from 60,000Rp) are a great way to get around. You'll find loads of rental outlets on the main strip.

Or maybe you'd rather mount a steed? **Stud Horse Riding Adventures** (📞0813 3960 0553; per hr 300,000Rp) will lead you on long rides down the north and west coasts and through the inland coconut groves.

Yoga, Fitness & Tennis

Gili Yoga (☑0878 6579 4884; www.giliyoga .com) A superb new yoga centre that runs twice-daily group classes (90,000Rp per session). Yoga styles practised include Prana Flow, Vinyasa and Ashtanga, and there are also meditation sessions.

Kelapa Villas (☑632 424; 2-hour session 80,000Rp) Offers yoga classes nightly at 7pm in an air-conditioned studio, and also has a good tennis court and gym.

🛏 Sleeping

Gili T has over 100 places to stay, and these range from thatched huts right through to sleek, air-conditioned villas with private pools. It's wise to arrive with a relaxed attitude – this is a tiny desert island and many places are owned by local families with little or no experience of running hotels.

The midrange *lumbung*, loosely modelled on a traditional Lombok rice barn, is a delightful thatched-roofed, bow-sided bungalow that has become Gili T's signature accommodation choice.

The cheapest digs are in the village, where the mosque is everyone's alarm clock. You'll pay more for a beachside address. Head to the north or west coasts to escape the crowds.

All budget and most midrange places have brackish tap water. Pure water is available in some upmarket bungalows.

The high-season rates quoted can drop up to 50% off-peak. Breakfast is included unless stated otherwise.

VILLAGE

The village (inland from the main drag) has at least 20 simple homestays and budget places.

Marta's HOTEL $$
(☑0812 372 2777; www.martasgili.com; s/d 650,000/750,000Rp, apt from 850,000Rp; ☻❉☲) Run by a very hospitable Sasak-English couple, Marta's offers very high-quality accommodation, from double rooms to family apartments; all mix Indonesian style (hand-carved furniture) with Western comforts (commodious beds). It's located on the edge of the village, and has a lovely private pool area.

Pondok Twins Garden BUDGET HOTEL $
(☑0817 570 8373; s/d 200,000/300,000Rp) A great place towards the top end of the budget sector. The eight rooms are well maintained and very tidy, all have a desk and ceiling fans and face the garden. There's a laundry machine and the friendly local family cooks up barbecues for guests.

Black Sand HOTEL $
(☑0812 372 0353; r/bungalow 250,000/ 400,000Rp; ❉) Tucked away on the inland side of the village, this is archetypal flashpacker terrain. Offers superb value,

---

SNORKELLING THE GILIS

Ringed by coral reefs and with easy beach access, the Gilis offer superb snorkelling. If you enjoy swimming and are reasonably fit, there's no better feeling than exploring a reef without the burden of a tank on your back. Masks, snorkels and fins are widely available and can be hired for as little as 40,000Rp per day. It's important to check your mask fits properly, just press it gently to your face, let go and if it's a good fit the suction should hold it in place.

The main (most-developed) strips of each island all have decent snorkelling offshore, but are likely to be busy with boat traffic – so take care and listen out for outboard motors while you're in the water. On Trawangan, turtles very regularly appear on the reef right off the beach. You'll likely drift with the current here, so be prepared to walk back to the starting line. Over on Air, the walls off the east coast are good too.

It's not hard to escape the crowds though. Each island has a less-developed side, usually where access to the water is obstructed by shallow patches of coral. Using rubber shoes it's much easier to get in the water near the lighthouse on Trawangan or on Gili Air's north coast. Try not to stamp all over the coral but ease yourself in, and then swim, keeping your body as horizontal as possible.

Top snorkelling spots include the Meno Wall and the jetty at the former Bounty resort (which has prolific marine life), the north end of Trawangan's beach, and Gili Air's Air Wall.

The Gili Islands are a superb dive destination as the marine life is plentiful and varied. Turtles and black- and white-tip reef sharks are common, and the macro life (small stuff) is excellent, with sea horses, pipefish and lots of crustaceans. Around the full moon, large schools of bumphead parrotfish appear to feast on coral spawn; at other times of year manta rays cruise past dive sites.

Though years of bomb fishing and an El Niño–induced bleaching damaged corals above 18m, the reefs are now in recovery. Dozens of electric currents run to Biorock reefs (p295), which are evolving into natural coral reefs.

The Gilis also have their share of virgin coral. Hidden Reef, a recently discovered site, pops with colourful coral life above 20m, and there's also an abundance of deep coral shelves and walls at around 30m, where the coral is, and always has been, pristine.

Safety standards are high on the Gilis – there are no dodgy dive schools, and instructors and training are professional. Rates are fixed (no matter what company you dive with) at US$38 a dive, with discounts for dive packages. A PADI open-water course costs US$350, the Advanced is US$275, Divemaster training starts at US$750. Nitrox and trimix courses are also available. For dive-school information, see individual island entries. Trawangan is also one of Asia's premier **freediving** destinations.

Some of the best dive sites include the following:

» **Bounty Pier** At 12m to 18m, this sunken pontoon site is ideal for beginners, and you can often glimpse rare frogfish here.

» **Deep Halik** A canyon-like site ideally suited to drift diving. Black- and white-tip sharks are often seen at 28m to 30m.

» **Deep Turbo** At around 30m, this site is ideally suited to nitrox diving. It has impressive sea fans and leopard sharks hidden in the crevasses.

» **Hans Reef** Great for macro life including frogfish, ghostfish, sea horses and pipefish.

» **Hidden Reef** It was never bombed and has vibrant, pristine soft coral and table coral formations.

» **Japanese Wreck** For experienced divers only (it lies at 45m), this shipwreck of a Japanese patrol boat (c WWII) is another site ideal for nitrox divers. You'll see prolific soft coral, and lots of nudibranches.

» **Shark Point** Perhaps the most exhilarating Gili dive: reef sharks and turtles are very regularly encountered, as well as schools of bumphead parrotfish and mantas. Look out too for cuttlefish and octopuses. At shallow depths there can be a strong surge.

» **Simon's Reef** The reef here is in excellent condition; from 16m to 30m you can see schools of trevally, and occasionally barracuda and leopard sharks.

» **Sunset (Manta Point)** Some impressive table coral and sharks and large pelagics are frequently encountered.

well-presented two-storey bungalows and rooms – all with good beds, high ceilings and wooden furniture – plus a great garden (with exotic pandan trees) to relax in.

Lisa Homestay HOMESTAY **$**
(☑0813 3952 3364; s/d 120,000/140,000Rp) All you could ask for in a budget place, this sweet spot has four very clean rooms, all with two beds, front verandas and good showers that face a pretty garden.

Rumah Saga HOTEL **$**
(☑648 604; www.rumahsaga.com; cottages 300,000/500,000Rp; ❄❄) A welcoming, relaxed place with neat, well-equipped cottages that are set around a lovely garden area with a nice pool.

Pondok Lita BUDGET HOTEL **$**
(📞648 607; d/tr from US$25; ❄️) Eight spacious rooms spread around a shady garden courtyard with beruga (open-sided pavilions) and Buddhas.

Pondok Sederhana BUDGET HOTEL **$**
(📞0813 3860 9964; r 140,000Rp) Run by a house-proud, friendly Balinese lady; the spotless rooms here face a neat little garden.

MAIN STRIP

Kokomo LUXURY VILLAS **$$$**
(📞642 352; www.kokomogilit.com; villas from 1,400,000Rp; ❄️🛜🏊) Offering beautifully finished and lavishly equipped modern accommodation, these mini-villas are set in a small complex at the (quiet) southern end of the main strip. All have private pools, contemporary decor and lovely indoor-outdoor living quarters. Also the home of Gili T's best restaurant.

🌿**Scallywags** ECO HOTEL **$$**
(📞645 301; www.scallywagsresort.com; 1,000,000Rp; ❄️🛜🏊) Directly behind Trawangan's busiest restaurant, this very well-designed, professionally run place has a gorgeous decked pool area and 10 immaculate rooms, each with a little front garden, bedroom with queen-sized bed and all mod cons, plus an outdoor shower area with volcanic stone and greenery. Scallywags uses solar power and recycled rainwater.

Hotel Vila Ombak RESORT HOTEL **$$**
(📞642 336; www.hotelombak.com; r US$110-170 plus 21% tax; ❄️🛜🏊@) Gili T's original resort occupies an attractive garden plot partly shaded by yuccas and palms. It offers smallish but cute A-frame bungalows (book 1 or 2 for sea views) and stunning, spacious, minimalist rooms. Huge pool, spa, diving academy and kids' activities are offered. Ombak is expanding south with dozens more high-spec bungalows due to be completed in 2011.

Some more good choices:

Big Bubble BUNGALOWS **$$**
(📞625 020; www.bigbubblediving.com; r with fan/air-con 450,000/500,000Rp; 🔄❄️🏊) Seven gorgeous wood-and-thatch bungalows facing a flowering garden, plus simple clean budget rooms. Breakfast is available anytime.

Blue Marlin BUNGALOWS **$$**
(📞632 424; www.bluemarlindive.com; d US$55; ❄️🏊) Simple and stylish, these double and twin rooms are just the ticket if you want a central location.

Manta BUNGALOWS **$$**
(📞643 649; www.manta-dive.com; bungalows US$70; ❄️🏊) Well-designed, good-value mod-bungalows at the rear of this popular dive school.

Tir na Nog BUNGALOWS **$$**
(📞639 463; www.tirnanogbar.com; r US$60; ❄️) Ten very spacious, well-appointed rooms in the heart of the action.

BEACHSIDE

Dream Village HOTEL **$$**
(📞664 4373; www.dreamvillagetrawangan.it; bungalows 800,000Rp; ❄️) Guests are well looked after, with five classic, well-equipped lumbung complete with gorgeous fresh-water outdoor bathrooms, and in a new block at the rear you'll find six immaculate, very tasteful and spacious rooms with huge contemporary bathrooms. There's a spa zone for massages too (from 100,000Rp).

Tanah Qita BUNGALOWS **$**
(📞639 159; martinkoch-berlin@hotmail.de; bungalows with fan/air-con 250,000/600,000Rp; ❄️) Another excellent set-up. Tanah Qita ('Homeland') has four large, immaculate lumbung (with four-poster beds) and also smaller fan-cooled versions that represent exceptional value. Cleanliness is taken very seriously. The garden is a bucolic delight.

Blu d'Mare TEAK BUNGALOWS **$$**
(📞0858 8866 2490; www.bludamare.it; villas 600,000-850,000Rp; ❄️) Eschewing the fad for lumbung living, the Italian owners here have reassembled four teak Javanese village houses in a Gili beachside location. Decor is shabby chic with a real eye for artistic detail, and there's a wonderfully warm welcome from Sandra and her mum Siva who run the place and the restaurant, one of Gili T's very best.

Kelapa Kecil BOUTIQUE ROOMS **$$**
(📞0812 3690 1421; www.kelapakecil.com; bungalows US$100; ❄️🏊) With the ocean just 50m away, it's easy to appreciate the appeal of these sleek, minimalist rooms where you can gaze at Gili Meno from your bed. You'll find nice extras like lovely cotton linen, security boxes, limestone baths and a plunge pool. Staff are very helpful.

Blue Beach Cottages HOTEL **$$**
(📞623 538; www.bluebeach.biz; r/lumbung 450,000/750,000Rp; ❄️) Stylishly presented

So you've paid your hotel bill, settled up with the scuba school and cleared that painful bar tab – why should you have to pay a tax on your stay? Well, you don't *have* to. Gili Trawangan's EcoTax (50,000Rp per person) is a voluntary scheme, set up by the pioneering **Gili Eco Trust** (www.giliecotrust.com) to improve the island's environment.

Though Gili T looks like a vision of paradise, there's been severe pressure on the island (intensive development and rubbish) and offshore reefs (fishermen using cyanide and dynamite to harvest fish) for years. Large swathes of coral were left in a shattered state and sea almost cleared of sea life. But several initiatives have tried to reclaim the reef.

Biorock, a coral regeneration project, has been staggeringly successful, reducing beach erosion and nurturing marine life. Loose pieces of living coral (perhaps damaged by an anchor or a clumsy diving fin) are gathered and transplanted onto frames in the sea. Electrodes supplied with low-voltage currents cause electrolytic reactions, accelerating coral growth and ultimately creating an artificial reef. There are now 42 Biorock installations (and many more planned) around the Gilis. You'll see them as you snorkel or dive; their shapes look quite startling in the water – flowers, an aeroplane, turtle, star, manta and even a heart – covered in flourishing coral and sponges. The reef's progress has been remarkable, and the Biorock installations now form vital nurseries for juvenile 'muck life' including razorfish, pufferfish, crocodile fish and sweetlips.

The second initiative, the creation of a widespread **fishing exclusion zone**, presented a cultural conundrum. Trawangan was first settled by Bugis fishing people, and fishing represented many senior islanders' identity and heritage. Today Trawangan's dive schools compensate local fisherman for loss of income and the scheme works well, with two areas set aside for fishing and most of the island's reefs protected. Top predators including reef sharks have returned and are regularly encountered, and Trawangan is now one of the best places to see turtles in Asia.

Since 2009 the Gili Eco Trust has also started to tackle **land issues**. Rubbish is a huge issue – as recently as 2007 plastic and waste littered the village's sandy lanes. An education program implemented in schools raised awareness. In May 2010 over 1000 recycling bins were introduced to the Gilis, you'll see the colour-coded bins everywhere on Trawangan, and some on Meno and Air. Plastic bags are another huge issue, so strong reuseable bags (you can purchase them for 20,000Rp) have been introduced and it's hoped a complete ban will be agreed on in the future.

Trawangan's hard-working (some would say flogged) *cidomo* horses are now getting medical care in a free clinic, and deworming treatment. A feral cat neutering program has started.

Big challenges lie ahead. The speed of development has been lightning-fast on Gili T, which has changed from a simple fishing settlement to one of the globe's most cosmopolitan corners in 15 years. Solar energy and rainwater collection is being adopted by some businesses. If you want to get involved you can join the island clean-up (first Friday of every month) and collect land or sea garbage; kids are very welcome to help out. Or if you're not around, you can pay your EcoTax.

lumbung with all mod cons and (hot) freshwater bathrooms. Cheaper rooms at the rear with cold-water bathrooms are also available. The beach is steps away.

Warna Homestay   HOTEL **$**
(☏623 859; r/bungalow 300,000/450,000Rp; ❄) Enjoying a terrific location just off the beach, these modern lumbung have style and space. The rooms here (with fan or aircon) are quite plain, but roomy.

H Rooms   CONTEMPORARY ACCOMMODATION **$$**
(☏639 248; www.thegiliislands.com; r from US$100; ❄) Offering an amazing space, these cleverly designed pads have sunken chill-out areas with TV/DVD, luxe bathrooms and private sun terraces. They're at the rear of Horizontal bar-restaurant.

Trawangan Dive BOUTIQUE BACKPACKERS $$
(⌖649 220, 0813 3770 2332; www.trawangan
dive.com; dm US$5, bungalows US$80; ✷ ▦) Un-
derstated yet comfortable, these well-kept
rooms boast beds with fine white linen, TV/
DVD and Indian limestone bathrooms. At
the rear is a new backpacker block with tiny
fan-cooled rooms with bunk beds.

Ozzy Homestay BUNGALOWS $$
(⌖0813 3770 2332; bungalow 600,000Rp; ✷)
Locally owned place with six very attractive, upmarket A-frame bungalows, each
with TV, safe and minibar. The outdoor
bathrooms are worthy of special mention:
each has a large volcanic stone sink, pebble
flooring and heated fresh water.

Oda Café ROOMS $
(⌖0859 3700 1081; r with fan/air-con 250,000/
350,000Rp; ✷) After beach on the cheap?
Good-quality, clean rooms with new beds
and a few artistic touches.

Good Heart HOTEL $
(⌖0812 239 5170; r 170,000Rp, bungalows from
400,000Rp; ✷) Budget rooms and stylish A-
frame bungalows with pebble-floored open-
air bathrooms.

Balenta BUNGALOWS $
(⌖0818 0520 3464; US$35-60; ✷) Next to a
great stretch of beach, the posh lumbung
and bungalows here have local style in
abundance.

NORTH & WEST COASTS, & INLAND

⌖TOP⌖ **Karma Kayak** RUSTIC HOTEL $$
CHOICE (⌖0818 0559 3710; www.karmakayak
.com; bungalows 550,000Rp; ✷) Simplicity
is the key here at this wonderful back-to-
nature retreat where everything seems to
exist in harmony with the tranquil rural
location. All the fine rooms adopt a less-
is-more uncluttered design, with soothing
natural colours, large windows and gener-
ous balconies or verandas. Kayak tours are
offered, and the beachside cafe is first-class.

Alam Gili HOTEL $$
(⌖630 466; www.alamgili.com; r US$55-95;
✷ ▦) A stunning mature garden, shaded
by soaring palms and casuarinas, and a
quiet beach location are the main draws
here, combined with very welcoming and
efficient service. Rooms and villas (some
are two-storey) boast lashings of old-school
Balinese style and hand-crafted furniture.
There's a small pool and a branch of Café
Wayan, so the food's excellent. But best of all,

it doesn't hike its prices for high season, so
get in quick.

Lutwala CONTEMPORARY ROOMS $$
(⌖693609; www.lutwala.com; r from 600,000Rp;
✷ ⠰ ▦) With an unrivalled position on a
lovely, tranquil north-coast beach, with good
snorkelling on your doorstep, Lutwala is an
exciting new hotel (and dive school). Seven
modern rooms, all with TV/DVD and giant
photographic prints, are scattered around
an imposing two-storey villa with an indoor-
outdoor pool. The young South African own-
er is a mine of info about the Gilis.

🌿 **Gili Eco Villas** ECO VILLAS $$$
(⌖0361 847 6419; www.giliecovillas.com; vil-
las US$140-220 plus 21% tax; ✷ ⠰ ▦) Classy vil-
las made from recycled teak, set back from
the beach on Trawangan's idyllic north
coast. Comfort and style (rattan sofas and
stone-walled outdoor bathrooms) are combined with solid green principles (water
is recycled, there's an organic vegetable
garden, and solar and wind energy provide
most of the power).

Luce d'Alma LUXURY HOTEL $$
(⌖621 777; www.lucedalmaresort.com; r from
US$115; ✷ ⠰ ▦) Extravagant luxury, includ-
ing huge living quarters with tribal art and
royal bathrooms, at very moderate rates
given the quality on offer. All rooms face
each other across a slimline 80m (yes...
that's correct) pool, so the layout is slightly
claustrophobic. It's about 500m inland
from the coast; free bicycles are provided.

Kelapa Villas LUXURY VILLAS $$$
(⌖632 424; www.kelapavillas.com; villas
US$195-620 plus 21% tax; ✷ ▦) Luxury devel-
opment in an inland location with a selection of commodious villas, all with private
pools, that offer style and space in abundance. There's a tennis court and gym in
the complex.

Desa Dunia Beda BUNGALOWS $$
(⌖641 575; www.desaduniabeda.com; bungalows
US$110-140 plus 21% tax; ▦) Astonishing Ja-
vanese Joglo teak houses kitted out with
colonial-style decor and antiques (though
their interiors are dark). No air-con and no
fresh water.

Villa Julias BOUTIQUE HOTEL $$
(⌖0878 6568 6584; www.villajulius.com; bunga-
lows r US$85; ✷ ▦) This is an architect-
designed modernist pad that ticks all the
right contemporary boxes. All seven rooms
have polished hardwood floors, veranda or

balcony. It's located in an isolated west-coast beach spot.

✖ Eating

Tiny Trawangan is extremely cosmopolitan and it's easy to munch your way around the world – from Mexico to Japan – here. In the evenings, several places on the main strip display and grill delicious fresh seafood.

Kokomo
TOP CHOICE GOURMET $$$
(☑642 352; www.kokomogilit.com; mains Rp60,000-160,000Rp)
Unquestionably top dog on the Gilis, Kokomo has really raised the bar in the culinary stakes and is the only genuine fine-dining restaurant in town. Standards are very high indeed, using hyper-fresh local seafood and select imported meats. Lots of fresh salads, wonderful steaks and pasta, but for the ultimate treat opt for a seafood or sashimi (with Atlantic salmon and yellowfin tuna) platter. Eat on the beachside terrace or in the air-conditioned dining room.

Blu d'Mare
ITALIAN $$
(☑0858 8866 2490; meals from 60,000Rp)
Wonderfully authentic, Italian-owned trattoria where they bake their own bread, make their own pasta and grill meat, fish and seafood to perfection. The simple seashack-style surrounds belie the quality of the cuisine here and you can count on the chef-patron for advice and suggestions. It's well away from the hullabaloo on the main strip on a lovely stretch of beach.

Karma Kayak
TAPAS $
(☑0818 0559 3710; tapas from 15,000Rp) Terrific tapas (including sardines, house-cured olives and tempura), sandwiches and salads are served up on a blissfully tranquil beach location. Wash it all down with a jug of sangria or a bottle of chilled wine. It's magical at sunset here, with the volcanoes of Bali filling the horizon.

Trawangan Dive
MEXICAN $
(☑649 220; meals from 40,000Rp) Genuine Mexican food (the chef is from Veracruz) is served beneath casuarina trees right on the beach. There are lots of delicious dishes to choose from – the *tostadas* are street-authentic and topped with chopped salad and fresh coriander. Lush margaritas and hotel delivery complete the picture. *¡Olé!*

Warung Indonesia
INDONESIAN $
(dishes from 12,000Rp) Tucked away at the rear of the village, this authentic Indo

> The Gili Islands may be a huge tourism destination but they are culturally very different from Bali. Virtually all locals are Muslim and visitors should dress appropriately away from the beach or hotel pool. It's not at all acceptable to wander the lanes of the village in a bikini, and nude or topless bathing anywhere is a no-no.
>
> Islamic law forbids drinking alcohol and although it's sold everywhere on the Gilis it's offensive to drink booze next to a mosque. During the month of Ramadan many locals fast during daylight hours and there are no parties on Gili Trawangan.

warung scores high marks for cheap local grub in no-nonsense surrounds. No alcohol served.

Scallywags
INTERNATIONAL $$
(☑631 945; meals 40,000-100,000Rp; 🛜)
Scallywags enjoys a prime beachfront location, with tables under Arabian-style canvas and an attractive shabby-chic interior. A lot of effort is made to source organic produce, and tempting specials are chalked up daily on blackboards. The menu covers everything from freshly grilled fish, through pasta, panini and wraps, to 'Full Monty' breakfasts.

Café Wayan
INDONESIAN $
(meals 30,000-65,000Rp) At the Alam Gili hotel, this fine place offers authentic Balinese and Indonesian dishes (try the steamed prawns) plus some good Western options (sandwiches with very fresh bread). Great service and a beachside garden location make it worth the trip up north.

Blue Marlin
FISH $
(mains 9000-35,000Rp) Blue Marlin is one of the best places to eat fresh fish on the island – just select yours from the glistening displays and enjoy it with a limitless buffet of salads and sides.

Beach House
INTERNATIONAL $$
(☑642 352; dishes 17,000-60,000Rp) This is a hugely popular place with a seafront terrace that's best for fresh fish (or grilled meats) and its comprehensive salad-bar selection.

Horizontal
ECLECTIC **$$**

(✆639 248; dishes from 40,000Rp) Lounge-bar-restaurant replete with luxe scarlet seating, sculptured white pods and a delicious menu of Western and Eastern grub, presented with elan.

Coco's
CAFE **$**

(drinks from 15,000Rp; sandwiches from 25,000Rp) Coco's is a stylish cafe ideal for a hit of Western-style city tucker. Great for breakfast (muesli, or try the English breakfast with Earl Grey tea) or a baguette, and the smoothies are heavenly.

Rumah Makan Kikinovi
INDONESIAN **$**

(meals from 12,000Rp) Run by a formidable *ibu*, this is Indonesian food at its tastiest. It's very inexpensive – a big feed is around 15,000Rp.

Ryoshi
JAPANESE **$$**

(✆639 463; meals from 60,000Rp) Japanese eatery renowned for its consistently good sushi and teriyaki dishes. Eat right by the waves.

🍷 Drinking & Entertainment

The island has more than a dozen great beachside drinking dens, ranging from sleek lounge bars with ubercool seating and decadent cocktail lists to simple shacks with nothing more than cold Bintang beer.

Round-the-clock partying may be a fading memory as Trawangan's identity shifts from rave-up central to boutique chic, but there's still plenty of life left in the island. Parties are held three nights a week, shifting between Blue Marlin (Monday), Tir na Nog (Wednesday), and Rudy's Pub (Friday). DJs mix house and trance (and increasingly some R 'n' B as the scene gets more commercial). During Ramadan the action is curtailed out of respect for local culture.

Sama Sama
MUSIC BAR

A premier-league reggae bar with a top-end sound system and a killer live band at least six nights a week. Good food is also served here.

Rudy's Pub
BAR

Rudy's hosts arguably the best party on the island, with a good mix of locals and visitors and legendary drinks specials. The huge dance floor at the rear is verging on meat-market terrain on party nights, rammed with young Gili Islanders chasing blondes.

GILI KNOW-HOW

Electricity supply is very limited on the Gilis and power cuts are common, but many of the top-end places have their own generators. **Salty water** is the norm as well, though again the more expensive places have freshwater tanks.

The Gilis have excellent **mobile phone** coverage, and all islands have a *wartel* and **internet** cafes (but surfing is often woefully slow). Several places now boast free **wi-fi** on Trawangan, as well as a couple on Gili Air.

Gili Trawangan has a couple of **ATMs** and foreign cards are accepted, the other islands do not. It's also wise to have a cash stash in case these ATMs are out of action. Shops and hotels on each island will **change money** and arrange cash advances from credit and debit cards but rates are poor and commissions are very high (around 10%).

Blue Marlin
CLUB

Of all the party bars, this upper-level venue has the largest dance floor and the meanest sound system – it pumps out trance and tribal sounds on Monday.

Tir na Nog
IRISH PUB

Known simply as 'The Irish', this barn-like place has a sports-bar interior with big screens ideal for the footy. Its shoreside bar is the probably the busiest meeting spot in the island, though you'll have to endure sounds from one of the worst DJs on planet earth.

ℹ Information

Emergencies

There's a health clinic just south of Hotel Vila Ombak. For security issues contact **Satgas**, a community organisation, via your hotel or dive school.

Internet & Telephone

Wi-fi is rare on Trawangan, though **Scallywags** restaurant has good connections. **Lightning** (internet per min 500Rp) is a decent cybercafe and also operates as a wartel.

Money

Gili Trawangan has two ATMs. Both accept foreign cards, though due to electricity shortages it's very advisable to have a cash back-up. Stores and hotels change cash and travellers cheques, but rates are poor. Cash advances on credit/debit cards involve a commission of up to 10%.

Post

There's no post office, but stamps and postcards are sold in the Pasar Seni.

Travel agent

Perama (✆638 514; www.peramatour.com) Slow- or fast-boat tickets to Bali, and connections to all locations on Lombok by shuttle bus. Trips to Komodo can also be arranged here (see the boxed text, p390).

Gili Meno

✆0370

Gili Meno is the smallest of the three islands and the perfect setting for your Robinson Crusoe fantasy. In high season Meno still feels delightfully tranquil; at any other time of year it's positively soporific. Most accommodation is strung out along the eastern coast, near the widest and most picturesque beach. Inland you'll find scattered homesteads, coconut plantations and a salty lake.

◉ Sights

Turtle Sanctuary TURTLE HATCHERY
(www.gilimenoturtles.com) Meno's turtle sanctuary consists of an assortment of little pools and bathtubs on the beach, bubbling with filters and teeming with baby turtles. Turtles are nurtured until they're around eight months old before being released. It's maintained by Boulong, a villager whose costs are considerable, so donations are very welcome.

Taman Burung BIRD PARK
(✆642 321; admission 50,000Rp; ◷9am-5pm) Taman Burung is home to over 200 exotic birds from Asia and Australia, and some Indonesian wildlife. After years of neglect the whole place is steadily being renovated and conditions improved.

✗ Activities

Snorkelling, Diving & Walking

It takes around two hours to stroll around Meno, and obviously you can just jump in the ocean to cool off on the way (take your snorkelling gear).

Snorkelling is good off the northeast coast near Amber House; on the west coast near Good Heart; and also around the former jetty of the (abandoned) Bounty resort. Gear is available from 40,000Rp per day. Always ask about currents first. For more on snorkelling and diving, see p293 and p292.

Blue Marlin Dive Centre (✆639 979; www.bluemarlindive.com) offers a full range of courses and fun dives.

🛏 Sleeping

Meno has a limited selection of rustic bungalows and very little in the way of fancypants luxury. It's essential to reserve well ahead in the high season. Prices quoted are high-season rates – reductions of up to 50% are possible the rest of the year.

TOP CHOICE **Shacks 58 & 59** CHIC SHACKS $$
(✆0813 5357 7045; www.shack58.com; villas €45-65 plus 21% tax; ✱) Here, you have tropical slumming as an art form, with two magnificently simple yet elegant one-room villas that offer a real opportunity to experience island life at its purest on a dream beach. Both have been decorated with a real eye for taste and design using natural materials, antique furniture and local textiles. Each 'shack' has a lovely private beach gazebo, ideal as a shady retreat from the heat of the day, complete with daybed. Local food and drinks are available at moderate rates. Shack 58 is right on the beach, 59 is 150m inland.

Good Heart BUNGALOWS $
(✆0813 3955 6976; s/d bungalows 200,000/250,000Rp) Offering superb value, this friendly Balinese-owned place is on the quiet side of a very quiet island. Offers five two-storey lumbung cottages, each with a bedroom upstairs and an open-air freshwater bathroom below. There's a good restaurant and fine snorkelling on the Meno Wall just offshore.

Sunset Gecko ECO PLACE $
(✆0813 535 66774; www.thesunsetgecko.com; s/d 110,000/160,000Rp, bungalows 220,000-550,000Rp) Eco-aware place that composts and collects and recycles rainwater. All the comfortable accommodation is well constructed from timber and you'll find a stylish shower block with bamboo screens and natural soap. There's a restaurant here too.

Jepun Bungalows BUNGALOWS $
(✆0819 1739 4736; www.jepunbungalows.com; bungalows US$45, family house US$75) A new

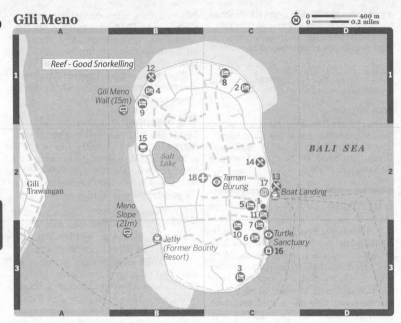

place 100m from the main beach strip and harbour with charming accommodation dotted around a garden. Choose from lovely thatched lumbung, bungalows, or book the family house; all have bathrooms with fresh (hot) water, fans and good-quality beds.

Villa Nautilus MODERN VILLAS **$$**
(☎642 143; www.villanautilus.com; r US$95; ❄)
Meno's only luxury option, these five well-designed detached villas enjoy a grassy plot just off the beach. They're finished in contemporary style with natural wood, marble and limestone and the hip bathrooms have fresh water.

Amber House BUNGALOWS **$**
(☎0813 375 69728; bungalows 200,000-300,000Rp) About as laid-back and peaceful as you could wish for, this humble place has five simple wooden bungalows with *alang-alang* (thatched) roofs and private bathrooms. The management is hospitable and can set up boat trips. Breakfast is extra.

Tao Kombo BUDGET BUNGALOWS **$**
(☎0812 372 2174; www.tao-kombo.com; hut €8, cottage €20) An innovatively designed place with two open-sided backpackers' huts that have bamboo screens for privacy, plus eight lumbung cottages with thatched roofs, stone floors and outdoor bathrooms.

It's also home to the Jungle Bar. It's 200m inland from the main strip.

Mallia's Child BUNGALOWS **$**
(☎622 007; www.gilimeno-mallias.com; bungalows 400,000Rp)
A row of thatch-and-bamboo bungalows that are ageing and pretty basic (cold-water bathrooms and fans) for the price quoted, but they do enjoy a prime beachfront location. There's a good restaurant here and the management is efficient.

Kontiki Meno COTTAGES **$**
(☎632 824; cottages with fan/air-con 300,000/400,000Rp; ❄) A faded resort-style place with dated but clean cinderblock cottages, some with four-poster beds. Right by a gorgeous stretch of beach.

Diana Café BUNGALOWS **$**
(☎081 3535 6612, bungalow 250,000Rp) Three simple, clean, thatched bungalows by the salt lake, a three-minute walk from the beach. As cheap as 120,000Rp in the low season.

Biru Meno BUNGALOWS **$**
(☎0813 365 7322; bungalows 450,000Rp)
Offers both wood-and-thatch and attractive newer concrete bungalows with coral walls, but service can be spotty and cleanliness is erratic.

Gili Meno

Eating & Drinking

Virtually all Meno's restaurants have sea views, which is just as well as service can be slow everywhere. Wood-fired pizza ovens are de rigueur on Meno for some reason.

Good Heart INDONESIAN $
(meals 15,000-70,000Rp) A Balinese-owned restaurant, so if you're bored of those standard-issue Indo dishes the flavours have a slight twist here. Excellent for fresh seafood: barbecued or steamed fish, prawns or squid (choose from six different accompanying sauces including lemon grass, ginger or chilli). Also perfect for a sunset cocktail (40,000Rp) or fresh juice (10,000Rp).

Diana Café BEACH BAR
(drinks 12,000-30,000Rp) If by any remote chance you find the pace of life on Meno too busy, head to this amazing little tropical shack par excellence. Diana couldn't be simpler: a wobbly-looking bamboo-and-thatch bar, a few tables on the sand, a hammock or two, reggae on the stereo and a chill-out zone that makes the most of the zillion-rupiah views. Like it so much you want to stay? Check out their bungalows.

Rust Warung FISH $
(642 324; mains 15,000-75,000Rp) The only 'proper' restaurant on Meno, this place has a large wooden deck by the harbour and *beruga* right by the water. It's renowned for its grilled fish (with garlic or sweet-and-sour sauce) served with corn, salad and potato.

Mallia's Child INTERNATIONAL $
(622 007; mains from 25,000Rp) Popular place with well-priced Western nosh (including tasty spaghetti and pizza from a wood-fired oven) and reliably good Indo food (try the gado gado), or they even knock up a decent Thai curry. Service is pretty organised.

Balenta Café INDONESIAN $
(mains from 20,000Rp) A wonderful location for a meal, Balenta has low tables right on the sand with turquoise water a metre or two away. It scores for omelettes, Sasak and Indonesian food like *kelak kuning* (snapper in yellow spice) and staff fire up a seafood barbecue most nights too. Service can be a tad relaxed though.

Ya Ya Warung INDONESIAN $
(dishes 10,000-20,000Rp) Ramshackle warung-on-the-beach that serves up Indonesian faves, curries, pancakes and plenty of pasta.

Jungle Bar BAR
(Tao Kombo) On busy nights this place can be a blast, especially when the traditional Gili band Badjang Kapung are playing.

Shopping

Island Life is a boutique and silver workshop; fine handmade jewellery is for sale or you can have a go at crafting something yourself for 250,000Rp (including 5g of silver). There's a large **handicrafts stall** just south of Kontiki Meno hotel with masks, Sasak water baskets, wood carvings and gourds.

Information

Minimarkets by the boat landing stock sunscreen and supplies; **internet** (per min 600Rp) and a wartel are here too. Money can be exchanged at the Kontiki Meno hotel, among others, at poor rates. For tours and shuttle-bus/boat tickets, contact **Perama** (☑632 824; www.peramatour.com) at Kontiki Meno. There's a **medical clinic** near the bird park, otherwise head to Mataram for emergencies.

Gili Air

☑0370

Closest to Lombok, Gili Air falls between Gili T's sophistication and less-is-more Meno. It's a rural island that still retains a strong local identity, and was the first Gili to be settled: Bugis and Sasak fishing families put down roots here around 1850. Although it feels delightfully empty at times, Air is still the most populous of the Gili islands (with around 1500 inhabitants). Tourism does dominate the island's economy today, but most Gili Air folk are eager not to ape Trawangan's route to riches: local customs have been preserved so there's only a small party scene, and coconuts and fishing remain a vital form of income.

Gili Air's ravishing white-sand beaches are arguably the best of the Gili bunch, a little broader than those of their neighbours. Snorkelling is good right from the main strip – a lovely sandy lane dotted with bamboo bungalows and little restaurants where you can eat virtually on top of a turquoise sea.

🏃 Activities

Snorkelling & Diving

The entire east coast has reef offshore with plenty of colourful fish; there's a drop-off about 100m to 200m from the coast. Snorkelling gear can be hired from Ozzy's Shop and a number of stores from 40,000Rp a day. Watch out for currents.

Scuba diving is excellent throughout the Gilis, and no matter where you stay, you'll dive the same sites. See p293 for more information.

Blue Marlin Dive Centre (☑634 387; www.bluemarlindive.com)

Dream Divers (☑634 547; www.dreamdivers.com)

Manta Dive (☑0813 377 89047; www.manta-dive.com)

Oceans 5 (☑0813 3877 7144; www.oceans5dive.com) Has a 25m training pool and freediving gear for rent.

Surfing

Directly off the southern tip of the island there's a long, peeling right-hand break that can get big at times. The dive schools will help you get your hands on a board.

Gili Air

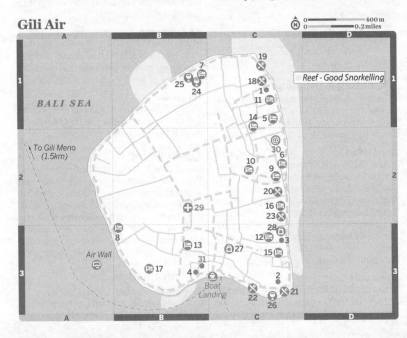

Cycling

Ozzy's Shop has bikes for hire from 35,000Rp a day. Pedalling on Air is fun and you're sure to roll into villagers' backyards if you explore the inland trails.

🛏 Sleeping

Gili Air's 40 or so places to stay are mainly located on the east coast, where the best swimming is. Prices double or even triple in high season, so expect to pay much less than the prices quoted here outside these times.

Biba
BUNGALOWS $
(📞0819 1727 4648; biba69@aliceit; bungalows 400,000Rp; ✳) Biba offers lovely, very spacious bungalows with large verandas and zany, grotto-like bathrooms that have walls inlaid with shells and coral. The gorgeous garden has little chill-out zones ideal for relaxing or reading a book. It's also home to a splendid Italian restaurant.

Sejuk Cottages
BUNGALOWS $
(📞636 461; sejukcottages@hotmail.com; bungalows 350,000-850,000Rp; ✳🖳) Very well-built, thatched lumbung cottages, as well as family rooms and pretty two-storey cottages (some have rooftop living rooms) scattered around a fine tropical garden. The French owner ensures service is efficient and welcoming.

Bintang
MODERN BUNGALOWS $
(📞0819 0773 0381; bungalows 120,000Rp) An excellent budget deal, these four attractive modern bungalows with comfortable beds, mosquito nets (and bathrooms with fresh water and Western toilets) are kept spick and span by the family owners, who also have a restaurant on the beach here. Very inexpensive long-term deals offered.

Manta Dive
BUNGALOWS $$
(📞0813 3778 9047; www.manta-dive.com; bungalows US$65; ✳🖳) Manta invented the Zen mod-hut motif that has been replicated throughout the Gilis. There are seven very well-finished bungalows with safes, quality linen, decks and outdoor baths.

Villa Karang
HOTEL $
(📞0813 3990 4440; www.villakarang.com; bungalows 250,000-800,000Rp; ✳🖳) A well-run, ever-expanding place that has four classes of accommodation, ranging from simple thatched huts to swankier modern air-con bungalows with TV/DVD. The pool is small (10m) but the central garden is attractive.

Casa Mio
ZANY BUNGALOWS $$
(📞646 160; www.giliair.com; cottages US$109; ✳🖳) Casa Mio is an unusual, quirky, Taiwanese-owned new place with four fine cottages that boast every conceivable

Gili Air

mod con, as well as a riot of knick-knacks (from the artistic to the kitsch). It boasts a lovely beach area, fresh-water showers, good Asian food and the fastest wi-fi on the Gilis.

Resota Bungalows BUDGET BUNGALOWS $
(☑0818 0571 5769; bungalows 300,000Rp) Very handy for the harbour, these four large, traditional-style thatched cottages all have two beds, mosquito nets and cold-water showers. Din, the owner, is a former *kepala desa* and very helpful. Rates can sink to a third of high-season rates quoted here.

Kaluku BUNGALOWS $
(☑636 421; bungalows 420,000Rp; ✸) Smart new place with seven posh A-frame bungalows, each with ocean views, TV, fridge and cool outdoor bathrooms. They're managed by Blue Marlin Dive Centre.

Corner Bungalows BUNGALOWS $
(☑0819 731 9200; bungalows 400,000Rp) Five large bungalows, each with bamboo furniture, mosquito nets and a large front deck with a hammock. They go for as little as 150,000Rp in the low season.

Vila Bulan Madu LUXURY BUNGALOWS $$$
(☑0819 0733 0444; www.bulan-madu.com; bungalows from €130; ✸) ⚲) Commodious bungalows that offer real comfort, though the decor is a little dated. Each has a very pretty front garden. A pool and restaurant are planned.

Sunrise Hotel BUNGALOWS $
(☑642 370; bungalows 300,000-400,000Rp) Two-storey lumbung-style thatched bungalows with outdoor living rooms set well back from the beach.

Abdi Fantastik BUDGET BUNGALOWS $
(☑636 421; r 200,000Rp) Simple thatched bungalows that enjoy a prime seafront location.

Gili Air Santay BUNGALOWS $
(☑0818 0375 8695; www.giliair-santay.com; d 280,000-550,000Rp) Austrian-Indo-owned place with traditional bungalows in a quiet coconut grove. A little overpriced.

✖ Eating

Most places on Gili Air are locally owned and offer an unbeatable setting for a meal, with tables right over the water facing Lombok's Gunung Rinjani. Standards don't vary that much. A few smarter Western-owned alternatives have opened in recent years.

Wiwin Café INDONESIAN $
(dishes 15,000-45,000Rp) A great choice for local dishes: grilled fish with yellow sauce, seafood fried-rice, gado gado or *cha kangkung* (water spinach) are all excellent. Has the most extensive veggie menu on the island (try the young papaya curry). Service is attentive and there's a nice bar area too.

Scallywags INTERNATIONAL $$
(☑639 434; meals from 40,000Rp; ⚲) Set on the island's best strip of sand, Scallywags is a Western-owned restaurant that offers what the other places don't: casual, yet elegant decor, polished glassware, switched-on service, free wi-fi and superb cocktails (though bland background music). The menu features amazing seafood – fresh lobster, tuna steaks, snapper and swordfish – plus sandwiches (British beef), a great salad bar, steaks and sweets.

Ali Baba INDONESIAN $
(dishes 10,000-50,000Rp) Beachside warung decorated with wacky sea- and coconut-shell sculpture. It serves up Indonesian and Western fare in a tranquil setting right by the waves.

Biba ITALIAN $$
(☑0819 1727 4648; meals from 50,000Rp) Book a table on the sand here for a memorable, romantic setting. Biba is Italian-owned and the delicious, filling pizzas and pasta are gloriously authentic.

Tami's Neverland CAFE $
(meals from 35,000Rp) A large bamboo space on the beach, this place serves hearty Western and Indo grub at fair prices: sandwiches, barbecued fish, burgers, steaks as well as curries and *cap cai* (stir-fried veggies).

Also good:

Munchies INDONESIAN $
(dishes 7500-26,000Rp) Come here for barbecued seafood, overflowing sandwiches and Sasak curries.

Gusung Indah INDONESIAN $
(dishes 15,000-40,000Rp) Scores for local food such as *opor ayam* (braised chicken in coconut milk), sandwiches or pasta.

🍷 Drinking

Gili Air is usually a mellow place, but there are occasional beach parties and things rev up a notch in high season.

Zipp Bar
BEACH BAR

Gili Air's premier drinking den, this large bar has tables dotted around a great beach setting and an excellent booze selection (try the fresh-fruit cocktails). Also serves up decent grub (try the fish of the day) and hosts a beach party every full moon.

Legend Pub
MUSIC BAR

Painted the requisite Rasta colours of red, green and gold, this reggae bar has a large dance party every dark moon.

Mirage
MUSIC BAR

The place to be on Friday, when there's live music, drinks specials and a sea of smiling faces.

Shopping

There's very little retail action on Gili Air. Check out the **Art Shop** behind the harbour for wooden masks. **Coconut Handicraft** stocks lovely coconut-shell necklaces, rings, bowls and cups.

Information

The Blue Marlin Dive Centre charges 8% for cash advances on credit cards. There's a **clinic** in the village for medical services.

Ozzy's Shop (✆622 179) Internet, telephone and money exchange.

Perama (✆637 816) Reliable travel agency.

Understand
〉 Bali & Lombok

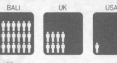

population per sq km

BALI UK USA

♟ ≈ 32 people

Bali & Lombok Today

» Population: Bali 3.6 million; Lombok 3 million

» Percentage of Bali's land used for rice production: 20%

» Average monthly wage of a tourism worker: US$70-150

» Down payment on motorbike purchase: US$30

» New motorbikes registered each month: 5000

» Area: Bali 5620 sq km; Lombok 5435 sq km

'This nation of artists is faced with a Western invasion, and I cannot stand idly by and watch its destruction.' A filmmaker, Andre Roosevelt, wrote this in 1930. Yet somehow the Balinese have always found a way to stay true to themselves, whether in the face of invasions from Java or volcanoes blowing their lid, or while welcoming two million visitors annually. Who can question the ingenuity of people who fly kites so they can have fun *and* talk to the gods?

Although concerns that Balinese culture is imperilled by tourism have been heard since Roosevelt's time (when visitors numbered fewer than 1000 yearly), the fears may finally be gaining wide traction with visitor numbers soaring into the millions.

Too Much of a Good Thing?

Although it's a problem far from unique to Bali, unconstrained development threatens some of the very qualities that make Bali a wonderful place to visit. The coast is especially vulnerable. In 2000, for example, rice fields extended north from Seminyak all the way to Pura Tanah Lot. Today this landscape is dotted with villas, illustrating the scope of the issue.

With the rice fields of Bali succumbing to development by 700 to 1000 hectares a year, solutions will be needed soon before the villa-spotted fields of Kerobokan and Canggu become the norm. These solutions may pose very hard questions for the Balinese, though, with the average youth now preferring a better-paying job in tourism over one that comes with the back-breaking conditions of the rice fields. Who would work the rice farms that are saved? And who would deny the farmers, who have never had anything, the money their land can bring them?

Top Books

» **Eat, Pray, Love** Hate it or love it, this best-seller lures thousands to Bali every year, hoping to capture something in Elizabeth Gilbert's prose.

» **Dragons in the Bath: Tales from Rural Bali** Cat Wheeler's accounts of daily life in Ubud ring more true than other recent books.

» **Island of Demons** A who's who of local luminaries in the 1930s, this novel focuses on Ubud expat artist Walter Spies. Nigel Barley brings to life a critical moment in Bali's past.

Top Downloads

Gamelan music is hypnotic, addictive and thoroughly Bali. The following are part of a best-of collection you can get from iTunes:

» 'Sekaha Ganda Sari Bona Kecak'

» 'Sadha Budaya Gamelan Gong'

» 'Gender Wayang Sukawati Sulendro'

belief systems
(% of population)

92
Hindu

6
Muslim

2
Other

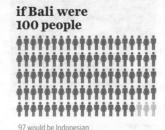

97 would be Indonesian
3 would be other

And Not a Drop to Drink

Warning signs of overcrowding and overdevelopment are everywhere. It's easy to dismiss the failing electrical grid as the expected outcome of a Third-World power supply with First-World demands, but the reality is that electrical consumption is going up faster than anyone predicted.

More ominous are the water shortages. On an island whose self image is based on bounteous, free-flowing water, it was a shock when 73 of Bali's normally always-flowing rivers ran dry during the extended dry season of 2009. Huge demands, from golf courses on the semi-arid Bukit Peninsula to all those villas with plunge pools, have stressed a supposedly bottomless resource. And climate change hasn't helped. (You can do your bit by following the advice on p359 and by patronising businesses highlighted in this book with the sustainable icon.)

Embracing Change

Every time you discover a tiny offering – even just an incense stick still smoking outside your hotel room – you're reminded that the Balinese get it. They never underestimate their power to flourish within the vicissitudes of modern life. That offering would have been in a small shrine amid rice 100 years ago; today the complex and rich belief system behind it has adapted to the current realities.

Responding to the south's horrible traffic congestion (which hits its nadir at the roundabout east of Kuta where the bypass road meets Sunset Rd), local religious leaders decided that outright opposition to 'stacking people' in a freeway overpass was wrong, because forcing people to sit in traffic was a greater indignity. How Bali will respond to ever-greater indignities is the question of the century.

And you're from?

Visitors to Bali in descending order:

» Australia (25% of arrivals, mate)
» Japan
» China
» Malaysia
» South Korea
» Taiwan
» France
» UK
» Netherlands
» Germany
» USA
» ...and the rest

Top Fruits

» **Mangosteen** It looks like a leathery ball, but inside are luscious sweet segments.

» **Langsat** The bland beige exterior belies a sharp sweet interior.

» **Rambutan** Hairy and scary outside, sweet and juicy inside.

Go Ahead

On Bali you can:
» Accidentally tread on an offering and nobody will take offence.

» Enjoy a beer during a serious dance performance.

» Wear something stupid that would get hoots at home.

» Find inner happiness through the sound of rice growing.

» Buy a souvenir so silly that you'll later claim it was slipped into your bag.

» Discover a culture unlike any you've known.

History

When Islam swept through Bali's neighbour Java at the beginning of the 12th century, the kings and courtiers of the embattled Hindu Maja-pahit kingdom began crossing the straits into Bali, making their final exodus in 1478. The priest Nirartha brought many of the complexities of the Balinese Hindu religion to the island, and established offshore temples, including Rambut Siwi, Tanah Lot and Ulu Watu.

From the early 1700s the Balinese sought to control Lombok with varying success until replaced by the Dutch for good in 1894.

Meanwhile in the 19th century the Dutch began to form alliances with local princes in north Bali. A dispute over the ransacking of wrecked ships was the pretext for the 1906 Dutch invasion of the south, which climaxed in a suicidal *puputan* (fight to the death). The Denpasar nobility burnt their own palaces and marched straight into the Dutch guns. Other rajahs soon capitulated, and Bali became part of the Dutch East Indies.

In later years Balinese culture was actually encouraged by many Dutch officials. International interest was aroused and the first Western tourists arrived.

After WWII the struggle for national independence was fierce in Bali. Independence was declared on 17 August 1945 (still celebrated as Independence Day), but power wasn't officially handed over until 27 December 1949, when the Dutch finally gave up the fight. The island languished economically in the early years of Indonesian sovereignty, but Bali's greatest national resource, beauty, was subsequently marketed to great effect.

The tourism boom, which started in the early 1970s, has brought many changes, and has helped pay for improvements in roads, telecommunications, education and health. Though tourism has had some marked adverse environmental and social effects, Bali's unique culture has proved to be remarkably resilient.

TIMELINE	**50 million BC**	**2000 BC**	**7th century**
	A permanent gap in the Earth's crust forms between Asia and Australia. The Wallace Line keeps Australian species from crossing to Bali until the invention of cheap Bintang specials.	A Balinese gentleman passes away. One of the first known inhabitants of the island, he rests peacefully until his bones are found and placed on display in Gilimanuk.	Indian traders bring Hinduism to Bali. Little is known about what was traded, although some speculate that they left with lots of wooden carvings of penises and bootleg *lontar* books.

The First Balinese

There are few traces of Stone Age people in Bali, although it's certain that the island was populated very early in prehistoric times – fossilised humanoid remains from neighbouring Java have been dated to as early as 250,000 years ago. The earliest human artefacts found in Bali are stone tools and earthenware vessels dug up near Cekik in west Bali, estimated to be 3000 years old. Discoveries continue, and you can see exhibits of bones that are estimated to be 4000 years old at the Museum Situs Purbakala Gilimanuk. Artefacts indicate that the Bronze Age began in Bali before 300 BC.

Little is known of Bali during the period when Indian traders brought Hinduism to the Indonesian archipelago, although it is thought it was embraced on the island by the 7th century AD. The earliest written records are inscriptions on a stone pillar near Sanur, dating from around the 9th century; by that time, Bali had already developed many similarities to the island you find today. Rice, for example, was grown with the help of a complex irrigation system, probably very like the one employed now (p327), and the Balinese had already begun to develop their rich cultural and artistic traditions.

If little is known about the earliest inhabitants of Bali, then even less is known about Lombok until about the 17th century. Early inhabitants are thought to have been Sasaks from a region encompassing today's India and Myanmar.

Oldest Sites

» Goa Gajah
» Gunung Kawi
» Tirta Empul
» Stone Pillar, Sanur

Hindu Influence

Java began to spread its influence into Bali during the reign of King Airlangga (1019–42), or perhaps even earlier. At the age of 16, when his uncle lost the throne, Airlangga fled into the forests of western Java. He gradually gained support, won back the kingdom once ruled by his uncle and went on to become one of Java's greatest kings. Airlangga's mother had moved to Bali and remarried shortly after his birth, so when he gained the throne, there was an immediate link between Java and Bali. It was at this time that the courtly Javanese language known as Kawi came into use among the royalty of Bali, and the rock-cut memorials seen at Gunung Kawi, near Tampaksiring, provide a clear architectural link between Bali and 11th-century Java.

After Airlangga's death, Bali remained semi-independent until Kertanagara became king of the Singasari dynasty in Java two centuries later. Kertanagara conquered Bali in 1284, but the period of his greatest power lasted a mere eight years, until he was murdered and his kingdom collapsed. However, the great Majapahit dynasty was founded by his son, Vijaya (or Wijaya). With Java in turmoil, Bali regained its au-

A Short History of Bali – Indonesia's Hindu Realm, by Robert Pringle, is a thoughtful analysis of Bali's history from the Bronze Age to the present, with excellent sections on the 2002 bombings and ongoing environmental woes caused by tourism and development.

9th century	1019	12th century
A stone-carver – the first of many! – creates an account in Sanskrit of now-long-forgotten military victories. Bali's oldest dated artefact proves early Hindu influence and ends up hidden in Sanur.	A future king, Airlangga, is born in Bali. He lives in the jungles of Java until he gains political power and becomes king of the two islands, unifying both cultures.	An amazing, incredible and stupendous series of 10 7m-high statues are carved from stone cliffs at Gunung Kawi north of Ubud. About 900 years later, Unesco notices...

» Shrines at Gunung Kawi

tonomy, and the Pejeng dynasty rose to great power. Temples and relics of this period can still be found near Ubud, in Pejeng.

Exit Pejeng

In 1343 the legendary Majapahit prime minister, Gajah Mada, defeated the Pejeng king Dalem Bedaulu, and Bali was brought back under Javanese influence.

Although Gajah Mada brought much of the Indonesian archipelago under Majapahit control, this was the furthest extent of their power. The 'capital' of the dynasty was moved to Gelgel, in Bali, near modern Semarapura, around the late 14th century, and this was the base for the 'king of Bali', the Dewa Agung, for the next two centuries. The Gelgel dynasty in Bali, under Dalem Batur Enggong, extended its power eastwards to the neighbouring island of Lombok and even westwards across the strait to Java.

The collapse of the Majapahit dynasty into weak, decadent petty kingdoms opened the door for the spread of Islam from the trading states of the north coast into the heartland of Java. As the Hindu states fell, many of the intelligentsia fled to Bali. Notable among these was the priest Nirartha, who is credited with introducing many of the complexities of Balinese religion to the island, as well as establishing the chain of 'sea temples', which includes Pura Luhur Ulu Watu and Pura Tanah Lot. Court-supported artisans, artists, dancers, musicians and actors also fled to Bali at this time and the island experienced an explosion of cultural activity that has not stopped to this day.

> Locks of hair from Nirartha, the great priest who shaped Balinese Hinduism in the 16th century, are said to be buried at Pura Rambit Siwi, an evocative seaside temple in west Bali.

Dutch Dealings

In 1597, Dutch seamen were among the first Europeans to appear in Bali. Setting a tradition that has prevailed to the present day, they fell in love with the island and when Cornelius de Houtman, the ship's captain, prepared to set sail from the island, two of his crew refused to come with him. At that time, Balinese prosperity and artistic activity, at least among the royalty, was at a peak, and the king who befriended de Houtman had 200 wives and a chariot pulled by two white buffalo, not to mention a retinue of 50 dwarfs, whose bodies had been bent to resemble the handle of a kris (traditional dagger). By the early 1600s, the Dutch had established trade treaties with Javanese princes and controlled much of the spice trade, but they were interested in profit, not culture, and barely gave Bali a second glance.

In 1710, the 'capital' of the Gelgel kingdom was shifted to nearby Klungkung (now called Semarapura), but local discontent was growing; lesser rulers were breaking away, and the Dutch began to move in, using the old strategy of divide and conquer. In 1846 the Dutch used

> Kuta was never a part of mainstream Bali. During royal times, the region was a place of exile for malcontents and troublemakers. It was too arid for rice fields, the fishing was barely sustainable and the shore was covered with miles of useless sand...

1292	1343	1520	1546
Bail gains complete independence from Java with the death of Kertanagara, a powerful king who had ruled the two islands for eight years. Power shifts frequently between the islands.	The legendary Majapahit prime minister, Gajah Mada, brings Bali back under Javanese control. For the next two centuries, the royal court is just south of today's Semarapura.	Java fully converts to Islam, leaving Bali in isolation as a Hindu island. Priests and artists move to Bali, concentrating and strengthening the island's culture against conversion.	The Hindu priest Nirartha arrives in Bali. He transforms religion and builds temples by the dozen, including Pura Rambut Siw, Pura Tanah Lot and Pura Luhur Ulu Watu.

ARTISTS IN CHARGE

The lasting wholesale change to Balinese life because of the mass exodus of Hindu elite from Javanese kingdoms in the 16th century cannot be overstated. It's as if all the subscribers to the opera were put in charge of a town – suddenly there would be a lot more opera. The Balinese had already shown a bent for creativity but once the formerly Javanese intelligentsia exerted control, music, dance, art and more flowered like the lotus blossoms in village ponds. High status was accorded to villages with the most creative talent, a tradition that continues today.

This flair for the liberal arts found a perfect match in the Hinduism that took full hold then. The complex and rich legends of good and evil spirits found ample opportunity to flourish, such as the legend of Jero Gede Macaling, the evil spirit of Nusa Penida (p130).

Balinese salvage claims over shipwrecks as a pretext to land military forces in northern Bali, bringing the kingdoms of Buleleng and Jembrana under their control. Their cause was also aided by the various Balinese princes who had gained ruling interests on Lombok and were distracted from matters at home, and also unaware that the wily Dutch would use Lombok against Bali.

In 1894, the Dutch, the Balinese and the people of Lombok collided in battles that would set the course of history for the next several decades. See the boxed text, p314.

With the north of Bali long under Dutch control and the conquest of Lombok successful, the south was never going to last long. Once again, it was disputes over the ransacking of wrecked ships that gave the Dutch an excuse to move in. In 1904, after a Chinese ship was wrecked off Sanur, Dutch demands that the rajah (lord or prince) of Badung pay 3000 silver dollars in damages were rejected and in 1906 Dutch warships appeared at Sanur.

For much of the 19th century, the Dutch earned enormous amounts of money from the Balinese opium trade. Most of the colonial administrative budget went to promoting the opium industry, which was legal until the 1930s.

Balinese Suicide

The Dutch forces landed despite Balinese opposition and, four days later, had marched 5km to the outskirts of Denpasar. On 20 September 1906, the Dutch mounted a naval bombardment of Denpasar and began their final assault. The three princes of Badung realised that they were completely outnumbered and outgunned, and that defeat was inevitable. Surrender and exile, however, would have been the worst imaginable outcome, so they decided to take the honourable path of a suicidal *puputan*. First the princes burned their palaces, and then, dressed in their finest jewellery and waving ceremonial golden kris, the rajah led

» Pura Tanah Lot

1579

Sir Francis Drake, while looking for spice, is thought to be Bali's first European visitor. However his postcard home is lost permanently so proof is elusive.

1580

The Portuguese also come sniffing around for spice but in a foreshadowing of today's surfers, they wipe out on rocks at Ulu Watu and give up.

the royalty, priests and courtiers out to face the modern weapons of the Dutch.

The Dutch implored the Balinese to surrender rather than make their hopeless stand, but their pleas went unheeded and wave after wave of the Balinese nobility marched forward to their death, or turned their kris on themselves. In all, nearly 4000 Balinese died. The Dutch then marched northwest towards Tabanan and took the rajah of Tabanan prisoner – he also committed suicide rather than face the disgrace of exile.

The kingdoms of Karangasem (the royal family still lives in the palaces of Amlapura) and Gianyar had already capitulated to the Dutch and were allowed to retain some of their powers, but other kingdoms were defeated and their rulers exiled. Finally, in 1908, the rajah of Semarapura followed the lead of Badung, and once more the Dutch faced a *puputan*. As had happened at Cakranegara on Lombok, the

THE BATTLE FOR LOMBOK

In 1894, the Dutch sent an army to back the Sasak people of eastern Lombok in a rebellion against the Balinese rajah (lord or prince) who controlled Lombok with the support of the western Sasak. The rajah quickly capitulated, but the Balinese crown prince decided to fight on.

The Dutch camp at the Mayura Water Palace was attacked late at night by a combined force of Balinese and western Sasak, forcing the Dutch to take shelter in a temple compound. The Balinese also attacked another Dutch camp further east at Mataram, and soon, the entire Dutch army on Lombok was forced back to Ampenan where, according to one eyewitness, the soldiers 'were so nervous that they fired madly if so much as a leaf fell off a tree'. These battles resulted in enormous losses of men and arms for the Dutch.

Although the Balinese had won the first battles, they had begun to lose the war. They faced a continuing threat from the eastern Sasak, while the Dutch were soon supported with reinforcements from Java.

The Dutch attacked Mataram a month later, fighting street-to-street against Balinese and western Sasak soldiers and civilians. The Balinese crown prince was killed, and the Balinese retreated to Cakranegara (Cakra). Rather than surrender, Balinese men, women and children opted for the suicidal *puputan* (a warrior's fight to the death) and were cut down by rifle and artillery fire. Their stronghold, the Mayura Water Palace, was largely destroyed.

In late November 1894, the Dutch attacked Sasari and, again, a large number of Balinese chose the *puputan*. With the downfall of the dynasty, the local population abandoned its struggle against the Dutch. The conquest of Lombok, considered for decades, had taken the Dutch barely three months.

beautiful palace at Semarapura, Taman Kertha Gosa, was largely destroyed.

With this last obstacle disposed of, all of Bali was under Dutch control and became part of the Dutch East Indies. There was little development of an exploitative plantation economy in Bali, and the common people noticed little difference between Dutch rule and the rule of the rajahs. On Lombok, conditions were harder, as new Dutch taxes took a toll on the populace.

WWII

In 1942, the Japanese landed unopposed in Bali at Sanur (most Indonesians saw the Japanese, at first, as anticolonial liberators). The Japanese established headquarters in Denpasar and Singaraja, and their occupation became increasingly harsh for the Balinese. When the Japanese left in August 1945 after their defeat in WWII, the island was suffering from extreme poverty. The occupation had fostered several paramilitary, nationalist and anticolonial groups that were ready to fight the returning Dutch.

With staff reviews, hard-to-find titles and stellar recommendations, *the* place for books about Bali is Ganesha Books in Ubud. The website (www.ganeshabooks bali.com) offers a vast selection and the shop does mail orders.

Independence

In August 1945, just days after the Japanese surrender, Sukarno, the most prominent member of the coterie of nationalist activists, proclaimed the nation's independence. It took four years to convince the Dutch that they were not going to get their great colony back. In a virtual repeat of the *puputan* nearly 50 years earlier, Balinese freedom fighters led by the charismatic Gusti Ngurah Rai (namesake of the airport) were wiped out by the Dutch in the battle of Marga in western Bali (p244) on 20 November 1946. The Dutch finally recognised Indonesia's independence in 1949 – though Indonesians celebrate 17 August 1945 as their Independence Day.

At first, Bali, Lombok and the rest of Indonesia's eastern islands were grouped together in the unwieldy province of Nusa Tenggara. In 1958 the central government recognised this folly and created three new governmental regions from the one, with Bali getting its own and Lombok becoming part of Nusa Tenggara Barat.

A woman of many aliases, K'tut Tantri breezed into Bali from Hollywood in 1932. After the war, she joined the Indonesian Republicans in their postwar struggle against the Dutch. As Surabaya Sue, she broadcast from Surabaya in support of their cause. Her book, *Revolt in Paradise*, was published in 1960.

Coup & Backlash

Independence was not an easy path for Indonesia to follow. When Sukarno assumed more direct control in 1959 after several violent rebellions, he proved to be as inept as a peacetime administrator as he was inspirational as a revolutionary leader. In the early 1960s, as Sukarno faltered, the army, communists, and other groups struggled for supremacy. On 30 September 1965, an attempted coup – blamed on the

1856	1891–94	1908	1912
Mads Lange, a Danish trader, dies mysteriously in Kuta after earning a fortune selling goods to ships anchored off the beach. His death is blamed on poisoning by jealous rivals.	Years of failed Sasak rebellions in eastern Lombok finally take hold after a palace burning. With Dutch assistance the Balinese rulers are chased from the island within three years.	The Balinese royalty commit suicide. Wearing their best dress and armed with 'show' daggers, they march into Dutch gunfire in a suicidal *puputan* or 'warrior's death' in Klungkung.	A German, Gregor Krause, photographs beautiful Balinese women topless. WWI intervenes, but in 1920 an 'art book' of photos appears and Dutch steamers docking in Singaraja now bring tourists.

Partai Komunis Indonesia (PKI, or Communist Party) – led to Sukarno's downfall. General Suharto emerged as the leading figure in the armed forces, displaying great military and political skill in suppressing the coup. The PKI was outlawed and a wave of anticommunist massacres followed throughout Indonesia.

In Bali, the events had an added local significance as the main national political organisations, the Partai Nasional Indonesia (PNI, Nationalist Party) and the PKI, crystallised existing differences between traditionalists, who wanted to maintain the old caste system, and radicals, who saw the caste system as repressive and were urging land reform. After the failed coup, religious traditionalists in Bali led

THE TOURIST CLASS

Beginning in the 1920s, the Dutch government realised that Bali's unique culture could be marketed internationally to the growing tourism industry. Relying heavily on images that emphasised the topless habits of Bali's women, Dutch marketing drew wealthy Western adventurers, who landed in the north at today's Singaraja and were whisked about the island on rigid three-day itineraries that featured canned cultural shows at a government-run tourist hotel in Denpasar. Accounts from the time are ripe with imagery of supposedly culture-seeking Europeans who really just wanted to see a boob or two. Such desires were often thwarted by Balinese women who covered up when they heard the Dutch jalopies approaching.

But some intrepid travellers arrived independently, often at the behest of members of the small colony of Western artists, such as Walter Spies in Ubud. Two of these visitors were Robert Koke and Louise Garret, an unmarried American couple who had worked in Hollywood before landing in Bali in 1936 as part of a global adventure. Horrified at the stuffy strictures imposed by the Dutch tourism authorities, the pair (who were later married) built a couple of bungalows out of palm leaves and other local materials on the otherwise deserted beach at Kuta, which at that point was home to only a few impoverished fishing families.

Word soon spread, and the Kokes were booked solid. Guests came for days, stayed for weeks and told their friends. At first, the Dutch dismissed the Kokes' Kuta Beach Hotel as 'dirty native huts', but soon realised that increased numbers of tourists were good for everyone. Other Westerners built their own thatched hotels, complete with the bungalows that were to become a Balinese cliché in the decades ahead.

WWII wiped out both tourism and the hotels (the Kokes barely escaped ahead of the Japanese), but once people began travelling again after the war, Bali's inherent appeal made its popularity a foregone conclusion.

In 1987, Louise Koke's long-forgotten story of the Kuta Beach Hotel was published as *Our Hotel in Bali,* illustrated with her incisive sketches and her husband's photographs.

1925	1936	1945	1946
The greatest modern Balinese dancer, Mario, first performs the Kebyar Duduk, his enduring creation. From a stooped position, he moves as if in a trance to the haunting melody of gamelan.	Americans Robert and Louise Koke build a hotel of thatched bungalows on then-deserted Kuta Beach. Gone is stuffy, starched tourism, replacing it is fun in the sun followed by a drink.	Following the Japanese surrender, nationalists, Sukarno among them, proclaim independence from the Netherlands.	Freedom fighter Ngurah Rai dies with the rest of his men at Marga. But this *puputan* slays the Dutch colonial spirit, and soon Indonesia is independent.

the witch-hunt for the 'godless communists'. Eventually, the military stepped in to control the anticommunist purge, but no one in Bali was untouched by the killings, estimated at between 50,000 and 100,000 out of a population of about two million, a percentage many times higher than on Java. Many tens of thousands more died on Lombok.

The 1963 Eruption

Amid the political turmoil, the most disastrous volcanic eruption in Bali in 100 years took place in 1963. Gunung Agung blew its top in no uncertain manner, at a time of considerable prophetic and political importance.

Eka Dasa Rudra, the greatest of all Balinese sacrifices and an event that takes place only every 100 years on the Balinese calendar, was to culminate on 8 March 1963. It had been well over 100 Balinese years since the last Eka Dasa Rudra, but there was dispute among the priests as to the correct and most favourable date.

Naturally, Pura Besakih was a focal point for the festival, but Gunung Agung was acting strangely as final preparations were made in late February. Despite some qualms, political pressures forced the ceremonies forward, even as ominous rumblings continued.

On 17 March, Gunung Agung exploded. The catastrophic eruption killed more than 1000 people (some estimate 2000) and destroyed entire villages – 100,000 people lost their homes. Streams of lava and hot volcanic mud poured right down to the sea at several places, completely covering roads and isolating the eastern end of Bali for some time. Driving the main road near Tulamben you can still see some lava flows.

Suharto Comes & Goes

Following the failed coup in 1965 and its aftermath, Suharto established himself as president and took control of the government. Under his 'New Order' government, Indonesia looked to the West for its foreign and economic policies.

Politically, Suharto ensured that his political party, Golkar, with strong support from the army, became the dominant political force. Other political parties were banned or crippled. Regular elections maintained the appearance of a national democracy, but until 1999, Golkar won every election hands down. This period was also marked by great economic development in Bali and later on Lombok as social stability and maintenance of a favourable investment climate took precedence over democracy. Huge resorts – often with investors in government – appeared in Sanur, Kuta and Nusa Dua during this time.

In early 1997, the good times ended as Southeast Asia suffered a severe economic crisis, and within the year, the Indonesian currency (the rupiah) had all but collapsed and the economy was on the brink of bankruptcy.

Bali's airport is named for I Gusti Ngurah Rai, the national hero who died leading the resistance against the Dutch at Marga in 1946. The text of a letter he wrote in response to Dutch demands to surrender ends with 'Freedom or death!'

For a different take on Bali, read Geoffrey Robinson's enlightening revisionist history *Bali, The Dark Side of Paradise*. He explores the iron Balinese will, which is often lost on outsiders who see only rice farmers and artisans.

1949

South Pacific, the musical, opens on Broadway and the song 'Bali Hai' fixes a tropical cliché of Bali in the minds of millions (even though it's based on Fiji).

1963

The sacred volcano Gunung Agung erupts, taking out a fair bit of east Bali, killing a thousand or more and leaving 100,000 homeless. The disastrous effects still echo decades later.

» Statue of Ngurah Rai

Bali Blues, by Jeremy Allan, tells of the struggle by locals to survive in Kuta during the year following the 2002 terrorist attacks. Using composite characters, it explores a side of Bali rarely seen by tourists.

Unable to cope with the escalating crisis, Suharto resigned in 1998, after 32 years in power. His protégé, Dr Bacharuddin Jusuf Habibie, became president. Though initially dismissed as a Suharto crony, he made the first notable steps towards opening the door to real democracy, such as freeing the press from government supervision.

Peace Shattered

In 1999 Indonesia's parliament met to elect a new president. The frontrunner was Megawati Sukarnoputri, who was enormously popular in Bali, partly because of family connections (her paternal grandmother was Balinese) and partly because her party was essentially secular (the mostly Hindu Balinese are very concerned about any growth in Muslim fundamentalism). However, Abdurrahman Wahid, the moderate, intellectual head of Indonesia's largest Muslim organisation, emerged as president.

Outraged supporters of Megawati took to the streets. In Bali, the demonstrations were typically more disruptive than violent and the election of Megawati as vice-president quickly defused the situation.

On Lombok, however, religious and political tensions spilled over in early 2000 when a sudden wave of attacks starting in Mataram burned

THE BALI BOMBINGS

On Saturday, 12 October 2002, two bombs exploded on Kuta's bustling Jl Legian. The first blew out the front of Paddy's Bar. A few seconds later, a far more powerful bomb obliterated the Sari Club.

The number of dead, including those unaccounted for, exceeded 200, although the exact number will probably never be known. Many injured Balinese made their way back to their villages, where, for lack of decent medical treatment, they died.

Indonesian authorities eventually laid the blame for the blasts on Jemaah Islamiyah, an Islamic terrorist group. Dozens were arrested and many were sentenced to jail, including three who received the death penalty (which was carried out in November 2008). But most received relatively light terms, including Abu Bakar Bashir, a radical cleric who many thought was behind the explosions. His convictions on charges relating to the bombings were overturned by the Indonesian supreme court in 2006, enraging many in Bali and Australia.

On 1 October 2005, three suicide bombers blew themselves up: one in a restaurant on Kuta Sq and two more at beachfront seafood cafes in Jimbaran. It was again the work of Jemaah Islamiyah, and although documents found later stated that the attacks were targeted at tourists, 15 of the 20 who died were Balinese and Javanese employees of the places bombed.

In 2008 Bashir formed a new group that is suspected of ties to hotel bombings in Jakarta in 2009. In 2010 he was arrested on new terrorism charges.

1960s	1965	1970	1972
The lengthening of the airport runway for jets, reasonably affordable tickets and the opening of the Bali Beach Hotel in Sanur mark the start of mass tourism.	Indonesia's long-running rivalry between communists and conservatives erupts after a supposed coup attempt by the former. The latter triumph and in the ensuing purges, tens of thousands are killed in Bali.	A girl ekes out a living selling candy in Kuta. Surfers offer advice, she posts a menu, then she builds a hut and calls it Made's Warung. She prospers.	Filmmaker Alby Falzon brings a band of Australians to Bali for his surfing documentary *Morning on Earth*, which proves seminal for a generation of Australians who head to Kuta.

Chinese and Christian businesses and homes across the island. The impact on tourism was immediate and severe, and the island is only now emerging from this shameful episode.

A Balinese Makes Good

After 21 months of growing ethnic, religious and regional conflicts, parliament had enough ammunition to recall Wahid's mandate and hand the presidency to Megawati.

Indonesia's cultural wars continued and certainly played a role in the October 2002 bombings in Kuta. More than 200 tourists and Balinese were killed, and hundreds more were injured. Besides the obvious enormous monetary loss (tourism immediately fell by more than half), the blasts fuelled the ever-present suspicions the Hindu Balinese hold regarding Muslims (that the Muslim Javanese are trying to muscle in on the profitable Bali scene, and the Muslims from Indonesia are, in general, looking to show prejudice against non-Muslim Balinese) and shattered the myth of isolation enjoyed by many locals. See the boxed text, p318.

Bali's history is reduced to miniature dramas with stilted dolls at the delightfully unhip Bajra Sandhi Monument in Denpasar. Meaning the 'Struggle of the People', the museum brings cartoon-like 3-D veracity to important moments in the island's history.

1979	1998	2000	2002
Australian Kim Bradley, impressed by the gnarly surfing style of locals, encourages them to start a club. Sixty do just that (good on an island where people fear the water).	Suharto, who always had close ties to Bali, resigns as president after 32 years. His family retains control of several Bali resorts, including the thirsty Pecatu Indah resort.	Indonesian rioting spreads to Lombok and hundreds of Chinese, Christian, and Balinese homes and businesses are looted and burned, particularly after a Muslim-sponsored rally to decry violence turns ugly.	Bombs in Kuta kill more than 200, many at the Sari Club. Bali's economy is crushed as tourists stay away and there is economic devastation across the island.

The Local Way of Life

The Local Spirit
Bali

Ask any traveller what they love about Bali and, most times, 'culture' – sometimes expressed as 'the people' – will top their list. Since the 1920s, when the Dutch used images of bare-breasted Balinese women to lure tourists, Bali has embodied the mystique and glamour of an exotic paradise.

For all the romanticism, there is a harsher reality. For most Balinese, as for Lombok's Sasaks, life remains a near hand-to-mouth existence, and the idea of culture can sometimes seem misplaced as overzealous touts test your patience in their efforts to make a living.

But there's also some truth to this idea of paradise. There is no other place in the world like Bali, not even in Indonesia. Being the only surviving Hindu island in the world's largest Muslim country, its distinctive culture is worn like a badge of honour by a fiercely proud people. After all, it's only a 100 years ago that 4000 Balinese royalty, dressed in their finest, walked into the gunfire of the Dutch army rather than surrender and become colonial subjects (see p313).

True, development has changed the landscape and prompted endless debates about the displacement of an agricultural society by a tourism-services industry. And the upmarket spas, clubs, boutiques and restaurants in Seminyak and Kerobokan might have you mistaking hedonism, not Hinduism, for the local religion. But scratch the surface and you'll find that Bali's soul remains unchanged.

The island's creative heritage is everywhere you look, and the harmonious dedication to religion permeates every aspect of society, underpinning the strong sense of community. There are temples in every house, office and village, on mountains and beaches, in rice fields, trees, caves, cemeteries, lakes and rivers. Yet religious activity is not limited to places of worship. It can occur anywhere, sometimes smack-bang in the middle of peak-hour traffic.

The book and movie *Eat, Pray, Love* has brought attention to Bali's traditional healers, known as *balians*. See p152 for details on these people, who play important roles in every village.

Offerings Here, Offerings There, Offerings Everywhere

No matter where you stay, you'll witness women making daily offerings around their family temple and home, and in hotels, shops and other public places. You're also sure to see vibrant ceremonies, where whole villages turn out in ceremonial dress, and police close the roads for a spectacular procession that can stretch for hundreds of metres. Men play the gamelan while women elegantly balance magnificent tall offerings of fruit and cakes on their heads.

There's nothing manufactured about what you see. Dance and musical performances at hotels are among the few events 'staged' for tourists, but they do actually mirror the way Balinese traditionally welcome visitors, whom they refer to as *tamu* (guests). Otherwise, it's just the Balinese going about their daily life as they would without spectators.

Balinese Tolerance

Luckily, the Balinese are famously tolerant of and hospitable towards other cultures, though they rarely travel themselves, such is the importance of their village and family ties, not to mention the financial cost. If anything, they're bemused by all the attention, which reinforces their pride; the general sense is, whatever we're doing, it must be right to entice millions of people to leave their homes for ours.

They're unfailingly friendly, love a chat and can get quite personal. English is widely spoken but they love to hear tourists attempt Bahasa Indonesia, or, better still, throw in a Balinese phrase such as *sing ken ken* (no worries); do this and you'll make a friend for life. They have a fantastic sense of humour and their easygoing nature is hard to ruffle. They generally find displays of temper distasteful and laugh at 'emotional' foreigners who are quick to anger.

A great resource on Balinese culture and life is www.murnis. com. Find explanations on everything from kids' names to what one wears to a ceremony, to how garments are woven.

Lombok

While Lombok's culture and language is often likened to Bali, this does neither island justice. True, Lombok's language, animist rituals and music and dance are reminiscent of the Hindu and Buddhist kingdoms that once ruled Indonesia, and of its time under Balinese rule in the 18th century. But the majority of Lombok's Sasak tribes are Muslim – they have very distinct traditions, dress, food and architecture, and have fought hard to keep them. While the Sasak peasants in western Lombok lived in relative harmony under Balinese feudal control, the aristocracy in the east remained hostile and led the rebellion with the Dutch that finally ousted their Balinese lords in the late 1800s. To this day, the Sasaks take great joy in competing in heroic trials of strength, such as the stick-fighting matches held every August near Tetebatu.

SMALL TALK

'Where do you stay?' 'Where do you come from?' 'Where are you going?' You'll hear these questions over and over from your super-friendly Balinese hosts. While Westerners can find it intrusive, it's just Balinese small talk and a reflection of their communal culture; they want to see where you fit in and change your status from stranger to friend.

Saying you're staying 'over there' or in a general area is fine, but expect follow-ups to get increasingly personal. 'Are you married?' Even if you're not, it's easiest to say you are. Next will be: 'Do you have children?' The best answer is affirmative: never say you don't want any. '*Belum*' (not yet) is also an appropriate response, which will likely spark a giggle and an 'Ah, still trying!'.

On Lombok, Sasak language does not have greetings such as 'good morning' or 'good afternoon'. Instead, they often greet each other with 'How's your family?'. Don't be surprised if a complete stranger asks about yours!

Lombok remains much poorer and less developed than Bali, and is generally more conservative. Its Sasak culture may not be as prominently displayed as Bali's Hinduism, but that can be its own reward as you peel away the layers.

A Day in the Life...

The pace of life in Bali is gloriously sloooow. So slow that before international time standards were adopted, the longest measure of time was *akejepan barong,* literally 'Barong's wink'. Since a Barong mask never winks, this is akin to saying 'don't hold your breath'. A common maxim in both Bali and Lombok is *jam karet* (rubber time).

Nothing, not even monetary gain, takes priority over community and religion. The Balinese don't work long hours, but neither do they have much time off. You may see them just hanging around a lot, but their whole lives centre on their village temple and household, within the framework of their complex Hindu calendar.

Family Ties

Through their family temple, Balinese have an intense spiritual connection to their home. As many as five generations share a Balinese home, in-laws and all. Grandparents, cousins, aunties, uncles and various distant relatives all live together. When the sons marry, they don't move out – their wives move in. Similarly, when daughters marry, they live with their in-laws, assuming household and child-bearing duties. Because of this, Balinese consider a son more valuable than a daughter. Not only will his family look after them in their old age, but he will inherit the home and perform the necessary rites after they die to free their souls for reincarnation, so they do not become wandering ghosts.

Motorbikes are an invaluable part of daily life. They carry everything from towers of bananas and rice sacks headed to the market, to whole families in full ceremonial dress on their way to the temple, to young hotel clerks riding primly in their uniforms.

KEEPING TRACK OF TIME

Wondering what day of the week it is? You may have to consult a priest. The Balinese calendar is such a complex, intricate document that it only became publicly available some 60 years ago. Even today, most Balinese need a priest or *adat* leader to interpret it in order to determine the most auspicious day for any undertaking.

The calendar defines daily life. Whether it's building a new house, planting rice, having your teeth filed or getting married or cremated, no event has any chance of success if it does not occur on the proper date.

Three seemingly incompatible systems comprise the calendar (but this being Bali that's a mere quibble): the 365-day Gregorian calendar, the 210-day *wuku* (or Pawukon) calendar, and the 12-month *caka* lunar calendar, which begins with Nyepi (p325) every March or April. In addition, certain weeks are dedicated to humans, others to animals and bamboo, and the calendar also lists forbidden activities for each week, such as getting married or cutting wood or bamboo.

Besides the date, each box on a calendar page contains the lunar month, the names of each of the 10 week 'days', attributes of a person born on that day according to Balinese astrology, and a symbol of either a full or new moon. Along the bottom of each month is a list of propitious days for specific activities, as well as the dates of *odalan* temple anniversaries – colourful festivals that visitors are welcome to attend.

In the old days, a priest consulted a *tika* – a piece of painted cloth or carved wood displaying the *wuku* cycle – which shows auspicious days represented by tiny geometric symbols. Today, many people have their own calendars, but it's no wonder the priests are still in business! See the boxed text, p326, for more on the popular commercial version of the calendar.

WHAT'S IN A NAME?

Far from being straightforward, Balinese names are as fluid as the tides. Everyone has a traditional name, but their other names often reflect events in each individual's life. They also help distinguish between people of the same name, which is perhaps nowhere more necessary than in Bali.

Traditional naming customs seem straightforward, with a predictable gender non-specific pattern to names: first-born Wayan, second-born Made, third-born Nyoman, and fourth-born Ketut. Subsequent children re-use the same set, but as many families now settle for just two children, you'll meet many Wayans and Mades. For those from the Sudra caste, these names are preceded by the title 'I' for a boy and 'Ni' for a girl. Upper-caste titles are Ida Bagus for a male and Ida Ayu for a female, followed by Co-korda, Anak Agung, Dewa or Gusti for both males and females.

Traditional names are followed by another given name – this is where parents can get creative. Some names reflect hopes for their child, as in I Nyoman Darma Putra, who's supposed to be 'dutiful' or 'good' *(dharma)*. Others reflect modern influences, such as I Wayan Radio who was born in the 1970s, and Ni Made Atom who said her parents just liked the sound of this scientific term that also had a bomb named after it.

Many are tagged for their appearance. Nyoman Darma is often called Nyoman Kopi (coffee) for the darkness of his skin compared with that of his siblings. I Wayan Rama, named after the *Ramayana* epic, is called Wayan Gemuk (fat) to differentiate his physique from his slighter friend Wayan Kecil (small).

The Dutch colonialists were so confused by the constant name-changing that they insisted each person stick to just one. The Balinese obliged, officially, but their naming customs remain an expression of their cultural identity. Today, most Balinese use formal names at school, work and when meeting strangers, and nicknames around their house and village.

A Woman's Work is Work

Men play a big role in village affairs and helping to care for children, and only men plant and tend to the rice fields. But women are the real workhorses in Bali, doing everything from manual labour jobs (you'll see them carrying baskets of wet cement or bricks on their heads) to running market stalls and almost every job in tourism. In fact, their traditional role of caring for people and preparing food means that women have established many successful shops and cafes.

In between all of these tasks, women also prepare daily offerings for the family temple and house, and often extra offerings for upcoming ceremonies; their hands are never idle. You can observe all of this and more when you stay at a classic Balinese homestay, where your room is in the family compound and everyday life goes on about you. Ubud has many homestays (see p354).

Name is the first indicator of where a Balinese person belongs in their family and society, revealing birth order and caste. Although the Balinese are easygoing and generally egalitarian, they still observe some rules of engagement defined by the ancient caste system. Those from the Sudra caste, which comprises over 90% of Balinese, use the highest form of the Balinese language when speaking to anyone from the three highest castes, composed of royalty, generals and priests.

Ceremonies & Rituals

Between the family temple, village temple and district temple, a Balinese person takes part in dozens of ceremonies every year, on top of their daily rituals. Most employers allow staff to return to their villages for these obligations, which consume a vast chunk of income and time (and although many bosses moan about this, they have little choice un-

CUSTOMS

less they wish for a staff revolt). For tourists, this means there are ample opportunities to witness ceremonial traditions.

Ceremonies are the unifying centre of a Balinese person's life and a source of much entertainment, socialisation and festivity. Each ceremony is carried out on an auspicious date determined by a priest and often involves banquets, dance, drama and musical performances to entice the gods to continue their protection against evil forces. The most important ceremonies are Nyepi (see the boxed text, p325), which includes a rare day of complete rest, and Galungan, a 10-day reunion with ancestral spirits to celebrate the victory of good over evil.

Under their karmic beliefs, the Balinese hold themselves responsible for any misfortune, which is attributed to an overload of *adharma* (evil). This calls for a *ngulapin* (cleansing) ritual to seek forgiveness and recover spiritual protection. A *ngulapin* requires an animal sacrifice and often involves a cockfight, satisfying the demons' thirst for blood.

Ceremonies are also held to overcome black magic and to cleanse a *sebel* (ritually unclean) spirit after childbirth or bereavement, or during menstruation or illness.

On top of all these ceremonies, there are 13 major rites of passage throughout every person's life. The most extravagant and expensive is the last – cremation.

Birth & Childhood

The Balinese believe babies are the reincarnation of ancestors, and honour them as such. Offerings are made during pregnancy to ensure the mini-deity's wellbeing, and after birth, the placenta, umbilical cord, blood and afterbirth water – representing the child's four 'spirit' guardian brothers – are buried in the family compound.

Newborns are literally carried everywhere for the first three months, as they're not allowed to touch the 'impure' ground until after a purification ceremony. At 210 days (the first Balinese year), the baby is blessed in the ancestral temple and there is a huge feast. Later in life, birthdays lose their significance and many Balinese couldn't tell you their age.

A rite of passage to adulthood – and a prerequisite to marriage – is the tooth-filing ceremony at around 16 to 18 years. This is when a priest files a small part of the upper canines and upper incisors to flatten the teeth. Pointy fangs are, after all, distinguishing features of dogs and demons. Balinese claim the procedure doesn't hurt, likening the sensation to eating very cold ice: it's slightly uncomfortable, but not painful.

Another important occasion for girls is their first menstrual period, which calls for a purification ceremony.

Marriage

Marriage defines a person's social status in Bali, making men automatic members of the *banjar* (see Local Rule Bali Style, p326). Balinese believe that when they come of age, it's their duty to marry and have children, including at least one son. Divorce is rare, as a divorced woman is cut off from her children.

The respectable way to marry, known as *mapadik*, is when the man's family visits the woman's family and proposes. But the Balinese like their fun and some prefer marriage by *ngrorod* (elopement or 'kidnapping'). After the couple returns to their village, the marriage is officially recognised and everybody has a grand celebration.

Death & Cremation

The body is considered little more than a shell for the soul, and upon death it is cremated in an elaborate ceremony befitting the ancestral

Traditionally, Balinese men do not cut their hair during their wives' pregnancies. This supposedly gives the baby good hair, while also giving the husband empathy for his wife's discomfort.

spirit. It usually involves the whole community, and for important people such as royalty, it can be a spectacular event involving thousands of people.

Because of the burdensome cost of even a modest cremation (estimated at around 5,000,000Rp), as well as the need to wait for an auspicious date, the deceased is often buried, sometimes for years, and disinterred for a mass cremation.

The body is carried in a tall, incredibly artistic, multi-tiered pyre on the shoulders of a group of men. The tower's size depends on the deceased's importance. A rajah or high priest's funeral may require hundreds of men to tote the 11-tiered structure.

Along the way, the group sets out to confuse the corpse so it cannot find its way back home; the corpse is considered an unclean link to the material world, and the soul must be liberated for its evolution to a higher state. The men shake the tower, run it around in circles, simulate

BALI PLAYS DEAD

Nyepi

This is Bali's biggest purification festival, designed to clean out all the bad spirits and begin the year anew. It falls around March or April according to the Hindu caka calendar, a lunar cycle similar to the Western calendar in terms of the length of the year. Starting at sunrise, the whole island literally shuts down for 24 hours. No planes may land or take off, no vehicles of any description may be operated, and no power sources may be used. Everyone, including tourists, must stay off the streets. The cultural reasoning behind Nyepi is to fool evil spirits into thinking Bali has been abandoned so they will go elsewhere.

For the Balinese, it's a day for meditation and introspection. For foreigners, the rules are more relaxed, so long as you respect the 'Day of Silence' by not leaving your residence or hotel. If you do sneak out, you will quickly be escorted back to your hotel by a stern *pecalang* (village police officer).

As daunting as it sounds, Nyepi is actually a fantastic time to be in Bali. Firstly, there's the inspired concept of being forced to do nothing. Catch up on some sleep, or if you must, read, sunbathe, write postcards, play board games...just don't do anything to tempt the demons! Secondly, there are colourful festivals the night before Nyepi.

I Go, You Go, Ogoh-Ogoh!

In the weeks prior to Nyepi, huge and elaborate papier-mâché monsters called *ogoh-ogoh* are built in villages across the island. Involving everybody in the community, construction sites buzz with fevered activity around the clock. If you see a site where *ogoh-ogoh* are being constructed, there'll be a sign-up sheet for financial support. Contribute, say, 50,000Rp and you'll be a fully fledged sponsor and receive much street cred.

On Nyepi Eve, large ceremonies all over Bali lure out the demons. Their rendezvous point is believed to be the main crossroads of each village, and this is where the priests perform exorcisms. Then the whole island erupts in mock 'anarchy', with people banging on *kulkuls (hollow tree-trunk drums),* drums and tins, letting off firecrackers and yelling *'megedi megedi!'* (get out!) to expel the demons. The truly grand finale is when the *ogoh-ogoh* all go up in flames. Any demons that survive this wild partying are believed to evacuate the village when confronted with the boring silence on the morrow.

Christians find unique parallels to Easter in all this, especially Ash Wednesday and Shrove Tuesday, with its wild Mardi Gras–like celebrations the world over.

In coming years, dates for Nyepi are 4 April 2011, 23 March 2012 and 12 March 2013.

THE LOCAL WAY OF LIFE VILLAGE LIFE

war battles, hurl water at it and generally rough-handle it, making the trip anything but a stately funeral crawl.

At the cremation ground, the body is transferred to a funeral sarcophagus reflecting the deceased's caste. Finally, it all goes up in flames and the ashes are scattered in the ocean. The soul is then free to ascend to heaven and wait for the next incarnation, usually in the form of a grandchild.

In classic Balinese fashion, respectful visitors are welcome at cremations. It's always worth asking around or at your hotel to see if anyone knows of one going on. The Ubud tourist office is a good source too.

Lombok

On Lombok, *adat* (tradition, customs and manners) underpins all aspects of daily life, especially regarding courtship, marriage and circumcision. Friday afternoon is the official time for worship, and government offices and many businesses close. Many, but not all, women wear headscarves, very few wear the veil, and large numbers work in tourism. Middle-class Muslim girls are often able to choose their own partners. Circumcision of Sasak boys normally occurs between the ages of six and 11 and calls for much celebration following a parade through their village.

The significant Balinese population on Lombok means you can often glimpse a Hindu ceremony while there; the minority Wektu Telu, Chinese and Buginese communities add to the diversity.

Village Life

Village life doesn't just take place in rural villages. Virtually every place on Bali is a village in its own way. Under its neon flash, chaos and otherworldly pleasures, even Kuta is a village; the locals meet, organise, celebrate, plan and make decisions as is done across the island. Central to this is the *banjar*, or neighbourhood organisation.

Local Rule Bali Style

Within Bali's government, the more than 3500 *banjar* wield enormous power. Comprising the married men of a given area (somewhere between 50 and 500), a *banjar* controls most community activities, whether it's planning for a temple ceremony or making important land-use decisions. Decisions are reached by consensus, and woe to a member who shirks his duties. The penalty can be fines or worse: banishment from the *banjar*. (In Bali's highly socialised society where your community is your life and identity – which is why a standard greeting is 'Where do you come from?' – banishment is the equivalent of the death penalty.)

Although women and even children can belong to the *banjar*, only men attend the meetings where important decisions are made. Women,

The Balinese tooth-filing ceremony closes with the recipient being given a delicious *jamu* (herbal tonic), made from freshly pressed turmeric, betel-leaf juice, lime juice and honey.

The Ubud tourist office is an excellent source for news of cremations and other Balinese ceremonies that occur at erratic intervals.

A GOOD DAY FOR...

Almost every Balinese home and business has a copy of the *Kalendar Cetakan* hanging on the wall. This annual publication tracks the various local religious calendars and overlays them on the 365-day Western calendar. Details are extensive. Most importantly, the calendar provides vital information on which days are most fortuitous for myriad activities, such as bull castration, building a boat, laying a foundation, drilling a well, starting a long trip and having sex. Many Balinese would not think of scheduling any activity without first checking the calendar, which can lead to inconveniences since many activities are only condoned for a few days a year (except sex, which is called for at least 10 days a month). For a full discussion of the numerous inputs that produce this calendar, see p322.

who often own the businesses in tourist areas, have to communicate through their husbands to exert their influence. One thing that outsiders in a neighbourhood quickly learn is that one does not cross the *banjar*. Entire streets of restaurants and bars have been closed by order of the *banjar* after it was determined that neighbourhood concerns over matters such as noise were not being addressed.

Rice Farming

Rice cultivation is the backbone of rural Bali's strict communal society. Traditionally, each family makes just enough to satisfy their own needs and offerings to the gods, and perhaps a little to sell at market. The island's most popular deity is Dewi Sri, goddess of agriculture, fertility and success, and every stage of cultivation encompasses rituals to express gratitude and to prevent a poor crop, bad weather, pollution or theft by mice and birds.

Subak: Watering Bali

The complexities of tilling and irrigating terraces in mountainous terrain require that all villagers share the work and responsibility. Under a centuries-old system, the four mountain lakes and criss-crossing rivers irrigate fields via a network of canals, dams, bamboo pipes and tunnels bored through rock. More than 1200 *subak* (village associations) oversee this democratic supply of water, and every farmer must belong to his local *subak*, which in turn is the foundation of each village's powerful *banjar*. It's a fascinating and democratic system; you can learn more at the Subak Museum in Tabanan (p245) or simply by following the coursing water from one field to the next.

Although Bali's civil make-up has changed with tourism from a mostly homogenous island of farmers to a heterogeneous population with diverse activities and lifestyles, the collective responsibility rooted in rice farming continues to dictate the moral code behind daily life, even in the urban centres.

Religion
Hinduism

Bali's official religion is Hindu, but it's far too animistic to be considered in the same vein as Indian Hinduism. The Balinese worship the trinity of Brahma, Shiva and Vishnu, three aspects of the one (invisible) god, Sanghyang Widi, as well as the *dewa* (ancestral gods) and village founders. They also worship gods of the earth, fire, water and mountains; gods of fertility, rice, technology and books; and demons who inhabit the world underneath the ocean. They share the Indian belief in karma and reincarnation, but much less emphasis is attached to other Indian customs. There is no 'untouchable caste', arranged marriages are very rare, and there are no child marriages.

Bali's unusual version of Hinduism was formed after the great Majapahit Hindu kingdom that once ruled Indonesia evacuated to Bali as Islam spread across the archipelago. While the Bali Aga (the 'original' Balinese) retreated to the hills in places such as east Bali's Tenganan to escape this new influence, the rest of the population simply adapted it for themselves, overlaying the Majapahit faith on their animist beliefs incorporated with Buddhist influences. A Balinese Hindu community can be found in west Lombok, a legacy of Bali's domination of its neighbour in the 19th century.

The most sacred site on the island is Gunung Agung, home to Pura Besakih and frequent ceremonies involving anywhere from hundreds to sometimes thousands of people. Smaller ceremonies are held across

Balinese culture keeps intimacy behind doors. Holding hands is not customary for couples in Bali, and is generally reserved for small children; however, linking arms for adults is the norm.

Huge decorated *penjor* (bamboo poles) appear in front of homes and line streets for ceremonies such as Galungan. Designs are as diverse as the artists who create them but always feature the signature drooping top – in honour of the Barong's tail and the shape of Gunung Agung. The decorated tips, *sampian,* are exquisite.

the island every day to appease the gods, placate the demons and ensure balance between *dharma* (good) and *adharma* (evil) forces.

Don't be surprised if on your very first day on Bali you witness or get caught up in a ceremony of some kind.

The ancient Hindu swastika seen all over Bali is a symbol of harmony with the universe. The German Nazis used a version where the arms were always bent in a clockwise direction.

Islam

Islam is a minority religion in Bali; most followers are Javanese immigrants or descendants of seafaring people from Sulawesi.

The majority of Lombok's Sasak people practise a moderate version of Islam, as in other parts of Indonesia. It was brought to the island by Gujarati merchants via the island of Celebes (now Sulawesi) and Java in the 13th century. The Sasaks follow the Five Pillars of Islam; the pillars decree that there is no god but Allah and Muhammad is His prophet, and that believers should pray five times a day, give alms to the poor, fast during the month of Ramadan and make the pilgrimage to Mecca at least once in their lifetime. However, in contrast to other Islamic countries, Muslim women are not segregated, head coverings are not compulsory, and polygamy is rare. In addition, many Sasaks still practise ancestor and spirit worship. A stricter version of Islam is beginning to emerge in east Lombok.

Black magic is still a potent force and spiritual healers known as *balian* are consulted in times of illness and strife. There are plenty of stories floating around about the power of this magic. Disputes between relatives or neighbours are often blamed on curses, as are tragic deaths.

Wektu Telu

Believed to have originated in Bayan, north Lombok, Wektu Telu is an indigenous religion unique to Lombok. Now followed by a minority of Sasaks, it was the majority religion in northern Lombok until as recently as 1965, when Indonesia's incoming president Suharto decreed that all Indonesians must follow an official religion. Indigenous beliefs such as Wektu Telu were not recognised. Many followers thus state their official religion as Muslim, while practising Wektu traditions and rituals. Bayan remains a stronghold of Wektu Telu; you can spot believers by their *sapu puteq* (white headbands) and white flowing robes.

Wektu means 'result' in Sasak and telu means 'three', and it probably signifies the complex mix of Balinese Hinduism, Islam and animism that the religion is. The tenet is that all important aspects of life are underpinned by a trinity. Like orthodox Muslims, they believe in Allah and that Muhammad is Allah's prophet; however, they pray only three

---

EARLY WAKE UP

Before hopping on the motorbike, going to work and joining the ever-more frenetic pace of modern Bali, locals still have time in the early morning to live life as it has been lived for generations. Get up with the sun, wander the streets of a village and you might see:

» Wiry tanned farmers riding ancient bicycles to their fields, or leading their ducks on foot, scythes in hand.

» Farmers sauntering home during a downpour, using enormous banana leaves as umbrellas.

» Young women making offerings around their village, tending to babies and cooking.

» Old women trudging up and down steep roads with baskets or sacks balanced on their heads, perhaps heading to market or taking snacks to their husbands in the fields.

» Children walking or cycling to school, or helping with chores in the village.

» People bathing by the side of the road, uninhibited, as they believe they are invisible while doing so.

» The biggest smiles from everyone you meet.

Bali has a well-deserved reputation for being mellow, which is all the more reason to respect your hosts, who are enormously forgiving of faux pas if you're making a sincere effort. Be aware and respectful of local sensibilities, and dress and act appropriately, especially in rural villages and at religious sites. When in doubt, let the words 'modest' and 'humble' guide you.

Dos & Don'ts

» An increasing number of younger Balinese now adopt the dress of visitors, which means you'll see shorts and skirts everywhere. Overly revealing clothing is still frowned upon though, as is wandering down the street shirtless quaffing a beer.

» Many women go topless on Bali's main beaches, but bring a top for less touristy beaches, as the Balinese are embarrassed by foreigners' gratuitous nudity.

» On Lombok, nude or topless bathing is considered very offensive anywhere.

» Don't touch anyone on the head; it's regarded as the abode of the soul and therefore sacred.

» Pass things with your right hand. Even better, use both hands.

» Beware of talking with hands on hips – a sign of contempt, anger or aggression (as displayed in traditional dance and opera).

» Beckon to someone with the hand extended and a downward waving motion. The Western method of beckoning is considered very rude.

» Don't make promises of gifts, books and photographs that are soon forgotten. Pity the poor Balinese checking their mailbox or email inbox every day.

Religious Etiquette

» If visiting a temple or mosque, cover shoulders and knees. In Bali, a *selandong* (traditional scarf) or sash plus a sarong is usually provided for a small donation.

» Women are asked not to enter temples if they're menstruating, pregnant or have recently given birth. At these times women are thought to be *sebel* (ritually unclean).

» Don't put yourself higher than a priest, particularly at festivals (eg by scaling a wall to take photos).

» Take off your shoes before entering a mosque.

times a day and honour just three days of fasting for Ramadan. Followers of Wektu Telu bury their dead with their heads facing Mecca and all public buildings have a prayer corner facing Mecca, but they do not make pilgrimages there. Similar to Balinese Hinduism, they believe the spiritual world is firmly linked to the natural; Gunung Rinjani is the most revered site.

THE LOCAL WAY OF LIFE RELIGION

Food & Drink

Bali is a splendid destination for food. The local cuisine, whether truly Balinese or drawn from the rest of Indonesia and Asia, draws from the bounty of fresh local foods and is rich with spices and flavours. At bamboo warung (simple local cafes) and top-end restaurants you can savour this fare. And for tastes further afield, you can choose from restaurants offering some of the best dining in the region.

Balinese Cuisine

Food, glorious food. Or should that be food, laborious food? Balinese cooking is a time-consuming activity, but no effort at all is required to enjoy it. That part is easy, and it's one of the best things about travelling around Bali: the sheer variety and quality of the local cuisine will have your taste buds dancing all the way to the next warung.

The fragrant aroma of Balinese cooking will taunt you wherever you go. Even in your average village compound, the finest food is prepared fresh every day. Women go to their local marketplace first thing in the morning to buy whatever produce has been brought from the farms overnight. They cook enough to last all day, diligently roasting the coconut until the smoky sweetness kisses your nose, painstakingly grinding the spices to form the perfect paste *(base)* and perhaps even making fresh fragrant coconut oil for frying. The dishes are covered on a table or stored in a glass cabinet for family members to serve themselves throughout the day.

A traditional Balinese kitchen has a wood-fired oven fuelled by bamboo or sometimes even coffee wood that creates a smoky sweetness and wonderful earthy flavour. While modern gas-powered stoves are now common, the freshness of ingredients and particular blend of spices remain defining characteristics of Balinese cuisine.

TOP FIVE RESTAURANTS

There are many, many excellent places for a memorable meal in Bali and Lombok. On any day, this list could be entirely different, the choice is so varied.

» **Bumbu Bali** (p105) Hands down the best Balinese food on the island in a traditional house set-up. Gorge on the *rijsttafel* (array of Indonesian dishes).

» **Biku** (p85) Balinese and Western cuisines merge in this beautiful cafe in an old antique store. Great desserts.

» **Damai** (p235) Organic foods from this boutique resort's own gardens are served on a hillside with sweeping views.

» **Kokomo** (p297) Fabulous seafood right on the water on Gili T.

» **Sardine** (p85) Seafood fresh from the Jimbaran market in a magical rice-field setting.

There's no better place to get acquainted with Balinese cuisine than the local market. But it's not for late sleepers. The best time to go is around 6am to 7am. If you're any later than 10am, the prime selections have been snapped up and what's left has begun to rot in the tropical climate.

Markets offer a glimpse of the variety and freshness of Balinese produce, often brought from the mountains within a day or two of being harvested, sometimes sooner. The atmosphere is lively and colourful with baskets loaded with fresh fruits, vegetables, flowers, spices, and varieties of red, black and white rice. There are trays of live chickens, dead chickens, freshly slaughtered pigs, sardines, eggs, colourful cakes, ready-made offerings and *base* (spice paste), and stalls selling *es cendol* (colourful iced coconut drink), *bubur* (rice porridge) or *nasi campur* (mixed rice) for breakfast. There are small packets of coffee, noodles and cleaning detergents, and cooking utensils made from natural materials, such as a stone spice grinder, coconut-wood spoons, coconut-shell ladles and bamboo steaming pots. There's no refrigeration, so things come in small packages and what you see is for immediate sale. Bargaining is expected.

Markets ideal for visits include the huge Pasar Badung (p119) in Denpasar, the village and fish markets (p92) in Jimbaran, and the produce market (p155) in Ubud. Market tours are usually included in cooking courses.

Six Flavours

Compared with other Indonesian islands, Balinese food is more pungent and lively, with a multitude of layers that make the complete dish. A meal will contain the six flavours (sweet, sour, spicy, salty, bitter and astringent), which promote health and vitality and stimulate the senses.

There's a predominance of ginger, chilli and coconut flavours, as well as the beloved candlenut, often mistaken for the macadamia native to Australia. The biting combination of fresh galangal and turmeric is matched by the heat of raw chillies, the complex sweetness of palm sugar, tamarind and shrimp paste, and the clean fresh flavours of lemon grass, musk lime, kaffir lime leaves and coriander seeds.

There are shades of South Indian, Malaysian and Chinese flavours, stemming from centuries of migration and trading with seafaring pioneers. Many ingredients have been introduced; the humble chilli was brought by the fearless Portuguese, the ubiquitous snake bean and bok choy by the Chinese, and the rice substitute, cassava, by the Dutch. In true Balinese style, village chefs selected the finest and most durable new ingredients and adapted them to local tastes and cooking styles.

Cooking courses are ever-more popular and are great ways to learn about Balinese food and markets. Recommended ones are in Seminyak, Tanjung Benoa and Ubud.

Revered Rice

Rice is the staple dish in Bali and Lombok and is revered as a gift of life from God (see p327). It is served generously with every meal – anything not served with rice is considered *jaja* (a snack). It acts as the medium for the various fragrant, spiced foods that accompany it, almost like condiments, with many dishes chopped finely to complement the dry, fluffy grains and for ease of eating with the hand. In Bali, this dish of steamed rice with mixed goodies is known as *nasi campur*. It's the island's undisputed 'signature' dish, eaten for breakfast, lunch and dinner.

There are as many variations of *nasi campur* as there are warung. Just like a sandwich in the West can combine any number of fillings, each warung serves its own version according to budget, taste and whatever ingredients are fresh at the market. There are typically four or five different dishes that make up a single serving, including a small

FOOD & DRINK BALINESE CUISINE

Lombok's Sasak people are predominantly Muslim, so Bali's porky plethora does not feature in their diet of fish, chicken, vegetables and rice. The fact that *lombok* means chilli in Bahasa Indonesia makes sense, as Sasaks like their food spicy; *ayam taliwang* (whole split chicken roasted over coconut husks served with tomato-chilli-lime dip) is one example.

Ares is a dish made with chilli, coconut juice and banana-palm pith; sometimes it's mixed with chicken or meat. *Sate pusut* is a delicious combination of minced fish, chicken or beef flavoured with coconut milk, garlic, chilli and other spices and wrapped around a lemon-grass stick and grilled. Three vegetarian dishes are *kelor* (hot soup with vegetables), *serebuk* (vegetables mixed with grated coconut) and *timun urap* (sliced cucumber with grated coconut, onion and garlic).

portion of pork or chicken (small because meat is expensive), fish, tofu and/or tempeh (fermented soy-bean cake), egg, various vegetable dishes and crunchy *krupuk* (flavoured rice crackers). Beef seldom features, as the Balinese believe cows are sacred. These 'side dishes' are arrayed around the centrepiece of rice and accompanied by the warung's signature sambal (paste made from chillies, garlic or shallots, and salt). The food is not usually served hot, as it has been prepared in the morning.

Sambal Joy

Cradle of Flavor is a mouth-watering treatise on Indonesian foods and cooking by James Oseland, the editor of *Saveur* magazine.

Heinz von Holzen, the chef-owner of Bumbu Bali restaurant (p105) and author of numerous books on Balinese cuisine, says many people mistakenly believe Balinese food is spicy. 'The food itself is not normally spicy, the sambal is', Heinz says. That said, the Balinese certainly like some heat, and relish a dollop of fiery sambal with every meal; you may want to taste it to gauge the temperature before ploughing in. If you're averse to spicy food, request *tanpa sambal* (without chilli paste); better for most though is *tamba* (more) *sambal!* One other note on sambal: if your request results in a bottle of the generically sweet commercial gloop, downgrade the establishment.

A Taste of Asia

Despite its name, mangosteen is not related to the mango. It is, however, a popular tropical fruit for the peach-like flavour and texture of its white centre, and is often called 'queen of fruit'.

Bali's multicultural population means many warung serve pan-Indonesian and Asian cuisine, offering a taste of different foods from across the archipelago. Common menu items are often confused with being Balinese, such as *nasi goreng* (fried rice), *mie goreng* (fried noodles), the ever-popular gado gado, which is actually from Java, and *rendang sapi* (beef curry), which is from Sumatra. There are many restaurants serving Padang fare (which originates from Sumatra) in the main tourist areas of Bali and Lombok, and Chinese food is especially common on Lombok. See the boxed text, p332, for some of Lombok's famous dishes.

Breakfast

Many Balinese save their appetite for lunch. They might kick-start the day with a cup of rich, sweet black coffee and a few sweet *jaja* at the market: colourful temple cakes, glutinous rice cakes, boiled bananas in their peels, fried banana fritters and *kelopon* (sweet-centred rice balls). Popular fresh fruits include snake fruit, named after its scaly skin, and jackfruit, which is also delicious stewed with vegetables.

The famous *bubuh injin* (black-rice pudding with palm sugar, grated coconut and coconut milk), which most tourists find on restaurant dessert menus, is actually a breakfast dish and a fine way to start the day. Another variation available at the morning market is the nutty *bubur kacang hijau* (green mung-bean pudding) fragrantly enriched by ginger and *pandanus* leaf and served warm with coconut milk. It's popular with pregnant women, as it's believed to bestow a good head of hair to the baby.

If the Balinese feel like a bigger breakfast, *nasi campur* is the standard fare they'll opt for. They may eat leftovers from the previous day while they await the fresh offerings at lunch, or grab a fresh *nasi bungkus* (takeaway meal wrapped in banana leaves or grease-proof paper) at a market stall or street cart.

The Food of Bali by Heinz von Holzen and Lother Arsana brings to life everything from *cram cam* (clear chicken soup with shallots) to *bubuh injin* (black-rice pudding). Von Holzen's books also include a forthcoming one on Balinese markets.

FOOD & DRINK BALINESE CUISINE

Lunch & Dinner

The household or warung cook usually finishes preparing the day's dishes midmorning, so lunchtime is around 11am when the food is freshest. This is the main meal of the day. Leftovers are eaten for dinner, or by tourists who awake late and do not get around to lunch until well and truly after everyone else has had their fill! Dessert is a rarity; for special occasions, it consists of fresh fruit or gelati-style coconut ice cream.

The secret to a good *nasi campur* is often in the cook's own *base*, which flavours the pork, chicken or fish, and sambal, and which may add just the right amount of heat to the meal at one place, or set your mouth ablaze at another. The range of dishes is endless. Some local favourites include *babi kecap* (pork stewed in sweet soy sauce), *ayam goreng* (fried chicken), *urap* (steamed vegetables with coconut), *lawar* (a dish not for the faint-hearted, which combines vegetables with chopped fried liver, fried entrails, a dollop of congealed pig's blood and coconut milk), fried tofu or tempeh in a sweet soy or chilli sauce, fried peanuts, salty fish or eggs, *perkedel* (fried corn cakes) and various satay made from chunks of goat meat, chicken, pork or even turtle (although there are laws against illegal turtle slaughter).

If you stay at a homestay, like the many in Ubud, you'll see family members busily preparing food throughout the day.

Reason to Celebrate

Food is not just about enjoyment and sustenance. Like everything in Balinese life, it is an intrinsic part of the daily rituals and a major part of ceremonies to honour the gods. The menu varies according to the importance of the occasion. By far the most revered dish is *babi guling* (suckling pig), presented during rites-of-passage ceremonies such as a baby's three-month blessing, an adolescent's tooth filing, or a wedding.

VEGETARIAN DREAMS

Bali is a dream come true for vegetarians. Tofu and tempeh are part of the staple diet, and many tasty local favourites just happen to be vegetarian. Try *nasi saur* (rice flavoured by toasted coconut and accompanied by tofu, tempeh, vegetables and sometimes egg), *urap* (a delightful blend of steamed vegetables mixed with grated coconut and spices), gado gado (tofu and tempeh mixed with steamed vegetables, boiled egg and peanut sauce), and *sayur hijau* (leafy green vegetables, usually *kangkung* – water spinach – flavoured with a tomato-chilli sauce).

In addition, the way *nasi campur* is served means it's easy to request no meat, instead enjoying an array of fresh stir-fries, salads and tofu and tempeh. When ordering curries and stir-fries such as *cap cay* in both Bali and Lombok, diners can usually choose meat, seafood or vegetarian.

Western-style vegetarian pasta and salads abound in most restaurants and many purely vegetarian eateries cater for vegans. Seminyak and Ubud are especially good for meat-free fare.

FAST FOOD BALI STYLE

Usually the most authentic Balinese food is found at street level (although Denpasar has some sit-down places that are excellent). Locals of all stripes gather around simple food stalls in markets and on village streets, wave down *pedagang* (mobile traders) who ferry sweet and savoury snacks around by bicycle or motorcycle, and queue for *sate* or *bakso* (Chinese meatballs in a light soup) at the *kaki-lima* carts. *Kaki-lima* translates as something five-legged and refers to the three legs of the cart and the two of the vendor, who is usually Javanese. You can see the carts winding through village streets and scurrying out of the way of buses and trucks on busy highways.

One note on health: food cooked up fresh from carts and stalls is usually fine but that which has been sitting around for a while can be dodgy at best or riddled with dubious preservatives.

Babi guling is the quintessential Bali experience. The whole pig is stuffed with chilli, turmeric, ginger, galangal, shallots, garlic, coriander seeds and aromatic leaves, basted in turmeric and coconut oil and skewered on a wooden spit over an open fire. Turned for hours, the meat takes on the flavour of the spices and the fire-pit, giving a rustic smoky flavour to the crispy crackling.

Short of being invited to a ceremonial feast, you can enjoy *babi guling* at the famous Warung Ibu Oka across from Ubud's royal palace. Other highly recommended *babi guling* specialists include Warung Dobiel in Nusa Dua and the eponymous warung in Gianyar.

> *Pedagang* (mobile traders) still carry baskets of snacks and drinks around towns, but these days they mostly use motorbikes rather than go by foot. Among the more popular are ones selling *ayam bakso* (chicken soup) made with fresh noodles.

Bebek or *ayam betutu* (smoked duck or chicken) is another ceremonial favourite. The bird is stuffed with spices, wrapped in coconut bark and banana leaves, and cooked all day over smouldering rice husks and coconut husks. Ubud is the best place to enjoy smoked duck – head to Bebek Bengil (it's actually the source for the many restaurants that offer *bebek betutu* if ordered in advance).

Often served at marriage ceremonies, *jukut ares* is a light, fragrant broth made from banana stem and usually containing chopped chicken or pork. The satay for special occasions, *sate lilit,* is a fragrant combination of good-quality minced fish, chicken or pork with lemon grass, galangal, shallots, chilli, palm sugar, kaffir lime and coconut milk. This is wrapped onto skewers and grilled. Big ceremonies will call for hundreds of *sate lilit,* which is becoming common in warung and restaurants.

This will be accompanied by towers of *sate* (satay), plaques of *sarad* (colourful rice cakes) and *nasi kuning* (pyramids of yellow rice flavoured with saffron, turmeric and ginger).

> For an exhaustive run-down of eating options in Bali, check out www.balieats.com. The listings are encyclopaedic, continually updated and many have enthusiastic reviews.

While women cook the daily food, only men are allowed to be ceremonial chefs. The action begins in the early hours, when preparations begin for a banquet of dishes that will be used as offerings to God. It's community work at its best, sometimes with hundreds of men pounding meat and grinding kilos of spices, chopping and slicing vegetables, boiling coconut milk and making hundreds of satays.

Drinks
Beer

Beer drinkers are well catered for in Bali thanks to Indonesia's ubiquitous crisp, clean national lager, Bintang. Locally produced Storm microbrews are excellent if somewhat uncommon. Bali Hai beer sounds promising, but isn't.

Wine

Wine connoisseurs had better have a fat wallet. The abundance of high-end eateries and hotels has made fine vino from the world's best regions widely available but it is whacked with hefty taxes. Medium-grade bottles from Australia go for US$50.

Of the two local producers of wine, the least objectionable is Wine of the Gods, which overcomes the import duties by bringing crushed grapes from Western Australia and processing and bottling the wine in Denpasar. Hatten Wine, based in north Bali, has gained quite a following among those who like its very sweet pink rosé.

Local Booze

At large social gatherings, Balinese men might indulge in *arak* (fermented wine made from rice or palms or...), but generally they are not big drinkers, and Lombok's majority Muslim population frowns upon alcohol consumption.

Fresh Juices

Local nonalcoholic refreshments available from markets, street vendors and some warung are colourful, tasty and even a little psychedelic without the hangover! One of Bali's most popular is *cendol,* an interesting mix of palm sugar, fresh coconut milk, crushed ice and various other random flavourings and floaties. Fresh coconut juice is enjoyed straight out of the shell through a straw at many tourist sites.

Coffee & Tea

Many Western eateries sell imported coffees and teas alongside local brands, some of which are very good. But the most expensive – and arguably most over-hyped – is Indonesia's peculiar *kopi luwak,* aka 'cat-poo coffee'. Around 200,000Rp a cup, this coffee is named after the cat-like civet *(luwak)* indigenous to Sulawesi, Sumatra and Java that feasts on ripe coffee cherries. Entrepreneurs with a nose for a gimmick collect the intact beans found in the civet's droppings and process them to produce an extra-bitter, strong brew. Tourist gift shops usually stock it, although this kind of profit means that much fakery is brewed.

Where to Eat & Drink

The most common place for dining out in Bali and Lombok is a warung, the traditional roadside eatery. There's one every few metres in major towns, and several even in small villages. They are cheap, no-frills hang-outs with a couple of well-worn bench seats and a relaxed atmosphere; you may find yourself sharing a table with strangers as you watch the world go by. The food is fresh and different at each, and

FOOD & DRINK WHERE TO EAT & DRINK

COFFEE

If you happen to be drinking coffee with a Balinese person, don't be surprised if they tip the top layer of their coffee on the ground. This is an age-old protection against evil spirits.

TOP FIVE WARUNG

The following list scratches the surface. Many more warung are listed in this book – find your own favourite.

» **Ayam Goreng Kalasan** (p119) Amazing chicken that's been marinated in a plethora of spices.

» **Cak Asm** (p119) Spotless place serving truly wonderful fare, especially seafood.

» **Nasi Ayam Kedewatan** (p158) The place for *sate lilit* (minced fish, chicken or pork satay) in a simple open-front dining room on the edge of Ubud.

» **Warung Sulawesi** (p85) Delicious dishes from across the archipelago, served in a shady family courtyard.

» **Warung Teges** (p157) Great Balinese fare loved by locals, just south of Ubud.

usually displayed in a glass cabinet at the entrance where you can create your own *nasi campur* or just order the house standard. Both Seminyak and Kerobokan are blessed in particular with numerous warung that are particularly visitor-friendly.

Otherwise your choices are pretty much boundless. There are the seaside seafood barbecues of Jimbaran and the open-air casual Balinese cafes of Denpasar. Cafes, usually with refreshing juices made with fruits direct from the market as well as excellent coffee, can be found across south Bali, Ubud and other traveller hang-outs. And restaurants, there's just too many to even categorise except to say that if your hope is for excellent food served in an evocative open-air tropical setting, you won't starve *or* be starved for choice (see p330 for a starter's list).

In this book, we've used the following price ranges in eating reviews:

Budget ($) Meals below US$7 (about 63,000Rp)
Midrange ($$) Meals from US$7 to US$20 (about 63,000Rp to 180,000Rp)
Top end ($$$) Meals over US$20 (over 180,000Rp)

Dining – or Not – Balinese Style

Eating is a solitary exercise in Bali and conversation is limited. Families rarely eat together; everyone makes up their own plate whenever they're hungry.

The Balinese eat with their right hand, which is used to give and receive all good things. The left hand deals with unpleasant sinister elements (such as ablutions). It's customary to wash your hands before eating, even if you use a spoon and fork; local restaurants always have a sink outside the restrooms. If you choose to eat the local way, use the bowl of water provided at the table to wash your hands after the meal, as licking your fingers is not appreciated.

Balinese are formal about behaviour and clothing, and it isn't polite to enter a restaurant or eat a meal half-naked, no matter how many sit-ups you've been doing or new piercings and tattoos you've acquired.

If you wish to eat in front of a Balinese, it's polite to invite them to join you, even if you know they will say 'No', or you don't have anything to offer. If you're invited to a Balinese home for a meal, your hosts will no doubt insist you eat more, but you may always politely pass on second helpings or refuse food you don't find appealing.

Every town of any size in Bali and Lombok will have a *pasar malam* (night market). You can sample a vast range of fresh offerings from warung and carts after dark.

The Arts

Bali's vibrant arts scene makes the island so much more than just a tropical destination. In the paintings, sculpture, dance and music, you will see the natural artistic talent inherent in all Balinese, a legacy of their Majapahit heritage. The artistry displayed here will stay with you long after you've moved on from the island.

But it is telling that there is no Balinese equivalent for the words 'art' or 'artist'. Until the tourist invasion, artistic expression was exclusively for religious and ritual purposes, and almost exclusively done by men. Paintings and carvings were purely to decorate temples and shrines, while music, dance and theatrical performances were put on to entertain the gods who returned to Bali for important ceremonies. Artists did not strive to be different or individual as many do in the West; their work reflected a traditional style or a new idea, but not their own personality.

That changed in the late 1920s when foreign artists began to settle in Ubud; they went to learn from the Balinese and to share their knowledge, and helped to establish art as a commercial enterprise. Today, it's big business. Ubud remains the undisputed artistic centre of the island, and artists still come from near and far to draw on its inspiration, from Japanese glass-blowers to European photographers and Javanese painters.

Galleries and craft shops are all over the island; the paintings, stone-carvings and woodcarvings are stacked up on floors and will trip you up if you're not careful. Much of it is churned out quickly, and some is comically vulgar – put that 3m vision of a penis as Godzilla in your entryway will you? – but you will also find a great deal of extraordinary work.

There are excellent crafts available on Lombok as well, including pottery in villages such as Banyumulek. There are also many good shops and galleries in Mataram and Senggigi.

The Bali Arts Festival showcases the work of thousands of Balinese each June and July in Denpasar. It is a major event that draws talent and audiences from across the island.

Dance
Bali

There are more than a dozen different dances in Bali, each with rigid choreography, requiring high levels of discipline. Most performers have learned through painstaking practice with an expert. No visit is complete without enjoying this purely Balinese art form; you will be delighted by the many styles, from the formal artistry of the Legong to crowd-pleasing antics in the Barong.

You can catch a quality dance performance at any place where there's a festival or celebration, and you'll find exceptional performances in and around Ubud (see p160 for a guide to some of the best). Performances are typically at night and can last several hours. Absorb the hypnotic music and the alluring moves of the performers and the time will, er, dance past. Admission is generally around 70,000Rp. Music, theatre and dance courses are also available in Ubud.

Women often bring offerings to a temple while dancing the Pendet, their eyes, heads and hands moving in spectacularly controlled and coordinated movements. Every flick of the wrist, hand and fingers is charged with meaning.

Balinese Dance, Drama And Music, A Guide to the Performing Arts of Bali, by I Wayan Dibia and Rucina Ballinger, is a lavishly illustrated and highly recommended in-depth guide to Bali's cultural performances.

With the short attention spans of tourists in mind, many hotels offer a smorgasbord of dances – a little Kecak, a taste of Barong and some Legong to round it off. These can be pretty abbreviated, with just a few musicians and a couple of dancers.

One thing Balinese dance is not, is static. The best troupes, like Semara Ratih in Ubud, are continually innovating.

Kecak

Probably the best-known dance for its spell-binding, hair-raising atmosphere, the Kecak features a 'choir' of men and boys who sit in concentric circles and slip into a trance as they chant and sing the 'chak-a-chak-a-chak', imitating a troupe of monkeys. Sometimes called the 'vocal gamelan', this is the only music to accompany the dance re-enactment from the Hindu epic *Ramayana,* the familiar love story about Prince Rama and his Princess Sita.

The tourist version of Kecak was developed in the 1960s. This spectacular performance is easily found in Ubud (look for Krama Desa Ubud Kaja with its 80 shirtless men chanting hypnotically) and also at the Pura Luhur Ulu Watu.

Legong

Characterised by flashing eyes and quivering hands, this most graceful of Balinese dances is performed by young girls. Their talent is so revered that in old age, a classic dancer will be remembered as a 'great Legong'.

A CLASSIC BALINESE DANCER

Besides its cultural importance, Balinese dance just may be a fountain of youth as well. Ask Nyoman Supadmi when she started teaching the art and she says '1970'. A quick mental calculation confirms that she looks at most half her age.

Lithe and lively, Nyoman has taught thousands of women the precise moves and elaborate choreography demanded by classic Balinese dances such as Legong. And the key word is classic, as she has become a major force against the dilution of the island's great dances by what she dismisses as 'modernity'.

And just what is this aberration that brings such a frown to her otherwise serene face, well she demonstrates. 'The basic moves of classic dance require enormous discipline,' she says as she slips into the rigid pose with splayed arms and wide eyes that is immediately recognisable to anyone who has seen a performance.

Continuing, she says, 'Modern is like this,' and slumps into a slouch that would do any slacker proud. Still she understands the allure of the modern. 'It's much easier to learn and people have so many distractions that they can't find the time to learn the old ways.

'My teachers emphasised the basics', says Nyoman – whose dancer mother provided her with a private tutor. 'Your hand went here and your bottom here,' a statement backed up by a seemingly simple shift of position in her chair which leaves no doubt of her meaning.

'Today people just approximate the position.'

In order to preserve classic Balinese dance, Nyoman promotes dance courses in schools for students from age five. She keeps her eye out for promising pupils, who can then be guided for the years needed to master the art. A niece is one of these stars and is now much in demand for temple ceremonies and other occasions where sponsors demand the best.

'But the best is expensive', she admits. There are the fees for large gamelan orchestras, the dancers, actors, transport, food and 'just getting people to commit the time needed to be the best'.

The Barong and Rangda dance rivals the Kecak as Bali's most popular performance for tourists. Again, it's a battle between good (the Barong) and bad (the Rangda).

The Barong is a good but mischievous and fun-loving shaggy dog-lion, with huge eyes and a mouth that clacks away to much dramatic effect. As the good protector of a village, the actors playing the Barong (who are utterly lost under layers of fur-clad costume) will emote a variety of winsome antics. But as is typical of Balinese dance, it is not all light-hearted as the Barong is a very sacred character indeed and you'll often see one in processions and rituals.

There's nothing sacred about the Barong's buddies, however. One or more monkeys attend to him and these characters often steal the show. Actors are given free rein to range wildly. The best aim a lot of high jinks at the audience, especially members who seem to be taking things a tad too seriously.

Meanwhile, the widow-witch Rangda is bad through and through. The Queen of Black Magic, the character's monstrous persona can include flames shooting out her ears, a tongue dripping fire, a mane of wild hair and huge, hanging breasts (obviously Rangda could use some time at Ubud's myriad spas).

The story features a duel between Rangda and Barong, whose supporters draw their kris (traditional dagger) and rush in to help. The long-tongued, sharp-fanged Rangda throws them into a trance though, making them stab themselves. It's quite a spectacle. Thankfully, the Barong casts a spell that neutralises the kris power so it cannot harm them.

Playing around with all that powerful magic, good and bad, requires the presence of a *pemangku* (priest for temple rituals), who must end the dancers' trance and make a blood sacrifice using a chicken to propitiate the evil spirits.

In Ubud, Barong and Rangda dance troupes have many interpretations of the dance, everything from eerie performances that will give you the shivers (until the monkeys appear) to jokey versions that could be a variety show or Brit pantomime.

Barong masks are valued objects; you can find artful examples in the village of Mas, south of Ubud.

Peliatan's famous dance troupe, Gunung Sari, often seen in Ubud, is particularly noted for its Legong Keraton (Legong of the Palace). The very stylised and symbolic story involves two Legong dancing in mirror image. They are elaborately made up and dressed in gold brocade, relating a story about a king who takes a maiden captive and consequently starts a war, in which he dies.

Sanghyang & Kekac Fire Dance

These dances were developed to drive out evil spirits from a village – Sanghyang is a divine spirit who temporarily inhabits an entranced dancer. The Sanghyang Dedari is performed by two young girls who dance a dreamlike version of the Legong in perfect symmetry while their eyes are firmly shut. Male and female choirs provide a background chant until the dancers slump to the ground. A *pemangku* (priest for temple rituals) blesses them with holy water and brings them out of the trance.

In the Sanghyang Jaran, a boy in a trance dances around and through a fire of coconut husks, riding a coconut palm 'hobby horse'. Variations of this are called the Kecak Fire Dance (or Fire and Trance Dance for tourists) and are performed in Ubud almost daily.

Other Dances

The warrior dance, the Baris, is a male equivalent of the Legong – grace and femininity give way to an energetic and warlike spirit. The highly skilled Baris dancer must convey the thoughts and emotions of a warrior first preparing for action, and then meeting the enemy: chivalry, pride, anger, prowess and, finally, regret are illustrated.

In the Topeng, which means 'pressed against the face', as with a mask, the dancers imitate the character represented by the mask. This requires great expertise because the dancer cannot convey thoughts and meanings through facial expressions – the dance must tell all.

Lombok

Lombok also has its own unique dances, but they are not widely marketed. Performances are staged in some top-end hotels and in Lenek village, known for its dance traditions. If you're in Senggigi in July, there are also dance and *gendang beleq* (big drum) performances (p284). The *gendang beleq,* a dramatic war dance also called the Oncer, is performed by men and boys who play a variety of unusual musical instruments for *adat* (traditional customs) festivals in central and eastern Lombok.

The music, lyrics and costumes of Rudat performances reveal a mixture of both Muslim and Sasak cultures. The Rudat is danced by pairs of men in black caps and jackets and black-and-white-chequered sarongs, backed by singers, tambourines and *jidur* (large cylindrical drums).

Music
Bali

Balinese music is based around an ensemble known as a gamelan, also called a *gong*. A *gong gede* (large orchestra) is the traditional form, with 35 to 40 musicians. The more ancient gamelan *selunding* is still occasionally played in Bali Aga villages like Tenganan.

The modern, popular form of a *gong gede* is *gong kebyar,* with up to 25 instruments. This melodic, sometimes upbeat and sometimes haunting percussion that often accompanies traditional dance is one of the most lasting impressions for tourists to Bali.

The prevalent voice in Balinese music is from the xylophone-like *gangsa,* which the player hits with a hammer, dampening the sound just after it's struck. The tempo and nature of the music is controlled by two *kendang* drums – one male and one female. Other instruments are the deep *trompong* drums, small *kempli* gong and *cengceng* cymbals used in faster pieces. Not all instruments require great skill, making music is a common village activity.

Many shops in south Bali and Ubud sell the distinctive gongs, flutes, bamboo xylophones and bamboo chimes; CDs are everywhere.

Lombok

The *genggong,* a performance seen on Lombok, uses a simple set of instruments, including a bamboo flute, a *rebab* and knockers. Seven musicians accompany their music with dance movements and stylised hand gestures.

Theatre

Drama is closely related to music and dance in Bali, with the sound effects and puppets' movements an important part of *wayang kulit* (leather shadow puppet) performances.

Wayang Kulit

Much more than sheer entertainment, *wayang kulit* has been Bali's candle-lit cinema for centuries, embodying the sacred seriousness of classical Greek drama. (The word drama comes from the Greek *dromenon,* a religious ritual.) The performances are long and intense – lasting six hours or more and often not finishing before sun-up.

Long before the gorilla appears (!), you know *Road to Bali* is one of the lesser 'road' movies of Bob Hope and Bing Crosby. Few last long enough to see the pair vie for the affections of 'Balinese princess' Dorothy Lamour.

An *arja* drama is not unlike *wayang kulit* puppet shows in its melodramatic plots, its offstage sound effects and its cast of easily identifiable goodies (the refined *alus*) and baddies (the unrefined *kras*). It's performed outside and a small house is sometimes built on stage and set on fire at the climax!

Originally used to bring ancestors back to this world, the show features painted buffalo-hide puppets believed to have great spiritual power, and the *dalang* (puppet master and storyteller) is an almost mystical figure. A person of considerable skill and even greater endurance, he sits behind a screen and manipulates the puppets while telling the story, often in many dialects.

Stories are chiefly derived from the great Hindu epics, the *Ramayana* and, to a lesser extent, the *Mahabharata*.

For performances in Ubud (attenuated to a manageable two hours or less), see p160.

Painting

Balinese painting is probably the art form most influenced by Western ideas and demand. Traditional paintings, faithfully depicting religious and mythological subjects, were for temple and palace decoration, and the set colours were made from soot, clay and pigs' bones. In the 1930s, Western artists introduced the concept of paintings as artistic creations that could also be sold for money. To target the tourist market, they encouraged deviance to scenes from everyday life and the use of the full palette of modern paints and tools. The range of themes, techniques, styles and materials expanded enormously, and women painters emerged for the first time.

A loose classification of styles is: classical, or Kamasan, named for the village of Kamasan near Semarapura; Ubud style, developed in the 1930s under the influence of the Pita Maha; Batuan, which started at the same time in a nearby village; Young Artists, begun post-war in the 1960s, and influenced by Dutch artist Arie Smit; and finally, modern or academic, free in its creative topics, yet strongly and distinctively Balinese.

Where to See & Buy Paintings

There is a relatively small number of creative original painters in Bali, and an enormous number of imitators. Shops, especially in south Bali, are packed full of paintings in whatever style is popular at the time – some are quite good and a few are really excellent (and in many you'll swear you see the numbers used to guide the artists under the paint).

Top museums in Ubud such as the Neka Art Museum, Agung Rai Museum of Art and the Museum Puri Lukisan showcase the best of Balinese art and some of the European influences that have shaped it. Look for the innovative work of women artists at Ubud's Seniwati Gallery.

Commercial galleries like Ubud's Neka Gallery and Agung Rai Gallery offer high-quality works; exploring the dizzying melange of galleries – high and low – makes for a fun afternoon or longer.

Richly illustrated, *The Art & Culture of Bali*, by Urs Ramseyer, is a comprehensive work on the foundations of Bali's complex and colourful artistic and cultural heritage.

Classical Painting

There are three basic types of classical painting – *langse, iders-iders* and calendars. *Langse* are large decorative hangings for palaces or temples that display *wayang* figures (which have an appearance similar to the figures used in shadow puppetry), rich floral designs and flame-and-mountain motifs. *Iders-iders* are scroll paintings hung along temple eaves. Calendars are, much as they were before, used to set dates for rituals and predict the future.

Langse paintings helped impart *adat* (traditional customs) to the ordinary people in the same way that traditional dance and *wayang kulit* puppetry do. The stylised human figures depicted good and evil, with romantic heroes like Ramayana and Arjuna always painted with small, narrow eyes and fine features, while devils and warriors were prescribed round eyes, coarse features and facial hair. The paintings tell a story in a series of panels, rather like a comic strip, and often depict scenes from the *Ramayana* and *Mahabharata*. Other themes are the Kakawins poems, and demonic spirits from indigenous Balinese folklore – see the ceilings of the Kertha Gosa (Hall of Justice) in Semarapura for an example.

A good place to see classical painting in a modern context is at the Nyoman Gunarsa Museum near Semarapura (p179), which was established to preserve and promote classical techniques.

The Pita Maha

In the 1930s, with few commissions from temples, painting was virtually dying out. European artists Rudolf Bonnet and Walter Spies, with their patron Cokorda Gede Agung Surapati, formed the Pita Maha (literally, Great Vitality) to take painting from a ritual-based activity to a commercial one. The cooperative had more than 100 members at its peak in the 1930s and led to the establishment of Museum Puri Lukisan in Ubud, the first museum dedicated to Balinese art.

The changes Bonnet and Spies inspired were revolutionary. Balinese artists such as the late I Gusti Nyoman Lempad started exploring their own styles. Narrative tales were replaced by single scenes, and romantic legends by daily life: the harvest, markets, cockfights, offerings at a temple or a cremation. These paintings were known as Ubud style.

Meanwhile, painters from Batuan retained many features of classical painting. They depicted daily life, but across many scenes – a market, dance and rice harvest would all appear in a single work. This Batuan style is also noted for its inclusion of some very modern elements, such as sea scenes with the odd windsurfer.

The painting techniques also changed. Modern paint and materials were used and stiff formal poses gave way to realistic 3-D representations. More importantly, pictures were not just painted to fit a space in a palace or a temple.

In one way, however, the style remained unchanged – Balinese paintings are packed with detail. A painted Balinese forest, for example, has branches, leaves and a whole zoo of creatures reaching out to fill every tiny space.

This new artistic enthusiasm was interrupted by WWII and Indonesia's independence struggle, and stayed that way until the development of the Young Artists' style.

The Young Artists

Arie Smit was in Penestanan, just outside Ubud, in 1956, when he noticed an 11-year-old boy drawing in the dirt and wondered what he could produce if he had the proper equipment. As the legend goes, the boy's father would not allow him to take up painting until Smit offered to pay somebody else to watch the family's ducks.

Other 'young artists' soon joined that first pupil, I Nyoman Cakra, but Smit did not actively teach them. He simply provided the equipment and encouragement, and unleashed what was clearly a strong natural talent. Today, this style of rural scenes painted in brilliant technicolour is a staple of Balinese tourist art.

I Nyoman Cakra still lives in Penestanan, still paints, and cheerfully admits that he owes it all to Smit. Other 'young artists' include I Ketut Tagen, I Nyoman Tjarka and I Nyoman Mujung.

Other Styles

There are some other variants to the main Ubud and Young Artists' painting styles. The depiction of forests, flowers, butterflies, birds and

---

A carefully selected list of books about art, culture and Balinese writers, dancers and musicians can be found at www.ganeshabooks-bali.com, the website for the excellent Ubud bookstore (with a second branch in Kerobokan).

The magazine/comic *Bog Bog*, by a Balinese cartoonist, is a satirical and humorous insight into the contrast between modern and traditional worlds in Bali. It's available in bookshops and supermarkets or online at bogbog.busythumbs.com.

other naturalistic themes, for example, sometimes called Pengosekan style, became popular in the 1960s. It can probably be traced back to Henri Rousseau, who was a significant influence on Walter Spies. An interesting development in this particular style is the depiction of underwater scenes, with colourful fish, coral gardens and sea creatures. Somewhere between the Pengosekan and Ubud styles sit the miniature landscape paintings that are popular commercially.

The new techniques also resulted in radically new versions of Rangda, Barong, Hanuman and other figures from Balinese and Hindu mythology. Scenes from folk tales and stories appeared, featuring dancers, nymphs and love stories, with an understated erotic appeal.

Literature

The Balinese language has several forms, but the only written kind is 'high Balinese', a form of Sanskrit used for religious purposes and to recount epics such as the *Ramayana* and the *Mahabharata*. Illustrated versions of these epics, inscribed on *lontar* (specially prepared palm leaves; see p228), are Bali's earliest books.

Although exact numbers are hard to come by, it's generally agreed that Bali has Indonesia's highest literacy rate.

One of the first Balinese writers to be published in Bahasa Indonesia was Anak Agung Pandji Tisna, from Singaraja. His second novel, *The Rape of Sukreni* (1936), adapted all of the features of traditional Balinese drama: the conflict between good and evil, and the inevitability of karma. It was a popular and critical success; an English translation is available in bookshops in Bali.

An important theme of modern Balinese writing is tradition versus change and modernisation, often depicted as a tragic love story involving couples of different castes. Politics, money, tourism and relations with foreigners are also explored. There are several anthologies translated into English, some by renowned author Putu Oka Sukanta. Other writers of note include Oka Rusmini, whose book *Tarian Bumi* follows the lives of generations of Balinese women; poet and novelist Pranita Dewi; and author Gusti Putu Bawa Samar Gantang.

INFLUENTIAL WESTERN ARTISTS

Besides Arie Smit, several other Western artists had a profound effect on Balinese art in the early and middle parts of the 20th century. In addition to honouring Balinese art, they provided a critical boost to its vitality at a time when it might have died out.

» **Walter Spies** A German artist, Spies (1895–1942) first visited Bali in 1925 and moved to Ubud in 1927, establishing the image of Bali for Westerners that prevails today.

» **Rudolf Bonnet** Bonnet (1895–1978) was a Dutch artist whose work concentrated on the human form and everyday Balinese life. Many classical Balinese paintings with themes of markets and cockfights are indebted to Bonnet.

» **Miguel Covarrubias** *Island of Bali*, written by this Mexican artist (1904–57), is still the classic introduction to the island and its culture.

» **Colin McPhee** A Canadian musician, McPhee (1900–65) wrote *A House in Bali*. It remains one of the best written accounts of Bali, and his tales of music and house building are often highly amusing. His patronage of traditional dance and music cannot be overstated.

» **Adrien Jean Le Mayeur de Merpes** This Belgian artist (1880–1958) arrived on Bali in 1932 and did much to establish the notions of sensual Balinese beauty, often based on his wife, the dancer Ni Polok. Their home is now an under-appreciated museum in Sanur.

It's striking how much has been published about Bali internationally, and (until recently) how little of it has been penned by Balinese – it says much about the Western fascination with the island.

Crafts

Bali is a showroom for crafts from around Indonesia. A nicer tourist shop will sell puppets and batiks from Java, ikat garments from Sumba, Sumbawa and Flores, and textiles and woodcarvings from Bali, Lombok and Kalimantan. The kris, so important to a Balinese family, will often have been made in Java.

On Lombok, where there's never been much money, traditional handicrafts are practical items, but are still skilfully made and beautifully finished. The finer examples of Lombok weaving, basketware and pottery are highly valued by collectors.

Menagerie 4, edited by John McGlynn and I Nyoman Darma Putra, features short stories, essays and poems by Balinese and other Indonesian writers, exploring modern issues surrounding this mystical island's age-old beliefs and traditions.

Offerings & Ephemera

Traditionally, many of Bali's most elaborate crafts have been ceremonial offerings not intended to last: *baten tegeh* (decorated pyramids of fruit, rice cakes and flowers); rice-flour cookies modelled into entire scenes with a deep symbolic significance and tiny sculptures; *lamak* (long, woven palm-leaf strips used as decorations in festivals and celebrations); stylised female figures known as *cili,* which are representations of Dewi Sri (the rice goddess); or intricately carved coconut-shell wall hangings. Marvel at the care and energy that goes into constructing huge funeral towers and exotic sarcophagi, all of which will go up in flames.

Textiles & Weaving
Bali

Textiles in Bali and Lombok are woven by women for daily wear and ceremonies, as well as for gifts. They are often part of marriage dowries and cremations, where they join the deceased's soul as it passes to the afterlife.

Bali Behind the Seen: Recent Fiction from Bali, translated by Vern Cork and written by Balinese authors, conveys much of the tension between deeply rooted traditions and the irresistible pressure of modernisation.

The most common thread in Bali is the sarong, which can be used as an article of clothing, a sheet or a towel, among other things. The cheap cottons, either plain or printed, are for everyday use, and are popular with tourists for beachwear.

For special occasions such as a temple ceremony, Balinese men and women use a *kamben,* a length of *songket* wrapped around the chest. The *songket* is silver- or gold-threaded cloth, hand woven using a floating weft technique, while another variety is the *endek* (like *songket,* but with pre-dyed weft threads).

The men pair the *kamben* with a shirt and the women pair it with a *kebaya* (long-sleeved lace blouse). A separate slim strip of cloth known as a *kain* (known as *prada* when decorated with a gold leaf pattern) is wound tightly around the hips and over the sarong like a belt to complete the outfit.

Where to Buy

Any market, especially in Denpasar, will have a good range of textiles, as does Jl Arjuna in Legian. Threads of Life in Ubud is a Fair Trade–certified textiles gallery that preserves traditional Balinese and Indonesian hand-weaving skills. Factories around Gianyar in east Bali have large showrooms.

BATIK

Traditional batik sarongs, which fall somewhere between a cotton sarong and *kamben* for formality, are handmade in central Java. The dyeing process has been adapted by the Balinese to produce brightly coloured and patterned fabrics. Watch out for 'batik' that's been screen-printed. The colours will be washed out and the pattern is often only on one side (the dye in proper batik should colour both sides to reflect the belief that the body should feel what the eye sees).

IKAT

Ikat involves dyeing either the warp threads (those stretched on the loom) or weft threads (those woven across the warp) before the material is woven. The resulting pattern is geometric and slightly wavy. The colouring typically follows a similar tone – blues and greens; reds and browns; or yellows, reds and oranges. Gianyar, in east Bali, has a few factories where you can watch ikat sarongs being woven on a hand-and-foot-powered loom. A complete sarong takes about six hours to make.

The nonprofit Lontar Foundation (www.lontar.org) works to get Indonesian books translated into English so that universities around the world can offer courses in Indonesian literature.

Lombok

Lombok is renowned for traditional weaving on backstrap looms, the techniques handed down from mother to daughter. Abstract flower and animal motifs such as buffalo, dragons, crocodiles and snakes sometimes decorate this exquisite cloth. Several villages specialise in weaving cloth, while others concentrate on fine baskets and mats woven from rattan or grass. You can visit factories around Cakranegara and Mataram that produce weft ikat on old hand-and-foot-operated looms.

Sukarara and Pringgasela are centres for traditional ikat and *songket* weaving. Sarongs, Sasak belts and clothing edged with brightly coloured embroidery are sold in small shops.

Balinese Textiles, by Hauser, Nabholz-Kartaschoff & Ramseyer, is a large and lavishly illustrated guide detailing weaving styles and their significance.

Woodcarving

Woodcarving in Bali has evolved from its traditional use for doors and columns, religious figures and theatrical masks to modern forms encompassing a wide range of styles. While Tegallalang and Jati, on the road north from Ubud, are noted woodcarving centres, along with the route from Mas through Peliatan, you can find pieces in any souvenir store.

OFFERINGS: FLEETING BEAUTY

Tourists in Bali may be welcomed as honoured guests, but the real VIPs are the gods, ancestors, spirits and demons. They are presented with offerings throughout each day to show respect and gratitude, or perhaps to bribe a demon into being less mischievous.

A gift to a higher being must look attractive, so each offering is a work of art. The most common offering is a palm-leaf tray little bigger than a saucer, artfully topped with flowers, food (especially rice, and modern touches such as Ritz crackers or individually wrapped lollies) and small change, crowned with a *saiban* (temple/shrine offering). More important shrines and occasions call for more elaborate offerings, which can include the colourful towers of fruits and cakes called *baten tegeh,* and even entire animals cooked and ready to eat, as in Bali's famous *babi guling* (suckling pig).

Once presented to the gods an offering cannot be used again, so new ones are made again and again, each day, usually by women. You'll see easy-to-assemble offerings for sale in markets, much as you'd find quick dinner items in Western supermarkets.

Offerings to the gods are placed on high levels and to the demons on the ground. Don't worry about stepping on these; given their ubiquity, it's almost impossible not to (just don't try to). In fact, at Bemo Corner in Kuta offerings are left at the shrine in the middle of the road and are quickly flattened by cars. Across the island, dogs with a taste for crackers hover around fresh offerings. Given the belief that gods or demons instantly derive the essence of an offering, the critters are really just getting leftovers.

The common style of a slender, elongated figure reportedly first appeared after Walter Spies gave a woodcarver a long piece of wood and commissioned him to carve two sculptures from it. The carver couldn't bring himself to cut it in half, instead making a single figure of a tall, slim dancer.

Other typical works include classical religious figures, animal caricatures, life-sized human skeletons, picture frames, and whole tree trunks carved into ghostly 'totem poles'. In Kuta, there are various objects targeting beer drinkers: penis bottle openers (which are claimed to be Bali's best-selling souvenir) and signs to sit above your bar bearing made-to-order slogans.

Almost all carving is of local woods including *belalu*, a quick-growing light wood, and the stronger fruit timbers such as jackfruit wood. Ebony from Sulawesi is also used. Sandalwood, with its delightful fragrance, is expensive and soft and is used for some small, very detailed pieces, but beware of widespread fakery.

The website www.lombok-network.com gives details of customs on Lombok, and the arts and crafts of different regions, including areas far off the beaten track.

On Lombok, carving usually decorates functional items such as containers for tobacco and spices, and the handles of betel-nut crushers and knives. Materials include wood, horn and bone, and you'll see these used in the recent trend: primitive-style elongated masks. Cakranegara, Sindu, Labuapi and Senanti are centres for carving on the island.

Wooden articles lose moisture when moved to a drier environment. Avoid possible shrinkage – especially of your penis bottle opener – by placing the carving in a plastic bag at home, and letting some air in for about one week every month for four months.

Mask Carving

Masks used in theatre and dance performances such as the Topeng require a specialised form of woodcarving. The mask master – always a man – must know the movements each performer uses so the character can be accurately depicted in the mask. These masks are believed to possess magical qualities and can even have the ability to stare down bad spirits.

Other masks, such as the Barong and Rangda, are brightly painted and decorated with real hair, enormous teeth and bulging eyes.

Mas is the centre of mask carving and the Museum Negeri Propinsi Bali in Denpasar has an extensive mask collection so you can get acquainted with different styles before buying.

Treasures of Bali, by Richard Mann, is a beautifully illustrated guide to Bali's museums, big and small. It highlights gems often overlooked by group tours.

Stone Carving

Traditionally for temple adornment, stone sculptures now make popular souvenirs ranging from frangipani reliefs to quirky ornaments that display the Balinese sense of humour: a frog clutching a leaf as an umbrella, or a weird demon on the side of a bell clasping his hands over his ears in mock offence.

At temples, you will see stone carving in set places. Door guardians are usually a protective personality such as Arjuna. Above the main entrance, Kala's monstrous face often peers out, his hands reaching out to catch evil spirits. The side walls of a *pura dalem* (temple of the dead) might feature sculpted panels showing the horrors awaiting evildoers in the afterlife.

Among Bali's most ancient stone carvings are the scenes of people fleeing a great monster at Goa Gajah, the so-called 'Elephant Cave' (p164), believed to date to the 11th century. Inside the cave, a statue of Ganesha, the elephant-like god, gives the rock its name. Along the road through Muncan in east Bali you'll see roadside factories where huge temple decorations are carved in the open.

Usually adorned with an ornate, jewel-studded handle and a sinister-looking wavy blade, the kris is Bali's traditional, ceremonial dagger, dating back to the Majapahit era. A kris is often the most important of family heirlooms, a symbol of prestige and honour and a work of high-end art. Made by a master craftsman, it's believed to have great spiritual power, sending out magical energy waves and thus requiring great care in its handling and use. Many owners will only clean the blade with waters from Sungai Pakerisan (Pakerisan River) in east Bali, because it is thought to be the magical 'River of Kris'.

Balinese men literally will judge each other in a variation of 'show me your kris'. The size of the blade, the number owned, the quality, the artistry of the handles and much more will go into forming a judgement of a man and his kris. Handles are considered separately from a kris (the blade). As a man's fortunes allow, he will upgrade the handles in his collection. But the kris itself remains sacred – often you will see offerings beside ones on display. The undulations in the blade (called *lok*) have many meanings. There's always an odd number – three, for instance, means passion.

The Museum Negeri Propinsi Bali in Denpasar has a rich kris collection.

THE ARTS CRAFTS

Much of the local work is made in Batubulan from grey volcanic stone called *paras,* so soft it can be scratched with a fingernail (which, according to legend, is how the giant Kebo Iwa created the Elephant Cave).

Other Crafts

To see potters at work, visit Ubung and Kapal, north and west of Denpasar respectively. Nearly all local pottery is made from low-fired terracotta and is very ornate, as are functional items such as vases, flasks, ashtrays and lamp bases. Pejaten, near Tabanan, also has a number of workshops producing ceramic figures and glazed ornamental roof tiles. Stunning collections of designer, contemporary glazed ceramics are produced at Jenggala Keramik in Jimbaran, which also hosts exhibitions of various Indonesian art and antiques.

Earthenware pots have been produced on Lombok for centuries. They're shaped by hand, coated with a slurry of clay or ash to enhance the finish, and fired in a simple kiln filled with burning rice stalks. Pots are often finished with a covering of woven cane for decoration and extra strength. Newer designs feature bright colours and elaborate decorations. Penujak, Banyumulek and Masbagik are some of the main pottery villages, or head towards Mataram to visit the Lombok Pottery Centre.

Architecture

It brings together the living and the dead, pays homage to the gods and wards off evil spirits, not to mention the torrential rain. As spiritual as it is functional, as mystical as it is beautiful, Balinese architecture has a life force of its own.

On an island bound by deep-rooted religious and cultural rituals, the priority of any design is appeasing the ancestral and village gods. This means reserving the holiest (northeast) location in every land space for the village temple, the same corner in every home for the family temple, and providing a comfortable pleasing atmosphere to entice the gods back to Bali for ceremonies.

So while it exudes beauty, balance, age-old wisdom and functionality, a Balinese home is not a commodity designed with capital appreciation in mind; even while an increasing number of rice farmers sell their ancestral land to foreigners for villa developments, they're keeping the parcel on which their home stands.

'For the Balinese, their house where they have the family temple represents the most prestige in their lives', says renowned architect Popo Danes. 'It's the house of their roots. Selling it would be like selling their ancestors.'

COCONUT CODE

The rule that no building shall exceed the height of a coconut palm dates back to the 1960s when the 10-storey Bali Beach Hotel caused much consternation. However, soaring land prices in the south and ineffectual enforcement of building codes mean that this 'rule' is being increasingly challenged.

Preserving the Cosmic Order

A village, a temple, a family compound, an individual structure – and even a single part of the structure – must all conform to the Balinese concept of cosmic order. It consists of three parts that represent the three worlds of the cosmos – *swah* (the world of gods), *bhwah* (the world of humans) and *bhur* (the world of demons). The concept also represents a three-part division of a person: *utama* (the head), *madia* (the body) and *nista* (the legs). The units of measurement used in traditional buildings are directly based on the anatomical dimensions of the head of the household, ensuring harmony between the dwelling and those who live in it.

The design is traditionally done by an *undagi*, a combination architect-priest; it must maintain harmony between god, man and nature under the concept of *Tri Hita Karana*. If it's not quite right, the universe may fall off balance and no end of misfortune and ill health will visit the community involved.

Building on the Bale

The basic element of Balinese architecture is the *bale,* a rectangular, open-sided pavilion with a steeply pitched roof of thatch. Both a family compound and a temple will comprise of a number of separate *bale* for specific functions, all surrounded by a high wall. The size and proportions of the *bale,* the number of columns and the position within the compound are all determined according to tradition and the owner's caste status.

The focus of a community is a large pavilion, called the *bale banjar*, used for meetings, debates and gamelan practice, among many other activities. You'll find that large modern buildings such as restaurants and the lobby areas of resorts are often modelled on the larger *bale,* and they can be airy, spacious and very handsomely proportioned. (See the boxed text, p326, for more on the *banjar.*)

During the building process, if pavilions get beyond a certain size, traditional materials cannot be used. In these cases concrete is substituted for timber, and sometimes the roof is tiled rather than thatched. The fancier modern buildings – banks and hotels – might also feature decorative carvings derived from traditional temple design. As a result of this, some regard the use of traditional features in modern buildings as pure kitsch, while others see it as a natural and appropriate development of modern Balinese style. Buildings with these features are sometimes described as Baliesque, Bali baroque, or Bali rococo if the decoration has become too excessive.

Humble Palaces

Visitors may be disappointed by Balinese *puri* (palaces), which prove to be neither large nor imposing. The *puri* are the traditional residences of the Balinese aristocracy, although now they may be used as top-end hotels or as regular family compounds. They're unimposing, as a Balinese palace can never be built more than one-storey high. This is because a Balinese noble could not possibly use a ground-floor room if the feet of people on an upper floor were walking above.

The Family Compound

The Balinese house looks inward – the outside is simply a high wall. Inside there is a garden and a separate small building or *bale* for each activity – one for cooking, one for washing and the toilet, and separate buildings for each 'bedroom'. In Bali's mild tropical climate people live outside, so the 'living room' and 'dining room' will be open veranda areas, looking out into the garden. The whole complex is oriented on the *kaja–kelod* (towards the mountains–towards the sea) axis.

Many modern Balinese houses, particularly in Denpasar and the larger towns, are arranged much like houses in the West, but there are still a great number of traditional family compounds.

Homes from Head to...

Analogous to the human body, compounds have a head (the family temple with its ancestral shrine), arms (the sleeping and living areas), legs and feet (the kitchen and rice storage building), and even an anus (the garbage pit or pigsty). There may be an area outside the house compound where fruit trees are grown or a pig is kept.

There are several variations on the typical family compound illustrated on p350. For example, the entrance is commonly on the *kuah* (sunset side), rather than the *kelod* side as shown, but *never* on the *kangin* (sunrise) or *kaja* side.

Traditional Balinese homes are found in every region of the island; Ubud remains an excellent place to see them simply because of the concentration of homes there. Many accept guests (see p354). South of Ubud, you can enjoy an in-depth tour of the Nyoman Suaka Home in Singapadu (p169).

Temples

Every village in Bali has several temples, and every home has at least a simple house-temple. The Balinese word for temple is *pura*, from a Sanskrit word literally meaning 'a space surrounded by a wall'. Similar to a

ARCHITECTURE

The various open-air *bale* in family compounds are where visitors are received. Typically drinks and small cakes will be served and friendly conversations will ensue for possibly an hour or more before the purpose of a visit is discussed.

By long tradition, Balinese doors are ornately carved and painted, and are typically in two halves that open inwards. Traditional houses will have a few.

TYPICAL FAMILY COMPOUND

The following are elements commonly found in family compounds. Although there are variations, the designs are surprisingly similar, especially given they occur thousands of times across Bali.

1 Sanggah or Merajan Family temple, which is always at the *kaja-kangin* corner of the courtyard. There will be shrines to the Hindu 'trinity' of Brahma, Shiva and Vishnu, and to *taksu,* the divine intermediary.

2 Umah Meten Sleeping pavilion for the family head.

3 Tugu Shrine to god of evil spirits in the compound but at the far *kaja-kuah* corner; by employing the chief evil spirit as a guard, others will stay away.

4 Pengijeng Small shrine amid the compound's open space, dedicated to the spirit who is the guardian of the property.

5 Bale Tiang Sanga Guest pavilion, also known as the *bale duah.* Literally the family room, it's used as a gathering place, offering workplace or temporary quarters of lesser sons and their families before they establish their own home.

6 Natah Courtyard with frangipani or hibiscus shade trees, with always a few chickens pecking about, plus a fighting cock or two in a basket.

7 Bale Sakenam or Bale Dangin Working and sleeping pavilion; may be used for important family ceremonies.

8 Fruit trees & coconut palms Serve both practical and decorative purposes. Fruit trees are often mixed with flowering trees such as hibiscus, and caged song birds hang from the branches.

9 Vegetable garden Small; usually just for a few spices such as lemongrass not grown on larger plots.

10 Bale Sakepat Sleeping pavilion for children; highly optional.

11 Paon Kitchen; always in the south, as that is the direction associated with Brahma, god of fire.

12 Lumbung Rice barn – the domain of both the precious grain and the Dewi Sri, the rice goddess. It's elevated to discourage rice-eating pests.

13 Rice-threshing area Important for farmers to prepare rice for cooking or storage.

14 Aling Aling Screen wall requiring visitors to turn a sharp left or right. This ensures both privacy from passers-by and protection from demons, which the Balinese believe cannot turn corners.

15 Candi Kurung Gate with a roof, resembling a mountain or tower split in half.

16 Apit Lawang or Pelinggah Gate shrines, which continually receive offerings to recharge the gate's ability to repel evil spirits.

17 Pigsty or garbage pit Always in the *kangin-kelod* corner, the compound's waste ends up here.

traditional Balinese home, a temple is walled in – so the shrines you see in rice fields or at 'magical' spots such as old trees are not real temples. Simple shrines or thrones often overlook crossroads, to protect passers-by.

All temples are built on a mountains–sea orientation, not north–south. The direction towards the mountains, *kaja,* is the end of the temple, where the holiest shrines are found. The temple's entrance is at the *kelod. Kangin* is more holy than the *kuah,* so many secondary shrines are on the *kangin* side. *Kaja* may be towards a particular mountain – Pura Besakih in eastern Bali is pointed directly towards Gunung Agung – or towards the mountains in general, which run east–west along the length of Bali.

Temple Types

There are three basic temple types, found in most villages. The most important is the *pura puseh* (temple of origin), dedicated to the village

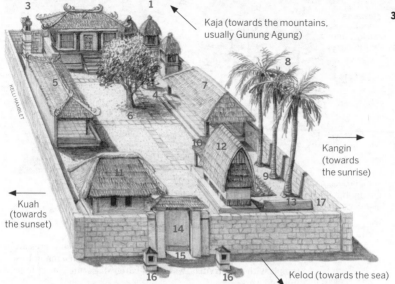

Kaja (towards the mountains, usually Gunung Agung)

Kangin (towards the sunrise)

Kuah (towards the sunset)

Kelod (towards the sea)

KELLI HAMBLET

founders and at the *kaja* end of the village. In the middle of the village is the *pura desa*, for the many spirits that protect the village community in daily life. At the *kelod* end of the village is the *pura dalem* (temple of the dead). The graveyard is also here, and the temple may include representations of Durga, the terrible side of Shiva's wife Parvati. Both Shiva and Parvati have a creative and destructive side; their destructive powers are honoured in the *pura dalem*.

Other temples include those dedicated to the spirits of irrigated agriculture. Because rice growing is so important in Bali, and the division of water for irrigation is handled with the utmost care, these *pura subak* or *pura ulun suwi* (temple of the rice-growers' association) can be of considerable importance. Other temples may also honour dry-field agriculture, as well as the flooded rice paddies.

In addition to these 'local' temples, there are a lesser number of great temples. Often a kingdom would have three of these temples that sit at the very top of the temple pecking order: a main state temple in the heartland of the state (such as Pura Taman Ayun in Mengwi, western Bali); a mountain temple (such as Pura Besakih, eastern Bali); and a sea temple (such as Pura Luhur Ulu Watu, southern Bali).

Every house in Bali has its house temple, which is at the *kaja-kangin* corner of the courtyard and has at least five shrines.

The gate to a traditional Balinese house is where the family gives cues as to its wealth. They range from the humble – grass thatch atop a gate of simple stones or clay – to the relatively grand, including bricks heavily ornamented with ornately carved stone and a tile roof.

Temple Decoration

Temples and their decoration are closely linked on Bali. A temple gateway is not just erected; every square centimetre of it is carved in sculptural relief and a diminishing series of demon faces is placed above it as protection. Even then, it's not complete without several stone statues to act as guardians.

The level of decoration inside varies. Sometimes a temple is built with minimal decoration in the hope that sculpture can be added when more funds are available. The sculpture can also deteriorate after a few years because much of the stone used is soft and the tropical climate ages it very rapidly (that centuries-old temple you're

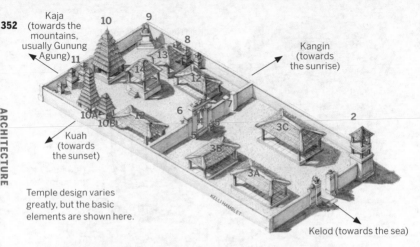

Kaja (towards the mountains, usually Gunung Agung)

Kangin (towards the sunrise)

Kuah (towards the sunset)

Temple design varies greatly, but the basic elements are shown here.

KELLI HAMBLET

Kelod (towards the sea)

looking at may in fact be less than 10 years old!). Sculptures are restored or replaced as resources permit – it's not uncommon to see a temple with old carvings, which are barely discernible, next to newly finished work.

You'll find some of the most lavishly carved temples around Singaraja in northern Bali. The north-coast sandstone is very soft and easily carved, allowing local sculptors to give free rein to their imaginations. As a result, you'll find some delightfully whimsical scenes carved into a number of the temples.

Sculpture often appears in set places in Bali's temples. Door guardians – representations of legendary figures such as Arjuna or other protective personalities – flank the steps to the gateway. Above the main entrance to a temple, Kala's monstrous face often peers out, sometimes a number of times, and his hands reach out beside his head to catch any evil spirits foolish enough to try and sneak in.

Elsewhere, other sculptures make regular appearances. The front of a *pura dalem* will often feature images of the witch Rangda, and sculpted relief panels may show the horrors that await evil-doers in the afterlife.

> Hard-wearing terracotta tiles have been the traditional roofing material since the Dutch era. Thatch in various forms or bamboo are now reserved for the most traditional and ceremonial sites.

Temple Design

Although overall temple architecture is similar in both northern and southern Bali, there are some important differences. The inner courtyards of southern temples usually house a number of *meru* (multi-roofed shrines), together with other structures, whereas in the north, everything is grouped on a single pedestal. On the pedestal you'll find 'houses' for the deities to use on their earthly visits; they're also used to store religious relics.

> Scores of open-air carving sheds supplying statues and ornamentation to temples and shrines are a highlight of the road between Muncan and Selat in east Bali.

While Balinese sculpture and painting were once exclusively used as architectural decoration for temples, you'll soon see that sculpture and painting have developed as separate art forms influencing the look of every aspect of the island. And the art of temple and shrine construction is as vibrant as ever: more than 500 new ones in all sizes are built every month.

Temple design follows a traditional formula. A temple compound contains a number of *gedong* (shrines) of varying sizes, made from solid brick and stone and heavily decorated with carvings.

No two temples on Bali are identical. Variations in style, size, importance, wealth, purpose and much more result in near infinite variety. But there are common themes and elements. Use this illustration as a guide and see how many design elements you can find in each Balinese temple you visit.

1 Candi Bentar The intricately sculpted temple gateway, like a tower split down the middle and moved apart, symbolising that you are entering a sanctum. It can be quite grand, with auxiliary entrances on either side for daily use.

2 Kulkul Tower The warning-drum tower, from which a wooden split drum (*kulkul*) is sounded to announce events at the temple or warn of danger.

3 Bale A pavilion, usually open-sided, for temporary use or storage. It may include a *bale gong* (3A), where the gamelan orchestra plays at festivals; a *paon* (3B), or temporary kitchen, to prepare offerings; or a *wantilan* (3C), a stage for dances or cockfights.

4 Kori Agung or Paduraksa The gateway to the inner courtyard is an intricately sculpted stone tower. Entry is through a doorway reached by steps in the middle of the tower and left open during festivals.

5 Raksa or Dwarapala Statues of fierce guardian figures who protect the doorway and deter evil spirits. Above the door will be the equally fierce face of a Bhoma, with hands outstretched against unwanted spirits.

6 Aling Aling If an evil spirit does get in, this low wall behind the entrance will keep it at bay, as evil spirits find it difficult to make sharp turns. (Also found in family compounds.)

7 Side Gate (Betelan) Most of the time (except during ceremonies), entry to the inner courtyard is through this side gate, which is always open.

8 Small Shrines (Gedong) These usually include shrines to Ngrurah Alit and Ngrurah Gede, who organise things and ensure the correct offerings are made.

9 Padma Stone Throne for the sun god Surya, placed in the most auspicious *kaja-kangin* corner. It rests on the *badawang* (world turtle), which is held by two *naga* (mythological serpents).

10 Meru A multiroofed shrine. Usually there is an 11-roofed *meru* (10A) to Sanghyang Widi, the supreme Balinese deity, and a three-roofed *meru* (10B) to the holy mountain Gunung Agung. However, *meru* can take any odd number of steps in between, depending on where the intended god falls in the pecking order. The black thatching is made from sugar palm fronds and is very expensive.

11 Small Shrines (Gedong) At the *kaja* end of the courtyard, these may include a shrine to the sacred mountain Gunung Batur; a Maospahit shrine to honour Bali's original Hindu settlers (Majapahit); and a shrine to the *taksu*, who acts as an interpreter for the gods. (Trance dancers or mediums may be used to convey the gods' wishes.)

12 Bale Piasan Open pavilions used to display temple offerings.

13 Gedong Pesimpangan A stone building dedicated to the village founder or a local deity.

14 Paruman or Pepelik Open pavilion in the inner courtyard, where the gods are supposed to assemble to watch the ceremonies of a temple festival.

The Birth of Bali Style

Tourism has given Balinese architecture unprecedented exposure and it seems that every visitor wants to take a slice of this island back home with them.

Shops along Ngurah Rai Bypass (the main road in south Bali, running from the airport around to Sanur) churn out prefabricated, knock-down *bale* for shipment to far-flung destinations: the Caribbean, London, Perth and Hong Kong. Furniture workshops in Kerobokan and handicraft villages near Ubud are flat out making ornaments for domestic and

ARCHITECTURE

export markets: wall sculptures, carved doors, statues and the ubiquitous Buddha images and handicrafts from all over Indonesia that have erroneously become synonymous with Balinese decor.

Local suppliers can't keep up with demand. *Alang-alang* farmers now use chemical fertilisers to harvest their crop of grass used in traditional thatched roofs several times a year instead of just once; craftspeople import wood and other materials from other provinces.

The craze stems back to the early 1970s, when Australian artist Donald Friend formed a partnership with Manado-born Wija Waworuntu, who had built the Tandjung Sari on Sanur beach a decade earlier. With a directive to design traditional, village-style alternatives to the Western multistoreyed hotels, they brought two architects to Bali: Australian Peter Muller and the late Sri Lankan Geoffrey Bawa. Some of the most iconic symbols of modern Balinese architecture are attributed to Bawa and Muller, credited with being the first to capture the spirit of traditional architecture and adapt it to Western standards of luxury. Many of their creations are on private estates, but you can see some examples of Muller's hotel work (see Contemporary Hotel Design, p355).

Before long, the cult movement known as 'Bali Style' was born. Then, the term reflected Muller and Bawa's sensitive, low-key approach, giving precedence to culture over style, and respect for traditional principles and craftspeople, local renewable materials and age-old techniques. Today, the development of a mass market has inevitably produced a much looser definition.

When you stay in a hotel featuring *lumbung* design, you are really staying in a place derived from rice storage barns – the 2nd floor is meant to be airless and hot!

Traditional Design in Modern Times

Architects are constantly being asked how Balinese architecture can be modified for an urban setting like London, or an apartment in India. The answer is: not easily. Bali Style can now often refer more to cosmetic touches – carved gates or an outdoor bathroom – rather than a walled-in compound with pavilions, communal courtyard and water gardens.

'I had a client in Costa Rica ask me to recreate Peter Muller's Amandari design for a multimillion dollar resort there', said Popo Danes. 'I had to say no – it just wouldn't have worked in that environment. People are crazy about Balinese architecture, but I would love to export the understanding of it, not just our architecture as a commodity.'

While several recent developments have prompted calls for stricter enforcement of regulations to preserve the island's heritage (see p98), all you need to do is venture off the main road and slip down a quiet *gang* to see that not much has changed in how the Balinese themselves live.

Foreigners may bend traditional principles to suit themselves, but the Balinese still take great pride in their architecture. Ubud is a notable tribute to how traditional design can survive modern development.

In more remote areas, many villages remain virtually untouched, such as Munduk in the central mountains and the ancient Bali Aga hamlet of Tenganan (p190), with neat rows of identical houses and a wall surrounding the whole village, which is closed to motor vehicles.

All over Bali, the architecture remains inextricably tied up in the religious, cultural and social rituals underpinning village life. The gods still get the best seat in the house, and they're not moving for anyone.

Contemporary Hotel Design

For centuries, foreign interlopers, such as the priest Nirartha, have played an intrinsic part in the island's myths and legends. These days, tourists are making an impact on the serenity of Balinese cosmology and its seamless translation into the island's traditional architecture. And while these visitors with large credit limits aren't changing the island's belief system – much – they are changing its look.

Most hotel designs on Bali and Lombok are purely functional or pastiches of traditional designs, but some of the finest hotels on the islands aspire to something greater. There is the sincere attempt to use highly sophisticated architecture to heighten, even exaggerate, the sensation of being not just on the islands but a part of their cultural fabric, albeit as part of a hedonistic escape.

Notable examples in rough order of completion:

Tandjung Sari (p110), in Sanur, is Wija Waworuntu's classic prototype for the Balinese boutique beach hotel.

Amandari (p154), near Ubud, is the crowning achievement of architect Peter Muller, who also designed the two Oberois. The inclusion of traditional Balinese materials, crafts and construction techniques, as well as Balinese design principles, respects the island's approach to the world.

Oberoi (p77), in Seminyak, was the very first luxury hotel and remains Muller's relaxed vision of a Balinese village. The *bale agung* (village assembly hall) and *bale banjar* form the basis for common areas.

Oberoi Lombok (p271), on Lombok, is both the most luxurious and the most traditionally styled hotel on the island.

Amanusa (p101), in Nusa Dua, avoids the over-grown, hackneyed approach of nearby resorts through the brilliant work of Kerry Hill, who drew on Balinese village design for this human-scaled hotel.

Alila (p189), near Candidasa, employs the typical buildings and spaces of Bali: the walled house and garden compound and the village with its *bale*.

Amankila (p189), in east Bali, adopts a garden strategy, with a carefully structured landscape of lotus ponds and floating pavilions that steps down an impossibly steep site.

Hotel Tugu Bali (p89), in Canggu, exemplifies the notion of instant age, the ability of materials in Bali to weather quickly and provide 'pleasing decay'.

Bambu Indah (p154), near Ubud, brings together seven century-old royal Javanese palaces that are visions of wood and bamboo.

Four Seasons Jimbaran Bay (p93), in south Bali, blends individualistic modern architecture with tiered, lavish gardens that accentuate views over the sea.

Four Seasons Resort (p154), near Ubud, is a striking piece of aerial sculpture, a huge elliptical lotus pond sitting above a base structure that appears like an eroded and romantic ruin set within a spectacular river valley.

Alila Villas (p99), in far south Bali, employs an artful contemporary style that's light and airy, conveying a sense of great luxury. Set amid hotel-tended rice fields, it embodies advanced green building principles.

Objects draped in black-and-white checked cloth (*poleng*) are empowered by the spirits. Such objects can be shrines, as you'd expect, but also statues, planters or seemingly everyday objects.

The ubiquitous open-air bathing area at more stylish hotels is based on the traditional *mandi* (literally bath), which is where you stand and take fresh water from a barrel or bucket and rinse off.

Look for carved wooden garudas, the winged bird that bears the god Wisnu, in the most surprising places – high up in pavilion rafters, at the base of columns, pretty much anywhere.

Lombok Architecture

Traditional laws and practices govern Lombok's architecture. Construction must begin on a propitious day, always with an odd-numbered date, and the building's frame must be completed on that day. It would be bad luck to leave any of the important structural work until the following day.

A traditional Sasak village layout is a walled enclosure. There are three types of buildings: the *beruga* (open-sided pavilion), the *bale tani* (family house) and the *lumbung* (rice barn). The *beruga* and *bale tani* are both rectangular, with low walls and a steeply pitched thatched roof, although, of course, the *beruga* is much larger. A *bale tani* is made of bamboo on a base of compacted mud. It usually has no windows and the arrangement of rooms is very standardised. There is a *serambi* (open veranda) at the front and two rooms on two different levels inside – one for cooking and entertaining guests, the other for sleeping and storage. There are some picturesque traditional Sasak villages in Rembitan and Sade (p279), near Kuta.

TOP TEMPLE VISITS

Hundreds of temples are found everywhere on Bali – from cliff tops and beaches to volcanoes – and are often beautiful places to experience. Visitors will find the following especially rewarding.

Directional Temples

Some temples are so important they are deemed to belong to the whole island rather than particular communities. There are nine *kahyangan jagat,* or directional temples, including the following four:

Pura Luhur Batukau (p221) One of Bali's most important temples is situated magically up the misty slopes of Gunung Batukau.

Pura Luhur Ulu Watu (p98) As important as it is popular, this temple has sweeping Indian Ocean views, sunset dance performances and monkeys.

Pura Lempuyang (p197) Near the old water palace at Tirta Gangga, this temple makes for an exhilarating and exhausting climb.

Pura Goa Lawah (p185) See Bali's own Bat Cave at this cliff-side temple filled with the winged critters.

Sea Temples

The legendary 16th-century priest Nirartha founded a chain of temples to honour the sea gods. Each was intended to be within sight of the next, and several have dramatic locations on the south coast. They include the following:

Pura Rambut Siwi (p248) On a wild stretch of the west coast and not far from where Nirartha arrived in the 16th century. Locks of his hair are said to be buried in a shrine.

Pura Tanah Lot (p243) Sacred as the day begins, it becomes a temple of mass tourism at sunset.

Other Important Temples

Some temples have particular importance because of their location, spiritual function or architecture. The following reward visitors:

Pura Maduwe Karang (p230) An agricultural temple on the north coast, this is famous for its spirited bas-reliefs, including one of possibly Bali's first bicycle rider.

Pura Pusering Jagat (p166) One of the famous temples at Pejeng, near Ubud, which dates to the 14th-century empire that flourished here. It has an enormous bronze drum from that era.

Pura Taman Ayun (p243) This vast and imposing state temple was a centrepiece of the Mengwi empire and has been nominated for Unesco recognition.

Pura Tirta Empul (p166) The beautiful temple at Tampaksiring, with holy springs discovered in AD 962 and bathing pools at the source of Sungai Pakerisan.

» *Architecture of Bali*, by Made Wijaya, contains stunning vintage photographs and illustrations, accompanied by informative personal observations from the Australian-born landscape designer.

» *Bali Style*, by Rio Helmi and Barbara Walker, details the clean and open-plan design ethos that's attracted a cult following.

» *Architectural Conservation in Bali*, by Edo Budihardjo, makes the case for preserving Bali's architectural heritage.

» *Architecture Bali: Birth of the Tropical Boutique Resort*, by Philip Goad, explores the origin and direction of contemporary Balinese design.

» *A House on Bali*, by Colin McPhee, is the classic account of the intricacies of building a traditional family compound.

Because it had a period under Balinese control in the 18th and 19th centuries, Lombok also features some fine examples of ancient Balinese architecture, such as the Mayura Water Palace (p259) and Pura Meru (p258). The magnificent temple compound Pura Lingsar (p262) is the holiest on Lombok and contains both a Balinese Hindu and a Wektu Telu temple, representing the relationship between the two religions.

Environment

The Landscape

Bali is a small island, midway along the string of islands that makes up the Indonesian archipelago. It's adjacent to the most heavily populated island of Java, and immediately west of the chain of smaller islands comprising Nusa Tenggara, which includes Lombok.

The island is visually dramatic – a mountainous chain with a string of active volcanoes, it includes several peaks around 2000m. The agricultural lands in Bali are south and north of the central mountains. The southern region is a wide, gently sloping area, where most of the country's abundant rice crop is grown. The northern coastal strip is narrower, rising rapidly into the foothills of the central range. It receives less rain, but coffee, copra, rice and cattle are farmed there.

Bali also has some arid, less-populated regions. These include the western mountain region, and the eastern and northeastern slopes of Gunung Agung. The Nusa Penida islands are dry, and cannot support intensive rice agriculture. The Bukit Peninsula is similarly dry, but with the growth of tourism, it's becoming quite populous.

Volcanoes

Bali is volcanically active and extremely fertile. The two go hand-in-hand as eruptions contribute to the land's exceptional fertility, and high mountains provide the dependable rainfall that irrigates Bali's complex and amazingly beautiful patchwork of rice terraces. Of course, the volcanoes are a hazard as well – Bali has endured disastrous eruptions in the past, such as in 1963, and no doubt will again in the future. Gunung Agung, the 'Mother Mountain', is 3142m high and thickly wooded on its south side. You can climb it or its steam-spewing neighbour, the comparatively diminutive 1700m Gunung Batur. The latter is a geographic spectacle: a soaring, active volcano rising from a lake that itself is set in a vast crater.

On Lombok, the 3726m Gunung Rinjani is Indonesia's second-tallest volcano. Within the huge caldera is an aquamarine lake, Danau Segara, which astounds those who spy it for the first – or even second – time.

Beaches

Bali is ringed by beaches. While not the whitest in Southeast Asia, they draw visitors by the score for surfing, playing and sunbathing. Locals and visitors alike pause on west-facing beaches at sunset and the Balinese hold purification and other ceremonies at the shore.

A brief guide to the sands of Bali includes the following:

Kuta Beach The original draw for tourists, the golden sand arcs in what seems an endless sweep past Canggu to the northwest. Raw surf hits here, delighting surfers.

Bukit Peninsula The west side has famous surf spots and beaches with names such as Balangan that feature little pockets of bright sand below limestone cliffs. The east side has reef-protected strands, such as the one at Nusa Dua.

East Bali A long series of open-water beaches begins north of reef-protected Sanur. Waves pound volcanic sand that ranges from a light grey to charcoal black. In the far east, on the Amed Coast, tiny coves of light sand front small fishing villages.

North Bali This grey-sand beach, protected by reefs, extends sporadically across the north at places such as Lovina and Pemuteran.

Gilis The whitest, sweetest sand draws the masses to the three little islands with offshore reefs.

Lombok It boasts all the variations of sand found on Bali, but the most popular with travellers are the beaches at Kuta (yes, Lombok has one, too) and Senggigi.

Responsible Travel

The best way to responsibly visit Bali and Lombok is to try to be as minimally invasive as possible. This is, of course, easier than it sounds, but consider the following tips:

» **Watch your use of water.** Travel into the rice-growing regions of Bali and you'll think the island is coursing with water, but demand outstrips supply. Take up your hotel on its offer to save itself big money, er, no, to save lots of water, by not washing your sheets and towels every day. Cynicism aside, this will save water. At the high end you can also forgo your own private plunge pool, or a pool altogether – although this is almost impossible at any price level.

» **Don't hit the bottle.** Those bottles of Aqua (the top local brand of bottled water, owned by Danone) are convenient but they add up. The zillions of such bottles tossed away each year are a major blight. Still, you're wise not to refill from the tap, so what to do? Ask your hotel if you can refill from their huge containers of drinking water. And, if your hotel doesn't give you in-room drinking water in reusable glass containers, tell them you noticed. In Ubud, stop

GROWING RICE

Rice cultivation has shaped the social landscape in Bali – the intricate organisation necessary for growing rice is a large factor in the strength of community life. Rice cultivation has also changed the environmental landscape – terraced rice fields trip down hillsides like steps for a giant, in shades of gold, brown and green, green and more green. Some date back 1000 years or more.

Subak (p327), the village assocation that deals with water rights and irrigation, makes careful use of all the surface water. The fields are a complete ecological system, home for much more than just rice. In the early morning you'll often see the duck herders leading their flocks out for a day's paddle around a flooded rice field; the ducks eat various pests and leave fertiliser in their wake.

A harvested field with its leftover burnt rice stalks is soaked with water and repeatedly ploughed, often by two bullocks pulling a wooden plough. Once the field is muddy enough, a small corner is walled off and seedling rice is planted there. When it is a reasonable size, it's replanted, shoot by shoot, in the larger field. While the rice matures, there is time to practise the gamelan (instruments used to play traditional Balinese orchestral music), watch the dancers or do a little woodcarving. Finally, the whole village turns out for the harvest – a period of solid hard work. While it's only men who plant the rice, everybody takes part in harvesting it.

In 1969, new high-yield rice varieties were introduced. These can be harvested a month sooner than the traditional variety and are resistant to many diseases. However, the new varieties also require more fertiliser and irrigation water, which strains the imperilled water supplies. More pesticides are also needed, causing the depletion of the frog and eel populations that depend on the insects for survival.

Although everyone agrees that the new rice doesn't taste as good as the traditional rice, the new strains now account for more than 90% of the rice grown in Bali. Small areas of trad rice are still planted and harvested in traditional ways to placate the rice goddess, Dewi Sri. Temples and offerings to her dot every rice field.

by the **Pondok Pecak Library & Learning Centre** (☎976 194; Monkey Forest Rd; ☺9am-9pm) – staff will refill your water bottle and tell you which other businesses offer this service. Elsewhere, simply ask; the service is slowly spreading. In restaurants, ask for '*air putih*', which will get you a glass of water from the Aqua jug out back, saving yet more plastic bottles.

» **Don't play golf.** The resorts will hate this, but tough. Having two golf courses on the arid Bukit Peninsula is environmentally unsustainable.

» **Support environmentally aware businesses.** The number of businesses committed to good environmental practices is growing fast in Bali and Lombok. Keep an eye out within this guide for the sustainable icon (S), which identifies environmentally savvy businesses.

» **Conserve power.** Sure you want to save your own energy on a sweltering afternoon, but using air-con strains an already overloaded system. Much of the electricity in Bali comes from Java and the rest is produced at the roaring, smoking plant near Benoa Harbour. Open the windows at night in Ubud for cool mountain breezes and the symphony of sounds off the rice fields.

» **Don't drive yourself crazy.** The traffic is already bad – why add another vehicle to it? Can you take a tourist bus instead of a chartered or rental car? Would a walk, trek or hike be more enjoyable than a road journey to an over-visited tourist spot? The beach is a fast and fun way to get around Kuta and Seminyak (often faster than a taxi in traffic). Cycling is more popular than ever, and you can hire a bike for US$3.

» **Bag the bags.** Bali's governor is trying to get plastic bags banned. Help him out by refusing them (and say no to plastic straws too).

Animals & Plants

Bali is geologically young, most of its living things have migrated from elsewhere and true native wild animals are rare. This is not hard to imagine in the heavily populated and extravagantly fertile south of Bali, where the orderly rice terraces are so intensively cultivated they look more like a work of sculpture than a natural landscape.

In fact, rice fields cover only about 20% of the island's surface area, and there is a great variety of other environmental zones: the dry scrub of the northwest, the extreme northeast and the southern peninsula; patches of dense jungle in the river valleys; forests of bamboo; and harsh volcanic regions that are barren rock and volcanic tuff at higher altitudes. Lombok is similar in all these respects.

Animals
Wild Animals

Bali has lots and lots of lizards, and they come in all shapes and sizes. The small ones (onomatopoeically called *cecak*) that hang around light fittings in the evening, waiting for an unwary insect, are a familiar sight. Geckos are fairly large lizards, often heard but less often seen. The loud and regularly repeated two-part cry 'geck-oh' is a nightly background noise that many visitors soon enjoy – it's considered lucky if you hear the lizard call seven times.

Bali has more than 300 species of birds, but the one that is truly native to the island, the Bali starling (see the boxed text, p253), is probably extinct in the wild, although thousands can be found in cages. Much more common are colourful birds such as the orange-banded thrush, numerous species of egrets, kingfishers, parrots, owls and many more.

Bali's only wilderness area, Taman Nasional Bali Barat (West Bali National Park), has a number of wild species, including grey and black monkeys (which you will also see in the mountains, Ubud and east Bali), *muncak* (mouse deer), squirrels, bats and iguanas.

The Indonesian Ecotourism Centre (www.indecon.or.id) is devoted to highlighting responsible tourism; Bali Fokus (http://balifokus.asia) promotes sustainable community programs on Bali for recycling and reuse.

One hawksbill sea turtle that visited Bali was tracked for the following year. His destinations: Java, Kalimantan, Australia (Perth and much of Queensland) and then back to Bali.

TURTLES

Domestic Animals

Bali is thick with domestic animals, including ones that wake you up in the morning and others that bark at night. Chickens and roosters are kept as food and as domestic pets. Cockfighting is a popular male activity, and a man's fighting bird is his prized possession. If you see a thicket of cars and motorbikes by the side of the road in rural Bali but don't see any people, they may all be at a cockfight 'hidden' behind a building.

Dogs (when not pampered pets) have hard lives – they're far down the social ladder, bedevilled by the rabies epidemic (see p394) and thought by some to be friendly with evil spirits (thus the constant barking). But some people are trying to improve the lives of feral mutts; see the boxed text, p163.

Ducks are another everyday Balinese domestic animal and a regular dish at feasts. Ducks are kept in the family compound, and are put out to a convenient pond or flooded rice field to feed during the day. They follow a stick with a small flag tied to the end, and the stick is left planted in the field. As sunset approaches, the ducks gather around the stick and wait to be led home again. The morning and evening duck parades are one of Bali's small delights.

Marine Animals

There is a rich variety of coral, seaweed, fish and other marine life in the coastal waters off the islands. Much of it can be appreciated by snorkellers, but you're only likely to see the larger marine animals while diving. The huge, placid sunfish and manta rays found off Nusa Penida lure divers from around the world.

SEA TURTLES

Both green sea and hawksbill turtles inhabit the waters around Bali and Lombok, and both species are supposedly protected by international laws that prohibit trade in anything made from sea turtles.

In Bali, however, green sea turtle meat (penyu) is a traditional and very popular delicacy, particularly for Balinese feasts. Bali is the site of the most intensive slaughter of green sea turtles in the world – no reliable figures are available, although in 1999 it was estimated that more than 30,000 are killed annually. It's easy to find the trade on the backstreets of waterside towns such as Benoa.

Still, some progress is being made. 'People in Kuta used to eat turtles, now they save them,' says Wayan Wiradnyana, head of ProFauna (www.profauna.org) in Bali, a group that works to protect animals across Indonesia. In Bali, the group has spurred police to enforce a 1999 ban on turtle killing and it has helped release turtles seized from poachers. But its biggest achievement has been in public education. 'In Kuta,' he says, '30 turtles a year lay eggs on the beach. The community now helps us guard them and make certain the babies hatch and get to the water'. ProFauna has erected a turtle information centre along the beach.

A broad coalition of divers and journalists supports the SOS Sea Turtles campaign (www.sos-seaturtles.ch), which spotlights turtle abuse in Bali. It has been instrumental in exposing the illegal poaching of turtles at Wakatobi National Park in Sulawesi for sale in Bali. This illegal trade is widespread and, like the drug trade, hard to prevent. Bali's Hindu Dharma, the body overseeing religious practice, has decreed that turtle meat is essential in only very vital ceremonies.

Turtle hatcheries open to the public, such as the sanctuary on – fittingly – Turtle Island (p114), do a good job of educating locals about the need to protect turtles and think of them as living creatures (as opposed to satay), but many environmentalists are still opposed to them because they keep captive turtles.

Dolphins can be found right around the islands and have been made into an attraction off Lovina (see p230).

Plants

Trees

Much of the island is cultivated. As with most things in Bali, trees have a spiritual and religious significance, and you'll often see them decorated with scarves and black-and-white chequered cloths (*poleng,* a cloth signifying spiritual energy). The *waringin* (banyan) is the holiest Balinese tree and no important temple is complete without a stately one growing within its precincts. The banyan is an extensive, shady tree with an exotic feature: creepers that drop from its branches take root to propagate a new tree. *Jepun* (frangipani or plumeria trees), with their beautiful and sweet-smelling white flowers, are found everywhere.

Bali's forests cover 127,000 hectares, ranging from virgin land to tree farms to densely forested mountain villages. The total is constantly under threat from wood poaching for carved souvenirs and cooking fuel, and from development.

Bali has monsoonal rather than tropical rainforests, so it lacks the valuable rainforest hardwoods that require rain year-round. Nearly all the hardwood used for carving is imported from Sumatra and Kalimantan.

A number of plants have great practical and economic significance. *Tiing* (bamboo) is grown in several varieties and is used for everything from satay sticks and string to rafters and gamelan resonators. The various types of palm provide coconuts, sugar, fuel and fibre.

Flowers & Gardens

Balinese gardens are a delight. The soil and climate can support a huge range of plants, and the Balinese love of beauty and the abundance of cheap labour means that every space can be landscaped. The style is generally informal, with curved paths, a rich variety of plants and usually a water feature. Who can't be enchanted by a frangipani tree dropping a carpet of fragrant blossoms?

You can find almost every type of flower in Bali, but some are seasonal and others are restricted to the cooler mountain areas. Many of

---

THE WALLACE LINE

The 19th-century naturalist Sir Alfred Wallace (1822–1913) observed great differences in fauna between Bali and Lombok – as great as the differences between Africa and South America. In particular, there were no large mammals (elephants, rhinos, tigers etc) east of Bali, and very few carnivores. He postulated that during the ice ages, when sea levels were lower, animals could have moved by land from what is now mainland Asia all the way to Bali, but the deep Lombok Strait would always have been a barrier. He drew a line between Bali and Lombok, which he believed marked the biological division between Asia and Australia.

Plant life does not display such a sharp division, but there is a gradual transition from predominantly Asian rainforest species to mostly Australian plants, such as eucalypts and acacias, which are better suited to long dry periods. This is associated with the lower rainfall as one moves east of Java. Environmental differences – including those in the natural vegetation – are now thought to provide a better explanation of the distribution of animal species than Wallace's theory about limits to their original migrations.

Modern biologists do recognise a distinction between Asian and Australian fauna, but the boundary between the regions is regarded as much fuzzier than Wallace's line. Nevertheless, this transitional zone between Asia and Australia is still called 'Wallacea'.

the flowers will be familiar to visitors – hibiscus, bougainvillea, poinsettia, oleander, jasmine, water lily and aster are commonly seen in the southern tourist areas.

Less-familiar flowers include Javanese *ixora (soka, angsoka),* with round clusters of red-orange flowers; *champak (cempaka),* a fragrant member of the magnolia family; flamboyant, the flower of the royal poinciana flame tree; *manori (maduri),* which has several traditional uses; and water convolvulus *(kangkung),* whose leaves are commonly used as a green vegetable. There are thousands of species of orchid.

Bali's climate means that gardens planted today look mature – complete with soaring shade trees – in just a couple of years. Good places to see Bali's plant bounty include Bali Botanical Gardens (p216), Botanic Garden Ubud (p135), Bali Orchid Garden (p107) and Plant Nurseries (north from Sanur and along the road to Denpasar).

National Parks

The only national park in Bali is **Taman Nasional Bali Barat** (p251). It covers 190 sq km at the western tip of Bali, plus a substantial area of coastal mangrove and the adjacent marine area, including the excellent dive site at Menjangan.

The **Taman Nasional Gunung Rinjani** (Gunung Rinjani National Park) on Lombok covers 413 sq km and is the water collector for most of the island. At 3726m, Gunung Rinjani is the second-highest volcanic peak in Indonesia and is very popular for trekking (see p276).

Environmental Issues

A fast-growing population in Bali has put pressure on limited resources. The tourist industry has attracted new residents, and there is a rapid growth in urban areas and of resorts and villas that encroach onto agricultural land.

Water use is a major concern. Typical top-end hotels use more than 500L of water a day per room, and the growing number of golf courses – the new one on the arid Bukit Peninsula in the Pecatu Indah development, for example – put further pressure on an already stressed resource.

Water pollution is another problem, both from deforestation brought on by firewood collecting in the mountains, and lack of proper treatment for the waste produced by the local population. Streams that run into the ocean at popular spots like Double Six Beach in Legian are very polluted, often with wastewater from hotels. The vast mangroves along the south coast near Benoa Harbour are losing their ability to filter the water that drains here from much of the island.

Air pollution is terrible, as anyone stuck behind a smoke-belching truck or bus on one of the main roads knows. The view of south Bali from a hillside shows a brown blanket hanging in the air that could be LA in the 1960s. And the problem is not just all those plastic bags and water bottles but the sheer volume of waste produced by the evergrowing population – what to do with it?

Just growing Bali's sacred grain rice has become fraught with environmental concerns. For details, see the boxed text (p359).

On the upside, there is a nascent effort to grow rice and other foods organically, reducing the amount of pesticide and fertiliser run-off into water supplies. Things may finally be moving forward on starting a sewage treatment program in the south (but it will take years and the money is not there). Even as businesses are offered recycling services, the cost – US$10 a month – is more than a small warung can afford.

On Lombok, environmental disaster in the gold rush town of Sekotong is ongoing. Gold mining using mercury in huge open-cast pits is causing enormous damage.

Balinese Flora & Fauna, published by Periplus, is a concise and beautifully illustrated guide to the animals and plants you'll see in your travels. The feature on the ecology of a rice field is excellent.

Each day Bali produces 150 tons of waste, at least 30% of which is nonbiodegradable and most of which is generated directly or indirectly by tourism. That is everything from plastic water bottles to your empty container of sunblock.

For organisations that have more info on the local environment and may be able to use your help in protecting it, see p376.

Survival Guide

Directory A-Z

Accommodation

Bali has a huge range of accommodation, primarily in hotels of every shape, size and price. It has great-value lodging no matter what your budget. The touristy areas of Lombok and the Gilis have the same range of options as Bali; elsewhere accommodation is simpler and more limited.

Accommodation attracts a combined tax and service charge (called 'plus plus') of 21%. In budget places, this is generally included in the price, but check first. Many midrange and top-end places will add it on, which can add substantially to your bill.

In this guide, the rates quoted include tax and are those that travellers are likely to pay during the high season. Nailing down rates is difficult, as some establishments publish the rates they actually plan to charge, while others publish rates that are pure fantasy, fully expecting to discount by 50%.

The range of prices used in this book are as follows:

» **Budget ($)** Most rooms cost less than 550,000Rp (around US$50) per night.

» **Midrange ($$)** Most rooms cost between 550,000Rp and 1,400,000Rp (around US$150).

» **Top End ($$$)** Most rooms cost more than 1,400,000Rp.

Rates are almost always negotiable, especially outside the main peak season. In the low season, discounts between 30% and 50% aren't uncommon at midrange and top-end hotels. With Bali enjoying record visitor numbers, prices are climbing sharply.

Rates are often given in US dollars (US$) – and sometimes euros (€) – as opposed to rupiah (Rp), especially at higher-end places.

Hotels

Pretty much every place to stay in Bali and Lombok can arrange tours, car rental and other services. Laundry service is universally available,

often cheap and sometimes free.

BUDGET HOTELS

The cheapest accommodation in Bali and Lombok is in small places that are simple, but clean and comfortable. Names usually include the word 'losmen', 'homestay', 'inn' or 'pondok'. Many are built in the style of a traditional Balinese home.

There are budget hotels all over Bali (less so on Lombok), and they vary widely in standards and price. Expect:

» Maybe air-con
» Maybe hot water
» Private bathroom with shower and Western-style toilet
» Often a pool
» Simple breakfast
» Carefree and cheery staff

International budget chains such as Tune Hotels are making a splashy entry into south Bali, but note that a tiny US$9 room quickly hits US$40 when you add the usual extras listed above.

MIDRANGE HOTELS

Midrange hotels are often constructed in Balinese bungalow style or in two-storey blocks and are set on spacious grounds with a pool. Many have a sense of style that is beguiling and may help postpone your departure. In addition to what you'll get at a budget hotel, expect:

» Balcony/porch/patio
» Satellite TV
» Small fridge
» Maybe wi-fi

TOP-END HOTELS

Top-end hotels in Bali are world-class. Service is refined and you can expect

---

BOOK YOUR STAY ONLINE

For more reviews by Lonely Planet authors, check out hotels.lonelyplanet.com/bali. You'll find independent reviews, as well as recommendations on the best places to stay. Best of all, you can book online.

decor plucked from the pages of a glossy magazine, along with the following:

» Superb service
» Views – ocean, lush valleys and rice fields or private gardens
» Spa
» Maybe a private pool
» Not wanting to leave

Villas

Like frangipani blossoms after a stiff breeze, villas are scattered around south Bali. They're often built in the middle of rice paddies, seemingly overnight. The villa boom has been quite controversial for environmental, aesthetic and economic reasons. Many skip collecting government taxes from guests, which has raised the ire of their luxury hotel competitors and brought threats of crack-downs.

Large villas can be bacchanal retreats for groups of friends and are typically found in Kerobokan and Canggu. Others are smaller, more intimate and part of larger developments – common in Seminyak – or top-end hotels. Expect the following:

» Private garden
» Private pool
» Kitchen
» Air-con bedroom(s)
» Open-air common space

Also potentially included:
» Your own staff (cook, driver, cleaner)
» Lush grounds
» Private beachfront
» Isolation (which can be good or bad, eg Canggu is a drive from everywhere)

Rates range from under US$200 per night for a modest villa to US$1200 per week and beyond for your own tropical estate. There are often deals, especially in the low season, and several couples sharing can make something grand affordable. You can sometimes save quite a bit by waiting until the last minute, but during the high season the best villas book up far in advance.

VILLA RENTAL QUESTIONS

It's the Wild West out there. There are myriad agents, some excellent, others not. It is essential to be as clear as possible about what you want when arranging a rental. Following are some things to keep in mind and ask about when renting a villa:

» How far is the villa from the beach and stores?
» Is a driver or car service included?
» If there is a cook, is food included?
» Is there an electricity surcharge?
» Are there extra cleaning fees?
» Is laundry included?
» What refunds apply on a standard 50% deposit?
» Is there wi-fi/internet access?

VILLA AGENTS

Bali Private Villas (☏0361-316 6455; www.baliprivate villas.com)

Bali Tropical Villas (☏0361-732 083; www.bali-tropical-villas.com)

Bali Ultimate Villas (☏0361-857 1658; www.baliultimatevillas.com) Also has wedding services.

Bali Villas (☏0361-703 060; www.balivillas.com)

Duncan & Edwards (☏0812 385 3337; www.duncan edwardsproperty.com)

House of Bali (☏0361-739 541; www.houseofbali.com)

Long-Term Accommodation

For longer stays, you can find flats for US$800 a month. Look in the Bali Advertiser (www.baliadvertiser.biz) and on notice boards, such as the one at Café Moka (p80) in Seminyak and those in Ubud (p80). If your tastes run simple, you can find basic bungalows among the rice fields in Ubud for US$300 a month.

Village Accommodation

A good way to arrange a village stay is through the JED Village Ecotourism Network; see Specialist Tours on p390. Another good option is the

FINDING A ROOM DEAL

For hotels, especially midrange and top-end places, you can often find the best deal online. Some hotels offer internet deals on their websites; many more work with agents and brokers to sell their rooms at discounts far below published rates.

Bali Discovery (www.balidiscovery.com) has discount rates for hundreds of places. The following sites are also good resources:

» www.asiarooms.com
» www.directrooms.com
» www.hotelclub.net
» www.otel.com
» www.zuji.com

Bali Homestay Program, north of Tabanan (p245).

Business Hours

In this book it is assumed that standard hours are as follows. Significant variations are noted in listings.

Banks 8am to 2pm Monday to Thursday, 8am to noon Friday, 8am to 11am Saturday

Government offices 8am to 3pm Monday to Thursday, 8am to noon Friday (although these are not standardised)

Post offices 8am to 2pm Monday to Friday, longer in tourist centres

Restaurants and cafes 8am to 10pm daily

Shops and services catering to visitors 9am to 8pm daily

Customs Regulations

Indonesia's list of prohibited imports includes drugs, weapons, fresh fruit and anything remotely pornographic.
Items allowed include:
» 200 cigarettes (or 50 cigars or 100g of tobacco)
» a 'reasonable amount' of perfume
» 1L of alcohol

Surfers with more than two or three boards may be charged a fee, and this can

apply to other items if the officials suspect that you aim to sell them in Indonesia.

There is no restriction on foreign currency, but the import or export of rupiah is limited to 5,000,000Rp. Greater amounts must be declared.

Indonesia is a signatory to the Convention on International Trade in Endangered Species (CITES), and, as such, bans the import and export of products made from endangered species. In particular, it is forbidden to export any product made from green sea turtles or turtle shells.

Electricity

220v/230v/50hz

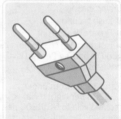

220v/230v/50hz

Embassies & Consulates

Foreign embassies are in Jakarta, the national capital. Most of the foreign representatives in Bali are consular agents (or honorary consuls) who can't offer the same services as a full consulate or embassy but can at least assist you with problems. A lost passport may mean a trip to an embassy in Jakarta.

The US, Australia and Japan have formal consulates in Bali (citizens from these countries make up half of all visitors). Unless noted, the following offices are open from about 8.30am to noon, Monday to Friday.

Indonesian embassies and consulates abroad are listed on the website of Indonesia's **Department of Foreign Affairs** (www.deplu.go.id).

Australia (Map p116; [☎]0361-241 118; www.bali .indonesia.embassy.gov.au; Jl Tantular 32, Denpasar; ⊙8am-4pm Mon-Fri) The Australian consulate has a consular sharing agreement with Canada.

Climate

Denpasar

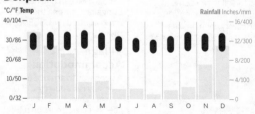

France (☏0361-285 485; consul@dps.centrin.net.id; Jl Mertasari, Gang II 8, Sanur)

Germany (☏0361-288 535; germanconsul@bali-ntb.com; Jl Pantai Karang 17, Batujimbar, Sanur)

Japan (☏0361-227 628; konjpdps@indo.net.id; Jl Raya Puputan 170, Renon, Denpasar)

Netherlands (Map p58; ☏0361-751 517; dutch consulate@kcbtours.com; Jl Raya Kuta 127, Kuta)

Switzerland (Map p58; ☏0361-751 735; swisscon@telkom.net; Kuta Galleria, Blok Valet 2, 12, Kuta)

UK (☏0361-270 601; www.ukinindonesia.fco.gov.uk; Jl Tirtanadi 20, Sanur)

USA (☏0361-233 605; amcobali@indosat.net.id; Jl Hayam Wuruk 310, Renon, Denpasar; ☉9am-3.30pm)

Gay & Lesbian Travellers

Gay travellers in Bali will experience few problems, and many of the island's most influential expat artists have been more-or-less openly gay. Physical contact between same-sex couples is acceptable and friends of the same sex often hold hands, though this does not indicate homosexuality.

There are many venues where gay men congregate, mostly in Kuta and Seminyak. There's nowhere that's exclusively gay, and nowhere that's even inconspicuously a lesbian scene. Hotels are happy to rent a room with a double bed to any couple. Homosexual

iPOD BROKE?

If your iPod or other Apple product breaks, iTube (☏0361-767 140; Jl Raya Kuta 100, Kuta) can fix it. Battery replacements are a fraction of Apple's prices.

behaviour is not illegal, and the age of consent for sexual activity is 18 years. Gay men in Indonesia are referred to as *homo* or *gay* and are quite distinct from the female impersonators called *waria*.

Many gays from other parts of the country come to live in Bali, as it is more tolerant, and also because it offers opportunities to meet foreign partners.

Gay prostitutes are mostly from Java, and some have been known to rip off their foreign clients. Gay Balinese men are usually looking for nothing more than adventure, though there is an expectation that the (relatively) wealthy foreign guy will pay for meals, drinks, hotels etc.

On Lombok, gay and lesbian travellers should refrain from public displays of affection (advice that also applies to straight couples).

The following are useful resources/organisations:

Bali Pink Pages (www.balipinkpages.com) Website by the Bali Gay & Lesbian Association.

Gaya Dewata (☏0361-780 8250; Denpasar) Bali's gay organisation.

Hanafi (☏0361-756 454; www.hanafi.net; Jl Pantai Kuta 1E) Kuta-based gay-friendly tour operator and guide; good for the low-down on the local scene.

Utopia Asia (www.utopia-asia.com) Not specific to Bali, but has excellent information about Bali's gay scene.

Insurance

Unless you are definitely sure that your health coverage at home will cover you in Bali and Lombok, you should take out travel insurance – bring a copy of the policy as evidence that you're covered. Get a policy that pays for medical evacuation if necessary. For more on health insurance, see p391.

Some policies specifically exclude 'dangerous activities', which can include scuba diving, renting a local motorcycle and even trekking. Be aware that a locally acquired motorcycle licence isn't valid under some policies. For more on vehicle insurance, see p387.

Worldwide travel insurance is available at www.lonelyplanet.com/travel_services. You can buy, extend and claim online anytime – even if you're already on the road.

Internet Access

Internet centres are common anywhere there are tourists in Bali. Expect to pay 300Rp to 500Rp per minute for access.

Speeds are usually fine for Skype and the like.

Many hotels have internet centres for guests. In-room wi-fi access is becoming common and many places are free. However, watch out for high charges pegged to time or data use (at one place two emails exhausted the 80,000Rp connection allowance). In south Bali and Ubud, wi-fi access in cafes is increasingly common and often free.

Indosat (www.indosatm2 .com) has a 3G data network across south Bali.

Internet access on Lombok tends to cost 400Rp to 500Rp per minute. Outside of Mataram and Senggigi, access is painfully slow.

In this book the @ icon is for hotels that have computers available for guest use. Wi-fi available at a hotel or a cafe gets a 🛜. Where coverage is not 100% this is noted, but you should always confirm independently if in-room access is vital to you.

Language Courses

Many visitors to Bali like to learn at least the basics of Bahasa Indonesia. Ubud is a good place to learn, as there are many private tutors. Formal schools include the following:

Indonesia Australia Language Foundation (IALF; ☎0361-225 243; www .ialf.edu; Jl Raya Sesetan 190, Denpasar) Well-regarded; offers a four-state 40-hour course (2,000,000Rp).

Seminyak Language School (☎0361-733 342; pelita_ater@yahoo.com; Jl Raya Seminyak, Seminyak) Popular with visitors, it is conveniently located down a footpath near the Bintang Supermarket.

Legal Matters

The government takes the smuggling, using and selling of drugs very, *very* seriously.

STOPPING CHILD-SEX TOURISM

Unfortunately, Indonesia has become a destination for foreigners seeking to sexually exploit local children. A range of socio-economic factors renders many children and young people vulnerable to such abuse and some individuals prey upon this vulnerability. The sexual abuse and exploitation of children has serious, life-long and even life-threatening consequences for the victims. Strong laws exist in Indonesia to prosecute offenders and many countries also have extraterritorial legislation that allows nationals to be prosecuted in their own country for these intolerable crimes.

For more information, contact the following organisations:

Child Wise (www.childwise.net) This is the Australian member of ECPAT.

ECPAT (End Child Prostitution & Trafficking; www.ecpat. org) A global network working on these issues, with over 70 affiliate organisations around the world.

PKPA (Center for Study & Child Protection; ☎061-663 7821 in Medan, Sumatra; pkpa@medan.wasantara.net. id) An organisation committed to the protection of Indonesia's children and the prevention of child-sex tourism.

Once caught, you may have to wait for up to six months in jail before trial. See Safe Travel (p373) for additional warnings. Gambling is illegal (although it's common, especially at cockfights), as is pornography.

Generally, you are unlikely to have any encounters with the police unless you are driving a rented car or motorcycle (see p388).

The age of consent is 18. Some governments (including the Australian government) have laws making it illegal for their citizens to use child prostitutes or engage in other paedophiliac activities anywhere in the world. Foreigners have been prosecuted and penalties are severe.

In both Bali and Lombok, there are police stations in all district capitals. If you have to report a crime or have other business at a police station, expect a lengthy and bureaucratic encounter. You should dress respectably, bring someone to help with translation, arrive early and be polite. You can also call the **Bali Tourist Police** (☎0361-224 111) for advice. Call ☎112 in an emergency in Bali.

Police officers often expect to receive bribes, either to overlook some crime, misdemeanour or traffic infringement, or to provide a service that they should provide anyway. Generally, it's easiest to pay up – and the sooner this happens, the less it will cost. Travellers may be told there's a 'fine' to pay on the spot, or some travellers offer to pay a 'fine' to clear things up. How much? Generally, 50,000Rp can work wonders and the officers are not proud. If things seem unreasonable, however, ask for the officer's name and write it down.

If you're in trouble, contact your consulate as soon as you can – they can't get you out of it, but they can recommend English-speaking lawyers and may have useful contacts.

Maps

For tourist resorts and towns, the maps in this guidebook are as good as you'll get. If you need a more detailed road map of the island, there are some OK sheet maps available in bookshops, but most are useless.

Periplus Travel Maps has a decent *Bali* contour map (1:250,000), with a detailed section on southern Bali, plus maps of the main town areas. However, the labelling and names used for towns are often incomprehensible. Periplus' *Lombok & Sumbawa* map is useful.

Money

Indonesia's unit of currency is the rupiah (Rp). There are coins worth 50, 100, 500 and 1000Rp. Notes come in denominations of 1000Rp, 5000Rp, 10,000Rp, 20,000Rp, 50,000Rp and 100,000Rp.

See Need to Know (p19) for an idea about current exchange rates of the rupiah. In recent times the currency has been fairly stable. Many midrange and all top-end hotels, along with some tourist attractions and tour companies, list their prices in US dollars, although you can usually pay in rupiah at a poorer exchange rate.

US dollars are the most convertible currency.

Always carry a good supply of rupiah in small denominations with you. People will struggle to make change for a 50,000Rp note or larger. And note that some shops will struggle with change period: chronic shortages of coins mean you'll often get small candies in lieu of 100Rp coins.

ATMs

There are ATMs all over Bali (with the notable exception of Nusa Lembongan). Most accept nonlocal ATM cards and major credit cards for cash advances. The exchange rates for ATM withdrawals are usually quite good, but check to see if your home bank will hit you with outrageous fees. Most ATMs in Bali allow a maximum withdrawal of 600,000Rp to 1.2 million rupiah. Avoid ones with a sticker saying '100,000Rp', as that's the denomination you'll get and you'll struggle to break those bills. Note: some Bank BRI ATMs get cranky with international ATM cards.

You'll find ATMs in Mataram, Praya and Senggigi on Lombok and now also on Gili Trawangan.

Banks

Major banks have branches in the main tourist centres and provincial capitals. Smaller towns may not have banks at all or have banks that don't exchange currency. Changing money in banks can be time consuming.

Cash

Changing money in Bali and Lombok isn't too difficult in tourist areas. It's easiest to exchange US banknotes, especially US$100 bills. However, make certain that your money is new and recent: older designs and damaged notes will often be refused.

Credit Cards

Visa, MasterCard and Amex are accepted by most of the larger businesses that cater to tourists. Conversions are at the interbank rate, though some banks add usage and exchange fees, which are strictly for their own profit. Be sure to confirm that a business accepts credit cards before you show up cashless.

Moneychangers

Exchange rates offered by moneychangers are normally better than the banks, plus they offer quicker service and keep much longer hours. The exchange rates are advertised on boards along footpaths or on windows out-

---

THE ART OF BARGAINING

Many everyday purchases in Bali require bargaining. Accommodation has a set price, but this is usually negotiable in the low season, or if you are staying at the hotel for several days.

Bargaining can be an enjoyable part of shopping in Bali, so maintain your sense of humour and keep things in perspective. Try following these steps:

» Have some idea what the item is worth.

» Establish a starting price – ask the seller for their price rather than making an initial offer.

» Your first price can be from one-third to two-thirds of the asking price – assuming that the asking price is not outrageous.

» With offers and counter-offers, move closer to an acceptable price.

» If you don't get to an acceptable price, you're entitled to walk – the vendor may call you back with a lower price.

» Note that when you name a price, you're committed – you must buy if your offer is accepted.

side shops. It's worth looking around because rates vary a little, but beware of places advertising exceptionally high rates – they may make their profit by short-changing their customers (see p373).

Tipping

Tipping a set percentage is not expected in Bali, but restaurant workers are poorly paid; if the service is good, it's appropriate to leave 5000Rp or more. Most midrange hotels and restaurants and all top-end hotels and restaurants add 21% to the bill for tax and service (known as 'plus plus'). This service component is distributed among hotel staff (one hopes), so you needn't tip under these circumstances, although handing the cash to individuals is the best way to see that they get it.

It's also a nice thing to tip taxi drivers, guides, people giving you a massage or fetching you a beer on the beach etc; 5000Rp to 10,000Rp is generous.

Travellers Cheques

Travellers cheques are hard to exchange, especially if they are not in US dollars. The exchange rates are often worse than for cash.

Photography

Bali is one of the most photogenic places on earth, so be prepared.

You can buy additional memory cards for digital cameras at shops in the major tourist centres, but you're really better off bringing what you need from home.

Practical matters to consider include the following:

» Photograph people with discretion and manners. Ask first: a gesture, smile and nod usually work.

» You may unobtrusively take photos of ceremonies in villages and temples.

» Ask before taking photos inside a temple.

» Never take photos at public bathing places; to do so is considered crass voyeurism.

Post

Every substantial town has a kantor pos. In tourist centres, there are also postal agencies, which are often open long hours and provide postal services.

Sending postcards and normal-sized letters (ie under 20g) by airmail is cheap, but not really fast.

Mail delivery times from Bali:

Australia Two weeks

UK & rest of Europe Three weeks

US Two weeks

Post offices will properly wrap your parcels over 20g for shipping for a small fee. Although goods usually arrive, don't use the post for anything you'd miss. Express companies offer reliable, fast and expensive service. These include the following:

FedEx (☎0361-701 727; Jl Bypass Nusa Dua 100X, Jimbaran) Located south of the airport.

UPS (☎0361-766 676; Jl Bypass Ngurah Rai 2005) Has a location near the Bali Galleria.

Public Holidays

The following holidays are celebrated throughout Indonesia. Many of the dates change according to the phase of the moon (not by month) or by religious calendar, so the following are estimates only.

Tahun Baru Masehi (New Year's Day) 1 January

Idul Adha (Muslim festival of sacrifice) February

Muharram (Islamic New Year) February/March

Nyepi (Hindu New Year) March/April

Hari Paskah (Good Friday) April

Ascension of Christ April/May

Hari Waisak (Buddha's birth, enlightenment and death) April/May

Maulud Nabi Mohammed/ Hari Natal (Prophet Mohammed's birthday) May

Hari Proklamasi Kemerdekaan (Indonesian Independence Day) 17 August

Isra Miraj Nabi Mohammed (Ascension of the Prophet Mohammed) September

Idul Fitri (End of Ramadan) November/December

SHIPPING LARGE ITEMS

For items that are shipped, you'll pay a 40% or 50% deposit and the balance (plus any taxes or import duties) when you collect the items at home. Arrange for delivery to your door – if you have to pick the items up from the nearest port or freight depot, you may be up for extra port charges.

Most stores selling furniture or heavy artwork can arrange packing, shipping and insurance. Shipping costs for volumes less than a full container load vary greatly according to the company, destination and quantity – think in terms of around US$150-plus per cubic metre. Be aware that packing costs, insurance, fumigation(!) and so on are included in some companies' prices but not others.

Rim Cargo (Map p74; ☎0361-737 670; www.rim cargo.com; Jl Laksmana 32, Seminyak) is a large company adept at dealing with the needs of Bali visitors.

Hari Natal (Christmas Day)
25 December

See Month by Month (p26) for additional holidays. The Muslim population in Bali observes Islamic festivals and holidays, including Ramadan. Religious and other holidays on Lombok are as follows:

Anniversary of West Lombok (Government holiday) 17 April

Ramadan Usually October

Founding of West Nusa Tenggara (Public holiday) 17 December

Safe Travel

It's important to note that compared with many places in the world, Bali is fairly safe. There are some hassles from the avaricious, but most visitors face many more dangers at home. Petty theft occurs but it is not prevalent.

Security increased after the 2002 and 2005 bombings but has tended to fade. The odds you will be caught up in such a tragedy are low. Note that large luxury hotels that are part of international chains tend to have the best security.

As for all destinations, it's a good idea to check your government's travel advisories before you depart.

Annoyances
HAWKERS & TOUTS

Many visitors regard hawkers and touts as *the* number one annoyance in Bali (and in tourist areas of Lombok). Visitors are frequently, and often constantly, hassled to buy things. The worst places for this are Jl Legian in Kuta, Kuta Beach, the Gunung Batur area and the over-subscribed temples at Besakih and Tanah Lot. And the cry of 'Transport?!?', that's everywhere. Many touts employ fake, irritating Australian accents ('Oi! Mate!').

Deal with hawkers by completely ignoring them from the first instance. Eye contact is crucial – don't make any! Even a polite *'tidak'* (no) encourages them. Never ask the price or comment on the quality of their goods unless you're interested in buying, or you want to spend half an hour haggling. Keep in mind, though, that ultimately they're just people trying to make a living, and if you don't want to buy anything, you are wasting their time trying to be polite.

In another scheme, some immigration officers are suspected of selling the names of visitors and the hotel they're staying at to timeshare sellers, who then call these people at their hotel.

Drugs

Numerous high-profile drug cases in Bali and on Lombok should be enough to dissuade anyone from having anything to do with illicit drugs. As little as two ecstasy tabs or a bit of pot have resulted in huge fines and multiyear jail sentences in Bali's notorious jail in Kerobokan. Try smuggling and you may pay with your life. Note that clubbers have been hit with random urine tests.

Scams

Bali has such a relaxed atmosphere, and the people are so friendly, that you may not be on the lookout for scams. It's hard to say when an 'accepted' practice such as overcharging becomes

an unacceptable rip-off, but be warned that there are people in Bali (not always Balinese) who will try to rip you off.

Most Balinese would never perpetrate a scam, but it seems that very few would warn a foreigner when one is happening. Be suspicious if you notice that bystanders are uncommunicative and perhaps uneasy, and one person is doing all the talking.

Common scams include the following.

CAR CON

Locals (often working in pairs) discover a 'serious problem' with your car or motorcycle – it's blowing smoke, leaking oil or petrol, a wheel is wobbling or a tyre is flat (problems that one of the pair creates while the other distracts you). Coincidentally, a brother/cousin/ friend nearby can help, and soon, they're demanding an outrageous sum for their trouble.

CASH SCHEMES

Many travellers are ripped off by moneychangers who use sleight of hand and rigged calculators. Always count your money at least twice in front of the moneychanger, and don't let them touch the money again after you've finally counted it. The best defence is to use a bank-affiliated currency exchange or ATMs (although there has been a rash of fake card skimmers attached to ATMs, so check authenticity).

GOVERNMENT TRAVEL ADVICE

Government advisories are often general; however, the following sites have useful tips:

Australia (www.smartraveller.gov.au)
Canada (www.voyage.gc.ca)
New Zealand (www.safetravel.govt.nz)
UK (www.fco.gov.uk)
US (www.travel.state.gov)

Swimming

Kuta Beach and those to the north and south are subject to heavy surf and strong currents – always swim between the flags. Trained lifeguards are on duty, but only at Kuta, Legian, Seminyak, Nusa Dua, Sanur and (sometimes) Senggigi. Most other beaches are protected by coral reefs, so they don't have big waves, but the currents can still be treacherous, especially along the coast running north and west from Seminyak and east from Sanur. Currents can also cause problems off the Gilis.

Water pollution is a problem, especially after rain. Try to swim well away from any open streams you see flowing into the surf.

Be careful when swimming over coral, and never walk on it. It can be very sharp and coral cuts are easily infected. In addition, you are damaging a fragile environment.

Theft

Violent crime is relatively uncommon, but bag-snatching, pickpocketing and theft from rooms and parked cars does occur in tourist centres. A few precautions:

» Secure money before leaving an ATM

» Don't leave valuables on a beach while swimming

» Use front desk/in-room safes

Traffic

Apart from the dangers of driving in Bali (see p387), the traffic in most tourist areas is often annoying and frequently dangerous to pedestrians. Footpaths can be rough, even unusable; gaps in the pavement are a top cause of injury. Carry a torch (flashlight) at night.

Telephone

Most public telephones, wartel and hotels block access to the toll-free ☏008 or ☏001 access numbers needed to use international

MORE SAFETY INFO

See p72 for warnings specific to the Kuta region. For information on Bali's notorious dogs and the rabies epidemic, see p163. See p392 for details on international clinics and medical care in Bali.

The many boat services between Bali and the surrounding islands are unregulated and there have been accidents. See p384 for information on how to improve your odds for a trouble-free journey.

phonecards or other home-billing schemes, and the few hotels and wartel that do permit it charge a fee for doing so. Calling internationally on a land line can easily cost from US$0.25 to US$1 or more a minute.

Internet Calling

Skype usage is common in south Bali and Ubud. Internet centres are hip to this and some allow it while others add a surcharge for the call to your connection time (perhaps 3000Rp per minute). If you're staying at a place with fast in-room wi-fi, you're set.

Mobile Phones

The cellular service in Indonesia is GSM; local providers include Telkomsel and Pro XL. Check with your mobile phone company to see if you can use your phone in Indonesia and – importantly – what the roaming rates will be (possibly outrageous).

Alternatively, a GSM mobile phone can be used cheaply if you purchase a prepaid SIM card in Bali. A mere 50,000Rp will give you your own local telephone

number. However, make certain your phone is unlocked, is OK with GSM frequencies of 900/1800 (eg Europe, Australia, some of the US) and is able to use SIM cards. Basic phones bought locally start at US$30.

Calls from a mobile with a local SIM card can be inexpensive. When you buy your SIM card, ask about special access codes that can result in international calls for as low as US$0.25 per minute.

Many shops are adept at getting your mobile access sorted. A convenient one is **Diamond Selular Center** (Map p74; ☏0361-736 779; Bintang Supermarket, Jl Raya Seminyak 17, Seminyak).

Phone Codes

Bali has six telephone area codes and Lombok two; these are listed in the relevant chapters of this book. Phone numbers beginning with ☏08 belong to mobile (cell) phones.

Useful numbers include the following:

Directory assistance	☏108
Indonesia Country Code	☏62
International Call Prefix	☏001/ 017
International Operator	☏102

Phonecards

The vast majority of public phones use phonecards. You can buy phonecards in denominations of 5000Rp, 10,000Rp, 25,000Rp, 50,000Rp and 100,000Rp at wartel, moneychangers, post offices and many shops.

Time

Bali and Lombok are on Waktu Indonesian Tengah or WIT (Central Indonesian Standard Time), which is eight hours ahead of Greenwich Mean Time/Universal Time or two hours behind Australian Eastern Standard

Time. Java is another hour behind Bali and Lombok.

Not allowing for daylight-saving time elsewhere, when it's noon in Bali and Lombok, it's 11pm the previous day in New York, 8pm in Los Angeles, 4am in London, 5am in Paris and Amsterdam, noon in Perth, 1pm in Tokyo, and 2pm in Sydney and Melbourne.

'Bali time' is an expression that refers to the Balinese reluctance to be obsessed by punctuality.

Toilets

You'll encounter Asian-style toilets only in the very cheapest accommodation. These toilets have two footrests and a hole in the floor – you squat down and aim. In almost every place catering for tourists, Western-style sit-down toilets are the norm. At some tourist attractions in Bali, there are public toilets that cost about 1000Rp per visit, but they can be filthy.

Apart from tourist cafes, restaurants and most accommodation, you won't find toilet paper, so bring your own. If there is a bin next to the toilet, it's for toilet paper to avoid clogged plumbing.

Tourist Information

The tourist office in Ubud is an excellent source of information on cultural events. Otherwise, the tourist offices in Bali are not useful.

Some of the best information is found in the many free publications and websites aimed at tourists and expats, which are distributed in south Bali and Ubud. These include the following:

Bali Advertiser (www.bali advertiser.biz) This newspaper and website has voluminous ads, comprehensive information and scores of idiosyncratic columnists.

Bali Discovery (www.balidis covery.com) Has an essential and first-rate Bali news section and a wealth of other island information.

Bali Times (www.thebalitimes .com) Weekly newspaper with provocative columnists.

Lombok Times (www.lombok times.com) A newspaper and website with tourist news and features.

The Beat (beatmag.com) Excellent bi-weekly with extensive entertainment and cultural listings.

Yak (www.theyakmag.com) Glossy, cheeky mag celebrating the expat swells of Seminyak and Ubud.

Travellers with Disabilities

Bali is a difficult destination for those with limited mobility. While some of the airlines flying to Bali have a good reputation for accommodating people with disabilities, the airport is not well set up. Contact the airlines and ask them what arrangements can be made for disembarking and boarding at the airport.

Public transport is not accessible; ditto the mini-buses used by shuttle bus and tour companies. Ramps and other disabled facilities at hotels and inns are uncommon. Your best bet are the international chains, but even then you should confirm your needs with the property. Out on the street, the footpaths, where they exist at all, tend to be narrow, uneven, potholed and frequently obstructed.

However, Bali can be a rewarding destination for people who are blind or vision impaired. Balinese music is heard everywhere, and the languages are fascinating to listen to. The smells of incense, spices, tropical fruit and flowers pervade the island. With a sighted companion, most places should be reasonably accessible.

Visas

The visa situation in Indonesia seems to be constantly in flux. It is essential that you confirm current formalities before you arrive in Bali or Lombok. Failure to meet all the entrance requirements can see you on the first flight out.

No matter what type of visa you are going to use, your passport *must* be valid for at least six months from the date of your arrival.

The main visa options for visitors to Bali and Lombok are as follows:

Visa in Advance Citizens of countries not eligible for Visa Free or Visa on Arrival must apply for a visa before they arrive in Indonesia. Typically this is a visitor's visa, which comes in two flavours: 30 or 60 days. Details vary by country; contact your nearest Indonesian embassy or consulate to determine processing fees and times. Note: this is the only way to obtain a 60-day visitor visa.

Visa on Arrival Citizens of over 50 countries may apply for a visa when they arrive at the airports in Bali and Lombok. The cost is US$25; be sure to have the exact amount in US currency. This visa is good for 30 days; for renewals, see p376. Eligible countries include Australia, Austria, Belgium, Canada, Denmark, France, Germany, Ireland, Italy, Japan, the Netherlands, New Zealand, Russia, South Africa, South Korea, Spain, Switzerland, Sweden, Taiwan, UK and the USA. Not all EU countries qualify.

Visa Free Citizens of Singapore and a smattering of other countries can receive a nonextendable 30-day visa for free upon arrival.

Whichever type of visa you use to enter Bali or Lombok,

RENEWING YOUR VISA

In 2010 it became possible to renew a 30-day Visa on Arrival once. However, the procedures have been poorly understood, especially by local bureaucrats. Here's what to do (according to a top local immigration official):

» At least seven days before your visa expires, go to the **Kuta Immigration Office** (Jl Airport Ngurah Rai), which is just off the main airport access road in Tuban (not actually Kuta).

» Bring a photocopy of your passport, your passport and a copy of your ticket out of Indonesia (which should be for a date during the renewal period).

» Pay a fee of 250,000Rp.

» Fill out the renewal form in black ink.

» List an address in Kuta (saying 'I'm staying in the Gilis', for instance, will get you sent to Lombok).

» Brave crowds and lines until you have your renewal.

you'll be issued with a tourist card that is valid for a 30- or 60-day stay (if you have obtained one of the coveted 60-day visas in advance, be sure the immigration official at the airport gives you a 60-day card). Keep the tourist card with your passport, as you'll have to hand it back when you leave the country. Note that some travellers have been fined for overstaying by only a day or so (officially it is US$20 per day for up to 60 days past your visa, after which it can mean jail) or for losing their tourist card.

Other Visa Matters

Note the following when applying for your visa (including Visa on Arrival) at the airport:

» Your passport *must* have six months of validity past the time of your stay. This is enforced.

» Visitors are often asked to show a return air ticket.

» Scruffy types may be asked to show up to US$1000 in cash.

If you want to spend more time in Indonesia beyond your visa period, you have to leave the country and then re-enter – some long-term foreign residents have been doing this for years. Singapore is the destination of choice for obtaining a new visa on the 'visa run'.

Complex visa matters may be referred to the main **Denpasar office** (✆0361-227 828; ◷8am-2pm Mon-Thu, 8-11am Fri, 8am-noon Sat) of the *kantor imigrasi*. Otherwise the airport office will suffice.

On Lombok, the **immigration office** (✆0370-632 520; Jl Udayana 2; ◷7am-2pm Mon-Thu, 7-11am Fri, 7am-12.30pm Sat) is in Mataram.

For visa advice and service, many expats in south Bali use the services of **Bali Mode** (✆0361-765 162; www.balimode-biz.com). Visa extensions (on legally extendable visas) average 500,000Rp.

Social Visas

If you have a good reason for staying longer (eg study or family reasons), you can apply for a *sosial/budaya* (social/cultural) visa. You will need an application form from an Indonesian embassy or consulate, and a letter of introduction or promise of sponsorship from a reputable person or school in Indonesia. It's initially valid for three months, but it can be extended for one month at a time at an immigration office within Indonesia for a maximum of six months. There are fees for the application and for extending the visa.

Volunteering

There's a plethora of opportunities to lend a hand in Bali and Lombok. Many people have found that they can show their love for these places by helping others.

Bali Spirit (www.balispirit.com/ngos) has information on a number of nonprofit and volunteer groups. For info on organisations helping Bali's dogs, see p163.

Local Organisations

The following organisations need donations, supplies and often volunteers. Check their websites to see their current status.

East Bali Poverty Project (✆0361-410 071; www.eastbalipovertyproject.org; Denpasar) Works to help children in the impoverished mountain villages of east Bali (see p206).

Helen Flavel Foundation (www.helenflavelfoundation.org) Always looking for people to help sponsor its students and its many projects in north Bali, which include education, senior care, health projects for women and animal-aid projects.

IDEP (Indonesian Development of Education & Permaculture; ✆0361-981 504; www.idepfoundation.org) A large Ubud-based organisation that works on environmental projects, disaster planning and community improvement.

JED (Village Ecotourism Network; ✆0361-735 320; www.jed.or.id) Organises highly regarded tours of small villages (see p390). Often needs volunteers to improve its services and work with the villagers.

PPLH Bali (Pusat Pendidikan Lingkungan Hidup; ☑0361-288 221; www.pplhbali.or.id; Jl Hang Tuah 24, Sanur) Organises a broad range of environmental and education programs.

ProFauna (☑0361-424 731; www.profauna.or.id) A large nonprofit animal-protection organisation operating across Indonesia; the Bali office has been aggressive in protecting sea turtles. Volunteers needed to help with hatchery releases and editing publications.

Smile Foundation of Bali (Yayasan Senyum; ☑0361-233 758; www.senyumbali.org) Organises surgery to correct facial deformities; operates the Smile Shop in Ubud (p161) to raise money.

SOS (Sumatran Orangutan Society; www.orangutans-sos.org) An Ubud-based group that works to save endangered species throughout Indonesia; has a good charity shop (p161).

WISNU (☑0361-735 321; www.wisnu.or.id; Jl Pengubengan Kauh, Kerobokan) An environmental group that teaches tourism-related industries how to be more green. It's set up community-based recycling programs with 25 hotels on the Bukit Peninsula, and always needs volunteers. It runs Warung Beten Gatep (p86).

Yakkum Bali (Yayasan Rama Sesana; ☑0361-247 363; www.yrsbali.org; Denpasar) Dedicated to improving reproductive health for women across Bali.

Yayasan Bumi Sehat (☑0361-970 002; www.bumisehatbali.org) Operates a clinic and gives reproductive services to disadvantaged women in Ubud; accepts donated time from medical professionals.

YKIP (Humanitarian Foundation of Mother Earth; ☑0361-759 544; www.ykip.org) Established after the 2002 bombings, it organises and funds health and education projects for Bali's children.

International Organisations

The following agencies are other possible sources of long-term paid or volunteer work in Bali or Lombok.

Australian Volunteers International (www.australianvolunteers.com) Organises professional contracts for Australians.

Global Volunteers (www.globalvolunteers.org) Arranges professional and paid volunteer work for US citizens.

Voluntary Service Overseas Canada (www.vsocanada.org); Netherlands (www.vso.nl); UK (www.vso.org.uk) British overseas volunteer program that accepts qualified volunteers from other countries.

Volunteer Service Abroad (www.vsa.org.nz) Organises professional contracts for New Zealanders.

Women Travellers

Bali

Women travelling solo in Bali will get a lot of attention from Balinese guys, but Balinese men are, on the whole, fairly benign. Generally, Bali is safer for women than many areas of the world, and with the usual care and common sense, women should feel secure travelling alone. (Although some recent high-profile attacks in south Bali have reminded people of the need for caution.)

If you are staying in Bali for longer than a short holiday, the **Bali International Women's Association** (BIWA; ☑0361-285 552; www.biwa-bali.org) can prove useful. It helps members integrate into local life and runs good charitable projects.

Lombok

Traditionally, women on Lombok are treated with respect, but in the touristy areas, harassment of single foreign women may occur. Would-be guides/boyfriends/gigolos are often persistent in their approaches, and can be aggressive when ignored or rejected. Clothes that aren't too revealing are a good idea – beachwear should be reserved for the beach, and the less skin you expose the better. Two or more women together are less likely to experience problems, and women accompanied by a man are unlikely to be harassed. Don't walk alone at night.

Kuta Cowboys

In tourist areas of Bali (and Lombok), you'll encounter young men who are keen to spend time with visiting women. Commonly called 'Kuta cowboys', beach boys, bad boys or gigolos, these guys think they're super-cool, with long hair, lean bodies, tight jeans and lots of tattoos. While they don't usually work a straight sex-for-money deal, the visiting woman pays for meals, drinks and accommodation, and commonly buys the guy presents.

While most of these guys are genuinely friendly and quite charming, some are predatory con artists who practise elaborate deceits. Many of them now come from outside Bali and have a long succession of foreign lovers. This long-established Bali phenomenon became the centre of scandal in 2010 when the movie *Cowboys in Paradise* was released (see p65).

Work

Quite a lot of foreigners own businesses in Bali – mostly hotels, restaurants, Seminyak shops and tour agencies. To do so legally, foreigners need the appropriate work or business visa, which requires sponsorship from an employer, or evidence of a business that brings investment to Indonesia. Many foreigners are engaged in buying and exporting clothing, handicrafts or furniture, and stay for short periods – within the limits of a 30- or 60-day tourist card. It's illegal to work if you've entered Indonesia on a tourist card, and you'll have to leave the country to change your visa status. Even if you do get work, typically teaching English, payment is often in rupiah, which doesn't convert into a lot of foreign currency. Under-the-table work, such as dive-shop and bar jobs, is typically poorly paid.

Transport

GETTING THERE & AWAY

Most international visitors to Bali will arrive by air, either directly or via Jakarta. For island-hoppers, there are frequent ferries between eastern Java and Bali, and between Bali and Lombok, as well as domestic flights between the islands. Most people visit Lombok via Bali.

Flights, tours and rail tickets can be booked online at www.lonelyplanet.com/travel_services.

Entering the Region

Arrival procedures at Bali's airport are straightforward, although it can take some time for planeloads of visitors to clear immigration; afternoons are worst, with waits of up to two hours to get through immigration. At the baggage claim area, porters are keen to help get your luggage to the customs tables and beyond, and they've been known to ask up to US$20 for their services – if you want help with your bags, agree on a price beforehand. The formal price is 5000Rp per piece.

Once through customs, you're out with the tour operators, touts and taxi drivers. The touts will be working hard to convince you to come and stay at some place in the Kuta area. If you go with these guys, you'll pay more than you would if you just show up on your own, as they get large commissions.

Passport

Your passport *must* be valid for six months after your date of arrival in Indonesia. Visas are the most nettlesome detail; see p375 for more.

Air

Although Jakarta, the national capital, is the gateway airport to Indonesia, there are also many direct international flights to Bali and a few to Lombok.

Airports & Airlines
BALI AIRPORT

The only airport in Bali, Ngurah Rai Airport (DPS) is just south of Kuta; however, it is sometimes referred to internationally as Denpasar or on some internet flight-booking sites as Bali.

The **international terminal** (☎0361-751 011) and **domestic terminal** (☎0361-751 011) are a few hundred metres apart. In the first, you'll find internet centres and shops with high prices. There is also a slew of private lounges where you can relax in far more comfort than in the crowded terminal. Although supposedly reserved for premium customers, 50,000Rp to an attendant often works for the lowly economy flyer.

The rates offered at the exchange counters at the international and domestic terminals are competitive, as good as the moneychangers in the tourist centres. There are ATMs in both terminals before and after immigration.

The **left-luggage room** (per piece per day 30,000Rp; ⊙24hr) is in the international terminal, behind the McDonald's near the departures area.

A doubling in size of the terminals began in 2010; the international terminal will eventually be relocated to a vast area near the present domestic terminal. Expect chaos for years. The oft-discussed scheme to lengthen the runway keeps running into hurdles, such as environmental concerns about destroying more of the mangroves. The present runway is too short for planes flying direct to/from Europe, so for these flights passengers need to change planes at places such as Singapore or Jakarta.

International airlines flying to and from Bali regularly change. Service is expanding, however, especially to Australia, where a new policy allows almost unlimited flying between Bali and Oz.

Airlines flying to/from the region include the following:

Air Asia (airline code AK; www.airasia.com) Serves Bangkok, Kota Kinabalu, Kuala Lumpur and Kuching in Malaysia, and Singapore, plus Darwin and Perth in Australia.

Cathay Pacific Airways (airline code CX; www.cathaypacific.com) Serves Hong Kong.

China Airlines (airline code CI; www.china-airlines.com) Serves Taipei.

Eva Air (airline code BR; www.evaair.com) Serves Taipei.

Garuda Indonesia (airline code GA; www.garuda-indonesia.com) Serves Australia (Darwin, Melbourne, Perth and Sydney), Japan, Korea and Singapore direct.

Jetstar/Qantas Airways (airline code QF; www.qantas.com.au) Serves Brisbane, Darwin, Melbourne, Perth and Sydney.

KLM (airline code KL; www.klm.com) Serves Amsterdam via Singapore.

Korean Air (airline code KE; www.koreanair.com) Serves Seoul.

Lion Air (airline code JT; www.lionair.co.id) Serves Singapore.

Malaysia Airlines (airline code MH; www.mas.com.my) Serves Kuala Lumpur.

Merpati Airlines (airline code MZ; www.merpati.co.id) Serves Dili in East Timor.

LOMBOK'S NEW AIRPORT

Lombok International Airport (Bandara Internasional Lombok), a new airport in the south of the island, is slated for a much-delayed official opening ceremony in 2011. Consult with your travel agent or airline about its opening. Access to the tourist areas of the north will probably be slow as road construction has been delayed. See p261 for more information.

Pacific Blue (airline code DJ; www.flypacificblue.com) Offshoot of Australia's Virgin Blue; serves Australia.

Qatar Airways (airline code QR; www.qatarairways.com) Serves Doha via Singapore.

Singapore Airlines (airline code SQ; www.singaporeair.com) Several Singapore flights daily.

Strategic Airlines (airline code VC; www.flystrategic.com.au) Serves Australia.

Thai Airways International (airline code TG; www.thaiair.com) Serves Bangkok.

Domestic airlines serving Bali from other parts of Indonesia change frequently. All have ticket offices at the domestic terminal, which you may need to use, as internet sales are difficult with some.

Air Asia (airline code AK; www.airasia.com) Serves Jakarta.

Batavia Air (airline code Y6; www.batavia-air.co.id) Serves Jakarta.

Garuda Indonesia (airline code GA; www.garuda-indonesia.com) Serves numerous cities, including Jakarta, Kupang, Makasar and Surabaya.

Lion Air (airline code JT; www.lionair.co.id) Serves Jakarta, Kupang, Makasar, Surabaya and Yogyakarta.

Mandala Airlines (airline code RI; www.mandalaair.com) Serves Jakarta and Surabaya.

Merpati Airlines (airline code MZ; www.merpati.co.id) Serves many smaller Indonesian cities, in addition to the main ones.

LOMBOK AIRPORT
Lombok's Selaparang Airport (AMI) is in north Mataram. See p260 for information about airlines flying to and from Lombok. Also see the boxed text on this page for details about Lombok's new airport.

Tickets
Deregulation in the Asian and Indonesian aviation markets means that there are frequent deals to Bali. Check major web-based travel agents and with the airlines for special promotions.

ROUND-THE-WORLD TICKETS
Round-the-world (RTW) tickets that include Bali are usually offered by an alliance of several airlines, such as **Star Alliance** (www.staralliance.com) and **One World** (www.oneworld.com). These tickets come in many flavours, but most let you visit several continents over a period of time that can be as long as a year. It's also worth investigating Circle Pacific–type tickets, which are similar to RTW tickets but limit you to the Pacific region.

These tickets can be great deals. Prices for RTW tickets are often under US$2000 – not much different from what you'd pay for the flight to Bali alone from North America or Europe.

Asia
Bali is well connected to major Asian hubs such as Hong Kong, Seoul, Singapore and Taipei. Lombok is now linked to Singapore.

Australia
Service to Australia is almost out of control, as scores of carriers rush to add flights after Australia and Indonesia deregulated service.

Canada
From Canada, you'll change planes at an Asian hub.

Continental Europe
None of the major European carriers can fly to Bali nonstop due to the length of the runway. Singapore is the most likely place to change planes coming from Europe, with Bangkok, Hong Kong and Kuala Lumpur also

DEPARTURE TAX

The departure tax from Bali and Lombok is 50,000Rp for domestic flights and 150,000Rp for international ones. Have exact cash ready for the collecting officer.

popular. You can switch to a score of airlines for the final hop to Bali in any of these cities.

New Zealand
You will have to change planes in Australia or Singapore.

Other Indonesian Islands
From Bali, you can get flights to major Indonesian cities, often for under US$50 and definitely for not much more than US$100. The ticket area at the domestic terminal is a bit of a bazaar. Deals to Jakarta put the price of a plane ticket in the same class as the bus – with a saving of about 22 hours.

From Lombok, you can get some decent deals but direct service is mostly limited to Bali, Surabaya and Jakarta.

UK & Ireland
From London, the most direct service to Bali is via Singapore, Bangkok, Hong Kong and Kuala Lumpur.

USA
The best connections are through any of the major Asian hubs with nonstop service to Bali. No US airline serves Bali.

Sea
You can reach Java, just west of Bali, and Sumbawa, just east of Lombok, via ferries. Through buses can take you all the way to Jakarta. Longer-distance boats serve Indonesia's eastern islands.

Java
When visiting Java from Bali and Lombok, some land travel is necessary.

FERRY
Running constantly, **ferries** (adult/child 6000/4500Rp, car & driver 95,000Rp, motorbike 31,000Rp; ⊗24hr) cross the Bali Strait between Gilimanuk in western Bali and Ketapang (Java). The actual crossing takes under 30 minutes, but you'll spend longer than this loading, unloading and waiting around. Car-rental contracts usually prohibit rental vehicles being taken out of Bali.

From Ketapang, bemo travel 4km north to the terminal, where buses leave for Baluran, Probolinggo (for Gunung Bromo), Surabaya, Yogyakarta and Jakarta.

BUS
The ferry crossing from Bali is included in the services

to/from Ubung terminal in Denpasar offered by numerous bus companies, many of which travel overnight. It's advisable to buy your ticket at least one day in advance from travel agents or at the Ubung terminal. Note, too, that fierce air competition has put tickets to Jakarta and Surabaya in the range of bus prices.

Fares vary between operators; it's worth paying extra for a decent seat and air-con. Typical fares/travel times include Yogyakarta 300,000Rp/16 hours and Jakarta 500,000Rp/24 hours.

On Lombok, public buses go daily from Mandalika terminal to major cities on Java. Most buses are comfortable, with air-con and reclining seats. Destinations include Surabaya (225,000Rp, 20 hours), Yogyakarta (310,000Rp, 30 hours) and Jakarta (415,000Rp, 36 hours).

TRAIN
Bali doesn't have trains but the **state railway company** (⊇0361-227131; www.kereta -api.com; Jl Diponegoro 150/ B4; ⊗8.30am-6.30pm) does have an office in Denpasar. From here buses leave for eastern Java where they link with trains at Banyuwangi for Surabaya, Yogyakarta and Jakarta, among other destinations. Fares and times are comparable to the bus, but the air-conditioned trains are more comfortable, even in economy class. Note: on

CLIMATE CHANGE & TRAVEL

Every form of transport that relies on carbon-based fuel generates CO_2, the main cause of human-induced climate change. Modern travel is dependent on aeroplanes, which might use less fuel per kilometre per person than most cars but travel much greater distances. The altitude at which aircraft emit gases (including CO_2) and particles also contributes to their climate change impact. Many websites offer 'carbon calculators' that allow people to estimate the carbon emissions generated by their journey and, for those who wish to do so, to offset the impact of the greenhouse gases emitted with contributions to portfolios of climate-friendly initiatives throughout the world. Lonely Planet offsets the carbon footprint of all staff and author travel.

the website *jadwal* means schedule.

Sumbawa

Ferries travel between Labuhan Lombok and Poto Tano on Sumbawa every 45 minutes (passenger 18,000Rp, motorbike 42,000Rp, car 322,000Rp). They run 24 hours a day and the trip takes 1½ hours. There are direct buses from Mandalika terminal to Bima (175,000Rp, 13 hours) and Sumbawa Besar (100,000Rp, six hours).

Other Indonesian Islands

Services to other islands in Indonesia are often in flux, although **Pelni** (www.pelni .co.id), the national shipping line, is reasonably reliable. It schedules large boats on long-distance runs throughout Indonesia.

For Bali, three Pelni ships stop at the harbour in Benoa as part of their regular loops throughout Indonesia. Schedules change often, so check for details locally, but in general, fares, even in 1st class, are very low, eg Benoa to Surabaya on Java costs US$35. You can inquire and book at the **Pelni offices** (📞0361-763 963, 021-7918 0606; www.pelni.co.id; Jl Raya Kuta 299; ⏰8am-noon & 1-4pm Mon-Fri, 8am-1pm Sat) in Tuban.

Pelni ships link Lembar on Lombok with other parts of Indonesia. Check schedules and buy tickets at Mataram's **Pelni office** (📞0370-637 212; Jl Industri 1; ⏰8am-noon & 1-3.30pm Mon-Thu & Sat, 8-11am Fri).

GETTING AROUND

Especially in Bali, the best way to get around is with your own transport, whether you drive, hire a driver or ride a bike. This gives you the flexibility to explore at will and allows you to reach many places that are otherwise inaccessible.

Public transport is cheap but can be cause for very long journeys if you're not sticking to a major route. In addition, some places are just impossible to reach.

There are also tourist shuttle buses, which combine economy with convenience.

Air

Batavia, Garuda Indonesia and Merpati have several flights daily between Bali and Lombok. The route is competitive and fares hover at around 600,000Rp – new entrants in the market keep fares low. See p260 for details of airlines flying between Bali and Lombok.

To/from the Airports

Bali's Ngurah Rai Airport is immediately south of Tuban and Kuta. From the official counters, just outside the terminals, there are supposedly fixed-price

---

METERED TAXI FROM THE AIRPORT

Avoid the airport taxi hassles and get a much cheaper – and better – **Bali Taxi** (📞0361-701 111; www .bluebirdgroup.com) just outside the airport exit. Walk from the international and domestic terminals across the airport car park to the right (northeast). Then continue for a couple of hundred metres through the vehicle exit to the airport road (ignoring any touts along the way), where you can hail a regular cab.

---

taxis. However, you may be charged at the high end of each range (eg you're going to the part of Seminyak that is supposed to cost 60,000Rp, but you might be charged 70,000Rp). Further, if you say you don't have a room booking, there could be heavy pressure to go to a commission-paying hotel. The costs are as follows (depending on drop-off point):

Jimbaran	60,000-75,000Rp
Kerobokan	70,000Rp
Kuta	45,000-50,000Rp
Legian	55,000-60,000Rp
Nusa Dua	95,000-110,000Rp
Sanur	95,000Rp
Seminyak	60,000-70,000Rp
Ubud	195,000Rp

If you have a surfboard, you'll be charged at least 35,000Rp extra, depending on its size. Ignore any touts that aren't part of the official scheme. Many hotels will offer to pick you up at the airport; however, there's no need to use these services if they cost more than the official rates.

If you're really travelling light, Kuta Beach is less than a 30-minute walk north.

Any taxi will take you to the airport at a metered rate that should be much less than what's listed here. (Regular taxis, as opposed to those that are part of the official airport scheme, are only allowed to drop passengers off at the airport, not pick them up.)

For transport details to/from Lombok's Mataram airport, see p261. Note, however, that a new airport in the south is due to open in 2011, so all details will change. Tourist hotels in Senggigi can usually provide transport.

Bemo

The main form of public transport in Bali and on Lombok are bemo. A generic term for any vehicle used as public transport, it's normally a minibus or van with a row of low seats down each side. Bemo usually hold about 12 people in very cramped conditions.

Riding bemo can be part of your Bali adventure or a major nightmare, depending on your outlook at that moment in time. You can certainly expect journeys to be lengthy and you'll find that getting to many places is both time-consuming and inconvenient. It's uncommon to see visitors on bemo in Bali.

See right for more on the troubled future of the bemo network.

On Lombok, bemo are minibuses or pick-up trucks and are a major means of transport for visitors.

Fares

Bemo operate on a standard route for a set (but unwritten) fare. The minimum fare is about 4000Rp. The fares listed in this book reflect what a tourist should reasonably expect to pay. If you get into an empty bemo, always make it clear that you do not want to charter it.

Terminals & Routes

Every town has at least one terminal (*terminal bis*) for all forms of public transport. There are often several terminals in larger towns. Denpasar, the hub of Bali's transport system, has four main bus/bemo terminals and three minor ones. Terminals can be confusing, but most bemo and buses have signs, and if you're in doubt, people will usually help you.

To travel from one part of Bali to another, it is often necessary to go via one or more terminals. For example, to get from Sanur to Ubud by bemo, you go to the Kereneng terminal in Denpasar, transfer to the Batubulan terminal, and then take a third bemo to Ubud. This is circuitous and time-consuming, two of the

LIFE AFTER THE BEMO

Long the sole means of public transport, bemo just haven't kept up with the times. As more and more Balinese get jobs, they find that bemo – which often stop running in the afternoon – can't get them to and from their employment. Routes remain geared to going to markets early in the morning. Places with high employment such as Legian, Seminyak and Kerobokan are poorly served, if at all.

Meanwhile, one-third of Balinese own motorbikes, with 5000 more being registered a month, and motorbikes are now the second major consumer purchase on the island after mobile phones. (These figures won't surprise anyone caught within the fish-like schools of the vehicles at traffic lights.) Given that it can cost US$2 a day for locals to endure multiple bemo getting to/from work (in the cases where this is even an option), compared with under US$50 a month to buy a motorbike, you can understand why many people aren't taking the bemo option.

In the meantime, the bemo system clings to the past and absurd practices continue, such as the need to transfer up to three times just to get across Denpasar. Not surprisingly, there are now calls to set up a modern public-transit system on the ever more traffic-choked island.

reasons so few visitors take bemo in Bali.

Bicycle

A famous temple carving at Kubutambahan in north Bali shows the Dutch artist W O J Nieuwenkamp pedalling through Bali in 1904. Bali's roads have improved greatly since then and more and more people are touring the island by *sepeda*. Many visitors are using bikes around the towns and for day trips in Bali and on Lombok. See p41 for more on how cycling can be a great part of your visit to Bali and Lombok.

Hire

There are plenty of bicycles for rent in the tourist areas, but many are in poor condition. The best place to rent good-quality mountain bikes in Bali is in the south and Ubud. On Lombok, you can find good bikes in Senggigi.

Ask at your accommodation about renting a bike; hotels often have their own. Prices are about 15,000Rp to 30,000Rp per day.

Touring

See Road Conditions (p387) for information on the state of the roads; make sure your bike is equipped for these conditions. Even the smallest village has some semblance of a bike shop – a flat tyre should cost about 5000Rp to fix.

If you don't have good maps, choose small roads and enjoy the scenery; locals are happy to help with directions.

Several companies organise full-day cycle trips in the back country.

Boat

Taking the boat is more relaxing than the hassle of flying between Bali and Lombok, and fast boats make it competitive time-wise, but note some important safety considerations in the boxed text on p384.

Public ferries travel slowly between Padangbai and Lembar on Lombok. **Perama** (www.peramatour.com) operates a daily boat service from Padangbai to Senggigi. See p188 for more details.

There are many fast boats operating between Bali and Lombok's Gilis. See p288 for details. New boats from Nusa Lembongan and Amed make for interesting itinerary possibilities.

Bus

Distances in Bali and on Lombok are relatively short, so you won't have cause to ride on many large buses unless you are transferring between islands or going from one side to another.

Public Bus
BALI

Larger minibuses and full-sized buses ply the longer routes, particularly on routes linking Denpasar, Singaraja and Gilimanuk. They operate out of the same terminals as the bemo. Buses are faster than bemo because they don't make as many stops along the way; however, with

---

TRAVELLING SAFELY BY BOAT

Fast boats linking Bali, Nusa Lembongan, Lombok and the Gilis have proliferated, especially as the latter places have become more popular. But in many cases these services are accidents waiting to happen, as safety regulations are definitely not up to scratch. In 2009 a boat between Bali and Nusa Penida sank, killing nine. In 2010 a boat between Lombok and Gili T capsized, killing three. Two fast boats between Gili T and Bali have sunk, and in both cases, the tourists and crew aboard were lucky to survive by swimming to shore or being rescued by other boats that happened to be passing by.

Crews on these boats may have little or no training: in one accident, the skipper freely admitted that he panicked and had no recollection of what happened to his passengers. And rescue is far from assured: a volunteer rescue group in east Bali reported that they had no radio.

Conditions are often rough in the waters off Bali. Although the islands are in close proximity and are easily seen from each other, the ocean between can get more turbulent than is safe for the small speedboats zipping across it.

With these facts in mind, it is essential that you take responsibility for your own safety, as no one else will. Consider the following points:

» **Bigger is better** It may add 30 minutes or more to your journey, but a larger boat will simply deal with the open ocean better than the over-powered small speedboats. Also, trips on small boats can be unpleasant because of the ceaseless pounding through the waves and the fumes coming from the screaming outboard motors.

» **Check for safety equipment** Make certain your boat has life preservers and that you know how to locate and use them. In an emergency, don't expect a panicked crew to hand them out. Also, check for lifeboats. Some promotional materials show boats with automatically inflating lifeboats that have later been removed to make room for more passengers.

» **Avoid overcrowding** Travellers report boats leaving with more people than seats and with aisles jammed with stacked luggage. If this happens, don't use the boat.

» **Look for exits** Cabins may only have one narrow entrance making them death traps in an accident.

» **Avoid fly-by-nighters** Taking a fishing boat and jamming too many engines on the rear in order to cash in on booming tourism is a recipe for disaster. Note that some outfits with safe boats will add unsafe boats to the fleet in order to make a quick profit.

» **Don't ride on the roof** It looks like care-free fun but travellers are regularly bounced off when boats hit swells and crews may be inept at rescue.

» **Use common sense** There are good operators on the waters around Bali but the line-up changes constantly. If a service seems sketchy before you board, don't. Try to get a refund but don't lose your life for the cost of a ticket.

everybody riding motorbikes, there are looong delays waiting for buses to fill up at terminals before departing.

LOMBOK

Buses and bemo of various sizes are the cheapest and most common way of getting around Lombok. On rough roads in remote areas, trucks may be used as public transport. Mandalika in Bertais is the main bus terminal for all of Lombok. There are also regional terminals at Praya and Pancor (near Selong). You may have to go via one or more of these transport hubs to get from one part of Lombok to another.

Public transport fares are fixed by the provincial government and displayed on a noticeboard outside the office of the Mandalika terminal. You may have to pay more if you have a large bag or surfboard.

Tourist Bus

Perama (www.peramatour. com) has a monopoly on this service in Bali. It has offices or agents in Kuta, Sanur, Ubud, Lovina, Padangbai and Candidasa. At least one bus a day links these Bali tourist centres. Services to Kintamani and along the east coast from Lovina to/from Candidasa via Amed are by demand. Perama also has a very limited service around Senggigi on Lombok.

Consider the following advantages and disadvantages when deciding whether to book your ticket (one day in advance is a good idea).

Advantages:

» Fares are reasonable (eg Kuta to Lovina is 125,000Rp)

» Buses have air-con

» Meet other travellers

Disadvantages:

» Perama stops are often outside the centre, requiring another shuttle/taxi

» Buses may not provide a direct service – stopping,

say, at Ubud between Kuta and Padangbai

» Like bemo, the service has ossified, resolutely sticking to the routes it ran years ago and not recognising popular new destinations such as Bingen or Seminyak

» Three or more people can hire a car and driver for less

Car & Motorcycle

Renting a car or motorbike can open up Bali and Lombok for exploration – and can also leave you counting the minutes until you return it. It gives you the freedom to explore myriad back roads and lets you set your own schedule. Most people don't rent a car for their entire visit but rather get one for a few days of meandering. In Bali, it's common to get a car in the south or Ubud and circumnavigate at least part of the island.

See Road Conditions for details of the at-times harrowing driving conditions on the islands.

Driving Licences

CAR LICENCES

If you plan to drive a car, you're supposed to have an International Driving Permit (IDP). You can obtain one from your national motoring organisation if you have a normal driving licence. Bring your home licence as well – it's supposed to be carried in conjunction with the IDP. Without an IDP, add 50,000Rp to any fine you'll have to pay if stopped by the police (although you'll have to pay this fine several times to exceed the cost and hassle of getting the mostly useless IDP).

MOTORCYCLE LICENCES

If you have a motorcycle licence at home, get your IDP endorsed for motorcycles too; with this you will have no problems. Otherwise you have to get a local licence – something of an adventure.

Officially, there's a 2 million rupiah fine for riding without a proper licence, and your motorcycle can be impounded. Unofficially, you may be hit with a substantial 'on-the-spot' payment (50,000Rp seems average) and allowed to continue on your way. Also, if you have an accident without a licence your insurance company might refuse coverage.

To get a local motorcycle licence in Bali (valid for a year), go independently, or have the rental agency take you, to the **Poltabes Denpasar** (Police Station; ☑0361-142 7352; Jl Gunung Sanhyang; ◷8am-1pm Mon-Sat), which is northwest of Kerobokan on the way to Denpasar. Bring your passport, a photocopy of same (just the page with your photo on it) and a passport photo. Then, follow these steps:

» Ignore the mobbed main hall filled with jostling permit seekers.

» Step around to the back of the parking lot and look for a building with a sign reading 'Pemohon Sim Asing/ Foreigner License Applicant' outside a 2nd-floor office.

» Find cheery English-speaking officials and pay 250,000Rp.

» Take the required written test (in English, with the answers provided on a sample test).

» Get your permit.

Sure it costs more than in the hall of chaos, but who can argue with the service?

Fuel & Spare Parts

Bensin is sold by the government-owned Pertamina company, and costs about 4500Rp per litre. Bali has scads of petrol stations. In remote areas, look for little roadside fuel shops that fill your tank from a plastic container (the same as the ones they use for *arak* – fermented rice wine – which seems

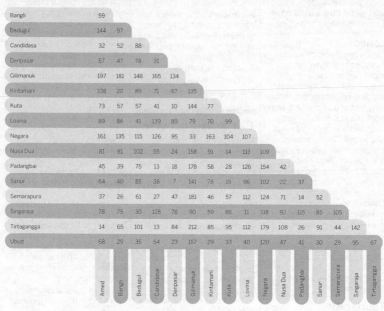

	Amed	Bangli	Bedugul	Candidasa	Denpasar	Gilimanuk	Kintamani	Kuta	Lovina	Negara	Nusa Dua	Padangbai	Sanur	Semarapura	Singaraja
Bangli	59														
Bedugul	144	97													
Candidasa	32	52	88												
Denpasar	57	47	78	31											
Gilimanuk	197	181	148	165	134										
Kintamani	108	20	89	71	67	135									
Kuta	73	57	57	41	10	144	77								
Lovina	89	86	41	139	89	79	70	99							
Negara	161	135	115	126	95	33	163	104	107						
Nusa Dua	81	81	102	55	24	158	91	14	113	109					
Padangbai	45	39	75	13	18	178	58	28	126	154	42				
Sanur	64	40	85	38	7	141	78	15	96	102	22	37			
Semarapura	37	26	61	27	47	181	46	57	112	124	71	14	52		
Singaraja	78	75	30	128	78	90	59	88	11	118	92	115	85	105	
Tirtagangga	14	65	101	13	84	212	85	95	112	179	108	26	91	44	142
Ubud	68	29	35	54	23	157	29	33	40	120	47	41	30	29	95	67

LOMBOK ROAD DISTANCES (KM)

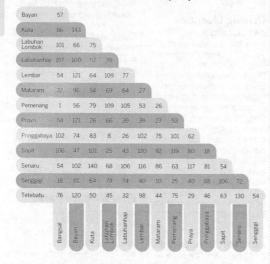

	Bangsal	Bayan	Kuta	Labuhan Lombok	Labuhanhaji	Lembar	Mataram	Pemenang	Praya	Pringgabaya	Sapit	Senaru
Bayan	57											
Kuta	86	143										
Labuhan Lombok	101	66	75									
Labuhanhaji	157	100	57	39								
Lembar	54	121	64	109	77							
Mataram	32	96	54	69	64	27						
Pemenang	1	56	79	109	105	53	26					
Praya	54	121	26	66	39	39	27	53				
Pringgabaya	102	74	83	8	26	102	75	101	62			
Sapit	106	47	101	25	43	120	92	119	80	18		
Senaru	54	102	140	68	106	116	86	63	117	81	54	
Senggigi	18	81	64	79	74	40	10	25	40	88	106	72
Tetebatu	76	120	50	45	32	98	44	75	29	46	63	130	54

fitting). On Lombok there are stations in major towns.

Make sure to check that the pump is reset to zero before the attendant starts to put petrol in your vehicle. Regular unleaded fuel is labelled Premium; diesel is labelled Solar.

Tyre repair services can be found in almost every town.

Hire

Very few agencies in Bali will allow you to take their rental cars or motorcycles to Lombok – the regular vehicle insurance is not valid outside Bali.

See Insurance for details on rental insurance.

CAR

The most popular rental vehicle is a small jeep – they're compact, have good ground clearance and the low gear ratio is well suited to exploring back roads. The main alternative is the larger Toyota Kijang, which seats six. Automatic transmissions are unheard of.

Rental and travel agencies in tourist centres rent vehicles quite cheaply. A Suzuki jeep costs about 180,000Rp per day, with unlimited kilometres and very limited insurance. A Toyota Kijang costs from 200,000Rp per day. These costs will vary according to demand, the condition of the vehicle, length of hire and your bargaining talents. Extra days often cost much less than the first day.

There's no reason to book rental cars in advance over the internet or with a tour package; doing it that way will almost certainly cost more than arranging it locally. Any place you stay can set you up with a car, as can the ever-present touts in the street.

Shop around for a good deal, and check the car carefully before you sign up.

MOTORCYCLES

Motorbikes are a popular way of getting around Bali and Lombok – locals ride pillion almost from birth. When you see a family of five all riding cheerfully along on one motorbike, it's called a Bali minivan.

Motorbikes are ideal for Lombok's tiny rough roads, which may be difficult or impassable by car. Once you get out of the main centres and off the main roads, there's not much traffic, apart from people, dogs and other motorbikes.

Motorbikes are easily rented. Ask at your accommodation or look for the inevitable offers on the street. The engines are modest (a fuel-stingy 125 cc is typical), so your chances of going fast are nil. Styles are more scooter than racy motorcycle.

Rentals cost 30,000Rp to 50,000Rp a day, less by the week. This should include minimal insurance for the motorcycle (probably with a US$100 excess), but not for any other person or property. Many have racks for surfboards.

Think carefully before renting a motorbike. It is dangerous and every year visitors go home with lasting damage – this is no place to learn to ride.

Other considerations:

» Some motorbikes are in very bad condition, so check carefully.

» Carry the motorbike's registration papers while riding.

» Helmets are compulsory; you can even be stopped for not having the chin-strap fastened.

» Standard helmets you get with rental bikes are lightweight. You may want to bring something more substantial from home or buy one locally.

» Shops in south Bali sell helmets with Viking horns and other fun stuff, but they may be flimsy.

Insurance

Rental agencies and owners usually insist that the vehicle itself is insured, and minimal insurance should be included in the basic rental deal – often with an excess of as much as US$100 for a motorcycle and US$500 for a car (ie the customer pays the first US$100/500 of any claim). The more formal motorcycle- and car-hire agencies may offer additional insurance to reduce the level of the excess, and to also cover damage to other people or their property, ie third-party or liability cover.

Especially with cars, the owner's main concern is insuring the vehicle. In some cases, a policy might cover the car for 30 million rupiah, but provide for only 10 million rupiah third-party cover. Your travel insurance may provide some additional protection, although liability for motor accidents is specifically excluded from many policies. The third-party cover might seem inadequate, but if you do cause damage or injury, it's usually enough for your consulate to get you out of jail.

A private owner renting a motorbike may not offer insurance. Ensure that your personal travel insurance

covers injuries incurred while motorcycling. Some policies specifically exclude coverage for motorcycle riding, or have special conditions.

Road Conditions

Bali traffic can be horrendous in the south, around Denpasar and up to Ubud, and is usually quite heavy as far as Padangbai to the east and Tabanan to the west. Finding your way around the main tourist sites can be a challenge, as roads are only sometimes signposted and maps are unreliable. Off the main routes, roads can be rough, but they are usually surfaced – there are few dirt roads in Bali.

Roads on Lombok are often very rough but traffic is lighter than on Bali.

Avoid driving at night or at dusk. Many bicycles, carts and vehicles do not have proper lights, and street lighting is limited.

Road Rules

Visiting drivers commonly complain about crazy Balinese drivers, but often it's because the visitors don't understand the local conventions of road use. For instance, the constant use of horns here doesn't mean 'Get the @£*&% out of my way!'; rather it is a very Balinese way of saying 'Hi, I'm here'.

The following information is useful:

» Watch your front – it's your responsibility to avoid anything that gets in front of your vehicle. In effect, a car, motorcycle or anything else pulling out in front of you has right of way.

» Often drivers won't even look to see what's coming when they turn left at a junction – they listen for the horn.

» Use your horn to warn anything in front that you're there, especially if you're about to overtake.

» Drive on the left side of the road, although it's often a

case of driving on whatever side of the road is available.

» Use seatbelts.

Traffic Police

Some police will stop drivers on very slender pretexts. If a cop sees your front wheel half an inch over the faded line at a stop sign, if the chin-strap of your helmet isn't fastened, or if you don't observe one of the ever changing and poorly signposted one-way traffic restrictions, you may be waved down.

The cop will ask to see your licence and the vehicle's registration papers, and they'll also tell you what a serious offence you've committed. They may start talking about court appearances, heavy fines and long delays. Stay cool and don't argue. Don't offer a bribe. Eventually they'll suggest that you can pay them some amount of money to deal with the matter. If it's a very large amount, tell them politely that you don't have that much. These matters can be settled for something between

10,000Rp and 100,000Rp, although it will be more if you argue. Always make sure you have the correct papers, and don't have too much visible cash in your wallet. If things deteriorate, ask for the cop's name and talk about contacting your consulate.

Hitching

You can hitchhike in Bali and on Lombok, but it's not a very useful option for getting around, as public transport is so cheap and frequent, and private vehicles are often full.

Bear in mind, also, that hitching is never entirely safe in any country. Travellers who decide to hitch should understand that they are taking a small but potentially serious risk.

Local Transport

Dokar & Cidomo

Small *dokar* (pony carts) still provide local transport in

some remote areas of Bali, and even in parts of Denpasar and Kuta, but they're uncommon, extremely slow and not particularly cheap.

The pony cart used on Lombok is known as a *cidomo* – a contraction of *cika* (a traditional handcart), *dokar* and *mobil* (because car wheels and tyres are used). They are often brightly coloured and the horses decorated with coloured tassels and jingling bells. A typical *cidomo* has a narrow bench seat on either side. The ponies appear to some visitors to be heavily laden and harshly treated, but they are usually looked after reasonably well, if only because the owners depend on them for their livelihood. *Cidomo* are a very popular form of transport in many parts of Lombok, and often go to places that bemo don't, won't or can't.

Fares are not set by the government on either island; prices start at 5000Rp per person for a short trip (3000Rp to 5000Rp on Lom-

---

HIRING A VEHICLE & DRIVER

An excellent way to travel anywhere around Bali is by hired vehicle, allowing you to leave the driving and inherent frustrations to others. If you're part of a group, it can make sound economic sense as well. This is also possible on Lombok but less common.

It's easy to arrange a charter: just listen for one of the frequent offers of 'transport?' in the streets around the tourist centres. Approach a driver yourself; or ask at your hotel, which is often a good method, as it increases accountability. Then consider the following:

» Although great drivers are everywhere, it helps to talk with a few.

» Get recommendations from other travellers.

» You should like the driver and their English should be sufficient for you to communicate your wishes.

» Costs for a full day should average 400,000Rp to 600,000Rp.

» The vehicle, usually a late-model Toyota Kijang seating up to seven, should be clean.

» Agree on a route beforehand.

» Make it clear if you want to avoid tourist-trap restaurants and shops (smart drivers understand that tips depend on following your wishes).

» On the road, buy the driver lunch (they'll likely eat elsewhere, so give them 20,000Rp) and offer snacks and drinks.

» Many drivers find ways to make your day delightful in unexpected ways. Tip accordingly.

bok) but are negotiable, depending on demand, number of passengers, nearby competition and your bargaining skills. The tourist price can be high if the driver suspects the tourist will pay big-time for the novelty value.

Ojek

Around some major towns, and along roads where bemo rarely or never venture, transport may be provided by an *ojek* (a motorcycle or motorbike that takes a paying passenger). However, with increased vehicle ownership in Bali, *ojek* are becoming less common. They're OK on quiet country roads, but a high-risk option in the big towns. You will find them in remote places such as Nusa Lembongan and Nusa Penida. *Ojek* are more common on Lombok.

Fares are negotiable, but about 10,000Rp for 5km is fairly standard.

Taxi

BALI

Metered taxis are common in south Bali and Denpasar (but not Ubud). They are essential for getting around Kuta and Seminyak, where you can easily flag one down. Elsewhere, they're often a lot less hassle than haggling with drivers offering 'transport!'.

The usual rate for a taxi is 5000Rp flag fall and 4000Rp per kilometre, but the rate is higher in the evening. If you phone for a taxi, the minimum charge is 10,000Rp. Avoid any driver who claims meter problems or who won't use the meter.

By far the most reputable taxi company is **Bali Taxi** (☎0361-701 111; www.blue birdgroup.com), which uses distinctive blue vehicles with a light on the roof bearing a stylised bluebird. Watch out for fakes – there are many – and also look for the phone number on the cab. Drivers speak reasonable English and use the meter at all times. There's even a number to call

if you have any complaints (☎0361-701 621). Many expats will use no other firm and the drivers are often fascinating conversationalists.

After Bali Taxi, standards decline rapidly. Some are acceptable, although you may have a hassle getting the driver to use the meter after dark. Others may claim that their meter is 'broken' or nonexistent, and negotiated fees can be over the odds (all the more reason to tip Bali Taxi drivers about 10%).

Rogue taxi drivers can be annoying with their constant honking to attract patrons. And men, especially single men, will find that some taxi drivers may promote a 'complete massage' at a 'spa'. Drivers will enthusiastically pantomime some of the activities that this entails. At the very least, insist that they keep their hands on the wheel.

There are plenty of bemo and taxis around Mataram and Senggigi. Drivers for **Lombok Taksi** (☎0370-627 000), owned by Bali Taxi's Blue Bird Group, always use the meter without you having to ask; this is the best choice. The only place you would need to negotiate a taxi fare is at the harbour at Bangsal (but not on the main road in Pemenang). See p271 for details.

Tours

Standardised organised tours are a convenient way to visit a few places in Bali. There are dozens and dozens of operators who provide a similar product and service. Much more interesting are specialised tour companies that can take you far off the beaten track, offer memorable experiences and otherwise provide you with a different side of Bali and Lombok. You can also easily arrange your own custom tour.

Tours originating on Lombok are based in Senggigi. You can usually book market visits in Mataram, a jaunt out to the Gilis or a trip down the south coast.

Standard Day Tours

Tours are typically in white eight- to 12-seat minibuses with air-con, which pick you up and drop you off at your hotel. Prices range from 50,000Rp to 200,000Rp for what are essentially similar tours, so it pays to shop around.

Consider the following:
» Will lunch be at a huge tourist buffet or somewhere more interesting?
» How much time will be spent at tourist shops?
» Will there be a qualified English-speaking guide?

TAXI TRAUMA

Bali Taxi's success at providing clean cabs, polite drivers and reliable use of meters has caused an uproar among some other taxi firms, who, unfortunately, have used their energy to fight Bali Taxi rather than emulate its fair business practices. Drivers of other firms managed to get a ruling ordering Bali Taxi to remove the name of its corporate owner, the Blue Bird Group, from the top of its cabs' windshields (which had made spotting genuine Bali Taxi cabs easier). Meanwhile some drivers have attacked Bali Taxis, while legions of others paint their cabs a similar colour. The logic of providing fair and reliable service in order to compete has yet to catch on.

BOAT TOURS TO FLORES

Travelling by sea from Bali and Lombok is a good way to get to Flores, an increasingly popular side trip. You get to see the region's spectacular coastline and dodge some seriously lengthy bus journeys and nonentity towns. Typical itineraries take in snorkelling at Pulau Satonda off the coast of Sumbawa, a dragon-spotting hike in Komodo and other stops for swimming and partying along the way.

However, this kind of trip needs careful consideration – a lot depends on the boat, the crew and your fellow travellers, who you are stuck with for the duration. Some operators have reneged on 'all-inclusive' agreements en route, and others operate decrepit old tugs without life jackets or radio.

The following reliable operators span the price categories.

SeaTrek (☎0361-283 358; www.seatrekbali.com) Has multiday luxury cruises aboard Bugus-style yachts (large wooden sailing vessels) to Flores and other eastern Indonesian islands. These memorable trips start at US$5000 per person.

Ikan Biru (☎0813 534 4511; www.goodwilldiving.com) This is a vintage Bugus-style sailing vessel operated by Trawangan Dive on Gili T. Eight-day trips include a lot of diving, are comfortable and cost from US$1500.

Perama (☎0361-751 170; www.peramatour.com) Offers fun budget trips that take six days return from Lombok and cost 4,000,000Rp per person in cabins (3,000,000Rp if you sleep on deck).

» Are early morning pick-ups for the convenience of the company, which then dumps you at a central point to wait for another bus?

The following are the usual tours sold around Bali. They are available from most hotels and shops selling services to tourists.

Bedugul Includes Sangeh or Alas Kedaton, Mengwi, Jatiluwih, Candikuning and sunset at Tanah Lot.

Besakih Includes craft shops at villages near Ubud, Gianyar, Semarapura (Klungkung), Pura Besakih, and return via Bukit Jambal.

Denpasar Takes in the arts centre, markets, the museum and perhaps a temple or two.

East Bali Includes the usual craft shops, Semarapura (Klungkung), Kusamba, Goa Lawah, Candidasa and Tenganan.

Kintamani–Gunung Batur Takes in the craft shops at Celuk, Mas and Batuan, a dance at Batubulan, Tampaksiring and views of Gunung Batur. Alternatively, the tour may go to Goa Gajah, Pejeng, Tampaksiring and Kintamani.

Singaraja–Lovina Goes to Mengwi, Bedugul, Gitgit, Singaraja, Lovina, Banjar and Pupuan.

Sunset Tour Includes Mengwi, Marga, Alas Kedaton and sunset at Tanah Lot.

Specialist Tours

Many Bali tour operators offer experiences that vary from the norm. These can include cultural experiences hard for the casual visitor to find, such as cremations or trips to remote villages where life has hardly changed in decades. Often you'll avoid the clichéd tourist minibus and travel in unusual vehicles or in high comfort.

See Bali & Lombok Outdoors (p33) for tours involving trekking, cycling and more; see p147 for details on the many tours around Ubud.

The following operators are recommended. Prices span the gamut but tend to be more expensive than the bog-standard tours.

JED (Village Ecotourism Network; ☎0361-735 320; www.jed.or.id) Organises highly regarded tours of small villages (from US$75), including coffee-growing Pelaga in the mountains, fruit-growing Sibetan in the east, seaweed farms on Nusa Ceningan and ancient Tenganan. You can even spend the night with a family in the villages (from US$105).

Bali Discovery Tours (☎0361-286 283; www.balidiscovery.com) Offers numerous and customisable tours that differ from the norm. One tour visits a small ricegrowing village in the west near Tabanan for hands-on demonstrations of cultivation. Can customise any kind of trip.

Suta Tours (☎0361-741 6665, 0361-788 8865; www.sutatour.com) Standard tours but also arranges trips to cremation ceremonies and special temple festivals, market tours and other custom plans.

Waka Land Cruise (☎0361-426 972; www.wakaexperience.com) Luxurious tours deep into rice terraces and tiny villages.

Self-Organised Tours

See the boxed text on hiring a vehicle and driver (p388), then use this book to plan a fun day out and off you go.

Health

make payments directly to providers or reimburse you later for overseas health expenditures. (In many countries doctors expect payment in cash at the time of treatment.) Some policies ask you to call back (reverse charges) to a centre in your home country where an immediate assessment of your problem is made.

Treatment for minor injuries and common traveller's health problems is easily accessed in Bali and to a lesser degree on Lombok. However, for serious conditions, you will need to leave the islands.

Travellers tend to worry about contracting infectious diseases when in the tropics, but infections are a rare cause of serious illness or death in travellers. Pre-existing medical conditions, such as heart disease, and accidental injury (especially traffic accidents) account for most life-threatening problems. Becoming ill in some way, however, is relatively common; ailments you may suffer include gastro, overexposure to the sun and other typical traveller woes.

It's important to note certain precautions you should take on Bali and Lombok, especially in regard to rabies, mosquito bites and the tropical sun.

The following advice is a general guide only and does not replace the advice of a doctor trained in travel medicine.

BEFORE YOU GO

Make sure all medications are packed in their original, clearly labelled containers. A signed and dated letter from your physician describing your medical conditions and medications (including generic names) is also a good idea. If you are carrying syringes or needles, be sure to have a physician's letter documenting their medical necessity. If you have a heart condition ensure you bring a copy of your electrocardiogram taken just prior to travelling.

If you happen to take any regular medication bring double your needs in case of loss or theft. You can buy many medications over the counter without a doctor's prescription, but it can be difficult to find some of the newer drugs, particularly the latest antidepressant drugs, blood-pressure medications and contraceptive pills.

Insurance

Even if you are fit and healthy, don't travel without sufficient health insurance – accidents do happen. If you're uninsured, emergency evacuation is expensive – bills of more than US$100,000 are not uncommon.

Find out in advance if your insurance plan will

Recommended Vaccinations

Specialised travel-medicine clinics are your best source of information; they stock all available vaccines and will be able to give specific recommendations for you and your trip.

Most vaccines don't produce immunity until at least two weeks after they're given. Ask your doctor for an International Certificate of Vaccination (otherwise known as the yellow booklet), which will list all the vaccinations you've received.

The World Health Organization recommendations for Southeast Asia include the following:

Hepatitis A Provides almost 100% protection for up to a year; a booster after 12 months provides at least another 20 years' protection.

Hepatitis B Now considered routine for most travellers.

Measles, Mumps & Rubella (MMR) Two doses of MMR are required unless you have had the diseases.

Typhoid Recommended unless your trip is less than a week and only to developed cities.

Required Vaccinations

The only vaccine required by international regulations is yellow fever. Proof of vaccination will only be required if you have visited a country in the yellow-fever zone (primarily some parts of Africa and South America) within the six days prior to entering Southeast Asia.

Medical Checklist

Recommended items for a convenient personal medical kit (more specific items can be easily obtained on Bali if needed):

» antibacterial cream (eg muciprocin)

» antihistamine – there are many options (eg cetirizine for daytime and promethazine for night)

» antiseptic (eg Betadine)

» contraceptives

» DEET-based insect repellent

» first-aid items such as scissors, bandages, thermometer (but not a mercury one) and tweezers

» ibuprofen or another anti-inflammatory

» steroid cream for allergic/itchy rashes (eg 1% to 2% hydrocortisone)

» sunscreen and hat

» throat lozenges

» thrush (vaginal yeast infection) treatment (eg clotrimazole pessaries or diflucan tablet)

Websites

There is a wealth of travel health advice on the internet.

World Health Organization (WHO; www.who.int/ith) Publishes a superb book called *International Travel & Health*, which is revised annually and is available online at no cost.

MD Travel Health (www.mdtravelhealth.com) Provides travel health recommendations for every country.

Centers for Disease Control & Prevention (CDC; www.cdc.gov) This website also has good general information.

HEALTH ADVISORIES

It's usually a good idea to consult your government's travel-health website before departure, if one is available:

Australia (www.smartraveller.gov.au)

UK (www.nhs.uk/nhsengland/healthcareabroad)

US (www.cdc.gov/travel)

Further Reading

Lonely Planet's *Asia & India: Healthy Travel* is a handy pocket-sized book that is packed with useful information, including pre-trip planning, emergency first aid, immunisation and disease information and what to do if you get sick on the road.

IN BALI & LOMBOK

Availability & Cost of Health Care

In south Bali and Ubud there are clinics catering to tourists and just about any hotel can put you in touch with an English-speaking doctor.

International Medical Clinics

For serious conditions, foreigners would be best served in one of two private clinics that cater mainly to tourists and expats. At both these places you should confirm that your health and/or travel insurance will cover you. In cases where your medical condition is considered serious you may well be evacuated by air ambulance to top-flight hospitals in Jakarta or Singapore; this is where proper insurance is vital as these flights can cost more than US$10,000.

BIMC (☎0361-761 263; www.bimcbali.com; Jl Ngurah Rai 100X, Kuta; ⊙24hr) On the bypass road just east of Kuta near the Bali Galleria. It's a modern Australian-run clinic that can do tests, hotel visits and arrange medical evacuation. Visits can cost US$100 or more.

International SOS Medical Clinic (☎0361-710 505; www.sos-bali.com; Jl Ngurah Rai 505X, Kuta; ⊙24hr) Near BIMC; offers similar services.

Hospitals

There are two facilities in Denpasar that offer a good standard of care. Both are more affordable than the international clinics.

BaliMed Hospital (☎0361-484 748; www.balimedhospital.co.id; Jl Mahendradatta 57, Denpasar) On the Kerobokan side of Denpasar, this private hospital has a range of medical services. A basic consultation is 200,000Rp.

Rumah Sakit Umum Propinsi Sanglah (Sanglah Hospital; ☎0361-227 911; Sanglah; ⊙24hr) The city's general hospital has English-speaking staff and an ER. It's the best hospital on the island and has a special wing for well-insured foreigners, **Paviliun Amerta Wing International** (☎0361-257 499).

Remote Care

In more remote areas facilities are basic – generally a small public hospital, doctor's surgery or *puskesmas*. In government-run clinics and hospitals, services such as meals, washing and clean clothing are normally provided by the patient's family.

The best hospital on Lombok is in Mataram, and there

are more basic ones in Praya and Selong.

Decompression Chamber

Divers should note that there is a decompression chamber in Sanur, which is a fast-boat ride from Nusa Lembongan. Getting here from north Bali can take three to four hours.

Pharmacies

In Bali, pharmacies are usually reliable. The **Kimia Farma** (☎0361-916 6509) chain is good and has many locations (you'll find several listed in the relevant sections of this book). Singapore's Guardian chain of pharmacies is also found in tourist areas. On Lombok you need to be more careful, as fake medications and poorly stored or out-of-date drugs are common. Check with a large international hotel for a recommendation of a good local pharmacy.

Infectious Diseases

Bird Flu

Otherwise known as avian influenza, the H5N1 virus has claimed more than 100 victims in Indonesia. Most of the cases have been in Java, west of Bali, although two people died in rural areas of Bali in 2007. Treatment is difficult, although the drug Tamiflu has some effect. Travellers to Bali and Lombok may wish to check the latest conditions before their journey.

Dengue Fever

This mosquito-borne disease is a major problem on Bali and Lombok, where many people have died from it in recent years. As there is no vaccine available it can only be prevented by avoiding mosquito bites. The mosquito that carries dengue bites day and night, so use insect avoidance measures at all times. Symptoms include high fever, severe headache and body ache (dengue was previously known as 'break-bone fever'). Some people develop a rash and experience diarrhoea. There is no specific treatment, just rest and paracetamol – do not take aspirin as it increases the likelihood of haemorrhaging. See a doctor to be diagnosed and monitored.

Hepatitis A

A problem throughout the region, this food- and water-borne virus infects the liver, causing jaundice (yellow skin and eyes), nausea and lethargy. There is no specific treatment for hepatitis A; you just need to allow time for the liver to heal. All travellers to Southeast Asia should be vaccinated against hepatitis A.

Hepatitis B

The only sexually transmitted disease that can be prevented by vaccination, hepatitis B is spread by body fluids, including sexual contact. In some parts of Southeast Asia up to 20% of the population are carriers of hepatitis B.

HIV

HIV is a major problem in many Asian countries, and Bali has one of the highest rates of HIV infection in Indonesia. Official HIV figures in Indonesia are unrealistically low, yet even these count 7100 HIV-positive people living on Bali. The main risk for most travellers is sexual contact with locals, prostitutes (the estimated infection rate on Bali is 40%) and other travellers.

The risk of sexual transmission of the HIV virus can be dramatically reduced by the use of a *kondom* (condom). These are available from supermarkets, street stalls and drugstores in tourist areas, and from the *apotik* in almost any town (from about 1500Rp to 3000Rp

each – it's worth getting the more expensive brands).

Malaria

The risk of contracting malaria in Bali is extremely low, but Lombok is viewed as a malaria risk area. During and just after the wet season (October to March), there is a very low risk of malaria in northern Bali, and a slightly higher risk in far western Bali, particularly in and around Gilimanuk. However, it is not currently considered necessary to take antimalarial drugs if you are sticking to the tourist centres in Bali, regardless of the season.

If you are going away from the main tourist areas of Lombok (Senggigi, the Gilis), or further afield in Indonesia, you should take preventative measures. The risk is greatest in the wet months and in remote areas.

Two strategies should be combined to prevent malaria: mosquito avoidance and antimalarial medications. Most people who catch malaria are taking inadequate or no antimalarial medication.

Travellers are advised to prevent mosquito bites by taking these steps:

» Use a DEET-containing insect repellent on exposed skin. Wash this off at night, as long as you are sleeping under a mosquito net. Natural repellents such as citronella can be effective, but must be applied more frequently than products containing DEET.

» Sleep under a mosquito net impregnated with permethrin.

» Choose accommodation with screens and fans (if not air-conditioned).

» Impregnate clothing with permethrin in high-risk areas.

» Wear long sleeves and trousers in light colours.

» Use mosquito coils.

» Spray your room with insect repellent before going out for your evening meal.

There are a variety of medications available:

Artesunate Derivatives of Artesunate are not suitable as a preventive medication.

Chloroquine & Paludrine The effectiveness of this combination is now limited in most of Southeast Asia. Generally not recommended.

Doxycycline This daily tablet is a broad-spectrum antibiotic that has the added benefit of helping to prevent a variety of tropical diseases, including leptospirosis, tick-borne disease, typhus and melioidosis. The potential side effects include a tendency to sunburn, thrush in women, indigestion, heartburn, nausea and interference with the contraceptive pill.

Lariam (Mefloquine) Lariam has received much bad press, some of it justified, some not. This weekly tablet suits many people. Serious side effects are rare but include depression, anxiety, psychosis and having fits.

Malarone This drug is a combination of Atovaquone and Proguanil. Side effects, most commonly nausea and headache, are uncommon and mild. It is the best tablet for scuba divers and for those on short trips to high-risk areas. It must be taken for one week after leaving the risk area.

Rabies

Rabies is a disease spread by the bite or lick of an infected animal, most commonly a dog or monkey. Once you are exposed, it is uniformly fatal if you don't get the vaccine very promptly. Bali had its first reported case of rabies in 2008 and by 2010 had a full-blown crisis. Initial government efforts to control the spread of the disease by culling dogs (some 200,000) went against all known protocols, which call for vaccination of dogs. Official counts

put the human death toll in the first two years at 100, but the real total is thought to be much higher.

To minimise your risk, consider getting the rabies vaccine, which consists of three injections in all. A booster after one year will then provide 10 years' protection. This may be worth considering given Bali's rabies outbreak. The vaccines are often unavailable on Bali, so get them before you go.

Also, be careful to avoid animal bites. Beware of Bali's ill-tempered strays – don't touch them. Especially watch children closely.

Having the pre-travel vaccination means the post-bite treatment is greatly simplified. If you are bitten or scratched, gently wash the wound with soap and water, and apply an iodine-based antiseptic. It would be a good idea to also consult a doctor.

Those not vaccinated will need to receive rabies immunoglobulin as soon as possible. Clean the wound immediately and do not delay seeking medical attention. Note that Bali is known to run out of rabies immunoglobulin, so be prepared to go to Singapore immediately for medical treatment.

Typhoid

This serious bacterial infection is spread via food and water. Its symptoms are a high and slowly progressive fever, headache and possibly a dry cough and stomach pain. It is diagnosed by blood tests and treated with antibiotics.

Traveller's Diarrhoea

Traveller's diarrhoea (aka Bali belly) is by far the most common problem affecting travellers – between 30% and 50% of people will suffer from it within two weeks of starting their trip. In over 80% of cases, traveller's

diarrhoea is caused by bacteria (there are numerous potential culprits), and therefore responds promptly to treatment with antibiotics.

Traveller's diarrhoea is defined as the passage of more than three watery bowel actions within 24 hours, plus at least one other symptom such as fever, cramps, nausea, vomiting or feeling generally unwell.

Treatment

Loperamide is just a 'stopper' and doesn't get to the cause of the problem. However, it can be helpful, for example, if you have to go on a long bus ride. Don't take Loperamide if you have a fever or blood in your stools. Seek medical attention quickly if you do not respond to an appropriate antibiotic. Otherwise:

» Stay well hydrated; rehydration solutions such as Gastrolyte are the best for this.

» Antibiotics such as Norfloxacin, Ciprofloxacin or Azithromycin will kill the bacteria quickly.

Giardiasis

Giardia lamblia is a parasite that is relatively common in travellers. Symptoms include nausea, bloating, excess gas, fatigue and intermittent diarrhoea. The parasite will eventually go away if left untreated but this can take months. The treatment of choice is Tinidazole, with Metronidazole being a second-line option.

Environmental Hazards

Diving

Divers and surfers should seek specialised advice before they travel to ensure their medical kit contains treatment for coral cuts and tropical ear infections, as well as the standard problems. Divers should ensure

DRINKING WATER

» Never drink tap water on Bali and Lombok.

» Widely available and cheap, bottled water is generally safe, however, check the seal is intact when purchasing. Look for places that allow you to refill containers, thus cutting down on landfill.

» Most ice in restaurants is fine if it is uniform in size and made at a central plant (standard for Bali's tourist areas). Avoid ice that is chipped off larger blocks (more common in rural areas).

» Avoid fresh juices outside of tourist restaurants and cafes.

their insurance covers them for decompression illness – get specialised dive insurance through an organisation such as **Divers Alert Network** (DAN; www .danseap.org). Have a dive medical before you leave your home country.

Heat

Many parts of Southeast Asia are hot and humid throughout the year. For most people it takes at least two weeks to adapt to the hot climate. Swelling of the feet and ankles is common, as are muscle cramps caused by excessive sweating. Prevent these by avoiding dehydration and excessive activity in the heat. Be careful to avoid the following conditions:

Heat Exhaustion Symptoms include feeling weak, headache, irritability, nausea or vomiting, sweaty skin, a fast, weak pulse and a normal or slightly elevated body temperature. Treatment involves getting out of the heat and/or sun, fanning the victim and applying cool wet cloths to the skin, laying the victim flat with their legs raised, and rehydrating with water containing one-quarter of a teaspoon of salt per litre. Recovery is usually rapid and it is common to feel weak for some days afterwards.

Heatstroke A serious medical emergency. Symptoms

come on suddenly and include weakness, nausea, a hot dry body with a body temperature of over 41°C, dizziness, confusion, loss of coordination, fits and eventually collapse and loss of consciousness. Seek urgent medical help and commence cooling by getting the person out of the heat, removing their clothes, fanning them and applying cool wet cloths or ice to their body, especially to hot spots such as the groin and armpits.

Prickly Heat A common skin rash in the tropics, caused by sweat being trapped under the skin. The result is an itchy rash of tiny lumps. Treat by moving out of the heat into an air-conditioned area for a few hours and by having cool showers.

Bites & Stings

During your time in Bali and Lombok, you may make some unwanted friends.

Bedbugs These don't carry disease but their bites are very itchy. They live in the cracks of furniture and walls and then migrate to the bed at night to feed on you as you sleep. You can treat the itch with an antihistamine.

Jellyfish Most are not dangerous, just irritating. Some jellyfish, including the Portuguese man-of-war, occur on the north coast of Bali, especially in July and August, and also between the Gili Islands and Lombok.

The sting is extremely painful but rarely fatal. First aid for jellyfish stings involves pouring vinegar onto the affected area to neutralise the poison. Do not rub sand or water onto the stings. Take painkillers, and anyone who feels ill in any way after being stung should seek medical advice.

Ticks Contracted after walking in rural areas, ticks are commonly found behind the ears, on the belly and in armpits. If you have had a tick bite and experience symptoms such as a rash at the site of the bite or elsewhere, fever or muscle aches, you should see a doctor.

Skin Problems

Fungal Rashes There are two common fungal rashes that affect travellers. The first occurs in moist areas that get less air such as the groin, armpits and between the toes. It starts as a red patch that slowly spreads and is usually itchy. Treatment involves keeping the skin dry, avoiding chafing and using an antifungal cream such as Clotrimazole or Lamisil. *Tinea versicolor* is also common – this fungus causes small, light-coloured patches, most commonly on the back, chest and shoulders. Consult a doctor.

Cuts & Scratches Easily infected in tropical climates, take meticulous care of any cuts and scratches. Immediately wash all wounds in clean water and apply antiseptic. If you develop signs of infection see a doctor. Divers and surfers should be careful with coral cuts as they become easily infected.

Sunburn

Even on a cloudy day sunburn can occur rapidly, especially near the equator. Don't end up like the dopey tourists you see roasted pink on Kuta Beach. Instead:

» Use a strong sunscreen (at least factor 30).

» Reapply sunscreen after a swim.

» Wear a wide-brimmed hat and sunglasses.

» Avoid baking in the sun during the hottest part of the day (10am to 2pm).

Women's Health

In the tourist areas of Bali, supplies of familiar-brand sanitary products are readily available. On Lombok the major-brand sanitary pads are not a problem to get hold of and are reasonably priced. Tampons, however, are like gold dust: they are hard to find and super expensive! Try to bring your own from home or stock up on them at the Hero supermarket in Mataram or in the supermarkets in Senggigi. Tampax and Lil-lets are available.

Birth-control options may be limited so bring adequate supplies of your own form of contraception.

Language

Indonesian, or Bahasa Indonesia as it's known to the locals, is the official language of Indonesia. It has approximately 220 million speakers, although it's the mother tongue for only about 20 million. Most people in Bali and on Lombok also speak their own indigenous languages, Balinese and Sasak respectively. The average traveller need't worry about learning Balinese or Sasak, but it can be fun to learn a few words, which is why we've included a few in this chapter. For practical purposes, it probably makes better sense to concentrate your efforts on learning Bahasa Indonesia.

Indonesian pronunciation is easy to master. Each letter always represents the same sound and most letters are pronounced the same as their English counterparts, with c pronounced as the 'ch' in 'chat'. Note also that kh is a guttural sound (like the 'ch' in Scottish loch), and that the ng combination, which is found in English at the end or in the middle of words such as 'ringing', also appears at the beginning of words in Indonesian.

Syllables generally carry equal emphasis – the main exception is the unstressed e in words such as besar (big) – but the rule of thumb is to stress the second-last syllable.

In written Indonesian there are some inconsistent spellings of place names. Compound names are written as one word or two, eg Airsanih or Air Sanih, Padangbai or Padang Bai. Words starting with 'Ker' sometimes lose the e, eg Kerobokan/Krobokan. Some Dutch variant spellings also remain in use, with tj instead of the modern c (eg Tjampuhan/Campuan), and oe instead of u (eg Soekarno/Sukarno).

Pronouns, particularly 'you', are rarely used in Indonesian. Anda is the egalitarian form used to overcome the plethora of words for 'you'.

WANT MORE?

For in-depth language information and handy phrases, check out Lonely Planet's *Indonesian Phrasebook*. You'll find it at **shop.lonelyplanet.com**, or you can buy Lonely Planet's iPhone phrasebooks at the Apple App Store.

BASICS

Hello.	Salam.
Goodbye. (if leaving)	Selamat tinggal.
Goodbye. (if staying)	Selamat jalan.
How are you?	Apa kabar?
I'm fine, and you?	Kabar baik, Anda bagaimana?
Excuse me.	Permisi.
Sorry.	Maaf.
Please.	Silahkan.
Thank you.	Terima kasih.
You're welcome.	Kembali.
Yes.	Ya.
No.	Tidak.
Mr/Sir	Bapak
Ms/Mrs/Madam	Ibu
Miss	Nona
What's your name?	Siapa nama Anda?
My name is ...	Nama saya ...
Do you speak English?	Bisa berbicara Bahasa Inggris?
I don't understand.	Saya tidak mengerti.

ACCOMMODATION

Do you have any rooms available?	Ada kamar kosong?
How much is it per night/person?	Berapa satu malam/orang?
Is breakfast included?	Apakah harganya termasuk makan pagi?
I'd like to share a dorm.	Saya mau satu tempat tidur di asrama.

campsite	tempat kemah
guesthouse	losmen
hotel	hotel
youth hostel	pemuda
a ... room	kamar ...
single	untuk satu orang
double	untuk dua orang
air-conditioned	dengan AC
bathroom	kamar mandi
cot	velbet
window	jendela

DIRECTIONS

Where is ...?	Di mana ...?
What's the address?	Alamatnya di mana?
Could you write it down, please?	Anda bisa tolong tuliskan?
Can you show me (on the map)?	Anda bisa tolong tunjukkan pada saya (di peta)?
at the corner	di sudut
at the traffic lights	di lampu merah
behind	di belakang
in front of	di depan
far (from)	jauh (dari)
left	kiri
near (to)	dekat (dengan)
next to	di samping
opposite	di seberang
right	kanan
straight ahead	lurus

EATING & DRINKING

What would you recommend?	Apa yang Anda rekomendasikan?
What's in that dish?	Hidangan itu isinya apa?
That was delicious.	Ini enak sekali.
Cheers!	Bersulang!
Bring the bill/check, please.	Tolong bawa kuitansi.
I don't eat ...	Saya tidak mau makan ...
dairy products	susu dan keju
fish	ikan
(red) meat	daging (merah)
peanuts	kacang tanah
seafood	makanan laut

KEY PATTERNS

To get by in Indonesian, mix and match these simple patterns with words of your choice:

When's (the next bus)?
Jam berapa (bis yang berikutnya)?

Where's (the station)?
Di mana (stasiun)?

How much is it (per night)?
Berapa (satu malam)?

I'm looking for (a hotel).
Saya cari (hotel).

Do you have (a local map)?
Ada (peta daerah)?

Is there (a toilet)?
Ada (kamar kecil)?

Can I (enter)?
Boleh saya (masuk)?

Do I need (a visa)?
Saya harus pakai (visa)?

I have (a reservation).
Saya (sudah punya booking).

I need (assistance).
Saya perlu (dibantu).

I'd like (the menu).
Saya minta (daftar makanan).

I'd like (to hire a car).
Saya mau (sewa mobil).

Could you (help me)?
Bisa Anda (bantu) saya?

a table ...	meja ...
at (eight) o'clock	pada jam (delapan)
for (two) people	untuk (dua) orang

Key Words

baby food (formula)	susu kaleng
bar	bar
bottle	botol
bowl	mangkuk
breakfast	sarapan
cafe	kafe
children's menu	menu untuk anak-anak
cold	dingin
dinner	makan malam
dish	piring
drink list	daftar minuman
food	makanan
food stall	warung
fork	garpu

Signs

Buka	Open
Dilarang	Prohibited
Kamar Kecil	Toilets
Keluar	Exit
Masuk	Entrance
Pria	Men
Tutup	Closed
Wanitai	Women

glass	gelas
highchair	kursi tinggi
hot (warm)	panas
knife	pisau
lunch	makan siang
menu	daftar makanan
market	pasar
napkin	tisu
plate	piring
restaurant	rumah makan
salad	selada
soup	sop
spicy	pedas
spoon	sendok
vegetarian food	makanan tanpa daging
with	dengan
without	tanpa

Meat & Fish

beef	daging sapi
carp	ikan mas
chicken	ayam
duck	bebek
fish	ikan
lamb	daging anak domba
mackerel	tenggiri
meat	daging
pork	daging babi
shrimp/prawn	udang
tuna	cakalang
turkey	kalkun

Fruit & Vegetables

apple	apel
banana	pisang
beans	kacang
cabbage	kol
carrot	wortel
cauliflower	blumkol
cucumber	timun
dates	kurma
eggplant	terung
fruit	buah
grapes	buah anggur
lemon	jeruk asam
orange	jeruk manis
pineapple	nenas
potato	kentang
raisins	kismis
spinach	bayam
vegetable	sayur-mayur
watermelon	semangka

Other

bread	roti
butter	mentega
cheese	keju
chilli	cabai
chilli sauce	sambal
egg	telur
honey	madu
jam	selai
noodles	mie
oil	minyak
pepper	lada
rice	nasi
salt	garam
soy sauce	kecap
sugar	gula
vinegar	cuka

Drinks

beer	bir
coconut milk	santan
coffee	kopi
juice	jus
milk	susu
palm sap wine	tuak
red wine	anggur merah
soft drink	minuman ringan
tea	teh
water	air
white wine	anggur putih
yogurt	susu masam kental

EMERGENCIES

Help!	Tolong saya!
I'm lost.	Saya tersesat.
Leave me alone!	Jangan ganggu saya!
There's been an accident.	Ada kecelakaan.
Can I use your phone?	Boleh saya pakai telpon genggamnya?
Call a doctor!	Panggil dokter!
Call the police!	Panggil polisi!
I'm ill.	Saya sakit.
It hurts here.	Sakitnya di sini.
I'm allergic to (antibiotics).	Saya alergi (antibiotik).

SHOPPING & SERVICES

I'd like to buy ...	Saya mau beli ...
I'm just looking.	Saya lihat-lihat saja.
May I look at it?	Boleh saya lihat?
I don't like it.	Saya tidak suka.
How much is it?	Berapa harganya?
It's too expensive.	Itu terlalu mahal.
Can you lower the price?	Boleh kurang?
There's a mistake in the bill.	Ada kesalahan dalam kuitansi ini.

credit card	kartu kredit
foreign exchange office	kantor penukaran mata uang asing
internet cafe	warnet
mobile/cell phone	hanpon
post office	kantor pos
signature	tanda tangan
tourist office	kantor pariwisata

TIME & DATES

What time is it?	Jam berapa sekarang?
It's (10) o'clock.	Jam (sepuluh).
It's half past (six).	Setengah (tujuh).

Question Words

How?	Bagaimana?
What?	Apa?
When?	Kapan?
Where?	Di mana?
Which	Yang mana?
Who?	Siapa?
Why?	Kenapa?

in the morning	pagi
in the afternoon	siang
in the evening	malam

today	hari ini
tomorrow	besok
yesterday	kemarin

Monday	hari Senin
Tuesday	hari Selasa
Wednesday	hari Rabu
Thursday	hari Kamis
Friday	hari Jumat
Saturday	hari Sabtu
Sunday	hari Minggu

January	Januari
February	Februari
March	Maret
April	April
May	Mei
June	Juni
July	Juli
August	Agustus
September	September
October	Oktober
November	Nopember
December	Desember

TRANSPORT

Public Transport

bicycle-rickshaw	becak
boat (general)	kapal
boat (local)	perahu
bus	bis
minibus	bemo
motorcycle-rickshaw	bajaj
motorcycle-taxi	ojek
plane	pesawat
taxi	taksi
train	kereta api

I want to go to ...	Saya mau ke ...
How much to ...?	Ongkos ke ... berapa?
At what time does it leave?	Jam berapa berangkat?
At what time does it arrive to ...?	Jam berapa sampai di ...?

Numbers

1	*satu*
2	*dua*
3	*tiga*
4	*empat*
5	*lima*
6	*enam*
7	*tujuh*
8	*delapan*
9	*sembilan*
10	*sepuluh*
20	*duapuluh*
30	*tigapuluh*
40	*empatpuluh*
50	*limapuluh*
60	*enampuluh*
70	*tujuhpuluh*
80	*delapanpuluh*
90	*sembilanpuluh*
100	*seratus*
1000	*seribu*

Does it stop at ...?	*Di ... berhenti?*
What's the next stop?	*Apa nama halte berikutnya?*
Please tell me when we get to ...	*Tolong, beritahu waktu kita sampai di ...*
Please stop here.	*Tolong, berhenti di sini.*
the first	*pertama*
the last	*terakhir*
the next	*yang berikutnya*
a ... ticket	*tiket ...*
1st-class	*kelas satu*
2nd-class	*kelas dua*
one-way	*sekali jalan*
return	*pulang pergi*
aisle seat	*tempat duduk dekat gang*
cancelled	*dibatalkan*
delayed	*terlambat*
platform	*peron*
ticket office	*loket tiket*
timetable	*jadwal*
train station	*stasiun kereta api*
window seat	*tempat duduk dekat jendela*

Driving & Cycling

I'd like to hire a ...	*Saya mau sewa ...*
4WD	*gardan ganda*
bicycle	*sepeda*
car	*mobil*
motorcycle	*sepeda motor*
child seat	*kursi anak untuk di mobil*
diesel	*solar*
helmet	*helem*
mechanic	*montir*
petrol/gas	*bensin*
pump (bicycle)	*pompa sepeda*
service station	*pompa bensin*
Is this the road to ...?	*Apakah jalan ini ke ...?*
(How long) Can I park here?	*(Berapa lama) Saya boleh parkir di sini?*
The car/motocycle has broken down.	*Mobil/Motor mogok.*
I have a flat tyre.	*Ban saya kempes.*
I've run out of petrol.	*Saya kehabisan bensin.*

LOCAL LANGUAGES

Balinese

How are you?	*Kenken kabare?*
What's your name?	*Sire wastene?*
My name is ...	*Adan tiange ...*
I don't understand.	*Tiang sing ngerti.*
How much is this?	*Ji kude niki?*
Thank you.	*Matur suksma.*
What do you call this in Balinese?	*Ne ape adane di Bali?*
Which is the way to ...?	*Kije jalan lakar kel ...*

Sasak

What's your name?	*Saik aranm side?*
My name is ...	*Arankah aku ...*
I don't understand.	*Endek ngerti.*
How much is this?	*Pire ajin sak iyak?*
Thank you.	*Tampak asih.*
What do you call this in Sasak?	*Ape aran sak iyak elek bahase Sasek?*
Which is the way to ...?	*Lamun lek ..., embe eak langantah?*

(m) indicates masculine gender, (f) feminine gender and (pl) plural

adat – tradition, customs and manners

adharma – evil

aling aling – gateway backed by a small wall

alus – identifiable 'goodies' in an *arja* drama

anak-anak – children

angker – evil power

angklung – portable form of the *gamelan*

anjing – dogs

apotik – pharmacy

arja – refined operatic form of Balinese theatre; also a dance-drama, comparable to Western opera

Arjuna – a hero of the *Mahabharata* epic and a popular temple gate guardian image

bahasa – language; Bahasa Indonesia is the national language of Indonesia

bale – an open-sided pavilion with a steeply pitched thatched roof

bale banjar – communal meeting place of a *banjar;* a house for meetings and *gamelan* practice

bale gede – reception room or guest-house in the home of a wealthy Balinese

bale kambang – floating pavilion; a building surrounded by a moat

bale tani – family house in Lombok; see also *serambi*

balian – faith healer and herbal doctor

banjar – local division of a village consisting of all the married adult males

banyan – a type of ficus tree, often considered holy; see also *waringin*

bapak – father; also a polite form of address to any older man; also *pak*

Barong – mythical lion-dog creature

Barong Tengkok – portable *gamelan* used for wedding processions and circumcision ceremonies on Lombok

baten tegeh – decorated pyramids of fruit, rice cakes and flowers

batik – process of colouring fabric by coating part of the cloth with wax, dyeing it and melting the wax out; the waxed part is not coloured, and repeated waxing and dyeing builds up a pattern

batu bolong – rock with a hole

belalu – quick-growing, light wood

bemo – popular local transport in Bali and on Lombok; usually a small minibus but can be a small pick-up in rural areas

bensin – petrol (gasoline)

beruga – communal meeting hall in Bali; open-sided pavilion on Lombok

bhur – world of demons

bhwah – world of humans

bioskop – cinema

bokor – artisans; they produce the silver bowls used in traditional ceremonies

Brahma – the creator; one of the trinity of Hindu gods

Brahmana – the caste of priests and the highest of the Balinese castes; all priests are Brahmanas, but not all Brahmanas are priests

bu – mother; shortened form of *ibu*

bukit – hill; also the name of Bali's southern peninsula

bulau – month

buruga – thatched platforms on stilts

cabang – large tanks used to store water for the dry season

candi – shrine, originally of Javanese design; also known as *prasada*

candi bentar – entrance gates to a temple

cendrawasih – birds of paradise

cengceng – cymbals

cidomo – pony cart with car wheels (Lombok)

cili – representations of Dewi Sri, the rice goddess

cucuk – gold headpieces

dalang – puppet master and storyteller in a *wayang kulit* performance

Dalem Bedaulu – legendary last ruler of the Pejeng dynasty

danau – lake

dangdut – pop music

desa – village

dewa – deity or supernatural spirit

dewi – goddess

Dewi Sri – goddess of rice

dharma – good

dokar – pony cart; known as a *cidomo* on Lombok

Durga – goddess of death and destruction, and consort of *Shiva*

dusun –small village

endek – elegant fabric, like *songket,* with pre-dyed weft threads

Gajah Mada – famous *Majapahit* prime minister who defeated the last great king of Bali and extended *Majapahit* power over the island

Galungan – great Balinese festival; an annual event in the 210-day Balinese *wuku* calendar

gamelan – traditional Balinese orchestra, with mostly percussion instruments like large xylophones and gongs; may have one to more than two dozen musicians; also used to refer to individual instruments such as drums; also called a *gong*

Ganesha – *Shiva's* elephant-headed son

gang – alley or footpath

gangsa – xylophone-like instrument

Garuda – mythical man-bird creature, vehicle of *Vishnu;* modern symbol of Indonesia and the national airline

gedong – shrine

gendang beleq – a war dance; like the Oncer dance

gendong – street vendors who sell *jamu,* said to be a cure-all tonic

genggong – musical performance seen in Lombok

gili – small island (Lombok)

goa – cave; also spelt *gua*

gong – see *gamelan*

gong gede – large orchestra; traditional form of the *gamelan* with 35 to 40 musicians

gong kebyar – modern, popular form of a *gong gede,* with up to 25 instruments

gringsing – rare double ikat woven cloth; both warp and weft threads are pre-dyed

gua – cave; also spelt *goa*

gunung – mountain

gunung api – volcano

gusti – polite title for members of the *Wesia* caste

Hanuman – monkey god who plays a major part in the *Ramayana*

harga biasa – standard price

harga turis – inflated price for tourists

homestay – small, family-run accommodation; see also losmen

ibu – mother; also a polite form of address to any older woman

Ida Bagus – honourable title for a male *Brahmana*

iders-iders – long painted scrolls used as temple decorations

ikat – cloth where a pattern is produced by dyeing the individual threads before weaving; see also *gringsing*

Indra – king of the gods

jalak putih – local name for Bali starling

jalan – road or street; abbreviated to *Jl*

jalan jalan – to walk around

jamu – a cure-all tonic; see also *gendong*

jepun – frangipani or plumeria trees

jidur – large cylindrical drums played throughout Lombok

Jimny – small, jeeplike Suzuki vehicle; the usual type of rental car

Jl – *jalan*; road or street

kahyangan jagat – directional temples

kain – a length of material wrapped tightly around the hips and waist, over a sarong

kain poleng – black-and-white chequered cloth

kaja – in the direction of the mountains; see also *kelod*

kaja-kangin – corner of the courtyard

kaki lima – food carts

kala – demonic face often seen over temple gateways

Kalendar Cetakan – Balinese calendar used to plan a myriad of activities

kamben – a length of *songket* wrapped around the chest for formal occasions

kampung – village or neighbourhood

kangin – sunrise

kantor – office

kantor imigrasi – immigration office

kantor pos – post office

Kawi – classical Javanese; the language of poetry

kebyar – a type of dance

Kecak – traditional Balinese dance; tells a tale from the *Ramayana* about Prince Rama and Princess Sita

kedais – coffee house

kelod – in the direction away from the mountains and towards the sea; see also *kaja*

kelurahan – local government area

kemben – woman's breast-cloth

kempli – gong

kendang – drums

kepala desa – village head

kepeng – old Chinese coins with a hole in the centre

kori agung – gateway to the second courtyard in a temple

kota – city

kras – identifiable 'baddies' in an *arja* drama

kris – traditional dagger

Ksatriyasa – second Balinese caste

kuah – sunset side

kulkul – hollow tree-trunk drum used to sound a warning or call meetings

labuhan – harbour; also called *pelabuhan*

laki-laki – boy

lamak – long, woven palm-leaf strips used as decorations in festivals and celebrations

lambung – long black sarongs worn by *Sasak* women; see also *sabuk*

langse – rectangular decorative hangings used in palaces or temples

Legong – classic Balinese dance

legong – young girls who perform the *Legong*

leyak – evil spirit that can assume fantastic forms by the use of black magic

lontar – specially prepared palm leaves

losmen – small Balinese hotel, often family-run

lukisan antic – antique paintings

lulur – body mask

lumbung – rice barn with a round roof; an architectural symbol of Lombok

madia – the body

Mahabharata – one of the great Hindu holy books, the epic poem tells of the battle between the Pandavas and the Korawas

Majapahit – last great Hindu dynasty on Java

mandi – Indonesian 'bath' consisting of a large water tank from which you ladle cold water over yourself

manusa yadnya – ceremonies which mark the various stages of Balinese life from before birth to after cremation

mapadik – marriage by request, as opposed to *ngrorod*

mata air panas – natural hot springs

meditasi – swimming and sunbathing

mekepung – traditional water buffalo races

meru – multiroofed shrines in temples; the name comes from the Hindu holy mountain Mahameru

mobil – car

moksa – freedom from earthly desires

muncak – mouse deer

naga – mythical snakelike creature

ngrorod – marriage by elopement; see also *mapadik*

Ngrupuk – great procession where *ogoh-ogoh* figures are used to ward off evil spirits

ngulapin – cleansing, often used to describe a ritual

nista – the legs

nusa – island; also called *pulau*

Nusa Tenggara Barat (NTB) – West Nusa Tenggara; a province of Indonesia comprising the islands of Lombok and Sumbawa

nyale – wormlike fish caught off Kuta, Lombok

Nyepi – major annual festival in the Hindu *saka* calendar, this is a day of complete stillness after a night of chasing out evil spirits

odalan – Balinese 'temple birthday' festival; held in every temple annually, according to the *wuku* calendar, ie once every 210 days

ogoh-ogoh – huge monster dolls used in the *Nyepi* festival

ojek – motorcycle that carries paying passengers

oong – Bali's famed magic mushrooms

open – tall red-brick buildings

padi – growing rice plant

padmasana – temple shrine resembling a vacant chair

pak – father; shortened form of *bapak*

palinggihs – temple shrines consisting of a simple, little throne

panca dewata – centre and four cardinal points in a temple

pande – blacksmiths; they are treated somewhat like a caste in their own right

pantai – beach

paras – a soft, grey volcanic stone used in stone carving

pasar – market

pasar malam – night market

pecalang – village or *banjar* police

pedagang – mobile traders

pedanda – high priest

pekelan – ceremony where gold trinkets and objects are thrown into the lake

pelabuhan – harbour; also called *labuhan*

Pelni – the national shipping line

pemangku – temple guardians and priests for temple rituals

penjor – long bamboo pole with decorated end, arched over the road or pathway during festivals or ceremonies

perbekel – government official in charge of a *desa*

perempuan – girl

pesmangku – priest for temple rituals

pitra yadna – cremation

plus plus – a combined tax and service charge of 21% added by midrange and top-end accommodation and restaurants

pondok – simple lodging or hut

prada – cloth highlighted with gold leaf, or gold or silver paint and thread

prahu – traditional Indonesian boat with outriggers

prasada – shrine; see also *candi*

prasasti – inscribed copper plates

pria – man; male

propinsi – province; Indonesia has 27 *propinsi* – Bali is a *propinsi*, Lombok and its neighbouring island of Sumbawa comprise *propinsi Nusa Tenggara Barat* (NTB)

puasa – to fast, or a fast

pulau – island; also called *nusa*

puputan – warrior's fight to the death; an honourable but suicidal option when faced with an unbeatable enemy

pura – temple

pura dalem – temple of the dead

pura desa – village temple for everyday functions

pura puseh – temple of the village founders or fathers, honouring the village's origins

pura subak – temple of the rice growers' association

puri – palace

pusit kota – used on road signs to indicate the centre of town

puskesmas – community health centre

rajah – lord or prince

Ramadan – Muslim month of fasting

Ramayana – one of the great Hindu holy books; these stories form the keystone of many Balinese dances and tales

Rangda – widow-witch who represents evil in Balinese theatre and dance

raya – main road, eg Jl Raya Ubud means 'the main road of Ubud'

rebab – bowed lute

RRI – Radio Republik Indonesia; Indonesia's national radio broadcaster

RSU or RSUP – Rumah Sakit Umum or Rumah Sakit Umum Propinsi; a public hospital or provincial public hospital

rumah makan – restaurant; literally 'eating place'

sabuk – Four-metre-long scarf that holds the *lambung* in place

sadkahyangan – 'world sanctuaries'; most sacred temples

saiban – temple or shrine offering

saka – Balinese calendar based on the lunar cycle; see also *wuku*

sampian – palm-leaf decoration

Sasak – native of Lombok; also the language

sate – satay

sawah – rice field; see also *subak*

selandong – traditional scarf

selat – strait

sepeda – bicycle

sepeda motor – motorcycle

serambi – open veranda on a *bale tani*, the traditional Lombok family house

Shiva – the creator and destroyer; one of the three great Hindu gods

sinetron – soap operas

songket – silver- or gold-threaded cloth, handwoven using a floating weft technique

stupas – domes for housing Buddha relics

subak – village association that organises rice terraces and shares out water for irrigation

Sudra – common caste to which the majority of Balinese belong

sungai – river

swah – world of gods

tahun – year

taksu – divine interpreter for the gods

tambulilingan – bumblebees

tanjung – cape or point

tektekan – ceremonial procession

teluk – gulf or bay

tiing – bamboo

tika – piece of printed cloth or carved wood displaying the Pawukon cycle

tirta – water

toya – water

transmigrasi – government programme of trans-migration

trimurti – Hindu trinity

triwangsa – caste divided into three parts *(Brahmana, Ksatriyasa and Wesia);* means three people

trompong – drums

TU – Telepon Umum; a public telephone

tugu – lord of the ground

tukang prada – group of artisans who make temple umbrellas

tukang wadah – group of artisans who make cremation towers

undagi – designer of a building, usually an architect-priest

utama – the head

Vishnu – the preserver; one of the three great Hindu gods

wanita – woman; female

wantilan – large *bale* pavilion used for meetings, performances and cockfights; community hall

waria – female impersonator, transvestite or transgendered; combination of the words *wanita* and *pria*

waringin – large shady tree with drooping branches which root to produce new trees; see *banyan*

warnet – warung with internet access

wartel – public telephone office; contraction of *warung telekomunikasi*

warung – food stall

wayang kulit – leather puppet used in shadow puppet plays; see also *dalang*

wayang wong – masked drama playing scenes from the *Ramayana*

Wektu Telu – religion peculiar to Lombok; originated in Bayan and combines many tenets of Islam and aspects of other faiths

Wesia – military caste and most numerous of the Balinese noble castes

WIB – Waktu Indonesia Barat; West Indonesia Time

wihara – monastery

WIT – Waktu Indonesia Tengah; Central Indonesia Time

wuku – Balinese calendar made up of 10 different weeks, between one and 10 days long, all running concurrently; see also *saka*

yeh – water; also river

yoni – female symbol of the Hindu god *Shiva*

behind the scenes

SEND US YOUR FEEDBACK

We love to hear from travellers – your comments keep us on our toes and help make our books better. Our well-travelled team reads every word on what you loved or loathed about this book. Although we cannot reply individually to postal submissions, we always guarantee that your feedback goes straight to the appropriate authors, in time for the next edition. Each person who sends us information is thanked in the next edition – and the most useful submissions are rewarded with a free book.

Visit **lonelyplanet.com/contact** to submit your updates and suggestions or to ask for help. Our award-winning website also features inspirational travel stories, news and discussions.

Note: We may edit, reproduce and incorporate your comments in Lonely Planet products such as guidebooks, websites and digital products, so let us know if you don't want your comments reproduced or your name acknowledged. For a copy of our privacy policy visit lonelyplanet.com/privacy.

OUR READERS

Many thanks to the travellers who used the last edition and wrote to us with helpful hints, useful advice and interesting anecdotes:

Jean, Nicola, Marco Agnitelli, Agung Anom, Rachel Ashton, Melinda Aw, Steve Bland, Yvonne Bohr, Danielle Bruggemann, Tony Bryant, William Butcher, Scott Coffey, Kathy Crow, Nol De Boer, Nick De Brett, Astrid De Bruijn, Hans De Ru, Suzanna Duffin, Nahia Ezkurdia, Nathalie Farigu, Mariola Fiedorczuk, Eveline Fortuin, Rachel Frampton, Laura Gordon-Hall, Vanny Gorissen, Christine Grant, Barbara Hasenoehrl, Sylvianne Helm, Erik Hoeksema, Ben Huiskamp, Marc Huisman, Thomas Husted, Kirsten Jackes, Cameron James, Irene Kaptein, Bruce Lawrence, Rhonda Lerner, Steve Lewis, Michael Luethi, Joanne Lynch, Silvie Marinovová, Trevor Mazzucchelli, Alois Müller, Eszter Nemeth, Isobel Parry, Kerry Powell, Stefano Rizzi, Stephan Schaller, Denise Schelbergen, Rainintha Siahaan, Bagus Sudiro, Andrew Taylor, Jenny Taylor, Ivan Todorovic, David Tran, Costanza Troini, Gijs Van Tol, Jaap Verheij, Ellen Wageneire, Martin 'Gung Made' Weinreuter, Erin Westerhout-Hanna, Horst Wilms, Kok Wing Kong, Voon Wong, Jens Zacho.

AUTHOR THANKS

Ryan Ver Berkmoes

This list just seems to grow. Many thanks to friends like Hanafi, Jeremy Allan, Eliot Cohen, Jamie James, arch-competitor Mary Justice Thomasson-Croll, Kerry and Milton Turner, Adyus, Kadek Gunarta, Ibu Cat, Patricia Miklautsch, Made Gunarta, Rucina Ballinger, Jack Daniels, Maura Murphey, Marilyn, Wayan Suarnata, Sara Morell, Chrystine Hanley, Marian Carroll (whose work last time was a huge help this time) and many more. Seeing my friends on Bali always makes me want to double my stay while tripling the fun (although when Janine Eberle is there that can prove fatal).

Iain Stewart

Thanks to Tashi, Ilaria and Ryan for making this such an enjoyable book to work on. Barbara Lucas Cahyadi, you are remarkable and your sheer bravado getting us an impromptu tour of the new airport was brilliant! Scott Coffey, Retno, Ewan, Dian, Glenn, Dee and Made in Kuta all helped me out considerably too. Thanks to Laely Farida for setting up the Rinjani hike (my knees are still paying for it). Over in the Gilis, ciao to the legend that is Guy Somers, Fern, Simon, Delphine, Amy and Diane Somerton. I'll be back!

This Book

This is the 13th edition of Lonely Planet's *Bali & Lombok*. We first visited Bali, the island of the gods, way back in the early '70s, when a floral-shirted Tony Wheeler came through while researching the inaugural *Across Asia on the Cheap*. Since then, an army of Lonely Planet authors has returned time and time again: following in Tony's sandalled footprints have been Mary Coverton, Alan Samagalski, James Lyon, Paul Greenway, Kate Daly, Ryan Ver Berkmoes, Lisa Steer-Guérard and Iain Stewart. For this edition, Ryan Ver Berkmoes returned once again to Bali, while the intrepid, island-hopping Iain Stewart researched and wrote the Lombok and Gili Islands chapters.

This guidebook was commissioned in Lonely Planet's Melbourne office, and produced by the following:

Commissioning Editors Shawn Low, Ilaria Walker, Tashi Wheeler

Coordinating Editors Michelle Bennett, Simon Williamson

Coordinating Cartographer Jacqueline Nguyen

Coordinating Layout Designer Wibowo Rusli

Managing Editor Bruce Evans

Senior Editor Helen Christinis

Managing Cartographers Shahara Ahmed, David Connolly Adrian Persoglia

Managing Layout Designers Indra Kilfoyle, Celia Wood

Assisting Editors Elisa Arduca, Susie Ashworth, Carolyn Bain, Adrienne Costanzo

Assisting Cartographers Xavier Di Toro, Jennifer Johnston

Cover Research Naomi Parker

Internal Image Research Sabrina Dalbesio

Language Content Annelies Mertens, Branislava Vladisavljevic

Thanks to Mark Adams, Imogen Bannister, Stefanie Di Trocchio, Janine Eberle, Joshua Geoghegan, Mark Germanchis, Michelle Glynn, Lauren Hunt, Laura Jane, David Kemp, Lisa Knights, Nic Lehman, John Mazzocchi, Wayne Murphy, Trent Paton, Piers Pickard, Averil Robertson, Lachlan Ross, Michael Ruff, Simon Sellars, Julie Sheridan, Laura Stansfeld, John Taufa, Sam Trafford, Juan Winata, Emily Wolman, Nick Wood

Acknowledgments

Climate map data adapted from Peel MC, Finlayson BL & McMahon TA (2007) 'Updated World Map of the Köppen-Geiger Climate Classification', Hydrology and Earth System Sciences, 11, 163344.

Cover photograph: Children dressed for full-moon procession, Bali, Indonesia/Bertrand Gardel, Photolibrary. Many of the images in this guide are available for licensing from Lonely Planet Images: www.lonely planetimages.com.

how to use this book

These symbols will help you find the listings you want:

👁 Sights	🎊 Festivals & Events	⭐ Entertainment
🏃 Activities	🛏 Sleeping	🛍 Shopping
🎓 Courses	🍴 Eating	ℹ Information/Transport
👉 Tours	🍷 Drinking	

These symbols give you the vital information for each listing:

🎵 Telephone Numbers	🛜 Wi-Fi Access	🚌 Bus
🕐 Opening Hours	🏊 Swimming Pool	⛴ Ferry
P Parking	🥗 Vegetarian Selection	M Metro
⊖ Nonsmoking	📖 English-Language Menu	S Subway
❄ Air-Conditioning	👪 Family-Friendly	⊖ London Tube
@ Internet Access	🐾 Pet-Friendly	🚋 Tram
		🚆 Train

Reviews are organised by author preference.

Map Legend

Sights
- 🏖 Beach
- 🔵 Buddhist
- 🏰 Castle
- ✝ Christian
- 🕉 Hindu
- ☪ Islamic
- ✡ Jewish
- 🔵 Monument
- 🏛 Museum/Gallery
- 🔵 Ruin
- 🍇 Winery/Vineyard
- 🦁 Zoo
- 🔵 Other Sight

Activities, Courses & Tours
- ⊜ Diving/Snorkelling
- ⊜ Canoeing/Kayaking
- 🎿 Skiing
- 🏄 Surfing
- ⊜ Swimming/Pool
- 🚶 Walking
- 🏄 Windsurfing
- • Other Activity/Course/Tour

Sleeping
- 🛏 Sleeping
- ⛺ Camping

Eating
- 🍴 Eating

Drinking
- ☕ Drinking
- ☕ Cafe

Entertainment
- ⭐ Entertainment

Shopping
- 🛍 Shopping

Information
- 🏦 Bank
- 🌐 Embassy/Consulate
- ➕ Hospital/Medical
- 🌐 Internet
- 👮 Police
- 📮 Post Office
- 📞 Telephone
- 🚻 Toilet
- ℹ Tourist Information
- • Other Information

Transport
- ✈ Airport
- ⊗ Border Crossing
- 🚌 Bus
- Cable Car/Funicular
- Cycling
- Ferry
- Ⓜ Metro
- Monorail
- P Parking
- Petrol Station
- Taxi
- Train/Railway
- Tram
- • Other Transport

Routes
- Tollway
- Freeway
- Primary
- Secondary
- Tertiary
- Lane
- Unsealed Road
- Plaza/Mall
- Steps
- Tunnel
- Pedestrian Overpass
- Walking Tour
- Walking Tour Detour
- Path

Geographic
- 🏠 Hut/Shelter
- 🗼 Lighthouse
- Lookout
- ▲ Mountain/Volcano
- Oasis
- Park
-)(Pass
- Picnic Area
- Waterfall

Population
- 🔵 Capital (National)
- ◉ Capital (State/Province)
- ● City/Large Town
- ○ Town/Village

Boundaries
- International
- State/Province
- Disputed
- Regional/Suburb
- Marine Park
- Cliff
- Wall

Hydrography
- River, Creek
- Intermittent River
- Swamp/Mangrove
- Reef
- Canal
- Water
- Dry/Salt/Intermittent Lake
- Glacier

Areas
- Beach/Desert
- Cemetery (Christian)
- Cemetery (Other)
- Park/Forest
- Sportsground
- Sight (Building)
- Top Sight (Building)

OUR STORY

A beat-up old car, a few dollars in the pocket and a sense of adventure. In 1972 that's all Tony and Maureen Wheeler needed for the trip of a lifetime – across Europe and Asia overland to Australia. It took several months, and at the end – broke but inspired – they sat at their kitchen table writing and stapling together their first travel guide, *Across Asia on the Cheap*. Within a week they'd sold 1500 copies. Lonely Planet was born.

Today, Lonely Planet has offices in Melbourne, London and Oakland, with more than 600 staff and writers. We share Tony's belief that 'a great guidebook should do three things: inform, educate and amuse'.

OUR WRITERS

Ryan Ver Berkmoes

Coordinating author, all chapters except Lombok and the Gili Islands Ryan Ver Berkmoes was first entranced by the echoing beat of a Balinese gamelan in 1993. On his visits since he has explored almost every corner of the island – along with side trips to Nusas Lembongan and Penida, the Gilis and Lombok. Just when he thinks Bali holds no more surprises, he finds, for example, a set of stairs leading to a beach on nobody's map. During research for this book, his 10th on the island for Lonely Planet, he confirmed the report of a friend who said that the wonders of snorkelling at Menjangan cause so many smiles you can't keep the water out of your mouth. Ryan never tires of Bali; sometimes his social calendar is busier on the island than it is anywhere else. Away from the gamelan, Ryan lives in Portland, Oregon, and writes about Bali and more at www.ryanverberkmoes.com.

Read more about Ryan at:
lonelyplanet.com/members/ryanverberkmoes

Iain Stewart

Lombok, Gili Islands Iain first visited Lombok and the Gilis in 1994, when the only dive shop was a shack on the beach and the parties could go on for weeks. Ah, the g_____ s returned many times to snorkel the reefs, hike the hills and enj_____ Asia's best cuisine. Highlights on this trip included a fascinating Chines_ ___mple, eating *ayam taliwang* (a spicy marinated chicken dish) in Kuta, surfing in Gerupuk and fine dining in Trawangan. Author of over 30 guidebooks, Iain specialises in tropical places far from his home in Brighton, England. He's co-written five books about Indonesia for Lonely Planet.

Read more about Iain at:
lonelyplanet.com/members/stewpot

Published by Lonely Planet Publications Pty Ltd
ABN 36 005 607 983
13th edition – March 2011
ISBN 978 1 74179 704 6
© Lonely Planet 2011   Photographs © as indicated 2011
10 9 8 7 6 5 4 3 2 1
Printed in Singapore

Although the authors and Lonely Planet have taken all reasonable care in preparing this book, we make no warranty about the accuracy or completeness of its content and, to the maximum extent permitted, disclaim all liability arising from its use.